0058917

D1154698

THOROTM 99

E
73
T46
1985

Thomas, Cyrus, 1825-
1910.

Report on the mound
explorations of the
Bureau of
Ethnology.

$27.50

Report on the

Mound Explorations

of the Bureau of Ethnology

Cyrus Thomas

Introduction by Bruce D. Smith

Smithsonian Institution Press
Washington, D.C.
1985

Originally published 1894
Reprinted 1985
New material for reprint edition
edited by Jeanne M. Sexton

**Library of Congress Cataloging in
Publication Data**

Thomas, Cyrus, 1825–1910.
Report on the mound explorations of
the Bureau of Ethnology.
Reprint. Originally published: 1st ed.
Washington, D.C.: U.S. G.P.O., 1894 as
accompanying paper to the 12th An-
nual report of the Bureau of American
Ethnology, 1890–1891. With Plate XX
omitted.
Bibliography: p.
1. Mound-builders. 2. Mounds.
3. Indians of North America—Antiqui-
ties. 4. United States—Antiquities.
I. Smithsonian Institution. Bureau of
American Ethnology. II. Title.
E73.T46 1985   973.1   84-600382

ISBN 0-87474-915-8 (pbk.)

Reprinted from the Twelfth Annual
Report of the Bureau of Ethnology
1890–91.

The paper in this book meets the
guidelines for permanence and dura-
bility of the Committee on Production
Guidelines for Book Longevity of the
Council on Library Resources.

Cover: The De Soto Mound, Jefferson
County, Arkansas, plate IX.

95 94 93 92 91 90 89   5 4 3 2

Contents

Publisher's Note

This volume is a photographic reprint of the first edition, which was published as the Accompanying Paper to the *Twelfth Annual Report of the Bureau of Ethnology*, 1890–91 (Washington, D.C.: Government Printing Office,1894). The original pagination has been kept. Plate XX, an oversized map showing the distribution of mounds in the eastern United States, does not relate directly to Thomas's discussion of mound distribution, and is not specifically referenced in the text. As a result, the map is not reproduced in this reprint edition. Interested readers are referred to either the initial issue of the *Twelfth Annual Report*, or to Cyrus Thomas, *Catalogue of Prehistoric Works East of the Rocky Mountains,* Bulletin 12 of the Bureau of Ethnology, Plate 1.

Introduction to the 1985 Edition

Bruce D. Smith

WITH WESTWARD EXPANSION IN THE UNITED STATES BEYOND the Appalachian wall in the late eighteenth century, settlers increasingly encountered the mysterious earthen mounds of the interior eastern woodlands. These mounds, and the identity of the mound builders, would remain at the center of archaeological interest and debate through much of the succeeding nineteenth century.

The Division of Mound Exploration of the Bureau of Ethnology, Smithsonian Institution, was established in 1881 to resolve the issue of the identity of the builders of the mounds. Published in 1894 as the accompanying paper of the *Twelfth Annual Report of the Bureau of Ethnology*, the final research report of the Division rejected the various speculative scenarios of vanished races and convincingly demonstrated that the forebearers of American Indian groups were the builders of the mounds. This final report is generally recognized as marking the beginning of modern archaeology in the Americas.

It is not just the presentation of a wealth of new information concerning the mounds, nor the resolution of the identity of the mound builders, however, that distinguishes the research of the Division of Mound Exploration as the first "modern archaeology" in the United States. Our level of understanding of the prehistory of the eastern woodlands has increased dramatically in the past 100 years, keeping pace with an ever-accelerating growth and development of archaeological theory, method, and technique. Yet the basic organizational and logical structure of present-day American archaeology can clearly be discerned in the work of the Division of Mound Exploration, from initial formation of research problems to be addressed, through design of the research program to recover relevant data, data recovery itself, and analysis, to preparation of the final report.

Formation of the Division of Mound Exploration

On February 24, 1881, the annual appropriation for the Bureau of Ethnology (later called the Bureau of American Ethnology) of the Smithsonian Institution for the coming fiscal year (1882) was considered by the House of Representatives. The proposed appropriation read as follows: "For the purpose of continuing ethnological researches among

5

the North American Indians, under the direction of the Smithsonian Institution, $25,000." When the clerk had finished reading this, Mr. J. Warren Keifer, from Ohio, offered the following amendment: "... add the following: 'five thousand dollars of which shall be expended in continuing archaeological investigations relating to moundbuilders, and prehistoric mounds'" (Rhees 1901:863).

From some of Mr. Keifer's remarks in the subsequent debate, it is clear that the motivation behind his proposed amendment earmarking funds specifically for mound exploration was meant to counter resistance from John Wesley Powell. The previous year Powell, the Bureau's director, had opposed using any of the Bureau's appropriation for the investigation of mounds in the eastern United States. Powell himself further clarifies the origin of Congressman Keifer's amendment in the following passage from the *Twelfth Annual Report*:

> *When the Bureau of Ethnology was first organized the energies of its members were devoted exclusively to the study of the North American Indians, and the general subject of archeology was neglected, it being the dominant purpose and preference of the Director to investigate the languages, arts, institutions, and mythologies of extant tribes rather than prehistoric antiquities; but certain archeologists, by petition, asked Congress to so enlarge the scope of the Bureau as to include a study of the archeology of the United States. . . . (Powell 1894:XL)*

By his own account, Powell was not aware that "such a movement was on foot" (Powell 1894:XLI), and when Keifer's amendment passed 51–29, the interest in mound exploration apparently came as a distinct surprise to him, and not a very pleasant one. Powell was not exactly inept at administrative tactics, however, and responded to this turn of events in predictable fashion:

> *In compliance with the terms of the statute the work of investigating the mounds of the eastern half of the United States was at once organized, and Mr. Wills de Haas was placed in charge, as he was one of the men who had interested himself to have the investigation enlarged. (Powell 1894:XLI)*

By placing one of the most outspoken of his critics in charge of the newly formed Division of Mound Exploration, Powell appears to have effectively headed off any further Congressional criticism of his administration of the Bureau of Ethnology, at least for the moment. At the same time, he brought one of the petitioners, Wills de Haas, inside his tent, so to speak, and under his thumb. De Haas resigned within a year. In his place, Powell appointed Cyrus Thomas, and the research program of the Division began in earnest.

Problem Orientation: Identification of the Research Questions to be Asked

When Congress earmarked the five thousand dollars for exploration of the mounds, it did not provide even the most general guidelines as to what kinds of research questions should be pursued under the appropriation—only that prehistoric mounds and mound builders should be investigated.

A general problem orientation, or identification of the research questions to be resolved, was quickly provided by Powell, however, who instructed Cyrus Thomas to settle the then still-unresolved debate over the identity of the mound builders:

> *The most important question to be settled is, "were the mounds built by the Indians?" The Director of the Bureau of Ethnology was desirous, therefore, that this important question, the origin of the mounds, should if possible be definitely settled, as it is the pivot on which all the other problems must turn. (Thomas 1894:21)*

The competing theories of the mound builder debate had been initially articulated seventy years earlier, with T. M. Harris presenting the pro-lost race position, and Bishop Madison making the case for the pro-Indian theory. Powell clearly did not consider this mound builder debate, which was still going strong in the 1880s, as an isolated issue that should be addressed solely because of its wide popularity. He placed the identity question within the larger context of the cultural development of the historically described Indian groups of the eastern United States. And when viewed in this context, the mound builder debate represented a major roadblock to Powell's driving interest in obtaining an accurate and detailed picture of North American Indians. It not only attracted too much of the time and efforts of researchers in eastern North America, but it also served to scatter their lines of investigation far too widely, and often in unproductive directions. It was Powell's hope that the Division of Mound Exploration could break this roadblock by once and for all demonstrating that the prehistoric mound builders and the historic tribes were part of the same fabric of unbroken cultural development.

If it could be proven that the prehistoric mounds had been constructed by the ancestors of the Indians,

> *the questions relating to the objects and uses of these ancient works would be merged into the study of the customs and arts of the Indians. There would then be no more blind groping by archeologists for the thread to lead them out of the mysterious labyrinth. The chain which links together the historic and prehistoric ages of our continent would be complete; the thousand and one wild theories*

7

and romances would be permanently disposed of; and the relations of all the lines of investigation to one another being known, they would aid in the solution of many of the problems which hitherto have seemed involved in complete obscurity. (Thomas 1894:21)

It is evident that even as Powell shaped the general problem orientation of Thomas's research he was also looking beyond the issue itself to the potential beneficial impact that its resolution would have on North American Indian studies in general.

Although it is difficult to determine the degree to which Powell subsequently provided the Division with advice or direction apart from his initial general instructions, he appears to have given Thomas free rein: "General lines of investigation were adopted by the Director and the details were intrusted to selected persons skilled in their pursuits" (Powell 1894: XXI).

Thomas considered the overall general goal of the Division to be "the collection of data necessary to an understanding of the more general and important problems relating to the mounds and the mound builders" (Thomas 1894:20). He was clear and explicit concerning what these more general and important research problems were, and expanded the Division's problem orientation beyond Powell's primary goal to include a number of related questions.

The "imperfect and faulty" (Thomas 1894:27) mound classification scheme developed by Squier and Davis (1848), with its inherent functional attributions (e.g., "mounds of sacrifice"), was still widely used in the 1880s and Thomas hoped that the Division's work would produce a more comprehensive classification system for prehistoric mound sites— one based on observed and documented characteristics that would "group the individual monuments according to types of form and external characters, reference being made to uses only where these were obvious" (Thomas 1894:28).

There was also an explicit interest in determining the geographical range of occurrence of the various "types" of mounds, with the aim of defining different archaeological districts (Thomas 1894:23).

In addition, Thomas was very concerned with accurately determining the mode of construction of mounds, not only in the hope of "acquiring a clear insight into the character and methods of mound-building and into the purpose of their builders," but also of providing further information on geographical variation in the occurrence of the various mound types: "Particular attention has been paid to the mode of construction and methods of burial in the ordinary conical tumuli, because these furnish valuable evidence in regard to the customs of the builders and aid in determining the different archeological districts" (Thomas 1894:20,23). This concern with developing a comprehensive taxonomy of mound types also applied to the artifactual assemblages recovered during the exploration of mounds. It was hoped that subsequent detailed analysis of the various classes of artifacts by specialists would produce the ordered descriptive classification schemes that were so badly needed.

The research of the Division of Mound Exploration was from the start explicitly problem oriented. Powell identified the primary goal of resolving the debate over the identity of the mound builders, and Thomas provided an interrelated set of four secondary objectives:

1) Identify the full range of variation in the form or external shape of prehistoric mounds, and develop a comprehensive mound classification system;
2) Investigate and accurately describe the mode of construction of mounds of various types;
3) Establish a system of regional archaeological districts that reflected the geographical range of the various mound types;
4) Obtain representative artifact assemblages from prehistoric mounds, not only for distinguishing between various mound categories and archaeological districts, but also for allowing subsequent taxonomic analysis of the various classes of artifacts.

In addition to these problem-oriented goals, Thomas established another, equally important goal—he was determined that the work of the Division would result in a detailed and objective data base that would be available and of value to future generations of archaeologists: "By following the plan adopted and using proper care to note the facts ascertained, without bias, not only would the facts bearing on this important question be ascertained, but the data would be preserved for the use of archeological students without prejudice to any theory" (Thomas 1894:21).

Research Design: Procedure for Recovering Relevant Information

The research design or data recovery plan of the Division of Mound Exploration was a logical extension of the problem orientation set out by Powell and Thomas, and can be seen to have been carefully and deliberately tailored to obtain information relevant to the research questions that had been defined.

The most obvious problem faced by Thomas in developing a research design was one of simple geography—prehistoric mounds were scattered in great numbers over most of the eastern United States. The limited financial resources available to the Division made it obvious from the start that it wasn't feasible to thoroughly examine all, or even a large number, of the mounds. Thomas rejected the option of thoroughly investigating those of a smaller and more manageable geographical area because it would not yield the information necessary to answer several of the defined research questions. Instead, a research design was instituted that involved the selection and detailed examination of a sample of mounds that represented the full range of known variation of form and mode of construction, and which were distributed over a wide geographical area.

> ... such mounds and groups as are believed to be typical of their class have been examined with care and thoroughness. By the method of a careful examination of typical structures in the various districts it is thought that the end aimed at has been secured—that is, the collection of data necessary to an understanding of the more general and important problems relating to the mounds and the mound builders. (Thomas 1894:20)

The process of selecting the prehistoric mounds to be examined, described, and possibly excavated was initially based on background research carried out by Thomas, who drew on published accounts of mounds (including newspapers) as well as the extensive unsolicited correspondence concerning mounds that had accumulated at the Smithsonian Institution over the years. Bulletin 12 of the Bureau of Ethnology, *Catalogue of Prehistoric Works East of the Rocky Mountains*, by Cyrus Thomas, provides a good indication of the total known universe of prehistoric mounds from which Thomas's sample was drawn. In addition, promising mound groups located during the course of field investigations were quite often added to Thomas's original sample.

In extending the research design to the actual process of data recovery, Thomas continued to keep the problem orientation of the Division clearly in mind. Each mound or mound group selected for examination was first described in a detailed manner: "The topography of the immediate locality, the form, characters, and dimensions of the works and their relations to one another was written out, accompanied by diagrams and figures illustrating these descriptions" (Thomas 1894:21). The descriptions were often accompanied by horizontal and vertical sections showing the location of skeletons and artifacts.

Specimens recovered during excavations were in turn assigned field numbers and were packed and shipped, together with a descriptive list, to the Washington offices of the Bureau of Ethnology, then located on the southwest corner of 14th and F Streets. When these field collections were unpacked in Washington, each specimen received a Bureau of Ethnology catalogue number, and this number was entered into the Division's catalogue ledger, along with the specimen's field number, the collector, the locality from which it was collected, provenience information, and a description of the object. This information was actually recorded twice because a dual ledger system was maintained, with one set going to the National Museum. The Bureau of Ethnology was an independent research branch of the Smithsonian Institution, separate from the National Museum, with no storage facilities of its own. Division of Mound Exploration specimens were, as a result, subsequently transferred to the National Museum (the original National Museum is now known as the Arts and Industries building and is located adjacent the Smithsonian Institution "Castle"). Since each specimen was also assigned a National Museum catalogue number most ended up with three catalogue numbers, often accompanied by the collector's name and site name.

The research design of the Division of Mound Exploration was formulated entirely by Cyrus Thomas. It included the following important aspects:

1) A sampling strategy was on the one hand designed to obtain systematic geographic coverage of mounds in the eastern United States, and was, at the same time, stratified in an attempt to obtain a representative sample of mounds from each of the various general "classes" or taxonomic categories of mounds.
2) Procedures of data recovery were standardized and involved detailed descriptions and plans of mound sites, descriptions and section drawings of the internal composition of mounds, and descriptions of the location of recovered materials.
3) Collections management procedures involved the field numbering and cataloging of recovered specimens, followed by their rapid shipment to Washington, where a detailed project catalogue was maintained.

Field Operations

In setting up the field operations of the Division, Thomas faced a variety of problems. The most obvious involved the sheer size of the defined geographical study area—it stretched from the Dakotas to Florida and from Texas to New York.

One way to approach this vast expanse of territory that needed coverage would have been to engage for short periods of time a variety of local researchers to investigate nearby mound sites. Thomas did in fact do this to a limited degree, but this approach had the obvious drawback of having to deal with, and rely upon, individuals of varied qualifications, levels of competence, and trustworthiness.

Largely for this reason, I suspect, Thomas channeled most of the funds and research efforts of the Division into the three permanent field assistant positions that he established. He needed field assistants who were willing to put up with constant travel, difficult logistical problems, and hard, dirty excavation work, and who would at the same time meet his high standards of providing accurate and detailed descriptions of mound sites, excavations, and artifacts. It is thus not too surprising that Thomas hired people whom he knew well, or whose work he admired. Table 1 lists the different individuals who filled, at one time or another, one of the three permanent positions. Also listed are those individuals who were temporarily engaged by the Division of Mound Exploration.

Except for an occasional foray into the field, Thomas stayed in Washington and directed the activities and movements of the three field assistants by mail.

To judge from the correspondence between Thomas and his men in the field, he was not an easy person to work for. His outgoing letters invariably contain comments, corrections, and admonitions concerning the last batch of artifacts or mound descriptions received from a particular field assistant, as well as instructions indicating where the field assistant should next proceed. The incoming letters from field assistants similarly share several common themes: responses to Thomas's most recent comments concerning the quality of their work; explanations as to why they were not proceeding as quickly as Thomas wanted; and requests for both the "vouchers" and money owed them. Thomas was apparently tightfisted with the funds of the Division, sending out the field assistants' salaries on a month-by-month basis, and making it clear that next month's check was dependent on continuing adequate performance. For the fiscal year 1883 (July 1882–June 1883) Thomas's salary was $2,400; while P. W. Norris earned $1,650 for eleven months; Edward Palmer received $1,500 for twelve months; and James Middleton was paid $1,375 for eleven months. Thomas was constantly pushing the field assistants to keep more detailed and accurate mound description and excavation records, to find more and better artifacts, and to cover more territory in a shorter period of time. This "stick and carrot" relationship between Thomas and his field assistants is, I think, the key to understanding their astounding accomplishments.

There are a number of ways of unraveling the movements of the field assistants, one of which is shown in Table 2. By going through the Division's artifact ledger, I was able to determine the geographical source of collections sent in by the different field assistants on a year-by-year basis. Table 2 does not tell the whole story, however, since field assistants often visited and described sites without sending back artifacts to Washington.

The 1882–1883 column of Table 2 indicates that in a twelve-month

Cyrus Thomas
June 26, 1825–June 26, 1910

Smithsonian Institution, National Anthropological Archives,
Portrait 67B

period, Edward Palmer sent back specimens from Alabama, Arkansas, Georgia, Indiana, Mississippi, North Carolina, South Carolina, and Tennessee. During the same fiscal year, P. W. Norris visited Arkansas, the Dakotas, Kentucky, Iowa, Minnesota, Missouri, Ohio, Texas, West Virginia, and Wisconsin. Clearly Thomas did not allow his field assistants to dawdle too long in one place. The bottom row of Table 2 lists the total number of catalogue numbers assigned each year and provides a rough index of the level of activity of the field assistants. The number of assigned catalogue numbers drops almost in half after the first two years, and then to almost nothing after the spring of 1886. In terms of excavation and collection acquisition the Division was active only during the four-year span 1882–86. Although some mounds were excavated after 1886, mostly to fill in gaps in the Division's geographical coverage, field assistants in these later years (Middleton and Reynolds) were primarily engaged in mapping mound sites and rechecking the accuracy of previous descriptions.

The field assistants of the Division managed to visit more than 140 counties, and to investigate more than 2,000 mounds:

> *Over 2,000 mounds have been explored, including almost every known type of form, from the low diminutive, circular burial tumulus of the north to the huge truncated earthen pyramid of the south, the embankment, the stone cairn, the house site, etc. Every variety of construction hitherto known, as well as a number decidedly different in detail, have been examined. (Thomas 1894:23)*

Preparation of the Twelfth Annual Report

In the final report of the Division of Mound Exploration the brief abstract, preface, and introduction by Cyrus Thomas is followed by a 486-page descriptive section on field operations. This field operations section is in essence composed of the annual reports written and submitted to Thomas by each of the various field assistants (Thomas 1894:24). These field reports were then edited and sometimes revised by Thomas, W. H. Holmes, and others, and finally organized and consolidated by state and county. Almost all of the 344 figures presented in this descriptive section are the work of W. H. Holmes.

Following the field operations section of the paper are two sections written entirely by Thomas. The first outlines his division of the eastern "mound area" into eight archaeological districts, while in the second he marshalls the evidence collected during the field operations of the Division, and addresses the question of the identity of the mound builders.

The Division of Mound Exploration and the "Birth of Modern American Archaeology."

Historians of American archaeology have invariably recognized the Division of Mound Exploration as playing a prominent role in the development of American archaeology. While viewing the world through crimson-tinted glasses, Willey and Sabloff nonetheless do allow Thomas and his assistants to share the stage with Frederic Ward Putnam and the Peabody Museum during the "dawning age of professional archaeology in the 19th century" (1974:48). Both Hallowell and Jennings, however, clearly give Thomas top billing:

> *It was under the auspices of the Bureau of American Ethnology, in short, that, through a series of widely gauged programs, the empirical foundations of archeology in the United States were established on a broad geographical scale. (Hallowell 1960:84)*

> *Thomas' huge report of a decade of mound exploration by the Bureau of American Ethnology can be thought of as marking the birth of modern American archeology. (Jennings 1968:33)*

Although both Jennings and Hallowell mention the broad geographic coverage of Thomas's mound research, they emphasize the results of the project, the resolution of the identity of the mound builders, as their primary reason for marking it as the first beginnings of modern archaeology.

The methodology employed by Thomas in formulating and carrying out the mound survey, however, also sets it apart as the first modern archaeology carried out in America. If the work of the Division of Mound Exploration is analyzed within the conceptual framework of present-day archaeology, as I have tried to do in this Introduction, it turns out to be surprisingly modern, even though it was begun over a century ago. It was a long-term regional research program and had a larger regional focus than any subsequent archaeological undertaking in North America. It was explicitly problem oriented, and the research questions that were addressed were among the most important ones facing eastern North American archaeology in the nineteenth century. There was also a clear and direct relationship between this problem orientation and the research design developed by Thomas. The sampling strategy for selecting sites to be investigated and the kinds and level of specificity dictated by Thomas's plan of standardized data recovery were carefully tailored to produce the information relevant to the research questions being addressed.

References

Hallowell, A. I.

1960 The Beginnings of Anthropology in America. In *Selected Papers from the American Anthropologist, 1888–1920,* ed. Frederica de Laguna, 1–90. Evanston.

Jennings, Jesse

1968 *Prehistory of North America.* New York.

Powell, John W.

1894 Report of the Director, In *Twelfth Annual Report of the Bureau of Ethnology, 1890–1891.* Washington, D.C.: Government Printing Office.

Rhees, William Jones, comp. and ed.

1901 *The Smithsonian Institution. Documents Relative to its Origin and History, 1835–1899.* Vol. 1, 1835–1887. Washington, D.C.: Government Printing Office.

Squier, Ephraim G., and E. H. Davis

1848 *Ancient Monuments of the Mississippi Valley.* Smithsonian Contributions to Knowledge, vol. 1. Washington, D.C.

Thomas, Cyrus

1891 *Catalogue of Prehistoric Works East of the Rocky Mountains.* Smithsonian Institution, Bureau of Ethnology Bulletin no. 12. Washington, D.C.: Government Printing Office.

1894 Report on the Mound Explorations of the Bureau of Ethnology. Accompanying Paper in *Twelfth Annual Report of the Bureau of Ethnology,* 1890–1891. Washington, D.C.: Government Printing Office.

Willey, Gordon R., and Jeremy A. Sabloff

1974 *A History of American Archaeology.* San Francisco: W. H. Freeman and Co.

Table 1 Duration of Employment of Regular Field Assistants (Division of Mound Exploration)

July 1882	Dr. Edward Palmer Washington, D.C.	Col. P. W. Norris Norris, Michigan	James D. Middleton Carbondale, Illinois
July 1883			
July 1884	John P. Rogan Bristol, Tennessee		
July 1985		J. W. Emmert Kingsport, Tennessee	
July 1886			
July 1887	Gerard Fowke New Madison, Ohio		
July 1888		Henry Reynolds Washington, D.C.	
July 1889			
July 1890			

Individuals "Engaged for Short Periods"

Rev. W. M. Beauchamp, Baldwinsville, New York
F. S. Earle, Cobden, Illinois
Gerard Fowke (also known as Charles M. Smith and Kentucky Q. Smith), New Madison, Ohio (became a regular field assistant)
William McAdams, Otterville, Illinois
Rev. J. P. McLean, Hamilton, Ohio
Rev. Stephen D. Peet, Clinton, Wisconsin
Henry L. Reynolds, Washington, D.C. (became a regular field assistant)
John P. Rogan, Bristol, Tennessee (became a regular field assistant)
L. H. Thing, Cobden, Illinois

Table 2 Location of Specimens Obtained by Field Assistants or from Other Parties, 1882–1890 (Division of Mound Exploration)

	July 1882 to June 1883	July 1883 to June 1884	July 1884 to June 1885	July 1885 to June 1886	July 1886 to June 1887	July 1887 to June 1888	July 1888 to June 1889	July 1889 to June 1890
Alabama	Palmer L. C. Jones	Palmer Norris	Burns Rogan Johnson Thibault					
Arkansas	Palmer Norris Thing Middleton	Palmer	Thing Middleton Norris Derositt	Derositt				
Dakotas	Norris	Norris						Reynolds
Florida	Rogan	Rogan	Babcock					
Georgia	Rogan Palmer	Rogan Palmer	Rogan	Rogan	McGlasham (collection)			Reynolds
Kentucky	Norris	Norris				Middleton Fowke	Middleton	
Louisiana								Smith Waddell
Illinois	Thing Middleton			Middleton		Fowke	Middleton	
Indiana	Palmer							Reynolds
Iowa	Norris							Reynolds
Michigan	Allis							

Minnesota	Norris							
Mississippi	Palmer			Smith			Rogan	
Missouri	Thing Baird Norris							
New York						Reynolds		
North Carolina	Palmer Emmert Rogan Spain Hour	Palmer Rogan						
Ohio	Norris	Rogan Smith Middleton		Fowke		Reynolds Fowke		
Pennsylvania			Thomas		Smith			
South Carolina	Palmer			J. W. Earle				Reynolds
Tennessee	Palmer Emmert Middleton	Middleton Emmert Rogan		McGill (collection)	Emmert		Emmert	
Texas	Norris							
West Virginia	Norris	Norris (Death 1-85)						
Wisconsin	Norris Middleton		Emmert Middleton					
Number of catalog numbers assigned	2168	2164	1175	1153	296	144	376	127

REPORT

ON THE

MOUND EXPLORATIONS

OF THE

BUREAU OF ETHNOLOGY.

BY

CYRUS THOMAS.

CONTENTS.

6   CONTENTS.

CONTENTS. 7

ILLUSTRATIONS.

10 ILLUSTRATIONS.

OUTLINE OF THIS PAPER.

For the benefit of those who desire to learn the more important conclusions reached in this treatise, without the necessity of a thorough examination of the entire report, an outline of them is here presented:

(1) That the mound-builders of the area designated consisted of a number of tribes or peoples bearing about the same relations to one another and occupying about the same culture-status as did the Indian tribes inhabiting this country when first visited by Europeans.

(2) That the archeological districts as determined by the investigations of the mounds and other ancient remains conform, in a general way, to the areas occupied by the different Indian tribes or groups of cognate tribes.

(3) That each tribe adopted several different methods of burial, these differences depending to some extent upon the relative position, social standing, and occupation of the individuals.

(4) The custom of removing the flesh before final burial prevailed very extensively among the mound-builders of the northern districts, and was not uncommon among those of the southern districts.

(5) Very often some kind of religious ceremony was performed at the burial in which fire played a conspicuous part. Notwithstanding the common belief to the contrary, there is no evidence whatever that human sacrifice in the true sense was practiced. It is possible that cremation may have been practiced to a limited extent.

(6) In some of the southern districts, especially those of the valley of the lower Mississippi, where the bottoms are much depressed, it was the custom to erect dwellings on low mounds apparently constructed for this purpose, and, when deaths occurred, to bury the remains in the floor of these dwellings, burn the houses, and heap mounds over them before they were entirely consumed, or while the embers were yet smoldering. The houses in these districts appear to have been constructed of upright posts set in the ground, lathed with cane or twigs, and plastered with clay, having the roofs thatched precisely as described by the early French explorers.

(7) The links directly connecting the Indians and mound-builders are so numerous and well established that archeologists are justified in accepting the theory that they are one and the same people.

(8) The statements of the early navigators and explorers as to the habits, customs, social condition and art, of the Indians when first visited by Europeans are largely confirmed by discoveries in the mounds and other ancient works of our country. This is especially true as regards the discoveries made by this bureau in Arkansas, Georgia, and other southern states. They bear out, even to details, the statements of the chroniclers of De Soto's expedition and of the early French explorers of the valley of the lower Mississippi.

(9) The evidence obtained appears to be sufficient to justify the conclusion that particular works, and the works of certain localities, are attributable to particular tribes known to history; thereby enabling the archeologist to determine in some cases, to a limited extent, the lines of migration. For example, the proof is apparently conclusive that the Cherokees were mound-builders and that to them are to be

12 ETH——2   17

attributed most of the mounds of eastern Tennessee and western North Carolina; it also renders it probable that they were the authors of most of the ancient works of the Kanawha valley in West Virginia. There are also strong indications that the Tallegwi of tradition were Cherokees and the authors of some of the principal works of Ohio. The proof is equally conclusive that to the Shawnees are to be attributed the box-shaped stone graves, and the mounds and other works directly connected with them, in the region south of the Ohio, especially those works of Kentucky, Tennessee, and northern Georgia, and possibly also some of the mounds and stone graves in the vicinity of Cincinnati. The stone graves in the valley of the Delaware and most of those in Ohio are attributable to the Delawares. There are sufficient reasons for believing that the ancient works in northern Mississippi were built chiefly by the Chickasaws, and those in the region of Flint River, southern Georgia, by the Uchees, and that a large portion of those of the Gulf states were built by the Muskokee tribes.

(10) The testimony of the mounds is very decidedly against the theory that the mound-builders were Mayas or Mexicans who were driven out of this region by the pressure of Indian hordes and migrated to the valley of Anahuac or plains of Yucatan. It is also as decidedly against Morgan's theory that they were related to the Pueblo tribes of New Mexico. It likewise gives a decided negative to the suggestion that the builders of the Ohio works were pushed south into the Gulf states and incorporated into the Muskokee group.

(11) Although much the larger portion of the ancient monuments of our country belong to prehistoric times, and some of them, possibly, to the distant past, yet the evidence of contact with European civilization is found in so many mounds where it can not be attributed to intrusive burial and in such widely separated localities, that it must be conceded that many of them were built subsequent to the discovery of the continent by Europeans.

PREFACE.

As the following report is based almost exclusively upon the results of explorations carried on by the Bureau of Ethnology since 1881, it seems desirable to set forth briefly the plan adopted and the methods pursued.

During the first season the archeological work of the Bureau was assigned to Dr. Willis De Haas, but no definite and comprehensive plan of operations was adopted. In 1882 the Director organized a small division in the Bureau to which he assigned the work of investigating the mounds and other ancient monuments in the United States east of the Rocky mountains. This division was placed under my charge with Dr. Edward Palmer, of Washington city; Col. P. W. Norris, of Norris, Michigan, and Mr. James D. Middleton, of Carbondale, Illinois, as regular field assistants. Subsequently Dr. Palmer left the division, and Mr. John P. Rogan, of Bristol, Tennessee, was engaged in his place. The division suffered the misfortune of being deprived of the valuable services of Col. Norris by death, in January, 1885, while he was engaged in exploration. His enthusiasm for the work kept him in the field, although he was suffering from the disease which finally proved fatal. Mr. J. W. Emmert, who had been temporarily employed, was then engaged as a regular assistant.

The following-named gentlemen have also been engaged for short periods in special fields: Mr. F. S. Earle and Mr. L. H. Thing, of Cobden, Illinois; Mr. William McAdams, of Otterville, Illinois; Rev. J. P. McLean, of Hamilton, Ohio; Mr. Gerard Fowke, of New Madison, Ohio; Rev. Stephen D. Peet, of Clinton, Wisconsin; Mr. Henry L. Reynolds, of Washington City, and Rev. W. M. Beauchamp, of Baldwinsville, New York. Mr. Rogan and Mr. Emmert having retired from the work, Mr. Fowke and Mr. Reynolds were appointed regular assistants.

The results of the explorations and field work of the division and a discussion of results with special reference to the authors of the ancient monuments of the area explored are given in the present volume. Special papers relating to the collections made will be presented in future reports or bulletins.

In attempting to formulate a systematic plan for a work of such magnitude as the exploration of the mounds, great difficulties were

encountered. The region occupied is vast, and the works are scattered over it in great numbers, not by hundreds only, but by thousands. It was at once perceived that to attempt a systematic and
thorough examination of them all, or even of a large number of them,
including surveys and mapping, would involve many years of labor and
the expenditure of a very large amount of money. Neither the force
nor the money necessary for a work of such vast magnitude was available, for the lines of research undertaken by the Bureau of Ethnology
are necessarily many, and none may be unduly pushed at the expense
of the others. On the other hand, to attempt the thorough investigation of the mounds of any single district to the neglect of the area as
a whole, could result only in a failure to comprehend the more important problems connected with the mounds and their builders. Moreover, it should not for a moment be forgotten that the mounds are fast
being leveled by the encroachments of agriculture and under the stim-
ulus of commercial enterprise. Archeologic relics of all kinds have
attained a new value in recent years because of the great increase in
the number of private collectors. Those who gather specimens merely
for sale rarely preserve any data in connection with them, and, although
relics gathered in this haphazard manner have a certain value as
examples of aboriginal art or as mere curiosities, their scientific value
is comparatively small. As a consequence of the leveling of the
mounds by the plow and their despoiling by the relic hunter, opportunities for acquiring a clear insight into the character and methods of
mound-building and into the purpose of their builders, are rapidly
diminishing.

Chiefly for the above reasons a plan was adopted which comprises
the advantage of thoroughness in the case of single mounds and single
groups, and yet permits the work to be carried over a large area. No
attempt has been made to exhaust the local problems of mound-building by a complete examination of the works of any given section.
Nevertheless, such mounds and groups as are believed to be typical of
their class have been examined with care and thoroughness. By the
method of a careful examination of typical structures in the various
districts it is thought that the end aimed at has been secured—that is,
the collection of data necessary to an understanding of the more general and important problems relating to the mounds and the mound
builders. The exhaustive examination of many single groups and the
study of local problems is left to the future. It is hoped that this
important work may be undertaken largely by local societies whose
resources, when inadequate, may be supplemented by state aid.

The questions relating to prehistoric America are not to be answered
by the study of its ancient monuments alone, but also by the study of
the languages, customs, arts, beliefs, traditions, and folklore of the
aborigines. If any of these monuments are the work of an extinct

people, this fact can be satisfactorily determined only by a comprehensive study of the subject; if all are attributable to the races found occupying the continent at the time of its discovery, the necessity for a broad scientific method is equally apparent.

The most important question to be settled is, "Were the mounds built by the Indians?" If a careful examination and study of the antiquities should result in deciding it satisfactorily in the affirmative, then the questions relating to the objects and uses of these ancient works would be merged into the study of the customs and arts of the Indians. There would then be no more blind groping by archeologists for the thread to lead them out of the mysterious labyrinth. The chain which links together the historic and prehistoric ages of our continent would be complete; the thousand and one wild theories and romances would be permanently disposed of; and the relations of all the lines of investigation to one another being known, they would aid in the solution of many of the problems which hitherto have seemed involved in complete obscurity. Should the result of the examination give a decided negative answer to the question, one broad field would be closed and investigation limited in the future to other lines. In either case a great step toward the ultimate solution of the problem would be taken and the investigations restricted within comparatively narrow limits.

The director of the Bureau of Ethnology was desirous, therefore, that this important question, the origin of the mounds, should if possible be definitely settled, as it is the pivot on which all the other problems must turn. By following the plan adopted and using proper care to note the facts ascertained, without bias, not only would the facts bearing on this important question be ascertained, but the data would be preserved for the use of archeological students without prejudice to any theory.

Premising that accuracy as to details and statements, without regard to their bearing on any special theory, has been considered the chief and all-important point to be kept constantly in view in all the operations of the division, the methods of work pursued (except during the first year, when want of experience caused some of the details of accurate work to be omitted), have been substantially as follows:

First, a full and correct description of the groups examined, giving the topography of the immediate locality, the form, characters, and dimensions of the works and their relations to one another was written out, accompanied by diagrams and figures illustrating these descriptions.

As a rule each mound explored was measured before being excavated, and, if it varied from the ordinary conical type, a figure of it was made. As the exploration proceeded the character and thickness of the strata and the exact positions of the skeletons and relics found in them were noted in a memorandum book. In many cases where there was promise of important finds, outline figures, both of the horizontal and vertical sections, were drawn on which the positions of the skeletons and relics were marked as found.

Every effort possible was made at the time of collection to obtain all the facts in reference to each specimen. The assistants made full notes in the field and attached a number to each specimen before packing and shipping. Descriptive lists, with corresponding numbers, were forwarded with each shipment. All collections thus made were sent direct to the Bureau of Ethnology, and there, after being opened, examined and compared with the field catalogue, the numbers of the Bureau series were attached, and the collections forwarded to the National Museum, where the Museum numbers were placed upon them. After this a comparison was made, in most cases by the collectors themselves, to see that the memoranda, numbers, and articles agreed and were given correctly. The final catalogues contain not only the collector's, Bureau, and Museum numbers, which form checks upon one another, but also the name of the article, the locality, the collector's name, and remarks indicating the conditions under which each was found. These particulars are, of course, incomplete for specimens purchased and donated.

As an illustration, the heading of the columns and one line from the general catalogue are given here:

Collector's number.	Bureau number.	Smithsonian number.	Name of article.	Locality.	Collector.	Remarks.
398	6832	116021	Boat-shaped pot.	Lenoir group, Loudon county, Tennessee.	John W. Emmert.	From mound No. 2, by skeleton No. 49.

Two copies of this catalogue were made, one to be retained by the Bureau, the other to be transmitted with the specimens to the Secretary of the Smithsonian Institution, for use in the National Museum.

Although the specimens are included in the general collection of the National Museum, they are so carefully marked and numbered that by reference to the catalogue any article can easily be found and the precise locality ascertained from which it was obtained, with the attendant circumstances. In order to accomplish this, the collections made by the Bureau were retained until this accuracy was assured and the duplicate catalogues made out and compared. By reference to the following report all the particulars known regarding them may be learned, also all the facts in reference to the works from which they were obtained.

The number of specimens collected by the division since its organization is not less than 40,000. Among those procured by the field assistants, which constitute by far the most valuable portion, will be found not only almost every variety of material, form, and ornamentation hitherto obtained in the United States east of the Rocky Mountains, but also many new and interesting kinds.

The chief value of the work to archeologists, however, it is believed will be found in the descriptions of the mounds explored and groups examined and surveyed. In order that students of American archeology may have as complete illustrations as possible of groups and forms, not only are figures given but in numerous instances the complete field notes of surveys and measurements are added.

The sections in which operations have chiefly been carried on are as follows: Southwestern Wisconsin and the adjoining sections of Minnesota, Iowa, and Illinois; the northeastern and southeastern parts of Missouri; the western part of southern Illinois; the eastern part of Arkansas; certain points in northern and western Mississippi; the Kanawha Valley of West Virginia; eastern Tennessee, western North Carolina, and northern Georgia. Some work has also been done in northern Florida, New York, Ohio, the Wabash valley, Kentucky, western Tennessee, Alabama, southwestern Georgia, and the Dakotas. Hundreds of groups have been examined and in most cases surveyed, platted, and described. Over 2,000 mounds have been explored, including almost every known type of form, from the low, diminutive, circular burial tumulus of the north to the huge truncated earthen pyramid of the south, the embankment, the stone cairn, the house site, etc. Every variety of construction hitherto known, as well as a number decidedly different in detail, have been examined. Some of the latter are very interesting and furnish important data. Particular attention has been paid to the mode of construction and methods of burial in the ordinary conical tumuli, because these furnish valuable evidence in regard to the customs of the builders and aid in determining the different archeological districts. Many ancient graves and cemeteries and also several caches and cave deposits have been explored.

Perhaps the most important portion of the collection from an archeo logical view is the pottery, of which some 1,500 specimens have been obtained, including most of the known varieties and several that are new in form and ornamentation. It is believed that this collection will be found to contain most, if not all, of the hitherto known types of textile impressions and some that are unusual. As the history of each specimen is known and its genuineness unquestioned, the collection will be of great value to antiquarians.

An unusually large number of polished and pecked celts has been secured, including every known pattern and variety yet found in the area investigated. Special value attaches to this collection of celts from the fact that it has been obtained mostly from mounds and hence affords a means of comparing true mound specimens with surface finds.

The number of stone pipes obtained is proportionally great, including a large percentage of the usual forms and some new ones. But the most important fact in relation to this part of the collection is, that it so supplements other collections that the archeologist is enabled to trace the evolution of the comparatively modern and historic form from the "Monitor," or supposed earliest mound pipe. Moreover the record of localities whence the pipes have been taken may indicate the geographical line of this evolution.

A number of copper articles, including nearly all the types hitherto known, are in the collection. In addition to these, among the new forms are specimens of two new types decidedly the most important yet discovered. These were obtained from both mounds and stone graves.

The collection of engraved shells obtained from mounds probably exceeds any other in the country in number, variety, and importance.

The specimens of textile fabrics and remnants of matting, though not numerous, are important and valuable. Among these is a large and well-preserved specimen of each class found in a cave deposit where the burial could not have taken place more than a hundred years ago; yet they are of precisely the pattern and stitch found in the mounds and impressed on typical mound pottery. With the cloth and matting were also the bone implements used in weaving the former.

The collection of chipped flint implements, stone axes, discoidal stones, gorgets, etc., is large. Among the stone articles are parts of three well-made stone images which must have been nearly one-half life size. Bone implements, shell, etc., are in fair proportion.

As it was important that the explorations should be carried on during the winter as well as the summer, it was found advantageous to work in the northern sections in the summer and move southward as the cold advanced. Each assistant at the close of the working year made a report of his operations during that time. These reports would have been incorporated as furnished, but, as in most cases they related to different sections investigated during the same year, this would have prevented a systematic presentation of results, and hence the idea was abandoned, and the data obtained have been arranged geographically by states and counties. This method, however, is subject to the objection that county lines are liable to frequent changes and seldom correspond with the natural lines which influenced primitive settlement. Notwithstanding this objection, the fact that these political divisions afford the only means of defining localities on the maps of the present day has governed in selecting the method for this report.

Mounds are frequently described and illustrations introduced which are seemingly unimportant. The object of this will be apparent to every archeologist, for seemingly unimportant works afford the student a means of comparison and furnish him with valuable negative evidence which otherwise would not be available. Moreover, in the preparation of the report, I have proceeded upon the theory that no fact should be omitted, however trivial it may now appear, as a time may come when it will supply needed evidence in archeological investigations.

The geographical order in which the report is arranged is as follows: First, the Mississippi valley proper, commencing with Minnesota and Wisconsin and proceeding southward; next, the Gulf States from Mississippi eastward, after which follows the Appalachian district, including North Carolina, eastern Tennessee, and West Virginia, then Ohio, Pennsylvania, New York, and Michigan.

The territory over which the explorations have been carried is large, and, from necessity, no one section has been exhaustively examined for reasons given above. Suffice it to say that the chief object kept constantly in view was the search for types. But this included types of form, of modes of construction and internal arrangement, of methods of burial, of contents, and of indications of uses, etc.

The illustrations are original with a few exceptions. Those which are copied are chiefly from previous publications of this Bureau. A few, however, are from the annual reports of the Smithsonian Institution, the electrotypes being kindly loaned for this purpose.

Before concluding this preface I wish to acknowledge the many favors the division has received both in prosecuting the field work and in preparing the report. We have been kindly received in all portions of the country to which our operations have extended, the citizens always showing a commendable desire to encourage our work and to give us all the information possible. Here and there permission to explore mounds has been refused, but such refusal has generally been based on valid reasons.

To the assistants who have carried on operations in the field I extend thanks for the zeal and faithfulness with which their work was performed. I am also indebted to Mr. W. H. Holmes, Rev. W. M. Beauchamp, and Mr. Gerard Fowke; and also to Mr. Reynolds for valuable papers, and to Mr. James D. Middleton for the plats and results of the surveys made by him of works in Ohio and elsewhere.

It is proper to state here that only a partial study of the articles collected has as yet been made. Papers by specialists, describing and discussing them, are being prepared and will appear hereafter.

C. T.

REPORT ON THE MOUND EXPLORATIONS OF THE BUREAU OF ETHNOLOGY

By CYRUS THOMAS.

INTRODUCTION.

Before introducing the report of field work it will not be amiss to call attention to the various kinds of ancient monuments found in the area over which the explorations extended.

It is somewhat strange that, notwithstanding the large number of works devoted wholly or partly to the antiquities of our country, which have appeared since the publication of the "Ancient Monuments," by Messrs. Squier and Davis, no attempt has been made to rectify their imperfect and faulty classification. Their division of these antiquities into "Constructions of Earth," "Constructions of Stone," and "Minor Vestiges of Art," is sufficient for practical purposes so far as it goes, and the same may be said of the division of the first class into "Enclosures" and "Mounds." But their further classification into "Enclosures for Defense," "Sacred and Miscellaneous Enclosures," "Mounds of Sacrifice," "Temple Mounds," etc., is unfortunate, as it is based on supposed uses instead of real character, and has served to graft into our archeological literature certain conclusions in regard to the uses and purposes of these various works that, in some cases at least, are not justified by the evidence. For example, there is not a particle of evidence that any inclosure was formed for religious or "sacred" uses, or that any mound was built for "sacrificial" purposes in any true or legitimate sense of the term. Yet author after author, down to the present time, has adopted this classification without protest. It is only in some very recent works that objections to it begin to appear.

Failure to correct this faulty classification is doubtless due to the difficulties which lie in the way of satisfactorily grouping the variety of forms presented and to our imperfect knowledge of the uses and objects of these works. Nadaillac, after alluding to the various forms, remarks that "these facts will show how very difficult, not to say impossible, is any classification,"[1] a statement which anyone who

[1] Preh. Amer. French Edn. p. 90-Engl. Edn. p. 87.

attempts a systematic arrangement will be disposed to accept as true. Any attempt in this direction must be, to a large extent, arbitrary and a tentative arrangement. Nothing more than this is claimed for the classification here presented, which is limited to the works of the area now under consideration. Were it not for the absolute necessity of grouping under designated heads in order to simplify the work, no attempt in this direction would be made at this time.

It is undoubtedly desirable to adopt some arrangement agreeing with the European classification if this be possible, but a comparison of European antiquities with those of North America will soon satisfy any one of its impracticability. The chronological arrangement into four classes, to wit, Paleolithic, Neolithic, Bronze, and Iron, is conceded to be inapplicable to America. Evidences of the two stone ages may possibly yet be found, and a copper age be substituted for the bronze, but the likeness will extend no farther. I may add that, personally, I doubt very much if this classification into ages has been of any advantage to archeology.

As the first step, all antiquities of this region are considered as belonging to three general divisions:

(1) *Monuments, or local antiquities.*—Those antiquities that are fixed or stationary, which necessarily pertain to a given locality or place, as earthworks, stoneworks, cave dwellings, mines, quarries, etc.

(2) *Movable antiquities, or relics and remains.*—Those which have no necessary connection with a given place or locality, such as implements, ornaments, and other minor vestiges of art; also human and animal remains, etc.

(3) *Paleographic objects.*—Inscriptions, picture writings, symbols, etc., whether on fixed stones or transportable articles.

Although this arrangement is confessedly an arbitrary one, it is adopted because it appears to be a practical working system by which the lines of distinction are somewhat rigidly drawn. Moreover, it is adapted to the two methods of investigation and study, viz, in the field and in the museum.

THE FIXED OR LOCAL ANTIQUITIES.

The fixed or local antiquities of the section under consideration consist chiefly of earthworks, stoneworks, cave deposits, mines and quarries, and might be classed under these heads but for the fact that some belong partly to one class and partly to another; for example, while most mounds are built entirely of earth, some consist wholly of stone and others are partly stone and partly earth; then there are other local antiquities which can not be properly classed under either of these headings. The nearest approach, therefore, which can be made to a satisfactory classification is to group the individual monuments according to types of form and external characters, reference being made to uses only where these are obvious.

The variety of ancient works so far as form and modes of construction are concerned, is almost endless, but all may be included, in a general way, under the following primary headings, viz, Mounds, Refuse Heaps, Mural Works (such as inclosures, embankments, etc.), Excavations, Graves and Cemeteries, Garden Beds, Surface Figures, Hearths or Camp Sites, Hut Rings or House Sites, and Ancient Trails. Besides these as belonging to separate heads are Mines and Quarries, Cave Deposits, and Petroglyphs.

MOUNDS.

The term "mound," as used throughout this report, is limited to the artificial tumulus and is not intended to include walls, embankments, refuse heaps, or other works not usually classed as "mounds" in this country, though the lines of distinction between the examples which approximate each other in form are apparently arbitrary.

The tumuli or mounds are the most common and most numerous of the fixed works, being found throughout the region under consideration, and, in fact, constituting the larger portion of most of the groups. The forms are so varied that it would tax the imagination to devise one that is not represented. There is probably one exception and a somewhat remarkable one, as it is that which enters into the idea of a true pyramid. The form alluded to is the pyramid with true successive stages. There has been, it is believed. no mound found in the United States east of the Rocky Mountains, with successive stages running entirely around the structure. In other words, the form figured by Pidgeon in the frontispiece to his "Decoodah" as the type of the "ancient American battle mound," is without a representative in the United States.

Although so varied, they may for convenience be arranged in four classes, as follows: Conical tumuli, elongate mounds, pyramidal mounds, and effigy mounds.

CONICAL TUMULI.

Under this head are placed all those rounded, artificial heaps or hillocks which seem to have been cast up with some special object in view— that is to say, are not such mere accumulations of rubbish as the refuse heaps. The form is usually that of a low, broad, round-topped cone, but as at present found, is, in consequence of wear by the plow and the elements, often that of an irregular heap distinguished from the refuse heap only by internal evidences.

Mounds of this type are the most common of our ancient monuments, being found throughout the region under consideration, sometimes isolated, but more usually in association with other works. There are, in fact, few groups of ancient works to be found where mounds of this kind are entirely wanting.

They vary in size from a slight, scarcely perceptible swell in the surface of the ground to elevations 80 or 90 feet high, and from 6 or 8 feet to 300 feet in diameter at the base.   As a general rule the burial mounds are of this form.

The term " conical," although used in its widest and most general sense, is scarcely broad enough to include all tumuli that are referred to this class.   The circular or nearly circular base is the usual form, but oval and pear-shaped mounds, especially the former, are not rare. Some two or three of a crescent shape have been observed, but these are exceptional cases.   There are also some irregular forms which must be placed in this class if we would avoid multiplying divisions in our classification to an unwarranted extent.   These are mostly irregular heaps, similar to " refuse heaps," but which, as internal evidence shows, can not be properly placed in the latter category.

As the further subdivision of the class must be determined chiefly, if not wholly, by what the interior of the works presents, this part of the subject will be left for a subsequent chapter.   However, it may be stated here that no attempt has been made to divide the conical tumuli into any further subclasses than burial mounds, and those not designed for burial purposes.

ELONGATE OR WALL MOUNDS.

This division is intended to include those singular elongate works which seem to be confined strictly to the effigy-mound district.   The only characteristic which distinguishes them from the conical type is their wall-like form; in fact many of them, as may be seen by referring to Dr. Lapham's "Antiquities of Wisconsin," might very properly be called walls.   This wall-like form is apparent even where the length is not great compared with the width; in other words, they seldom assume the oval shape.   The width varies from 20 to 40 feet; the length from 50 to 900 feet, though the height seldom, if ever, exceeds 4 feet. They appear to be simple lines of earth cast up from the adjoining surface, and are seldom used for burial purposes, and even in these few cases it is evident the burial in them was a subsequent thought, their construction having no reference to this use.   The object in building them is yet an unsolved riddle.

PYRAMIDAL MOUNDS.

The typical form of this class is the truncated, quadrangular pyramid.   In some examples these are so reduced in height, compared with extent, as to assume the appearance of mere earthen platforms; others have a terrace extending outward from one or two sides.   Although the mounds of this class are usually four-sided, some are circular or rounded, and a few pentagonal, but all are flat on top.   The wearing by the plow and the elements has in most cases destroyed the sharp outlines of the original form, so that it is difficult, sometimes, to determine this satisfactorily.   In such cases the statements of the early observers become important.   But few works of this class are found in the northern districts.

These are the singular earthen structures designed to represent animal figures, the human form, or some inanimate object. They are limited almost exclusively to the Wisconsin district, the only known exceptions being two or three in Ohio and two in Georgia. It is more than probable that most of those to which the name "Man-mound" has been applied are really bird effigies.

Although not belonging strictly to the mound class in the restricted sense, yet, as being nearest allied thereto, we may arrange here the refuse heaps and house sites.

REFUSE HEAPS.

Although the ancient heaps of rubbish in America are composed chiefly of marine and fresh-water shells, the more comprehensive term refuse heap is given here, as under it may be placed not only the accumulations of shells but other heaps known as kitchen-middens and open-air workshops or accumulations of flint chips. The heap is distinguished from the mound by the fact that the former is a mere accumulation of rubbish, while the latter is constructed with a specific design in view.

HOUSE SITES AND HUT RINGS.

The works to which the latter of these names is applied are usually small rings or circles of earth from 15 to 50 feet in diameter, the inclosed area being more or less depressed. This name is given them because it is now conceded that they are the remains of circular houses or wigwams. In Arkansas and some other southern sections these rings appear to be replaced by low, flattened, mostly circular mounds in which are found the indications or remains of houses which in most cases appear to have been consumed by fire. To these and other similar remains, though not covered by mounds, the name "house sites" has been applied.

CAIRNS.

With the exception of two or three effigies and the accumulations of flint chips the only stone mounds found in the United States east of the Rocky Mountains are of the conical type. The term "cairn" is sometimes applied to the smaller and more regular ones, though "mound" is the word usually employed in this country in referring to them.

INCLOSURES, WALLS, ETC.

The works included in this class are inclosures, usually formed by a more or less complete surrounding wall of earth or stone; lines of walls, sometimes single, sometimes in pairs forming parallels; embankments, and other mural works.

INCLOSURES.

In this class are included some of the most important and most interesting ancient monuments of our country. In form they are circular, square, oblong, oval, octagonal, or irregular. Those which approach regularity in figure and symmetry in their parts are either circular, square, or octagonal, and with a few exceptions are found in Ohio and in the immediately adjoinining sections of Kentucky and Indiana, and in West Virginia.

Of the irregular in form there are several types; some, especially those located on level ground where the space is ample, are irregularly circular and in most cases are flanked by a ditch. This form is common in the region bordering the northern lakes; others, often of stone or stone and earth combined, are found on elevated points, the figure being determined by the boundaries or character of the area inclosed. Inclosures of this type are frequently incomplete, a steep bluff, river, or lake shore forming one or two of the sides.

In this class are included a few works where there is in reality no wall, a ditch or line of picket holes alone marking the boundary.

WALLS AND EMBANKMENTS.

Double or parallel lines of walls are in most, if not all, cases connected with other works. Single lines of wall are mostly those of earth or stone built across the neck of some projecting bluff or promontory or across some peninsula formed by the bend of a river or curve in a lake shore. These are evidently works thrown up for defensive purposes, often to protect a temporary or permanent village.

EXCAVATIONS.

This term is usually applied to those basin-shaped or irregular, artificial depressions often observed in connection with the more extensive groups. It is apparent in many cases that they have been dug with no other object in view than to obtain dirt with which to build a mound or construct a wall. But in other cases they have evidently been made for some specific purpose.

CANALS AND DITCHES.

Indications of what may be properly designated as "ancient canals" have been discovered at a few points, mostly in the south.

Ditches are seldom found except in connection with inclosures or defensive works. Yet, a few instances occur where they seem to replace the walls of inclosures, one of the most important groups of the South being thus surrounded.

PITS AND CACHES.

Pits as a matter of course are excavations and in a strictly systematic arrangement should be placed under that head, nevertheless as the present object is to indicate the various works by the terms which have come into use in this country, they are given separately. They are funnel-shaped or deep, cup-shaped excavations, the depth being greater in proportion to the diameter than the ordinary basin-shaped excavations. Those works, to which the term is applied, appear to be of two classes: First, the holes or pits made in digging for flint, which are usually known locally as "Indian diggings," and which, as a matter of course, are irregular as to form and size; second, the regularly formed pits of but a few feet in diameter and depth, and used chiefly as places for secreting food and other articles, and hence often called "caches."

GRAVES AND CEMETERIES.

The ancient graves of the area under consideration in this report are of various types, nevertheless there are one or two of these which form such important factors in discussing the question of the origin and builders of our ancient monuments that it is proper they should be mentioned here.

One of the most common and most important types is the "box-shaped stone grave" or cist. This is in the form of an oblong box, constructed of unhewn stone slabs. Graves of this kind are found isolated, in groups forming cemeteries and also in mounds.

Stone graves of other forms occur usually in mounds, but as these will be noticed hereafter it is unnecessary to describe them here.

The term "cemetery" is, of course, used in its ordinary sense.

GARDEN BEDS.

These are certain surface indications, found chiefly in Michigan and Wisconsin, leading to the conclusion that the limited areas covered were formerly under cultivation. These indications are generally low, parallel ridges, as though made in planting corn in drills. They average about 4 feet in width, and the depth of the space between them a few (6 to 8) inches. They are generally arranged in beds or plats.

OTHER FEATURES.

Fire beds or hearths are nothing more than the indications of local fires, found in mounds and in the ground. Camp-sites are usually indicated by marks of fire and other signs of temporary camps found near the surface of the ground.

Ancient trails are sufficiently indicated by the name.

Surface figures are outline figures of the human or animal form or of some object formed on the surface of the ground with pebbles or bones.

Cave deposits are sufficiently indicated by the name.

So far as ascertained the ancient mines of this country were limited to those of copper, flint, and other stone and mica.

12 ETH——3

FIELD OPERATIONS.

MANITOBA AND THE DAKOTAS.

Within the area embraced by the province of Manitoba and the two states of Dakota five distinct types of prehistoric works have been observed. First, the mounds of the Red river valley, extending from Grand Forks, North Dakota, down to Selkirk, Manitoba. Secondly, the mounds along the Souris river in Manitoba and North Dakota, and in Benson, Ramsey, and Walsh counties, North Dakota. Thirdly, the mounds along the Big Sioux river in southeast Dakota and Iowa associated with bowlder circles. Fourthly, the bowlder circles found upon the highest lands of the Missouri and James rivers and their tributaries, associated with bowlder outlines of animals. Fifthly, the house sites in the form of basin-shaped depressions found along the Missouri river from the mouth of the Niobrara to 10 miles north of Bismarck.

Of the first class, namely, the mounds bordering the Red river of the North, there are but few, scarcely more than twenty now visible. Those visited by the Bureau agent were in the vicinity of Grand Rapids, North Dakota, St. Andrews, and East Selkirk, Manitoba. All had been explored. They occur singly rather than in groups. The soil of which they are composed appears to be that of the surrounding land. They are conical in form, and none at present exceed nine feet in diameter, though originally, before they were cultivated and excavated, they were doubtless higher. Human burials were found in all.

SOURIS RIVER MOUNDS.

Along the Souris river, in southwestern Manitoba and south of the junction of the South Antler, numerous mounds were discovered. They extend over an extensive area up the river, and it is not improbable that they may be found following the stream across the border into Dakota.

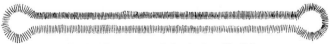

Fig. 1.—Elongate mound, Souris river, Manitoba.

They occur in large groups, are conical in form, and range from 1 to 5 feet in height and from 30 to 40 feet in diameter. In their midst were seen the two forms of elongate mounds, one as shown in Fig. 1, the other the ordinary oblong form. As the discovery of these mounds was incidental, and our assistant carried no instruments upon the trip, no survey of any of the groups could be made. The elongate mounds or embankments range from 1 to 2½ feet high and from 100 to 300 feet long. In the form showing expansions or mounds at the ends, no perceptible difference was noticed between the height of the mounds at the ends and the bank between them. They are composed of gravelly soil and in size are, as a rule, quite low and broad. Seven of these peculiar mounds were noticed just south of the junction of the South Antler, within 1 mile of Sourisford post-office. Two or more of this form sometimes occur either in an imbricated position or at right angles to one another, as in Fig. 2. Their positions and appearance are such as to preclude the idea that they were used for defense.

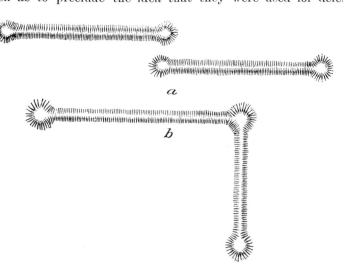

FIG. 2.—Elongate mounds, Souris river, Manitoba.

Some are situated along the brink of the precipitous river bluff, while others lie farther inward upon the prairie level. The mounds or expansions at the extremities of one were dug into but without any result.

Mounds of this character were also seen down the Souris river across the South Antler. Large numbers of them lie between that stream and the junction of the North Antler, 1½ miles distant. They range from 2 to 8 feet in height. The larger ones had been explored by settlers. One, 5 feet high, situated near the left bluff of the South Antler, was composed throughout of the gravelly prairie soil, intermingled considerably with buffalo bones. The bones of four skeletons were found in a confused condition in a pit dug in the original surface of the ground. A catlinite pipe of the tubular variety, curving towards the base, and many pieces of broken pottery were found with them. These pottery fragments are ornamented with straight incisions, and are composed of a mixture of clay tempered with fine sand or pulverized granite.

In another, 8 feet high, composed, like the last, of the gravelly prairie soil, the bodies or bones of five skeletons were found buried beneath the original surface. They appeared to have been originally placed in a sitting posture in a circle facing one another. The bones bore no signs of decay. The decayed remains of timbers were found just above them. Five catlinite pipes of the tubular variety, a polished sandstone tablet engraved on one side with the rude figure of a turtle, and two small clay cups about the size of an ordinary finger bowl, accompanied the skeletons. The pottery has an incised spiral ornamentation extending all around the bowl and a corrugated rim. The composition is a mixture of clay with fine sand or pulverized granite. Quite a fresh piece of bark, apparently bearing the marks of a steel knife along one edge, was also found accompanying these remains.

In front of the residence of Mr. Amos Snyder and near the junction of the North Antler with the Souris there is a mound 3½ feet high. This, not having been previously disturbed, was examined by Mr. Reynolds. He found the mound composed throughout of the uppermost prairie soil, very compact and hard, and the remains of a single skeleton on the original surface of the ground. The bones, which were extremely well preserved, were disarticulated and piled together, as though interred after having been denuded of the flesh, and the cranium placed on top. Fragments of buffalo bones and pottery, similar in type to that above described, except that some of it was ornamented with straight parallel incisions, were found mingled among the earth. Also, three fine specimens of arrow heads of a light grayish flint and a portion of some polished implement of bone, ornamented with straight incised lines which appear to have been produced with a sharp steel knife.

Another mound, 4 feet high, about 50 rods westward from the last, was opened the same day. A trench 3 feet wide was cut through it to the original surface, but no burial remains were found. Many broken buffalo bones, and pieces of pottery similar in description to those found in the other mounds, were intermingled in the earth throughout. A cross trench was abandoned for lack of time.

Other mounds similar to these in appearance were seen on the opposite or right bank of the Souris river on the Rumball farm, 3 miles from Sourisford post-office. One situated near the dwelling is 3 feet high and 30 feet in diameter. It appeared to be composed, like those just described, of the soil of the surrounding land. Not far from the dwelling were also four oblong mounds, similar in form to that shown in Fig. 1. One of them measured 225 feet long and 24 feet broad. Their height is scarcely more than 1 foot above the surrounding level.

While at Grand Forks, North Dakota, it was learned from Prof. Henry Montgomery that elongate, conical, and connected mounds, resembling these in character, and containing specimens of the types found in the mounds of this region, exist in Benson, Ramsey, and Walsh counties, North Dakota.

SIOUX RIVER MOUNDS.

Along the Big Sioux river, within 10 miles south of Sioux Falls, and principally where the river forms the boundary line between Minnehaha county, South Dakota, and Lyon county, Iowa, there are said to be about 275 mounds. Many of these our assistant visited. They were found situated on both sides of the river in clusters or groups upon the highest points of the river hills, or upon the broad terraces of the valleys. One of the groups visited demands special attention. It is situated in the extreme northwest corner of Lyon county, Iowa, and comprises about 50 mounds of the simple conical type, averaging about 4 feet in height. In the midst of the mounds, at times touching the skirt of them, are seen stone rings, circular and oblong, made with the granite bowlders of the prairie. It is evident that these mark the site of an old village, the circles and oblong outlines indicating the positions of the lodges, the skin coverings of which were held down by stones. With probably one or two exceptions every circle or oblong form presents a break, namely, a place about 3 or 4 feet wide where the continuity of the figure is broken by the absence of stones. This appears to have been the entrance, and in most instances it is at the southeast, or the point most protected from the cold northwest winds. They average about 30 feet in diameter. The number of lodges constituting the original village could not be counted, since about half of the group lies in a field, the original prairie sod of which has been disturbed by the plow of the settler and the stones utilized by him upon his farm. In the undisturbed portion they outnumber the mounds about three to one. The mounds are so intermingled with the stone figures as to show that the two were constructed by the same people. In some instances, where the stone circles nearly touch the skirt of a mound, the wash from the latter has covered the stones upon that side while those on the other side are fully exposed. This seems to indicate that the mounds had been constructed after the circles or lodges had been placed. These boulders are, as a rule, half imbedded in the prairie sod, but this fact does not necessarily imply great antiquity. Investigations had been made among these mounds by Mr. F. W. Pettigrew, of Sioux Falls, but the result did not indicate that they were used for burial.

About half a mile up the valley, on the same river terrace, there is another large village site consisting of mounds and circles similar in all respects to those just described. Each of these groups is upon a most beautiful and expansive terrace peculiarly adapted for a permanent village. Groups of mounds, fewer in number and smaller in size, are to be seen in the vicinity upon the most commanding points of the river heights, and in these human interments have been discovered. These may therefore be considered as the burial places of this people.

About 100 rods to the south of the village remains above described there is an irregular earthen inclosure somewhat octagonal in outline,

formed by throwing up the dirt from the inside. At one point it inter-
sects a low mound, seated upon the original surface, in which the owner
of the land discovered a skeleton. The inclosure embraces about 10
acres, but no survey could be made at the time it was visited on account
of the high corn crop that covered it. The group of mounds and stone
circles above described has been accurately surveyed by Mr. F. W. Pettigrew, of Sioux Falls.

BOWLDER CIRCLES.

In addition to the bowlder circles above described there are some of
another class, which, from all accounts, appear to be quite common
throughout the Dakota country. They differ from the others in that
they are unaccompanied by mounds, and average as a rule only
17 feet in diameter. The bowlders are much smaller and are scattered about irregularly instead of approximating a perfect circle like
the others. They are, however, like these, half imbedded in the soil.
Formerly they were doubtless much more common, but now they are
found principally, if not altogether, upon the highest ridges or buttes
overlooking the valleys. Those visited by the Bureau agent were situated on Medicine Butte, near Blunt, South Dakota, and Snake Butte,
6 miles up the Missouri river from Pierre, South Dakota. They occupy
the most commanding points of the buttes. In fact their locations are
the very best in all those regions for grand, extensive views. No relics
of any description are found about them, and everything seems to point
to temporary occupation only. Their positions and character indicate
that they are the sites of old teepees, and this is confirmed by the testimony of all the old Indians and "squaw men" who were questioned
as to their origin. In former times, they say, bowlders were the chief
means by which the Indians held down the skins of their lodges, and
even now it is resorted to in some of their temporary camps. Each of
these groups of stone circles is accompanied by the outline figure of an
animal, made with such small bowlders as are available upon the site,
and similar to those composing the circles about them. Like the latter, they are half embedded in the ground. The figure accompanying
the group upon Medicine Butte is a snake outlined with two rows of
bowlders. These boulders vary in size, those of the body being larger
than those of the tail, and that forming the nose or mouth larger than
those forming the head. The curvature of the body, the head, and the
eyes are all well defined. A sketch of this snake figure is given with
others of the same type by Mr. T. H. Lewis in the American Anthropologist, vol. 9. His description is full and accurate. The figure accompanying the group on Snake butte above Pierre is that of a turtle,
the figure of which, with dimensions as ascertained by our assistant, is
given herewith (Fig. 3). It is 15 feet in length, and 7 feet across the
body, and is composed of 83 stones varying somewhat in size, though
not as much so as those forming the snake above described. A num-

ber of smaller stones, as seen in the figure, ran from the neck through the body, which probably was intended to represent the "life line," thus giving the figure a mythical significance. This effigy lay in a direction S. 38° E. and was situated not far from the bluff of the Missouri river, to which it lay parallel. Tepee remains, or stone circles, are to be

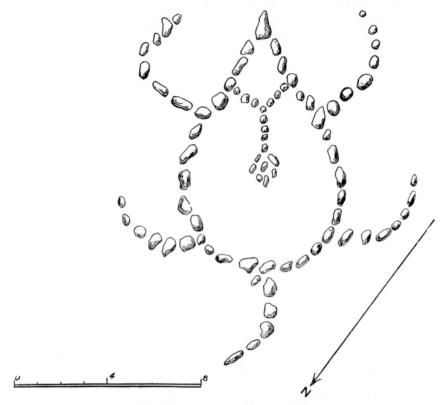

FIG. 3.—Turtle figure, Hughes county, South Dakota.

seen between it and the edge of the bluff, and on the other side, to the east, commencing about 150 feet to the south, is a long line of bowlders of similar description, which extend northerly fully 200 rods. In some places these stones are compact and set closely together, but towards each end they thin out by becoming farther and farther apart. At the north end this line terminates in a small heap of stones. This was torn down, and the earth beneath dug into, but without result. There are about 35 stone circles in this group, and the turtle figure lies in the midst of them, as does also the line of bowlders just described. They are seen on both sides of it to a certain distance. Some are also to be seen upon the high crest of the butte. These circles are of the same dimensions as those seen on Medicine butte, but the stones did not seem to be so deeply buried, in fact, they were as much above the surface as could be expected. Ashes were found upon digging in the center of one of the circles, though no such traces were seen in others that were examined here and upon Medicine Butte. The animal figures on each of these sites are poorly situated, and in each case there are circles that almost touch them. Indeed, their position with reference to the latter is such as to make them seem incidental to the prior location of the tepees. If they were intended as objects of veneration and worship, as has been conjectured, there are sites in the immediate vicinity of each better adapted for such purposes—sites where the archeologist more naturally expects to find them.

HUT RINGS.

Many old village sites, resembling each other in every respect, are to be seen on either side of the Missouri river from the mouth of the Niobrara to about 10 miles above Bismarck. Unlike the house sites of this type in southeast Missouri and Illinois no mounds accompany them, though kitchen-middens, resembling mounds, are seen among those farther up the river. Two of these village sites were examined by the agent of this Bureau near the town of Pierre, South Dakota. They occupied the second terrace of the river and were indicated by numerous basin-shaped depressions, sometimes, especially in the larger cases, with a distinct rim or bank around the edge. They are, at present, from 1 to 2 feet deep and 75 feet in diameter. Occasionally one is seen fully 4 feet deep and 75 feet in diameter. In some instances the entrance was indicated by a graded depression leading outward. At least fifty such hut rings were counted on each of these sites. It was apparent, however, that originally there were many more, for many had disappeared before the encroachments of the town. Numerous signs of former occupation abound, and refuse heaps are seen about almost every depression. Some of these refuse heaps were examined and found to consist chiefly of river loess, and to contain invariably much fragmentary pottery, discarded stone implements, and the broken bones of the buffalo and other food animals. Indications of fire were discovered in the center of the depressions or house sites. The ornamentation of the pottery is, as a rule, similar to that of the Mandans, except that it appears to be a trifle ruder. The characteristic incised lines of the Mandan pottery are constantly met with. The tempering material employed is also the same, it being a fine silicious sand. Quite a large group of these remains is to be seen farther down the river at the mouth of Chappelle creek, accompanied by the remains of an earthen inclosure. It was situated on the edge of the bank of the creek near its junction with the river. A distinct outside ditch was apparent on the side unprotected by the bank. It had a single entrance way and the interior was well filled up with house sites of the above description. The number of these depressions within and without the fort indicate a much larger population than is known of any of the villages of the Missouri when first visited by whites. Another very large group, similar to these in every respect, is, according to Mr. J. C. Collester, of Redfield, South Dakota, to be seen at the mouth of the Moreau river. These are doubtless the remains of the Arikara village that was visited by Lewis and Clarke in their passage up the Missouri in 1802. The houses of the Arikaras were described by these explorers as circular dome-like structures, the floor of which was about 3 feet below the level of the surrounding land. But in house-building, as in the manufacture of pottery and other things, the customs of the Arikaras, though somewhat ruder, resembled those of the Mandans, and the similar remains farther up the river may therefore be due to that people. Some are probably the remains of the Mandan villages described by Lewis and Clarke in 1802, and by Catlin in 1833.

MINNESOTA.

The only explorations made in this state on behalf of the Bureau were at and about the noted Pipestone quarry in Pipestone county and in the extreme southeastern county.

PIPESTONE COUNTY.

The only group known in this county is that in the vicinity of the sacred Pipestone quarry.

A sketch and description of the locality as it formerly appeared, together with an account of the Indian traditions relating to it, may be found in Catlin's "North American Indians."[1] These works consist of low mounds and an irregular inclosure in the vicinity of Pipestone.

One of these mounds, which for convenience is designated No. 1, is of the usual low conical form, 28 feet in diameter and 3 feet high. An exploration revealed nothing but the dark, adhesive soil of which it was chiefly composed, and stone-fragments, a few of which were catlinite, bearing traces of tool marks. No bones, ashes, or charcoal were observed. Possibly it was nothing more than a refuse heap.

No. 2 is the mound represented in Catlin's sketch[2] of which he gives the history, and which, according to his statement, was built two years before his visit, probably in 1836 or 1837. He does not give the diameter, but estimates the height at 10 feet. Nicollet saw and noted it in 1838. Col. Norris noticed it in 1857, when, although apparently undisturbed, it was but little over 6 feet in height. When he saw it again in 1877 it bore the marks of having been opened, and he then learned that a cranium and some of the weapons and trinkets deposited with the Indians buried had been unearthed and carried off. He found a perforated bear's claw and some glass beads among the angular fragments of rock lying in the excavation. Making a thorough excavation when he visited it in 1882 on behalf of the Bureau, he found near the center some decayed fragments of wood, one of them apparently the

---

[1] Vol. 2, p. 144.   [2] North American Indians, Vol. 2, p. 164, Pl. 270.

short, thick, perforated stock or handle of an Indian whip. With the dirt of the mound were mingled many fragments of stone.

No. 3, composed of earth and angular fragments of stone, was probably a refuse heap from the diggings.

Nos. 4 and 5, similar to No. 3.

No. 6 is a conical tumulus on the bank of the creek about a hundred yards above the falls, and is 6 feet high. Projecting through the sod was a stone slab 2 feet long, nearly as wide, and 9 inches thick, standing nearly perpendicular in the center; beneath it, lying flat, was another of similar form and size. Beneath the latter was a pile of broken stones, mostly of smaller sizes, among which were pieces of pipestone, badly decayed fragments of human and coyote bones, but no entire skeleton. In this were found charcoal and ashes, the only instance of their presence in any of the mounds at this place. They were underneath the pile of stones. A small stone drill was found with them.

No. 7, which is nearer the cliff than No. 6, is about 30 feet in diameter and 4 feet high. It was but little else than a pile of angular stones.

No. 8 is simply a bastion-like enlargement of the large circular earthwork at one of its numerous angles (see No. 8, Fig. 4), about 4 feet high. Nothing was found in it, not even the angular stones so common in the other mounds.

No. 9 is a circular mound inside the earthwork, 20 feet in diameter and 4 feet high. In this was found a single skeleton lying at full length upon the right side, head north, on the original surface of the ground. It was covered with a layer or pile of stones about 2 feet thick, and was so much decayed that the bones and even the teeth crumbled to dust when exposed to the air. No implements or ornaments were found with it except a flint lance head, some arrow points, and two or three rude scrapers which were near the breast.

No. 10 is merely an enlargement of the west horn of one of the circular works lying east of the large inclosure, of which more particular mention is made hereafter. Its diameter was found to be 20 feet; height, 3 feet. Nothing of interest was found in it.

CIRCULAR AND CRESCENT EARTHWORKS.

These interesting works are situated about 2 miles a little north of east from the quarry; a plan of them is given in Fig. 4. It is not certain that Catlin saw these works, although they are situated near the great war trail from Flandreau and the pipestone quarry to the Minnesota (formerly St. Peters) river. Nicollet, however, noted them in 1838, and makes special mention of two circular inclosures, or "camps," as he calls them, estimating the circumference of one at 2,000 feet.[1]

The shape of this inclosure, which appears to be the only complete one in the locality is shown at *a*. The circumference, according to

---

[1] Senate Report No. 237, 26th Congress, 2d session, p. 14.

Col. Norris's measurement, is 2,386 feet, the wall varying in height from a few inches to 4 feet. It has two well-marked and distinct openings, or gateways, one at the north, the other at the southeast, besides smaller and less evident ones. In the southern half is mound No. 9, heretofore mentioned.

The crescent-shaped embankments, which are roughly sketched in the figure, are about half a mile east of the large inclosure. They are simply earth embankments of slight elevation and are possibly parts of unfinished works.

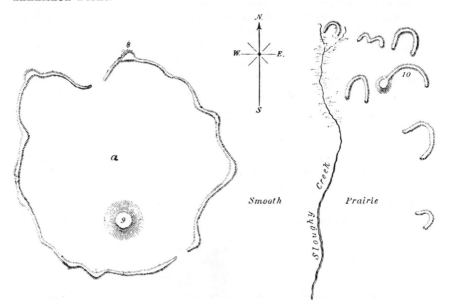

FIG. 4.—Inclosures and mounds, Pipestone county, Minnesota.

Nicollet's statement in regard to the works is as follows:

After having reconnoitered distinct marks of a buffalo path, we unexpectedly fell upon a circular breastwork of about 2,000 feet in circumference and sufficiently elevated to protect the bodies of those who are defending themselves within. The principal entrance is still marked by the places where the chiefs or principal personages of the nation had their lodges, the situation of these always indicating not only the main access to the camp but also the direction whence the enemy was advancing.

Two miles further on, accordingly, we met with another camp of a similar character. As the system of defense was on neither side more complicated than just described, it would seem that they had been erected during a long talk the result of which might lead to a war; whilst the small number of tumuli that are found within the breastwork would seem to imply that both parties remained in presence for some time, though there was no important battle fought.

The Sioux have lost the reminiscences of these camps, and merely conjecture that they were occupied during the settlement of difficulties between the Tetons and Yanktons.

Col. Norris thinks he saw in 1842 the second inclosure mentioned by Nicollet, but did not find it in 1882.

HOUSTON COUNTY.

The extreme southeast corner of this county, which is also the southeast point of the State, is just north of the town of New Albin, Iowa, at the confluence of Winnebago creek with the Mississippi river. About 1 mile north of this point, upon the summit of a cliff rising vertically 400 or 500 feet from the eastern or Mississippi valley side, and barely accessible for a pedestrian up the steep and somewhat rocky slopes on the south, west, and north sides, three mounds were found and excavated, with the following results:

No. 1, about 30 feet in diameter and 6 feet high, of the usual conical form, on the summit of the cliff, had already been opened sufficiently to remove therefrom the skeleton of an Indian warrior, together with his gun, hatchet, etc. The excavation which had been made was still partly open, and extending downward only about half the depth of the mound. Digging down about a foot farther into the hard, light-colored earth, apparently a mixture of clay and ashes, a stone slab was encountered something over 2 feet long, something less in width, and 5 inches thick, of the same kind of rock as that found in the cliff. This was lying flat upon others of various sizes, which were placed edgewise, so as to form an oblong cist or coffin, but so small that its contents, the decayed bones of an adult, were nearly in a heap, as though the skeleton had been folded and deposited after the flesh was removed. No implements or other vestiges of art were found.

FIG. 5.—Mound vault, Houston county, Minnesota.

No. 2. This interesting mound, situated about 50 feet south and somewhat down the slope from No. 1, is circular, about 25 feet in diameter and 6 feet high. An excavation had been made in the top to the covering or top slabs of a stone vault or chamber which further exploration showed the mound to contain. The form of this vault is shown in Fig. 5. It was about 6 feet in diameter throughout, and before it was disturbed probably reached nearly or quite to the top of the mound. Some of the top rocks had been thrown down, and, with some small human bones, were lying on the slope of the mound. The floor of the inner area was filled to the depth of about 2 feet with charcoal, ashes, and split bones of animals, among which were found two roughly chipped scrapers or skinners. This accumulation had not been disturbed by those who made the first partial opening above, and who, as was learned, had unearthed the skeleton of an Indian child, with some modern beads and other trinkets.

No. 3 is situated about 100 feet north but much below No. 1, and is about 20 feet in diameter and 4 feet high. Nothing whatever of interest was found in it.

Nothing was observed in relation to these works differing from the usual conical mounds found in this region except the peculiar com-

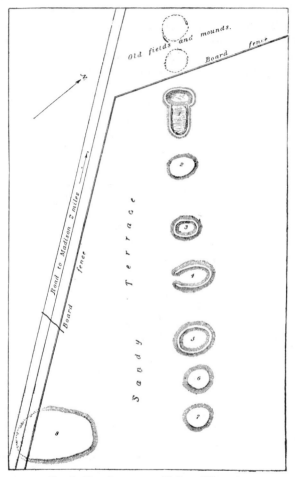

Fig. 6.—Mound group near Madison, Wisconsin.

manding position they occupy and the walled structure in No. 2. Of the numerous bluffs in this region no other affords such a clear and extensive view of the surrounding country as this. An unobstructed view of the Mississippi for a considerable distance above and below, also up the Little Iowa, Winnebago, and other streams, is here obtained. From this position can be seen the mouth of Root river on the west, and on the east the deep-gorged Badaxe, and the last battlefield on which Black Hawk fought. It must therefore have always been a favorite lookout point or station

Mound No. 2 seems to have been purposely built upon the sunny slope of the cliff just below the summit, so as to be sheltered from the cold northwest winds and partly also from observation, while its occupants had a nearly unobstructed field for observation and signals. Unlike the other mounds near it which were opened, it was composed wholly of the rock and soil taken from around it. Possibly it may have been used as a sentry post or signal station. The charcoal, ashes, and split bones of animals were doubtless the remains of the feasts and fires of the watchmen; the burial of a child in the mound was intrusive and by modern Indians. Not a fragment of pottery was found at this locality, although within 10 miles of the pottery circle in Iowa, which will be noticed hereafter.

WISCONSIN.

The explorations in this State were confined chiefly to the southwestern counties, though brief visits were made to some other localities, where a few mounds were opened and some interesting groups sketched.

DANE COUNTY.

One group near Madison, which does not appear to have been noticed by other explorers, was examined. This is situated about 2 miles southeast of the capital and just beyond the mounds near Lake Wingra, described by Dr. Lapham. The works consist chiefly of earthen circles and ovals, which in some cases surround excavations, and are shown in the annexed Fig. 6. As will be observed, with the exception of No. 8, which is a low mound, situated a short distance southwest of No. 7, they are in a single straight line running northwest and southeast. No. 1 is a double excavation, one portion oval, the other in the form of a horseshoe and surrounded by a ring of earth 1 foot high; depth of excavation from 3 to 6 feet. Nos. 2, 6, and 7 are low mounds, but the others, which are rings of earth, are about 5 feet high on the outside and 4 feet on the inside, the surface of the inner area being raised about a foot above the surrounding level. The respective diameters are as follows: No. 2, 32 feet; No. 3, 34 feet; No. 4, 36 feet (greatest diameter); No. 5, 28 feet; No. 6, 26 feet; No. 7, 28 feet. No. 1 is 45 feet long. No. 4 is not a complete circle, having a wide opening toward the southwest.

These are certainly not the work of the white man, as they present nothing in common with his habits or customs. They appear now just as they did in 1844, except that some of those in the field at the northwest end of the row have since been nearly obliterated by the plow.

CRAWFORD COUNTY.

The first group of mounds of this county noticed here is found on the bluff just above the confluence of the Wisconsin and Mississippi rivers, and about 5 miles southeast of Prairie du Chien. The bluffs at this

point form a sharp promontory jutting out toward the west, with remarkably steep and partially precipitous sides on the south and west, rising
about 150 feet above the general level. This is capped by a sharp
sandy ridge, rising in the central portion another hundred feet. On
the crest of this ridge are four mounds, which may be numbered 1, 2, 3,
and 4. Between 1 and 3 is a somewhat broad and flattened depression, in which mound No. 2 is situated. The ridge beyond the point
gradually descends toward the east, becoming broadened and flattened
as it recedes. On this portion there are 10 small circular mounds in a
single line.

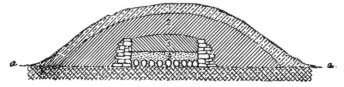

FIG. 7.—Walled vault in mound, Prairie du Chien, Wisconsin.

Mound No. 1 (Fig. 7) was opened in 1876 by Judge Bronson, who
found at the base of it some six or eight skeletons lying stretched out
horizontally, and covered by a dry, light colored mortar, which had run
between and incased the bones and even filled some of the crania. As
only the southern portion had been opened, the remainder was carefully

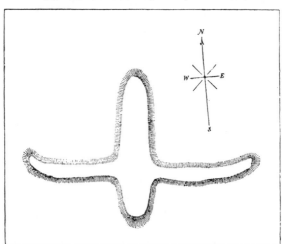

FIG. 8.—Bird mound, Prairie du Chien, Wisconsin.

explored. The dried mortar was very hard and difficult to dig through,
but the pick soon struck some flat limestone rocks, which, when
fully exposed, were found to be parts of a rough wall about 3 feet high,
from the natural surface of the ground, and 8 feet long. In the opposite side of the mound, about 12 feet from this and parallel to it, was
another similar wall.

The ends of these walls are shown in Fig. 8. Between them on the
natural surface had been placed side by side a number of skeletons

lying flat and lengthwise, parallel with the walls. The heads of these are indicated by the row of little circles at the bottom. Immediately over these was the layer of mortar; next above this, between the walls and also over the vault forming the body of the mound, was a layer of very hard, light-colored clay mixed with ashes, but no charcoal. The top covering was of sand and soil to the depth of 18 inches. Before it was disturbed this mound was about 35 feet in diameter and 6 feet high. There was no evidence of fire, but much tending to show that the builders intended to incase the skeletons in a water-tight covering of mortar, which, when originally placed there, must have been sufficiently soft to run into all the interstices between the skeletons, these all being filled, as were also some of the crania.

On the depression of the ridge heretofore mentioned, between mounds 1 and 3, is mound No. 2. This is an effigy representing a bird (see Fig. 8), the dimensions of which are as follows: Length of body, 42 feet, or total length, including the head and neck, 60 feet; of each wing, 42 feet; greatest width of body, 18 feet, and greatest elevation 3 feet. Several pits dug in it proved it to have been constructed wholly of the yellow

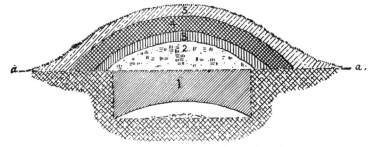

FIG. 9.—Section of mound and pit, Prairie du Chien, Wisconsin.

sand and soil of the ridge. No bones or relics of any kind were found in it. The indications lead to the belief that it was carved out of the ridge, rather than thrown up, the wings still forming the crest from which the head and body slope gradually in opposite directions.

Mound No. 3 (Fig. 9) is a few paces to the west of No. 2 and on slightly higher ground. This was also partially explored by Judge Bronson in 1876, and, with the further examination by the Bureau agent, gave the following results: First, a covering of soil and sand a foot or more in depth (No. 5), next a layer (No. 4) of calcined human bones nearly 2 feet in depth, without order, mingled with charcoal, ashes, and reddish brown mortar (clay and sand), burned as hard as a brick. Immediately below this was a layer (No. 3) 1 foot thick of mortar consisting largely of sand burned to a brick-red color. Below this in the layer marked 2 were found the skeletons of 15 or 16 individuals without any arrangement, mingled with which were charcoal, firebrands, and ashes. The bones were charred and portions of them glazed with melted sand. The mass appears to have been first covered with

12 ETH——4

soft mortar, which filled the spaces, and the burning done afterward. Scattered through the mass were lumps of clay apparently molded in the hands, which the fire had converted into rude bricks. The bottom of this layer corresponded with the original surface of the ground. Further excavation to the depth of 2 or 3 feet revealed a circular pit in the original soil (marked 1 in the figure) about 6 feet in diameter, the bottom of which was covered an inch deep with fine chocolate-colored dust. The strangest fact regarding this pit is that, although the intermediate filling between the 1-foot depth at the bottom and the layer above (the bottom of the mound proper) was similar in appearance to the ordinary soil of the ridge, yet the under portion of it remained arched over the 1-foot space beneath. It was probably hardened by the fierce fire above.

Eleven paces west of this mound, situated on the brow of the bluff, is No. 4, only 12 feet in diameter and 4 feet high. This mound, like the others, was built up chiefly of very hard material resembling mortar. In it was a single skeleton lying on its right side; placed in the form of a circle on the left hip were 140 shell beads. The left arm lay extended along the upper side; the knees were drawn up at right angles to the body. Although now so dry and hard, the mortar at some former time had made its way into and filled the skull and fitted neatly around the bones which were all well preserved and had not been disturbed since they were first placed there. Around the neck were 12 shell beads and 5 small perforated sea shells.

On the lower, broadened portion of the ridge, in its eastern extension, as before remarked, is a row of ten small circular mounds, which vary in height from 2 to 4 feet and in diameter from 19 to 32 feet. In addition to these there are also here two elongate mounds or embankments in a line with each other, their nearer ends being about 3 paces apart. The longest of these is 192 feet in length, the other 45 feet. Two of the circular ones were opened, in both of which were found some indications of their having been used for burial purposes, but in one only were any bones obtained. No relics of any kind were discovered. From the larger ones which had been previously opened a number of stone and copper implements were obtained.

A short distance to the northwest of the foregoing group are traces of many circular mounds, some long earthworks, and effigy mounds. In fact nearly the whole area of the valley of Prairie du Chien township appears to have been once literally dotted over with ancient works. Many of these are effigy mounds representing deer, bears, rabbits, etc., apparently in droves, sometimes with and sometimes without other works intermingled. But in all cases the effigies are heading southwest, trending with the general course of the river in this section.

At the upper end of the prairie are a number of effigy mounds and long works as yet but little injured, while others in the fields are nearly obliterated. Some of these have been opened and various relics obtained, mostly those accompanying intrusive burials.

The greater number of a row of large circular mounds, situated on a high bottom between the old bayou and the river, have been removed to make way for buildings, railroad tracks, etc., this being the only part of the immediate area which is not overflowed when the water is very high. Many articles of stone, copper, iron, and silver were found, but mainly from intrusive burials, though obtained at or beneath the base.

One large mound, 70 feet in diameter and 10 feet high, was still unexplored. This was opened. It had been considerably defaced, especially on the western side. According to tradition it was a noted burial place of the Indians, which was certainly confirmed by the result. The surface or top layer was composed mainly of sand and alluvial earth to the depth of some 3 or 4 feet. Scattered through this in almost every part of the mound were found human skeletons in various stages of decay and in different positions, but mostly stretched horizontally on the back. Mixed with these remains were fragments of blankets, clothing, and human hair; one copper kettle, three copper bracelets, one silver locket, shown in Fig. 10; ten silver bracelets similar to the one shown in Fig. 11, one having the word "Montreal" stamped on it; and another the letters "A. B.;" two silver ear-rings; six silver brooches similar to Fig. 12; one copper finger ring; one double silver cross (Fig. 13); one knife handle; one battered bullet, and one carved wooden pipe similar to those at present in use. In fact, the

FIG. 10.—Silver locket from mound, Prairie du Chien, Wisconsin.

top layer to the depth of 3 or 4 feet seemed to be packed as full of skeletons as possible without doubling them, and even that had been resorted to in some cases.

FIG. 11.—Bracelet of silver from mound, Prairie du Chien, Wisconsin.

FIG. 12.—Silver brooch from mound, Prairie du Chien, Wisconsin.

Carrying the trench down to the original surface of the ground there was found, near the center, at the bottom, a single skeleton of an adult, in the last stages of decay, and with it a stone skinner, stone drill, scraper, fragments of river shells, and fragments of a mammoth's tooth.

The earth below the thick upper layer was mixed with clay and ashes or some other substance evidently different from the surrounding soil, but not so hard as the mortar-like material found in the mounds on the bluff.

The main road from Prairie du Chien to Eastman follows chiefly the old trail along the crest of the divide between the drainage of the Kickapoo and Mississippi rivers. Along this are a number of effigy mounds; some of them in cultivated fields, but the larger number in the forest, the trees upon them being of the same size as those on the surrounding ground. Most of these, which are in part referred to in Mr. Strong's notes and figures,[1] were surveyed and platted. A plat of the southwest part of Crawford county showing the location of the groups mentioned is given in Fig. 14.

FIG. 13.—Silver cross from mound, Prairie du Chien. Wis.

The first group measured is situated about a quarter of a mile north of Eastman, on Sec. 18, T. 8 N., R. 5 W. These mounds lie west of the road, partly in the woods and

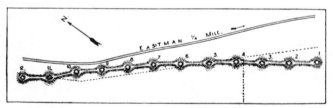

FIG. 15.—Earthworks near Eastman, Crawford county, Wisconsin.

partly in the field. The group is in fact a series or chain of low, small circular tumuli extending in a nearly straight line northwest and southeast, connected together by embankments as shown in Fig. 15. They are on the top of the ridge.

---

[1] Smithsonian Report of 1877, pp. 239-246.

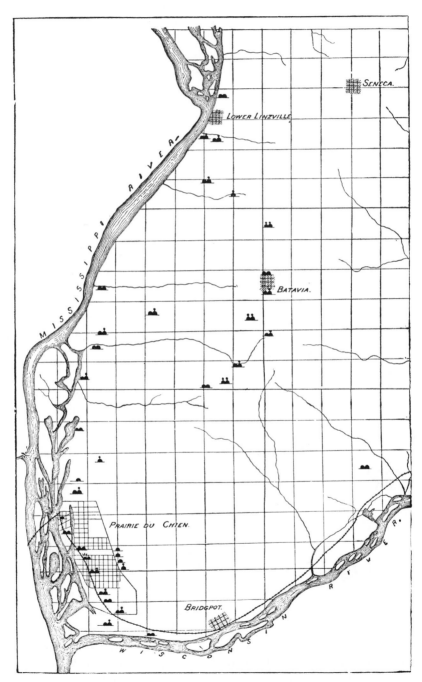

FIG. 14.—Plat of southwest part of Crawford county, Wisconsin.

Commencing with mound No. 1, at the southern end of the line, the direction and distances from center to center and the diameters and heights are as follows:

Number of mound.	Course.	Distance.	Diameter, north and south.	Diameter, east and west.	Height.
		Feet.	Feet.	Feet.	Feet.
1..			22	25	3
1 to 2..	N. 37° W..	55	18	22	3
2 to 3..	N. 33° W..	55	19	23	3
3 to 4..	N. 25° W..	56	18	22	2½
4 to 5..	N. 36° W..	56	23	24	3
5 to 6..	N. 31° W..	56	22	25	3
6 to 7..	N. 34° W..	56	20	21	2½
7 to 8..	N. 43° W..	53	23	27	2½
8 to 9..	N. 36° W..	56	20	18	1½
9 to 10..	N. 36° W..	57	23	25	2
10 to 11..	N. 39° W..	58	27	25	2
11 to 12..	N. 30° W..	57	22	18	1

In the same section, at the village of Eastman (or Batavia), are the remains of two bird-shaped mounds, both on top of the watershed and both heading southward.

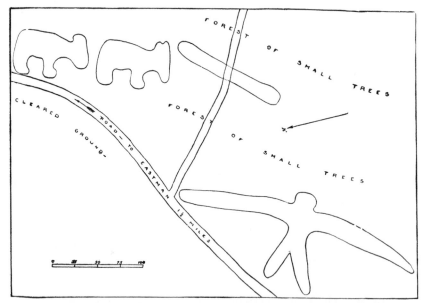

FIG. 16.—Mounds on northeast quarter of Sec. 24, T. 8 N., R. 6 W., Wisconsin.

About 2 miles from Eastman, in the direction of Prairie du Chien, just east of the Black River road, on Sec. 24, T. 8 N., R. 6 W., are three effigy mounds and one long mound, shown in Fig. 16. They are situated in a little strip of woods near the crest, but on the western slope of the watershed and near the head of a coulee or ravine.

This is the group which Mr. Strong represents in his Figs. 12, 13, and 14.[1] The two effigies representing quadrupeds (bears) are headed toward the south, while the other (probably representing some swallow-tailed bird) is headed eastward; the long mound runs northeast and

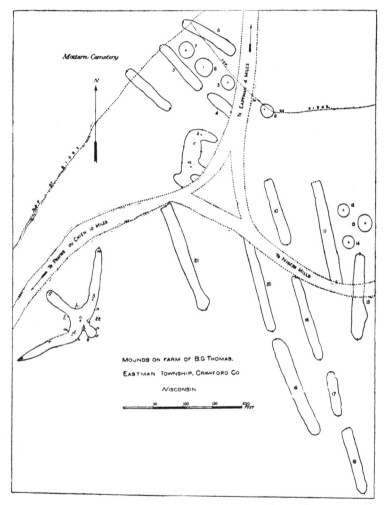

Fig. 17.—Mound group at Hazen Corners, Crawford county, Wisconsin.

southwest. The dimensions of these are as follows: The total length of each of the quadruped figures is about 80 feet, greatest height about 2 feet. The expansion of the wings of the bird from tip to tip is 267 feet; length of the body from top of the head to the tip of the longer branch of the tail, 110 feet; height of the center of the body, 3 feet.

[1] Smithsonian Report, 1877, p. 244.

As will be seen by reference to Mr. Strong's figures, these measurements differ considerably from his. This is due in part, but to no great extent, to the wearing down and consequent expansion since the date of his examination.

The length of the long mound is 120 feet, average width 15 feet, and height from 12 to 15 inches.

HAZEN CORNERS GROUP.

The next group surveyed is situated on Mr. B. G. Thomas's farm, Sec. 36, T. 8 N., R. 6 W., at what is known as Hazen Corners. The mounds are on the crest of the ridge heretofore mentioned and on both sides of the Black River road, 9 miles from Prairie du Chien.

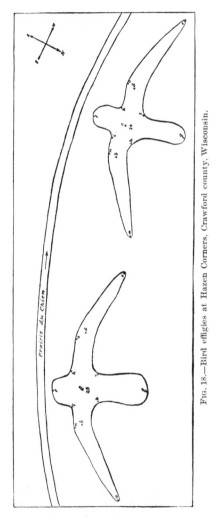

Fig. 18.—Bird effigies at Hazen Corners, Crawford county, Wisconsin.

This is the group represented in Mr. Strong's Fig. 4. It is mostly covered with a growth of small trees, which confirms Mrs. Thomas's statement that when her family first came to this place the ridge here was almost bare of trees.

The main ridge runs a little east of north before reaching this point, but here it curves and branches, one branch running north, the other eastward. A few of the mounds are on the crest, the rest on the southern slope of the ridge that runs eastward and on the eastern slope of the main ridge close to the junction of the branches.

The group consists of 24 mounds, 1 quadruped, 3 birds, 13 long and 7 round mounds, all of which, except two of the birds, are shown in the diagram (Fig. 17); the latter are shown in Fig. 18.

The dimensions of mound No. 1 (quadruped) are as follows: Total length, 98 feet; width over the shoulder to the fore foot, 41 feet; width of body between the legs, 27 feet; width of fore leg near the body, 23 feet; width of the hind leg near the body, 17 feet; distance between the legs at the body, 32 feet; height at highest point, 3 feet. The natural curves of the animal's body are remarkably true to nature.

The following table gives the dimensions (length and width of the long and diameter of the round mounds) of those numbered 2 to 21.

No.	Diameter or length.	Width.	Height.*	Remarks.
	Feet.	Feet.	Feet.	
2	90	13 to 18	3	
3	93	15 to 15	2½	
4	50	14 to 18	2½	This is the measurement of the part remaining.
5	24	....	3	
6	31	....	2½	
7	28	... .	4	
8	102	15 to 19	3	
9	22	....	2	
10	110	14 to 17	....	
11	166	18 to 19	2½	
12	21	....	2	
13	28	....	2½	
14	21	....	2½	
15	136	11 to 17	3	
16	138	14 to 18	3	
17	74	12 to 16	2½	
18	110	13 to 18	2	
19	173	18 to 22	2½	
20	155	13 to 18	2	
21	180	16 to 23	3	

* Approximate.

The dimensions of bird mound (22) are as follows, commencing with the end of the north wing:

	Feet.		Feet.
a to b	84	Width of north wing at tip	8
b to c	44	Width of north wing between tip and curve	15
c to d	27	Width of north wing between tip and curve	15
d to e	100	Width of north wing at curve	18
e to f	34	Width of north wing at body	35
e to g	74	Width of body and tail	15
f to g	108	Width of body at h to l	17
a to e	228	Width of neck, i to k	18
c to h	23	Width of head, p to q	15
c to i	16	Width of south wing at body, k to l	32
c to k	15	Width of south wing at curve, m to o	19
c to l	20	Width of south wing between curve and tip, at r	14
c to m	26	Width of south wing between curve and tip, at r	14
c to n	36	Width of south wing at tip	4
c to o	29		

This effigy lies with head down hill, and the washing from the ridge has filled in between the body and the wings until they are probably lower and narrower than when they were first built. The outline of the south wing is filled with this washing for a distance of 38 feet, and hence its dimensions here could not be accurately determined. It and the mounds numbered 17, 18, and 19 stand on the lowest ground of any of the group. It is about 3 feet high at the point *c* if the measurement is taken from the surface about the head, but only about a foot and a half if taken under the right wing. The surface of the wings and body is rough and rounded, the slopes to the surface of the ground abrupt to the east and gradual to the west. The wings taper and decrease in height to the tips, but the body keeps its height and form.

Mound No. 23 (Fig. 18) is also in the form of a bird with outstretched wings. It lies to the southwest of 22, on top of the ridge, with the head lying crosswise of the highest point.

Mound No. 24 is close to the right or east, on the high part of the ridge, extending in the same direction as 23.

The outlines of both are clear and the slopes to the surface abrupt. The wings curve and taper and decrease in height to their tips, while the bodies of both preserve their height and form. They are covered by a thick growth of young trees. The dimensions of No. 23 are as follows, commencing at the end of the left wing:

	Feet.		Feet.
a to *b*	94	Width of left wing at tip	9
b to *c*	37	Width of left wing midway between	
c to *d*	56	tip and curve	18
d to *e*	90	Width of left wing at body	25
e to *f*	37	Width of body at tail	31
e to *g*	72	Width of body at *h* to *l*	29
f to *g*	109	Width of neck at *i* to *k*	25
a to *e*	240	Width of head at end	24
c to *h*	22	Width of right wing at body	30
c to *i*	23	Width of right wing at curve	25
c to *k*	28	Width of right wing midway be-	
c to *l*	25	tween curve and tip	18
c to *n*	44	Width of wing at tip	7
c to *o*	56		

The measurements of mound 24, also commencing with the left wing, are as follows:

	Feet.		Feet.
a to *b*	94	*c* to *o*	46
b to *c*	35	Width of left wing at tip	6
c to *d*	45	Width of left wing midway between	
d to *e*	95	tip and bend	18
c to *f*	39	Width of left wing at bend	21
c to *g*	71	Width of left wing at body	25
f to *g*	110	Width of body at tail	23
a to *e*	230	Width of body at *h* to *l*	29
c to *h*	26	Width of neck	27
c to *i*	23	Width of head	23
c to *k*	22	Width of right wing at body	25
c to *l*	24	Width of right wing at bend	23
c to *n*	35	Width of right wing at tip	6

The nearest spring is some 300 or 400 yards northeast of the group at the foot of the ridge.

Three of the round mounds of this group were explored, in each of which were found skeletons much decayed. In two of them no specimens, but in the other, on the original surface of the ground at the center, a small stone celt, some pieces of melted lead, and a regularly formed gunflint. These articles were close together and about 2 feet from the skeleton.

Trenches were also cut through the long mounds, which showed that the first 10 or 12 inches were of the ordinary vegetable mold, but the remainder to the original surface, of yellow clay. In one or two places small pieces of charcoal were observed, but nothing indicating burial. The result was the same in all the trenches.

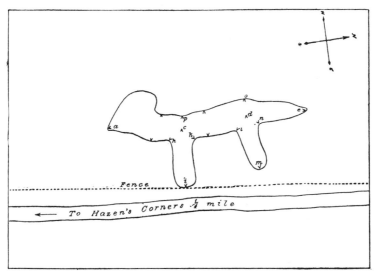

FIG. 19.—Quadruped effigy on Sec. 36, T. 8 N., R. 6 W., Wisconsin.

Northward of this group some 400 yards there is a mound in the form of a quadruped, probably a fox (Fig. 19), partly in the woods and partly in the field on the west side of the road. It is built on the crest of the ridge with the head to the south. The outlines of the body are clear, but those of the head are somewhat indistinct. It gradually decreases in height from the head, where it is about 18 inches, to the end of the tail and legs. It is in the same section as the mounds at Hazen Corners. The nearest water is the spring before mentioned.

The ridge slopes to the east and west from the mound and also falls slightly to the north and south. A partial exploration has been made, but nothing save a good sized rock was dug out of it.

The measurements of this mound are as follows:

	Feet.		Feet.
Length of nose to end of tail, *a* to *e*..	145	Width of tail at body	17
Length of body, *h* to *n*	62	Width of tail at end	3
Length of tail, *n* to *e*	35	Width of body at fore leg, *k* to *p*	21
Length of fore leg	32	Width of body between legs	19
Length of hind leg	30	Width of body at hind legs	20
Width of fore leg at body, *h* to *k*	18	Distance between legs at body, *k* to *l*	31
Width of fore leg at end	16	Distance between legs at toes, *i* to *m*.	50
Width of hind leg at body, *l* to *n*	19	Tip of nose to fore leg, *a* to *i*	64
Width of hind leg at end	13		

The tail is pointed and the ends of the legs are round.

MOUNDS ON SECTION 35, T. 8 N., R. 6 W.

About a mile southward of Hazen Corners on the Blake river road

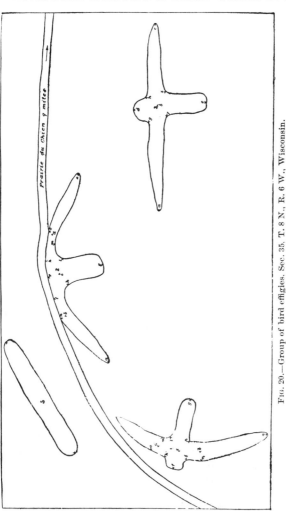

Fig. 20.—Group of bird effigies. Sec. 35, T. 8 N., R. 6 W., Wisconsin.

is a group of four bird-shaped a n d one long mound situated o n t h e NE. of sec. 25, T. 8 N., R. 6 W., at the cross roads. The effigy mounds are west of the road and the long one is east of it. They are all situated on the northern slope of the ridge not far from the top; the heads of the effigy mounds a r e, a s usual, to the south and up the hill.

Three of these ef- figies are of about the same form, the only difference be- tween No. 3 and the others being in the shape of the w i n g s, w h i c h stretch nearly at right angles with the body instead of curving like the o t h e r s. T h e i r bodies are shorter than those at Hazen Corners; otherwise there is but little difference.

The tops of all the mounds in this group are rounded and the slopes abrupt. Like the others they gradually narrow and descend to the tips of the wings.

No. 1 (Fig. 20) is about 3 feet high; No. 2, 3½ feet; No. 3, 2½ feet; No. 4 (Fig. 21) 2½ feet, and No. 5 (Fig. 20) (the long mound), 2 feet.

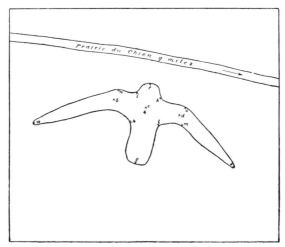

Fig. 21.—Bird effigy, Sec. 35, T. 8 N., R. 6 W., Wisconsin.

The dimensions of No. 1, commencing with the tip of the left wing, are as follows:

	Feet.		Feet.
a to b	82	Width of left wing at tip	7
b to c	28	Width of left wing midway between	
c to d	27	bend and tip	21
d to e	59	Width of left wing at body	26
a to e	161	Width of body immediately under the	
c to f	25	wings	25
c to g	56	Width of tail	20
f to g	81	Width of head at the front	18
c to h	21	Width of right wing at body	23
c to i	20	Width of right wing at bend	21
c to k	21	Width of right wing between bend	
c to l	17	and tip	17
c to m	24	Width of right wing at tip	8
c to n	37	Width of left wing at bend	22
c to o	36		

In No. 2, they are as follows:

	Feet.		Feet.
a to b	71	f to g	69
b to c	40	c to h	18
c to d	48	c to i	29
d to e	74	c to k	22
a to e	209	c to l	18
c to f	15	c to m	34
c to g	54	c to n	56

	Feet.
c to o	54
Width of left wing at tip	5
Width of left wing between tip and bend	17
Width of left wing at road	18
Width of left wing at body	23
Width of body at butt of wings	41

	Feet.
Width of body at tail	23
Width of right wing at body	18
Width of right wing at road	12
Width of right wing between bend and tip	15
Width of right wing at tip	6

In No. 3, they are as follows:

	Feet.
a to b	121
b to c	98
b to d	28
b to e	56
b to f	18
b to g	21
b to h	17
b to i	20
Width of left wing at tip	4
Width of left wing between tip and body	17

	Feet.
Width of body at butt of wings	25
Width of body near the end	26
Width of head	20
Width of right wing at body	25
Width of right wing between body and tip	16
Width of right wing at tip	5
a to c	219

Of No. 4, the measurements are:

	Feet.
a to b	88
b to c	36
c to d	39
d to e	83
a to e	214
c to f	24
c to g	61
c to h	22
e to i	20
c to k	23
c to l	25
c to m	44
c to n	35
c to o	44

	Feet.
Width of left wing at tip	7
Width of left wing between tip and bend	18
Width of left wing at bend	24
Width of left wing at body	30
Width of body at butt of wings	30
Width of body at tail	22
Width of neck at butt of wings	25
Width of head at front	17
Width of right wing at body	28
Width of right wing at bend	23
Width of right wing between bend and tip	17
Width of right wing at tip	5

No. 5, the long mound, is 152 feet long and 19 feet wide at the north end, 22 in the middle, and 20 at the south end.

The tips of the wings, the heads, and tails of the effigy mounds and the ends of the long mound are rounded.

These mounds do not appear to be included in those mentioned in Mr. Strong's paper.

MOUNDS ON SLAUMER'S LAND.

This is a small group consisting of but two mounds, an effigy, and a long mound. They are situated west of the Black river road, just north (10 or 15 rods) of the line between Prairie du Chien and Eastman townships, on SW. ¼ Sec. 35, T. 8 N., R. 6 W., on the top of the ridge in the woods. The ridge slopes from them to the east and west. The group is shown in Fig. 22. No. 1 (the long one) is 142 feet long, 21 feet wide at the north end, 20 in the middle, and 13 at the south end. It is about 2 feet high and extends northwest and southeast.

No. 2, the effigy, 410 feet south and a little west of No. 1, is about 3 feet high, the top round, and the surface tolerably even, with highest point on the back; the slopes to the east abrupt. It measures from—

	Feet.
a to *b*	75
b to *c*	38
c to *d*	41
d to *e*	72
e to *f*	36
e to *g*	70
f to *g*	106
e to *h*	22
e to *i*	20
e to *k*	24
e to *l*	26
e to *m*	49
e to *n*	42
e to *o*	45
Width of left wing at tip	8
Width of left wing between tip and bend	17
Width of left wing at bend	21
Width of left wing at body	23
Width of body at end	20
Width of body at butt of wings.	30
Width of neck at butt of wings.	28
Width of head from *p* to *q*	31
Width of head at end	14
Width of right wing at body	24
Width of right wing at bend	21
Width of right wing between bend and tip	19
Width of right wing at tip	7
Expanse of wings, from *a* to *e*	200

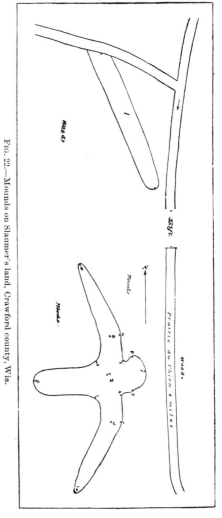

Fig. 22.—Mounds on Slaumer's land, Crawford county, Wis.

The ends of the wings and body are roughly semicircular.

THE COURTOIS GROUP.

About 3 miles north of Prairie du Chien is a group of ordinary conical mounds situated on Sec. 12, T. 7 N., R. 7 W., the general plan of which is seen in Fig 23. The mounds numbered 1 to 9 are on a long, narrow, sandy swell, about 70 or 80 feet wide, which runs north and south, and is just high enough to place them out of reach of the high water of the Mississippi; the others, numbered 10 to 33, are in the adjoining fields.

No. 1. Circular in outline, rounded on top, 60 feet in diameter at the base and 3 feet high. Made of black sandy loam.

No. 2. An oblong, flat-topped mound; length, 60 feet; width, 35 feet, and height, 3 feet. As it was occupied in early times by the house of a Frenchman, and looks as though it had been plowed or graded down, the present form is probably not the original one.

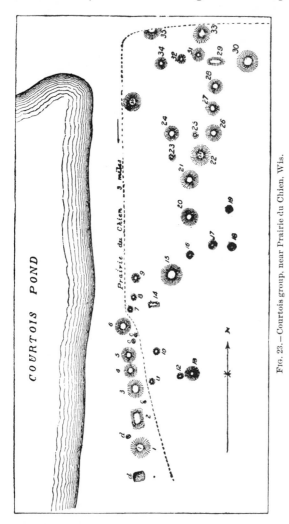

FIG. 23.—Courtois group, near Prairie du Chien, Wis.

No. 4. Similar in size and form to No. 1; 5 feet high. A partial examination of this mound had previously been made, when some specimens were found, but no particulars could be learned in regard to them. It consisted of three layers; first, a top layer, $2\frac{1}{2}$ ft. thick, of black sandy loam; next a thin stratum of silver sand, and a bottom layer, 2 feet thick, of dark muck, slightly mixed with sandy loam. The reexamination revealed nothing save a few fresh-water shells.

No. 5. Conical, 40 feet in diameter and $3\frac{1}{2}$ feet high, had previously been opened by a trench through it from north to south. A further examination brought to light some badly decayed human bones, which had been partially disturbed by the previous explorers, but enough remained in position to show that the bodies, or skeletons, had been folded when buried. These lay on the gravelly substratum of the ridge; hence it is presumed that the thin surface soil had been removed before burial. Nothing more, save a few decayed shells scattered here and there through the mound, was observed.

No. 6. Similar in size and form to No. 1; 4 feet high and composed throughout of dark sandy loam, similar to the surrounding surface soil. The plan of this mound, showing the relative positions of the skeletons and articles discovered, is given in Fig. 24.

In the western side (at *f*), about 2 feet below the surface, was a small deposit of fresh-water shells, but so far decayed that no specimens were saved. At *e* a folded adult skeleton was discovered, with head south and face west; under it lay a small stone perforator and above it a small arrow head. The bones were broken and very soft and the skull was crushed flat; from the indications it would seem that they had been broken before burial.

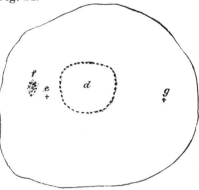

FIG. 24.—Mound No. 6, Courtois group, Prairie du Chien, Wis.

At *d* the original surface of the ridge had been excavated to the depth of a foot and over an area about 12 feet in diameter. In this layer were some 6 or 7 adult skeletons, all folded, with the heads in various directions, but all so soft and badly decayed that none of the skulls could be saved. At *g*, near the eastern side, at the depth of 2 feet, was part of an iron knife blade.

Nos. 3, 7, 8, and 10 were found to consist of dark loam throughout, but furnished no specimens or any evidence of having been used as burial places.

No. 16 is a very small and insignificant mound, scarcely exceeding 20 feet in diameter and not more than a foot in height, though it has evidently been considerably worn down by the plow. Nevertheless it is important as presenting the characteristics of a somewhat peculiar class of mounds quite common in this State, but seldom met with elsewhere; for this reason the figures and details are given more fully than would otherwise be required.

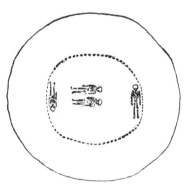

FIG 25.—Plan of mound No. 16, Courtois group, Prairie du Chien, Wis.

Circular in form, as shown by the plan given in Fig. 25, low, rounded, but somewhat flattish, it was constructed of material similar to the surrounding soil, and of the same character throughout, without any indications whatever of stratification. A circular, basin-shaped excavation had first been made in the ground to the gravel, in this case to the depth of 2 feet. The boundary of this excavated portion is indicated by the dotted circle.

Four skeletons were found at the points indicated in the figure, all lying horizontally at full length; 2 side by side near the center on the gravel, with heads south and faces up; 1 at the north side on the gravel, with head west and face northeast, and the other on the south side, with head to the east. No implements or ornaments of any kind were observed. It is probable that tumuli of this character are the burial places of the common people.

No. 17 was similar in every respect to No. 16 except that the excavation was only to the depth of 1 foot, and that in it were 8 folded skeletons in no regular order, heads being in all directions. On the margin of the excavation and rather above the natural surface of the ground was a broken skull.

No. 18, 20 feet in diameter and 2 feet high, unstratified, was composed of earth similar to the surrounding soil. There were no indications that the original surface had been hollowed out in this case, as in most of the others of the group, nevertheless 2 broken skulls were found a little south of the center at the depth of 3 feet, hence 1 foot below the original surface. A few feet northwest of the center, scarcely a foot below the surface of the mound, were 3 folded skeletons, and in the center another lying at full length, head west and face up. The height of the mound had been reduced by plowing.

FIG. 26.—Mound No. 20 (section), Courtois group, Prairie du Chien, Wis.

No. 19, 25 feet in diameter and 2 feet high, was similar to No. 18. Broken human bones were found in this tumulus to the depth of 6 inches, and 3 folded skeletons at different depths in no regular order of burial. But, what is somewhat singular, the skull in each case had been disconnected from and placed on top of the bundled bones of the skeleton.

No. 20, 70 feet in diameter and 5 feet high. This mound, as will be seen by the section shown in Fig. 26, was stratified as follows: Top layer of soil, 18 inches; next a hard mortar-like substance, or clay mixed with ashes, 2½ feet; below this a layer of black, sticky, wet earth, 1 foot, and a bottom layer of sand 1 foot thick, extending to the gravel 1 foot below the original surface of the ground. On the west side, in the top layer, at the depth of from 9 to 12 inches, were 6 folded skeletons, and at the head of each a single sandstone of considerable size. Other human bones occurred in the same layer at a depth of from 6 to 9 inches,[1] which had been disturbed by the plow. In this layer was also a small pile of lead ore, on it some burned

---

[1] The measurements indicating the depth of skeletons and articles are always to be understood to the upper surface thereof from the top of the mound.

bones, and on these a folded skeleton with the head west, a lance head by one shoulder, and a stone implement near by.

Near the center, in the hardpan or mortar-like layer (No. 2) immediately under layer No. 1, was a folded skeleton with head east. By the head was a broken clay vessel. Directly under this, in layer No. 3, was a broken clay pot. At the west side, in the bottom or sand layer, was an extended skeleton, head east. Under the body a spearhead, and under the head a few copper beads. Some copper beads were also found around the ankles.

No. 21. Sixty feet in diameter and 3 feet high. The first stroke of the spade brought to light broken human bones, which lay close to the surface and appeared to have been disturbed by the plow, as they were not in regular order. Near the center, a foot down, lay a folded skeleton with head west, and by it a broken pot. A little to the east of the last, and 3 feet down, was another skeleton stretched at full length, with the head and face up. Under the head were a few copper beads. South of this, and at the same depth, was a small copper ornament, and a short distance southeast of the center, also at the same depth, a fine lance head.

No. 22. Sixty feet in diameter and 5 feet high. First foot, soil; the rest black, mucky earth, with a slight admixture of sand. At the depth of 2 feet were seven skeletons, with heads in various directions, some stretched out with the faces up, others folded, also other bones. At the center, about 3 feet down, were a few rib bones, apparently the remains of a skeleton, over which lay a copper plate. At the same depth, a little south of the center, three silver beads were discovered.

Although the excavation in this case, as in the rest of the mounds, was carried down into the gravel beneath, nothing was found below the depth indicated.

No. 26. Sixty feet in diameter and 5 feet high. Composed of earth similar to the surrounding soil. Near the center, 2 feet down, were two folded skeletons, with the heads northeast. At the heads were two pots, one with the mouth up, the other on its side, and in it a lump of lead ore. Under one of the skulls were two perforated bear's teeth. Several soft sandstones were found in the southwest portion, and under them some very soft human bones, the remains of a body buried here.

Southeast of the mound, and almost adjoining it, is a long, narrow, pear-shaped pile of dirt (not shown in the plat) about 40 feet long, 10 feet wide at the widest point and 2 feet high. A broad trench across the middle revealed nothing except the fact that it was composed of earth similar to the surrounding soil.

No. 23. A small mound 15 feet in diameter, 1 foot high, and of the same type as No. 16. In the excavation originally made in the natural surface was a single skeleton stretched at full length, head southeast and face up and near by it a broken pot.

The surface of the field around the mounds is uneven and looks as though the latter had been heaped up with dirt taken from about them, leaving irregular depressions.

THE DOUSEMAN MOUND.

A mound of the usual conical form, about a mile and a half north of Prairie du Chien, 75 feet in diameter and 5 feet high, situated on the land of Mr. H. L. Douseman, was opened with the following result: It was composed throughout of a black sandy loam, like the surface soil of the field in which it stands, the material probably coming from what seems to be an artificial depression immediately southeast of it. The annexed figure (Fig. 27) is a horizontal plan showing the relative positions of the skeletons and other things discovered therein. Fig. 28 is a vertical section. About 6 feet east of the center (at

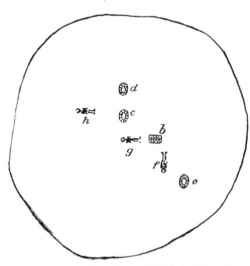

FIG. 27.—Douseman mound (plan), Prairie du Chien, Wis.

b), and 2 feet below the surface, was a regularly built, solid, oblong pile of small rough sandstone and limestone fragments 2 feet long east and west, 18 inches wide, and 15 inches high. Under it were portions of a human skeleton, but the skull was wanting; the bones were very soft and badly decayed.

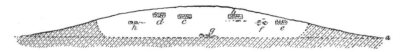

FIG. 28.—Douseman mound (section), Prairie du Chien, Wis.

North of the center, at c, 2 feet below the surface, was another pile of similar dimensions, but oval and hollow. At d was a third of similar size and form, and at e a fourth. These three were regularly built of soft, coarse-grained sandstones, which bear indications of fire, though no charcoal or ashes were on or about them. No bones were seen in or under either of these three piles or little vaults. Quite a number of shell beads were found some 10 or 12 inches below the surface, immediately under which was a folded skeleton f, head south, face west. Remains of two other skeletons were found, one in the center at g, at the base of the mound. This was so completely decayed that fragments of the skull only were left. The other, at *h*, 2 feet below the surface, was similarly decayed.

THE VILAS MOUNDS.

This group, shown in Plate I, is a large one, containing 56 mounds, and is situated on the area bounded by the Mississippi and Wisconsin rivers and the Chicago, Milwaukee and St. Paul Railroad, on Secs. 7 and 8, T. 6 N., R. 6 W., about 3 miles south of Prairie du Chien. They stand on the high sandy bank of the Wisconsin river, in a growth of small trees, some of them being flush with the brink, some on a small table land 10 or 15 feet higher than the others, and the rest on the general level of the prairie, all above high water.

The river banks are about 40 feet higher than the usual water level, the slopes steep, the surface where most of the mounds are situated comparatively flat, but to the northwest it rises in a small table some 10 or 15 feet higher than the prairie that borders on the Mississippi river, and commands an extensive view of the bottoms. The soil is sandy and easy to work, although not deep nor very productive. The trees appear to be of recent growth.

No. 48, S. 77° E. of 49, 62 feet long, extends east and west, and was intended to represent some kind of a quadruped, probably a bear. The eastern end at the time of examination was covered by a heavy growth of corn, and has been so plowed down that its form could not be fully ascertained.

Nos. 23, 24, and 33 were carefully excavated, but furnished no indications of having been used for burial purposes; nor were ashes, charcoal, or relics of any kind found in them; yet under each there was an excavation to the depth of a foot or more. They were composed of dark, sandy soil. Others were examined, but nothing discovered.

THE POLANDER GROUP.

This group is about a mile up the Mississippi river from Lynxville, Crawford county, on Lot 2, Sec. 14, T. 9 N., R. 6 W., at the mouth of a deep, narrow ravine.

The mounds are located partly on top of a narrow bench that runs around the foot of the bluff to the northwest and partly on its western slope. One of them is in the bed of a small creek (now dry) that drains the ravine. A plan of the group is given in Fig. 29. They are mostly simple conical heaps of earth, although there are some long ones in the group. Two of the large ones, close to the foot of the slope, are connected by a long, low embankment, like those found on the Souris river in Manitoba. The majority of them are small and low. The bank upon which they stand is probably 75 feet higher than the road that runs close to its foot on the west side. The bench is covered by a growth of trees, which the owner says have grown up within the last twenty-seven years.

Mound No. 3, situated on the western slope of the bench, is conical in form, about 45 feet in diameter and 7 feet high. Commencing at the top, there was first a thin layer of vegetable mold 2 inches in thickness (*a*, Fig. 30); next a layer, mostly of clay, slightly mixed with sand, which had probably washed from the bluffs, 3½ feet thick (*c*); below this a layer of clay, very hard, 18 inches (*d*); then a layer (*b*) of loose, fine, dry dust, which gave out a peculiar odor; and lastly,

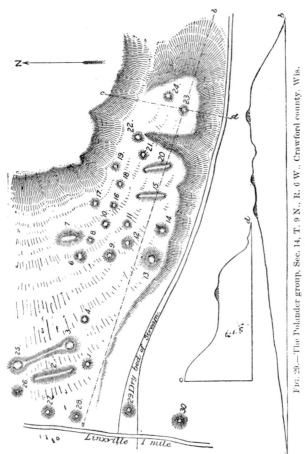

corresponding to the original surface of the ground, a thin layer, apparently composed of decayed vegetable matter (*e*). Beneath this was an excavation about 1 foot in depth, 8 feet wide, and 12 feet long. Owing to the slope on which the mound was placed, this had been cut into so as to make a level bed, on which the bodies were deposited. Here were twelve skeletons—ten of adults and two of children. The two children were in the northeast corner of the pit; the bones were in confusion. Three of the adult skeletons were in the middle

Fig. 29.—The Polander group, Sec. 14, T. 9 N., R. 6 W., Crawford county, Wis.

of the platform; the bones were disarticulated, but those of each skeleton formed into a bundle. Two skulls and a few of the bones of the body were found between the children and the other three, one of the skulls lying on top of the other. In the south end of the pit were three skulls in fragments and the remains of five skeletons in a confused heap. A single skull, but no other bones with it, was found in connection with a few flat stones in the hard clay layer at the depth of 2 feet.

Mound 9, 26 feet in diameter and between 2 and 3 feet high, stood on the same slope as the preceding and, like it, had an excavation in the original surface of the ground, but much smaller, the length being only 4 feet, the width a little less, and the depth 1 foot. A foot from the top, near the center of the mound, lay a bundled skeleton, apparently an intrusive burial. Nothing was discovered in the pit except what were supposed to be decayed remains of two bundled skeletons.

Mound 8, one of the smaller tumuli of the group, presented some marked variations from those described. The diameter was scarcely 20 feet and height 3 feet. In the central portion, 2 feet distant from each other, were two stone graves, oval in outline, each 3½ feet long by 3 feet wide, built up of cobblestones, and had probably been closed over dome-fashion at the top, though this portion had apparently fallen in. Over these, covering the tops about 6 inches and filling the spaces between and each side of them, was a layer of surface soil, and covering this a single layer of loose sandstones about 6 inches thick. In one grave were two bundled skeletons; in the other, three.

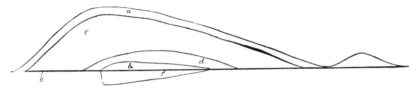

FIG. 30.—Mound No. 3 (section), Polander group, Crawford county, Wis.

Mound 6, circular, 23 feet in diameter and 3 feet high, was constructed as follows: Commencing at the top, there was first a layer, 2 inches thick, of vegetable mold, then a foot of surface soil; next a single layer of rough stones of various sizes; next a layer of earth 1 foot thick. Immediately under the layer of stones, nearly in the center of the mound, were two folded or bundled skeletons, lying on some loose stones. These stones were found to be part of a wall lining a pit in the original soil. This pit was 4 feet long by 3 feet broad between the walls, which were of a single thickness of cobblestones, the sides somewhat flaring, the corners nearly square, 18 inches deep, and sides lined entirely around with stones. Lying on the bottom were the skeletons of three adults and one child, all folded.

In mound No. 1 nothing was found save three good-sized stones. In No. 17 were three folded skeletons. In 29 there was a pile of stones somewhat in the form of an inverted cone, measuring 10 feet across the upturned base and tapering to a point at the depth of 3 feet; a few coals lay on the upper surface. At the bottom of the mound, on the original surface of the ground, were a copper drill and an arrow point.

Trenches were cut across the long mounds, but nothing observed, except that they were formed of loose surface soil.

No. 4 measured 26 feet in diameter and 3 feet high. In the center was a kind of vault formed by a circular stone wall 6 feet in diameter from outside to outside, and 4 feet inside, built in a pit dug in the original surface to the depth of a foot or 18 inches. In this vault or grave was a skeleton very well preserved, doubled up and lying on the right side, at the depth of 4 feet from the top of the mound. The vault was covered very carefully with flat limestones like those of which the wall was built. No implements, ornaments, or relics of any kind were found.

No. 11 was about the same size as No. 4. Lying on the natural surface of the ground near the center were four large flat stones, placed so as to form a square. These bore distinct evidences of having been burned. In the area between them lay a single skeleton, folded and placed on its side. There were coals and ashes immediately about and on the stones, but none in direct contact with the skeleton.

Mound No. 12 was like No. 4 throughout, with stone vault and single skeleton, differing only in the fact that the skeleton was stretched out horizontally and that the covering of stones over the vault was less complete.

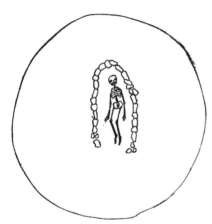

FIG. 31.—Mound No. 16 (horizontal section), Polander group.

No. 16, though a small mound only 17 feet in diameter and 2½ feet high, presented some interesting features. It also contained an incomplete stone vault (Fig. 31), which, though only about 3½ feet wide, and of the form shown in the figure, extended from the top of the mound down a foot or more below the natural surface of the ground. This contained a single skeleton in a half upright position, the head being only about 2 feet below the surface of the mound while the feet were down some 3½ or 4 feet below the surface, or nearly 2 feet lower than the head. The head was southwest, the feet northeast. Near the right hip was a discoidal stone. There were no traces of coals or ashes in this mound.

No. 30 contained neither stones, vault, nor skeleton, the only things found in it were a few badly decayed *Unio* shells near the bottom.

THE FLÜCKE MOUNDS.

This group, shown on plat (Pl. I) in connection with the Vilas group, is on the farm of Mr. Joseph Flücke, 2 miles south of Prairie du Chien, and in the vicinity of the Vilas group. It contains twelve circular mounds, the relative positions of which are shown in the figure. Of these, numbers 1, 2, 3, 4, and 5 were opened with the following result:

No. 1, 65 feet in diameter and 6 feet high, was composed of dark, sandy soil throughout, except near the bottom, where there were some

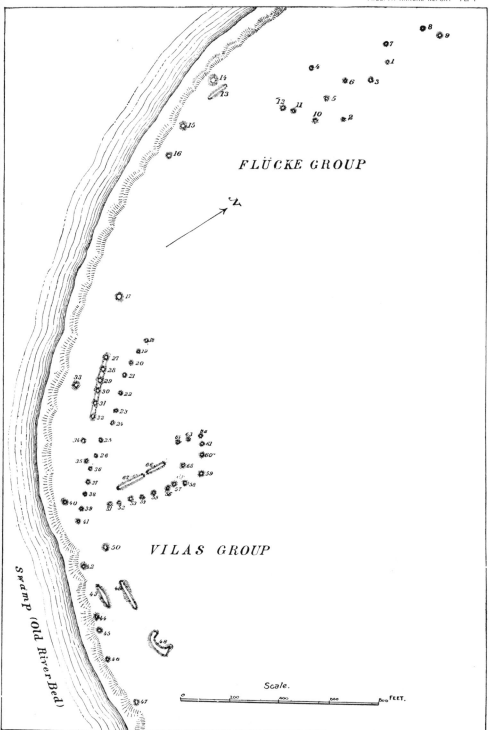

FLÜCKE GROUP

VILAS GROUP

Swamp (Old River Bed)

Scale.

0　　　　200　　　　400　　　　600　　　800 FEET.

PLAN OF THE VI'　　　FLUCKE GROUPS, CRAWFORD COUNTY, WISCONSIN.

very thin layers of black earth, but these were of limited extent, not reaching across the mound, and not exceeding 2 inches in thickness. Beneath the central portion was an excavation in the natural soil, about 12 feet in diameter and extending down to the yellow sand, a depth of something over a foot. On the bottom of this excavation were three skeletons, all lying in a horizontal position. No. 1, on the back, head east, elbows out and hands turned towards the head; near each hand was a fine, large obsidian spearhead, one of which is 9 inches long. Near the head, on each side, were two spool-shaped articles of copper. From the position in which these were found, relative to the head, it is presumed they had been used as ear ornaments. Skeleton 2 was lying close to and on the north side of No. 1, the bones much decayed; no relics with it. No. 3 lay with the head northeast. The bones were partially burnt and charred from the head to the hips and more or less covered throughout with charcoal and ashes. The skull was crushed to pieces and charred until it was black; near it were several large copper beads, or perhaps ear pendants, made of sheet copper rolled into the form of long cones, varying in length from three-fourths of an inch to an inch and a half.

Mound 2 stands on the same elevation as No. 1. It measured about 60 feet in diameter, and a little less than 6 feet high. This, like the other, had beneath it a slight excavation in the natural soil. In this were the bones (except the skull) of an adult, in a close, compact bundle; with them were some of the teeth, but no part of the skull. The flesh had evidently been removed before burial here. Near by was a single arrowhead, the only article found in the mound.

Mounds 3 and 4, each 3 feet high, and respectively 42 and 36 feet in diameter, were similar in construction to 1 and 2, with the usual excavation beneath, but without any evidences of burial in them.

No. 5, a beautiful mound measuring 68 feet in diameter and 7 feet high, stands on the same elevation as 1 and 2. In the center was a circular or inverted conical mass of yellow sand and gravel, extending from the top of the mound to the depth of 3 feet. In this mass were the much decayed bones of a child. One side of the skull was colored by copper; a small copper bracelet made of two pieces of slender copper wire twisted together and a coil of copper wire were found with the bones. As these are evidently of European manufacture this may have been an intrusive burial. At the bottom of the mound, in an excavation in the original surface, were other human bones, but so decayed that it was impossible to tell whether they belonged to one or two bodies.

THE ARMSTRONG GROUP.

This group, which is situated near the Mississippi, one-fourth of a mile below Lynxville, at the mouth of a deep and narrow ravine, and consists of eleven round mounds and one effigy, is represented in Fig. 32.

Mound No. 11, somewhat oval in form, measured 48 feet in diameter from north to south, 33 feet from east to west, and a little over 4 feet high. Near the center was a skeleton lying on a circular platform of stones. This platform or layer of stones was about 5 feet in diameter and rested on the original surface of the gound. The skeleton was so far decomposed that it was impossible to determine precisely its position.

No. 12 occupies the lowest point in the group and is only about 200 yards from the river's edge, on a level about 20 feet above the usual water mark. It measured only 26 feet in diameter and 4 in height, and was composed almost wholly of stones, packed so tightly that it was

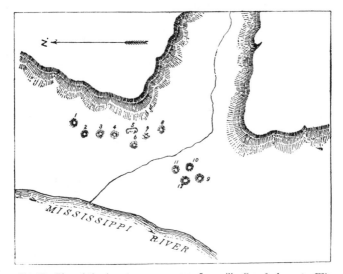

FIG. 32.—Plan of the Armstrong group, near Lynxville, Crawford county, Wis.

difficult to remove them. The stones being removed to the depth of 2½ feet, a layer of dark earth was reached, though still filled with stones. At the bottom of this layer, which extended downward 18 inches, was a mass of human bones so closely packed that but little earth was mixed with them. They occupied a space about 6 feet in diameter and rested on a platform or layer of stones which extended under the larger portion of the mound. As there were nine skulls, there were at least nine individuals or rather skeletons buried here. Among the bones were two bear's teeth, a few bone articles, some fragments of pottery, a piece of deer's horn, and the claw of some bird.

On top of the high bluff immediately back of this group is another larger group of mounds, some of which are effigies.

MOUND IN PRAIRIE DU CHIEN.

This mound, which is situated just below Old Fort Crawford, and measures 60 feet in diameter and nearly 5 feet in height, is noticed here on account of the excavation beneath it. This was 12 feet in diameter, extending 5 feet below the original surface of the ground, and was filled with dark, sandy earth similar to that of which the mound was composed. No specimens of any kind, charcoal, ashes, or indications of burial were discovered.

This group, a plat of which is given at A in Fig. 33, is situated near the Mississippi river at the mouth of the ravine known as "Sue Coulee." It consists of eighteen beautiful round mounds, standing on a level bench or table, some 30 feet high, which runs back to the bluff. They have been plowed over for about sixteen years. Several of them had been partially explored previous to the visit of an employé of this Bureau, but nothing could be learned of the result.

At B, Fig. 33, is shown a cross section of Sue Coulee at *a–b*; 1 is the creek channel; 2, the table or bench on which the mounds are located; 3, the bluff on the south side; and 4, the bluff on the north side.

Mound 1, 42 feet in diameter and 5 feet high, was composed of yellow, sandy soil similar to that of the surrounding surface, unstratified and no excavation beneath it. Near the center on the original surface were ten skeletons all piled together, with their heads in almost every direction, the leg and arm bones crossing one another. Some stones were lying immediately on them. Among them was a very large flint spear-head and some bear teeth.

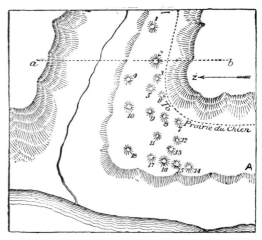

FIG. 33.—Plan of the Sue Coulee group, Crawford county, Wis.

Mound 4, 44 feet in diameter and 4 feet high, was composed of the same yellow, sandy soil as No. 1. In the center, lying on the natural surface, were three skeletons, two of them side by side, heads east, the third with the head northeast, the feet of the latter touching the feet of the other two, and all stretched at full length in a horizontal position. They were covered with stones as those in No. 1.

Mound 9, but 30 feet in diameter and 2½ feet high, was composed of darker earth than those already mentioned. A single skeleton, very much decayed, probably of a comparatively young person, was found lying on the natural surface of the ground near the center of the mound. Some scattering pieces of charcoal were observed, but no stones.

Mound 12, 48 feet in diameter and 8 feet high, was composed throughout of the yellow earth heretofore mentioned, but the portion extending from the depth of 3 to 5 feet was packed very hard and tight, much more so than that above or below it. No articles or indications of burial were observed.

No. 16 is the middle one of the row (see Fig. 33) of five mounds running parallel to and on the side next the Mississippi. It measured 45 feet in diameter and 4 feet in height. In the central portion, at the bottom, were eleven skeletons close together, with the heads in every direction; no implements or ornaments accompanied them, but at some distance from them, and about a foot above the level at which the skeletons lay, was a large broken pot. At the bottom a pit had been dug to the depth of 3 feet in the natural soil, in which were four skeletons, two lying with heads southeast and the other two, one a child, with heads northwest. Near the head of the former lay a copper plate. This is $10\frac{3}{4}$ inches in length and $2\frac{3}{4}$ inches in width at the widest part, a thin sheet less than one-twentieth of an inch thick, but slightly uneven. Near each end, on one side, are four rows of small, circular indentations (some of them entirely through), which must have been made with a metallic instrument, as is evident from the raised points on the opposite side of the plate. This lay just below the skull and near the under jaw. Near the hand of the same skeleton were two long, slender, square copper drills or spindles, one about 9 inches long and one-fourth of an inch thick, pointed at one end and chisel-shaped at the other; the other 7 inches long and pointed at both ends, shown in Fig. 34. Near the head of one of these skeletons was a thin, cup-shaped ornament of copper, probably part of an ear-pendant.

FIG. 34.—Copper spindles from the Sue Coulee group, Crawford county, Wis.

Mound 7, which stands on the highest ground of any of the group, is quite symmetrical, 60 feet in diameter and 8 feet high, and, with the exception of a column running down in the center, it consisted of yellow, sandy soil. The column, circular in outline, 5 to 6 feet in diameter, and composed of loose dark earth, extended from the highest central point to the original surface of the ground. The yellow earth immediately surrounding it was very hard.

In this column, at the depth of 5 feet from the top, lay a mass of human bones about 2 feet thick which spread over the entire circuit of the pit. Although but slightly decayed, they were mostly broken into pieces; even the skulls were in fragments, and all were heaped together in such confusion that it was impossible to determine the number of individuals represented, but there could not have been less than 10 or 12.

Immediately below them a small copper spindle was discovered similar to those already mentioned, and some split bear teeth with holes through them. At the bottom of the mound was a complete skeleton, lying at full length on the original surface, face up, head east, and arms by its side. Near the left hand lay a fine copper ax, weighing 1 pound 9 ounces, a little over 9 inches in length. By the side of this was a large round implement of chipped obsidian, and near the right hand were 67 small copper beads, a bear tooth, and the jaw bone and some teeth of a small quadruped.

The respective distances of the mounds of this group from one another, measuring from center to center, are as follows: From 1 to 2, 365 feet; from 2 to 3, 88 feet; from 3 to 5, 88 feet; from 5 to 4, 210 feet; from 5 to 6, 55 feet; from 6 to 7, 238 feet; from 7 to 8, 105 feet; from 8 to 9, 108 feet; from 9 to 10, 112 feet; from 7 to 12, 200 feet; from 12 to 11, 180 feet; from 12 to 13, 90 feet; from 13 to 15, 95 feet; from 15 to 14, 65 feet; from 15 to 16, 101 feet; from 16 to 17, 80 feet; and from 17 to 18, 85 feet.

During the grading of a street that runs by Old Fort Crawford in Prairie du Chien, in a rise near the fort, a number of skeletons were unearthed. One of these had been buried in a small canoe about 9 feet long. Most of the skeletons lay with the head to the southeast; with some were brass or copper kettles with iron bails; on the arm bone of some were bracelets made of thick copper wire. Among the articles found was a fine catlinite pipe and one or two other stone pipes.

VERNON COUNTY.

There are several mounds on the foot hills or lower benches of the bluffs in Sec. 15, T. 11 N., R. 7 W., in the extreme southwest corner of the county. The bluffs are very high and steep with a narrow strip of land between them and the Mississippi river, sloping, but not too steep to cultivate, the soil being very productive. A diagram showing the relative positions of those examined is given in Fig. 35.

No. 1, 40 feet in diameter and 5 feet high [1], unstratified. Near the center, a foot and a half below the surface of the mound, was an irregular layer of burned sandstones, some flat and others irregular in form. Immediately beneath these lay some partially burned human bones,

---

[1] When no reference is made to the form it is to be understood that the mounds are of the simple conical type.

and near them a single chipped stone hoe. A little northwest of the center, at the depth of 5 feet and apparently resting on the natural surface of the ground, were the remains of five folded skeletons, heads north and faces west. Under one of these was a single perforated bear-tooth. The skeletons had been covered with a mortar-like substance which was dry and very hard.

No. 2, 100 feet northwest of No. 1 (measuring from base to base), 75 feet in diameter and 7 feet high. This was composed throughout (except the surface layer) of blue clay mixed with sand, very hard and tough. Large sandstones, weighing from 10 to 100 pounds, occurred at all depths, but not placed with any regularity or according to any perceptible plan. At the depth of 8 feet, and hence slightly below the original surface of the ground and a little southwest of the center, were

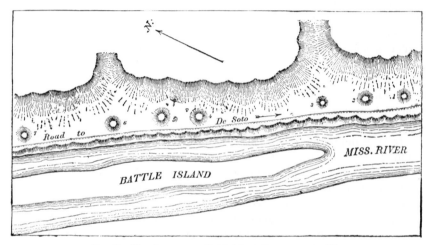

Fig. 35.—Mound group near Battle island, Vernon county, Wis.

six folded skeletons, lying on the bottom with the heads east and faces north. As soon as they were uncovered the bones fell to pieces so that not even the skulls could be saved. The dirt immediately around them was wet and sticky.

No. 3, 60 feet north of No. 2, 40 feet in diameter and 3½ feet high. The top layer, 1½ feet in depth, consisted of black, rich loam, the remainder of blue clay. The original soil had evidently been removed to the depth of a foot or more—in one portion to the depth of 2 feet—before burial. On the north side, not far from the margin, the clay, for a considerable space, was very hard and dry, immediately beneath which were some four or five folded skeletons, with heads, so far as could be determined, in various directions. Near the southeast margin, at the depth of 6 feet, lay six other skeletons at full length with heads in different directions. Under one of them were three bears' teeth. The owner in a previous examination found near the center, at the depth of 15 or 18 inches, a long string of glass beads.

No. 4, 300 feet north of No. 3, 65 feet in diameter and 4 feet high. At the depth of 4 feet eight skeletons were lying at full length on the natural surface of the ground, with heads east and faces up. They lay on the natural slope of the bench, so that the heads were higher than the feet. Their relative positions are given in Fig. 36 (a horizontal section of the mound), the larger figures indicating adult skeletons and the small one that of a child. Under the one at the northern end of the row were several bear teeth, and near them and at the same depth lay the under jaw of some animal. At the head of each skeleton was a large, irregular piece of sandstone. The composition of this tumulus was chiefly a mixture of sand and light yellow clay unstratified.

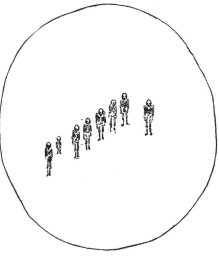

FIG. 36.—Plan of Mound No. 4, Battle island, Vernon county, Wisconsin.

No. 5, 30 feet northwest of No. 4, was 80 feet in diameter, 5 feet high, and more flattened on top than is usual with tumuli of this type. On the northern side, at a depth of 3 feet, two folded skeletons were discovered, under one of which were several copperbeads, and under all bears' teeth. About the center and near the bottom was a single skeleton also folded and under the head were several bears' teeth. In the southern side, at the depth of 5 feet, a single very fine lance head was discovered; no bones were near it.

No. 6, 125 feet northwest of No. 5, 85 feet in diameter and 4 feet high, was composed of rich black earth interspersed with sandstones. Near the center, at the bottom, lay a single badly-decayed skeleton, over which was heaped an irregular pile of sandstones of various sizes.

No. 7, 20 yards northwest of No. 6, 50 feet in diameter and 5½ feet high, consisted chiefly of dry, yellow clay. In the northern side at the depth of 5 feet were three or four much decayed skeletons, apparently folded, with heads east and faces north and in the southern portion at the depth of 2 feet the fragments of a stone pipe. Under the latter was an irregular pile of burned sandstones; but no ashes or coals were discovered, from which fact it is inferred that the stones were placed here after having been subjected to fire.

WHITE'S GROUP.

In the northwest corner of the county, in Sec. 28, T. 14 N., R. 7 W., on land owned by Mr. H. White, is a group of small circular mounds extending in a nearly straight line along the margin of the sandy level known locally as "Sand Prairie," where it descends to the lower bottom lands of Raccoon river. This level extends to the bluffs about a half mile distant, which are here very high and steep. A plan of the group is given in Pl. II, from which it will be seen that it contains 22 mounds of various sizes.

No. 1 of this group, 35 feet in diameter and 3½ feet high, was composed throughout of black, sandy soil similar to that around it. Six inches below the surface, at the center, fragments of a red earthenware vessel were found, but so rotten that they fell to pieces on being handled. A little north of the center, at the bottom, lying on the natural sand stratum, were the remains of four skeletons, heads north. Another skeleton was found in the southern side at the same depth, folded, head south, face east; over the skull was a small lance head.

No. 2, immediately north of No. 1, touching it at the base, was 45 feet in diameter and 3 feet high. It was composed throughout of earth similar to the surrounding soil. Five skeletons were found at various depths, from 2 to 4 feet. Some were lying at full length, others folded with heads in various directions, but were all so soft that none could be saved.

No. 3, 160 feet north of No. 2, 40 feet in diameter and 4 feet high, was not stratified. The skeleton of a child was lying near the center at the depth of 18 inches, head west. Under the head was a brass ornament wrapped in cotton cloth, and about the position of the breast the fragments of another metallic ornament, also a few glass beads. This skeleton had evidently been incased in a wooden coffin of some kind, but whether of bark or boards could not be determined. In the southwestern side the skeleton of an adult was discovered at the same depth, folded, with head south. Nothing else was observed, save a few fragments of pottery near the surface.

No. 4, about 100 feet northeast of No. 3, measured 50 feet in diameter and 4 feet high, unstratified. Nothing was discovered in this mound.

No. 6, 160 feet northwest of No. 5, oblong, 50 feet in diameter north and south, and 4 feet high, was composed of black, sandy soil from the fields. In the northern side, at the depth of 2 feet, were ten skeletons, some folded and others stretched out on their backs, heads in every direction. A little west of the center, at the depth of 4 feet, two more were found folded, with the heads west. On the skull of each of these was a thick copper plate, apparently beaten out of native copper with rude implements. The larger, over the southern skull, represented in Fig. 37, is 8 inches long by 4½ inches wide. About 6 inches above it was a fine large lance head. The other plate is nearly square, 4½ inches by 4½ inches. The bones were so rotten and soft, except immediately under the copper plates, that none of them could be preserved. Freshwater shells were scattered through the mound at various depths.

In No. 7, 25 feet in diameter and 3 feet high, nothing was discovered save a single skeleton near the northern edge, a foot below the surface, and a few fragments of pottery near the head.

No. 8, diameter, 65 feet; height, 6 feet; unstratified; disclosed nothing.

No. 9, diameter, 60 feet; height, 5 feet; unstratified; contained nothing worthy of notice.

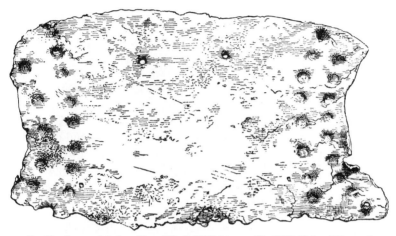

FIG. 37.—Copper plate from Mound No. 6, White's group (No. 88336, National Museum).

No. 10, 50 feet in diameter and 4½ feet high. A vertical section of this mound is shown in Fig. 38. The top layer, 2 feet thick, consisted of black, loose, sandy loam similar to the surrounding soil of the field. Six skeletons were lying in this near the center, some folded, others stretched at full length, heads in different directions. The next or lower layer, 3 feet thick, and extending downward slightly below the original surface, consisted of red clay very largely mixed with sand. Skeletons were found in this at various depths. A little south of the center the original soil, below layer No. 2, had been hollowed out to the

FIG. 38.—Section of Mound No. 10, White's group.

gravel. This excavation was about 7 feet long, 3 feet wide, and 1 foot deep. In it were the remains of a single adult skeleton, stretched at full length, face up, and covered with a layer of hard black muck. The bones were nearly all gone, but their forms and positions could be traced. Under the skull was a fine lance head, and about 2 feet south, in the same excavation, a magnificent chipped implement of obsidian, represented in Fig. 39.

12 ETH——6

No. 11, touching No. 10 at the northeast, 50 feet in diameter and 4 feet high, was composed chiefly of a dark, sandy soil, about 10 feet of the central portion being of yellow clay and sand mixed.   In the southern portion, at the depth of 2 feet, were two very soft, folded skeletons, heads west.   A little southwest of the center, at the depth of 3 feet, a few human bones were found incased in hard, black muck or mortar-like substance, and immediately under them some copper beads.   Near the center, at about the same depth, was a folded skeleton, with the

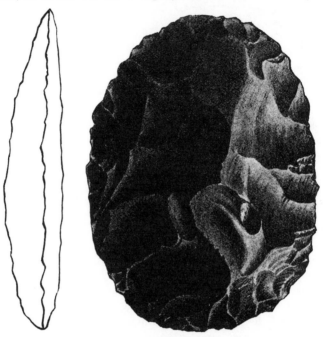

Fig. 39.—Obsidian implement from Mound No. 10, White's group.

head northeast, also incased in the hard, black muck.   By the skull was a broken earthen pot and a bottle-shaped vase, short neck and flat bottom.   The broken pot, which has been partially restored and is represented in Fig. 40, is equal, if not superior in the quality of the ware, to any mound pottery discovered in the Mississippi valley.   A jasper lance head was discovered a little north of the center near the base. The other mounds of the group, which are small, simple tumuli of the conical type, were not opened.   Their sizes are as follows:

No.	Diameter.	Height.	No.	Diameter.	Height.
	Feet.	Feet.		Feet.	Feet.
12	45	4	17	50	4
13	35	3	18	35	2
14	25	3	19	20	2
15	20	2	20	50 by 35	4
16	50	4½	21	40	3½

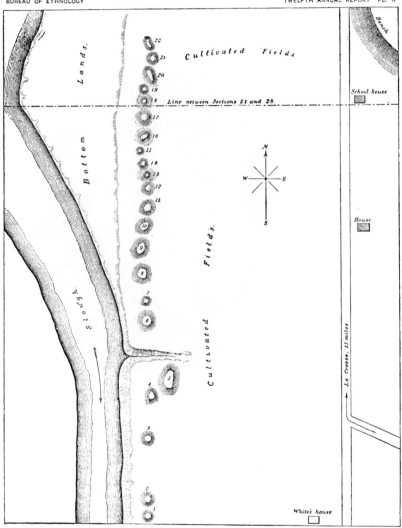

PLAT OF WHITE'S GROUP, VERNON COUNTY, WISCONSIN.

About half a mile south of No. 1 of this group, on Sec. 33, same township, stands an isolated mound of the same type, which, upon opening, proved to be unstratified, as most of the others already mentioned. Diameter about 50 feet and height 7 feet. On the west side a few soft and badly decayed human bones were discovered at the depth

FIG. 40.—Pot from Mound No. 11, White's group.

of 2 feet. On the east side similar bones were found at the depth of 4 feet, and on the southwest, at the same depth, the fragment of a large sea shell (*Busycon perversum*).

GRANT COUNTY.

On the bluffs north of Sinepy creek are the remnants of two groups or lines of mounds. These were visited in 1880 by Col. Norris, and in 1890 a second visit was made. Such portions of the groups as have been subject to cultivation have entirely disappeared. On the narrow promontory overlooking the river is a row of small conical mounds, composed largely of rough stones from the adjoining bluff. Five of these mounds were opened in 1880. All contained human bones, which in two cases were charred.

Many of the bones in these mounds were disconnected and often broken as though deposited after the flesh had been removed, probably after exposure of the bodies on scaffolds or after previous burial.

On a second promontory, east of the first, across a deep ravine, is a group of works consisting of two effigy mounds and one oblong mound.

Other oblong mounds, said to have been situated to the north of these, have been obliterated by the plow. The most southern of the effigy mounds would seem never to have been finished. The body is represented by a well-rounded ridge, and the head and forelegs are present, but only a trace of one of the hind legs appears. These mounds are in a forest and have not been disturbed by the whites. The other animal figure is somewhat larger, the body being 90 feet long. The legs are unusually long, the length from the toes to the back line being upwards of 40 feet. The head is merely a heavy rounded projection, and the tail is so obscure as to be barely traceable.

WORKS NEAR CASSVILLE.

About 1 mile south of Cassville the road traverses a bench or level bottom, which is seldom overflowed, extending from the bluffs to a bayou, a distance of nearly 1 mile. Near this road on one side, when visited in 1880, were two lines of works, consisting of effigy, circular, and elongate mounds, and on the other a single row of circular mounds. These, except 1 and 2, are shown in their respective forms and positions in Fig. 41.

No.	Length.	Height.	Shape.	Remarks.
	Feet.	Feet.		
1	10 by 20	3	Oblong	Ordinary earth mound.
2	10 by 30	3	....do	Opened; nothing found.
3	90	4	Effigy	Probably represents an elk.
4	90	4	....do	Do.
5	....	....	Circular	
6	....	....	....do	
7	150	5	Effigy	Lizard; head and body 90 feet, tail 60 feet.
8	45	3	Oblong	Ordinary earth mound.
9	72 by 84	4	Effigy	A well-formed bird.
10	20	2	Circular	Opened; nothing found.
11	120 by 84	4	Effigy	Probably an eagle.

Nos. 12 to 15 are small circular and oval mounds on the eastern side of the road in a line south of the Eagle's head; Nos. 16 to 28 the row of circular mounds on the west side of the road. The latter vary in diameter from 15 to 40 feet and in height from 3 to 5 feet. Quite a number of these had previously been opened, and, as was ascertained, presented evidences of intrusive burials.

Excavations were made in a number of the mounds of this and adjacent groups, but nothing was discovered save human bones in the last stages of decay.

This locality was revisited in 1890, when slight traces of these works were seen. The railroad had been carried directly through the group and an immense gravel pit now occupies the site. About three-fourths of one of the bird figures remain and some shapeless hillocks mark the line of conical mounds.

Stone cairns containing fragments of decaying human bones were found on top of the adjacent bluff; and upon the bank of the bayou near Cassville is a circular mound 40 feet in diameter and 4 feet high, in the base of which, beneath the hard earth, were four skeletons of adults in a much better state of preservation.

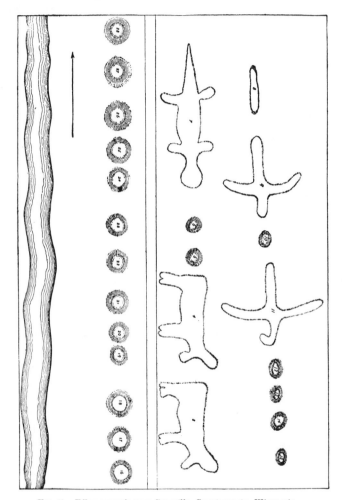

FIG. 41.—Effigy mounds near Cassville, Grant county, Wisconsin.

The large Dewey farm, now owned by Gen. Newberry, extending from 1 to 3 miles north of Cassville, is literally dotted over with mounds and other works. This was a favorite haunt of the modern Indians, who used these earthen structures as depositories for their dead, hence intrusive burials are very common here. In a number explored, of which only the bottom central core remained undisturbed, nothing was found except decaying human bones and very rude stone implements.

A remarkable series of mounds is situated upon the bluffs about 3 miles north of Cassville. These, remarks Mr. Holmes, may be taken as an illustration of the earthworks of this region. The bluffs are here upwards of 300 feet in height and are very abrupt on the margins overlooking the river. The horizontal beds of massive magnesian lime-stone outcrop along the brink, giving a series of gray escarped promontories, between which are notch-like recesses cut by the drainage. The steep faces of the bluff are without timber, but the recesses and the upper surfaces are covered with forests; this, together with the dense growth of underbrush, make exploration extremely difficult.

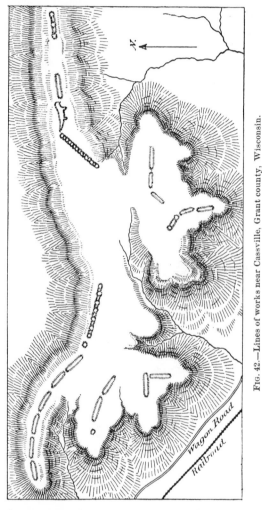

FIG. 42.—Lines of works near Cassville, Grant county, Wisconsin.

Between Muddy creek, which comes out of the bluffs at right angles to the river escarpment and the Sandy, a rivulet emerging three-fourths of a mile farther south, there is a tongue of the plateau divided into several parts at the outer end and connected by a narrow ridge with the main plateau. This outstanding mass is a mile in length and at the widest part not more than one-fourth of a mile wide. Mounds are found upon the main crest as well as upon most of the spurs. This distribution in groups was determined apparently by the topography, as will be seen by reference to the accompanying map. (Fig. 42.)

The main lines of works occupy the crest of the principal ridge, which borders Muddy creek on the south. Beginning at the outer point we follow the curved ridge encountering first six oblong mounds of the usual character, then a conical mound standing somewhat alone, and beyond this a series of eight conical mounds connected into a chain by low ridges. Traversing a distance of about 700 feet a second chain-group is encountered, and at the eastern extremity of this lies the only effigy mound of the system so far as observed. East of this a broken series of oblong and chain mounds continues indefinitely. On the southern spurs of the promontory are three additional groups of conical and oblong mounds following the crests of the ridges and terminating near the escarped points.

All of these works are in an excellent state of preservation. A few have been dug into by relic hunters. The two isolated conical mounds are of average size, being about 25 feet in diameter and between 3 and 4 feet high. The oblong mounds are straight even ridges, ranging from 80 to 125 feet in length and from 10 to 20 in width, and in height rarely exceeding 3½ feet.

The chain mounds are of particular interest. They have been built with much care and are wonderfully preserved. The cones average less than 20 feet in diameter and are from 2 to 4 feet in height. The distance from center to center varies from 30 to 40 feet and the connecting ridges of earth are about 16 feet wide and from 2 to 3 feet high.

The most noteworthy member of the series is the effigy mound. It is perhaps more suggestive of the puma than of any other quadruped. This work is well preserved, but the loose vegetable mold of which it is composed does not admit of the preservation of more than a generalized form, no matter to what extent the individuality of the original shape was developed.

The full length of the figure may be given as 144 feet, although the tail is very indistinct toward the extremity. The head is toward the east and exhibits no other feature than a slight projection for the nose. The characters of the animal have received proper attention. The body is full and rounded and the extremities fall off gradually in width and height. The curves of the back and legs are well rendered, and the whole conception is presented with sufficient spirit. The distance from the toes to the back line is 36 feet. The body, at the point of greatest relief, is not over 3½ feet high.

The mounds of this group appear to be composed mainly of vegetable mold obtained on the spot.

The conical mound, situated upon the very brow of the bluff, is 25 feet in diameter and 4 feet high. A broad trench carried through it revealed only the decayed bones of a child, extended at full length beneath the central core of hard, dry earth. Pits sunk in the oblong mounds brought nothing to light. A number of circular mounds on the adjacent bluffs was also opened, but nothing save decayed human bones was found in them.

WORKS NEAR WYALUSING.

Four excellent illustrations of the remarkable mound groups of Wisconsin are to be seen near Wyalusing, a station on the Burlington and

Northern Railroad. The village of Wyalusing is picturesquely situated on a narrow strip of alluvial land between the Mississippi river and the bluff, which here rises abruptly in a single step to the height of 350 feet. These bluffs, as those elsewhere in Grant county, are the margin of a plateau which extends eastward from the escarpment. The margin of this plateau is cut by numerous streams and is for the most part too rugged for cultivation. In the marginal region the ridges separating the streams are often narrow, but have rounded and somewhat level crests, which were favorite resorts of the mound builders.

Upon the steep timbered bluff that rises above the village of Wyalusing is found a line of earthworks following the crest of a nearly straight ridge. The principal work of the group is an animal effigy, a quadruped. It is of large size and is in an excellent state of preservation. Singularly enough it does not occupy the crest of the ridge which runs parallel to the river, but lies in a shallow depression in the slope between the crest and the margin of the steep bluff overlooking the village. The head is toward the south and the legs extend down the gentle slope toward the river. The form is perfectly preserved, the body is well rounded and the outline is everywhere distinct. So perfect is the preservation that the extension representing the ears or horns shows a slight parting at the outer end, and the two legs of each pair are separated by a shallow depression throughout their entire length. The feeling for correct form possessed by the builders even in this rude method of realization is indicated by the outline which defines the forehead, by the curves of the back and belly, and of the gambrel joints of the legs, as well as by the relief which expresses something of the rotundity and relative prominence of the parts. What additional details of form have been effaced by the lapse of time can not be determined.

The length of the work from the forehead to rump is 115 feet; the length of the head is 47 feet; the distance from the feet to the back, representing the full height of the figure, is 50 feet; the width of the body is 28 feet, and the width of the legs about 20 feet. The relief does not exceed $3\frac{1}{2}$ feet at any point, the ears, nose, and legs not exceeding half that.

Some years ago Mr. D. W. Derby, an enthusiastic collector of mound relics, dug into the body of this effigy about the locality of the heart, and found human bones and an earthen vessel about the size of the crown of an ordinary hat. The vessel had a flat bottom, but was so fragile from decay that no part of it could be preserved.

Running approximately parallel with the greatest length of the animal figure and occupying the crest of the ridge is a row of oblong mounds. These vary from a straight line to accommodate themselves to the crest, and in orientation vary from S. 25° E. to S. 15 W. The largest one is 100 feet in length and the shortest 60 feet. The width averages about 20 feet and the height is in no case greater than 3½ feet. On the rounded surface of the north end of the ridge is a number of small circular depressions that may represent old dwelling sites; others are seen on a level space about 100 feet north of the animal figure. The ridge terminates at the north in a rounded point and at the south in a long narrow one, and is con-

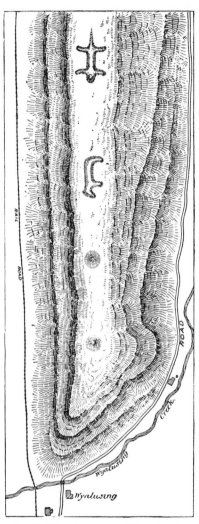

nected with the chain of ridges on the east by a broad saddle; along this, and extending for an indefinite distance, is an almost continuous series of mounds mostly of the oblong type. In the older cultivated fields only traces of the works are found, but in the new ground, and in the wooded areas, the forms are fully preserved. There is no telling what was the original extent of these wonderful lines of mounds, or what their connection with the other series, the remnants of which are found on nearly every part of the bluffs where tillage has not destroyed them.

A second group of more than usual interest is located upon the promontory that overlooks the village on the north. This promontory extends to the northward, as a narrow ridge with an uneven crest, to the residence of Mr. Derby and beyond. Its trend is parallel with the river, from which it rises at an angle of 40 degrees or more. On the opposite side it falls off with abruptness to a little stream which runs to the southward and passes out at the north end of the village. From the railroad bridge at the cross-ing of the stream we ascend the

Fig. 43.—Mound group near Wyalusing, Grant county, Wisconsin.

point of the promontory by a series of slopes and cliffs to the height of about 200 feet; beyond this point the ridge extends to the northward and is narrow, and for about one-quarter of a mile nearly horizontal.

Upon the level crest, which is forest covered, are four mounds; at the south are two conical mounds and at the north two mounds repre-

senting animals, distributed as shown in Fig. 43. All are in an excel
lent state of preservation save where recent excavations conducted by
Mr. Derby have mutilated them. The southern mound was conical in
shape and about 20 feet in diameter and 6 feet high. When Mr. Derby
began his excavations the eastern half of the cone was covered with
rough stone slabs obtained from the vicinity. In digging into the center of the mound four stones as large as a human head were found near
the surface. At the depth of a foot a circle of stones was encountered,
having a diameter of 4 feet; at a depth of about 2 feet the top of a cistern, 3½ feet in diameter, of well laid stones, was uncovered. This was
3 feet deep and had been built upon the surface of the limestones of
the bluff. The well was filled with black earth, in which were found
seven oblong shell beads, a copper celt of ordinary shape, and a red
pipestone, platform pipe; outside of the well a flake of flint was found,
and some curious lines of colored sand were observed. These seemed
to radiate roughly from the center of the mound and were followed to
the circumference by the explorers. Wide trenches were carried across
the mound from east to west and from north to south.

The second mound was much like the first and is still perfect, save
for the sinking of a pit in the center. Nothing of interest was found.
The present diameter is over 30 feet in the line of the ridge and somewhat less across it. The height is 6 feet.

A little over 100 feet to the north of this mound is the first animal
mound. The creature, possibly a bear, is represented as lying upon its
side with the head to the south and the feet to the east. The body is a
neatly rounded ridge 70 feet long and nearly 25 feet wide, and has a
relief of nearly 4 feet. The head is about 30 feet long, the projection
representing the ears being very slightly indicated and difficult to
define. The low ridge representing the forelegs is straight, while that
for the hinder ones is bent, thus defining the gambrel joint. The distance from the toes to the back line is a little less than 40 feet. This
figure is of the most frequently occurring type of effigy works.

The other effigy mound, 150 feet to the north, is of a form somewhat
unusual. It is spread out upon the ridge, after the fashion of a lizard
or alligator. The head is toward the south, and is merely a rounded
projection of the body embankment. The tail at the opposite end is
upwards of 35 feet long, but is very attenuated and indistinct toward
the tip. The body is a rounded ridge 3½ feet high and less than 20
feet wide, and the legs, extended to the right and left, are low embankments of earth, the forelegs being bent forward and the hinder ones
backward, as shown in the illustration.

Passing north along this ridge, another series of mounds is encountered. The first member is an oblong mound, about three-fourths of a
mile beyond the residence of Mr. Derby. This is followed by a series
of works in which are oblong, conical, and animal mounds, some of
which are almost obliterated by the plow.

On the crest of the bluff, north of the last mentioned mounds and just south of the Wisconsin river, is a continuous straight line of mounds, all of which, except two, are elongate, embankment-like structures, giving to the line the appearance of an interrupted wall. Of the two exceptions one is oval and the other is an effigy mound, probably intended to represent an elk. Several of these mounds were opened, but in none, except the third from the south end of the line, was anything found. This is somewhat oval, 24 feet in diameter, and 4 feet high. In the center was a rude, irregular stone coffin or vault of flat sandstones, so arranged around the single skeleton that a large one sufficed to cover it from animals. The bones were in the last stages of decomposition.

The top of this bluff, for the distance of half a mile, is literally covered with these works, which are uniformly placed so near the brink of the descent to the Mississippi as to present a clear cut outline, except where the view is obstructed by trees. As the position is a commanding one, and as very few of the works were intended or used for burial purposes, it is difficult to conceive of any other object the builders could have had in view in their construction than that of defense. But how they were made available for this purpose without encircling any area or without closing the numerous openings is difficult to understand.

On the NW. ¼ of Sec. 20, T. 6 N., R. 6 W., about 1 mile east of the works just mentioned, is another group of considerable interest. This consists of one continuous line of circular and effigy mounds, numbering 36 in all.

THE ELEPHANT MOUND.

This effigy, of which so much has been said and written, is situated on the southeast quarter of Sec. 21, T. 5 N., R. 6 W., in Bloomington township, 4 miles south of Wyalusing. It lies on the right side, head south, in a depression between two drift sand ridges, in what is known as the Cincinnati bottom. This bottom extends from the bluff on one side to a large bayou on the other, and is just above the overflows of the Mississippi. Although the mound has been under cultivation for five years, the outlines are yet distinct. " By a hasty measurement," says Col. Norris, who incidentally visited it while engaged by the Bureau in the northwest, " I made its entire length to the front of the head 135 feet, the width across the body from 55 to 60 feet, the height varying from 3 to 6 feet. I made a rude sketch of it on the spot with pencil, for the purpose of showing the so-called trunk as I saw it. There is a depression some 4 or 5 feet deep between the trunk and breast, and a kind of slight platform or apron-like extension on the upper or back part of the head, from 2 to 3 feet high, or half as high as the rest of the head. Whether the resemblance to an elephant, which arises almost wholly from the proboscis-like extension to the head, is due to intentional work done by the builders or has resulted from the drifting of the loose, sandy soil, of which it is mainly composed, is a question difficult to decide. I can only say that I represent it as I found it." This sketch, which is not reproduced here, shows the trunk somewhat distinctly as curved inward toward the fore legs. It is very doubtful whether this should be considered a part of the effigy. If both Mr. Warner and Col. Norris show correctly what they saw, the trunk was evidently a shifting line of sand.

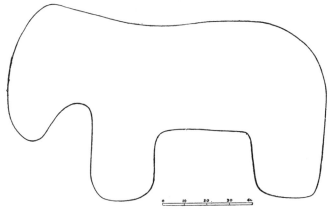

FIG. 44.—Elephant mound, according to Middleton's survey in 1884.

In November, 1884, Mr. Middleton was directed to call to his assistance a civil engineer and make a regular and careful survey of this mound for the purpose of modeling it for the New Orleans Exposition. This was very carefully done, and the result is shown in outline in Fig. 44. His report in reference to it, as seen at that time, is as follows:

"The 'Elephant mound' is located on the southeast quarter of Sec. 21, T. 5 N., R. 6 W., Bloomington township, in a long rectangular depression or rather cul de sac as shown in Pl. III, the level of which is a few feet only above high water. The immediate spot on which it stands is a little higher than the general level around it. For 200 yards north the surface is even, with a slight rise to the foot of the bank. This bank is about 20 feet higher than the mound level. Going east along line *a b* (Pl. III) the ground at first dips slightly, but rises a little as it approaches the foot of the bank, which is here about 30 feet above the mound level. South towards *c* the surface is flat for more than 600 yards. The bank on the west is about the same height as that on the east. About 200 yards south is an effigy mound, a bird with outspread wings, head south. Near by there are a number of round mounds placed in a line and two or three long mounds.

"Plowing over it for a number of years has considerably reduced the height of the elephant effigy, and has rendered the outlines of portions of the head and back somewhat indistinct, but the body between the legs is quite plain. It is gently rounded on the surface, the highest points being at the hip, where it is nearly 4 feet high. Entire length, 140 feet; width across the body to the farther end of the hind leg, 72 feet; across the body between the legs, 55 feet; across the body and fore leg, 77 feet; across the neck, 40 feet; length of head from back to nozzle, 60 feet; width of hind leg at the body, 32 feet; at the foot, 15 feet; length of hind leg, 22 feet; across the fore leg at the body, 28 feet; at the foot 15 feet; length of fore leg, 28 feet."

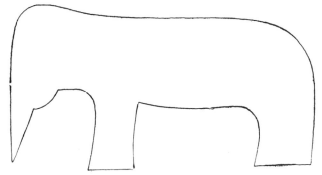

FIG. 45.—Elephant mound, after Warner's figure.

Fig. 45 is another view of this mound, which is an exact copy, reduced to half size, of the original manuscript pencil sketch by Jared Warner, from which the figure in the Smithsonian Report for 1872 was made.

SHEBOYGAN COUNTY.

MANITOWOC AND SHEBOYGAN MOUNDS.

There are some scattering mounds on the hills bordering the Sheboygan marshes on the north. These are usually isolated, simple conical tumuli, though some are in irregular groups on elevated situations.

The only one opened (the rest had been previously explored) was situated on a sandy ridge half a mile north of the marsh and 100 feet above it. It was about 50 feet in diameter at the base and 5 feet high. After passing through 18 inches of surface soil the central mass was struck, which appeared to be composed of earth mingled with firebeds, charcoal, ashes, and loose stones. Near the center of this mass, at the bottom of the mound, a large human skeleton in a sitting posture was discovered, apparently holding between its hands and knees a large clay vessel, unfortunately in fragments. These were covered over by an irregular layer of flat bowlders. Nothing else worthy of notice was found.

About 2 miles west of this, on a bluff overlooking the marsh, was another mound of similar form and slightly larger, which had been previously opened by Mr. Hoissen of Sheboygan. It was found literally filled, to the depth of 2½ feet, with human skeletons, many of which were well preserved and evidently those of modern Indians, as with them were the usual modern weapons and ornaments. Beneath these was a mass of rounded bowlders aggregating several wagon loads, below which were some 40 or 50 skeletons in a sitting posture, in a circle, around and facing a very large sea shell. This specimen, which with the other articles taken from this mound is in Mr. Hoissen's collection, measures 21 inches in length and 29 in circumference at its greatest girth.

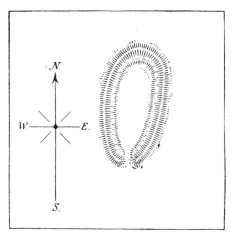

FIG. 46.—Inclosure near Sheboygan. Sheboygan county, Wisconsin.

Just south of the outlet of the marsh is a small, oval inclosure, with an opening at one end of some 4 or 5 feet. It consists of a single wall 3 feet high and a ditch about two feet deep (shown in Fig. 46).

BARRON COUNTY.

THE RICE LAKE MOUNDS.

The only explorations in this county were around Rice lake. This group, a plat of which is given in Pl. IV, is situated at Rice lake village, on sec. 16, T. 35 N., R. 11 W., about half a mile above Red Cedar river. The land at this point is somewhat broken, and the area occupied by the group is cut by a small ravine that runs northeast to the lake. Some of the mounds are on gravely knolls, a few in the ravine, some on the slope up to the level which runs back to a ridge a quarter of a mile distant and some on this level. The location was well chosen for hunting, fishing, and procuring a supply of food, as game and fish are still abundant and wild rice formerly grew on the lake.

The group consists of fifty-one mounds, chiefly of the ordinary conical form. There are no effigies or long slender embankments in it. Two of the long type, however, were found at the other end of the village.

The construction varies so little that few only will be described as samples of the rest, No. 1, for instance, as representing Nos. 24, 26, 35, 39, 46, and 45. This stands in the bottom of a ravine about 10 feet above the water level and about 500 feet from the shore of the lake; diameter, 28 feet; height, 4 feet. The construction, as shown in figure 47, was as follows, commencing at the top: First, a layer of dark vegetable mold (*a*), 2 inches thick which had formed since the mound was abandoned, next, a layer (*b*) of sandy loam with a slight admixture of clay; third, the core (*c*), forming the central and remaining portion of

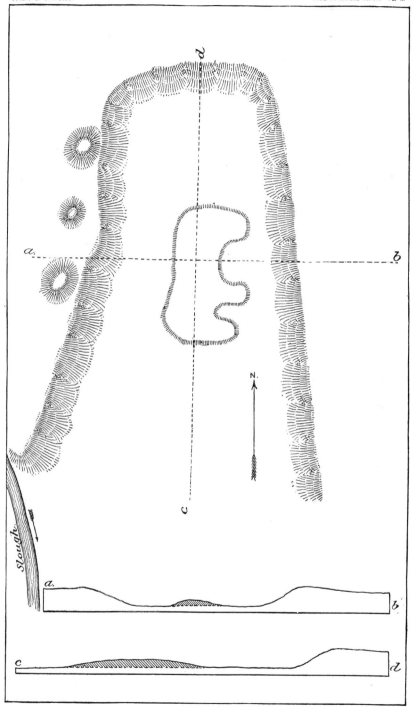

ELEPHANT MOUND AND SURROUNDINGS, GRANT COUNTY, WISCONSIN.

the structure and resting on the original surface of the gully. This consisted of clay mixed with sand and was very hard. It appeared to be composed of small, rounded masses about 16 to 18 inches in diameter and 6 to 10 inches thick, doubtless representing the loads deposited by the builders. Lying on the original surface of the ground, underneath the core, were two skeletons (1 and 2) bundled, as was the case with nearly all found in this group. The bundling was done by placing the long bones together as closely as possible around the ribs, the vertebral bones being placed here and there so as to render the bundle as compact as possible. Close to these were the charred remains of another skeleton (3) pressed into a layer scarcely exceeding an inch in thickness, but, as there were no signs of fire, ashes, or coals on the surface beneath, burning must have taken place before burial. As all the skeletons were under the core, and the small masses heretofore mentioned showed no signs of disturbance, they must have been buried at one time.

Mound 24 measured but 22 feet in diameter and 3 in height. It differed from No. 1 only in containing four skeletons, none of them charred.

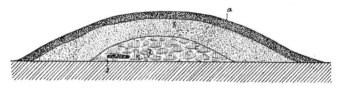

FIG. 47.—Mound No. 1, Rice lake group.

Mound 26, but 25 feet in diameter and 4 feet high, contained four skeletons of the original burial and three of intrusive burial, as did also No. 35.

In No. 46 there had been seven original burials, at the base of the core, as usual, one of a child,—no intrusive burials.

No. 8, oval in outline, 36 feet long, 26 feet wide, and 5 feet high, differed from the others, as it lacked the core and layer of sandy loam. With the exception of the top layer of vegetable mold it consisted of yellowish clay mixed with sand, probably taken from the immediately surrounding surface. Six skeletons were found in it; the first, 3 feet south of the apex and at a depth of 2 feet. No. 2 a foot and a half south of the first. These two appeared to have been buried at the same time, or nearly so, and most likely were intrusive burials. No. 3 was at the bottom, on the original surface, under No. 1; No. 4 a foot northeast of 3; No. 5 two feet east of the last; and No. 6 a foot north of No. 5. The last four skeletons were probably the first interments in the mound, and appear to have been buried about the same time from the fact that they were bundled, and the bones clean and white, although so soft as to fall in pieces when exposed to the atmosphere.

Mound No. 11, standing east of No. 8, is also oblong, 35 feet long, and 23 feet wide. The construction the same as the preceeding. There had been five original and five intrusive burials, the latter in the center at the depth of 3 feet, the others at the bottom of the mound, in the north end. All of the skeletons were bundled, those near the surface being in a better state of preservation than those in the bottom. A large pine stump was standing over the latter, the roots of which had broken them up to a considerable extent.

Mound 42, standing in the ravine, measured 27 feet in diameter and 4 feet high. The construction was found to be similar to that of No. 1; first, the thin layer of vegetable mold; then sandy loam and the clay core; but here was a pit in the original soil, rectangular in form, 3 feet long, 2 feet wide, and 1 in depth, the sides and ends flaring. In this mound there had been three intrusive and two original burials. Two skeletons of the former were in the southwest part, at the depth of 2 feet; the third in the center at the depth of 4 feet, a cut having been made in the top of the core to receive it. The material of the layer over it had a disturbed appearance; indicating that these were intrusive burials.

Two other skeletons were found on the bottom of the pit, bundled as usual. The bones of these two are larger than those of any of the other skeletons of this group. Mounds numbered 41, 47, and 48 were so similar in every respect to 42 as to need no further notice.

Mound 49 stands on the lower margin of the gravelly ridge south of the gully, 20 or 25 feet above the water level of the lake; its diameter being 26 feet and height 5 feet. It was found to consist, except the top layer, of an unstratified mass of dark brown loam with a considerable mixture of sand and gravel, having the same appearance as the soil of the ridge on which it stands; an occasional lump of clay, similar to the load masses heretofore spoken of, was observed. Under this main layer or body of the mound, near the center, was an oval pit, diameters 2 and 2½ feet, and 1 foot in depth. This mound furnished evidence as usual of both intrusive and original burials. The original burials were two adults in the pit; these, as also the skeletons of the intrusive burials, being bundled, an indication that the two peoples who buried here belonged to the same race. Mounds 28 and 36 were similar throughout to No. 49.

GROUP ON SEC. 10, T. 35 N., R. 11 W.

These mounds, which are on the opposite side of the lake from the preceding, are all of the round or conical type and are located on a point of land some 25 feet above and overlooking the lake and the other village just described. No. 8, one of the largest of the group, measured 45 feet in diameter and 5 feet high. Commencing at the top, the first 3 feet was a layer of sandy loam; the remainder was a hard core of clay mixed with sand, made up of small masses, like those heretofore described. The latter rested on a layer, about an inch thick, of what

RICE LAKE

seemed to be the decayed vegetable material of the original surface of the ground. A skeleton was discovered southeast of the center, only 3 inches below the surface, bundled. Fragments of a skull were found near the center at the depth of 2 feet. Here there were evidences that a grave had been dug in the mound after it had been completed, and a body buried in bark wrappings, but all save these fragments of the skull had completely decayed. A third was at the same depth. Four feet east of the center was another at the depth of 3 feet, but the skull in this case was wanting from the bundle. In the apex of the central core, in which a cut had been made for its reception, was a fifth at a depth of 3½ feet from the top and 6 inches in the core. No skeletons were found in the lower part of the mound, though at two points the earth was similar in character to that which results from decayed bodies and probably marked burial places. At the bottom of the mound, south of the center, was the only relic obtained, a copper drill or spindle, similar to that shown in Fig. 34; this is 7½ inches long, a little over one-fourth of an inch square, and pointed at each end. When found it was upright.

Mound 12, situated west of No. 8, in a thicket, measured 32 feet in diameter and 3½ in height. The upper layer consisted of loose sandy loam, like the surrounding surface. The remainder, of sand and clay, very hard, rested on the original surface of the ground. Under this was a pit, length 7 feet, width at one end 4 feet, at the other 5½, depth 2 feet, its walls perpendicular and bottom flat. Three bundled skeletons, the only ones found in the mound, were in this pit. With one were a few copper beads.

Mound 14, standing 120 feet from the lake shore, measured but 26 feet in diameter and a little over 3 feet in height. The construction was similar to that of No. 8; first a layer of sandy loam, 1 foot thick, then the core, 2 feet thick; but in this case there was, immediately below the second layer, a stratum of charcoal 4 inches thick, covering an area 6 feet in diameter, and immediately below it a layer of burned earth 3 inches thick and covering the same area. Underneath this, on the original surface, were the remains of three bundled skeletons partially burned. The remains of two logs, which had been nearly consumed by fire, could be traced in the layer of burned earth. They must have been about 6 feet long and 4 or 5 inches in diameter. They were parallel, within a foot of each other, and had evidently been laid on the earth covering the skeletons, but there were no indications of a wooden vault. The evidence seemed conclusive that the fire had been kindled here after the skeletons and logs were in place. The first skeleton was in the center under the two burned logs, and the indications were that it had been wrapped in birch bark, parts of which, although both wrappings and bones were charred, were obtained. The other two skeletons were north and west of this central one, and one of them showed but little of the effects of the fire, while the other was nearly consumed.

12 ETH——7

Southward, outside of this burned area, but under the core or layer, were two other skeletons, which seemed to have been buried at the same time as the other three.

ROCK COUNTY.

In 1886 Rev. S. D. Peet explored an effigy mound, probably representing a turtle, in the group near the waterworks at Beloit. The results of this examination he reports in substance as follows:

This mound was found by measurement to be 80 feet long, the length of the body and tail being equal, each 40 feet; the width of the body across the middle 15 feet, and across the ends 30 feet.

Other parties had taken off the top before his examination. A broad trench running through the middle, lengthwise, was carried down to the original surface of the ground. Here he found 8 skeletons, bundled, lying on the original surface of the mound. The dirt over them showed evidences of fire, but was not baked. The particulars, which resemble closely those observed in another effigy of the same kind belonging to the same group opened by Prof. S. Eaton, may be summarized as follows: First, the mound consisted of black loam; second, the earth was packed tightly about the bones; third, no gravel was found above the skeletons, but the original gravel of the bluff was immediately below them, indicating that the top soil had been removed before burial; fourth, the bodies were laid on the surface and the material of the mound, scraped from the surrounding area, thrown over them; fifth, the bodies or skeletons were evidently not interred in an extended position, for the bones of each individual were folded or heaped together, pieces of the skull in some instances resting upon them; they were probably "bundled" skeletons, buried after the flesh had been removed; sixth, there were no implements or ornaments of any kind with them; seventh, some of the bones were tolerably well preserved, others much decayed; and eighth, all of the skeletons were those of adults.

The bones of each skeleton were in a separate pile or bundle, those of the lower extremities being doubled up along the trunk, but the skull in most cases placed on top. It is, therefore, evident that the burial had taken place after the flesh had been removed, probably by exposure on platforms or scaffolds—a custom which seems to have been followed by the mound-building clans of this section. Under one body there was a small layer of stones. These stones were burned, smoked, and cracked, as if they had been subjected to great heat. Two or three pieces of dirt were taken out which were flat on one side, as though the dirt had been wet and packed down upon bark and then left to dry out, or, possibly, a fire had been kindled upon it, so as to take the color out of it. It was difficult to tell where the fire had been placed. Pieces of coal were scattered through the dirt and some of the bones showed signs of fire, though it was apparent that the bodies could not have been cremated.

IOWA.

The explorations made in this state on behalf of the Bureau were confined to the counties bordering on or adjacent to the Mississippi river, and chiefly in the extreme northeastern section.

Some of the works of this section evidently belong to the same type as those of Wisconsin, effigy or figure mounds being found in one or two of the extreme northeastern counties of the state, showing that the tribes which reared the singular structures in Wisconsin were not limited geographically by the Mississippi, although they extended beyond it but a short distance and over a comparatively small area.

As we proceed southward a change in the mode of construction and in other respects becomes apparent, indicating the presence of different tribes; yet there is sufficient resemblance in the two classes of works to indicate ethnic relationship, or at least that they belong to the same culture state.

ALLAMAKEE COUNTY.

This northeastern county of the state is bordered on the east by the Mississippi river, and much of it watered by the Little Iowa and its branches, all of which have worn deep channels through the Potsdam sandstone, which, whether remaining as castellated cliffs 300 or 400 feet high or rounded off to bold bluffs or terraced slopes, results in giving the charming contour and sheltered valleys of a mountain region.

POTTERY CIRCLE AND OTHER WORKS.

About 7 miles above New Albin, on the Little Iowa river, is an extensive group of earthworks, consisting of inclosures, lines of small mounds, excavations, etc., situated on the farm of Mr. H. P. Lane, and represented in Pl. v. The largest work is an inclosure, marked A, and shown on a larger scale in Fig. 48, to which the name "pottery circle" has been applied. It is situated on the margin of a bluff overlooking the Little Iowa river and an intervening bog beyond, probably the former channel of the river. It is almost exactly circular in form with clear indications of straight stretches (not shown in the figure), as though somewhat polygonal, the curve being broken on the eastern side, where it touches the brink of the bluff, is there made to conform to the line of the latter. The ends at the southeast overlap each other for a short distance, leaving at this point an entrance way, the only one to the inclosure. A ditch runs around the inside from the entrance on the south to where the wall strikes the bluff on the north, but is wanting along the bluff side and overlapping portion. The north and south diameter, measuring from center to center of the wall, is 251 feet; from east to west, 235 feet; the entire outer circumference, 807 feet; the length of the straight portion along the bluff,

100 feet, and of the overlapping portion at the entrance, 45 feet. The wall is quite uniform in size, about 4 feet high and from 25 to 27 in width, and the ditch about 8 or 10 feet wide and from 1 to 3 feet deep. The entrance is 16 feet wide, but there seems to have been no ditch along this portion. On the north, adjoining the wall on the outside

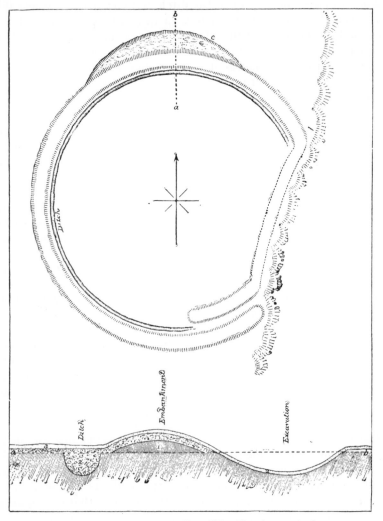

FIG. 48.—Circular inclosure near New Albin, Allamakee county, Iowa.

and extending along it for about 100 feet, is an excavation, Fig. 48 (see plan and section), 35 feet wide at the widest point and 3 deep.

As this ground, including the circle, has been under cultivation for fifteen years, it would be supposed that the height of the wall is considerably less than originally, but this is doubtful. On the contrary, it is probable it was originally about 20 feet wide and not more than 3 feet high, composed mainly of yellowish-brown clay, obtained, in part at least, from the ditch, but that, during occupancy, the accumulation of numerous bones of animals used for food, stone chips, river shells, broken pottery, and dirt, and since abandonment the accumulation of sand, drifted by the winds from the crumbling sandstone butte over-looking it, have not only filled the ditch, but elevated the whole inte-rior area and the wall 2 feet or more. This accumulation of sand is so great and so uniform over the adjacent plateau that fifteen years of cul-tivation has not reached the clay of the original natural surface, nor has it unearthed or penetrated to the bones, pottery fragments, and other refuse matter covering the original surface in the circle.

Three trenches 4 feet wide were dug through this wall from side to side and down to the original soil. The first was run through the northern portion opposite the large excavation. Here was found, first a layer of sand about 1 foot thick; next, an accumulation of refuse material mixed with earth, forming a layer from 1 to 2 feet thick; and below this the original clay embankment 2 feet thick, resting on the original surface. A section of the ditch, embankment, and excavation at this point is shown in Fig. 48. The dotted line *a b* indicates the natural surface; No. 1, the original clay layer of the embankment or wall; No. 2, the layer of earth and refuse material with which the ditch is filled; and No. 3, the top layer of sand.

In No. 2 were found charcoal, ashes, fragments of pottery, fractured bones, etc.

Trench No. 2, opened through the west side, gave a similar result. No. 3, in the southern part, across the lap of the walls and entrance way, varied in showing less clay and no distinct ditch.

A broad belt of the inner area on the east side next the bluff wall was excavated and carefully examined. It was found to consist of the same kind of accumulations as No. 2 in the first trench, except that here the shells were more numerous and there were many burnt stones.

SQUARE EARTHWORK.

D, Pl. V, is situated at the southwest corner of the plateau, on the margin of the bluff, facing west. It consists of a wall from 12 to 15 feet broad and 2 to 4 feet high, along three sides of a nearly regular par-allelogram. The length of the wall on the south is 175 feet, that on the east 150, with traces of a ditch on the outside; that on the north, 200 feet.

About 30 feet east of the northeast corner, which is the highest point adjacent to the work, and above the inclosed area, is an excavation now about 3 feet in depth.

Within this square inclosure are three small mounds, which were opened with the following results:

No. 1, 30 feet long by 20 wide and 4 high, was found to consist of a top layer of loose sand 1 foot thick, the remainder of hard yellowish clay.

In the latter were several flat sandstone fragments, and beneath them, on the original surface of the ground, a much decayed human skeleton, with a few stone chips, *Unio* shells, and fragments of pottery.

No. 2, 18 feet in diameter and 3 feet high, was mainly a loose cairn of sandstones, covering traces of human bones, charcoal, and ashes.

No. 3, 15 feet in diameter and 3 feet high, a stone pile or cairn covered with earth and heaped over a mass of charred bones, charcoal, ashes, and some fragments of pottery.

This inclosure is about half a mile from the pottery circle, and, like it, well situated for defense, but not so well constructed and apparently more ancient.

THE OBLONG WORK.

This is an oblong inclosure, situated south of the group just mentioned, and just across an impassable slough, and is the one marked E in Pl. v. It is on a sloping terrace at the foot of a bluff, which rises abruptly behind it to the height of 200 feet. The end walls run from this bluff to the margin of the slough, where there is also another descent. Along this margin runs a connecting wall some 300 feet in length. The wall at the west end is 160 feet long; that at the east end 175. The height varies from 1 to 3 feet and the width from 10 to 15 feet. On the outside of each end wall is a washout, possibly marking the ditches from which the dirt to form the walls was taken.

MOUNDS.

Extending southward from the pottery circle to the bluff bank that margins the slough, a distance of about half a mile, and expanding at the southern end to an equal extent, is a dry, undulating plateau. On the eastern half of this area are six parallel lines of mounds running northeast and southwest (marked B in Pl. v), mostly circular in form, varying in diameter from 15 to 40 feet and in height from 2 to 6 feet. A few, as indicated in the figure, are oblong, varying in length from 50 to 100 feet. The number in the group exceeds 100.

An examination revealed the fact that, in addition to the mounds, much of the area between them was used as a burying place, and that scattered here and there between the graves were charcoal and ashes, stone chips, shells, etc. Both in the mounds and these graves there was a compact layer of hard, light-colored earth, having much the appearance of lime mortar, probably clay and ashes mixed together, which had undergone the action of fire. As the burials in these intermediate spots were seldom over 18 inches deep, the only soil above the hard layer which covered them was the sterile sand from the sandy butte marked C on the plate, while the mounds were uniformly covered with a layer of richest soil, although below this and covering the skeletons was the layer of hard, light colored earth.

A trench cut through the oblong mound of this group (No. 1) revealed near the center an oblong pile of loose sandstones, beneath

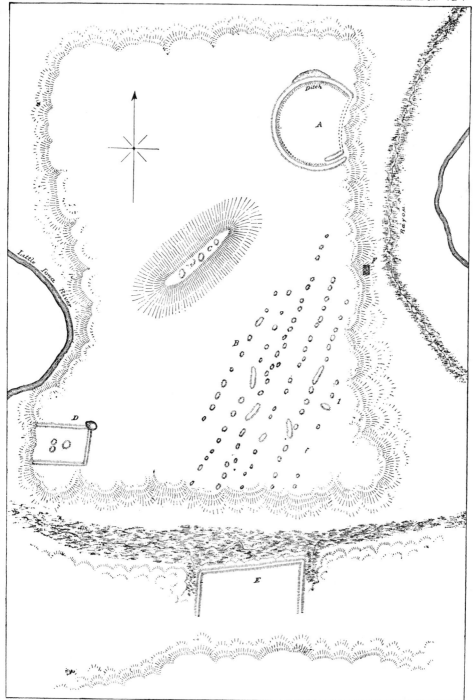

ANCIENT WORKS NEAR NEW ALBIN, ALLAMAKEE COUNTY, IOWA.

which was found a crypt or rude stone coffin about 6 feet long and 18 inches wide, formed by first placing flat sandstones on the natural clay surface of the ground, then other slabs edgewise at the sides and ends, and a covering of similar stones. Within this, extended at full length, with the head nearly west, was the skeleton of an adult, but too much decayed for preservation. With it were some stone chips, rude stone scrapers or skinners, a *Unio* shell, and some fragments of pottery similar to those found in the pottery circle.

THE SAND BUTTE.

This prominent feature of the area (marked C in Pl. v), which, by the eroding influence of wind and rain, has covered the plateau to the depth of a foot or more with sand since the works were constructed, is about 100 feet high at its northern end and 150 at the southern extremity. On the narrow crest are three small circular mounds, in which were found human bones, fragments of pottery, etc. The same compact earth as found elsewhere was also encountered in these, showing them to be the work of the same people.

WALLED VAULT.

In the side of the eastern bluff, about half way down from the top, is a somewhat singular work (marked F). This is a room or vault about 11 feet square, excavated in the face of the bluff and roughly walled up with flat sandstones. Although many of these stones are too large to be handled by an ordinary man, they were evidently brought by some means from the sand butte, and several are still on the top of the bluff above the vault. The back and most of the end walls are sustained by the bank, standing from 4 to 6 feet high, but the front, although built of the larger pieces, especially about the doorway, is only about half as high. A careful examination of the interior revealed nothing but charcoal, ashes, and decaying firebrands, which might possibly have resulted from the burning of a timber roof. The regularity with which the walls were built, and the square corners, aside from all other indications, suggest that this is of comparatively recent date, and the work of a different people from those who constructed the circle and mounds of the plateau. It was probably made by some white or half-breed trapper within the past two centuries.

Among the results of the exploration of this interesting group may be noted the following: That, although human skeletons and bones were found in great numbers in the mounds and under the surface of the plateau, none were found within the pottery circle or nearer than 200 yards of it. Those found were sometimes mingled promiscuously with charcoal and ashes, but were usually whole skeletons, frequently, but not always, lying horizontally near the natural surface of the ground, without any apparent system, except that they were uniformly covered with from 1 to 3 feet of very hard earth, seemingly mixed with ashes or something of a similar nature and color, giving this covering the appearance of dried lime or mortar.

Fragments of pottery were found in abundance in the circle, in the mounds, in the washouts, and in fact at almost every point in the area covered by the group. Judging by the fragments, for not a single entire vessel was obtained, the prevailing forms were the ordinary earthen pot with ears, and a flask or gourd-shaped vase with a rather broad and short neck. The latter were the larger ones and were usually too thin for use in cooking, or even for holding liquids. The paste of which this pottery was made had evidently been mixed with pounded shells. The only ornamentation observed consisted in the varied forms given the handles or ears, and indentations or scratched lines.

Nearly all the implements found were of stone, exceedingly rude, being little lse than stone flakes with one sharp edge, many of which appear to have been resharpened and used as knives, scrapers, and skinners. Some had been worked into moderately fair perforators or drills for making holes in horn, bone, or shell, specimens of all these with holes having been found.

The immense quantity of charred and fractured bones, not only of fishes, birds, and the smaller quadrupeds, such as the rabbit and fox, but also of the bear, wolf, elk, and deer, shows that the occupants of this place lived chiefly by the chase, and hence must have used the bow and arrow and spear; yet, strange to say, less than a dozen arrow or spear heads were found, and these so rude as scarcely to deserve the name. A single true chipped celt, three sandstones with mortar-shaped cavities, and a few mullers or flat stones used for grinding or some similar purpose, were obtained. The specimens of other materials obtained consist of fragments of horn, evidently cut around by some rude instrument and then broken off at about a finger's length and possibly intended to be shaped into more perfect implements, or probably handles for knives. Several horn and bone punches and awls were also found, and among them one that is barbed, and another with a perforation through the larger end.

ANCIENT INCLOSURE ON HAYS'S FARM.

On the farm of Mr. A. D. Hays, 2 miles southwest of New Albin, is the circular inclosure shown in Fig. 49. This is situated on the lower bluff just above the point where the Little Iowa river enters the Mississippi. The bluff here is about 100 feet higher than the bottoms which border these streams, and continues along the Mississippi for some distance at about the same height, with small circular mounds scattered over its surface; but the plateau slopes gradually to the margin of a deep ravine which enters the Little Iowa upon the western side. This area, including the circle, has been under cultivation for twenty-one years; but, notwithstanding the wear, the lines of the works were distinctly traceable throughout.

The circle consists of three parallel ditches and two intermediate earthen walls. The inside ditch (before the works were disturbed) was probably 5 or 6 feet deep and 12 feet wide; the inner wall the same width; the middle ditch 4 feet deep and a little over 12 feet wide; and finally, the outer ditch 4 feet deep and about the same width as the wall. As will be seen from the figure, the inclosure is circular, with a

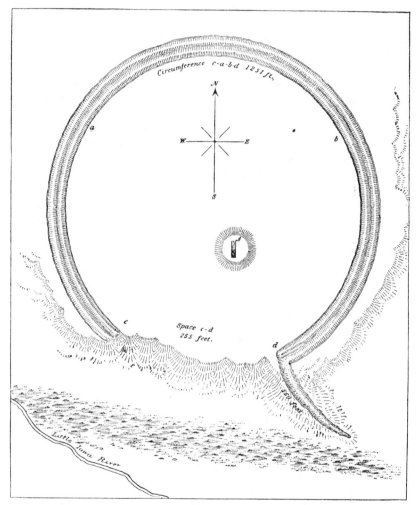

FIG. 49.—Inclosure on Hays's farm, near New Albin, Allamakee county, Iowa.

break on the side where it strikes the southern margin of the bluff overlooking the slough that runs into the Little Iowa river. The circumference of the circle, exclusive of the break, is 996 feet, and the extent of the break along the bluff 225 feet. At the southeast an embankment some 10 or 12 feet wide and from 3 to 5 feet high runs down the crest of a narrow spur about 150 feet, gradually tapering to a point. The slope on which this work is situated, like that at the pottery circle, is considerable, but very smooth and even. The location is a good one for defense and was in all probability selected by the ancient people who erected the works on this account.

The most singular parts of the works at this place are three stone structures, to which the name "furnaces" has been applied by the people of this locality. One of these was found in a small mound within the inclosure (marked A in Fig. 49) and two not in mounds, outside and about 80 or 90 paces from the northwestern part of the circle. Light traces of those outside of the wall remain, while of that in the inclosed mound only about 1 foot of the wall was visible. But Mr. Hays, who has owned and occupied the land for twenty-one years and since it was first opened for cultivation, gave the following information in regard to them: The one in mound A, and the other, not shown in the figure, were each 18 feet long, each formed of two parallel walls about 3 feet high and 3 feet apart, composed of flat sandstones (yet to be seen close by), roughly laid up, and gradually drawn in near the top until one layer would cover the opening left in the top near that end. The inner stones stood fire well, as shown by the indications on them.

Mound A in the circle is 24 feet in diameter, and now only about 1 foot high. Fragments of pottery, stone chips, *Unio* shells, and pieces of bone are still abundant in and about the work, and especially among the stones in the mound.

FISH'S MOUNDS.

These are situated on the lands owned by Mr. Fish, near the Mississippi river, a short distance below the point where the Little Iowa joins it. Those of one group are placed along the crest of a ridge running parallel with the river, and about one-fourth of a mile therefrom. They number about 30; circular in form, and varying from 20 to 40 feet in diameter. One singular feature was observed; those on the higher and sandy ground having a core of clay about the same size and form as those on the firm clay portion of the ridge, though to the latter a layer of several feet of sand was added, making them appear much larger and more recent than the others; yet upon opening the two classes, the contents, consisting of decaying human bones, fragments of pottery, and rude stone implements, showed no perceptible differences.

In one of the mounds opened two skeletons were found, lying horizontally side by side, facing each other. They were at the base of the hard clay core, which seemed to have formed a perfect roof, while the sand, upon a sharp ridge, formed the flooring, thus protecting them from moisture and preserving them longer from decay than where less favorably situated; the skulls were obtained almost uninjured.

Many mounds similar to these were found along the foothills of these rocky bluffs.

Upon the terrace below these mounds, where the railroad track has been graded lengthwise, was a line of comparatively large mounds, the remaining portions of which show that, although from 6 to 15 feet high, and composed mainly of sand similar to that around them, they had a hard central core of clay mixed with ashes, from 2 to 4 feet high, under which was generally found at least one skeleton. Several stone hatchets, arrow and spear heads, and a few copper chisels, were found by the first explorers. One of the mounds, 32 feet in diameter and 8 feet high, contained a walled circular vault, represented in Fig. 50; this, like the stonework in the furnaces, did not have the true arch, but, as the main portion of it, which still remains standing shows, it was built of flat stones, and gradually lessened in diameter as it rose,

FIG. 50.—Walled mound, Fish group, Allamakee county, Iowa.

being covered at the top by a single stone. It contained a single adult skeleton in a squatting posture, with which was a small earthen vase of the usual globular form.

FISH'S CAVE.

This is simply a fissure in the vertical face of the sandstone bluff facing the Mississippi, about 6 miles south of New Albin, which by the action of the river or other means has been enlarged to a cave or rock house 40 or 50 feet long and 12 feet high. The elevation is so little above the Mississippi that it must be at least partially flooded during high water. The walls and ceiling are literally covered with rude etchings, representing quadrupeds, birds, turtles, bird tracks, totems, and symbolic or fanciful objects. These figures range in length from 2 or 3 inches to 2 or 3 feet, and proportionally in width, and are cut into the soft rock from one-fourth to a full inch in depth, the width of the lines exceeding their depth. The width of these lines appears to have been increased by a crumbling process which must have gone on for a time after they were cut, but was checked by the formation of a dark-colored and hard crust over the surface, which now protects them.[1] The floor was covered to the depth of 2 feet with a mass of refuse material consisting of fish and other animal bones, fragments of pottery and stone, charcoal, and ashes mingled with dirt.

---

[1] A tracing of the figures was made and handed to Col. Garrick Mallery, for use in his study of Sign Language.

CLAYTON COUNTY.

The ancient remains of this county are chiefly effigy mounds or emblematic works similar in character to those found in Wisconsin, and evidently attributable to the authors of those singular structures. So far as could be ascertained, these works are only found on the west side of the Mississippi, between Yellow river on the north and the Maquoketa on the south and westward, a distance of some ten or twelve miles. As will be seen by reference to a map of this region, this small belt is directly opposite that portion of Wisconsin which seems to have been the chief home of the effigy mound-builders, where, as well as in this small portion of Iowa, they have left enduring evidences of a dense population or long occupancy, as the bluffs, the terraces, and even higher bottoms of the river subject to occasional overflow are alike dotted over with effigies and the usual accompanying small circular mounds and lines of earthworks.

ELKPORT EFFIGY.

This is situated on a bluff overlooking Turkey river near Elkport, about 10 miles west of the Mississippi, and is 120 feet long, nearly one-half its length consisting of an extremely elongated tail, which is in strong contrast with the short legs. It is probably intended to represent the otter. The greatest height of the body is 5 feet, the main portions of the extremities from 2 to 3 feet, but the tail tapers to a point.

There are many other interesting works along Turkey river and upon high bluffs above McGregor, notably effigies of antlered elks, uniformly in lines or groups heading southward. Unfortunately the sketches made of these were so defaced by subsequent exposure to a heavy rain as to render them valueless for reproduction.

Near the town of Clayton is another group of these works, which consists of an extended line of effigy and circular mounds.

DUBUQUE COUNTY.

Near the town of Peru, immediately south of the mouth of Maquoketa creek, situated on a dry, sandy bench or terrace some 20 feet or more above a bayou which makes out from the Mississippi, is a group, mostly of small circular tumuli. As the relative positions may possibly furnish some aid to the archeologist in studying their several uses, a sketch of the group is given in Fig. 51. Fifty years ago, according to the old settlers, this ground was covered with a heavy growth of timber, which was removed for the purpose of cultivation; but the larger portion having afterwards been abandoned, most of the mounds are again covered with a young forest growth. A number were opened, but only detached portions of a skeleton were found, as a skull in one, a leg, arm, or other part in another, four or five adjacent ones apparently aggregating one entire skeleton. Some of these bones are charred and all are much decayed, indicating great age. Otherwise nothing peculiar was observed in this group, except the arrangement of the mounds, which is shown in the sketch. Nos. 34, 35, 36, and 37 are four oblong mounds, varying in length from 40 to 110 feet, and from 1½ to 4 feet in height. The inner portions were found to be of hard, compact earth, as is usual in this region.

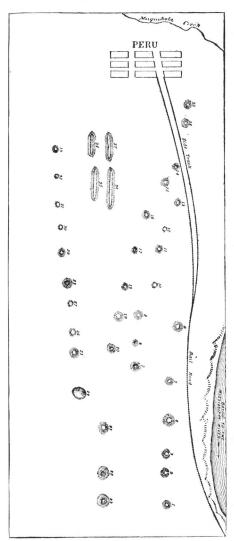

EAGLE POINT GROUP.

This group is about 3 miles above Dubuque on the bluffs and terrace fronting the Mississippi. The larger number of the mounds—about 70—all of which, except two oblong ones, are small and conical, are on a level terrace about 50 feet above high-water mark. On a bluff immediately west of these is a single embankment or mound about 300 feet long, 20 feet broad, and 3 feet high; and on Eagle point proper, immediately north, which is the point of a bluff some 200 feet high overlooking the river, are several low circular and two long mounds and a stone cairn.

Eleven of the small circular mounds on the terrace were opened thoroughly, but nothing found in them except some charcoal, stone chips, and fragments of pottery.

FIG. 51.—Group near Peru, Dubuque county, Iowa.

In an excavation made in the center of the long mound on the western bluff two decayed skeletons were found. Near the breast of one of them were a blue stone gorget (shown in Fig. 52) and five rude stone scrapers; with the other, thirty-one fresh-water pearls, perforated and used as beads.

An excavation was made in one of the long mounds on the point, and also in one of the circular ones. Both were found to be composed of a very hard cement or prepared earth, which could be broken up only with the pick, when it crumbled like dry lime mortar, and was found to be traversed throughout with flattened horizontal cavities. These cavities were lined with a peculiar black felt-like substance, specimens of which were carefully preserved. There is scarcely a doubt that these cavities mark the spaces occupied by a body or bodies buried here, and it is possible that this felt-like substance is the remnant of the fleshy portion of the bodies. An examination for the purpose of deciding this point will be made and reported hereafter.

WAPELLO COUNTY.

The diagram of the area between Eldon and Iowaville along the Des Moines river, shown in Fig. 53, is constructed from a careful examina-

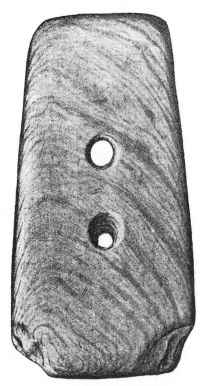

tion of the ground and the statements of Mr. J. H. Jordan, who has r e s i d e d here since the close of the Black Hawk war, and was the Indian agent to the Sacs and Foxes from the time of their removal thither after the war until Black Hawk's death, Sept. 15, 1838. Between the two points named stretches the noted Iowa bottom, which is at least 2 miles wide at the middle, about which point formerly stood the old agency; near the same point is the present residence of Mr. Jordan. The position of Black Hawk's grave, the

FIG. 52.—Stone gorget, Dubuque county, Iowa.

race tracks, the mounds of the Iowas, the mounds of the Pottowatamies, and the place where the scaffolds for their dead stood are also indicated on the plat.

This valley had long been a famous haunt for the Indians, but at the time of Mr. Jordan's first acquaintance with it was in possession of the Iowas, whose main village was around the point where his house stands.

The race course consisted of three parallel hard-beaten tracks nearly a mile in length, where the greater portion of the Iowa warriors were engaged in sport when surprised by Black Hawk and a large portion of them slaughtered, in 1830. After Black Hawk and his warriors had departed with their plunder the remaining Iowas returned and buried

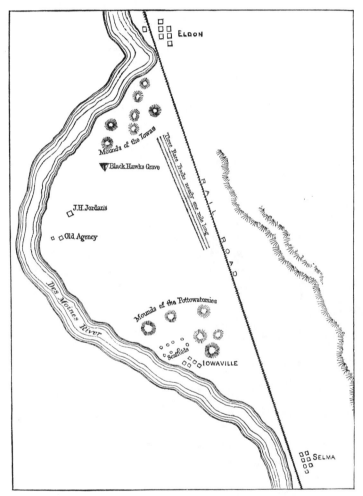

FIG. 53.—Diagram of Indian battle ground, Wapello county, Iowa.

their dead in little mounds of sod and earth from 2 to 4 feet high at the point indicated in the diagram.

After the Black Hawk war the remnant of the Iowas, by a treaty, formally ceded their rights in this valley to the Sacs and Foxes. Here this noted chief was buried, in accordance with his dying request, in a full military suit given him by President Jackson, together with the various memorials received by him from the whites, and the trophies won from the Indians. He was placed on his back on a puncheon slanting at a low angle to the ground, where his feet were sustained by another, and covered with several inches of sod. Then a roof-shaped covering of slabs or puncheons, one end elevated and the other lowered, was placed above. Over all was thrown a covering of earth and sod to the depth of a foot or more, and the whole surrounded by a line of pickets some 8 or 10 feet high. The subsequent stealing of his bones and their return to his friends have been recorded by the historian and poet, and need not be repeated here.

VAN BUREN COUNTY.

MOUNDS NEAR DOUD.

These mounds are some 18 in number, circular in form, of rather small size, and placed in a nearly straight line upon the very crest of a remarkably straight and sharp ridge, 30 or 40 feet higher than the plateau upon which the town is built.

One denoted No. 1, about 25 feet in diameter and 5 feet high, had been previously opened by Mr. Doud, and yielded two gray disks each 4 inches in diameter, a grooved stone axe and stone chips.

No. 7, about 20 feet in diameter and $3\frac{1}{2}$ feet high, was explored and found, as usual, to contain a core of hard earth, but nothing else.

No. 12, diameter 25 feet and height 4 feet, was found to contain, beneath the hard core and lying on the original surface of the ground, decayed human bones and three fragments of dark colored pottery.

No. 14, opened, nothing found.

No. 15, same size as No. 12. In this, beneath a very hard core and lying horizontally on the original surface with head north, were the remains (scarcely more than traces) of a human skeleton.

LEE COUNTY.

Upon the bluffs near the junction of the Des Moines river with the Mississippi were many circular mounds, most of which have been opened and numerous articles mostly of intrusive burials obtained therefrom. Several were opened by the Bureau agent, but nothing found in them save decayed human bones, fragments of pottery and stone chips.

ILLINOIS.

JOE DAVIESS COUNTY.

Overlooking the city of East Dubuque (Dunleith) is a line of bluffs whose grassy slopes and summits are dotted over with ancient mounds of unusual symmetry, some of them above the usual size for this section of the country. The relative positions of these mounds to one another, to the bluffs, and to the river are shown in the diagram (Fig. 54).

The following list gives the respective sizes and a brief statement of the results of the explorations made in them. They are all of the usual conical form:

No.	Diameter.	Height.	Remarks.
	Feet.	Feet.	
1	12	3	Stone cairn. Coals, ashes, etc.
2	42	5	Human bones.
3	43	4	Nothing found.
4	46	8	Contained a stone crypt.
5	70	12	Large skeleton, copper ornaments, etc.
6	40	8	Opened, but result unknown.
7	40	4	Do.
8	32	5	Human bones.
9	34	4	Opened, but result unknown.
10	20	3	Nothing found.
11	25	3	Result unknown.
12	60	9	Vault and human bones.
13	45	4	Reopened, result given hereafter.
14	25	3	Skeletons.
15	45	6	Bones.
16	65	10	Vault found.
17	50	8	Opened, result unknown.

Nos. 18 to 26, inclusive, form a line of nearly connected mounds, from 30 to 50 feet in diameter and 4 to 7 feet high.

A section of the bluff through the line of mounds No. 13 to No. 17 is shown in the lower part of Fig. 54, in which is seen the general slope of the upper area.

No. 5, the largest of the group was carefully examined. Two feet below the surface, near the apex, was a skeleton, doubtless an intrusive Indian burial. Near the original surface of the ground, several feet north of the center, were the much decayed skeletons of some 6 or 8 persons, of every size, from the infant to the adult. They were placed horizontally at full length, with the heads toward the south. A few perforated *Unio* shells and some rude stone skinners and scrapers were found with them. Near the original surface, 10 or 12 feet from the center, on the lower side, lying at full length upon its back, was one of the largest skeletons discovered by the Bureau agents, the length as proved by actual measurement being between 7 and 8 feet. It was all clearly traceable, but crumbled to pieces immediately after removal from the hard earth in which it was encased. With this were three thin, crescent-shaped pieces of roughly hammered, native copper, respectively 6, 8, and 10 inches in length, with small holes along the convex margin; a number of elongate copper beads made by rolling together thin sheets; and a chert lance-head over 11 inches long. Around the neck was a series of bear teeth, which doubtless formed a necklace; there were also several upon the wrists. Lying across the thighs were dozens of small copper beads, which perhaps once adorned

12 ETH——8

the fringe of a hunting shirt. These were formed by rolling slender wire-like strips into small rings.

A partial exploration of No. 4 was made in 1857, revealing masses of burned earth and charred human bones mingled with charcoal and ashes. A further examination revealed, on the lower side, the end of a

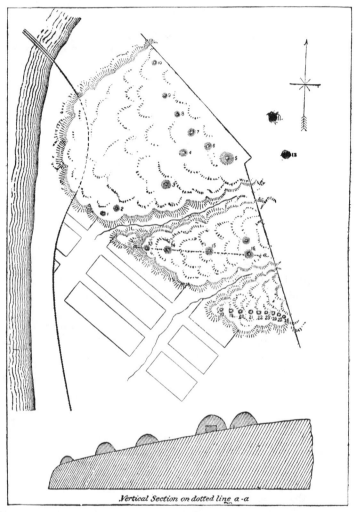

Vertical Section on dotted line a -a

Fig. 54.—Mound group, Dunleith, Illinois.

double line of flat stones set on edge, about a foot apart at the bottom and adjusted so as to meet at the top in a roof-shaped arch or drain (for which it was probably intended). This extended inward nearly on a level, almost to the center, at which point it was about 3 feet beneath the original surface of the ground. Here a skeleton was discovered in a vault or grave which had been dug in the ground before the mound was cast up. Over that portion below the waist and the dislocated right arm, which was drawn below the waist, were placed flat stones so arranged by leaning as to support each other and prevent pressure on the body; no traces of fire were on them, yet when the upper portions were reached, although extended in a natural position, they were but charred remains, scarcely traceable amid the charcoal and ashes of a fire that had nearly consumed them.

It was apparent that a grave had first been dug, the right arm of the skeleton dislocated and placed beside it below the waist, and this part covered; then the remainder burned to a cinder and over all a mound raised, which covered, in addition thereto, a pile of charred human bones, charcoal and ashes. The mound, vault, and drain are represented in Fig. 55. (1, outline of the mound; 2, the vault, and 3, the drain.)

A partial examination was made of mound No. 13 in 1857, showing it to be similar to the preceding, so far as then explored. Further exploration brought to light a circle of stone slabs 10 feet in diameter, set on

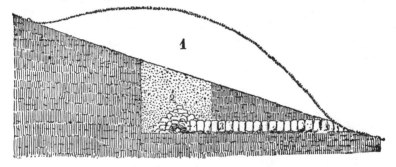

FIG 55.—Vault in Mound No. 4, Dunleith, Illinois.

edge at the natural surface of the ground. Within this circle, at the depth of 3 feet, were five skeletons, two of adults, two of children, and one of an infant. They were all lying horizontally side by side, heads south, the adults at the outside and the children between them.

No. 15, except a roof or arched stratum 2 feet thick of prepared earth or mortar, so firm as to retain its form for several feet unsupported, was found to be an ossuary or heap of human bones in a promiscuous mass, many of them decayed. Only an ankle bone which had reunited after being broken was saved.

The most interesting feature of the group was found in No. 16, a symmetrical mound 65 feet in diameter and 10 feet high.

The first 6 feet from the top consisted of hard gray earth, seemingly a mortar-like composition, which required the use of the pick. This covered a vault built in part of stone and in part of round logs. When fully uncovered this was found to be a rectangular crypt, inside measurement showing it to be 13 feet long and 7 feet wide. The four straight, surrounding walls were built of small unhewn stones to the height of 3 feet and a foot or more in thickness. Three feet from each end was a cross wall or partition of like character, thus leaving a central chamber 7 feet square, and a narrow cell at each end about 2 feet wide and 7 feet long. This had been entirely covered with a single layer of round logs, varying in diameter from 6 to 12 inches, laid close together side by side across the width of the vault, the ends resting upon and extending to uneven lengths beyond the side walls.

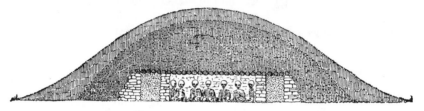

FIG. 56.—Section of Mound No. 16, Dunleith, Illinois.

In the central chamber were 11 skeletons, 6 adults, 4 children of different sizes, and 1 infant, the last evidently buried in the arms of one of the adults, presumably its mother. They had all apparently been interred at one time as they were found arranged in a circle in a sitting posture, with backs against the walls. In the center of the space around which they were grouped was a fine large shell, *Busycon perversum*, which had been converted into a drinking cup by removing the columella. Scattered around this were quite a number of pieces of broken pottery.

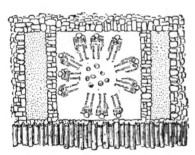

FIG. 57.—Vault in Mound No. 16, Dunleith, Illinois.

The end cells, walled off as heretofore stated, were nearly filled with a fine chocolate-colored dust, which, when first uncovered, gave out such a sickening odor that it was found necessary to suspend operations until the next day in order to give it time to escape. This dust may be the ashes resulting from burning the fleshy portions of the individuals buried in the central chamber. A bottle of it was saved for future examination.

A vertical section of the mound and vault, lengthwise of the latter, is shown in Fig. 56. In this can be seen the end and partition walls of the vault, the cells, the skeletons, the ends of the logs forming the cover and the hard central mass of the mound. Fig. 57 shows the plan of the vault, the positions of the skeletons, and the projecting ends of the logs on one side. The covering consisted of oak logs, nearly all of which had been peeled and some of the larger ones somewhat squared by slabbing off the sides before being put in place. The slabs and bark thus removed, together with reeds and twigs, had been laid over the logs to fill the crevices. It was not possible to decide from the indications what kind of implement had been used in peeling and slabbing the logs. The larger logs extended a foot or more, irregularly, beyond the side walls. Over the whole vault had been spread layer after layer of mortar-like material evidently containing lime or ashes, a foot or more of ordinary soil, forming the outer or top layer, completing the mound.

No. 12 was opened some years ago by Dr. Campbell, who found in it a vault similar in character to the one described.

PIKE COUNTY.

On the spur of the ridge upon which the Welch mounds of Brown county, hereafter noticed, are situated, and about midway between them and Chambersburg, in Pike county, is a group of circular mounds, possibly the work of another people than those who built the effigies.

They are mainly on the farm of Mr. W. A. Hume, who assisted in opening eight of them, of which but two are specially noticed here.

The first was 5 feet high and but 25 in diameter, of true conical form. It was composed of the usual hard "burial earth" throughout, with nothing of interest at the bottom; but near the top, scarcely covered with earth, was found the skeleton of an adult, doubtless an Indian intrusive burial.

The other, situated on the point of a commanding bluff, was also conical in form, 50 feet in diameter and 8 feet high. The outer layer consisted of sandy soil, 2 feet thick, filled with slightly decayed skeletons, probably Indians of intrusive burials. The earth of the main portion of this mound was a very fine yellowish sand which shoveled like ashes and was everywhere, to the depth of from 2 to 4 feet, as full of human skeletons as could well be stowed away in it, even to two and three tiers. Among these were a number of bones not together as skeletons, but mingled in confusion and probably from scaffolds or other localities. Excepting one, which was rather more than 7 feet long, these skeletons appeared to be of medium size and many of them much decayed. Some feet beneath all these was a single skeleton of ordinary size, much decayed, and with it a bone and skull of some quadruped.

The other mounds of the group are circular, varying in diameter from 30 to 50 feet and in height from 4 to 8 feet. In the six opened the only things found were the bones of intrusive burials near the top and sides, with a few arrow points and rude, chipped stone implements, probably scrapers.

From a line of ancient fire beds and kitchen heaps along a rivulet that runs into McGee creek, near these mounds, some pieces of bones, a number of rude stone implements and fragments of pottery were obtained.

BROWN COUNTY.

THE WELCH GROUP.

This group, of which a plan is given in Fig. 58, is on the farm of Mr. Edward Welch, 3 miles west of Perry Springs station, Wabash and St. Louis Railroad, on a narrow ridge some 200 feet above the bottom lands. It consists of six mounds (Nos. 1 to 6 in the plan) and a number of small saucer-shaped basins surrounded by low, earthen ridges, doubtless the sites of ancient dwellings or wigwams. The latter are indicated on the plan by small circles.

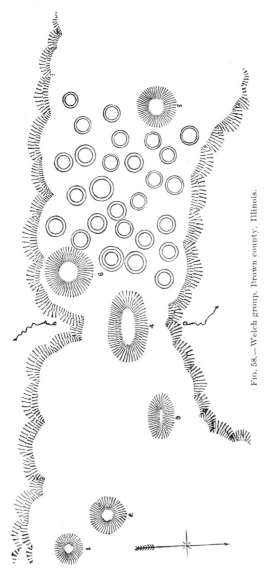

FIG. 58.—Welch group, Brown county, Illinois.

Mound No. 2, about 100 feet in diameter and 8 feet high, had a very marked depression in the top. A pit 6 feet square carried down to the natural surface brought to light three fire beds at different depths. Numerous fragments of pottery, stone chips, pieces of sandstone, which had been used as tool-sharpeners, and a flat sandstone nearly 2 feet square, on one side of which were several long, deep grooves, probably made in sharpening tools, were also found.

No. 6 was also opened, but only disclosed the fact that it consisted of an outer layer of soil 1 foot thick and the remainder, soil, clay, stone chips, and fragments of pottery commingled.

As the land was in wheat at the time of examination, permission to make further excavations in the mounds was refused.

The dwelling sites vary considerably in size, some being as much as 70 feet in diameter, and some of them 3 feet deep in the center after fifty years of cultivation.

Mound No. 4 is oblong in form, the longer diameter 165 feet and the shorter 90, height 15 feet; regularly truncated, with flat top, the length on top about 100 feet.

ANCIENT WORKS NEAR LAGRANGE.

These works are on the top of the bluff facing the Illinois river, just below the mouth of Crooked creek. The principal area occupied is the top of a spur flanked by a ravine on each side and extending back from the river with a level plateau. At the back, where the side bluffs cease to form a sufficient natural defense, an embankment has been thrown up. This extends across the area from one ravine to the other, measuring 597 feet in length, leaving a slope of 48 feet to a ditch 30 feet wide and 8 or 10 feet below the level of the plateau beyond. Immediately within the wall was evidently the main village, as here are numerous saucer-shaped depressions or hut rings, and between these and the margin of the bluff in a nearly straight line are three mounds, one oblong, the others circular. With or without palisades the place must have been easily defended in this direction.

The only other assailable part of the bluff is a sloping ridge extending down toward the river on the left. This is fortified by an earthen wall, breast high, which follows the windings of the crest and which has a mound-like enlargement at each turn or change of slope.

The length of the nearly level area from the rear wall to the oblong mound or embankment is 492 feet; thence to the mound which is on the very edge of the bluff the slope is marked and the distance is 315 feet. There are other mounds outside of the fort on the point of a spur across the ravine to the right.

A considerable collection of stone implements, mostly in fragments, was made at this place, gathered from the surface. Only four mounds were examined, as the remaining ones had been opened by others, who found a number of fine stone hatchets, pipes, arrowheads, gorgets, etc., mostly at the tops of the mounds. The dwelling sites are from 30 to 50 feet in diameter and from 1 to 3 feet deep.

The four mounds opened yielded only human bones and a few fragments of stone implements.

In one, diameter 50 feet, height 15 feet, lay a human skeleton at the bottom, much decayed.

In the second, diameter 40 feet, height 10 feet, were decaying bones, stone chips, and fragments of pottery.

No. 3, diameter 60 feet, height 15 feet, full of bones.

No. 4, diameter 50 feet, height 15 feet, many bones.

As all the human bones found in the last were near the surface, at the top or sides, they are presumably those of modern Indians, and the mounds may have been built for other than burial purposes. But those upon the bluff to the right are probably all burial mounds. They are mainly of very hard prepared earth, and one of those explored was certainly a depository of skeletons removed from elsewhere.

Upon the level bottom between the bluff and a lake or bayou connecting with the Illinois river, and about 2 miles south of Lagrange, is a small group of mounds, very interesting from the fact that here we see the pyramidal form so common in the south, but so rare in this northern region.

The dimensions of these mounds are as follows (the numbers are given merely as means of designating them):

No. 1, circular; diameter, 100 feet; height, 5 feet.

No. 2, rectangular; base, 198 by 117 feet; top, 111 by 30 feet; height, 30 feet; regularly truncated; top level.

No. 3, rectangular; base, 165 by 82 feet; top, 105 by 30 feet; height, 24 feet; regularly truncated; top level.

No. 4, circular; diameter, 96 feet; height, 15 feet.

No. 5, circular; diameter, 33 feet; height, 6 feet.

The size, form, appearance, and surroundings of these mounds seemingly indicate that they are the work of southern mound-builders.

The neighboring bluffs are covered with the ordinary circular mounds, 20 to 60 feet in diameter and 4 to 8 feet high. The tops of these had already been rifled of the intrusive burials of Indian skeletons, stone, and occasionally iron implements and other modern articles. Further exploration of the hard central core of many of them revealed only decaying human bones and unimportant articles. But those on the bottom are of a very different type from those on the bluffs, and probably are the work of a different people. The bottom on which these stand is subject to occasional overflows. Many acres of a dry, sloping terrace 2 miles south of this point are strewn with the finest lance and arrow heads and other stone implements found in the valley of the Illinois river. Fragments of a better quality of pottery were also abundant, but no entire vessels were found.

ADAMS COUNTY.

Upon the east bank of the Mississippi opposite Canton, Missouri, is an irregular line of mounds, nearly all of which are circular and vary in diameter from 30 to 120 feet, and in height from 4 to 10 feet. Two of these were opened with the following result:

No. 1, about 100 feet in diameter and 10 feet high, was composed of, first, a layer of soil 2 feet thick, the remainder of compact earth so hard as to require the use of the pick. At a depth of 1 foot in the latter, or 3 feet from the top, was a much-decayed skeleton of ordinary size lying horizontally with the head toward the west, about which were some fragments of pottery. Nothing else of interest was found.

No. 2, 60 feet in diameter and 5 feet high, was of similar construction, but nothing was found in it.

INDIAN GRAVE PRAIRIE.

About 5 miles southeast of the preceding on the western shore of a small lake is a spot known as "Indian Grave prairie," which in former times was a favorite haunt of the Indians. It is a circular area containing some 50 acres, rising about 5 feet above the surrounding lands, with a steep descent all around the margin, and is now a part of the levee. Mr. R. R. Thorn, who now occupies and cultivates it, says there is neither trace nor tradition of timber having ever grown upon it, but that he has found abundant evidence of long-continued occupancy prior to its possession by white men.

Excavations made in several oval-topped mounds brought to light nothing except the fact that they were composed mainly of sand like the surrounding soil, although decayed human bones are said to have been found in some of them.

Three or four feet in depth of the bank fronting the lake is, in fact, a refuse heap mixed with charcoal, ashes, stone chips, and other evidences of long occupancy. However, a single bone awl and some pieces of pottery were the only articles obtained by the Bureau assistant.

A small image of pottery, found while plowing near one of the mounds on this area, is in possession of one of the residents.

CALHOUN COUNTY.

This county is a long narrow belt of land lying between the Illinois and Mississippi rivers immediately above their junction. It consists chiefly of an elevated ridge from 250 to 300 feet high, flanked on each side by rich alluvial bottoms bordering the two rivers, its sides being cut by numerous deep ravines. The upland is irregular and broken, some of it too much so for cultivation, though the soil is rich.

Mounds are comparatively numerous over this area, the larger portion being found on the uplands.

The first group examined was one consisting of four mounds situated on the NW. ¼, Sec. 34, T. 10 S., R. 2 W. These are placed along the top of a spur of the ridge, about 250 feet above the bottoms; the immediate position being flanked on the east and west by deep ravines. The following table shows the respective sizes of the tumuli and their courses and distances from one another, commencing with No. 1 at the northwest end of the series and measuring from center to center:

No. of mound.	Bearings.	Distance.	Diameter.	Height.
		Feet.	*Feet.*	*Feet.*
1			55 by 35	4
1 to 2	S. 47° E	342	15 by 16	1
2 to 3	S. 75° 30′ E	310	40	6
3 to 4	S. 57° 30′ E	103	39 by 29	6
4 to 5	S. 45° E	94	28 by 20	4
5 to 6	S. 33° 45′ E	71	33 by 22	3½
6 to 7	S. 25° E	100	61 by 34	6
7 to 8	S. 31° E	120	34 by 28	4

The construction of No. 1, which stands on the highest point occupied by the group, proved to be very simple. Passing through the vegetable mold Fig. 59, *c*, some 3 inches thick, a layer of earth *d* was reached which formed the mass of the mound, and was similar in character to the soil of the surrounding surface of the ridge. Under this

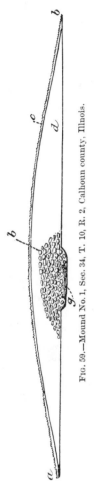

Fig. 59.—Mound No. 1, Sec. 34, T. 10, R. 2, Calhoun county, Illinois.

was a pile of stones *b* resting on the original surface, except where excavated, the area covered measuring 13 by 9 feet. Below this at *g* was an excavation in the original soil, 7 feet long by 2 feet wide, and a little more than a foot deep. In the bottom of this grave was a single badly decayed skeleton lying at full length on its back. Over it was earth mixed with stones, which filled the grave. There were no indications that bark or any other wrapping had been used.

Mound No. 2 was in fact nothing more than a single layer of stones covering an area of about 16 feet in diameter, placed here doubtless to shield from the wild beasts the half dozen bodies or skeletons buried beneath them. On top of the stones was a fire bed, showing that a fire had been built immediately after the stones were placed, as it lay on the stones but not on the mold which covered them.

Mound No. 4 was found to consist—after passing through the vegetable mold (*e*)—chiefly of yellow clay from the surrounding surface. This was interrupted only by two small heaps of stone, as shown in Fig. 60 (plan and section), *f* indicating the clay layer and *g* and *h* the stone heaps; *m* is an excavation in the original surface. In this grave, which was but little more than 6 inches deep, was a single skeleton, resting on the right side, head northwest. There were no indications of wrappings or other covering than earth.

Mound No. 5, which stands on the edge of the ridge, had been partially opened before. Its construction was similar to that of No. 1, except that the stone heap was smaller, and the form and arrangement of the grave beneath different. This grave was nearly 6 feet by 5, and 18 inches deep. Slabs of limestone were set on edge around the sides. It contained a single skeleton, resting on the left side, accompanied by a shell needle, and surrounded by a quantity of light ash-like substance almost filling the grave. The bones were slightly decayed and the skull was crushed.

The next group examined is situated on the SE. ¼ Sec. 29, T. 10 S., R. 2 W., on the main ridge, probably 300 feet higher than the river bottoms. This consists of 12 mounds, two of which were excavated with the following results:

Mound No. 1, between 3 and 4 feet high, diameters 31 and 22 feet, is oval in outline and somewhat flattened. It proved to be a simple heap of earth covering a single grave or slight excavation, in which lay a single skeleton at full length on the back.

Mound No. 2 of this group presented the same method of construction as No. 1.

In Fig. 61 is presented the plat of a group on the NE. ¼ Sec. 31, T. 10 S., R. 2 W., the land of Mr. William I. Wilkinson. It consists of twelve mounds, situated on the top of a ridge some 200 feet above the river bottoms. They are all of the ordinary conical type, varying in diameter from 20 to 50 feet, and in height from 2 to 5 feet, as will be seen by reference to the following table (measurements from base to base).

No.	Bearing.	Distance.	Diameter.	Height.
		Feet.	Feet.	Feet.
1	....	....	33 by 30	4
1 to 2	N. 50° W..	40	30 by 26	3½
2 to 3	N. 55½° W.	41	30 by 30	3
3 to 4	N. 84° W..	62	33 by 31	3½
4 to 5	N. 80½° W.	44	32 by 29	....
5 to 6	N. 81¼° W.	114	45 by 37	....
6 to 7	N. 62° W..	10	28 by 21	4
7 to 8	N. 41½° W.	130	50 by 20	....
8 to 9	N. 34° W..	66	40 by 23	5
9 to 10	N. 34¾° W.	95	50 by 32	5½
6 to 11	N. 62° W..	55	35 by 24	3
7 to 12	N. 41° W..	62	20 by 20	2

No. 1 is on west edge of ridge.
No. 2 is 40 feet from edge of ridge.

No. 2, 3 feet high, was nothing but a simple heap of earth covering five skeletons, two of which were bundled, the others stretched at full length. These lay at different depths, from 1 to 3 feet, those at the latter depth being on the original surface of the ground. There was no excavation or grave beneath this mound. A *Unio* shell and two chipped implements were found with two of the skeletons.

Mounds Nos. 3, 4, 5, 9, and 11 were of the same type, the only difference being that some of them contained but one skeleton, while others contained two or four.

No. 7, standing near the edge of the ridge, presented some slight variations from the six mentioned. In this, which was 4 feet high, was found, at the depth of a few inches, a dark sticky mass about 2 feet in diameter and 1 foot thick, seemingly of burned animal matter, which contained fragments of burned human bones, charcoal, and ashes. Under this was a layer of burned earth some 10 or 11 feet in diameter. Lower down and nearer the margin of the mound was another similar, but smaller, dark mass also mixed with burned human bones and charcoal. A single skeleton rested on the original surface, near the southwest edge of the tumulus. Two bird-shaped stone pipes (Nos. 134766 and 134767) were taken from the layer of burnt earth and three chipped implements were also found in the same layer.

No. 8, a section of which is shown in Fig. 62, also presents some variations worthy of notice. In this figure, *e* is the surface accumulation of vegetable mold, 3 inches thick; *f* the yellow clay body of the mound, 2 feet thick; *h* a mass of burned clay; *k* a layer about 2 inches thick of dark, greasy earth; *m* an excavation in the original soil. The clay mass *h* had been burned to a brick red, and in the center was as hard as a brick. The grave was about 6 feet long by 2½ in width, and con-

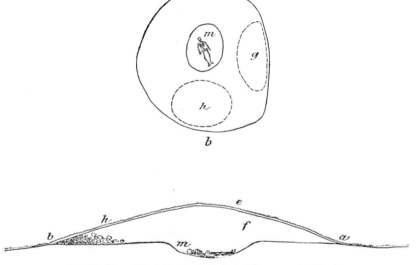

FIG. 60.—Mound No. 4, Sec. 34, T. 10, R. 2, Calhoun county, Illinois.

tained the skeleton, probably of a female, lying on its back at full length. Immediately under the southwest end of the burned clay mass were the charred remains of three skeletons; and at *g* fragments of charred animal and human bones.

A mound on the NE. ¼ Sec. 15, T. 10 S., R. 2 W., standing on the brink of a bluff, presented the following features: It measured a little over 4 feet high and 30 feet in diameter, and was composed entirely of clay from the surface of the ridge immediately to the west, as was apparent from an excavation at this point some 2 feet deep. Contrary to the rule, this contained no covering of vegetable mold. The northern, eastern, and southern margins were strengthened by flat stones (see Fig. 63), probably to prevent washing, as the surface of the ridge sloped rapidly away in these directions.

The important feature of the mound was the number of skeletons found scattered through it, most of them intrusive and at various depths. The mode of burial was somewhat different from the usual custom in this region, though resembling that in mound No. 2 of the first group mentioned. The first three were in the eastern side at the depth of 12 inches, lying at full length; the fourth at the depth of 9 inches, the

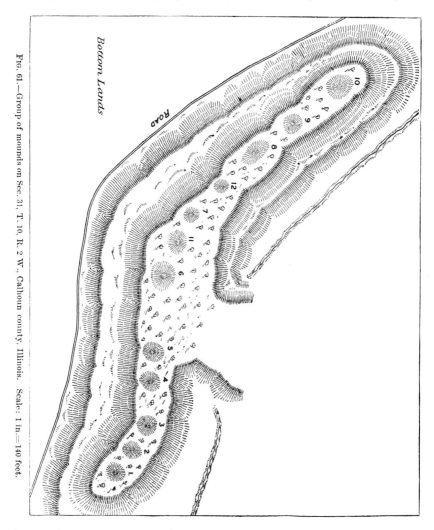

FIG. 61.—Group of mounds on Sec. 31, T. 10, R. 2 W., Calhoun county, Illinois. Scale: 1 in.= 140 feet.

bones of which had been charred before burial; the fifth at the depth of 6 inches, bundled, lying on one flat stone and covered by another. At another point were three skeletons, at the depth of 9 inches, one of them at full length, the other two bundled. Four other skeletons, at the depth of a foot, were lying at full length on one layer of stones and covered by another. Nine others were scattered through the mound at various depths, some between stones and most of them bundled.

Underneath the mound were two excavations in the original soil, the one marked *a* being but 2½ feet long, 2 feet wide, and 18 inches deep. In this were the bones of a single skeleton, but in such confusion as to make it evident they were buried after the flesh had been removed. The other excavation, *b*, 7 feet long by 2½ wide and 2½ feet deep, contained a single male skeleton lying at full length, face up and head south. The bottom of the grave under this skeleton was covered with decayed vegetable matter to the depth of 2 or 3 inches.

Several relics were found in this tumulus, all with the skeletons. These were as follows: Two arrow points, a banner stone (134776); a broken pot (134772) with the skeleton in grave *b;* a stone celt (134775), a shell, a lot of bone beads (134770); a piece of lead ore (134773); and a grooved stone axe (134771).

The next group examined, consisting of twenty mounds, is in the northwest quarter of Sec. 2, T. 9 S., R. 2 W., located along the narrow crest of a ridge rising from 125 to 300 feet above the Illinois river. The distance from 1 to 20 (at the opposite ends of the line), following the bend, is above three-sevenths of a mile. The following table gives the courses and distances of the mounds from one another, measuring from center to center, and the size of each:

Number.	Direction.	Distance.	Diameters.	Height.
		Feet.	*Feet.*	*Feet.*
1	....	....	65 by 45	5
1 to 2	N. 21° 33′ W...	86	25 by 20	1½
2 to 3	N. 23° 39′ W...	313	31 by 27	2
3 to 4	N. 5° 02′ E.....	74	39 by 32	4
4 to 5	N. 34° 10′ E....	93	55	5
5 to 6	N. 19° 33′ E....	45	17	3
6 to 7	N	30	20 by 17	1
7 to 8	N. 14° 05′ E....	149	57 by 19	3½
8 to sta. *a*	N. 2° 03′ E.....	512	....	....
Sta. *a* to 9	E	49	40 by 25	7
Sta. *a* to 1⁰	N. 2° 40′ E.....	143	44 by 30	5
10 to 11	N. 2° 31′ W	103	38 by 30	6
11 to 12	N. 25° 23′ W...	58	26 by 16	2
12 to 13	N. 18° 37′ W...	72	26 by 21	2
13 to 14	N. 17° 22′ W ...	95	31 by 22	3½
14 to 15	N. 24° 29′ W ...	42	32 by 24	3
15 to 16	N. 26° 53′ W...	93	22 by 20	2
16 to 17	N. 22° 50′ W...	99	50 by 40	7
17 to 18	N. 18° W	86	23 by 14	2
18 to 19	N. 28° W......	190	24 by 15	2½
19 to 20	N. 38° 08′ W...	149	59 by 45	9

No. 1 stands on the southern end of the ridge, occupying the full width of the top, which is here about 125 feet above the river. The structure, positions of skeletons, etc., are shown in Fig. 64, in which are presented vertical sections both of the length and width.

In these, *e* is the surface sod, 2 inches thick; the remainder, *f*, down to the natural ground, consisted of yellow clay taken from the top of the ridge; *g-g*, the line of the original surface; Nos. 1 to 10 skeletons, *h*, a small fire bed, and *k*, a flat stone resting on it. Skeleton 1, 6 inches below the sod, lay at full length, face up, head south; 2 and 3, at full length, faces up, heads northeast, at the depth of 10 inches; 4, on the original surface of the ridge, stretched out, head northwest, face toward the river. The bones in this case were more decayed than those further up in the mound; and near by was the fire bed, *h* also on the original surface. This was small, measuring but 2 feet in diameter,

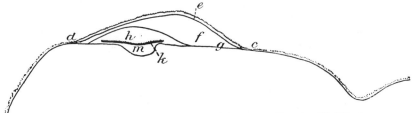

FIG. 62.—Vertical section of Mound No. 8, NE. ¼ Sec. 31, T. 10. R. 2 W., Illinois.

and not more than 2 inches thick; it was covered by a flat stone, *k*, which bore no indications of fire. No. 5, a skeleton at the depth of 9 inches, face up, head southwest; 6, at the depth of 15 inches, head southwest, face down, an unusual position; 7, at a depth of 3 feet, bones in a heap with the skull on top, the heap resting on the natural surface. No 8, but 3 inches below the sod, at full length, face up, head southwest; 9 and 10, at the depth of 10 inches, heads northeast.

Most of the burials in this mound seem to have been intrusive or made at different periods. A few shell beads with skeleton No. 1 were the only relics found.

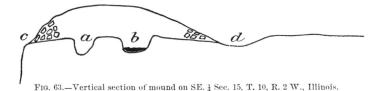

FIG. 63.—Vertical section of mound on SE. ¼ Sec. 15, T. 10, R. 2 W., Illinois.

Mounds 2 and 5 were constructed much like No. 1; the former containing no skeletons; the latter, which had been partially opened before, containing several skeletons, three of which remained. These were intrusive, all at full length, faces up.

Mound 6 was similar in construction to the preceding. Under the northern end and resting on the natural surface of the ridge was a fire bed some 6 inches thick and 3 feet in diameter, of charcoal, ashes, and burned human bones. Judging by all the indications Mr. Middleton, the explorer, concluded that the body or skeleton of a medium-sized person had been placed on the surface of the ridge, face up, head eastward, and a fire kindled over the middle portion, consuming the larger bones. The skull does not seem to have been affected by heat. Another fact worthy of notice is that the earth immediately over the bones showed no indications of fire.

In the southern end of the mound lay another skeleton at full length on the surface of the ridge, with the head south.

Mound 7 was not thoroughly explored because of a large hickory tree standing on it. The construction so far as it could be made out was as follows: 2 inches of sod, then the body of clay as usual; below this, resting on the surface of the ridge, was a layer of thoroughly burnt clay stretching nearly across the mound; this was covered with coals and ashes to the depth of 2 inches. Under this layer of burnt clay were the charred remains of a skeleton. The indications were that the body in this case had been buried in the flesh.

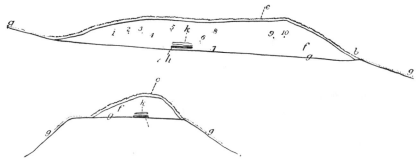

FIG. 64.—Vertical section of Mound No. 1, NW. Sec. 2, T. 9, R. 2 W., Illinois.

Another group examined is situated on the W. $\frac{1}{2}$ of Sec. 2 and E. $\frac{1}{2}$ of Sec. 3, T. 9 S., R. 2 W. This consists of 5 mounds varying in diameter from 30 to 60 feet and in height from 3 to 6 feet; on the crest of a ridge as usual.

All except one had been previously explored, and in one of them a box-shaped stone grave found.

No. 4, the smallest of the group, the one which had not been disturbed consisted of a top layer of vegetable mold and a body of clay as usual. Resting on the surface of the ridge near the center was a pile of flat limestones, which were probably brought from the eastern end of the ridge near by. This pile covered a space 12 feet in diameter, being 2$\frac{1}{2}$ feet high in the center. The spaces were filled with decayed vegetable material, and the outer stones bore indications of weathering as though the pile had remained uncovered for some time after it was built. At the northern base of the heap, partly surrounded by it, was a box-shaped stone grave 5 feet long and 2 feet wide. It was complete, having stones both at bottom and top, though the latter had fallen in. In it were two skeletons apparently of young persons, on their backs, but faces turned towards each other, heads east. They were surrounded by decayed vegetable or animal matter. Immediately east of the center of the mound and partially covered by the stone pile was a decayed skeleton lying at length on its back, head to the south.

There are a number of groups on the western side of the county in the vicinity of Hamburg, most of which have been explored; one, however, appears to have been overlooked. This is located on the NW. ¼ Sec. 1, T. 10 S., R. 3 W., on the crest of a ridge some 200 feet or more above the river level, and consists of six mounds.

The dimensions of these are as follows: No. 1, diameters 61 by 23 feet; height, 4 feet. No. 2, diameters, 50 by 34 feet; height, 5 feet. No. 3, diameters, 66 by 37 feet; height, 6 feet. No. 4, diameter, 25 feet; height, 4 feet. No. 5, diameters, 60 by 35 feet; height, 6 feet. No. 6, diameters, 57 by 30 feet; height, 3 feet. .

In No. 4 nothing was observed of interest except a small fire-bed on the natural surface of the ridge under the center of the mound. There were no indications of burials.

The construction and contents of No. 5 were as follows: A layer of vegetable mold 3 inches thick; then 2 feet of clay surface soil very hard and difficult to work; under this, conforming to the shape of the mound and resting on the surface of the ridge, was a layer of earth about 9 feet in diameter. This covered a mass of burnt clay 5 feet long, 3 feet wide, and 18 inches thick, which had been burned to a brick red and was in fragments. At the south end was a small heap of ashes which had probably been raked off the fire beds, and in the same locality but at the depth of 18 inches, was a skeleton resting at full length face up, in or under a small fire-bed. Judging from the indications, clay had been placed over the middle part of the body on which a fire had been kindled. As the bones were not charred it is probable the flesh had not been removed before burial. In the northern part, at the depth of 3 feet, was another badly decayed skeleton.

Mixed in the fire bed were a number of charred human bones; parts of two skeletons, apparently intrusive burials, were found in the upper layer.

Another group situated a short distance north of Hardin on the NE. ¼ Sec. 27, T. 10 S., R. 2 W., stands on the margin of a bluff, about 200 feet above the Illinois river. Directly in front of the mounds the bluff breaks down perpendicularly for about 40 feet.

The dimensions are as follows:

No.	Diameters.	Height.
	Feet.	Feet.
1	93 by 100	19
2	47 by 26	3
3	93 by 84	16
4	25 by 21	1½
5	21 by 15	2

No. 1, the only one of the group explored, proved to be very interesting. As will be seen by reference to Fig. 65, showing a vertical
section, it is located on the very brink of the precipice.

The upper portion (*a*) to the depth of 14 feet was a single layer composed chiefly of yellow clay obtained from the surrounding surface of
the bluff. Near the center, at the depth of 4 feet, was a horizontal
bed (*b*) of hard, gray earth—apparently muck from the river, 8 inches
thick and covering an area about 20 feet in diameter, and three feet
lower another bed (*c*) of burnt clay about the same thickness and
extent as the preceding. Although particles of charcoal were mixed
through the latter no ashes were observed on or about it.

At the depth of 14 feet the top of what seems to have been the nucleus
or original mound was reached, over which the heavy mass of clay had
been cast at some subsequent period. Over this lay a thin covering of

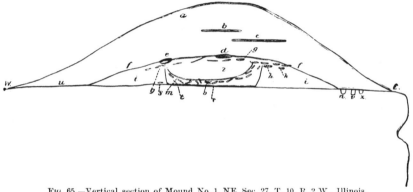

FIG. 65.—Vertical section of Mound No. 1. NE. Sec. 27, T. 10, R. 2 W., Illinois.

white, ash-like material (*ff*) not more than 2 inches thick and extending
on all sides to the original base. This rested, for the most part, on a
single layer of stones (*g g*), the latter lacking several feet of extending
to the outer margin. Examining carefully the stones which formed
this layer, evidences of weathering on the upper side were distinctly
visible, showing that the mound must have remained undisturbed at
this height for a considerable length of time. The thin stratum of ash-
like material seems to confirm this view as the decayed stems of grass
found near the outer margin show that it was produced by burning a
covering of grass which had probably grown over it. The dark spots
(*d* and *e*) indicate two small fire beds resting on the layer of stones.

Removing the stones and cutting a trench through the low, broad
original mound or nucleus to the natural surface of the bluff, the construction was found to be as shown in the figure. By *z* is indicated
an oval basin, 10 by 13 feet, lined throughout with a layer of stones (*m*),
similar to those above. It was filled with the yellow surface soil of the
ridge and covered with the layer of stones *g g*. The stones below also
bore distinct marks of weathering, and were covered with a thin layer

of a white material like ashes mixed with decayed leaves and grass. Under these stones and resting on the natural surface of the ridge was a thin layer of decayed vegetable matter (r). The slopes i i surrounding the basin were of yellow clay similar to that of the thick upper layer of the mound. The dark spots h and k indicate small fire beds.

Partly under and partly in the bottom layer of decayed vegetable matter and exactly in the center of the mound was a single skeleton (o) lying on the back at full length, the feet to the south, but the head was wanting. Not a tooth or particle of the jaw or skull was to be found, though careful search was made. As all the other bones were well preserved and comparatively sound, except that the pelvis and some of the ribs were broken, it is presumed that the head must have been removed before burial. This is the second instance observed in which the head had been thus removed. The first was noticed at Pecan Point, Arkansas.

Six feet south of the center of the mound was a small deposit of burned bones lying on the natural surface of the bluff. Seven feet west of the center, lying on the original soil, were the remains of an infant (s), which had been doubled up until the knees touched the chin, wrapped in a grass covering, and placed upon its left side.

A seashell (*Busycon perversum*) from which the columella had been removed, converting it into a drinking cup, which was at the right shoulder of the skeleton, and a fragment apparently of another similar shell, were the only relics found in the mound. The latter was in a stone box or cist 2½ feet square and 1 foot deep, resting on the natural surface of the ridge. Not a fragment of bone was found in this box.

Another singular feature observed consisted of three small pits (n, v, x) under the eastern base of the upper layer. These were three holes, from 15 to 18 inches in diameter and 1 foot deep. One of them contained particles of rotten wood. There were several intrusive burials in the thick upper clay layer which presented nothing of special interest.

It would seem from the facts and figure given that we have in this tumulus a specimen of the Ohio "altar mound" type, as what we have called the nucleus or original mound is in fact one of the so-called "altars" of the type described by Messrs. Squier and Davis.

MADISON AND ST. CLAIR COUNTIES.

On the line separating these two counties is the celebrated Cahokia group, which includes the giant structure known as the Cahokia or Monk's mound.

In the fall of 1882 Mr. William McAdams was engaged by this Bureau to make an exploration and preliminary survey of this interesting region, but his work was suddenly cut short at the end of a month by severe winter weather.

The first mounds visited were those on Wood river where it emerges from the highlands and enters the bottom. This bottom, which extends southward from Alton along the Mississippi, is generally known as the "American bottom." Many small mounds are found on the bluffs in this vicinity, as shown in the accompanying map. (Fig. 66.) An oval-shaped one some 5 feet in height, situated on the sloping bluff between the forks of the stream, was of a yellowish clay much more compact and tenacious than the loess of the bluff. At the depth of 5 or 6 feet were the crumbling bones of a human skeleton. The body had evidently been buried extended, with the face upward. With the bones were some ashes, but none of the bones showed any indications of having been burned. No relics of stone or other material were found.

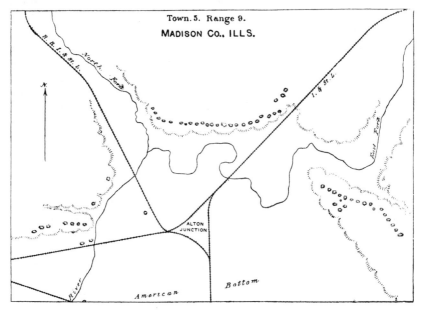

Fig. 66.—Wood river mounds, Madison county, Illinois.

An adjoining mound on the west and of nearly the same size was opened, but presented nothing materially different from the first. Subsequently, however, in a small mound on the bluff above the railroad track, on the west side of Wood river, a human skeleton was discovered, at the depth of about 2 feet, much decayed; the skull, however, was preserved.

On this bluff there had been, in times not very remote, numerous burials without the erection of mounds. Some of the bones were but a few inches beneath the surface of the ground.

The next excavation of any importance was made in a mound on the bluff in St. Clair county, near the line between St. Clair and Madison counties and nearly east of the Great Cahokia mound. This was conical in shape and formed a landmark for some distance around. At the depth of about 3 feet the earth, which was a yellowish clay, became dry and very hard and quite different in character from the loess of the bluff on which the mound stands. At the depth of about 12 feet a layer of ashes, nearly an inch thick, was disclosed, and a foot below this another layer of ashes a foot or more in thickness. Excepting some thin, flat pieces of sandstone there were no relics nor other remains, not even a portion of bone. Below the ashes the earth showed the effect of heat for a few inches, but seemed to be the undisturbed surface of the bluff.

Near this mound the projecting point of the bluff has been changed to form a flat circular platform that might, in times past, have served for some aboriginal purpose, possibly an outlook or signal station, as it occupies one of the highest points and overlooks the whole plain of the Cahokia. Numerous excavations in this vicinity revealed the fact that at one time the top of the bluff had been a burying place, and from a small elevation in the loess, that might originally have been a mound of some dimensions—for the place is under cultivation—a tolerably well-preserved skull was obtained. There were three entire skeletons in the mound, the skulls of two being crushed.

These burials were made by laying the bodies on their sides or backs, with the limbs straight. The form of the skull seems to be a common one on the bluff, but, as the explorer thinks, somewhat different from those found by him in the bottom or low lands. No relics of any kind were found with these bones.

It is worthy of note that nearly all the relics found at the Cahokia group of mounds have been taken from the low ground between the mounds. The remarkable find of pottery, implements, and shells made by Mr. McAdams in the winter of 1881 was in the low land a short distance from the northeast corner of the great mound. The articles were nearly all taken from a square rod of ground. This has been to some extent Dr. Patrick's experience in making his fine collection of pottery.

The real burial place of the builders of the Cahokia mounds probably is yet to be discovered.

The bank of Cahokia creek during the occupation of the mounds was evidently more to the south than its present line along the eastern part of the group. The old bank is still plainly visible, as shown in Pl. VI. The low land between this old bank and the creek is now covered with forest trees. All along this bank, which forms the edge of the plateau on which the mounds stand, are abundant evidences of occupation in remote times. In digging 2 or 3 feet at almost any point along this bank indications of fireplaces are found, with numerous river shells, broken pottery, and kitchen refuse. As all the arable ground about the mound has been in cultivation many years, it is quite possible that some of the burial places, which are usually quite shallow, have been destroyed, as pieces of human bones are very common in the plowed fields.

The location, forms, and heights of the various mounds of the Cahokia group as given in the annexed diagram (Pl. VI) are from Mr. McAdams's survey and are believed to be strictly correct. The figures on or by the mounds indicate the height.

The next excavations were made in the mounds at Mitchell, on Long lake. The principal digging was done in the base of the large mound through which the railroad tracks run. Bones and sea shells had been discovered here by some workmen in digging a trench through the base of the mound between two railroad tracks for the purpose of laying a water pipe to the lake. This ditch was reopened, then widened out, and the spot fully explored. There seemed to have been 4 or 5 skeletons of adults, which lay east and west. A great number of whorls of sea shells had been buried with them, probably taken out in forming drinking cups or water vessels. These shells are from a few inches to a foot or more in length and belong mostly to the genus *Busycon*.

The mound from which these shells were taken was nearly square in shape, 100 paces on each of its sides, 25 or 30 feet in height, with a flat, level summit. It is now, with the exception of a small portion in the center between two railroad tracks, obliterated, a part only of the base remaining.

In removing the western side of the mound a few years ago, to make a road across Long lake, many human remains were found and, with them, implements of stone, bone, and copper. The mound was composed principally of black dirt or soil, and wherever excavations were made in the base, at the depth of 3 or 4 feet, the original under soil of the surrounding prairie, a yellowish sandy loam, was reached. This is the mound from which Mr. Henry R. Howland obtained the copper articles described and figured in his paper in the bulletin of the Buffalo Academy of Sciences, 1877.

In addition to the maps already given, Mr. McAdams prepared a map of the western part of Madison county, including one range of sections in the northern part of St. Clair county, showing the location and relative positions of the various groups of mounds named. This map is shown (on a reduced scale) in Pl. VII.

RANDOLPH COUNTY.

STONE GRAVES ON THE MILL TRACT.

These are situated about half a mile north of Prairie du Rocher, on a long ridge that runs in a westerly direction nearly across the narrow bottom of a small creek that flows through the village. This ridge, which is about 25 feet higher than the bottom land, descends gradually from the hills to the west, having a steep slope on each side. The soil is yellow, tenacious clay. The graves were on the rounded top,

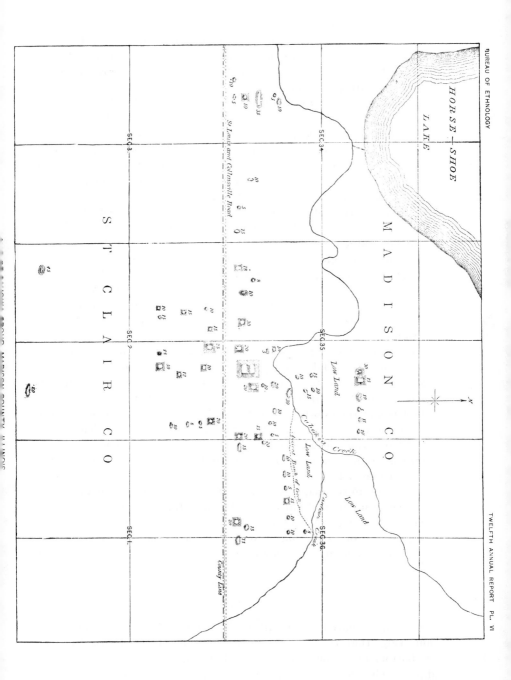

HORSE—SHOE LAKE

MADISON CO.

ST. CLAIR CO.

SEC.34

SEC.3

SEC.35

SEC.2

SEC.36

SEC.1

St. Louis and Collinsville Road

Cahokia Creek

Low Land

Low Land

Low Land

County Line

some little distance back of the point. All were of the usual box shape and all but one more than 6 feet long; some of them were so near the surface as to leave the tops exposed. The position of the head of the skeleton could easily be determined in all but three of them before the cover was removed, by the form of the grave, as the cists were wider at one end than the other, and somewhat coffin-shaped. They usually measured from 2 to 2½ feet in width at the head, but only a foot or even less at the other end, the depth from a foot to 18 inches. In fact, it seems that in some cases the body must have been placed in position and the side and end stones fitted to it. In these cases slabs of limestone were first placed in the bottom of the excavation, as the pieces forming the sides and ends rested edgewise on these, usually two pieces

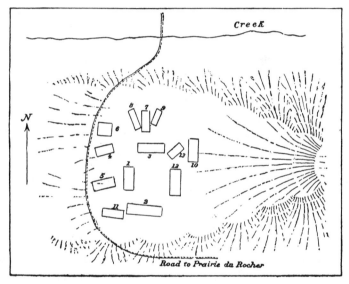

Fig. 67.—Stone graves on Mill tract, Randolph county, Illinois.

to a side and one at each end. Where the two pieces at the sides joined, there was a smaller piece thrust at right angles between them, the main projection being outward. The cover consisted of a single layer of these slabs, in some instances without breaking the joints, in others overlapping each other. In other cases the pieces forming the walls and ends appear to have been put into position before the bottom was lined. In some of them a single slab formed one side; if more than one slab was used, they either overlapped or another was added to strengthen the joint. The stones were obtained from the hillside a few rods farther up the ridge.

The bodies buried in these graves were covered to a depth of 2 or 3 inches with the yellow clay of the ridge; the covering over the graves consisted of limestone. The respective positions are shown in Fig. 67.

The positions of the bodies in the graves were as follows:

Grave No. 1: Skeleton on the back at full length, head to the south, face up.

Grave No. 3: Skeleton on the back at full length. A small earthen pot was buried with it, but was so soft when found that it could not be moved before it had crumbled to pieces.

Grave No. 4: Skeleton at full length on the back, head to the east, but face turned over toward the south.

Grave No. 6: Skeleton bundled, but the skull in the east side of the cist with the face up.

Grave No. 7: Skeleton at full length on the back, head south, but face turned toward the west.

Graves Nos. 8 and 9: Skeletons at full length on the back, faces up, heads to the south.

Graves Nos. 11 and 2: Skeletons at full length on the back, heads east.

With the exception of that in grave No. 6, the bodies appear to have been buried without removing the flesh.

THE DE FRENNE STONE GRAVES.

These graves are just outside of the limits of the village of Prairie du Rocher, on the steep point of a ridge of dry, yellow clay, which terminates at the junction of the two branches of the creek, about half a mile below the graves previously mentioned. The ridge at this point is about 30 feet higher than the road which runs along the side of the creek.

Although a plan of the cemetery and a section of the ridge was obtained, as shown in Fig. 68, the respective positions of only a part of the skeletons can be given, as several of the graves had been opened by other parties. All the cists were built in the same manner as those heretofore described, and differed from them only in having the head and foot of the same width, and a few of them also contained more than one skeleton. Five of them—Nos. 21, 22, 23, 26, and 28—were graves of infants. The largest of these, No. 21, was only 15 inches long; the smallest, No. 26, only 9 inches long, 5 inches wide, and 4 inches deep (inside measurement in all cases). Mrs. Morude, an old Belgian lady, who lives here, informed Mr. Middleton that when they were grading for the foundation of their house she saw skulls with the hair still hanging to them taken from these graves. It is therefore more than probable, and, in fact, is generally understood by the old settlers of this section, who derived the information from their parents, that these are the graves of the Kaskaskia and other Indians who resided here when this part of Illinois began to be settled by the whites.

At the point of the hill the graves were but slightly covered with earth. In some instances this covering was not more than 6 inches

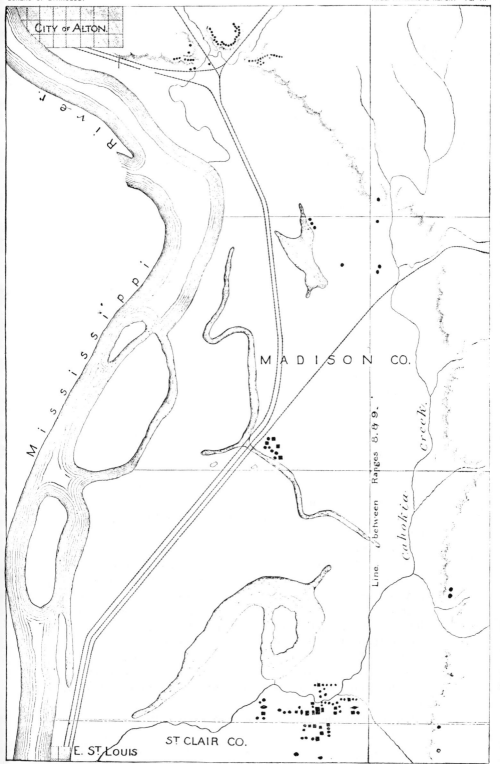

MAP OF THE WESTERN PART OF MADISON COUNTY ILLINOIS.

deep, but toward the back part of the cemetery it reached a depth of 4 feet. This was probably due in part to washings.

In grave No. 1 the skeleton lay at full length on its back, head west. The skull was saved in good condition.

Grave No. 2: There were two skeletons in this grave, heads west, both at full length on the back. Both skulls were saved.

Grave No. 4: Skeleton at full length on the back, head west.

Grave No. 6: This proved to be the largest grave in the cemetery measuring 6 feet in length, 5 in width, and 18 inches in depth (inside measurements to be understood in all cases). As seen by reference to the diagram (Fig. 68), this grave occupies a central position in the

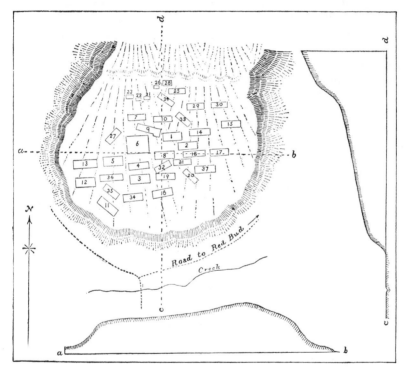

Fig. 68.—The De Frenne stone graves, Randolph county, Illinois.

cemetery. It contained five skeletons, four of adults and one of an infant; one of the larger was that-of a female. They all lay at full length on their backs, faces up, and heads north.

Grave No. 7: This contained two adult skeletons, both at full length, on their backs, heads east, but faces turned toward each other. Both skulls were secured in good condition. A clay muller was found with the skeleton on the north side and a stone muller with the other.

Grave No. 9: The skeleton, apparently of a female, at full length, face up. With it were four bone implements, one a tube, one an awl or perforator, one stone chisel, one stone drill, a shell ornament, a stone implement, the fragment of an unusually fine flint knife, some green paint, red paint, lead ore, and a chipped celt.

Grave No. 10: Skeleton at full length on the back, face up, head east.

Grave No. 14: Skeleton at full length on the right side, head east, face north. With it were six bone implements, some shell spoons, and two shell pendants, the last from the sides of the head.

Grave No. 16: Skeleton at full length on the back, face up, head west. With it were two earthen bowls by the head, and a single shell bead in the right hand.

Grave No. 18: The skeleton in this grave appeared to be that of a half-grown person. It was, as usual, at full length on the back, head east, face north. With it was a single quartz crystal, apparently from the region of Hot Springs, Arkansas.

Graves Nos. 21, 22, 23: The skeletons in these graves all lay on their backs with heads east. A pot and shell spoon were found by the right cheek of the one in No. 23. The pot stood upright, with the spoon in it.

Grave No. 24: A single skeleton occupied this grave. It was, as usual, at full length on the back, head northwest. Two pots were by the head, one on each side, in an upright position.

Grave No. 27: In this grave there were two skeletons, at full length, heads northeast. Nine bone implements were found with them.

Grave No. 29: A single skeleton and with it a pot.

Grave No. 31: A single skeleton and with it a piece of lead ore.

No particulars were ascertained in reference to other graves which had been opened by other parties, except that all the skeletons were lying at full length, as those mentioned.

STONE GRAVES ON THE BLUFF.

These are situated on the bluff, just within the Randolph county line, at the mouth of the first large ravine on the road from Glasgow to Prairie du Rocher. They are probably the graves mentioned by Dr. Wislizenus.[1]

They are located more than 100 feet above the bottom lands, on the point of a narrow steep spur. The cliffs immediately south of them are perpendicular. Their respective positions, with sections of the spur, are shown in Fig. 69.

As all but three of these graves had been opened previous to the visit of the Bureau agent, and nothing peculiar was observed, a detailed description is deemed unnecessary. In one of the three which was undisturbed the skeleton was bundled, in the other two they lay at full length, heads east, faces up. The skull of the bundled skeleton was in the east end of the grave.

[1] Trans. St. Louis Acad. Sci., Vol. I, p. 66.

Southeast of Prairie du Rocher, on the bluffs, is another cemetery of stone graves situated much as the one last mentioned, and near by is a fine spring. These had all been examined by previous explorers. The arrangement was found to be much like the last, one large grave with the others around it.

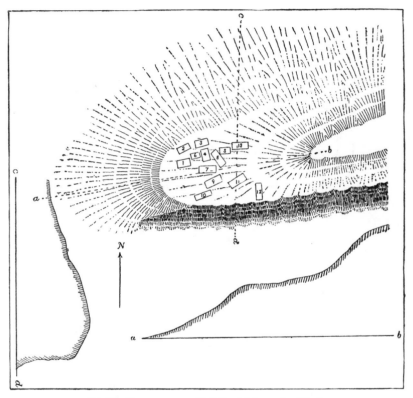

FIG. 69.—Stone graves on bluff, Randolph county, Illinois.

STONE GRAVES AT ROCKWOOD.

These are situated close to the village of Rockwood on the land of Mr. Reed, on a high bench or terrace that stands about 75 feet above the bottom lands.

The larger portion of them had been explored; some had been carried down by a caving of the bank near which they were placed and others removed to make way for foundations of houses. This must have been a very extensive cemetery, as the area over which the remaining graves extend is comparatively large. The surface, which was level originally, seems to have been rounded up somewhat, as though intended for a low, broad mound, but so much excavating had been done that no positive conclusion could be reached on this point.

The graves were of the usual box shape, and all those which remained, except one, measured 5 feet or more in length. The small one, which had not been disturbed, was 2 feet square and 18 inches deep, but in place of bones were four uninjured earthen pots.

In addition to the works mentioned, the following antiquities are found in this county:

MOUNDS.

At Rockwood; at Prairie du Rocher; 3 miles south of Prairie du Rocher, on the Simpson place; on the Mudd place; above Old Lafay-

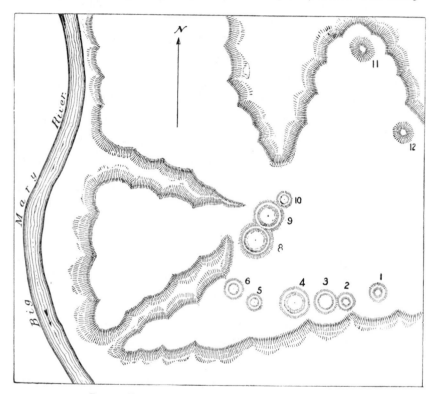

FIG. 70.—Hut rings near the bank of Big Mary river, Illinois.

ette on the Kaskaskia river; at Chester; 3 miles south of Sparta, along Big Mary river, and at Evansville.

STONE GRAVES.

At the Bluff ferry; 1 mile south of Rockwood; on the West fork of Degognia creek, 1½ miles from the bridge near the Brown farm; 7 miles west of Sparta; 3 miles southeast of Sparta; on Henderson's place on Nine-mile creek west of Sparta; on William Cox's old place on the Kaskaskia river below the Mobile and Ohio railroad bridge, and on the Widow Boyd's place, 3 miles south of Baldwin.

Three miles southeast of Sparta, on the left bank of Big Mary river, near the stone graves and mounds mentioned above, are the hut rings shown in Fig. 70. These are situated upon a flat-topped ridge about 30 feet higher than the creek bottoms. They are low, with the usual depression in the center, but the outlines are rather indistinct. Mr. Gault, of Sparta, who has long resided here, states that when he first moved to this section the Indians lived in houses or wigwams which, when decayed, left such remains as these. They hollowed out a shallow circular cavity in the surface soil, then, standing poles around the margin of this basin, brought them together at the top, and having covered them with bark or other material—in other words, having constructed wigwams of the usual circular form—covered them in whole or in part, especially the lower portion, with earth. He also said that after a camp was abandoned and the wood rotted away it left these rings of earth. Another of these camping places is situated 8 miles west of Sparta.

JACKSON COUNTY.

THE SORRELS MOUND.

This is situated 1 mile directly north of Carbondale, on the upper level bordering a small creek, at the margin or break where the land descends to the lower level and has been in constant cultivation for 15 or 20 years. It is now nearly circular in outline, a little over 150 feet in diameter, 3 feet high, and composed throughout of dark sandy loam, with a slight admixture of clay, similar to that of the surrounding surface of the ground, without any indications of stratification.

Two skeletons were discovered in the central portion at the depth of 2½ feet and about 10 feet apart. Both were closely folded and lying on the side, one with the head north, the other with the head southwest. Judging from the manner in which they were folded it was evident they were buried after the flesh had been removed, as it would have been impossible to press the bones so closely together with the flesh on them, nor could they have assumed this condition in consequence of the decay of the flesh and the pressure of the earth.

Considerable pottery in fragments and varying in quality was found in and on the mound. Some of the pieces in the mound were so situated in relation to one another as to indicate that the vessels of which they had formed parts had been intentionally broken before they were buried. Most of the pottery found in the mound was very rude and coarse, made of materials not well pulverized and but slightly burned. By putting the pieces together one of the vessels proved to be a small jar with a flat bottom and, although the form gives it a decidedly modern appearance, it is probably the rudest piece of pottery in the National Museum. It bears on the outside marks of the grass with which it was surrounded before being burned. The chief interest which attaches to this rude specimen (shown in Fig. 71) is its close resemblance in form and material to an undoubted specimen of Iroquois pottery in the National Museum and its marked contrast with the pottery usually found in this part of the immediate valley of the Mississippi. One other vessel of similar character and closely resembling it was obtained by Mr. Perrine from a mound in Union county, and another similar in

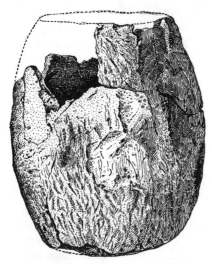

form but of better quality was found by Dr. Palmer in eastern Arkansas; it is believed that these are the only ones of this type which have been found in the immediate valley of the Mississippi. The two found in southern Illinois are made of dark-colored clay, very slightly mixed with pulverized shells.

On the surface of the mound were many small pieces of pottery which had probably been turned up by the plow, some of them undoubtedly attributable to the mound-builders. These were of much better quality than those found near the skeletons, showing some attempt at ornamentation;

FIG. 71.—Pot from Jackson county, Illinois.

some bearing traces of the red coloring often observed in southern mound pottery.

Arrowheads, fragments of flint and greenstone implements, nodules of red and yellow paint, two bone awls, part of the carapace of a tortoise, *Unio* shells common in the streams of this section, and fragments of deer's horn, were also found.

MOUNDS NEAR AVA.

Two of these, small and circular, were discovered on the land of Mr. Henry Thompson, 5 miles southeast of Ava. One of them, about 3 feet high and 20 feet in diameter, contained two empty box-shaped stone graves of the usual form, but without cover or bottom. They measured 3 feet in length and 2½ in width. In the other mounds nothing was found except a pile of stones thrown together without order or arrangement. They probably formed a stone grave which had been disturbed, as the mound had previously been opened.

On the bank of Rattlesnake creek, a short distance from the preceding, another small conical mound, which was thoroughly explored, revealed nothing except a small piece of charcoal. An ancient grave close by was excavated with a similar result.

Three small circular mounds on Mr. Dempsey Williamson's place were next examined. These are similar in size and form to those above mentioned, each being about 25 feet in diameter and 3 feet high. In one two empty stone graves without covering or bottom were found. They were about 10 inches below the surface, one of them 2 feet 3 inches long by 2 feet wide and 16 inches deep. In the other was a single stone grave 2 feet 5 inches long, 20 inches wide, and 15 inches deep. This, like the others, was empty. In the third nothing was discovered but some flat stones.

That these graves formerly contained human bones can not be doubted, but whether they were removed by explorers of modern times or not could not be determined. Though of such small size, it does not follow that they were used as depositories of children only, as it is not uncommon to find in the stone graves of southern Illinois adult skeletons crowded into as small a space as indicated by the measurements above given.

THE VOGEL GROUP.

This group, consisting of eleven mounds, is situated on the farm of Mr. Henry Vogel, about 3 miles from the following, both groups being in the Mississippi bottom near Fountain bluff. The relation of these mounds to each other is shown in Fig. 72.

The largest of the group, No. 1, is 12 feet high and 190 feet long by 130 wide. A trench 15 feet long and 4 feet wide, through the central portion, was carried down 12 feet, to the original surface. Considerable broken pottery and also a number of animal bones, most of them split and broken, were found between 8 and 11 feet from the top. At the depth of 11 feet was a bed of ashes mixed with earth and charcoal. In this fragments of pottery and bones were more abundant than elsewhere.

The surrounding land, which is subject to frequent overflows, is composed of a black waxy soil to the depth of 2 feet, and below this of sand. The mound was built entirely of this stiff waxy soil; at the depth of 12 feet the sand was reached. A wild-cherry tree 6 feet 3 inches in circumference, stands on the east end. On No. 2, which is 200 feet in circumference and 4 feet high, there is a walnut stump 9 feet 6 inches in circumference.

No. 3, about 150 feet southwest of No. 1, is 4 feet high and 120 feet long by 75 in width.

No. 4 is 250 feet in circumference and 6 feet high. In this a trench 22 feet long was dug through the center. For most of the length it was carried down to a depth of 9 feet, or 3 feet below the original surface of the ground. Human bones in considerable numbers were found at various depths from 6 inches down to 6 feet. Below this no human bones were observed, but at the depth of 9 feet some animal bones were obtained. As many as 12 skeletons were unearthed, but only 1 whole skull was obtained.

At the depth of 3 feet, and lying by a skeleton, were the spool-shaped copper ornaments shown in Fig. 73.   At the depth of 5½ feet, immediately under a root about 2 inches in diameter, a small earthen pot was discovered near a skeleton.   At the same depth, near the feet of

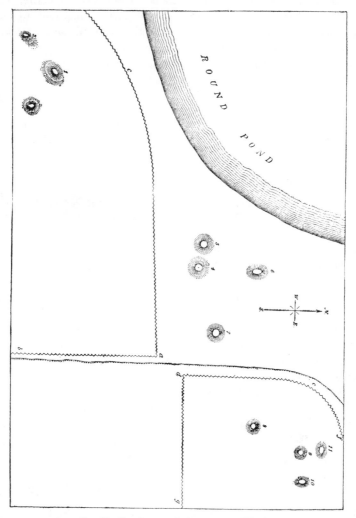

FIG. 72.—Vogel group, Jackson county, Illinois.

another skeleton, were the skull and teeth of some large animal. At the depth of 6 feet, by the knee of a large skeleton, was a lozenge-shaped gorget of slatestone 4 inches long and 1½ inches wide in the middle.   Under the head of this skeleton was a whole shell and some pieces; also a small curiously-wrought stone which was probably an ear ornament, as it was at the side of the head.   The skull of the skeleton, though damaged, was saved.

Fragments of pottery, also a few shells (*Unios*), were scattered through the mound at various depths. The earth in this mound was more sandy than that of those in the field, and was in alternate layers of black soil and sand.

Mound No. 5 is a little north of west from No. 4, the bases of the two approaching within 10 feet of each other. This is about 180 feet in circumference and something over 5 feet high. On the southern part stands a walnut stump 16 feet in circumference, and on the north side an ash 7 feet in circumference. Two trenches were carried down about a foot below the original surface of the ground. At one point, 5½ feet below the surface, a skeleton lay immediately beneath roots from both trees. One of the roots from the walnut, although 12 feet from the stump, was 4 inches in diameter. At another point, at the depth of 4 feet, were two small flint implements, and a foot below this some

FIG. 73.—Spool-shaped ornament of copper.

human teeth, but no bones, though by looking carefully at the earth indications of the other parts of the skeleton, which had decayed, were discovered.

GROUP ON SCHLIMPERT'S PLACE.

These mounds are situated on Mr. Joseph Schlimpert's land—the W. ½ of the NW. ¼ of Sec. 22, in Fountain Bluff township—and are located in reference to each other as shown in the annexed plat (Fig. 74). The soil around them is of a black waxy character, from 1 foot to 18 inches in depth, underlaid by sand. They lie near a slough which borders the farm on the north side, as shown in the plat. Nos. 1, 2, 3, 4, 5, 6, and 7 are mounds, No. 8 a sink or excavation, and No. 9 a platform or terrace.

No. 6, circular in form, is 60 feet in diameter, a little over 4 feet high, and has growing on it several trees, the largest a hackberry 7 feet in circumference. It was excavated to and slightly below the original surface of the ground, but nothing was found except a few small sand-stones. The interesting feature of this mound is its internal structure, which will be understood by reference to the vertical section shown in Fig. 75.

In the first place a central core of sand *c* appears to have been thrown up 40 feet in diameter at the top (1 to 2), and about 4 feet high. Around this apparently in order to secure it, was placed a ring of the black waxy soil (*bb*), so as properly to round it off. The V-shaped depression in the top (*d*) measured 3 feet in diameter at the top and extended downward about 2 feet. It was filled with a mass of hard white sand. Over the whole was a layer of sand about 1 foot thick.

The structure of this mound is suggestive of the so-called "altar mounds" of Ohio. Squier and Davis speak in one place of an altar or altar-shaped mass of sand found in a mound.[1]

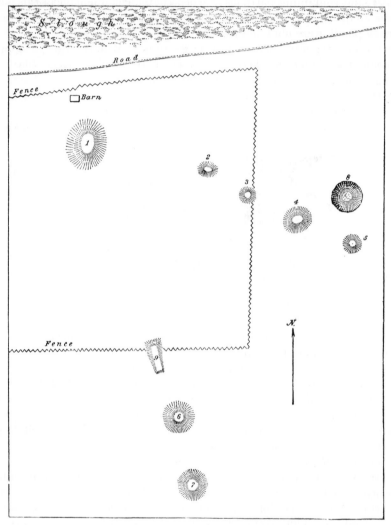

FIG. 74.—Schlimpert mounds, Jackson county, Illinois.

No. 7, 60 feet in diameter and 5 feet high, was composed almost wholly of the black waxy soil, with here and there small masses of sand. Nothing was found in it.

No. 4 was composed entirely of sand except the top layer; nothing was found in it.

[1] Ancient Monuments, p. 156.

No. 5, a small mound, was composed wholly of sand; No. 2, of the black waxy soil; No. 1, the largest of the group and somewhat oval in form—longest diameter, 110 feet; shortest, 100 feet, about 8 feet high—bore a strong resemblance in its construction to No. 6.

The central portion of the last was filled with black waxy soil mixed with sand containing particles of wood coal. The diameter of this portion was 44 feet. A few flint implements such as spear heads and arrow points were obtained from the surface of this mound.

A very interesting feature of this group is the platform or low, flat, rectangular mound, marked No. 9 on the plat. This is about 100 feet long, 50 feet wide, and 2 feet high. It is quite level on top and stands on the edge of a low bench, so that the eastern side is somewhat higher than the western. The sides run a little west of north.

A short distance northeast of mound No. 4 is a circular sink (No. 8 on the plat), about 80 feet in diameter and 1½ feet deep, which appears to be an artificial excavation.

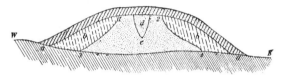

FIG. 75.—Section of mound on Schlimpert's place, Jackson county, Illinois.

Some small mounds on Big Muddy river, in Sec. 22, T. 10 S., R. 3 W., were also examined.

No. 1 is about 75 feet in diameter, 4 feet high, and flat on top. At the depth of 4 feet, on the natural surface of the ground, but at different points, were two skeletons of adults extended, with the heads west and faces up. Several layers of stone were placed over them, in fact the mound, to the depth of 3 feet, was composed in great part of flat stones, some of which would weigh probably 150 pounds. The only relic found in this mound was a broken flint implement.

No. 2, a quarter of a mile south of No. 1, although only 3 feet high and of the same diameter as the preceding, was largely occupied by stone graves.

Grave No. 1, 2½ feet long and 9 inches wide, contained the badly decayed bones of a child.

Grave No. 2, 3 feet long and 10 inches wide, also contained the bones of a child; badly decayed.

Grave No. 3, 3½ feet long and 1 foot wide, was occupied by the bones of an adult. There was no stone layer in the bottom of this cist.

Grave No. 4 was 6 feet long and 1 foot wide; No. 5, 4 feet long and 1 foot wide; No. 6, same size as No. 5, and No. 7, 2½ feet long and 1 foot wide; each contained the bones of a single adult.

About half a mile below the little village of Mill Creek, Union county (but just across the county line), a long ridge extending southeast terminates in the low ground in the angle at the junction of Cooper with Mill creek.   On the top of this ridge, at its lower terminus, are two or three low mounds and many stone graves, some of which had been previously opened and pottery, beads, and other articles taken from them. These appear to be in the midst of, or rather on, an immense refuse

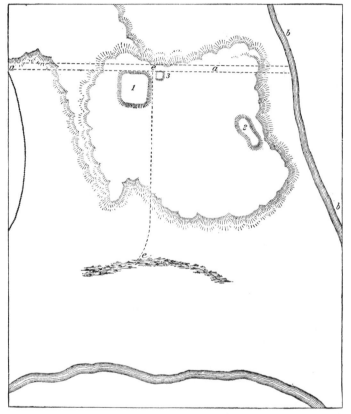

FIG. 76.—Mounds on Hale's place, Jackson county, Illinois.

heap; in fact, the whole top of the ridge appears to be covered to a depth of from 3 to 6 feet with an accumulation of flint chips, broken deer bones, broken pottery, mussel shells, etc.   Charcoal, burned limestone, and other evidences of fire are plentifully scattered throughout the mass.   The locality would probably be better described as a "kitchen heap," averaging 4 or 5 feet in depth and covering several acres.

The works and the grounds are shown in the annexed diagram (Fig. 76).   The line *a a* running across the ridge marks the boundary line at this point between Union and Alexander counties; and Mill creek *b b* the boundary line between Alexander and Pulaski counties. The remains are, therefore, at the point where these three counties meet, but in Alexander. The line *e e* represents the fence which separates the land of Mr. Hale on the right (Sec. 5, T. 14 S., R. 1 W.) from that owned by Mr. Hileman on the left. The boundary of the refuse heap is designated by the heavy shadings, the mounds by the Figs. 1, 2, and 3. No. 1 is nearly square and some 6 or 8 feet high; on it Mr. Hileman has built his dwelling house. No. 3 is a small pile of flint chips. No. 2 is irregular in outline, as shown in the figure, and about 4 feet high. Permission was granted to make excavations on the east side of the fence only.

Mound No. 2, as before stated, is about 4 feet high. Its length was found to be about 100 feet and average width 40 feet. The direction of the length is a little west of north. The surface was covered with loose flat stones thrown out by former explorers who had made a partial examination. A trench about 5 feet wide was carried obliquely across the middle directly east and west. Scattered through the soil to the depth of 5 or 6 inches were flint chips, fragments of stone and pottery and bits of bones. Lying lengthwise with the ditch, about 6 feet from the east end, was an open stone grave or cist, the side stones reaching to the surface of the mound but still in place. This we called by way of distinction "Grave No. 1." It was 3½ feet long and 14 inches wide (inside measurement). The top had been removed. The sides and ends were of limestone slabs from 1 to 2 feet long by 1 to 1½ wide and from 1 to 2 inches thick. The contents of the grave had been removed by previous explorers.

Immediately west of this, and 1 foot below the surface, were four large, roughly worked flint implements.

No. 2, immediately east of No. 1, had been partially rifled, but some bits of a skull and other bones and some small fragments of pottery were found in it. Below the bottom layer of stone, which was still in place, was a layer of charcoal and other evidences of fire; the charcoal stratum rested on a layer of rich black dirt about 10 inches thick, which lay on the yellow clay 2 feet below the surface. In this were some *Unio* and turtle shells and bits of pottery.

No. 3, immediately west of No. 1, was near the surface, but had been rifled.

No. 4, by the side of No. 3, but at a lower level, 6 feet long, 1 foot wide by 7 inches deep at the foot, and 14 inches wide by 12 deep at the head, had the boxing stones all in place, those of the cover laid on like shingles, beginning at the foot. This contained a single skeleton, stretched full length on the back, feet to the east; the head was supported on deer horns. The skull was secured entire as were also most of the long bones. Two roughly dressed flints were found near the head, and in the same locality a small perforated bone.

No. 5, above and just west of No. 4, and near the surface, measured but 2 feet and 10 inches in length. It had been disturbed and, besides the dirt, contained nothing but some small bones.

No. 6 lay obliquely across the trench; the feet of the skeleton toward the southeast at the surface of the ground and uncovered. The bones were much decayed. Length of the grave, 6¾ feet.

No. 7, just west of No. 6, parallel to it, and less than 6 inches from it, was 7 feet long; width, from 12 to 16 inches.

No. 8 lay with head resting below the feet of Nos. 6 and 7; length, 6 feet 9 inches. It was covered with several layers of thin flat stones, the lowest of which rested directly on the bones; skeleton at full length lying on the back. The skull was crushed by the weight of the stones that lay upon it. A few waterworn pebbles were noticed in this grave and also in No. 7. Signs of fire were observed immediately under the layer of stones forming the bottom, indicating that a fire had been kindled here and the stones afterward laid on the ashes. Some bits of charcoal were mixed with the dirt in nearly all the graves.

No. 9, immediately north of the east end of No. 8, formed in part by the same side stones and covered by the same slabs, was evidently the grave of an infant, being but 2½ feet long by 14 inches wide. The bones were mostly decayed. Near the head in a triangular cavity between two stones was a quantity of peculiar pinkish material which contained bits of lead ore. At the foot were four or five roughly worked flints and as many smaller ones at the head.

No. 10 was on the north side of No. 9, and very near it, and measured 2½ feet in length by 9 in width. A few infant bones were found in it, but mostly decayed. Under these were two rough flints.

No. 11, near the surface, contained the bones of a child that had not lost its first teeth.

No. 12, also near the surface, contained an adult skeleton lying on the back with feet to the south; the skull was broken. A small pot, with handle on one side, stood near the back of the head.

No. 13 was the grave of an infant, being 2¼ feet long and 8 inches wide. This was under No. 5 and on the same level as No. 14.

No. 14.—This was immediately below No. 8, the sides almost corresponding with the latter, and on the same level as No. 13, that is to say, 3 feet below the surface. Length, 5 feet 8 inches. Two fragments of fossil wood, placed near the neck of the skeleton, were the only objects found.

Below this grave was black soil several inches thick, and then yellow clay. The latter lay 4 feet below the surface of the mound. The size of this grave and the small rounded skull render it probable that this was the resting place of a woman.

Nos. 15 and 16.—No 16 was on the same level as No. 14, but lay with its foot toward the head of the latter. It contained the remains of an adult. No. 15 lay in the same direction as and immediately above No.

16. It also contained the well-preserved skeleton of an adult, the skull of which was secured.

No. 20, near the surface was 6 feet long and 16 inches wide at the head. This grave contained two skeletons the bones of which were very well preserved; they were lying side by side, the head of one a few inches nearer the end than that of the other. A quantity of red paint had been deposited near the chin of the one nearest the end while some flat, circular beads, made of mussel shells, placed between their breasts.

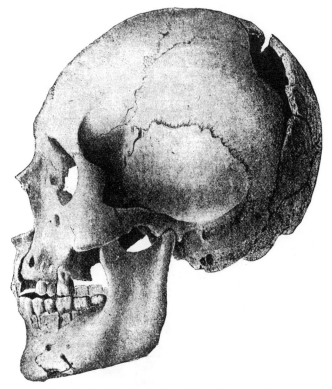

FIG. 77.—Skull from mound on Hale's place (side view).

From about the foot of grave No. 20, trench No. 1 was carried through a kitchen heap consisting of an immense number of flint chips, showing charcoal, burned limestone, broken bones of animals, broken pottery, etc. This was $2\frac{1}{2}$ feet deep here and rested on yellow clay. In a prospect hole sunk just west of the foot of grave No. 20, the clay proved to be only a layer less than a foot thick, resting on a layer of pure charcoal. There were no flints in either of these layers, but some broken bones, deer horns, and pottery were found in the charcoal stratum. A short distance west of this prospect hole, about 18 inches below the surface, the trench cut through some human bones that were not inclosed in stone cists; the femora and shin bones were lying side by side and some fragments of the skull and lower jaw bones with them.

About 12 feet west of pit No. 1, in another prospect pit, the flint layer was from 1½ to 2 feet thick and contained fewer bones and pottery; at a depth of about 3 feet were some pockets of charcoal but no continuous layer.

A few graves were found immediately south of trench No. 1, from one of which, that of a child, were obtained some univalve shells that had been perforated and worn around the neck. This small grave, only 23

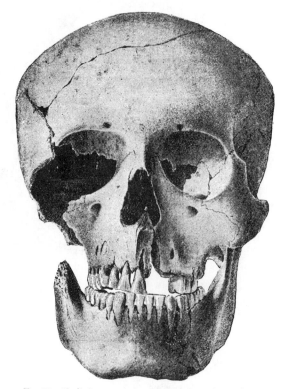

FIG. 78.—Skull from mound on Hale's place (front view).

inches long by 6 inches wide, contained some bits of a heavy mineral, perhaps pulverized lead ore.

Another child's grave contained a single gasteropod shell at the chin, another the skeletons of two children; the skull of the lower one of these two skeletons was filled with pure light-colored sand, the only sand seen in the mound.

Trench No. 3 was run from near the northeast corner of the mound. Graves 1 and 2 of this trench had been disturbed.

In grave 3 about a foot below the surface, the skeleton was well preserved. Here a number of shell beads were obtained which had been worn around the waist. A skull and some other bones were found in the same grave at the feet of this skeleton.

No. 4 lay directly below No. 3. From this was obtained a nearly perfect skull. It is small and the front narrow. (See Figs. 77 and 78.) This grave was one of the lowest tier, as it rested on the natural clay.

No. 5 was also in the bottom layer. Near the head of the skeleton which this contained were two wooden trinkets in the form of elongate beads perforated lengthwise. They are about 1 inch long and half an inch thick and bear copper stains, rendering it probable they were originally covered with a thin plate of this metal. Their position near the head probably justifies the belief that they were used as ear pendants.

No. 6 was on the same level as No. 5, and close by the side of it. There were no indications that this grave had been disturbed, yet the skull was standing upright facing the feet, and directly in front of it, lying across the skeleton, were the femora and shin-bones. The lower jaw had been dislocated, and placed at the left side of the skull. The other bones were in their proper position. A long bone needle was sticking up above the jaw, and some flakes of copper marked with flutings or ridges, like a piece taken from this mound by Mr. Bankstone, were found scattered through the dirt. On the bottom of the grave, to the left of the skull and under the lower jaw, were the remains of some woven bark matting stained with copper, and near the elbow of the right arm was an oblong bead of wood coated with oxide of copper similar to those heretofore mentioned.

FIG. 79.—Bone plate from mound on Hale's place.

No. 7 was near the surface of the mound. From it was obtained a very perfect skull and other bones; one femur is curiously deformed. No implements or ornaments accompanied the skeleton.

No. 8 was about 1 foot below the surface with top open. This small grave, which was only 18 inches long and 12 inches wide, contained the bones of a single skeleton closely packed. The lower jaw, however, was missing. The skull was marked on both sides with copper stains.

Trench No. 4 was run from near the southeast end of the mound, revealing two or three disturbed graves. In one of these was a skull with jaws open; in another the feet were lying in the wrong direction, the only case of the kind noticed. Near the head stood a small mug in the shape of some animal. Some thin plates of bone or turtle shell, each about 2 inches long, 1½ inches wide, very thin, a little cup-shaped, and drilled with four or more holes (see Fig. 79), were found lying closely packed together in a separate stone grave or box hardly a foot long. There was nothing else in the box.

In a grave a little to the west of this trench, near the surface, lay a skeleton stretched at full length. The skull was small and curiously flattened at the back and lying face down.

The northwestern end of this mound is its highest point, but there were no burials in this portion. From the dirt thrown out of one of these graves was obtained the Catholic medal shown in Fig. 80.

Subsequently to the examination of the works on the Hale place above referred to, some further explorations were made in the large mound, which was not completely worked over by the agent who first visited it. Two additional trenches were carried through it, running north and south. These revealed the fact that the south side was composed of refuse matter, mostly flint chips, with some fragments of pottery, bones, deer horns, etc. In this part there were no stone graves.

FIG. 80.—Catholic medal from mound on Hale's place.

In a child's grave in the upper tier near the center of the mound was

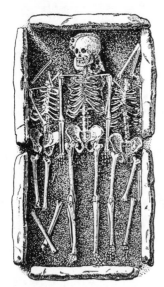

a small pot placed by the head of the skeleton. In the same part of the mound, 3 feet below the surface and immediately beneath a small walnut tree, was a stone coffin 7 feet long, of the usual width, which contained three skeletons. The heads of two of the skeletons had been separated from the bodies to which they belonged and laid side by side at the end of the coffin, and the other bones placed at the sides near the foot. The head of the third skeleton lay on the other skulls. (See Fig. 81.) The head of this coffin, like most of the others in the mound, was toward the west. The three skulls were saved. One of them is somewhat broken, but was preserved because of a singular protuberance on the top. In this coffin were some yellow paint, *Unio* shells, and two round stones, all lying near the upper skull.

FIG. 81.—Stone grave on Hale's place.

Several other graves were explored—all in fact which had not been previously disturbed, but nothing found except skeletons and a few river shells.

INDIAN DIGGINGS.

Not far from the little town of Mill Creek, and situated on Secs. 35 and 36, T. 13 S., R. 2 W. are the so-called Indian Diggings. These consist of numerous pits which have been dug at some distant day along the sides and on the tops of narrow ridges in quarrying the flint or chert found here. They are now partially filled up and covered by the forest growth no way differing from that about them. Scattered all over the ground in the vicinity of these pits are immense numbers of flint or chert nodules, nearly all of which are broken; two only were discovered that were unbroken. Several large flint implements were also found.

There are several places in this neighborhood where the flint taken from these pits was manufactured into implements, as large beds of flint chips of the same stone occur in which are many unfinished tools some of them showing good workmanship.

In the same neighborhood as the preceding, on Sec. 30, T. 13 S., R. 1 W., a number of stone graves were found and explored, but presented nothing different from those already described. However, a discovery was made here which deserves notice.

In the immediate vicinity, in fact but a few feet from some of the graves, a stone pavement was discovered about a foot below the surface of the ground. When fully exposed by removal of the earth this proved to be level, nearly circular, and about 9 feet in diameter. It was composed of flat pieces of limestone so neatly and closely fitted together that it was difficult to find a place where the steel prod could be thrust down between them. These showed the effect of fire, some of them crumbling into lime when disturbed; mingled with and scattered through the earth which covered them were ashes, charcoal, and charred fragments of human bones. In this earth was also discovered a small clay pot. The graves and pavement are not in or near a mound, but on the highest point of a hill and in a cultivated field.

A number of rude stone implements were found on the surface of the ground. There is also one point on the farm where these discoveries were made, where the surface is covered with flint chips to such an extent that it is difficult to plow it. As the flint diggings are near by, it is probable that stone implements were manufactured here, many unfinished and imperfect specimens being scattered over the ground.

UNION COUNTY.

ANCIENT WORKS ON LINN'S PLACE.

The first published notice of these interesting works was given by Mr. T. M. Perrine, of Anna, Illinois, in the Smithsonian Report for 1872.[1]

They are situated in the southwest part of Union county (Sec. 30, T. 13 S., R. 2 W.), on the bottom land of the Mississippi, a mile or more from this river. The immediate spot upon which they are located is a portion of the upper level of the bottom land, which is here some 10 or 12 feet above the swamp land which surrounds it on the west and

_____
[1] Pp. 418–420.

northwest. This area, however, was overflowed in the great rise of 1844, and also in 1882, the large mound hereafter described being the only part not under water. A creek runs along the east and northeast, separating the area from the bluff. The soil is a rich deep alluvium, underlaid by sand, with neither rock nor gravel in place.

Referring to the annexed plat (Fig. 82) made by Prof. Hull from a

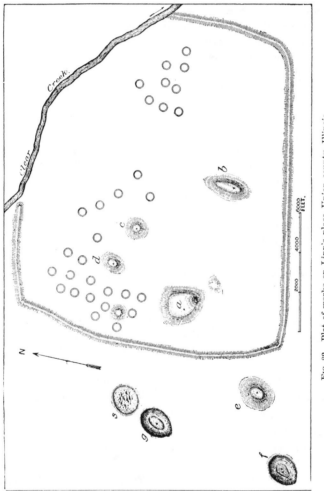

FIG. 82.—Plat of works on Linn's place, Union county, Illinois.

careful survey taken by him during our visit, we see that a wall, starting on the west side of the creek at the east end of the inclosure, runs thence southward to the bend, a distance of 400 feet, where it curves southwestward 126 feet. From this point it runs almost directly west to the corner 1,168 feet; thence north 1,036 feet to the northwest corner, thence east to the bank of the creek 569 feet, embracing in these boundaries about 28 acres.

The portion of the wall in the field, where it is much worn down, is not more than 2 feet high, while that part north of the fence and in the woods is from 4 to 5 feet high with indications of a ditch along the inside, though nothing of the kind is observable in the field. The width in the field varies from 20 to 25 feet, but is somewhat less in the woodland where not so much worn down. On this part there are a number of oak trees from 1 to 2 feet or more in diameter.

A rough outline figure of the large mound (marked *a* in the plat) as seen from the east at a distance of about 300 yards is shown in Fig. 83. The little rise at *c* is a low flat mound composed chiefly of fragments of limestone partly calcined, situated a few yards immediately south of the large mound. The length of the eastern side of the large mound, from 1 to 2, is 160 feet; the height at *a* is 13 feet; at *b* 11½ feet and at *m* 12 feet. These letters, *a*, *b*, and *m*, also mark the places where pits were sunk during the first examination. The circumference of the base is 544 feet.

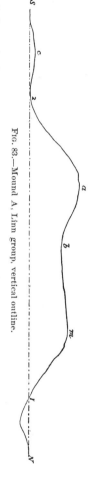

FIG. 83.—Mound A. Linn group, vertical outline.

At *a*, the highest point, a pit about 4 feet wide and 10 feet long was sunk to the depth of 10 feet; some pieces of burnt clay, small fragments of human bones and flakes of flint were found scattered irregularly through it for the first 5 feet, but below this only sand.

Three other pits were sunk in the depressed portion (*b*). In the first, at the depth of 3 feet, a bed of light, dry ashes was discovered, nearly a foot thick but only a few feet in extent horizontally. In this were two rather large fragments of pottery, one inside of the other, as though they had been so placed originally. At the depth of 4 feet a pot with ears was found, mouth upward. It still retained, in part, its original reddish-brown color.

Below this was a layer of sand similar to that found in pit *a*. Near the surface were some small irregular pieces of burnt clay. In the second pit, some 3 feet northwest of the first, nothing of interest was found until a depth of 4 feet was reached. At this point a considerable quantity of charred grass and ashes was observed.

In the third of these three pits a number of rather large irregular pieces of burned clay, similar to that already mentioned, were found near the surface. About 3 feet from the surface lay a flat rock of considerable size. A foot below this a layer of burned clay was encountered, the upper surface of which was as smooth and even as pottery. This proved to be part of an arch, the central portion of which had been broken and thrown down.

As the pit sunk by Mr. Perrine was very near this point there can be no doubt that this was a portion of the arch he speaks of. He also speaks of a wall of stone. This was not found, unless the large stone mentioned formed a part of it.

This arch or dome of clay had evidently been spread over the surface of the mound when it had reached a height of 5 or 6 feet and over this dry grass and brush had been spread and burned. A large quantity of the charred grass and bits of wood-coal were found around the margin of this arch as far as explored, making it apparent that the fire had been extinguished probably by throwing dirt upon it before the grass and brush were entirely consumed. Immediately below the arch we came upon a thick loose bed of ashes.

In another pit the strata were as follows: First, a layer of earth with particles of charcoal mixed through it, 3 feet 8 inches; next, a layer of burnt sand and clay with evidences of straw having been used, 3 inches; then another layer of earth 1 foot 10 inches; then a second layer of burnt sand and clay 4 inches thick, with indications of straw; next, a layer of sand 5 inches; then a third layer of burnt sand and clay 3 inches (similar to the others); a layer of sand, 3 feet; and last a layer of ashes, 3 inches.

But few things were found during these excavations; still they are of some importance in our efforts to learn the method and object of building this mound. They consist of burnt straw, grass, and charcoal found on the upper side of each layer of burnt clay, the clay itself showing evidence of having grass mixed with it. Possibly this admixture may have resulted from tramping the grass into the soft clay while spreading it over the surface previous to firing it.

Fragments of burnt, cherty limestone, similar to that composing the little mound at the south end, marked c in Fig. 83, were found all through the second trench. Numerous fragments of pottery and several fragments of human bones; irregular pieces of burnt clay resembling brick; a few fragments of river shells (*Unio*); and some rude flint implements were also found. Among the ashes at the bottom were some fragments of bone and pottery; one of the pieces of bone was found in the concave side of a large fragment of pottery. At another point in the same layer were fragments of pottery, bones, and shells.

Firmly imbedded in the middle layer of burnt clay, was a broken pot and with it were pieces of bone. Three feet from the surface and above the upper layer of clay, another broken pot was obtained; this was filled with ashes, firmly packed and mixed with particles of charcoal. Under the second layer of clay was a small pot filled with sand with a thin layer of ashes on the top. At one point between the upper and middle layers of clay was a small bed of ashes mixed with fragments of pottery, animal bones, and a piece of shell. In a small bed of ashes under the middle layer of clay were potsherds and some broken and split bones.

At a point between the upper and middle layers of clay, with fragments of pottery, pieces of bone and charcoal, was discovered a piece of charred wood.

Mound *b*, about 450 feet east of *a*, of the form shown in the plat, is 190 feet long by 66 in width, and 5 feet high. Two pits were dug in this and a few detached pieces of human bones found.

Mound *c* is 100 feet in diameter and 9 feet high; *d*, a little smaller and 6 feet high; *e*, about 150 feet in diameter and a little over 4 feet high; *f* and *g* are circular excavations outside of the wall; the former 120 feet in diameter and 5 feet deep; the latter with the longer diameter 154 feet; depth, 7 feet. Excavations made in the bottom of these indicate that they were artificially lined with a coating of stiff clay. At *s* is another sink, apparently artificial, but now partially filled with mold of decaying vegetation, leaves, etc.

The "hut rings" or small circular depressions surrounded by slight earthen rings, indicated in Fig. 82 by little circles, are scattered irregularly over the wooded portion of the inclosure, the number exceeding 100. They vary in diameter from 20 to 50 feet, and in depth from 1 to 3 feet and are often but a few feet apart.

MOUND ON RUNNING LAKE.

This mound, or rather remnant of a mound, is near Running lake in the southwestern part of Union county. A part of it had been removed for filling purposes on the line of the Mobile and Ohio railroad, which runs near it. It appears to have been about 9 feet high, and 60 feet in diameter and composed of sand, with the exception of 2 feet of top soil. At one point, about 2 feet below the surface, the leg bones of a single individual were found; no other bones were with them; at another and about the same depth were the bones of two feet and a deer's horn. Some pots and other implements were obtained from it by parties who had previously examined it. The parts of the skeleton found scattered through the mound appear to have been separated previous to burial.

MOUNDS ON ROUND POND.

These mounds are situated by the side of the public highway near the Reynolds place 2 miles from the Mississippi river and on the bank of a little lake known as Round pond. Two of them are so close together that one appears partially to overlap the other as shown in the accompanying sketch (Fig. 84).

No. 1 is 40 feet in diameter, 6 feet high, and of the usual conical form. Two trenches near the middle carried down to the original surface showed it to be composed entirely of sand except the top layer of soil 1½ feet thick, but no bones or remains of any kind were observed. The top had been nearly covered with graves, but they were empty, having been rifled of their contents by previous explorers.

No. 2 is only about 25 feet in diameter and 3 feet high, and, like the other, is composed entirely of sand, except the top layer. On the west side, near the middle, were two empty stone graves (*c c*), each 7 feet long, 18 inches wide, and about 1 foot in depth, covered with a thin layer of soil. In the road where it crosses the connecting portions of the two mounds were three stone graves (*a a a*). These, like the two in the mound, lay east and west, but were much smaller, being only 20 inches long, 16 inches wide, and 15 inches deep, and were at the surface of the ground. Two were empty, but in the other was a skeleton doubled up, the skull and trunk lying on the left side, the lower jaw touching the

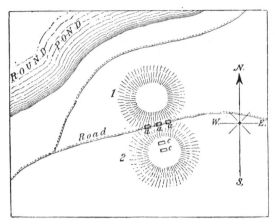

FIG. 84.—Round pond mounds, Union county, Illinois.

west end of the grave; the trunk was bent double, the backbone touching the south side. Although confined in this narrow space, this was the skeleton of an adult.

A few flint specimens were picked up from the surface of the ground about the mounds.

ANCIENT GRAVES.

These box-shaped stone cists are on a spur of the bluffs which bound the Mississippi bottoms in the NW. ¼ Sec. 16, T. 13 S., R. 2 W. This spur is about 400 feet high, has steep sides and a narrow top.

Grave No. 1, 2 feet under the surface, lay northeast and southwest; length, 6 feet; width, 2 feet; depth, 1 foot; bottom formed of two flat stones; each side of five similar stones and each end of two; the cover was in three layers, each formed of two rather thick flat stones. In the grave were two skeletons, an adult and a child, stretched at full length, faces up, and heads southwest. Under the skull of the adult were a bone needle and two stone implements. At the feet was a long-necked bottle-shaped vase. These remains were covered with very dry, yellow earth which well-nigh filled the grave.

No. 2, 10 feet north of No. 1, was of the same size and form, but the top in this case had fallen in. It was 3 feet under the surface, lay east and west, and contained one skeleton, at full length upon its back, head west, bones comparatively sound. Under and near the skull were a small, circular, shell ornament, bone awl, bone needle, and bone punch. Two small pieces of thin copper plate were discovered, but were so corroded and fragile that they fell into minute particles when handled. This grave was very dry, and nearly full of a loose, dry, yellowish earth.

Four other stone graves were opened in section 20, same township and range. These were on a stony bench, east of the bottom, about 30 feet high. They were of the same form and size as the others, but were only about 6 inches under the surface. These graves contained nothing but rotten bones.

Another ancient cemetery is situated on the brow of a high, abrupt hill, NW. ¼ Sec. 16, T. 10 S., R. 2 W., at the foot of which is the "Upper Bluff lake." The graves are of stone, similar to those mentioned. Quite a number had been previously opened by Mr. T. M. Perrine.

Grave No. 1 contained the skeleton of an adult, extended, face up, head west. The cover to the coffin, which had not been disturbed, was 2 feet below the surface.

In this grave were one discoidal stone, one shell, and several pieces of copper plates. One of the latter, badly corroded, bears the impressed figure of a bird, similar to that shown further on in Pl. XVIII, but wanting the head; the other, bearing dancing figures, is fortunately but slightly corroded; it measures 6 by 6½ inches, and is shown in Fig. 85. The latter plate was lying flat on the bottom rock of the grave at the left of the skull immediately above the shoulder.

FIG. 85.—Copper plate bearing dancing figures. Union county, Illinois.

No. 2, only 2 feet long, was evidently the grave of a child, as indicated by the skeleton. In it was an earthen bowl.

No. 3 contained all the bones of a full-sized adult, but they were piled together in a coffin only 2 feet long. Most of them were quite firm, but the skull was broken. With them was an earthenware pot with two handles or ears.

No. 4 was the grave of a child and contained, besides the skeleton, two earthern vessels, one a small dish, at the head, the other, a bowl, at the feet. Over this grave stands a black oak 9 feet in circumference which has evidently grown there since the grave was made, as some of the largest roots ran into it. Immediately under the trunk was another grave which was partially explored through the large hollow of the base. From it was obtained a broken dish. Upon one of the graves had been piled as much as a wagonload of stones. This was a few feet down the slope of the hill, and contained three skeletons and one long-necked water vessel.

In the majority of the graves opened at this place the skulls were

12 ETH——11

broken. Although most of the stone coffins were from 5 to 7 feet long and the skeletons in them lying at full length, others did not exceed 2 feet in length and 1 in width. In the latter the bones were in a confused heap, showing that the flesh must have been removed before burial.

In section 29, same township, on land belonging to Mr. Joseph Hindman, is another cemetery of stone graves. It is on a bench about 50 feet above the creek bottom. Fifteen of these graves were examined. The bones in most of them were comparatively firm and well preserved.

Grave No. 1, 2 feet 3 inches long and 18 inches wide, contained all the bones of an adult and a water vessel.

No. 2 contained only a few badly decayed bones.

No. 3, 2½ feet long and 15 inches wide, contained all the bones of an adult, rather firm but the skull broken.

No. 4, 2 feet long, 18 inches wide, and 15 inches deep, contained the bones of an adult.

No. 5, 6½ feet long and 15 inches wide, contained a single, extended skeleton, head west, face up.

No. 7, 2 feet 4 inches long, 2 feet wide, and 15 inches deep, was filled with bones, apparently of three adults, as there were three skulls; they were piled in without order.

In grave No. 9, 5½ feet long and only 15 inches wide, were two extended skeletons, quite firm, the skulls of which were secured.

Nos. 6, 8, and 10 contained only badly decayed bones.

No. 12, 5½ feet long, 18 inches wide, contained one skeleton, extended, head west. Bones firm, but skull broken; by the latter stood a small water jar.

No. 13 was of the same length as No. 12, but only 1 foot wide (inside measurement in all cases); skeleton extended and bones badly decayed.

No. 14, length 4½ feet, contained the skeleton of a child, extended; near the skull a small water jar and a bowl.

No. 15, 6 feet long, 16 inches wide, contained a single skeleton, extended, head west, face up.

The graves here were not so deep in the ground as those in section 16, the tops of some of them being only 6 inches below the surface and the deepest only 18 inches.

In the cemetery situated on the NW. ¼ Sec. 16, T. 13 S., R. 2 W. is a circular stone grave south of the black oak tree. This grave, about 5 feet in diameter, was formed by standing on end short slabs of stone around the circle. The sides of the grave were slightly flaring. There are some reasons for believing that this pertains to an earlier period than the other graves, though nothing positive on this point could be ascertained.

The graves on the Hindman place are only about half a mile from the Linn mounds, those on the Hileman farm about 2 miles from them, and those on the hill 3 miles. It is possible, therefore, that the people who lived at the Linn farm and built the mounds and other works there buried their dead at one or more of those places.

LAWRENCE COUNTY.

It was ascertained by the Bureau agent that some of the supposed mounds on the bluff or ridge opposite Vincennes, in which skeletons have been found are natural hillocks but used as burying grounds by the aborigines.

BROWN'S MILL MOUNDS.

These are on Embarrass river 6 miles west of Vincennes, on the farm of Dr. F. R. Austin. There are but two in the group, one 4 and the other 6 feet high. Excavations to the base revealed nothing but sand, though stone implements and fragments of pottery have been plowed up here, some of which were obtained.

MOUNDS NEAR RUSSELLVILLE.

These are situated near the bank of the Wabash about a mile southeast of the town on the farm of Mr. William Wise. One had been opened a short time before the Bureau investigation and a skeleton found at the depth of 2 feet; a flat rock was lying over it, but no relics of any kind with it. Two others formerly stood near it, but have been removed. According to local information several skeletons were found at the bottom and with them two iron tomahawks, some pipes, some shells and glass beads, and parts of three pairs of beaded buckskin moccasins.

Another mound on the Lawrenceville road, about 3 miles southeast of Russellville, had also been opened and several skeletons found about 2 feet below the surface, with heads outward and feet toward the center. No articles of any kind were with them.

Near the town of Russellville formerly stood several mounds, but they were excavated in repairing the road. In these were found arrowheads, a silver breast ornament, two iron tomahawks, a crescent-shaped earring, two stone turtles, two copper kettles, a brass ring, and several skeletons, all at the bottom of the mound.

MISSOURI.

CLARK COUNTY.

Between Fox river and Sugar creek a sharp dividing ridge, about 100 feet high, extends for a distance of nearly 2 miles, in a northwesterly direction, from where these streams debouch to the open bottoms of the Mississippi.

At an abrupt turn to the east, near the middle, there is a bold point much higher, capped by an ancient mound which is surmounted by a station of the U. S. Coast Survey. This is one of a line of circular mounds scattered irregularly along the crest of this ridge, as shown in the accompanying diagram (Fig. 86). These range in size from 15 to 50 feet in diameter at the base and from 2 to 6 feet high. The entire ridge is now covered with scattering large red and white oaks and dense thickets.

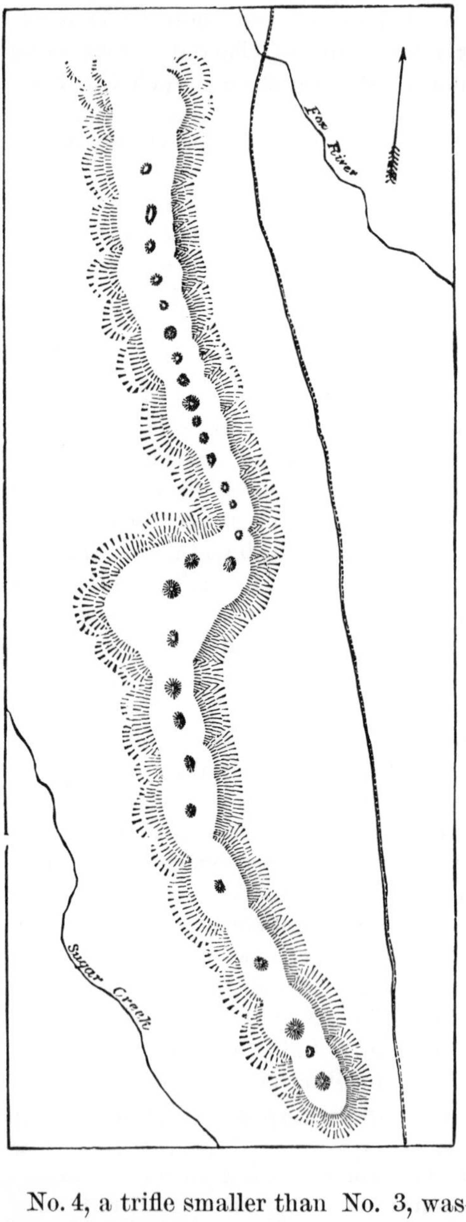

The following circular mounds, numbering from the south end of the line, were opened:

No. 1, 30 feet base, 3 feet high, in which were found only fragments of rude pottery.

No. 2, very small; nothing found in it.

No. 3, diameter 35 feet, height 5 feet. In the central part of this was a box-shaped stone coffin, or cist, 2 feet wide and 7 feet long. This was covered by stone slabs, as usual, and then with enough rougher ones to form a heap over it. Over this was hard earth which filled the interstices as though it had been a mortar when placed there. Over all was a foot or more of yellowish earth similar to that forming the ridge. In the coffin was the skeleton of an adult, lying horizontally on the back, but too much decayed for removal. No stone implements or other articles of any kind were with it.

FIG. 86.—Mound group, Clarke county, Missouri.

No. 4, a trifle smaller than No. 3, was opened by running a trench from the eastern side. For a distance of 15 or 16 feet only ordinary earth was encountered, with which the whole mound to the depth of 2 feet appeared to be covered; then a layer of rough stones, charcoal, and ashes, with bones intermixed. In fact, the indications were that one or more bodies (or the bones) had been burned in a fire upon the natural surface of the earth near the center; the coals and brands then covered with rough stones thrown on without system to the depth of 3 feet over a space 10 or 12 feet in diameter, and these covered with hard, light-colored earth. Only fragments of charred human bones and rude pottery and stone chips were found commingled with the charcoal and ashes of the fire.

Several of the next (and larger) mounds had been previously opened by other parties.

Nos. 16, 23, 25, and 26 were excavated, but nothing of interest was obtained from them. All except the last (No. 26) had a hard core in the center at the base, but this (No. 26) was composed wholly of ordinary earth similar to that about it, and was easily spaded to the bottom.

ANCIENT WORKS ON J. N. BOULWARE'S PLACE.

These are in Clark county, but near the line between it and Lewis county, and on the land of Mr. John N. Boulware, 10 miles north of Canton. Ordinary circular mounds are found scattered along the bluffs and terraces of the Mississippi for 7 miles southward from those heretofore mentioned near Fox river, to the group on Mr. Boulware's place. This group is on a bench or terrace, from 20 to 40 feet above the open bottoms of the Mississippi, and extending less than half a mile therefrom to the bluffs, which rise nearly 100 feet higher. Of these, fifty-one are in a woods pasture from which the undergrowth has been removed, affording a fine opportunity for exploration. A diagram of this group is given in Pl. VIII.

No. 4 was opened, and in it, near the top, were found the much decayed fragments of a human skeleton and some broken pottery encircled by a row of flat stones, set up edgewise and covered by others lying flat above them. Beneath these was a layer of very hard, light-colored earth, scattered through which were fragments of charred human bones, pottery, charcoal, and stone chips.

No. 5 was examined, but nothing was found except a core of hard earth having the appearance of dried mortar, in which were patches of soft charcoal, fragments of pottery, and flakes of stone.

The road runs near No. 50, and has cut away the eastern portion. A trench through the remainder brought to light the femora of an ordinary sized skeleton, but no trace of the other portions could be found. With this were some rude stone scrapers, fragments of pottery, charcoal, and ashes.

No. 46 is about 60 feet in diameter and 6 feet high, conical and unusually symmetrical. A trench 6 feet wide was carried entirely across it. The exterior layer, scarcely a foot thick, consisted of ordinary top soil; the remainder was unmistakably composed of dried mortar, in which fragments of charred human bones, small rounded pieces of pottery, stone scrapers, and fleshers were commingled with charcoal and ashes.

As all the mounds opened here presented this somewhat singular feature, a very careful examination was made of this mortar-like substance. It was found that there was a difference between different portions in the same mound, sufficiently marked to trace the separate masses. This would indicate that the mounds had been built by successive deposits of mortar thus mixed with charred bones, etc., not in strata, but in masses.

All the facts seem to indicate that the builders of these mounds burned their dead, and that possibly each family mixed together the charred remains, ashes, etc., forming one of these masses, 1 or 2 bushels in amount, and then deposited it with others to form the central part of the mound.

The following is a list of the mounds of this group, showing the size and form of each:

No.	Diameter.	Shape.	Height.	Remarks.
	Feet.		*Ft. In.*	
1	33	Circular ..	3 0	
2	30	....do	3 0	
3	42	....do	3 6	
4	45	....do	4 6	Dug; human skeleton, fragments of pottery, etc.
5	54	....do	2 0	Dug; hard earth like dried mortar.
6	46	....do	5 0	Dug; very hard light-colored earth; no remains.
7	45	....do	4 0	Dug; no remains in the hard earth.
8	35	....do	2 6	
9	30	....do	2 0	
10	30	....do	2 6	
11	60	....do	6 0	Dug; fragments of human bones and round pieces of pottery in a matrix of dried mortar.
12	25	....do	2 0	
13	20	....do	1 6	
14	20	....do	1 6	
15	20 by 15	Oblong ...	1 6	
16	75 by 20	Wall-shaped..	2 0	
17	35	Circular ..	3 0	
18	15	....do	1 6	
19	15	....do	1 6	
20	54	....do	5 0	
21	20	....do	2 0	
22	60	...do	5 0	
23	66	...do	6 0	
24	35	...do	3 0	
25	50	...do	5 0	
26	50	...do	5 0	Dug; only fragments of charcoal, ashes, small rounded pieces of bones and pottery.
27	15	...do	2 0	
28	30	...do	2 0	
29	20	...do	1 6	
30	20	...do	1 6	

No.	Diameter.	Shape.	Height.	Remarks.
	Feet.		*Ft. In.*	
31	20	Circular ..	1 6	
32	20	...do	1 6	
33	20	...do	2 0	
34	21	...do	1 6	
35	15	...do	1 6	
36	23	...do	1 6	
37	23	...do	1 6	
38	22	...do	2 0	
39	20	...do	2 0	
40	15 by 11	Oblong....	2 0	
41	25	Circular ..	2 0	
42	25	...do	2 0	
43	45	...do	5 0	
44	40	...do	4 0	Dug; dried mortar in appearance.
45	20	...do	2 0	
46	60	...do	6 0	Dug; see description.
47	40	...do	4 0	Dug; found only fragments of human bones, and pottery.
48	30	...do	3 6	
49	50	...do	5 0	
50	60	...do	5 0	Dug; found human bones.
51	45	...do	4 0	
52	....	...do	....	These four mounds are on the Mississippi bottoms, cultivated over for fifty years and much flattened but said to have resembled No. 51 in size and form.
53	....	...do	....	
54	....	...do	....	
55	....	...do	....	

Excavation, 75 by 100 feet, 5 feet deep; nearly full of water.

LEWIS COUNTY.

The only work examined in this county was a mound 2 miles north of Canton on the point of a bluff facing the Mississippi bottom. It is oblong, the longer diameter being 46 feet and the shorter 32 feet; height, 6 feet. A trench through the middle resulted in bringing to light decayed human bones commingled with charcoal, ashes, a few fragments of rude pottery, and stone chips. These were upon the natural surface near the center, covered, first with nearly 3 feet of hard earth, over this earth similar to the surrounding soil. An oak tree 3 feet in diameter was growing on the northern slope.

The character of this mound and its contents connect it with those of Clarke county.

ST. LOUIS COUNTY.

"SALT-KETTLE POTTERY."

This is found near the Clifton Springs, 4 miles south of Kirkwood and about 16 miles southwest of St. Louis.

Following a country road between the low rounded bluffs of a winding valley, we cross the brook twice within a distance of 400 yards, and upon the point of a terrace, between these crossings, we find numerous fragments of pottery fully an inch thick, being the heaviest ancient pottery yet discovered in this country. As may be seen by the form of specimens collected, the vessels were of unusually large size. No entire vessels, however, have been found, but the fragments show that they were low and shallow, like a salt pan or kettle, and destitute of ears or handles.

As its popular name, "Salt-kettle pottery," indicates, it is generally supposed to have been used in making salt.

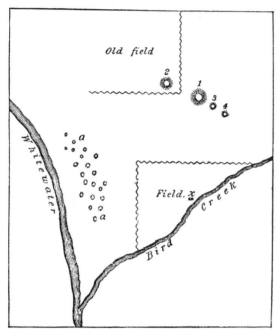

A careful examination of the pottery was made and the channel of the brook enlarged and deepened above and below, and a large drain made through the low land beyond it, without discovering a fragment of the pottery or of the charcoal or ashes of any ancient fires. As no indications of a change in the location of these springs or of the quality of their waters, which are as near sulphur as salt, were found, it is very doubtful whether the pottery was ever used for salt-making purposes here or elsewhere, as it was too heavy to carry without canoes, which could not have been used at this locality, or horses and wagons, which the pottery makers did not possess. Besides this, no traces of salt are observed on the fragments seen, and according to Prof. Collett, none has ever been found on them by chemical analysis. It is stated that at various localities in this valley, including one not remote from this point, crypts or rude stone coffins containing human skeletons, weapons, and ornaments of considerable interest have been found, but none were observed by the Bureau agent.

FIG. 87.—The Ben Proffer mound, Cape Girardeau county, Missouri.

CAPE GIRARDEAU COUNTY.

THE BEN PROFFER MOUNDS.

These are situated partly on the end of a high ridge, at the point where Bird creek unites with Whitewater river, and partly on the river bottom, as shown in Fig. 87.

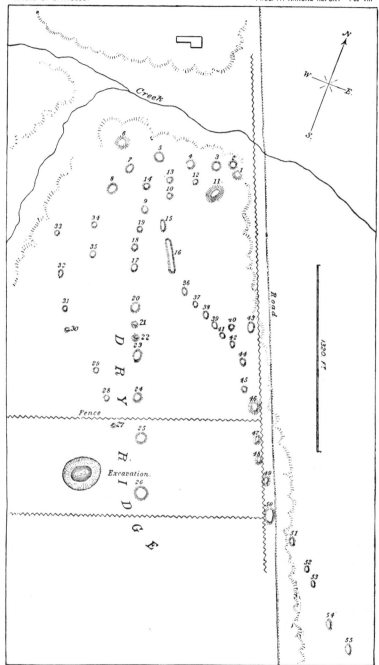

ANCIENT WORKS ON BOULWARE'S PLACE, CLARKE COUNTY, MISSOURI.

No. 1, the largest, occupies a commanding position overlooking the valleys of both streams. Though not large, being only about 35 feet in diameter and 5 feet high, it is quite a conspicuous object, and has some local notoriety. It is rounded with steep slopes that contrast strongly with the low flat outline of the small mounds of the valley below (at *a a*). A number of chert stones were observed embedded in its surface. No. 2 is forty paces from No. 1 in an open field; it is 30 feet in diameter by 2 in height. There are two piles of stone on it, but these were probably placed there recently to get them out of the way of the plow. Flint chips are scattered around it in considerable numbers.

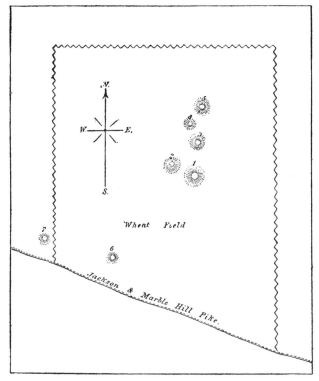

FIG. 88.—The Witting mounds, Cape Girardeau county, Missouri.

Nos. 3 and 4 are quite small and near to No. 1. The mounds in the bottom at *a a* are circular, quite small, low, and flattened on top. They are probably the sites or foundations of former dwellings or wigwams.

THE WITTING MOUNDS.

These compose a small group on the farm of Mr. August Witting, 5 miles west of Jackson, and seem to differ somewhat from the ordinary type. Their position is also peculiar, as they are near the top of the divide between Cane and Bird creeks and on the north slope of the hill, the only instance of this kind noticed. Their relative positions are shown in Fig. 88. Some two years ago a trench was dug through No.

1, but no specimens or remains, except some broken stones, were found. A few sandstones and chert fragments are still lying in the trench.

The following measurements, though made in haste and without strict accuracy, are probably of sufficient value to be recorded here:

No. 1: 40 feet in diameter, 4½ feet high.

No. 2: 55 feet northwest of No. 1; 35 feet diameter, 2½ feet high.

No. 3: 85 feet north of No. 1, and same distance from No. 2; 30 feet diameter, 2 feet high.

No. 4: 55 feet north and a little west of No. 3; 25 feet diameter, 2 feet high.

No. 5: 55 feet northeast of No. 4; 35 feet diameter, 2½ feet high.

No. 6: 80 paces southwest of No. 1; 20 feet diameter, 1½ feet high.

No. 7: 70 paces west of No. 6: 20 feet diameter, 2 feet high.

BOLLINGER COUNTY.

This county lies west of Cape Girardeau county, and like the latter is nearly all high land, but the southern end extends a short distance into the swamps. In the southeast corner is one of the inclosed "settlements," which is here named after the owner of the land.

THE PETER BESS SETTLEMENT.

This is situated 5 miles west of Lakeville, on the western bank of the Castor river, near where the line of the Cape Girardeau and State-Line railway crosses that stream. The "settlement," as these groups are locally named, is a small one, the embankment inclosing only about 12 acres. With the exception of a small strip on the east side, it has been under cultivation for forty years, so that the rings or residence sites have long since been obliterated. The wall extends entirely around the inclosure, excepting a small space at the northeast corner, where it is open toward the stream. A plat of it is given in Fig. 89, on which 1, 2, 3, etc., indicate mounds, *a a* embankments, and *c c* places where human bones were exposed.

From the direction of the current of the river it seems quite possible that the wall once entirely surrounded the area, but that the northeast corner has been washed away. In the strip of woods on the eastern side the wall is a little over 3 feet high. In the field it is considerably worn down by the plow, but the line of it can still be easily traced. The land inside of it is fully 2 feet higher than that outside, and is so much richer that the owner says it yields 75 bushels of corn per acre in favorable seasons, while that outside yields but 50. Frequent traces of burned earth and ashes are seen in the fields, and great quantities of broken pottery are scattered about. Where the land slopes a little, in the northeast and southeast corner (at *c c*), fragments of human bones have been washed out in considerable numbers. The large mound, No. 1, is situated a little north of the center of the inclosure. It is 150 feet across and about 10 feet high, nearly circular, but has been worn so much by forty years' tillage that its original outline can not be satisfactorily determined. An old log house and some out-

buildings occupy the nearly level top. In digging post holes some
bones and pottery were found, but no excavations have been made in
it deeper than 2 or 3 feet.

Mound No. 2, near the east wall, is circular in outline, 75 feet across,
and 6 feet high. It has never been explored.

Nos. 3 and 6 are quite small. A few stones have been plowed up on
No. 3. In the same field, some little distance south of the inclosure,
are two small mounds, Nos. 4 and 5. Mr. Bess stated that a few years

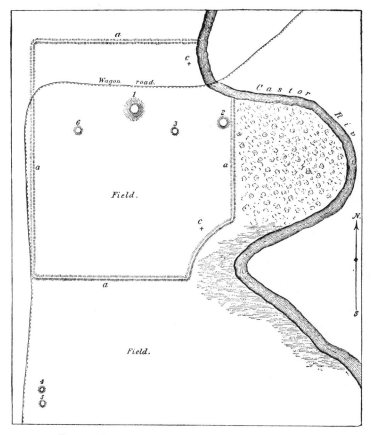

FIG. 89.—The Peter Bess settlement, Bollinger county, Missouri.

ago, while plowing over No. 4, his plow struck something and on digging down he found two stone coffins, each containing a skeleton. In
one of them he found a gourd-shaped vessel, ornamented with red
stripes and filled with lead ore so pure that he afterwards made bullets
from a part of it. An examination of this mound confirmed Mr. Bess's
statement, as the disturbed remains of the stone cists were found.
These were of the box-shaped type. Portions of a skeleton, including
a well-preserved lower jaw and a few bits of painted pottery, were
also discovered here.

STODDARD COUNTY.

Although this county lies wholly within what is known as the "swamp region," the central portion of it consists of a high clay ridge or table-land which may be considered a spur from the Ozarks. This table-land is separated from the bluffs of Cape Girardeau and Bollinger counties to the north by a strip of lowland known as the Mingo swamp. During high water a portion of the overflow from the Castor reaches the Whitewater through this swamp.

The county is bordered on the east by the Whitewater or Little river, which flows through an extensive tract of low, sandy swamp, which in places is as much as 20 miles wide. It is known to the people of Stoddard and Dunklin counties as the "East swamp," and the Bureau agent heard no other name for it. Mr. Potter, in his report,[1] refers to it as "West swamp" and "West lake" in his description of New Madrid and Sikeston ridge. This is confusing, since the name of "West swamp" is given to a similar tract along the St. Francis, which forms the western boundary of the county.

A little south of Dexter city the clay hills come to an end, and the divide between the East and the West swamps consists only of a low, sandy ridge. Under the local names of the "Rich woods" and the "West prairie" this extends in a southerly direction to the state line. Through Dunklin county it is crossed by sloughs that impede travel during wet weather. The swamps in this county consist of parallel sloughs of no great depth, with low, sandy ridges between them, which are for the most part above overflow. They are crossed at intervals by lower places that are covered during high water, thus converting the higher portions into islands. A good many farms have been cleared up on these ridges, so that the swamps support a scattered population. The sloughs are filled with a heavy growth of cypress (*Taxodium distichum*) and Tupelo gum (*Nyssa uniflora*). On the ridges the timber is principally different species of oak and hickory and sweet gum (*Liquidamber styraciflua*).

Earthworks of different kinds are very numerous throughout this county. Two settlements were examined during the preliminary visit, one near Lakeville, in the northern part, and the other in the extreme south, on the county line.

Groups of small mounds are to be found along most of the little streams among the hills. Several were observed on the low ridges in the East swamp, south of the railroad.

What is said to be the most extensive system of mounds in southeast Missouri is found 7 miles south of Dexter city, on that portion of the sandy divide between the swamps, which is known as the "Rich woods." There seems to have been, as is shown further on, no wall or ditch here, and there are few circular depressions or lodge sites.

---

[1] Contributions to the Archæology of Missouri (1880) pp. 5–8.

THE LAKEVILLE SETTLEMENT.

This settlement or group of works, which is shown in Fig. 90, is located 2 miles southwest of the village of Lakeville, on a narrow but rather high east-and-west ridge, between two cypress swamps. It consists of an inclosing wall, and includes mounds and hut rings. The inclosure is oblong, but when complete was probably rectangular; it extends, however, at each end into fields which have been cultivated so long that the traces of it are lost here. The central portion (that shown in the figure), extending east and west about 360 yards, is still covered by heavy timber and a thick growth of underbrush and briers. Here the walls and other works are uninjured.

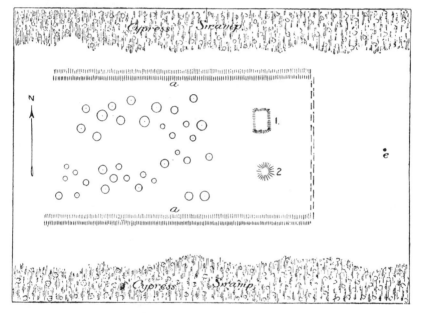

FIG. 90.—The Lakeville settlement, Stoddard county, Missouri.

A wall extends along each flank of the ridge facing the swamp that borders the latter on either side. They are 200 paces apart and run nearly parallel to each other in an east-and-west direction. Slight enlargements at irregular intervals are seen, and there are a few short breaks, but these may have been made by rainwater which had accumulated on the inside. Whether these two lines were once connected by cross-end walls, can not now be determined, but it seems quite probable that such was the case. These walls, measured on the outside, average about 3 feet in height, varying but little in this respect; but the inside has been so filled up by the garbage and débris of the village or otherwise that this portion is now within 1 foot of the top of the wall.

Nearly the whole space between the walls is occupied by the hut-rings or circular depressions. They are of the usual size, 20 to 50 feet across, and 1 to 3 feet deep. In all that were excavated, beds of ashes, containing broken pottery, burned clay, bits of bone, mussel and turtle shells, etc., were found at the depth of from 6 inches to 1 foot. In one of these, near the southwest corner of the wooded portion, the sandstone pipe shown in Fig. 91 was discovered.

FIG. 91.—Stone pipe, Lakeville settlement.

SETTLEMENT AT THE COUNTY LINE.

This settlement, shown in Fig. 92, on which *a a* denote the county line between Stoddard and Dunklin counties, is situated in an oak opening on West prairie, 500 yards east of the Dexter and Malden road. It borders on East swamp and is surrounded on the other three sides by a ditch (*b b*) that averages 10 feet wide and 3 feet deep. The dirt seems to have been thrown out about equally on each side, but there is nothing that can be called a wall or an embankment. The inclosure is 330 yards long by 220 in width, and contains about 15 acres. Nearly the whole of this space is occupied by circular depressions or hut-rings of the usual size and appearance, containing the usual amount of ashes, broken pottery, bones, etc. There are

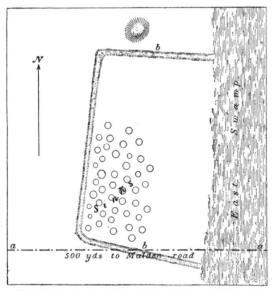

FIG. 92.—County line settlement, Stoddard county, Missouri.

no mounds in the inclosure, but just outside, near the northwest corner, is a low, circular one about 4 feet high and 100 or more feet in diameter.

RICH WOODS MOUNDS.

These mounds; shown in Fig. 93, are located 7 miles south of Dexter city on the road leading from that place to Malden, and are doubtless the ones referred to in the Summary of Correspondence, Smithsonian Report, 1879, as reported by Mr. Q. C. Smith.

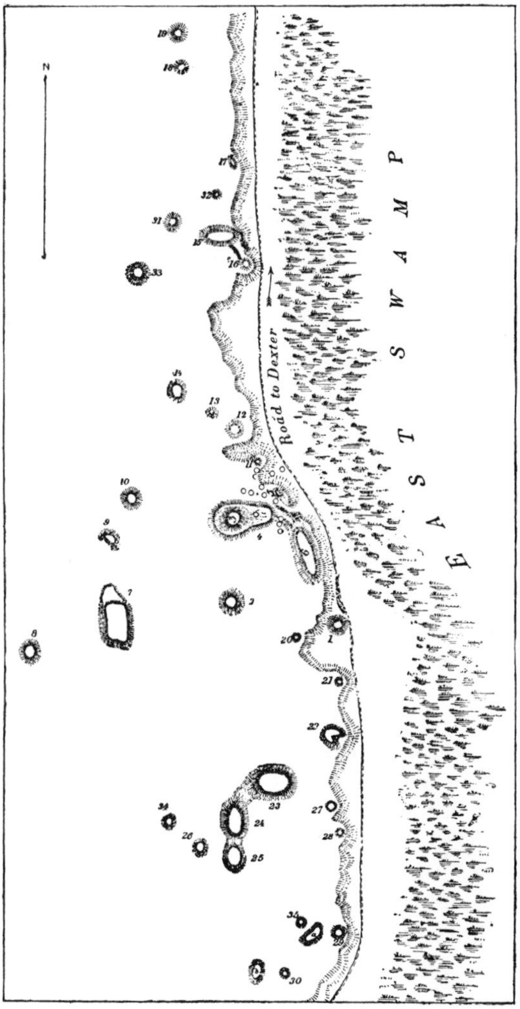

The low sandy ridge, known as the Rich Woods, is here between 1 and 2 miles wide. The surface, which is quite level, stands generally about 15 feet above the ordinary water line of the swamp and is composed chiefly of sand. The swamp bordering it on the east is known here as East swamp. The margin of the general level, which breaks abruptly down, as is usual with the banks of Western rivers, is somewhat irregular, as shown in the figure, the indentations being numerous, yet the general course is almost directly north and south. The mounds are principally located along or near the margin, the distance between the extreme northern one of the group and the most southern being about 1,600 yards, or a little less than 1 mile, and the greatest width of the belt occupied, about 500 yards.

FIG. 93.—The Rich Woods mounds, Stoddard county, Missouri.

All of the mounds except No. 1 stand on the upper or general level. Nos. 1, 2, and 3, near the central part of the group, are large, varying in height from 20 to 26 feet, obscurely pentangular in outline and flattened on top. No. 3 forms, with 4, what may be called a composite mound. This appears to be the case also with 15 and 16 and with 23,

24, and 25, which will be described further on. No. 6 is oval in shape, the diameter 266 by 110 and the height nearly 8 feet. There are some indications that it was formerly connected at its northern extremity with the double mound 3 and 4 by a graded way, though there are hut rings there now. Between this and No. 1 the ground suddenly descends to the lower level, as is seen by the abrupt bend in the hachured line marking the margin, which here makes a sudden turn to the west.

No. 7, which lies directly west of No. 2, is the longest tumulus of the group, irregularly oblong in form, the diameters being 340 and 200 feet and height 15 feet, the top flat. The south end is irregularly pointed, but this condition may have resulted wholly or in part from washing, as the surface has been in cultivation for several years and was for some years the location of a schoolhouse. At the north end is an apron 6 feet high, extending northward about 60 feet. This is irregularly rounded at the extremity. It is possible, and, in fact, probable, that this was a regular oblong mound, with a rectangular apron, as are many mounds in eastern Arkansas. The top is perfectly level. No. 8, west of 7, is circular, flat on top, and about 7 feet high.

No. 9, immediately north of 7, is peculiar in form, being a regular crescent, as shown in the plat, the distance between the tips of the horns about 75 feet, height 6 feet. Nos. 10, 11, 12, and 14 are circular mounds, ranging from 8 to 12 feet high. Nos. 13, 17, 18, 19, 31, 32, 33, 20, 28, 29, 30, 26, 27, 34 are small, circular mounds, varying from 1 to 4 feet in height. The shape of 22 is peculiar. It appears as if a broad ditch had been dug from the east side to the center. A large oak stump in the middle of this supposed ditch shows that it is certainly not a recent excavation. Possibly the mound was for some reason thrown up in this form. The figure is too small to bring out the evident difference between this and the crescent.

No. 21, near the road, is of the ordinary conical form, 45 feet in diameter and 5 feet high.

No. 15, about 230 paces northeast of 14, is a large, oblong, flat-topped mound, the length east and west 170 feet and width 110 feet, height nearly 11 feet. There is a graded way running east from this and curving south to mound 16, which is circular and 6 feet high.

Mounds 23 and 24 are oval in outline and of considerable size, the former measuring 223 by 180 feet and 8 feet high, the latter 213 by 112 feet and 9 feet high. The line between their approximate ends is somewhat higher than the surface of the surrounding area, and may be the remains of a connecting graded way.

No. 3, the tallest of the entire group, is fully 25 feet high. It is conical in form and very steep, except on the side toward the ramp. This elevated way or ramp, commencing on the side some distance below the summit, descends regularly eastward to No. 4, which appears to be a landing or halting place rather than a true mound, and is, in fact, but

an enlargement of the ramp or way at this point, with a flat or level
top. This ramp seems to have extended to No. 5, and, as before stated,
to No. 6, forming here a grand platform. The hut rings which are so
scattered around and over this immediate area are probably the
remains of a subsequent occupancy to that by the builders of the
mounds. Mound 6 presents more the appearance of an elongated plat-

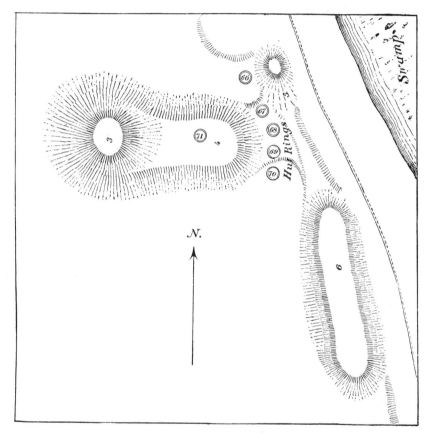

FIG. 94.—Plan of Mounds Nos. 3. 4. 5. and 6. Rich Woods mounds.

form than a true mound. A plan of these four mounds and the graded
way, prepared from a careful survey, is given in Fig. 94, and a section
of 3, 4, and 5 in Fig. 95.

As the surface of the area occupied is comparatively level it was
thought best to make the survey of the group dependent upon one
base and one auxiliary line. These in the reduction of the plat have
been omitted. The base runs north and south, east of the group along
the margin of the swamp, and makes three bends, on account of the
changes in the direction of the margin of the upland and the obstruc-

12 ETH——12

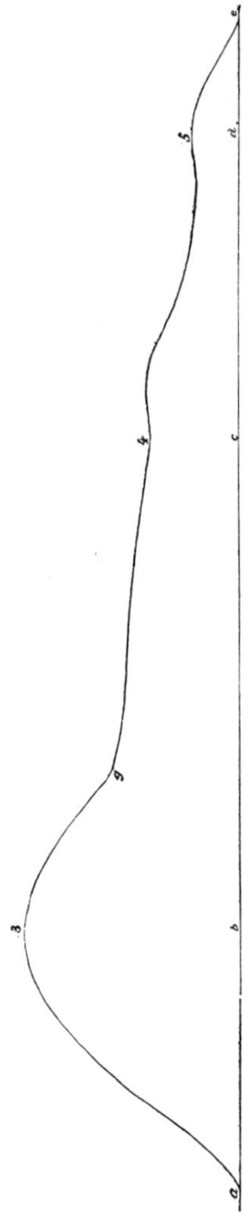

FIG. 95.—Section of Mound No. 3 and adjuncts, Rich Woods mounds.

tions which would have to be encountered in the attempt to run a single straight line. The auxiliary line runs westward from station 46 on the chief base. The stations on these lines are numbered from 35 to 58, respectively, No. 36 being taken as the starting point, 35 simply indicating an after northern extension to connect with mound 18. The positions of the mounds nearest these bases are indicated by lines running at right angles therefrom. The other mounds more distant are located by courses and distances from those determined by means of the base lines.

Measurements are in all cases to the center of the mound, hut ring, or other work, unless otherwise expressly mentioned. The various measurements made are shown in the following tables.

Table I contains the measurements of the chief base line; II, those of the auxiliary line; III, the positions of the mounds by the offsets from the base line; IV, the positions of the mounds by offsets from the auxiliary line; V, the positions of the mounds as determined by lines from one to the other; VI, the courses and distances locating the hut rings; VII, the positions of the excavations; VIII, the sizes of the mounds; IX, the diameter of the hut rings; and X, the sizes of the excavations. In order to make a plat of the group, start from the center of Mound 17 and run a line 57 feet N. 88° 30′ E. This will locate Station 36, from which all the other stations and mounds can be determined.

TABLE I.—BASE LINE.

Station.	Bearing.	Distance.	Remarks.
		Feet.	
36			Northern end of line offset for mound 17.
36 to 37	S. 1° 22′ E....	373	Offset for mound 15.
37 to 38	S. 1° 22′ E.....	137	Offset for mound 16.
38 to 39	S. 1° 22′ E	349	Bend in line.
39 to 40	S. 4° 00′ E.....	414	Offset for mound 12.
40 to 41	S. 4° 00′ E.....	86	Bend in line.
41 to 42	S. 23° 49′ E....	59	Offset for mound 11.
42 to 43	S. 23° 49′ E....	83	Offset for hut-ring 59.
43 to 44	S. 23° 49′ E....	91	Offset for mound 5.

TABLE I.—BASE LINE—Continued.

Station.	Bearing.	Distance.	Remarks.
		Feet.	
44 to 45 .	S. 23° 49′ E....	204	Offset for mound 6.
45 to 46 .	S. 23° 49′ E....	416	Beginning of auxiliary line.
46 to 47 .	S. 23° 49′ E....	71	Offset for mound 1.
47 to 48 .	S. 23° 49′ E....	24	Bend in line.
48 to 49 .	S. 0° 45′ W	289	Offset for mound 21.
49 to 50 .	S. 0° 45′ W	238	Offset for mound 22.
50 to 51 .	S. 0° 45′ W	336	Offset for mound 27.
51 to 52 .	S. 0° 45′ W	130	Offset for mound 28.
52 to 53 .	S. 0° 45′ W ...	477	Offset for mound 29.
53 to 54 .	S. 0° 45′ W	35	Southern end of line.

TABLE II.—AUXILIARY LINE.

46 to 55 .	S. 84° 49′ W ...	263	Offset for mound 20.
55 to 56 .	S. 84° 49′ W ...	302	Offset for mound 2.
56 to 57 .	S. 84° 49′ W ...	581	Offset for mound 7.
57 to 58 .	W	434	Offset for mound 8.

TABLE III.—OFFSETS TO MOUNDS ALONG THE BASE LINE.

36 to 17 .	S. 88° 38′ W ...	57	To station on mound.
37 to 15 .	S. 88° 38′ W ...	105	To station on eastern end of mound.
38 to 16 .	S. 88° 38′ W ...	40	To station on mound.
40 to 12 .	S. 86° 00′ W ...	197	Do.
42 to 11 .	S. 86° 00′ W ...	101	Do.
43 to 59 .	S. 86° 00′ W ...	57	To station in hut-ring.
44 to 5 ..	S. 86° 00′ W ...	75	To station on mound.
45 to 6 ..	S. 86° 00′ W ...	66	To station on northern end of mound.
47 to 1 ..	S. 86° 00′ W ...	84	To station on mound.
49 to 21 .	S. 66° 11′ W ...	84	Do.
50 to 22 .	S. 66° 11′ W ...	131	Do.
51 to 27 .	S. 66° 11′ W ...	140	Do.
52 to 28 .	S. 66° 11′ W ...	99	Do.
53 to 29 .	S. 66° 11′ W ...	110	Do.

TABLE IV.—OFFSETS TO MOUNDS ALONG THE AUXILIARY LINE.

55 to 20 .	S. 5° 11′ E.....	125	To station on mound.
56 to 2 ..	N. 5° 11′ W ...	79	Do.
57 to 7 ..	N. 5° 11′ W ...	46	Do.
58 to 8 ..	S	61	

TABLE V.—BEARINGS AND DISTANCES FROM MOUND TO MOUND.

7 to 9 ...	N. 3° 00′ W ..	416	To station on mound.
9 to 10 ..	N. 28° 35′ E....	227	Do.
12 to 13 .	N. 56° 29′ W ..	147	Do.
12 to 14 .	N. 56° 29′ W ..	343	Do.
29 to 30 .	S. 54° 30′ W ...	338	Do.
27 to 23 .	N. 66° 00′ W ..	307	Do.

TABLE V.—BEARINGS AND DISTANCES FROM MOUND TO MOUND—Continued.

Station.	Bearing.	Distance.	Remarks.
		Feet.	
23 to 24 .	S. 49° 50′ W ...	253	To station on mound.
24 to 26 .	S. 54° 29′ W ...	226	Do.
24 to 25 .	S. 4° 55′ W	190	Do.
15 to 32 .	N. 22° 15′ W ..	214	Do.
15 to 31 .	N. 75° 45′ W ..	312	Do.
15 to 33 .	S. 70° 15′ W ...	510	Do.
15 to 18 .	N. 14° 15′ W ..	9/5	Do.
5 to 4 .	S. 39° 40′ W ...	135½	Do.
4 to 3 .	S. 84° 00′ W ...	152½	Do.
24 to 34 .	S. 88° 00′ W ...	150	Do.

TABLE VI.—BEARINGS AND DISTANCES FROM THE MOUNDS AND HUT RINGS TO THE HUT RINGS.

11 to 60 .	S. 22° 30′ W ...	44	To station in hut-ring.
60 to 61 .	S. 0° 45′ W	27½	Do.
60 to 62 .	S. 19° 15′ E....	89	Do.
60 to 63 .	S. 40° 00′ E ...	66	Do.
62 to 64 .	S. 52° 00′ W ...	41	Do.
62 to 65 .	S. 25° 00′ W ...	61	Do.
62 to 66 ⁻	S. 19° 30′ E....	35	Do.
5 to 67 .	S. 17° 16′ W ...	60	Do.
5 to 68 .	S. 0° 44′ E.....	83½	Do.
5 to 69 .	S. 1° 28′ W	115	Do.
5 to 70 .	S. 2° 16′ E.....	143	Do.
4 to 71 .	N. 80° 19′ W ..	30	Do.

TABLE VII.—BEARINGS AND DISTANCES OF THE EXCAVATIONS FROM THE MOUNDS

29 to *a* ..	S. 86¼° W	140	To station in excavation.
30 to *b* ..	S. 69½° W	120	Do.

TABLE VIII.—SIZES OF THE MOUNDS.

No.	Diameter.	Height.	Remarks.
		Feet.	
1	150	20	
2	150 by 140	20	
3	185	26	Slopes steep.
4	150 by 140	....	
5	84	....	
6	266 by 109	7½	Extends north and south.
7	339 by 200	15	{ Has apron about 6 feet high at northern end extending 60 feet from base northward.
8	134 by 114	6½	Crescent-shaped.
9	....	6	
10	130 by 125	10	
11	44 by 48	5	
12	60 by 65	8	

TABLE VIII.—SIZES OF THE MOUNDS—Continued.

No.	Diameter.	Height.	Remarks.
		Feet.	
13	50 by 40	1	
14	124 by 96	5	
15	109 by 171	10½	Extends east and west.
16	75	6	
17	100 by 69	4	Extends northwest and southeast.
18	60 by 65	3	Circular.
19	60	....	Estimated.
20	40 by 35	3	Circular.
21	45	5	Do.
22	....	5½	
23	181 by 223	8	Extends east and west.
24	213 by 112	9	Extends north and south.
25	65 by 60	5	Circular.
26	78	3½	Do.
27	40	4	Do.
28	50	4	Do.
29	64 by 40	3	Do.
30	60 by 56	3½	Do.
31	100 by 110	3	Do.
32	70 by 65	3½	Do.
33	100	3	Do.
34	60	2½	Do.

TABLE IX.—DIAMETER OF THE HUT RINGS.

No.	Diameter.	No.	Diameter.	No.	Diameter.
60	22 by 29	64	27	68	28
61	28	65	24	69	24
62	29	66	21	70	25
63	29	67	27	71	34

TABLE X.—SIZES OF THE EXCAVATIONS.

Excavations.	Diameter.	Depth.	Remarks.
a	70 by 35	4	Extends northeast and southwest.
b	55	3½	Circular.

The first examination of this interesting group on behalf of the Bureau was made by Mr. Earle during his visit to this part of the state. Subsequently I visited them in company with Mr. Earle and Dr. Robert Allyn, president of the Southern Illinois Normal University. I found Mr. Earle's description and the plat he furnished quite correct, though the latter has been replaced by the more accurate survey made by Mr. Middleton; but descriptions and plats, though critically correct, fail to convey a true conception of this magnificent group.

Exploring No. 1 (Fig. 93), which by a careful remeasurement was ascertained to be 150 feet in diameter at the base and 20 feet high, we found it to consist of an external layer of surface soil, varying in depth from 2 to 3 feet, and an inner core of hard clay. This inner core, which evidently constituted the original mound, consisted of dry compact clay so hard that an ax was used to cut it. It was almost as dry as powder and of an ash-gray color, having here and there as we descended the appearance of being slightly mixed with ashes. At the depth of 5 feet a broken pot-shaped jar, of ware similar to that usual to this region, was discovered. At this point a few ashes and some slight indications of fire were noticed. The same dry hard clay continued to the bottom of the pit (which was carried down to the depth of 17 feet), except one thin layer of sand about 6 inches thick at the depth of 10 feet. Other pits dug in the sides and near the base revealed ample evidence of fire, indicating that after the central core was completed a quantity of brush and leaves had been burned over it, the coals and ashes sliding down, as it is quite steep, so that near the base a layer of charcoal several inches thick was formed. A thin layer of surface soil must have been thrown over it while burning, as considerable quantities of charred leaves were found mixed with the charcoal. In one of the pits some human bones were discovered before reaching the clay, doubtless an intrusive burial.

This mound, as will be seen by reference to the plat, is outside of the hachured line which represents the edge or break of the general level, and is some 6 feet lower and on the same level as the road and not more than 6 or 7 feet above the usual water level of the swamp.

Pits were sunk in No. 22 to the original surface without finding anything of interest save some fragments of pottery. The height of this mound was found to be a little over 5 feet, and the composition, after passing through the surface soil, a uniform mixture of yellow clay and sand. On this mound is an oak stump 2 feet in diameter.

No. 21 was examined with similar results, except that in it were found some small pieces of burned clay, flint chips, and traces of charcoal.

No. 26 and a small tumulus west of it were found to consist wholly of sandy clay. A few fragments of human bones, small pieces of pottery, and some flint chips were discovered in them.

An opening was made in the large mound No. 15 in a depression near the center where the height is between 9 and 10 feet. The pit was carried down to the original surface of the ground through yellow sandy clay. Nothing of interest was obtained.

No. 32, a low mound but little more than 3 feet high, was, like most of the others, built of a mixture of sand and clay. It contained human bones and fragments of pottery, which were scattered irregularly through it. The ground was damp and soft, and most of the bones were soft, falling to pieces when any attempt was made to lift them up. We were unable to trace out a single complete skeleton or to find a whole vessel.

Nos. 29, 30, and 31 were also explored, but nothing of special interest was observed in them, the construction being the same and of similar material as those already referred to.

No. 6 was subsequently partially explored. A trench was carried down only to the depth of 5 feet. Nothing was found in it at a greater depth from the surface than 3½ feet. Near the foot of the mound and 2 feet below the surface was a skeleton with the bones rather firm; probably an intrusive burial, as they are not uncommon in this particular locality. This was extended, head south; near it was a *Unio* shell. About 2 feet west of this skeleton and lying parallel with it was another of smaller size, probably of a female; bones firm, but the skull broken when found. Near the skull was a bottle-shaped water vessel. Other vessels were found at different points and at the depth of only 1 or 2 feet.

About 2 feet down on the top and side of the mound were lumps of burnt clay, which appear to be fragments of plastering with which the walls of a dwelling or other house had been coated. As further evidence of this is the following fact, given in the words of the last explorer: "In the top of the mound, in a small circular depression, I dug down about 2 feet, when I came to a sort of platform of burnt clay. It seemed to be made of irregularly shaped pieces, one side being smooth and the other rough. And what was peculiar, the smooth side was down. I did not dig enough to ascertain the extent of the platform."

It is easy enough to account for the smooth side being down if we suppose it to have been (as we shall hereafter see there is reason for believing) plastering from the walls of a house, for when the building was burned it would not be unlikely that the stiff and thick coat of plastering should fall over in a sheet and that pieces of it should roll down the side of the mound.

Numerous other objects were discovered in this mound, as pieces of *Unio* shells, some of which had holes bored through them, and were apparently unfinished beads; many fragments of pottery scattered promiscuously through the outer layer, and quite a number of animal bones, from the skull of a deer down to the delicate bones of very small birds.

Permission could not be obtained to make further exploration in this interesting and important group, nor to complete the excavation of the mounds partially examined.

SCOTT AND MISSISSIPPI COUNTIES.

In 1879 and 1880 the people in the neighborhood of Charleston, Mississippi county, discovered that the pottery, in which the mounds of this region seem to have been unusually rich, had a considerable commercial value. A regular mining fever at once broke out and spread so rapidly that in some instances as many as twenty-five or thirty men, women, and children could be seen digging for pottery in one field at the same time.

The specimens obtained were taken to Charleston and sold to the merchants, who in turn sold them to various museums, scientific institutions, and relic hunters. It is said that this trade brought to town several thousand dollars.

Some 10 or 12 miles southwest of the battlefield of Belmont is one of the peculiar sand ridges of this swampy region, called Pin Hook ridge. This extends 5 or 6 miles north and south, and is less than a mile in width; both of its tapering ends hook round in a westerly direction, as shown in Fig. 96. There is abundant evidence here that the entire ridge was long inhabited by a somewhat agricultural people, with stationary houses, who constructed numerous and high mounds, which are now the only place of refuge for the present inhabitants and their stock from the frequent overflows of the Mississippi. About one-half of the ridge is under cultivation ; the remainder is covered by a native forest of oak, ash, gum, and other trees, which are as large upon these mounds and residence circles as elsewhere.

BAKER'S MOUND.

This (No. 2 on the diagram) is situated nearly a mile southwest of Beckwith's Fort (marked No. 1, in Fig. 96), and hereafter more fully

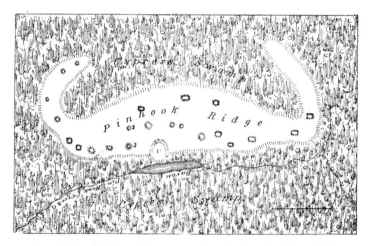

FIG. 96.—Pin Hook Ridge mounds, Mississippi county, Missouri.

described; it is circular in form, about 50 feet in diameter and 4 feet high. The peculiar feature of this mound is the mode of its construction, which is shown in Fig. 97. The lower stratum, marked No. 2, consists of bluish swamp muck mixed with ashes, which, as a matter of course, when deposited was soft and pliable as dough, though now so hard as to require the use of a pick to penetrate it. Instead of the top's being leveled as usual, it was depressed in the middle, so as to form a saucer-shaped basin, the rim on the south side being higher than on the opposite side, as the mound stands on a natural slope. This was filled with sandy loam (No. 1) and rounded over, completing the mound. Near the upper part of this sandy layer Mr. Baker, who had previously opened it, found two skeletons, placed horizontally, with heads north, below which was a layer of decayed skeletons, and with them a number of vessels of pottery of forms usual to this region. Several of these vessels which were discovered in this first excavation were fractured; yet Mr. Baker obtained thirty u n i n j u r e d specimens. Further excavation in t h e hard bottom layer revealed the parts of several skeletons, a number of broken

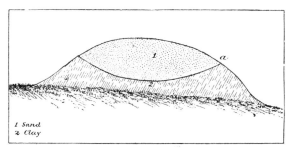

Fig. 97.—Baker's mound, Mississippi county, Missouri.

vessels, and also one small pot or cup with scalloped rim, and one bottle-shaped water vessel, which were obtained whole. A few rude stone scrapers were also found.

GUM TREE MOUND.

This is situated nearly to the east of the preceding, is circular in form, 60 feet in diameter, and 8 feet high. It is No. 3, of Fig. 96, and stands on the crest of a low ridge fronting upon a cypress swamp. It was found to consist of five or six distinct layers, as follows, counting from the bottom upwards: Layer No. 1, 30 inches of clear white sand, probably the natural crest of the ridge. No. 2, 16 inches of dark colored, hard clay, through which were scattered fire-beds, c h a r c o a l , ashes, stone chips, fragments of pottery, and split animal bones. No. 3, 12 inches of yellow sand, containing but few relics of any kind. No. 4, 8

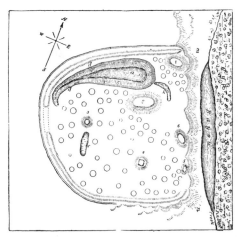

Fig. 98.—Beckwith's fort, Mississippi county, Missouri.

inches of hard gray mortar, doubtless made of blue muck and ashes mixed and covered with kitchen refuse similar to that found in No. 2. No. 5, 18 inches of loose gray sand, containing few relics; but all the central portion of this layer had been previously examined by others who found it and the top layer (No. 6) literally filled with decayed human bones and a number of whole and broken vessels of clay.

Half a mile north of the last mentioned mound, and upon the highest point of the bank fronting Pin Hook bayou, is a remarkable earthen inclosure (marked 1, in Fig. 96), to which the name Beckwith's fort is given, after that of the owner. An enlarged view of this work is given in Fig. 98.

As will be seen by reference to this figure, the inclosure is nearly a semicircle in form, with the open base facing the swamp or bayou. The length of this open base from point to point of the wall (m to n) is 1,041 feet, and the circumference along the wall from m around to n, 2,700 feet. The location was wisely chosen, as it is the only point within an area of many miles square where the natural surface of the ground was not covered by the great flood of 1882. The bank facing the swamp is here quite steep and fully 30 feet high.

Mounds Nos. 1, 5, and 6, and some small burial mounds not shown in the figure, are so nearly in a line as to form a strong breastwork along this front, except about 200 feet opposite mound No. 2, where there is no embankment, mound, nor the marks of ancient dwellings; thus, as is usual in this kind of fort, leaving an open court adjoining one side of the great flat-topped mound.

The height and width of the wall vary at different points, in some places being as low as 2 feet, while at others it is fully 8 feet high; in some places it is not more than 15 feet wide, while at others it is 30 or more.

Running close along the outside of the wall is a ditch varying in width from 20 to 40 feet, and in depth from 4 to 8 feet, except where filled up by floods and frosts, especially the former, some of which may have broken through the walls to the great interior excavation. The area within the inclosure is almost entirely occupied by earthworks of one kind or another, those marked 1, 2, 3, 4, 5, and 6 being mounds, those marked a, b, and c being excavations, and the numerous small circles scattered over it the little saucer-shaped depressions supposed to be house sites or hut rings.

Mound No. 1 is situated in the extreme northern corner, where the wall ends on the bank next the swamp or bayou. It is 120 feet long from northwest to southeast, 100 feet broad, and about 10 feet high at the highest point. The central portion of the top had been lowered, either originally or subsequently, by a circular depression about 15 feet in diameter and 2 feet deep. Permission to excavate could not be obtained.

Mound No. 2, or the so-called Temple mound, is situated almost directly south of No. 1 and near the central portion of the area. Its northern base comes directly to the margin of the great excavation a, while but a short distance away, a little to the northeast, is the small crescent excavation b. The dimensions, as nearly as could be ascertained, are as follows: Length on top (northeast and southwest), 165 feet; width, 105 feet; height, about 25 feet. Near each end, on the flat top, is a saucer-shaped depression 3 to 4 feet deep, reaching to a heavy deposit (in each) of charcoal, ashes, bones, etc., resting upon a layer of earth 3 or 4 inches thick, burned as hard as brick. Permission could not be obtained to make further excavations in this mound.

Mound No. 3 is circular, 75 feet in diameter and 8 feet high, having a saucer-shaped depression on the top, and below this a fire-bed, charcoal, ashes, etc., as usual.

No. 4 is almost circular at the base, but square on the top, which is flat, each side measuring 30 feet. It is 15 feet high, the sides very steep and each bearing with the cardinal points. It was doubtless originally a regularly truncated pyramidal mound, the washings having rounded the base.

No. 5 is an oval mound with sloping sides, 10 feet high and 90 feet across the top, which is flat. It was composed, in part at least, of black swamp mud and blue clay and had in it several fire-beds, beds of clay burned brick red, stone chips, *Unio* shells, and fragments of pottery.

No. 6 is 75 by 100 feet a⁺ base, 8 feet high, and now surmounted by the log house of the colored man who cultivates this portion of the extensive Beckwith plantation.

Between 5 and 6 is a long low mound not marked on the diagram, the surface of which was strewn with fragments of human bones, pottery, and stone chips.

Excavation *a* is somewhat pear-shaped, the large end being near the northeast corner and the curved side running along the northern wall for fully 1,000 feet. The width at the widest part is 320 feet and the greatest depth 10 feet, but the depth decreases with the width toward the southwest point. The most of it is now a bushy swamp, though the larger end is an open pond never dry.

Excavation *b* is small, the length along the convex side not exceeding 200 feet, narrow and crescent shaped. It lies just beyond the eastern end of the large excavation, one of its horns touching the latter.

Excavation *c* is in the southwestern part of the area, and now a rectangular swamp, 300 feet long by 100 wide, 8 feet deep at the greatest depth, and seldom dry.

HOUSE SITES OR HUT RINGS.

These almost literally cover the remainder of the area, the only open space of any considerable size being the 200 feet square just east of the large mound (No. 2, Fig. 98). They are not confined to the natural level of the inclosure, as some are found on the level tops of the mounds. They are circular in form, varying from 30 to 50 feet in diameter, measuring to the tops of their rims, which are raised slightly above the natural level. The depth of the depression at the center is from 2 to 3 feet. Near the center, somewhat covered with earth, are usually found

the baked earth, charcoal, and ashes of ancient fires, and around these
and beneath the rims split bones and fresh-water shells.   Often mingled
with this refuse material are rude stone implements and fragments of
pottery.

The similarity in the size, form, and general appearance of these depressions and earthen rings to those of the earth lodges of the abandoned Mandan towns along the Missouri river, leaves no doubt that they
mark the dwelling sites of the people who formerly occupied this locality.

Upon the top of the great mound, fully 35 feet above the bed of the
adjacent excavation, stands a white oak tree 4 feet in diameter; also

Fig. 99.—Image vessel from Beckwith's ranch.   Fig. 100.—Bowl from Beckwith's fort.

the stumps of several others, little if any smaller.   On the wall back
of the excavation is another white oak 16 feet 9 inches in circumference,
4 feet from the ground, also a sassafras 30 inches in diameter at breast
height, and other trees of similar dimensions.   The annual growth-rings
of several white oak and ash stumps on No. 6 and other mounds near
the house, were counted and ranged in number from 350 to 500 each.
The following is a list of the whole or nearly whole clay vessels obtained
from various openings made in the mounds and elsewhere on Pin Hook
ridge:

1 image vessel (Fig. 100.)   1 double-headed vessel.
1 water vessel with human head.   1 pot (already mentioned.)
1 water vessel with eagle head.   1 bowl with lip (Fig. 102.)
3 water vessels with hooded heads.   Eleven others of various forms.
1 flat open lamp.

BECKWITH'S RANCH.

Although the ancient works at this place are less than 2 miles from the inclosure and other works just described, they are differently

FIG. 101.—Water vessel from Beckwith's ranch, Mississippi county, Missouri.

occupied and appear to have been differently constructed. The area of the site is least subject to overflow of any in this region except the "Fort," but there is no trace of wall or ditch, nor is there a pyramidal

FIG. 102.—Water vessel from Beckwith's fort, Mississippi county, Missouri.

mound in the group, the only works here being low, flattish, circular mounds and long oval ones, resembling so closely the low, natural swells of the level area as to require a practical investigation to determine whether they are natural or artificial. They appear to belong to two classes, those used for dwelling sites and those used for burial purposes, the former being the higher and the color of the surface layer darker than that of the other class. This darker color of the surface layer is probably due to the fact that immediately below it are found fire-beds with burnt earth, charcoal, ashes, and the bones of animals, (mostly split). There are seldom any human skeletons or entire vessels of pottery in the mounds of this class though the earth is filled with fragments of broken vessels. In these tumuli, which are so close

Fig. 103.—Gourd-shaped vessel from Beckwith's ranch, Mississippi county, Missouri.

together as sometimes to form an almost continuous ridge, are often found two or three, and sometimes even four, fire-beds in succession, at different depths, ranging from 1 to 4 feet down to the natural surface.

The skeletons, among which were a number of clay vessels, were of medium size, lying at full length horizontally upon the back or side, without any apparent regularity as to direction, except so far as was necessary to avoid overlapping, which was seldom done in the same layer. The vessels were invariably placed by the side of or over the skull, which was often found indented or crushed. Many, and in places a majority or all, of the skeletons of a layer were without an accompanying entire vessel, but seldom without the fragments of a broken one where the entire one was wanting.

As a rule, but one vessel was found to a skeleton, though occasionally two and even three were observed; but when this was the case they were of different forms and evidently intended for different purposes. Thus, if a long-necked water cooler was found on one side of the skull, the vessel on the other side, if any, would be a cup or basin or other food dish, and if a third were present it would be an effigy or ornamented vessel placed at the crown or above it. No fire-beds, charcoal, or split bones of animals were found among the skeletons.

Fig. 104.—Owl image vessel from Beckwith's ranch.

The mounds of this class were often so low as to be scarcely apparent. Indeed, it is evident that the people who once occupied this locality buried their dead about 2 feet deep in the natural earth, and that the elevation of portions of their cemetery is the result of subsequent burials on the same site, as in such cases we found two or three layers of skeletons.

At this place some 45 or 50 whole vessels were found of which the following were obtained for the Bureau, the owner of the place, Col. Beckwith, who assisted in the work, retaining the rest:

1 water vessel, female image (Fig. 99).
1 long-necked water vessel with three legs (Fig. 101).
1 water vessel, female image.

1 gourd-shaped vessel with animal head (Fig. 103).
1 owl image (Fig. 104).
1 fish-shaped bowl (Fig. 105, *a* and *b*).
1 vessel with animal head.
1 vessel with human head.
1 bowl with human head.

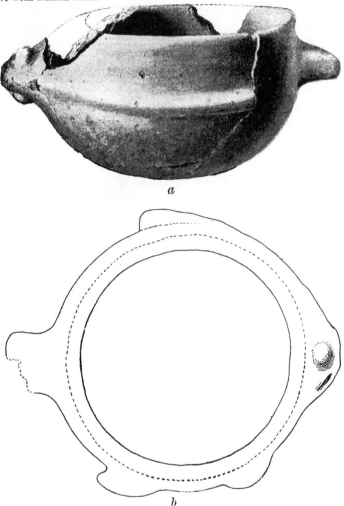

a

b

Fig. 105.—Fish-shaped vessel from Beckwith's ranch. *a*. view; *b*. plan

1 shell-shaped bowl.
1 pottery ornament.
1 pottery ornament.
Seventeen other vessels, besides 5 pottery mullers and some stone implements.

MEYERS MOUNDS.

These, 2 in number, are situated on the county road from Cairo, Illinois, by way of Bird's Point, to Charleston, about midway between the two points. They are on the highest ground in that immediate section and fronting a cypress swamp. One is double or terraced, and the other much lower and oval in outline. The latter is 73 feet long, 50 feet broad, and 10 feet high, sides straight, but the ends rounded and flat on top, where Mr. John Meyers, the owner, has placed his dwelling house. The large one (Fig. 106) consists of a higher portion or main part, which is pyramidal in form, 50 feet square on the level top, and 25 feet high, and a level terrace 63 feet long, 50 feet broad, and 15 feet high, extending northward.

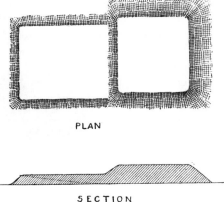

PLAN

SECTION

FIG. 106.—Meyers' mound, Scott county, Missouri.

A regular ancient cemetery which had been worked over by previous explorers, was found about 100 yards east of the main works. The area around the large mound, to the extent of several acres, except a small spot on the north side near the swamp, was formerly thickly covered over with small circular depressions or house sites, but these are now mostly obliterated by cultivation.

Several low mounds in the vicinity had been so thoroughly upturned as to be now barely traceable. As a matter of course nothing was found in these but the fragments left by others; but in excavations made in other parts of the farm several vessels and images of pottery of the character and designs common in this section were obtained. No indications of a surrounding wall were observed.

BUTLER COUNTY.

Along the railroad from St. Louis to Iron mountain few mounds were observed, but from there to Poplar bluff they are numerous on the low valley lands, almost always circular in form, from 30 to 50 feet in diameter, and from 3 to 4 feet high. So far as they have been opened, little else has been found in them than decaying human bones, often commingled with charcoal and ashes, and occasionally fragments of pottery.

Four of this class found on the bottoms of Big Black river, about 2 miles above Poplar bluff, were explored. They, like many others of similar appearance, are on land subject to overflow at ordinary high water. All are circular and some of them very flat, those excavated being the highest and situated in the midst of a dense growth of swamp oak, ash, elm, and other timber growing on the mounds the same as elsewhere.

Mound No. 1 measured but 25 feet in diameter and 4 feet in height. Nothing was found in it except a hard, central, or inner core of light-colored clay which, when thrown out, appeared like dry mortar mixed with charcoal, ashes, and stone chips. No traces of bones or indications of burial were observed.

No. 2, 30 feet in diameter, 4 feet high; resembled No. 1 in internal arrangement and contents.

No. 3, 40 feet in diameter and 4 feet high; gave the same results as 1 and 2.

No. 4, similar in size, differed from the others only in the fact that at the bottom, in the center, was found a bushel or more of charcoal and ashes.

In Fig. 107 is presented a group of this character near Harviell, which is given as a type of the groups of this class of mounds which

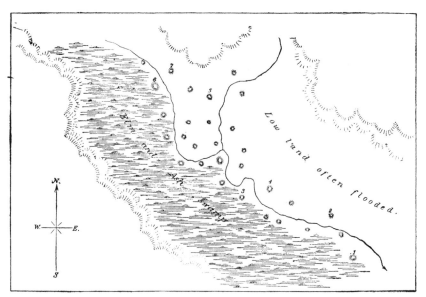

Fig. 107.—Mound group near Harviell, Butler county, Missouri.

literally dot all the land in this region except the cypress swamps. They are uniformly circular, seldom exceeding 50 feet in diameter, or 4 feet in height.

The seven of this group marked 1, 2, 3, 4, 5, 6, and 7 and quite a number of other groups were excavated, the uniform result being to find the main portion composed of very hard clay with charcoal and ashes mixed in greater or less quantities and frequently, but not always, fragments of very rude pottery and rude stone scrapers or skinners.

POWER'S FORT.

This is an ancient inclosure, connected with other works on the farm of Mr. Power, on a low ridge which runs between Little Black river

and Cypress swamp, near the Ripley county line. A plat of the group
is given in Fig. 108, from which it will be seen that it consists of a quadrangular (nearly square) inclosure with embankments or walls on three
sides, and an outside ditch along the entire length of the walls, an
excavation at each western corner outside, and four mounds on the
interior area. The western wall, which runs exactly north and south,
is 750 feet long and, as it is still covered by the original forest growth,

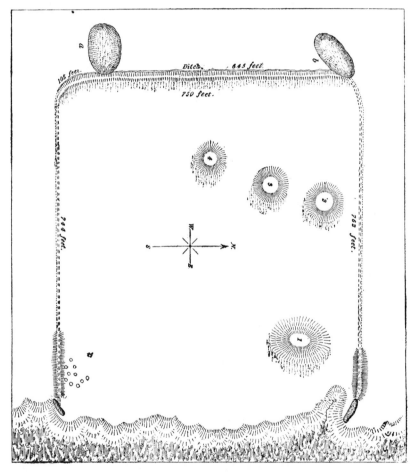

FIG. 108.--Power's fort. Butler county. Missouri.

is quite distinct. The ditch, which runs along the outside is also very
distinct, being from 3 to 5 feet deep and about twice as wide. The
northern and southern walls and ditches in the cultivated area are
almost obliterated; still they can be traced throughout from where they
connect at the corners with the western wall, to the undisturbed
extremities near the swamp. The northern line measures 762 feet and
the southern 744.

The excavation connecting with the ditch near the southwest corner (*a*) is about 150 feet long, 100 feet wide and 15 feet deep at the lowest point. The excavation at the northwest corner (*b*) is somewhat longer, rather narrower, and not quite so deep, but both always contain water.

The four mounds in the inclosure are located as indicated at 1, 2, 3 and 4, No. 1, which is the largest, being nearly 150 feet long, north and south, 120 feet broad at base, and 20 feet high. The length and width have evidently been increased and the height lowered by the continued cultivation of fifty years. A thorough examination of this was made and the construction found to be somewhat peculiar, as will be seen by reference to Fig. 109, which shows a vertical section through the length.

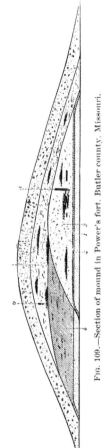

FIG. 109.—Section of mound in Power's fort. Butler county. Missouri.

The bottom layer (1) is a circular platform about 100 feet in diameter and 2 feet high, formed of yellow sand similar to the original surface beneath and around it.

The next layer, marked 2, is only 6 inches thick and consists of dark blue, adhesive clay, or muck, from the swamp; which has become very hard. It was strewn with burnt earth, charcoal, ashes, fragments of split bones and pottery, stone chips and *Unio* shells. The next layer (3) is 8 feet thick at the central point of what appears to have been the original mound, of which it was the top stratum. But it is not uniform, and, although showing no distinct strata, was not all formed at one time, as in it there were, at different depths, at least three distinct fire-beds of burnt earth and heavy accumulations of ashes, charcoal, and charred animal bones.

In this layer, a little south of the center, were found the charred fragments of long poles and small logs, all lying horizontally, and also a post (*a*), probably of locust wood, 6 inches in diameter and 5 feet long, still erect, but the upper end shortened by fire and the lower end haggled off by some rude implement.

The layer marked 4 is an addition to the original plan. At this stage the occupants or builders, for some reason, made an addition to the original mound, extending it northward some 40 feet, apparently in this wise: the lower layer was built on the north end precisely as in the original mound and of the same height; then the layer corresponding to No. 2 of the original mound, which is No. 4 in the figure, was built up of bluish clay irregularly mixed with fire-beds, ashes, charcoal, yellow sand, and calcined bones to the height of No. 3 and somewhat overtopping it. Having thus obtained the desired form, layer No. 5, 6 feet thick, chiefly of dark swamp-muck, was heaped over the original mound and addition. But this layer was probably formed by additions made to it from time to time, as it presents considerable variety in the appearance of the material and also contains large masses of yellow sand, charcoal, ashes, fragments of pottery, and charred bones, among which were found the head of a deer and of an elk, with portions of the charred horns still attached. Many rude stone knives, scrapers, and perforators, a few rude lance-heads and fragments of a better class of pottery were scattered through it. Northwest of the center, in this layer, were some charred timbers lying horizontally and one post (*b*) standing erect, resembling the timber post found in No. 3.

The external layer, 4 feet thick, and of a heterogeneous character, was apparently formed of various sized masses of bluish clay, yellow sand, and charcoal combined.

Mound No. 2 is much smaller than No. 1, not exceeding 100 feet in diameter and 6 feet in height, and is flat on top. It consisted of four layers, the first or upper stratum of sandy soil, 2 feet thick, mixed with fragments of pottery; the second, about the same thickness, chiefly yellow sand, with patches of blue clay, charcoal, ashes, fragments of pottery, and human bones mostly unbroken but soft as pulp; the third, 6 inches thick, was made up of blue clay and fragments of pottery; and the fourth, 18 inches thick, of yellow sand, well filled with decayed human bones, though some of them were plump and soft. Scattered among them were charcoal and ashes.

Mound No. 3, also flat on top, 80 feet in diameter and 4 feet high, was without regular layers; but the base was found to be composed chiefly of yellow sand, containing fire-beds, patches of bones, charcoal, ashes, fragments of pottery, etc.

Mound No. 4 resembled No. 3 in form, size, composition, and contents. Fragments of pottery, stone chips, lance-heads, scrapers, and perforators were scattered over the area of the inclosure, and at one point there was an almost solid deposit of them.

Mound No. 5, standing outside the inclosure in a grove of large oak timber and dense underbrush, is 40 feet in diameter and 8 feet high, circular and symmetrical in form. An opening 6 feet in diameter and 3 feet deep had been made in the top so long ago that oak saplings have since grown up in it. Further excavation revealed nothing but the fact that it was composed of four parallel, horizontal[1] strata, the first or top one of yellow sand 1 foot thick, the second, 1 foot of dark muck, the third, 4 feet of yellow sand, and the bottom, 1 foot of dark muck.

---

[1] As a general rule throughout this part of the Report "horizontal" when applied to strata is to be understood in the strict sense of the term and as implying that the stratum does not conform to the curve or contour of the mound.

ARKANSAS.

Although explorations were made in other parts of this state, much the larger portion of the ancient works referred to are in the northeastern part, or, in other words, the lands bordering the Mississippi and lower Arkansas and the area drained by the White and St. Francis rivers. This area, if extended southward so as to include Desha and Chicot counties, is known as the Mississippi alluvial region of Arkansas. With the exception of Crowley's ridge, which breaks its monotonous uniformity, it consists chiefly of broad bottom lands interrupted in places by swamps, sloughs and wet prairies, through which, or separating which, are generally low, broad swells or ridges (as they are called, though of but few feet in height) of rich sandy loam heavily timbered.

Crowley's ridge, which runs through Green, Craighead, Poinsett, and St. Francis counties, forming the divide between the waters of White and St. Francis rivers, terminates in Phillips county just below the city of Helena. The top, throughout its entire extent in Arkansas, is composed for the most part of siliceous clay and marl of quaternary date, usually resting on a bed of waterworn gravel. Numerous springs of good cool water flow from beneath this gravel bed along the eastern foot of the ridge near Helena. Most of the bottom lands are overflowed during high water.

CLAY COUNTY.

This, the extreme northeastern county of the state, is comparatively level and is drained by the St. Francis river on the east, Cache river in the center, and Black river on the west. These rivers are bordered by low, flat, bottom lands heavily timbered and subject to overflow. Between Black and Cache rivers is a low ridge, which extends southwestward through several counties. Between the Cache and St. Francis rivers is a still more prominent and wider elevation, which is the beginning of Crowley's ridge.

The only group of mounds examined in this county is situated in the immediate vicinity of Corning, the county seat, on a sandy ridge that rises some 20 feet above the cypress swamp flanking it on the east.

A few of these were measured and opened with the following results:

No. 1, oblong, measured 90 feet in length by 65 in width at the base and 9 feet high. About 20 feet of the north end had been removed by the townspeople. The only things of interest observed were fire beds of swamp muck, charcoal, ashes, stone chips, and a few charred bones. An examination of the remaining portion revealed nothing additional except the indications of long-continued occupancy and the fact that it had been built up by successive layers.

No. 2, oblong, 40 by 35 feet at base and 5 feet high, was explored with similar results.

No. 3 measured 100 by 80 feet at base, but the height could not be determined, as it had been partially removed for grading the railroad track. From the number of decayed human bones and fragments of pottery found in the remaining portion, it is supposed to be the principal burial place of the mound-builders who occupied the village located here.

The small circular mounds were composed chiefly of sandy soil similar to that of the surrounding surface, but the fire beds, burned clay, stone chips, and bones discovered in them render it evident that they had been used as dwelling sites and that the custom of burying in the floor of the cabin had been followed here to some extent.

GREENE COUNTY.

The topographical features of this county are very similar to those of Clay county, its eastern boundary being the St. Francis river, which through this and the two counties south is a continuous lake-like swamp, being the section known as the "Sunken lands of the St. Francis." The western portion consists of the flat Cache river lands, partly black sandy levels and partly wet post-oak flats. Between the lowlands of the two extremes and occupying a large portion of the area, is Crowley's ridge, with its sandy lands.

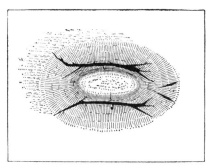

On the plantation of Mr. Robert Law, 9 miles east of Paragould, fronting the cypress borders of the St. Francis lake, is a group of interesting mounds. They are chiefly in a forest of oak, ash, gum, and other heavy timber.

FIG. 110.—Effect of earthquake of 1811 on mound, Greene county, Arkansas.

The spot they occupy is in the "Sunken land region," or that section so terribly shaken by the great earthquake of 1811.

At this particular locality the sand ridge and cypress swamp seem still to retain their original relative elevations, but the ridge is so cut up with trenches, narrow ridges, sink holes, and "blow-outs" of fine sand as to render the original size and even number of these mounds very uncertain. There are some indications of a surrounding wall, though not sufficient to justify the positive statement that there ever was one.

The largest mound, which is flat on top, measured 120 feet long by 72 feet broad on top, 192 by 145 at the base and 25 feet high. Several medium-sized trees are still standing on it, and there is evidence of larger ones having been overturned, possibly during the earthquake, or by some previous or subsequent severe windstorm. Be this as it may, the effects of the earthquake are still visible in this artificial structure, after a lapse of eighty years, in two very distinct and peculiar fissures, as shown in Fig. 110. These are from 4 to 6 feet deep and fully as wide, partially disclosing the character of the mound, permission to explore it being refused by the owner.

The small group bearing this name consists of but two mounds, situated in Sec. 36, T. 16 N., R. 2 E., of the fifth principal meridian, in the southeast corner of the county on a low ridge between Cache river and a cypress swamp.

Mound 1 is of the ordinary round or conical form, 65 feet in diameter and 7 feet high, composed chiefly of earth similar to the surrounding soil. About halfway down from the top was found a thin layer of burnt clay reaching from 2 feet east of the middle to the western margin, which did not conform horizontally to the curve of the mound, but to the level of the ground on which the mound stands. A few inches above this layer were two small deposits of burnt clay. It is doubtful whether they were burnt where they were found, there being no coals or ashes about them and the earth in contact with them showing no indications of heat. They were scarcely more than a foot square and 3 inches thick.

Two skeletons found were probably intrusive burials, as they were placed only 12 and 16 inches below the surface. The most interesting thing observed in this simple, ordinary mound was the size of some of the supposed "load masses." Near the bottom, in the central part, the clayey portion increased and the mottled appearance, supposed by mound explorers to be due to the deposits of individual loads, became quite distinct and some of these masses were apparently too heavy loads for even two persons, as they were 3 feet across the face and from a foot to 20 inches thick.

The other mound had already been opened.

The topographical features of this county are much the same as those of Greene, the only important difference being that its area embraces a larger proportion of the lowlands of the St. Francis valley.

According to Col. Norris, who visited the northeast part of the county, the entire region along this part of the St. Francis lake is so cut up with sink holes, "blow-outs," sand hillocks, and trenches (trending northeast and southwest), the effect of earthquakes, that the ancient works are scarcely traceable except in certain favored localities. One of these he found at Carpenter's landing on the St. Francis lake, 12 miles east of Brooklyn. Even this sandy ridge is much marred by the effects of the earthquake but there are unmistakable evidences that this locality was occupied in former times by a large mound-builder's village and cemetery. A long line of circular and oblong mounds—some nearly square and flat on top—is still traceable in what is now a swamp back of the ridge.

Several of these, much shattered by the earthquake, were examined and others uninjured were opened. All were formed of irregular layers of swamp muck on which were fire-beds, charcoal, ashes, fragments of pottery, and charred animal bones, as is usual in this region.

In a conical mound on the ridge, at the depth of 3 feet from the top, was the skeleton of a child not more than 3 feet long, and by the side of the skull a dark scallop-rimmed basin, and close to it another vessel, light colored. At the bottom, on the natural surface of the ground, was a fire-bed. The main body of the mound was composed of gray loam, such as that of the soil around it, but the top was covered with a layer of soft, yellow sand, 20 inches thick at the center, and thinning out each way.

A small circular mound, 25 feet in diameter and 7 feet high, found on Cane island in St. Francis lake, was explored. This had a rather mod-

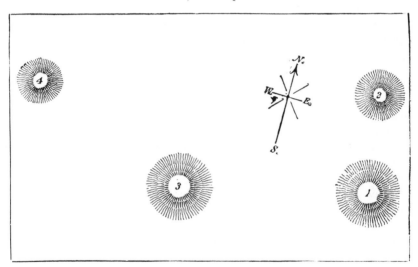

Fig. 111.—Webb group, Craighead county, Arkansas.

ern appearance and had evidently been built up at intervals. Passing through a top stratum of gray, sandy soil, something over a foot thick, the explorer reached a layer of charcoal and ashes about 6 inches thick, covering an area of about 6 feet in diameter, in which were the charred fragments of animal bones. Next below this was a layer, 2 feet thick, of sand so loose as to shovel like ashes. This lay on a fire-bed of similar size, and at least a foot in depth of charcoal, in which were decayed firebrands. This was, in fact, a coalpit in which were several bushels of excellent charcoal, but little ashes and no bones. About a foot or so below this was another similar charcoal bed. Not a particle of clay, mud, or a piece of stone or pottery was seen in any part of the mound.

The group shown in Fig. 111 is situated in the southern part of the county, on Sec. 16, T. 13 N., R. 5 E., on the land of Mr. Jasper Webb, about 10 miles southeast of Jonesboro.

No. 1, the largest of the group, is 85 feet long by 75 broad on the flat top and 13 feet high; but being occupied as a graveyard could not be explored.

No. 2, conical in form, measured about 150 feet in diameter at the base and very nearly 20 feet high. It was examined but revealed nothing of interest.

No. 3, conical in form, 65 feet in diameter and 7½ feet high, contained four skeletons, but so far decayed that they could only be partially traced. One was near the center at a depth of 5 feet, another on the west side 3 feet below the surface. Two feet and a half below the latter was a broken pot with some badly decayed shells in it. Pottery was discovered at all depths from 6 inches to 6½ feet below the surface and in all conditions from unbroken vessels to those in fragments. All the whole vessels were sitting right side up and in most cases near the surface; those lower down were generally in fragments. Some parts of the mound appeared to be entirely barren of specimens while in other parts several were found near together. In one place on the south side, in a space of 3 feet square by 2 feet deep, were five pots. Thirty-four specimens of the Bureau collection are from this mound.

Mound No. 4 was but partially explored, the work being stopped by water rising in the trenches. In this were two skeletons and a number of clay vessels. With one of the skeletons were six pots.

None of the specimens found in this mound were buried more than 2 feet deep and some of them were within 6 inches of the surface. This tumulus is situated close to a slough and is surrounded by water in times of great freshets.

There are a few places near these mounds elevated about a foot above the surrounding land. One near mound No. 1 was examined and at the depth of a foot charcoal and fragments of very firm pottery were discovered; but further examination was stopped by the water which rose in the trenches.

Mound No. 5 (not shown in the figure), circular, rounded on top, 40 feet in diameter and 2½ feet high, was composed entirely of sand and unstratified. Although it stands on low, wet ground, graves had been dug in the natural soil, or excavations made before it was built, as remains and specimens were found at the depth of 4½ feet below the surface of the mound.

Comparatively few human bones were discovered and these so badly decayed that none of them could be saved, but the number of pottery vessels was unusually large, over forty being found in the mound. Usually these vessels were in groups or nests; that is to say, from two to four would be found together, though occasionally one would be by itself; and as a general thing the mouths were up. The ware is throughout of very inferior quality, usually thin and imperfectly burned. It consists of cooking pots, some with ears and some without, and some showing evidences of usage; long-necked water bottles, gourd-shaped water vessels; bowls, one large with a flaring rim; dipper or skillet-shaped vessel with short handles; two clay pipes, etc.

A limestone celt, lance head, and arrow point were the only stone implements discovered in it. Some coals and ashes, rough, burned stones, and lumps of burned clay were observed.

POINSETT COUNTY.

The topography of this county is throughout similar in every respect to that of Craighead county which lies immediately north of it. It has the same dividing ridge, the same low flat belt and the same bounding streams.

TYRONZA STATION.

This is a mere siding about 1 mile east of the point where the Kansas City, Springfield, and Memphis railroad crosses the Tyronza river, constructed as a means of access to a large and valuable gravel bed underlying the sandy ridge, which is something less than a mile wide at this point and between 3 and 4 miles long. Although the summit of this ridge is from 10 to 15 feet above the swamp around it, only the tops of the larger and higher ancient mounds upon it remain above the water during the heavy overflows of the Mississippi river. Fig. 112 shows the relative positions of the mounds and their relation to the railroad.

The following list gives the numbers, the shape, diameter at the base, and the height of each of the mounds shown in the figure and remarks in regard to the contents of those explored.

No.	Shape.	Diameter.	Height.	Remarks.
		Feet.	*Feet.*	
1	Circular	120	12	Flat-topped. Long occupied by a house.
2	....do	100	8	Used as a cemetery by the whites.
3	....do	70	5	Bones and fragments of pottery.
4	....do	60	5	Do.
5	....do	100	6	Ancient fire-bed, ashes, and bones.
6	Oblong	100 by 40	3	Found nothing.
7	Circular	75	5	Two tiers of fire-beds and ashes.
8	....do	80	5	Opened thoroughly, finding the burned clay and plaster for the floor and walls of a dwelling 12 by 13 feet. Fig. 113 shows vertical section.
9	....do	100	6	Cut away by the railroad men; dotted with red fire-beds, black earth above them filled with human bones and pottery.
10	....do	60	3½	Charred remains of a dwelling seemingly about 12 feet square.
11	....do	60	3	Partly cut away by railroad men. Fire-beds, charcoal, ashes, and pottery.
12	....do	90	4	Ruins of dwelling; Fig. 114 shows a vertical section.
13	....do	40	2	Fire-bed and clay burned to a brick red.
14	....do	50	3	Do.
15	....do	100	4	Do.
16	....do	80	7	In the woods; contained three tiers of fire-beds and in the upper, 2 feet from the surface, one skeleton and pot.
17	....do	120	9	Contained two fire-beds, ashes, and bones.

Three other similar mounds were seen in the woods but not excavated.

Fig. 115 is a representation of the face of the cut made by the rail-road in the gravel pit; or, in other words, a vertical section of the ridge to the depth of from 5 to 6 feet below the normal surface; also of the mounds on the line of the section. The length of the section shown in

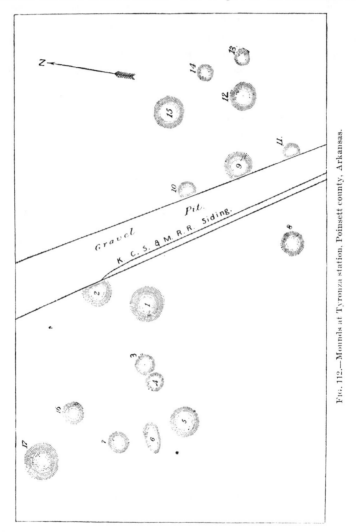

Fig. 112.—Mounds at Tyronza station, Poinsett county, Arkansas.

the figure is 1,100 feet. The heights, distances, and in fact all the fig-ures given are from actual careful measurements.

It will be seen from this, that not only were the mounds occupied as dwelling sites, but that the entire ridge, so far as the cut for the rail-road extends, and to the depth of from 2 to 3 feet, has, scattered through it, burnt clay beds which in Arkansas are sure marks of house sites. The short, heavy, black, horizontal dashes mark the locations of fire-beds or indications of fire, as beds of ashes, charcoal, etc.; the cross-hatched, or shaded, short, horizontal dashes represent the burnt clay beds, some of which formed the hard floors of dwellings and some the fragments of plastered walls which have fallen over when the dwelling was burned, as appears to have been the case in most instances. The positions and relations of these beds, as shown in the figure, make it evident that upon the site of one burned dwelling another was usually constructed, not infrequently a third, and sometimes even a fourth, the remains of each being underlaid and usually overlaid in part by very dark, adhesive clay or muck from the adjacent excavations which are found in the swamp as well as upon the ridge, and contain water and occasionally fish.

FIG. 113.—Section of Mound No. 8, Tyronza station, Poinsett county, Arkansas.

The peculiar black color of these beds is chiefly in consequence of the large proportion of charcoal with which they are mixed, some of it doubtless the fine particles of burned grass and reed matting with which the cabins appear to have been thatched. In and immediately beneath these are found the deposits of human skeletons, pottery and other relics.

In mound A (Fig. 115), and at the second red clay bed from the top was found a water vessel which is neatly ornamented with red figures, and in the next bed below an image vessel.

On the bottom hearth of mound B was a layer of what had the appearance of hand-molded brick, well burned, and as red and hard as modern brick. These bricks, as a matter of course, were irregular in form and proportion, but seemed to have been intentionally formed

FIG. 114.—Section of Mound No. 12, Tyronza station, Poinsett county, Arkansas.

before burning. Upon this floor, commingled with the burned plaster, which had formed the walls of the dwelling and which still showed the casts of cane, brush, and grass, were found balls or rounded masses of burned clay, containing the remarkably clear and distinct casts of small ears of maize (Fig. 116). This is judged from the casts to be the variety known in the South as the "gourd seed corn," which has the outer end of the grain very thin. Of these A is the original clay with the grain impressions in it; B is a cast of another piece showing the reverse of the impressions.

Mound No. 8 is circular, 80 feet in diameter at the base, 5 feet high, and quite flat on top. It contained two beds of burned clay, indicating two successive dwellings.

In No. 12, a vertical section of which is shown in Fig. 114, were found the ruins of a dwelling, the plan of which, so far as it could be made out, is given in Fig. 117.   There seems to have been three rooms (*a, b* and *d*), each as nearly square as the builders were capable of making

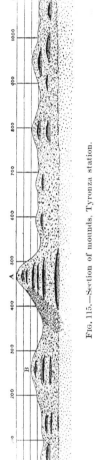

Fig. 115.—Section of mounds, Tyronza station.

it, the floor consisting of a layer of clay, burned when formed. The floor of room *a* was in pieces, somewhat as represented in the figure.

The floor of room *b* was smooth clay, hardened and partially burned. The sizes of these rooms were as follows: *a*, 11 feet 6 inches front by 12 feet 2 inches back; *b*, 11 feet 7 inches front by 11 feet 9 inches back; *d*, 12 feet 3 inches front, the part remaining, 6 feet back, but showing indications of about 6 feet more, making the depth about 12 feet.

The black dots along the lines of the walls indicate the upright posts which supported the roof and to which the reed lathing for holding the plastering was attached. Remains of a sufficient number of these posts were found to show how far apart they were placed, which appears to have been a little less than 2 feet.

From the burned fragments of the walls found it would seem that the cane lathing was worked in between the posts, as shown in Fig. 118, and was held in position by interwoven twigs until the plaster was applied, both inside and out. The semicircular figures (*c c c*) are supposed to represent fireplaces. The back room (*d*) may or may not have been square.

As will be seen further on, the floor of another dwelling, somewhat similar in form to the one here shown, was discovered at another point (see Fig. 136).

In digging away the gravel bank numerous skeletons were discovered, usually in a deposit of swamp mud, charcoal, and ashes, either immediately beneath or just above the layer of the hearth and burned plastering of the ancient dwellings. All the indications go to confirm the theory that the dead were interred in a deposit of clay, swamp mud, or charcoal and ashes, or a mixture of them, either in or immediately beneath the dwellings, which were then burned over them. Frequently several skeletons of different sizes were found in these places as though members of a family; but whether they were all interred at one time or were buried there one at a time, as they died, is not clear, as the evidence seems to point to both methods, and perhaps both were practiced. But there can be no doubt that it was a custom among the mound-builders of this section to spread a layer of fresh earth upon the charred remains of one dwelling, often while yet smouldering, to the depth of 1, 2, or 3 feet, and subsequently use it as the site of another dwelling, and sometimes even a third, thus increasing the height of the mound; each layer becoming the burial place of some, at least, of the occupants of the dwellings destroyed. In this way many, if not most of the smaller and medium-sized tumuli of this region, then as now subject to overflow, have been built up. A great majority of the mounds of this character in this region are now and always were subject to overflow; but no instance is known where the large, flat-topped mound of a group is not now above all ordinary floods. Although the latter also contain fire beds, these are not so common as in the smaller ones, from which we may perhaps justly conclude that the people realizing their situation, built up more rapidly one large central

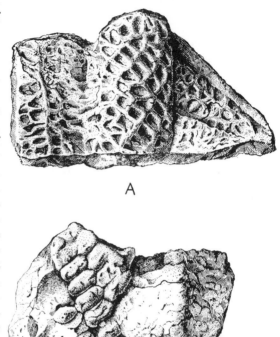

A

B

Fig. 116.—Clay casts of ear of maize, or Indian corn.

mound above the floods as a site for several dwellings or a large communal house, as well as a refuge for the villagers in times of floods.

MILLER MOUNDS.

This group, which is shown in Fig. 119, is situated in Sec. 10, T. 10 N., R. 6 E. on land owned by Mr. William Davis on the west side of the St. Francis river.

The large mound, No. 1 (probably in part a natural formation) and part of the surrounding lands are under cultivation; the rest of the group is yet in the forest, which consists of oak, pecan, cottonwood, hackberry, haw, gum, and hickory trees and scattering stalks of cane.

The bottom land is a black, sticky soil, very rich, producing fine crops of cotton, corn, and tobacco. Mounds 1, 2, and 3 remain uncovered during overflows, the rest being submerged to the depth of 3 or 4 feet or more. Quantities of potsherds, broken stone implements, burned clay, bones, and arrowheads are plowed up every season and are scattered over the surface of the large mound and fields.

Mound No. 1, if in fact it be throughout an artificial structure, is long, flat-topped, though not level, and irregular in form, the greatest length being about 900 feet and the greatest width about 225 feet. The height varies from 4 feet at the northern end to 12 at the southern (see vertical section, Fig. 120).

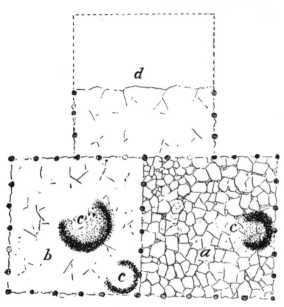

FIG. 117.—Clay floor of a three room house.

At m (Fig. 119) there is a considerable depression, as though it had not been filled up at this point or had been washed out, this portion being raised only 2 feet. On the surface at c and d are two small mounds about 3 feet high and 20 feet in diameter, composed of hard clay. The soil is sandy and quite rich.

Although designated a mound, this may be in part a natural formation, possibly the remnant of a former ridge which has been swept away by the overflows; but that the height has been artificially increased at the southern end can not be doubted, though permission to dig here was not granted, as this dwelling and other houses were located here.

No. 2, near the north end of No. 1, is about 110 feet in diameter and 18 feet high; conical and symmetrical. The surface layer proved to be a sandy soil and quite different from that of the woodland in which it stands, which is black and sticky. Several large trees are growing on the sides and near the top.

No. 3 is 60 yards from No. 2, oval and flat on top; diameter north and south, 105 feet, east and west 75 feet, and height 12 feet.

No. 4 is about 50 yards east of No. 3, 25 feet in diameter, 3 feet high, and circular. In this little mound was a mingled mass of human bones in every conceivable position, covering an area of about 10 feet in diameter. All the skulls were soft and in pieces. Among the bones were several whole earthen vessels and numerous fragments of pottery This is the only one of the group examined in which neither charcoal nor ashes were found.

No. 5 is 40 yards southwest of No. 3, diameter 20 feet, height 2 feet.

No. 6 is 70 yards west of No. 3, diameter 40 feet, height 3 feet. About 2 inches of the top consisted of vegetable soil. Under this was a layer of burnt clay extending across the mound, but not reaching the

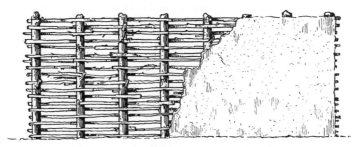

FIG. 118.—Mode of lathing houses by Mound-builders.

margins. This was not in a compact layer, but consisted of broken fragments bearing the imprint of grass and twigs and in some places the casts of split cane. In most cases the smooth side was down. The layer conformed to the surface of the ground and not to the curve of the mound, and in the central portion was slightly depressed. Below this, as far as the excavation extended (water stopping the work) was dark muck. Immediately below the burnt clay were four small ash beds on the same level. On and immediately below the large layer of burnt clay were several whole earthern vessels, two water bottles, two pots, and three bowls, and in the clay bed a large number of fragments of pottery.

No. 7, 100 yards west of No. 2, stands on low, wet ground with water all around it; diameter 60 feet, height 5 feet. After passing through a top layer of vegetable mold some 2 or 3 inches thick an unusually heavy layer of burnt clay, some 15 feet in diameter, was reached, which, in the center, measured 18 inches thick, but thinning out toward the margin, where it consisted of scattering fragments. The middle portion

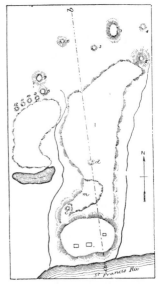

FIG. 119.—The Miller mounds, Poinsett county, Arkansas.

of the underside curved slightly upward, where it pressed upon a layer of ashes immediately below it. This layer of clay had the appearance of having been made by laying down irregularly shaped chunks of burnt

12 ETH——14

clay, some of them very hard, and filling in between them with smaller pieces. Although not solid, it seems that it was intended it should be as compact and smooth on top as it could be made with such material·

Under this was a layer of ashes some 2 or 3 inches thick; below this, dark muck or sticky clay. Other small ash beds were also found· Eight pots were found in the large burnt clay layer, two of them at the bottom of the layer by the side of an adult skeleton which lay in a horizontal position.

No. 8, 35 yards south of No. 7, measured only 20 feet in diameter and 2 feet in height. This, like the preceding, was composed chiefly of the

FIG. 120.—Vertical section of mound No. 1, Miller group, Poinsett county, Arkansas.

black, sticky soil or muck of the swamp areas around the group. A trench across it revealed nothing except a layer of burnt clay, about 6 inches thick, occupying about two-thirds of the area of the mound

No. 9 is only about 15 feet southwest of No. 8, diameter 30 feet, height, 4 feet; circular, and flat on top; a large pecan tree stands on

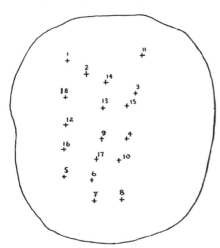

FIG. 121.—Mound No. 9, Miller group. Poinsett county, Arkansas.

the northeast slope. The top layer, 6 inches thick, consisted of loose, sandy soil, followed by a layer of burnt clay, quite hard, 9 inches thick; the rest of the mound to the original surface of the ground consisted of black muck.

Fig. 121 is a plat of this mound showing the relative positions of the articles found in it: 1, a chipped celt at the depth [1] of 6 inches; 2, a folded skeleton, head east, at the depth of 6 inches, and by the side of it a pot; 3, another skeleton at the depth of 9 inches, and by its side a bowl; 4, a clay disk at the depth of 6 inches; 5 and 6, two folded skeletons, depth 2½ feet, heads west; 7 and 8, two folded skeletons, depth 18 inches, heads east, with a bowl by the side of one and a jug by the other; 9 and 10, folded skeletons with jug and pot; 11, a pottery disk at the depth of 2 feet; 12, stone disk at 18 inches; 13, 14, and 15, folded skeletons, heads southeast, depth 2½ feet, by them a three-legged jug, a bowl and pot; 16 and 17, a jug and bowl at the depth of 3½ feet, no skeletons with them; 18, a single bowl, very small, depth 1 foot. A bone punch was also found here.

---

[1] Measurements of depth are always to the upper side of the article mentioned as it lies in the mound.

Some of the clay vessels were quite soft at the time they were found, but the larger number were strong, well made, and of comparatively good material. Fragments of pottery, broken stone, clay, ashes and charcoal were found at various depths. The bones of the skeletons were soft and fell to pieces as soon as they were uncovered.

No. 10, a small, circular mound, 3 feet high, was made up of several irregular layers as follows: First a top layer of soil 3 inches thick; below this a layer of burnt clay similar to that of the other mounds, about 5 inches thick; next, a foot of soil similar to that of the surrounding surface; and the remainder, to the original surface of the ground, a mixture of ashes, burnt clay, and soil. At the center of this was a considerable bed of ashes occupying its entire thickness, in which lay a single skeleton and with it four pots, two of them under the head of the skeleton.

No. 11, 20 feet west of No. 10; diameter 35 feet, height 3½ feet; circular.

A broad trench was cut through it, carrying away the larger portion to the original earth. In Fig. 122 the positions of the articles found are marked. After passing through a very thin layer of surface soil a bed of hard-burned earth 4 inches thick was reached which covered the greater portion of the mound; the remainder consisted of black muck from the bottom lands around; at the depth of 5½ feet, or 2 feet below the original surface of the ground, was a layer of ashes and charcoal. Quantities of broken mussel shells, charcoal, potsherds and chunks of burned clay were found at various depths.

FIG. 122.—Plan of mound No. 11, Miller group.

At 1 lay a very soft folded skeleton, head north, 2 feet below the surface; by the head a single earthen pot. Pots 2 and 3, and a bowl (4), were all immediately under the usual layer of burned earth. Nos. 5 and 6—clay pipes—were discovered at the depth of 2½ feet; 8, a pot, at the depth of 2 feet; a clay pipe (not shown in the figure) at the depth of 18 inches.

Several pieces of burned clay bearing the impressions of split canes were secured. These probably were pieces of plastering from the walls of a dwelling which stood here and was destroyed by fire. The layer of burned earth or clay mentioned was quite hard. It was full of the impressions of grass and twigs, and looked as though grass and clay had been mixed together. Some small trees, varying from 6 inches to a foot in diameter, stood on the top and sides of the mound.

No. 12, 25 feet southwest of No. 11, diameter 25 feet, height, 3 feet; circular; was composed of black, sticky muck, except a layer of burned clay 9 inches thick which covered the top.

Fig. 123 shows the positions of the following articles found in it. Nos. 1 and 2, pots at the depth of 9 inches, or immediately under the bed of burned clay; 3, clay disk, depth, 9 inches; 4, a folded skeleton, head north, depth, 1 foot, with a pot on each side of it; 5, a pot, depth, 2 feet; 6, a soft skeleton and a pot, depth, 2 feet; 7, a broken bowl at the depth of 2½ feet; 8, a bowl at a depth of 2 feet; 9, 10, 11, three skeletons, heads in different directions, at the depth of 2 feet; 12, a clay pipe immediately under the top layer of burned clay.

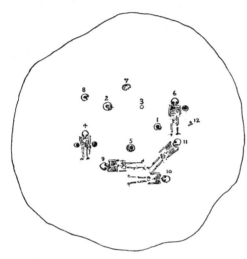

FIG. 123.—Plan of Mound No. 12, Miller group.

Most of the pottery in this mound was very soft, hence it was only with great care that the vessels could be taken out whole. The bones were so wet and soft that they went to pieces when handled. Several small, hardwood trees, such as hackberry, hickory, pecan and walnut, grew on the mound, but none exceeded 6 or 8 inches in diameter. Soft mussel shells, chunks of burned clay, charcoal, burned stones, ashes and fragments of charred cane were found at various depths.

THORNTON GROUP.

This group is situated in T. 11 N., R. 6 E., on the east bank of Little river, about 3 miles above its junction with the St. Francis.

The bottom land on which the mounds stand, although under cultivation, is low and subject to overflow. The plan of the group is given in Fig. 124.

Fragments of pottery, broken stone implements, mussel shells, stone chips, broken bones, and chunks of burned clay are scattered over a portion of the ground. A clay pipe was the only whole article that rewarded a careful search of the surface.

Owing to continued rains and abundance of water but two mounds of the above group were examined and very little of interest found in them.

The following list gives the respective sizes and forms of the mounds of this group:

No. 1. Seventy-five feet long north and south, 65 feet wide, and 2 feet high.

No. 2. Ninety feet long north and south an 40 feet east and west.

No. 3. Thirty feet in diameter and 2 feet high.

No. 4, 25 feet across the widest point and 2 feet high.

No. 5, apparently double, 75 feet long north and south, 35 feet across at the widest point, and 3 feet high.

No. 6, 50 feet long east and west, 30 feet wide, and 2 feet high.

No. 7, which is but 20 feet in diameter and 2 feet high, was opened and found to consist throughout of sandy soil like that in the field around it. It was full of ashes, charcoal, burned clay, broken mussel shells, fragments of pottery, and stone chips. A soft, folded skeleton, with head north, was found on the northern side at the depth of 18 inches; under it was a discoidal stone. A few large fragments of pottery, very soft, were at the center near the surface. The clay pipe heretofore mentioned was found on the surface of this mound.

No. 8, diameter 35 feet and height 2 feet, is situated in a depression, and at the time of examination was surrounded by water.

In No. 9, which is 25 feet in diameter and 3 feet high, was a folded skeleton at the depth of 1 foot, with head south; no relics of any kind with it.

THE TAYLOR SHANTY GROUP.

This group, shown in Fig. 125, is situated in the southern part of T. 11 N., R. 6 E., on the right bank of the St. Francis river, about 3 miles below where the Kansas City, Fort Scott and Memphis railroad crosses this stream. This part of the county lies within the bounds of what are known as the "Sunken lands of the St. Francis river;" hence the present condition is proba-

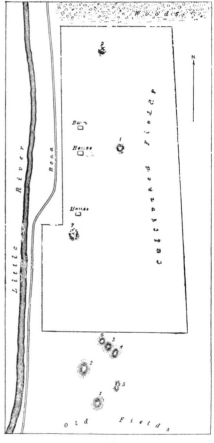

Fig. 124.—Plat of Thornton group, Poinsett county, Arkansas.

bly quite different from what it was previous to 1811, though it must have abounded in swamps and sloughs as far back as the time of De Soto's visit. The land on which the mounds stand is subject to overflow, and in 1882, 1883, and 1884 was inundated to the depth of 10 or 12 feet, only the tops of the highest mounds remaining uncovered.

Mound No. 1, shown on a larger scale in Fig. 126, is at this time but a remnant of what it was, the overflow and wash of the St. Francis river having worn away a considerable portion of it. The length at present is 150 feet, greatest width 75, and height 6 feet, the top flat. On this were two small mounds shown at *a* and *b*, each about 26 feet in diameter and 2 feet high. Trenches 20 feet wide were dug through

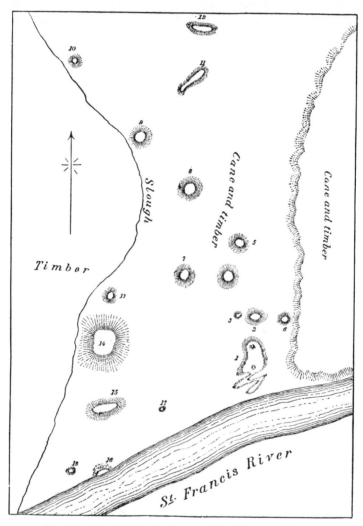

FIG. 125.—Plat of Taylor Shanty group, Poinsett county, Arkansas.

these small mounds to the depth of 5 feet. In that (*c d*) running through the little mound *a*, seven skeletons of adults were found, all extended and lying on their backs, and with each (save two) were two earthen vessels lying near the skulls, in most cases a bowl and jar. With one of the exceptional cases was one vessel; with the other, three. At one point two skeletons were lying close together side by side, but with the feet of one to the head of the other. Shells and animal bones were observed; of the latter those of the deer were the most common. Burnt clay and ashes were scattered through the earth, but not in beds.

In the trench (*e f*) running through mound *b* were also several skeletons, all lying horizontally, at full length, each with one or more earthen vessels close by it; with one there were four, two at the knees and two at the head. In one of the pots found in this trench were a number of small animal bones. At the depth of 2 feet was a bed of burnt clay and immediately beneath it a bed of charcoal and ashes, in which was found a single clay pipe.

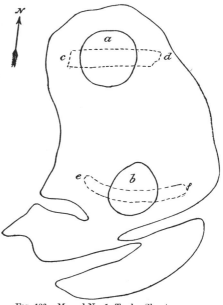

Mound No. 2 lies a few feet north of No. 1, and is somewhat oval in outline; north and south diameter, 41 feet; east and west diameter, 58 feet; and height, 5 feet. It was covered with a dense growth of cane, and a large tree had grown on the top near the center, but, having fallen, its trunk lay buried in

FIG. 126.—Mound No. 1, Taylor Shanty group.

the top of the mound and was covered with vegetable mold to the depth of 2 inches.

The construction of this mound as shown in Fig. 127, which represents an east and west cross section, is as follows, commencing at the top: First, a top layer of soil, *a*, 3 inches thick; next, a layer of burnt clay, *b*, 15 inches thick in the central portion and thinning out to the margins, smooth on top, but rough beneath, with the usual indications

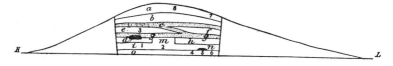

FIG. 127.—Section of mound No. 2, Taylor Shanty group.

of admixture with straw and twigs. Immediately under this was a continuous layer of ashes and charcoal (*c*), equal in extent to the layer of burnt clay above it and about 2 inches thick. The remains of partly burned cane were found mixed through it; also fragments of pottery and burned stones. Under this were layers of burnt clay, *e* and *f*, 8 inches thick, placed as shown in the figure, with a thin layer of ashes between their overlapping edges. There were no indications of grass or twigs in the clay of these layers, as in that of the upper one, *b*. Beneath these was another horizontal and continuous layer of fine coal and ashes, *g*, about 2 inches thick. This had the appearance of burnt cane, as fragments of cane partially burned were found in it. Under this was still another layer of burnt clay (*h*) equal in extent to those above it and, like them, horizontal. Its upper side was comparatively smooth and flat. In the central portion it was rather more than a foot thick, but thinning out toward the margins. This had been cut at *m* in a north and south direction for the purpose of burying a single individual, whose skeleton was found immediately below at 2. This layer appears to have been solid, and contained no indications of grass or weeds. Near the northern edge, at *d*, were a small bed of gray ashes, quite a quantity of coals, fragments of pottery and stones, and among them human bones slightly discolored by the ashes, but not burned. This deposit was some 4 or 5 inches thick, covering an area about 6 feet in diameter and lying chiefly in the layer *g*. Immediately under this burnt clay was a layer (*i*) of gray, waxy soil about 1 foot thick, horizontal,[1] extending over the area of the mound, and of nearly uniform thickness throughout. On the south side of the mound in this layer, at *n*, was a small bed of ashes. Next and last, resting on the original surface of the ground, was another layer of burnt clay (*o*) some 7 inches thick in the center. This, to all appearances, had been burned where it lay; nevertheless it was in fragments, and indications of grass and twigs to a very limited extent were observed in it. It is possible, therefore, that it may have been plastering from a house.

Skeletons and fragments thereof were found as follows: Bones (3) in the ash heap at *d;* skeleton lying at full length (1) in the layer of earth *i;* with this was a red-striped earthen bowl close to the head. No. 2 was in the same layer as No. 1, but judging by the indications was buried subsequent to it, as the latter lay immediately under the undisturbed portion of the clay layer (*h*), while 2 was under the opening which had evidently been made in the clay layer for its reception. This burial had taken place previous to the deposit of the layer of ashes, *g*, as this had not been disturbed. By the side of the latter, near the head, stood a water bottle and a bowl containing shell beads. Three skeletons (4, 5, and 6) lay at the bottom, on the original surface of the ground. By No. 4 was an earthen canteen; by 5, a red and white striped water bottle; and by 6, a bowl.

A wide mouthed water bottle and some human bones were discovered near the surface of the mound at 7, but these appear to have been brought up from some deeper position by the roots of the tree mentioned when it fell. A spoon-shaped clay vessel was buried in the ashes at *d*, and scattered through the dirt of the mound were fragments of

---

[1] Horizontal, when used in this connection, implies that the bed or stratum does not correspond with the curve or vertical contour of the mound, but is level, or horizontal.

pottery, fresh-water shells, and animal bones, chiefly of the deer and raccoon.

Mound 3 is a small circular tumulus, standing near No. 2 on the west, 14 feet in diameter and 2 feet high. Being nearly covered by water it was not explored.

Mound 4 is about 60 feet from the margin of No. 2; diameter 66 feet, height nearly 6 feet. The construction was as follows, commencing at the bottom and going up: The line *a a* in Fig. 128 indicates the original surface of ground; *b*, a layer of burnt clay, which lay chiefly on the right side, extending only a short distance to the left of the center, averaging about 5 inches in thickness. The impressions of grass and weeds were very abundant in it. The top was much smoother than the underside. The soil immediately beneath showed, to the depth of 2 or 3 inches, the effect of heat, from which it would seem that the clay was burnt on the spot where it lay.

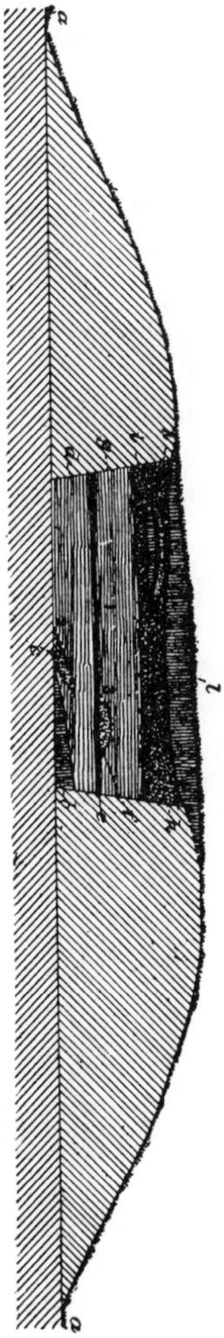

Overlapping the northern end of this layer was a bed of ashes and coals (*c*) a little beyond the center of the mound. This covered an area about 6 feet in diameter and was about 10 inches thick where deepest. Over this was a nearly horizontal layer (*d*) of clean surface soil, stretching entirely across the mound. On this lay a thin stratum (*e*) of burnt cane, but little more than an inch thick, on which, or rather in which, not far from the center, were the remains of a few fires, marked by the ash bed (*f*). Over the layer of burnt cane (*e*) was a thick layer of surface soil, marked *g*, including and covering the bed of ashes (*f*). Over this was a second layer of black, loose soil (*h*), 13 inches thick, in which at *i*, lay a small bed of burnt clay, occupying an area about 5 feet in diameter, covered by a layer of ashes extending somewhat beyond its margins. Next above was another layer of burnt clay (*l*), 15 inches thick in the central portion, but thinning out to the margins, as shown in the figure, and covering an area of 36 by 27 feet. This was composed of chunks of burnt clay that appeared to have been placed on top of the mound, and the crevices filled up with smaller fragments.

FIG. 128.—Section of mound No. 4, Taylor Shanty group.

Three skeletons were found in this mound; first (1), that of a person under medium size in the layer of soil (*g*), immediately on the stratum of burnt cane. It lay at full length face up, head east; the bones were very soft and the skull was much flattened, but not crushed. Near the head stood two clay vessels, a water bottle, and a bowl. Under the skull and part of the neck was a kind of pillow of burnt clay 13 inches long, 10 wide, and 3 thick. Although showing the form, the moisture had so affected it that it crumbled on exposure. The corners were rounded and the form was appropriate to the use to which it was applied.

The second skeleton (2) was in the bottom of the mound on the original surface of the ground and partly covered by the ash bed *c*, though not charred. It lay extended, face up and head southeast, resting on a clay pillow similar to that already described. Near the right shoulder was a water bottle and close to it a bowl. The bottle stood erect and was about two-thirds full of water, which had probably soaked in during an overflow.

The third skeleton (3) was in the southern part of the mound in the ash bed (*f*), and, though resting on the layer of burnt cane, the bones were not charred. It lay horizontally, the head resting on a clay pillow, as the others, and near it stood a water bottle and bowl; with these was also a chipped celt.

Mound 5 stands 25 feet north of 4, measuring from base to base, and is similar in size and form to 3. On it is a black walnut stump, 16 feet in circumference. No. 6, 35 feet east of No. 2, is circular; diameter 26 feet, height 3 feet. No. 7, 45 feet west of 4, is somewhat oval; diameter 52 and 61 feet, height 6 feet. Although neither of these three was explored, burnt clay was observed near the surface of each.

No. 8 is 127 feet north of 7; diameter 50 feet; height about 3 feet. Two feet below the surface was a water bottle in the form of a fish, and near it a bowl. Nothing else was observed, except a few fresh-water shells, fragments of pottery, and a few coals.

The positions and sizes of the remaining mounds of the group, which were not excavated, are given in the following table:

No.	Position.	Form.	Diameter.	Height.
			Feet.	*Feet.*
9	100 feet northwest of No. 8	Circular	55	4
10	200 feet northwest of No. 9	....do	30	2
11	93 feet northeast of No. 9	(Double) oblong ..	83 by 30	2½
12	90 feet north of No. 11	Oblong	75 by 25	3½
13	145 feet southwest of No. 7	Circular	35	3
14	25 feet south of No. 13	Nearly square	150 by 112	6
15	75 feet south of No. 13	Oblong	87 by 44	5
16	125 feet south of No. 15	Circular	Part only.	3
17	80 feet east of No. 15	....do	10	1
18	15 feet west of No. 16	....do	30	3½

Other mounds which presented little of interest may be briefly mentioned as follows:

One in Sec. 9, T. 12 N., R. 2 E., conical, 60 feet in diameter and 2½ feet high, except the southeast quarter, which was raised a foot higher. Under the latter portion at the depth of 3 feet, was a single skeleton lying at full length, face up, head east. Fragments of pottery, shells, ashes, coals, bones, stones and burned earth were scattered through it.

One on Sec. 35, T. 12 N., R. 2 E., conical, 35 feet in diameter and 4 feet high, was situated on low wet land. Two folded skeletons occurred at the depth of 2 feet, and the usual amount of fragments of pottery, shells, coals, etc.

One in SW. ¼ Sec. 26, T. 12 N., R. 2 E., 75 feet in diameter, 4½ feet high, circular and nearly flat on top. Near the center, at a depth of 2½ feet, lay a bed of ashes covering an area about 5 feet in diameter. A little to the north of this bed, at the same depth, were four folded skeletons, without order as to direction, and a little north of them another fire bed, to the right of which at the depth of 3 feet, was another skeleton, lying at full length, head west. Shells, stones, bones, fragments of pottery, etc., were scattered through it.

One near the preceding, 25 feet in diameter and nearly 3 feet high, composed of dark brown loam, similar to the soil around it, contained only the usual mixture of shells, coals, ashes, etc. This and the one preceding it are subject to overflow, and like many of the others, probably most of the low circular ones were house sites.

A conical and unusually steep mound on the SW. ¼ Sec. 32, T. 11 N., R. 4 E., which had been partially explored, was examined. It was composed of the sandy soil of the bottom land on which it stands, and covered with a layer of dark vegetable mold, about 9 inches thick. Two large poplars (tulip trees), each about 3 feet in diameter, stand on the northern slope. A folded skeleton, accompanied by three clay pots, was found near the apex at a depth of 1 foot under an old stump, and another at the depth of 9 inches, accompanied by three pots. Burned human bones occurred at three points, two at a depth of 2 feet and one at the depth of 5 feet. Fragments of pottery, stones, and mussel shells were scattered through the earth. In the center, at the base, was a hard layer of sand, several feet in extent and 2 feet deep. Under it lay five folded skeletons, all placed in the same direction.

A third mound in the same locality, about 200 yards from the last and similar in form and size, was partially explored. A badly decayed skeleton, with head west and accompanied by a small water jug, was discovered at a depth of 18 inches, and another at a depth of 2 feet, by which stood a pot and bowl. Another pot and another bowl were also found.

MISSISSIPPI COUNTY.

This county, which is bounded on the east by the Mississippi river and on the west by the Tyronza and Little rivers, is low and flat throughout, and the northern, middle, and western portions much cut up by lakes, bayous, and cypress swamps.

PECAN POINT.

This is one of the most elevated points which the Mississippi, in its many bends and windings, has left as a part of its west bank along this portion of its course; yet it is but a high bank. Nearly a mile northwest of the present landing at this place is an oblong, oval-topped mound, 150 feet long, north and south, by 80 broad at the base and 15 feet high. This is on the southern bank of a bayou where the river probably ran when it was built. As it is covered with modern graves of negroes and whites no excavations were allowed to be made in it. The people of the neighborhood state that in digging graves they bring up the remains of as many people as they bury.

But the chief point of interest at this place is the old cemetery or burying ground of the ancient mound-builders, which lies immediately east of the mound mainly along the slough.

A plat of the locality is given in Fig. 129; *m* indicating the mound, and the space *c*, surrounded by the dotted line, the cemetery.

Although many individuals are buried in mounds, and, in this section, in the dwelling sites, yet it is evident from the indications of long

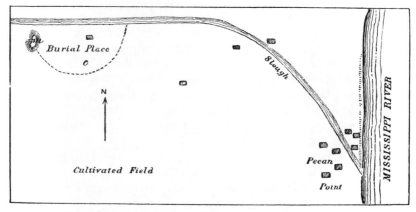

FIG. 129.—Plat of Pecan point works, Mississippi county, Arkansas.

occupancy and a numerous population, in many localities, that a large portion of the dead must have been buried elsewhere. Occasionally these burying grounds can be found. In the present case the cemetery furnishes the chief evidence that there was formerly an extensive village here. It is possible the mounds and other works may have been swept away by the Mississippi changing its bed; possibly they never existed.

The usual mode of burial here was horizontal—at full length upon the back or side, in a bark coffin placed from 1 to 3 feet below the surface. There are, however, exceptions to this mode, as some are placed with the face down, some with the legs drawn up, or, in other words, folded, some in a sitting or squatting posture; but this last is usually where a group of various sizes, as of a family, are found huddled together around some rare and highly prized object. There is no uniformity as to the direction in which they were placed, either in regard to the points of the compass or their relation to one another. It was under circumstances of this kind that the vessels representing the human head, one of which, shown in Fig. 130, was found here.

Usually in the graves of the horizontal skeletons there was found with each a pot, bowl, or jug near the head, at the feet, or by the hips; often two and sometimes all three with one skeleton, but it was seldom that two vessels of the same kind or intended for the same use were with one skeleton. The human headed vessels were not together, but adjacent to each other, and, although the large one (shown in Fig. 130) was encircled by skeletons, none was nearer than 2 or 3 feet of it. In some places there were as many as three or four tiers of burials, the lower tiers being considerably deeper than the average mentioned.

FIG. 130.—Image vessel, Pecan point, Mississippi county, Arkansas.

Scattered through this cemetery were fire-beds, ashes, charcoal, burned stones, and mussel shells from 6 inches to 2 feet below the surface. The fire beds were layers of burned earth from 6 inches to a foot thick and usually about 10 feet in diameter, with ashes and charcoal on and under them. Skeletons without accompanying relics were sometimes found near these fire beds.

Figures of some of the interesting and rare forms of clay vessels obtained at this place have been published.

In the central portion of this county, back of Osceola, there is a group of mounds on Frenchman's bayou, 6 miles west of Golden Lake post-office.

These are all of the simple, ordinary, conical type, the highest not exceeding 8 feet elevation. The plow and previous explorers had cut them to pieces and all the valuable specimens had been removed. A large number of pieces of clay, burnt to a brick-like substance, were observed together with ashes, animal bones and mussel shells, indicating that most of them were house sites.

JACKSON MOUNDS.

These are situated on the farm of Mr. B. F. Jackson, on the Little river cut-off, about 16 miles northwest of Osceola.

No. 1, oval in form, 4 feet high, and the longest diameter 60 feet, was partially occupied by the graves of three white persons, but permission to dig so as not to disturb these was obtained. Three pits were carried to the original surface. The first passed through a top layer of black surface soil 2½ feet thick, then a layer of burnt clay 10 inches thick, and below this a layer of charcoal and ashes 6 inches deep. Here, associated with the charcoal and ashes, was a skeleton, with pots at each side of the head.

In the second pit the results were much the same, except that in this, below the skeleton a hard floor of well-burnt clay was encountered, which was covered with 2 feet of ashes, in which were some specimens of pottery, but no skeleton or bones.

In the third the layers passed through were as the first, but no skeleton was found.

The other mound (there were but two mounds in the group) was somewhat higher than No. 1, but so occupied by modern graves that no examination of it could be made.

About 30 yards from this, immediately under the surface of the ground, commences a level floor of hard clay, which, so far as examined, was burned to a brick red, and varied from 6 inches to nearly 2 feet in thickness. This layer extended more or less continuously over an area almost or quite 300 feet square. As a part of it is covered by a dwelling and outbuildings, and permission to examine only certain portions was given, it was not possible to determine the extent of the spaces thus continuously covered. Breaking through this at the points where digging was allowed, the Bureau explorer discovered, in each case at the depth of from 1 to 3 feet, skeletons and pottery. In one place two skeletons of adults were found a few feet apart, and close by one of a child. With each adult skeleton were five pots, and with the child one pot and two toy vessels; all were more or less embedded in ashes, but the bones were not charred.

Several separate house sites were found in which ashes and broken pottery occurred. One of the vessels found here is represented in Fig. 131. This was beneath the clay floor.

Mr. R. B. Evans visited this county on his archeological tour in 1881, in behalf of the Chicago Times. He describes a mound on the land of a Mr. Sherman, at the head of Young's lake, midway between Osceola and Pitman's landing. The special reasons for calling attention to it here are because of the reference made by Mr. Evans to the supposed brick discovered in it, and the peculiar form of the mound, shown in Fig. 132, copied from the Times of April 9, 1881, which, as will be seen elsewhere, is almost identical with one observed by Col. Norris in Phillips county, Arkansas (see Fig. 145).

FIG. 131.—Vessel from Jackson mounds, Mississippi county, Arkansas.

The dimensions given are as follows: Altitude of the first terrace 11 feet, width 129 feet, length 158 feet; altitude of second terrace 3 feet 7 inches, width 60 feet, length 93 feet; altitude of third terrace 6 feet, width 63 feet, length 78 feet.

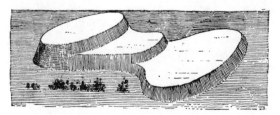

FIG. 132.—The Sherman mound, Mississippi county, Arkansas.

Digging into the top he found, near the surface, fragments of burned clay, which increased in amount a little farther down, where they formed a layer apparently over the upper terrace. These lumps of burned clay, which he supposed to be brick, are evidently the fragments of plaster from the walls of a dwelling, as they were, in some cases, marked with the fluting elsewhere mentioned as occurring in the mounds of Arkansas.

INDEPENDENCE COUNTY.

The surface of this county is broken and hilly, and is crossed from the northwest to the southeast by White river. The Oil Trough bottom in the southwest part, where the mounds mentioned are situated, is a rich alluvial tract lying along the west side of White river.

FIG. 133.—Engraved shell (*Busycon perversum*) from mound, Independence county, Arkansas.

The only works reported in this county are two mounds near Akron and 9 miles northwest of Jacksonport.

The first of these is about 300 feet in diameter, 7 feet high and circular in outline. It is covered over with the graves of the townspeople to its very skirts, and hence could not be disturbed. It was ascertained, however, that in digging the graves numerous articles had been found, among them a very fine specimen of *Busycon perversum*, engraved, which was obtained from Mr. M. A. Mull, of Jacksonport, for the National Museum, and is shown in Fig. 133. A figure or image of some kind made of clay was taken out at the same time and sold to Messrs. Dodd, Brown & Co., of St. Louis, Mo.; also a number of shell beads which were obtained by the Bureau.

The second mound is much smaller, being only about 4 feet high and 50 feet in diameter. One foot below the surface a 6-inch stratum of burnt clay was encountered, then 5 inches of ashes and charcoal. The base was composed of clay and sand. Only a few broken vessels and some fragments of pottery were obtained.

JACKSON COUNTY.

On the farm of Mr. Rindman, a mile and a half north of Jacksonport, on a narrow strip of land bordering a slough, are evidences of an ancient settlement. These consist of three small mounds and patches of burned clay, or "brick-like substance," as the explorer terms it, immediately under the surface of the surrounding soil. An examination of this burnt clay showed it to be in patches, forming a layer from 6 to 10 inches thick, much of it bearing the impressions of grass, roots, and cane; occasionally mud-daubers' nests, burnt as hard as a brick, were found still sticking to it, from which it is evident that it had formed the plastering of dwellings.

FIG. 134.—Stone spool from mound, Jackson county, Arkansas.

The mounds varied from 15 to 25 feet in diameter, and from 18 to 36 inches in height. In one, at the bottom, was a hard burnt clay floor, very smooth, covered with ashes; in another, some broken pots with ashes, and in the third only ashes.

One mile east of Jacksonport, on the banks of White river, there stood, until last year, a mound, but it was carried away by the flood, which also washed off the top soil from the land for a considerable space around it, revealing fragments of pottery, bones, stone implements, and much burnt clay scattered about in patches.

In a mound, 5 feet high and about 30 feet in diameter, 6 miles south of Newport, on the farm of Mr. G. R. Stevens, two skeletons were found lying in opposite directions, face down, and with them two small stone spools, one of which is shown in Fig. 134, marked with copper stains; also a shell pin, and a clay pipe.

CRITTENDEN COUNTY.

The topographical features of this county are similar to those of Mississippi county, which joins it on the north. The works in it which were examined are situated 1 mile from Oldham (formerly Bradley's landing), near the Mississippi river, on land belonging to the Bradley

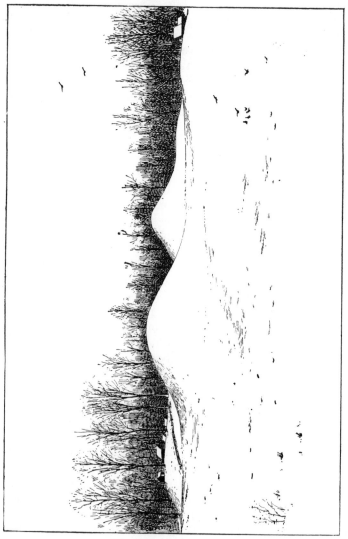

FIG. 135.—Bradley mounds, Crittenden county, Arkansas.

estate. A view of part of the group is given in Fig. 135. Unfortunately the explorer's report on these interesting works is very brief.

The land is not now subject to overflow, but an examination of the portion outside of the field shows that a stream formerly ran here and that then it was probably subject to occasional inundation, as, where it has not been disturbed by the plow, the strata of sand and vegetable remains are quite distinct. The Mississippi is one-fourth of a mile distant; this land seems therefore to have been made since the river ran by the field. The old river bed is probably the former channel of the Wappanoke creek which now runs some distance back of the field in which the mounds are situated. Many of the trees on this land are 5 feet in diameter and 80 feet high. The human and other remains found in this field are from 3 to 5 feet deep. The mounds occupy the highest point and the greater the distance from them the deeper are the remains, as would be the case with deposits made by overflows.

The mounds had already been worked over, so attention was turned to the house sites scattered over the area around them. A number of these had also been previously examined, but several remained undisturbed. As an almost universal rule, after removing a foot or two of top soil, a layer of burnt clay in a broken or fragmentary condition would be found, sometimes with impressions of grass or twigs, which easily crumbled but was often hard and stamped apparently with an implement made of split reeds of comparatively large size. This layer was in places a foot thick and frequently burned to a brick red or even to clinkers.

Below this, at a depth of 3 to 5 feet from the surface, were more or less ashes, and often 6 inches of charred grass, immediately covering skeletons. The latter were found lying in all directions, some with the face up, others with it down, and others on the side. With these were vessels of clay, in some cases one, sometimes more.

From the excavations made here about seventy whole vessels and numerous fragments were obtained; also rubbing stones, hammer stones, celts, cupped stones, horn and bone implements, etc.

ST. FRANCIS COUNTY.

The surface of this county is quite level, with the exception of Crowley's ridge, which runs through the western portion north and south. East of the ridge is the broad region of alluvial lands of the White and Mississippi rivers.

About 4 miles southeast of Forest city, and near Crow creek, some singular remains were discovered, called by the people of the neighborhood the "Old Brick House," or "Fort," from the quantity of bricklike material or burnt clay found there. These appear to be house sites. There are three of them, rectangular in form, the larger one 30 feet long by 10 feet wide, consisting of a floor of burned clay 8 inches thick. The outer edges consisted of broken fragments forming ridges and presenting the appearance of being the remnants of a clay wall which had fallen down during the destruction of a building by fire. The area occupied is about 2 feet higher than the surrounding level. Immediately below the clay floor was a layer of ashes 6 inches thick, and below this black loam. Some large trees are growing on these sites, one a poplar (tulip tree)[1] 3 feet in diameter and 100 feet high.

The other squares have been more or less obliterated by a roadway made through them. Some years ago a large oak on one of them was blown down, revealing the bones of a skeleton, some pottery, and a pipe.

Near by is a mound 10 feet high, oblong in shape and flat on top, the width of the upper surface 36 feet. It consisted of three strata, the first or top layer of soil about 10 inches thick; next a layer of yellow clay 1 foot thick, and the remainder, to the bottom, white clay. No relics or evidences of its having been used for burial purposes were observed.

CROOK'S MOUND.

This is situated on the farm of Capt. W. J. Crook, 10 miles southeast of Forest city and near the bank of Tunic creek. It is oval in form, 408 feet long, 150 feet wide, and 15 feet high, flat on top.

Thorough examination was not allowed by the owner, as it is the only retreat for his farm stock in time of high water. Three small pits revealed the fact that the first or top layer of loam was about 1 foot thick; next below this a layer of ashes of variable depth; the remainder, to the base, consisted of clay. It had been very deeply plowed and a skeleton or two and some pots taken out.

LAKE ANDERSON MOUNDS.

This group of mounds is on the bank of Lake Anderson or Mud lake, some 2 miles northeast of Forest city. The largest one is oblong in form, flat on top, with unusually steep sides; height, 12 feet; width on top, 30 feet. Permission to excavate it was refu ed because of the owner's wish to utilize it in times of freshets. Two small circular mounds on the immediate bank of the lake were composed of loam, clay, ashes, and burnt, brick-like material, mingled in a confused mass by the tramping of cattle in times of high water.

A short distance from these were patches of burnt clay, slightly raised above the natural surface of the ground. But they had been so badly cut up by the passage of vehicles, the public road crossing directly over them, that nothing satisfactory could be ascertained in reference to their original form or condition.

REMAINS ON THE ROBERT ANDERSON FARM.

These are on the bank of the St. Francis river, 2 miles northeast of those last mentioned.

At this place, on the immediate bank of the St. Francis river, is a projecting point, which was formerly much larger, but has been cut away by the river until but a few feet of the projecting portion remain. During this process of wearing away, many skeletons, much pottery, and numerous stone implements have been washed out. The point now

---

[1] In the South the name " poplar " is universally applied to the tulip tree—*Liriodendron tulipifera.*

presents the appearance shown in Fig. 136, the squares indicating the remains of houses. In this, 1 is the St. Francis river; 2, 2, parts of the floors of two rooms or houses, the rest having been washed away; 3, a complete square or house floor. These squares are composed, as usual, of a layer of brick-like substance, with the impressions of grass and twigs in it. The edges are all higher and have a thicker layer of this material than the inner areas. The surface soil has been washed away, leaving these hard floors naked. This layer of burnt clay, except at the edges, is usually about 8 inches thick. Immediately beneath it is a layer of charcoal and ashes, of about the same thickness, and beneath this black loam. No. 4 in the figure indicates the public road, and 5, a small clear space between the square and the river.

Two small circular mounds near by were partially examined. Permission for further work in them could not be obtained. In one were

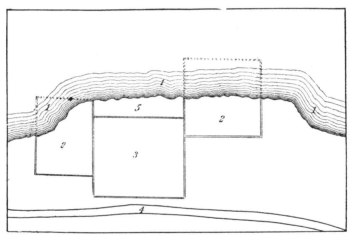

FIG. 136.—House site, St. Francis county, Arkansas.

found burnt clay and ashes commingled, the body of the mound below this consisting of sand. The other contained no burnt clay or ashes, the top layer, 3 feet thick, being black loam, the remainder yellow clay.

ARKANSAS COUNTY.

One of the most remarkable mounds in this state is that called "the Menard hill" (*a*, Fig. 137, which is a plat of the group), on the farm of Mr. N. Menard, 7 miles west of Arkansas post. Its peculiarity consists in its unusual steepness, being, according to Dr. Palmer's measurement, 50 feet high and only 150 feet in diameter at the base. It is flanked by two wings, indicated at *b* and *c*. The larger of these wings is 150 feet long, 60 feet wide, and 20 feet high; the smaller is 75 feet long and 7 feet high.

A slight examination of the main mound, carried down only to the depth of 10 feet, showed that it was composed of a mixture of sandy loam, decayed vegetable matter and clay, but there can be scarcely a doubt that the central core is hard clay which has preserved its form.

An opening was made in the larger wing near the top. After passing through a top layer of sandy loam 6 inches thick, a layer of burnt clay of the same thickness was reached. Immediately below this was a layer of burnt matting 3 inches thick, scattered through which were grains of parched corn. In an opening previously made on the oppo-

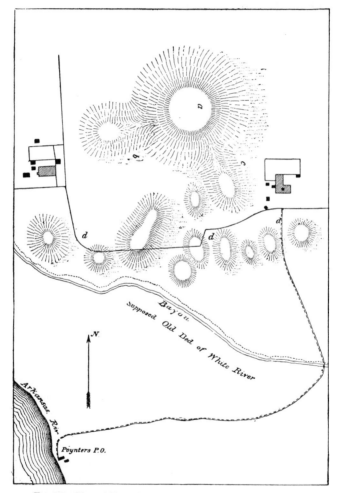

Fig. 137.—Plan of Menard mounds, Arkansas county, Arkansas.

site side of the same wing a thick layer of burnt clay was encountered and a number of broken pots were found.

The small flat-topped mounds *d d d*, none of which are more than 2 feet high, are probably house sites. They consisted of a top layer of soil, next a layer of burnt clay, and below this ashes, in which were skeletons and pottery. It was in these house sites that Dr. Palmer made the large find of pottery previous to his connection with the Bureau of Ethnology.

As Dr. Palmer's report of his previous work has not been published, I copy from it his remarks in regard to this group:

I found that this mound (the Menard hill) had been previously dug into, and I learned that a metal cross was found 4 feet below the surface. A field of 20 acres surrounds it, in which are numerous remains of ancient dwellings. In these, ashes were discovered under a layer of burnt clay, which I presume formed the roofing of the dwellings. Close to (under) the ashes a skeleton was usually found with from one to three pieces of pottery by the side of the skull.

The most important result of the exploration was finding the remains of a large house. About 2 feet under the surface was a thick layer of burnt clay, which probably formed the roof. In tracing out the circumference a hard clay floor was found beneath, and between the two several inches of ashes, but no skeletons. There were a great many pieces of broken dishes so situated as to lead one to believe they were on top of the house at the time it was burned. When restored most of these vessels proved to be basin-shaped bowls.

LEE COUNTY.

The topographical features of this county are very similar to those of St. Francis county, which joins it on the north.

GREER'S MOUND.

This is a very regular, oblong truncated or flat-topped mound, situated upon the point of a second or upper terrace of the L'Anguille river 2 miles above its confluence with the St. Francis. It is rectangular, measuring on the top 87 feet in length and 51 feet in width and is 30 feet high; the slope of the sides is very steep, being about 45°.

A shaft sunk in it near one end some years ago revealed, as is stated by the parties who made the exploration, the stump of a small tree and a stake 4 or 5 feet long near the bottom, the former growing in the natural soil. Layers of swamp mud and fire beds were found at irregular distances through the whole depth.

Permission to make further exploration was not obtained.

ANCIENT DWELLING SITES AND CEMETERIES.

A careful examination was made of the bluffs and valleys both of the L'Anguille and St. Francis rivers above their confluence for a distance of fully 20 miles, from which it was found that scarcely a terrace or hillock was without evidences of ancient occupancy, such as brick-red fire-beds, charcoal, ashes, etc., indicating camps or dwellings.

For more than fifty years the Priest and Forest farms, where these evidences appear in greatest abundance, have been noted for the amount of ancient pottery of superior quality frequently unearthed in cultivating the land and recently by relic hunters. Quite a number of whole vessels of this pottery were obtained by the Bureau.

There is usually sufficient space between the bluffs and the irregular line of hillocks, which slope off from them to the lower bottoms, for a roadway. The upper or highest portion of each hillock seems to have been occupied as a dwelling place until the accumulation of dark earth, fire-beds, and refuse material has reached a depth of from 2 to 10 feet, which gradually thins out with the slope in all directions. Shafts and trenches in these disclosed the fact that the material is in irregular layers or patches, in which are intermingled charcoal, charred bones of animals, as well as many split bones not charred, also the never absent stone chips, rude scrapers, and other implements. Occasionally one or more human skeletons are found, always beneath a fire-bed and usually accompanied by pottery. These are generally in low, oblong mounds, where the peculiar color of the earth indicates their presence, and the uppermost ones are at a slight distance below the surface. There are often two or three tiers of skeletons, apparently deposited without any other system than simply to avoid overlapping and so as to arrange them parallel with each other and at full length.

The crania, which are not crushed, vary greatly, both in size and form, but are usually of the brachycephalic type. Occasionally one is found which shows very distinctly the effects of artificial compression of the front.

Many of the skeletons observed had only fragments of pottery by the side of the cranium; some had a vessel, usually a water bottle; others a cup, bowl, or other open-mouthed vessel, and, perhaps, in addition, a human or animal effigy.

Col. Norris, who made the explorations in this locality, says that he " rarely found more than three vessels with one skeleton, and one of them was always a water bottle. They were usually, but not always, found in the proper position to contain water, food, or other presents for the dead. I found a number of the bottles closed with stoppers made of clay, some of the latter in the form of mullers, and others simply rounded off and made to fit; but no relic of any kind in these bottles; while, on the contrary, polishing stones, shells, bones of birds, and red paint were frequently found in cups, basins, and other open-mouthed vessels. Although so similar in general form and finish, there are often such marked peculiarities in the finish, color, or ornamentation of vessels of neighboring villages but a mile or two apart as to enable a close observer to readily distinguish them. For instance, the Forest and Priest farms extend less than 2 miles each, yet any person, by close observation could soon learn to distinguish the pottery found at one extremity from that obtained at the other."

At one point the skull of a skeleton was found crushed beneath ten platters, seven of which were placed edgewise above it on one side and three, slightly differing in form, on the other. Most of them, however, fell to pieces on being removed.

MONROE COUNTY.

No explorations were made in this county, but two large stone pipes were obtained, shown in Figs. 138, 139, 140, and 141, which are reported to have been found in the upper part of a large truncated mound near Clarendon.

The former (Figs. 138–140) is of quartzite, smoothed and partially polished, 8 inches high to the top of the head, 7 inches long and 3 inches thick. It represents a kneeling, naked individual; Fig. 138 is a side view; Fig. 139 a front view, and Fig. 140 a view of the top of the head showing the carving. The latter (Fig. 141) is of a species of white

FIG. 138.—Image pipe, Monroe county, Arkansas.

marble, polished, 4 inches high, 4½ long and 2½ thick, a squatting figure with pipe bowl in the lap. There is no doubt as to their authenticity and that they were obtained as reported.

PHILLIPS COUNTY.

Several miles of the lower portion of the St. Francis river valley are included in this county. In portions of this stretch, especially opposite Phillips bayou, the river, in cutting into the high bottom, is constantly unearthing ancient pottery and human bones, many of the latter being in such a state of preservation as to indicate that they, as well as many found on the west side above the bayou, pertain to a comparatively modern period. It is even stated by some of the oldest settlers of the locality that when first occupied by the whites it was not an unusual thing to plow up fragments of bark boxes or coffins, together with bones and pottery.

OLD TOWN WORKS.

These are situated on a sandy ridge between the Mississippi river and Old Town lake, at the point where they make their nearest approach to each other and near the

ancient outlet of the latter, which is now closed by the levee. They consist of earthen walls or embankments, mounds, and the saucer-shaped depressions supposed to be house sites, as shown in Fig. 142. The works to the left, marked *a*, consist of an inclosing wall surrounding a space somewhat in the form of a quadrant of a circle; a large, truncated, pyramidal mound with terrace (No. 3 in the figure) and other smaller conical or oval mounds and numerous saucer-shaped house sites. Those at the right must have been very extensive, but have been to a large extent removed for the purpose of forming the levee.

The preservation of the wall around the western works is largely due to the fact that it has, in part, been utilized as a portion of the levee.

FIG. 139.—Image pipe, Monroe county, Ark.

No. 1, at the right and forming a part of the group marked *b*, is the remnant of a wall which extended from the old bank of the river 400 feet diagonally toward the head of the former outlet of the lake and terminated in a small rectangular inclosure 15 by 30 feet.

Whether this wall and inclosure are wholly the work of aborigines or partly of the whites is a question the Bureau assistant was unable to decide, but thought the latter view possible, judging from the size and rectangular form of the work. According to local tradition they were built by Moscosa and the remnant of De Soto's army while preparing their brigantines for the descent of the Mississippi river.

Much of mound No. 2 has been removed for levee purposes, but traces of the edges still remaining prove it to have been 600 feet long and about 200 broad at its greatest width and oval in form. Its height, however, was only some 8 or 10 feet. It appeared from information obtained that it contained from one to three tiers of skeletons and that several hundred vessels of clay have at different times been taken from it. From the excavations made by the Bureau assistant in the remnants it was ascertained that it was built of the surrounding soil, with the usual admixture of fire-beds, charcoal and ashes. Several skeletons were unearthed and some vessels obtained, one of which is shown in Fig. 143. These skeletons were uniformly buried at full length upon their backs or sides without regard to the cardinal points and a number of them in bark coffins, which were unmistakably of cypress and in no way differing from others found near the surface and supposed to be intrusive burials of modern Indians. In one of these was a water bottle close by the side of the skull.

FIG. 140.—Image pipe, Monroe county, Arkansas. FIG. 141.—Image pipe, Monroe county, Arkansas.

Mound No. 3, in the large inclosure (*a*), is a truncated pyramid, nearly square, 96 feet long by 86 in width at the base; the first or lower platform is 4 feet high, and forms a terrace 36 feet wide on two connecting sides of the mound proper; this rises 8 feet above this terrace, and is 50 by 60 feet at its base and 20 by 30 feet on the flat top. It is shown in Fig. 144 restored (*a* the elevation and *b* the ground plan). Excavations were made, but nothing of interest was revealed.

There was, as usual, a space fronting this mound destitute of the circular house sites. Excavations in the house sites revealed the usual fire-bed, charcoal, and fragments of pottery.

BARNEY MOUND.

This singular and interesting earthwork is shown in Fig. 145, *a* the ground plan and *b* the elevation. As will be seen, it consists of an oval platform constricted near the middle so as to appear like two conjoined, unequal circles, the larger of which is surmounted by an oval truncated mound. The platform averages throughout about 15 feet high, the diameter of the smaller end being about 200 feet and of the larger 338 feet. The mound rises about 20 feet above the platform or terrace and is flat on top, its larger diameter here being 108 feet.

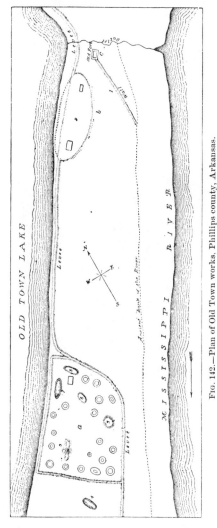

FIG. 142.—Plan of Old Town works, Phillips county, Arkansas.

The whole is entirely surrounded, as shown in the figure, by a ditch varying in depth from 10 to 15 feet and in width from 50 to 75 feet.

Excavations made at points on the summit and sides, both of the mound proper and platform, brought to light patches or beds of clay burnt to a brick red.

ROGER'S MOUNDS

This is the name given to a group a mile distant from the Barney mound, just described. The mounds are all of the ordinary conical or oval form, except the largest one of the group, which is flat on top and surmounted near one end by another small hemispherical mound, as shown in Fig. 146. This is oval in outline, the longer diameter (at the base) 247 feet, and the shorter nearly 200 feet; height of the platform or terrace 20 feet, the longer diameter on the top 150 feet, and the shorter 90. The little mound on the top is about 50 feet in diameter, 5 feet high, and rounded off in the ordinary form. On the terrace are the ruins of a modern house and barn overgrown by brush and small trees. A very heavy fire-bed was found immediately below the surface of the upper mound; others were also found at various points on the terrace and on the sides of the main mound.

Near the surface of another mound, the next in size, was a bed of clay burned to a brick red, and so hard that it could not be cut with a spade, but had to be undermined and taken out in blocks like irregular bricks. A portion of this was removed and an excavation made through charcoal, ashes, and flakes of mortar burned to a bright brick red, but retaining the casts of the stems of grass and cane. Two feet below this was another fire-bed.

DESHA COUNTY.

This county, which lies along the Mississippi and includes the mouths of Arkansas and White rivers, is embraced in the Mississippi alluvial region of the state.

Fig. 147 represents a mound situated on a level bottom 1 mile north of Arkansas city. It is 108 feet long, 72 feet wide on top, and 12 feet high. There is a slope of about 35 feet at the east end, produced by a

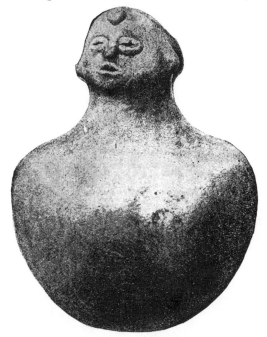

FIG. 143.—Pottery vessel from Old Town works.

slide which carried down some of the upper level. During the overflow of 1882, which was of unusual height, the top of this mound was never less than 5 feet above the water. It has, on this account, been utilized as a burying ground by the citizens of Arkansas City, where they bring their dead in boats in times of overflow.

A conical mound at Walnut lake station, 40 feet in diameter and 8 feet high, was composed wholly of sandy loam. Fig. 148 represents an ancient fort on what is known as the "Turner Place." It is near the Arkansas river, which formerly ran within 400 yards of this fortification. Although evidently constructed by whites its history is unknown to the people of that section, who have the usual tradition of its being the work of De Soto and his army. It was probably built

by the French to protect a trading post. As confirmatory of this
theory there is a ridge near by on which are found the indications of
houses such as were built by the whites.

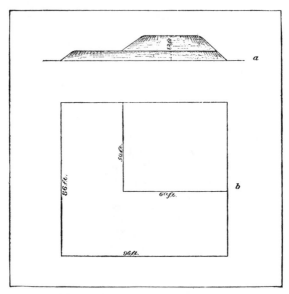

FIG. 144.—Mound No. 3, Old Town works.

Trees a foot through were cut from it twenty-two years ago; but Dr.
Palmer was informed by Mr. Bezzell, who lives near by, that thirty-six
years ago the trees now growing on the new-made lands along the river
some of which are 3 feet in diameter, were small saplings.

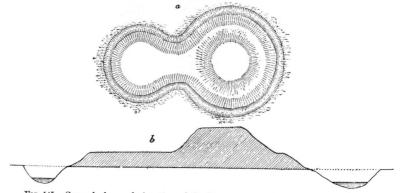

FIG. 145.—Ground plan and elevation of the Barney mound, Phillips county, Arkansas.

The fort is square, measuring 150 yards from side to side. On the
west side extends a graded or covered pathway a distance of 250 yards,
ending near the former bank of the river. The height of the wall of the
fort is at present 4 feet. In one corner, as shown in the figure, is a hole
6 feet deep supposed to be the site of the magazine.

The articles picked up here from time to time and found in the process of cultivating the soil belong both to the days of the first settlement of the county and to very modern times. They are thimbles, pipes, broken dishes, parts of pistols and guns, pieces of silver coin, probably used as gun-sights, a Chinese coin, a toy pistol of stone, articles of Indian origin, stone bullet molds, etc. The remains of an old forge were uncovered here a few years ago.

THE WYENN MOUNDS.

This is a group of mounds situated on the bank of Mound lake, 16 miles from the present mouth of the Arkansas river. The large one is 18 feet high, oval in form, flat on top, and 130 feet long, exclusive of the apron-like appendage at one end, which is 140 feet long, 60 feet wide, and 3 feet high. As this is used as a graveyard it could not be explored nor was permission granted to examine the others which are small and of the usual conical form.

FIG. 146.—Roger's mound, Phillips county, Arkansas.

CHOCTAW MOUND.

This is a small circular mound, 10 feet high and 40 feet in diameter, situated at the junction of Choctaw bayou and Walnut lake. It was found by excavation to consist of a top layer of sandy loam 1 foot thick and the remainder, to the base, of hard tough clay. No charcoal, ashes, or other evidences of occupancy or use, save a few fragments of pottery, were discovered in it.

Near this point there are evidences of two ancient trails running in different directions.

DREW COUNTY.

THE TAYLOR MOUNDS.

This interesting group is located on the land of Dr. J. M. Taylor, 4 miles west of Winchester railroad station. A view showing the larger portion of the group is given in Fig. 149. It consists of several comparatively large mounds, of the usual conical form, several small mounds, and numerous slight elevations which are supposed to be house sites. There is one large mound, with flat top and terrace, not shown in the figure, which is 30 feet high. The others range from 5 to 14 feet in height.

Along the left margin of the field, not shown in the figure, is a row of what are believed to be artifical ponds made by removing the dirt for the mounds.

The mounds and house sites had been opened and rifled of their treasures previous to the visit of the Bureau agent; but he was fortunate in obtaining from the owner of the property, Dr. Taylor, several fine specimens of pottery taken out of them. Some of these have been figured by Mr. Holmes.

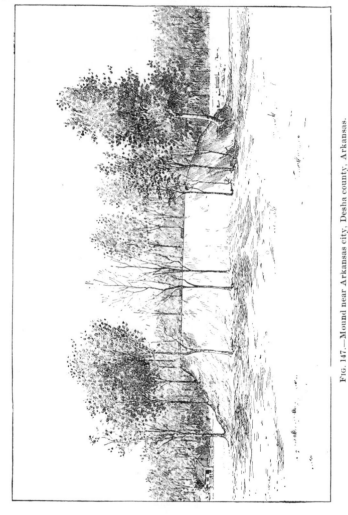

FIG. 147.—Mound near Arkansas city, Desha county, Arkansas.

THE TILLER MOUND.

This mound, of the ordinary conical form, 9 feet high and rather less than 50 feet in diameter, is situated on the farm of Mr. J. T. Tiller, 2½ miles southwest of Winchester station. It was found, by the thorough excavation made, to be composed of sandy soil similar to that of the surrounding ground, with a single, heavy layer of human bones, pottery, etc., closely packed in a confused mass. This layer was struck at the depth of 1 foot from the surface of the mound and proved to be something over 2 feet thick in the center but thinner toward the margins.

The skeletons lay in every direction and without any noticeable order; in many cases the bones of one body lay across those of another. It was difficult, in fact impossible in some cases, to trace the different skeletons. Fifty-eight skulls were observed and sufficient bones to correspond therewith. The pots and other vessels of clay were scattered irregularly through the deposit, but always near to and apparently associated with some cranium. Near one head were four pots, close by another two pots and a pipe, and one or more by others. Several mussel shells were obtained, generally near the heads, and two turtle shells

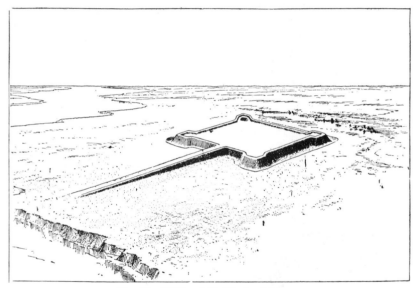

FIG. 148.—Old French Fort Desha, Arkansas.

were discovered inside of a pot, but no burnt clay, charcoal, or ashes were found in or about the mound. Twenty-three whole vessels, a number of pipes, shells, animal bones, etc., were obtained here.

LINCOLN COUNTY.

A mound on the farm of Mr. Felix Smith, and another on the farm of Mr. J. D. Adams, both in R. 7 W., were examined and found to be composed of a top layer of loam and the rest of hard, stiff clay. No burnt clay, charcoal, ashes, fragments of pottery, or bones were observed in either. One was 7 feet high and 90 feet in diameter, the other 20 feet high and 90 feet in diameter.

Another group of small, conical mounds is situated near Heckatoo, in which burnt clay or brick-like material was observed, usually about 18 inches under the soil.   Broken pottery and some rude stone implements were also found; but a thorough examination was not allowed, as the field was covered with cotton.

JEFFERSON COUNTY.

A mound on land belonging to the estate of Mr. Snuggs, 1 mile south of Garrettson's landing, was explored. This was composed wholly of sand except the thin layer of surface soil. No specimen of any kind nor any indications of life or use were discovered in it, yet its form and appearance were such as to show clearly that it was artificial.   Height, 10 feet; diameter, 40 feet.

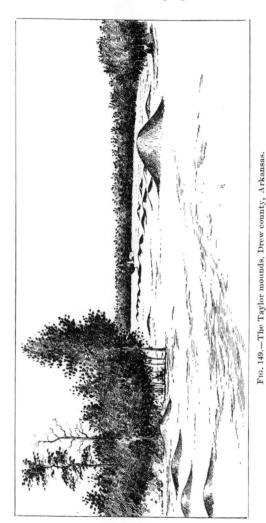

FIG. 149.—The Taylor mounds, Drew county, Arkansas.

A group of three fine conical mounds, something over a mile north of Linwood station, was visited, but as they were covered with graves permission to excavate them could not be obtained. The average height is about 15 feet, the three being very nearly of the same size and form.

A short distance from these, on the Houson farm, are two other tumuli of similar form, one 25 and the other 30 feet high, but being also covered with graves, digging was prohibited.

Excavations for the graves do not appear to have brought to light any pottery, bones, or burnt clay.

THE CLAYTON MOUNDS.

This group, situated on the lands of Hon. Powell Clayton, in Sec. 36 T. 6 S., R. 7 W., and 16 miles southeast of Pine Bluff, consists of four

THE DE SOTO MOUND, JEFFERSON COUNTY, ARKANSAS.

THE KNAPP MOUNDS, PULASKI COUNTY, ARKANSAS.

mounds. The most interesting of these is oblong in shape, rectangular, 125 feet long exclusive of the terrace or apron-like extension, 65 feet broad, and 30 feet high, and resembles the following, shown in Plate IX. It is used by the neighborhood as a burying ground, and hence could not be disturbed.

THE DE SOTO MOUND.

The mound, which is shown in Pl. IX, is on the land of Mr. H. G. De Priest, 13 miles southeast of Pine Bluff and 2½ miles northwest of the Clayton mound, which it resembles in form but exceeds in magnitude. It is 60 feet high at the west end, but somewhat less at the end to which the terrace is attached; the top, which is flat, as represented in the figure, is 144 feet long by 110 in width (exclusive of the terrace); back of the mound (from the house) is a large excavation, now a pond, from which the earth was taken for its construction. A part of the top is planted in forest trees; the rest is in cultivation.

It is known in this locality as the "De Soto mound" from current tradition that this distinguished explorer camped here for some time.

PULASKI COUNTY.

THE KNAPP MOUNDS.

These works form, without doubt, the most interesting group in the state, and, in fact, one of the most important in the United States. A plat of the group and surrounding wall is given in Pl. X, and a sketch in Pl. IX. They are situated on the farm of Mr. Gilbert Knapp and directly on the east bank of Mound lake, a crescent-shaped bayou, 16 miles southeast of Little Rock.

As seen by reference to the plat, the area inclosed by the wall is oblong, or somewhat oval, the length north and south about 170 rods, and width east and west, 80 to 85 rods, containing 85 acres. The wall appears to have formed the defense on three sides, the lake being relied on for protection on the fourth.

The lake is 3 miles long and about one-fourth of a mile wide. The field, in which the group is situated, is from 2 to 6 or 8 feet above average water level, and has been under cultivation for more than thirty years. The surrounding earthen wall reaches 5 or 6 feet in height where best preserved, but where most reduced by cultivation is about obliterated. It is a little over a mile in length and starts at the very margin of the lake on the south, circles around the field, and comes to the lake again on the north side. It is broken in three places, as shown on the plan. In two places deep trenches, probably of artificial origin, pass through the wall. They contain water for the greater part of the year. The other opening is not complete and may have been cut for a roadway by the whites. The curve of the northern half of the wall is very even, but near the middle portion there is a slight reverse curve some hundreds of feet in length and the southern segment is quite uneven.

In 1844, the period of the greatest overflow known in this section, these mounds were clear of the water, and it is said that many people came here for safety, bringing their household effects and stock with them.

The largest mound (*a*, Pl. x.) is 48 feet high, 280 feet long from north to south, and 150 feet wide. The nearly level summit is about 50 feet wide by 90 long. The whole surface is densely covered by forest trees and undergrowth. The slopes are even and rather steep, about 35 or 40 degrees. It stands in front, a little to the right, in Plate ix. Permission was given by the owner to sink a shaft into this mound. After descending 10 feet the clay became so hard that the work was abandoned. The first 2 feet passed through consisted of vegetable mold, in which were some animal bones and fragments of pottery; then 8 feet of sandy loam mixed with clay, the proportion of clay increasing until at this depth it became wholly clay, exceedingly hard and tough. A tunnel was carried in the side for 10 feet with a like result. No brick-like substance was found in it anywhere.

Mound *b*, the second in size, is oblong and slightly rectangular in outline. The slopes are gentle, save where interfered with by the plow, which has encroached upon the base at the sides and ends. The base measures about 175 by 200 feet, and the height is 38 feet. A shaft 8 feet square and 10 feet deep was sunk in the top, showing the first 2 feet to be a black, waxy clay or muck, and the rest of the distance a yellow, greasy clay. Nothing was observed except two fine quartz crystals 2 feet beneath the surface and some fragments of pottery. The top is about 80 by 100 feet in extent, and has been used as a garden for a number of years. Fifty feet from the base is a shallow depression about 260 feet long and 150 in width which is now overgrown with trees and underbrush. This contains water during a part of the year and may have been excavated by the ancient inhabitants to contain a water supply.

Mounds *c*, *d*, and *e* lie to the southeast of the large one. The largest of these (*c*) is 12 feet high, about 100 feet long and 90 feet broad at the base. A shaft 11 feet deep was made in the center of it. For the first 4 feet it passed through sandy loam, with here and there a piece of pottery and an animal bone; at the depth of 5 feet, in yellow sand which continued for 3 feet, was a broken pot; at a depth of 7 feet the sand became very wet and continued so to the bottom. Nothing else was found.

Mound *d* is 5 feet high, about 100 feet long, and 75 feet wide at the base. In four places were patches of burnt clay, doubtless the remains of former dwellings; in five other places were deposits of ashes and human bones, but no burnt clay. These were generally 1½ or 2 feet below the point reached by the plow in cultivating the soil. In these

PLAT OF THE KNAPP MOUNDS, PULASKI COUNTY, ARKANSAS.

places a few stone implements were obtained, one of which is shown in Fig. 150; also a small Catholic medal of copper. Ten other mounds, in most cases very much reduced by the plow, were observed. The circular mounds range from 2 to 10 feet in height, and from 25 to 100 feet in diameter, and the oblong ones are from 40 to 350 feet in length. All bear evidence of having been used as residence sites, as pottery, stone tools and the refuse of chipped stonework are found associated with them.

THIBAULT MOUNDS.

On the farm of Mr. J. K. Thibault, 8 miles southeast of Little Rock, are a number of small mounds averaging only about a foot and a half in height and 18 feet in diameter. These belong to the class "house

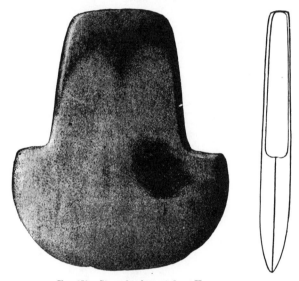

FIG. 150.—Stone implement from Knapp group.

sites," as examination showed that, under a top layer of soil 1 foot thick, a layer of burnt clay was always to be found; immediately beneath this a layer of ashes with which human remains and pottery were usually associated.

They had been partially rifled of their contents by the owner of the ground, who, however, kindly donated most of the specimens to the Bureau, some of which are represented in Mr. Holmes's papers.

SALINE COUNTY.

On the farm of Mr. J. D. Chidester, 3 miles southeast of Benton, is a space of about 10 acres covered with house sites in which are the usual layers of burnt clay, ashes, human bones, etc. They however had already been explored.

This work, a sketch of which is given in Fig. 151, is situated on the
farm of Mr. George Hughes, 3 miles southwest of Benton and within
100 yards of Saline river, though the bank was formerly within 50 feet
of it. Some low mounds, probably house sites, formerly surrounded it,
but they have been removed. In these were skeletons, pottery and
stone implements under ashes and burnt clay.

FIG. 151.—The Hughes mound, Saline county, Arkansas.

The large work yet remaining consists of two parts, the mound
proper, which is somewhat circular and a wing or extension on one side.
The former is 25 feet high, flat on top, 124 feet in diameter at the base
and 34 on the top. The wing, which runs northeast, is about 120 feet
long, 80 feet broad at the point where it joins the mound and 54 at the
northeast end, the height varying from 10 to 12 feet.

A shaft, 10 feet deep, in the center of the mound reached the hard core without bringing to light any relics, clay, ashes or bones. At several places on the top and sides of the wing, layers of burnt clay were found at the depth of 2 feet from the surface and, under each, a layer of ashes and charcoal. At four points charcoal and ashes occurred, but without the layer of burnt clay. No human remains or indications of them were observed.

CLARK COUNTY.

WORKS ON SALINE BAYOU.

According to tradition, when this section was first visited by the white settlers, the Indians were discovered here making salt. They were driven away by the whites, who, for many years, made salt here, and during the war the Confederate government utilized the saline waters for the same purpose.

There are numerous salt wells and remains of evaporators and also several round mounds of small size. Those explored were very similar to one another; in each was a top layer of soil, then a layer of burnt clay, and beneath this, ashes. One, about 3 feet high, consisted of a top layer of loam 2 feet thick, then 4 inches of burnt clay, and beneath this 5 or 6 inches of ashes. In the last were parts of a skeleton and a bowl.

The strata in another mound, about 4 feet high, were as follows: Top layer, 2 feet of black soil; next, 5 inches of burnt clay, and below this, 8 or 9 inches of ashes, resting on a hard clay floor 1½ inches thick and 5 feet in diameter. Specimens of this floor were obtained.

THE TRIGGS MOUND.

This is a small mound on the farm of Mr. W. A. Triggs, 4 miles northwest of Arkadelphia, on the bank of Caddo creek. It was partially washed away by the overflow of the creek, bringing to light two layers of burnt clay, ashes, and human bones, together with pottery and stone implements. The Bureau agent was fortunate enough to find it in this condition, and before the things had been carried away. Among the specimens of pottery found here are the following:

Fig. 152, an ornamented water-bottle, one of the finest specimens of the kind ever obtained.

Fig. 153, a flat-bottomed jar of unusual shape, partly broken.

Another mound on the same farm was examined. This was 9 feet high with a wing on one side 6 feet high, and another on the opposite side 4 feet high. Three excavations in the main portion showed it to be composed entirely of loam, without a trace of fire, burial or relics of any kind. Two feet under the surface of the wings were traces of ashes and burnt clay.

Two others opened were composed entirely of ashes and yellow clay; no relics.

OUACHITA COUNTY.

The only explorations made in this county were of some groups near Camden.

About 3 miles north of Camden, in Sec. 9, T. 13 S., R. 17 W., on the Piles plantation, is a group consisting of one large and two small mounds. It formerly contained another, which has been dug away to aid in filling a railroad embankment. The plantation on which they are situated has been in cultivation for thirty years or more. The soil is a reddish, sandy loam, not very productive, and subject to occasional

FIG. 152.—An ornamented water bottle. Clark county, Arkansas.

FIG. 153.—Flat-bottomed jar, Clark county, Arkansas.

overflows. Broken bones, small pieces of pottery, broken stone implements, and mussel shells lie scattered over the surface. A few pitted stones, a number of arrowheads, a pestle or two, and a stone celt were also found on the surface.

A plat of the group and its immediate surroundings is shown in Fig. 154. As will be seen by this, the largest of the three mounds stands on the bank of a small slough. It is oblong, and nearly flat on top, 12 feet high, length on the top, east and west, 70 feet, and width 60 feet. Abutting against it on the east end is a long, apron-like extension running out for 175 feet, 100 feet wide, and 4 feet high. Both mound and terrace are composed of sandy loam, but the latter is much harder and

firmer than the former.   As the mound is used at the present time for a
burying place, permission was granted to sink only a single shaft in it,
which revealed nothing worthy of notice.

Mound No. 2, situated about 200 yards south of the large mound (No.
1), is circular in form, 2 feet high, and 25 feet in diameter. A thorough

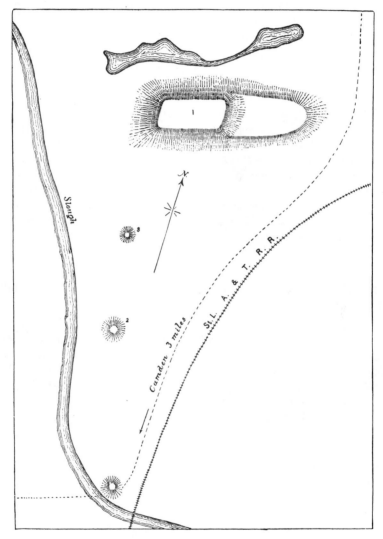

FIG. 154.—Mound group near Camden, Arkansas.

excavation showed that the upper portion to the depth of 14 inches con.
sisted of sand similar to that of the surrounding surface, and the remainder to the depth of 9 inches, of rich black loam.   In the latter were three
much decayed skeletons, the head of one toward the east, that of another north, and that of the third west.   No relics of any kind were

observed, though some fragments of pottery were picked up from the surface, which had probably been turned out by the plow.

No. 3, about the same size as No. 2, though carefully explored, revealed nothing worthy of notice.

Another conical mound near this group, 35 feet in diameter and 3½ feet high, was also examined. It was composed of loose, black loam, through which were scattered fragments of pottery and mussel shells. In the south side, at a depth of 2½ feet, was a fire bed about 10 feet in diameter and 6 inches thick. This was covered with ashes, charcoal, fragments of pottery, and mussel shells. In the south side, at the depth of 3 feet, was a single skeleton, by which lay a broken clay pipe. An oak tree, 3 feet in diameter, stands on this mound.

About 150 feet east of the last mound is a small circular tumulus with a flat top. This was composed throughout of very hard, dry, yellow clay, but contained no indications of burial, no evidences of fire, nor relic of any kind. This is somewhat remarkable, as the form and material render it more than probable, judging by what has been ascertained in regard to the mounds of this state, that it was built for a house site, and hence, according to the rule, should have contained firebeds and ashes. Possibly it was the site of a baracao or storehouse, or was built for a house site, but not used.

LOUISIANA.

The explorations in this state were confined to Washita, Catahoula, and Tensas parishes.

THE PARGOUD GROUP.

This group, located in Washita parish, consists of two mounds situated on a point of land between Washita river and Chauvin bayou. The larger one, about 28 feet high and flat on top, has had the sides cut away to obtain material for repairing the road that runs by its base. From this (as permission to explore it was refused) it was ascertained that it consists of several strata; first, a top layer, 2 feet thick, of black sandy soil, next 15 inches of yellow sand and black loam intermixed; then 18 inches of black sandy loam; next 2 feet of yellow sand, and below this, yellow sand and black loam intermixed. In the last were some pieces of pottery. The layers on the opposite side differed somewhat from the order and thickness given, though the material was the same.

The smaller mound is conical in form and only 6 feet high.

Evidences of house sites were found in the surrounding area, such as beds of burnt clay and ashes.

TROYVILLE MOUNDS, CATAHOULA PARISH.

This interesting group, a plat of which is given in Fig. 155, is located at the junction of the Tensas, Washita, and Little rivers, where the three unite to form Black river, and consists, as shown in the plat, of six mounds, an inclosing wall or embankment, and artificial ponds and canals.

The wall which incloses the area on the south and west is very nearly or quite 1 mile in length, and at the points where least disturbed from 7 to 8 feet high and 20 to 25 feet wide. The inclosed area contains about 100 acres.

The large mound (1), which is near the center of the inclosure and about

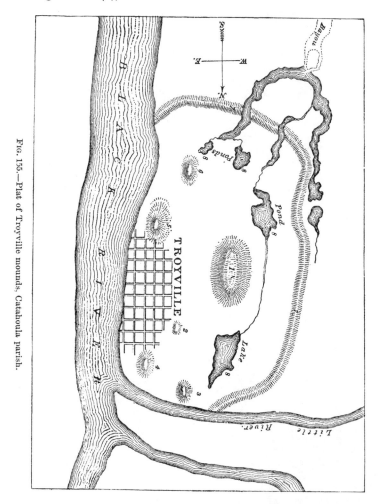

FIG. 155.—Plat of Troyville mounds, Catahoula parish.

300 yards from Black river, was originally about 250 feet long, 160 feet wide at base, and probably 60 feet high, though persons who saw it before it was disturbed say it was 75 feet high, with a nearly sharp summit. At present it is so gashed and mutilated, having been used during the war as a place for rifle pits, that its original form can scarcely be made out. It is now 45 feet high, 270 feet long, and 180 feet wide. The top can be seen back of the house in Fig. 156. From the

gashes in the side, one of which is 25 feet deep, it could be seen that it was composed chiefly of red and yellowish clay. In one of these cuts was exposed a layer of charred cane 1 foot thick extending back into the mound.

Fig. 156 shows mound 6. This is 15 feet high, 90 feet long, and 75 feet wide. Two excavations made in it proved it to be composed of a very hard, greasy clay.

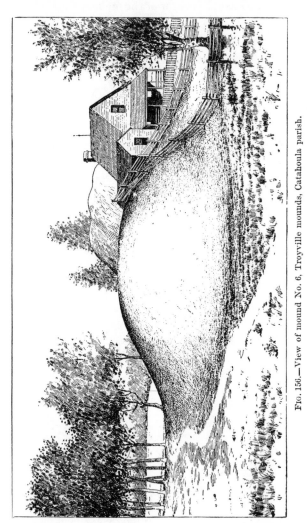

FIG. 156.—View of mound No. 6, Troyville mounds, Catahoula parish.

Mound No. 5 is 200 feet long, 90 feet wide, and 8 feet high, and covered with modern graves. In digging these, skeletons and pottery are frequently thrown out.

Mound No. 4 is nearly destroyed, but according to local information was originally 20 feet high.

Mounds 2 and 3 are also nearly destroyed. Numbers 8, 8, 8, 8 indicate four artificial ponds which were, and to a certain extent are still, connected with each other and with the bayou on the southwest by canals which are still from 10 to 12 feet wide and 5 feet deep.

As the bayou connects with the river 3 miles below, it is apparent that canoes could reach the inclosure by this route.

Two conical mounds, one 12 and the other 7 feet high, are situated on the plantation of Mrs. Brisco, in Tensas parish, 4 miles southeast of St. Joseph; but as they are occupied, one as a graveyard and the other as a rain-water cistern, they could not be excavated.

MISSISSIPPI.

COAHOMA COUNTY.

Col. P. W. Norris, who visited this section of the state, thinks that at some former period the Mississippi river ran 6 or 8 miles southward from Friars point, and then returned to where the present channel cuts across the bend westward toward Old Town. Along the eastern bank of the old channel, on the plantation of the Carson brothers, 6 miles south of Friars point, is an interesting group of mounds and earthworks. The illustrations are by Mr. Holmes, who subsequently visited the group.

The general plan of these works is shown in Pl. XI. In the northwest is an inclosure surrounded by an earthen wall and a ditch. Nos. a to f are mounds. There are also several excavations. The area embraced in the plat is about 1 mile east and west and something over half a mile north and south.

The inclosure fronts west for a distance of 738 feet on a cypress swamp, probably an open bayou or one channel of the Mississippi when these works were constructed. It is in the form of a parallelogram, the wall on three sides measuring 1,173 feet long, and embracing an area of about 5 acres. This wall is from 15 to 30 feet wide at the base, and from 3 to 5 feet high. A ditch is distinctly traceable along the whole length of the outside, but it is not exhibited on the plate.

Within this area, a little northwest of the center, is a circular mound (a), 192 feet in diameter at the base, 15 feet high, and 66 feet across the nearly flat top. There appears to have been originally a platform some 5 or 6 feet high, on which the mound proper was built. Several excavations made in the top and on the sides showed that it was composed of earth from the bottom land, probably obtained from the excavation near the southeast corner of the inclosure. A number of fire-beds of burnt clay were found near the summit and at different elevations throughout the mound. Charcoal, ashes, and fragments of pottery and stone were also discovered, but no bones. It is probable, therefore, that these spots mark the sites of houses.

Some slight elevations noticed within the inclosure were not explored but are shown on the plate.

Just outside of the southwest corner is an artificial excavation about 100 feet in diameter, but now partially filled and converted into a bog.

Mound b, shown in detail in Pl. XII, is double. There are at the bottom indications of an oval platform, probably 10 feet high, with a length of 240 feet at the base. On this, two truncated cones, which occupy the entire length, but not the entire width of the platform, rise jointly for 18 feet, and above the union rise separately 8 feet higher. The entire height of the mound from the natural surface of the land is therefore 36 feet. The cones are level on top, the one being 42 feet in diameter at this point and the other 48. On this mound, near the top of the northern cone, stands a thrifty black oak, 5 feet in diameter.

Little excavating was done in this mound and nothing of interest found, except the ever present fire-beds of burnt clay, stone chips, and fragments of pottery.

Mound c is oval and rounded on top, 210 feet long, 150 broad at the base, and 16 feet high. This mound and several smaller ones near it are so nearly masses of fire-beds, burnt clay, fragments of stone and pottery, together with more or less charcoal and ashes, as to indicate clearly that they are the sites of ancient dwellings thus elevated by accumulation of material during long continued occupancy.

Mound d, Pl. XIII, the finest of the group, is roughly pentangular and very symmetrical, level on the top, 25 feet high (including the platform), 310 feet in diameter at the base, and 210 feet across the top. Besides the broad, sloping platform, 5 feet high, on which the mound rests, there is near by, almost adjoining, a small mound which, as in many other groups, forms a kind of appendage to the large one. This is about 100 feet long, 75 feet wide, and 8 feet high, rounded on top.

Not only are beds of hard burned clay (the fragments of which show the casts of cane and grass running through it) abundant upon the surface and sides of the mound, but are also found in the wells and cisterns and in other excavations made in digging cellars and for the foundations of buildings. It is evident from this that it was used as a dwelling place or as a location for a temple or some other public building.

Mound e is double and similar in almost every respect to b. The platform is 5 feet high and 120 by 80 feet on top. Near the top of one cone is a red oak tree, 4 feet in diameter, and near the top of the other a black oak, 6 feet in diameter. In the depression between the two cones a partially decayed skeleton was found in digging a grave for a person now interred there. This skeleton was under a bed of burnt clay, and other similar beds are found near the surface of the sides and summit.

Mound f is oval, rounded on top, 150 feet long by 75 feet wide and between 5 and 6 feet high, differing but little from several others not shown on the plat. A thorough examination of this mound revealed the fact that from base to summit it was composed of burnt clay, mud, or alluvial earth in irregular layers formed of lumps or little masses burned to a brick red or actually melted into slag. Much of the top of this mound is a deposit resembling mud or clay plastering, from which the sustaining canes and timbers had been burned out, leaving their casts. It seems evident, therefore, that mud-walled and perhaps partitioned dwellings, stood here which were destroyed by fire.

PLAT OF THE CARSON MOUNDS

COAHOMA COUNTY, MISSISSIPPI.

ROAD

CARSON MANSION

THE CARSON MOUNDS, COAHOMA COUNTY, MISSISSIPPI.

EXCAVATIONS.

The places from which a part at least of the dirt was taken that was used to form the mounds are shown by the unevenness of the surface of the ground immediately around them. But there are several excavations which must have furnished a large portion of the material for this purpose. They are still so deep as to form swamps, bogs, or open ponds, some of the last being well stocked with fish.

During all the excavations made and digging done by the present proprietors, who have made all the improvements there are on the plantation, but few skeletons have been unearthed and no whole vessels of pottery found. Still, it is possible that more extensive explorations of the small mounds may reveal these, but the owner will not allow them to be disturbed.

The solid material of which the mounds are composed, together with their numerous fire beds or patches of burnt clay, are so well calculated to withstand the erosion of the elements in a region but little subject to frosts, that the lapse of time has had but little effect upon their appearance. Still, the rounding off of the parts not protected by fire-beds, the boggy character of the excavations, and the considerable accumulation of soil upon the works suggest that the town of the mound-builders located here was upon the bank of the Mississippi when this river flowed in its ancient channel, but was abandoned when it changed its bed.

The more recent works at Old Town, built apparently by people having the same customs, seem to favor this supposition.

THE DICKERSON MOUNDS.

On the Dickerson farm, 4 miles east of Friars point, is another interesting group of mounds. These are situated on the dry, gravelly bank of the Sunflower river. There is no inclosure, but several fields of the farm are literally strewn with stone chips and fragments of ancient pottery, and upon long oval hillocks are found numerous fragments of human bones.

The Sunflower is here scarcely a creek during low water and its gravelly banks are high above the floods; yet the mounds are mostly oblong or oval and flat on top, like those found on the bottoms subject to overflows. They are built as usual of the material from adjacent ground, which, being gravel instead of clay or mud, rendered the outlines of the beds of burned clay distributed through them more distinct than usual. Most of them seem to have been the sites of dwellings, the same as those upon the bottoms; yet on the intermediate areas are saucer-shaped depressions, indicating that the earth lodge so common farther north had been in use here.

Of the numerous mounds explored only one was found to be a true cemetery of the ancient inhabitants. This was, as usual, one of the least conspicuous of the group. The first tier of skeletons was barely covered and the vessels, which are usually a little higher than the skeletons, were broken into fragments, only one whole one being found in this tier. The next tier was about 2 feet below the first and the bones more decayed. Relatively fewer vessels were found and these so badly broken that but two bowls were obtained entire. The third tier was 2 feet below the second, or 5 feet from the top, and slightly below the original surface of the ground.

As less than a hundred skeletons were found here, there are doubtless other burying places in this group, but there are so many modern burials in these mounds that it was impossible to sink a pit without disturbing the skeletons of whites and negroes.

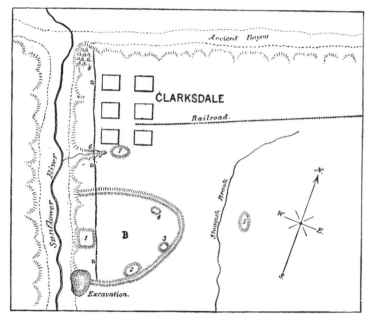

FIG. 158.—Clarksdale works, Coahoma county, Mississippi.

At Clarksdale on the Sunflower river, is a group consisting of an inclosure and six mounds. The plan of these works is presented in Fig. 158. At B is a semicircular inclosure fronting the river, the surrounding earthen wall partially obliterated by the plow, though sufficient remains to trace satisfactorily the line. The length following the curve, as ascertained by pacing, is 2,004 feet; the height where least disturbed is from 3 to 5 feet. Nos. 1, 2, 3, 4, 5, and 7 are mounds; No. 6 a wash-out, revealing a cemetery; No. 8, house sites, and in the southwest corner at the end of the wall an excavation.

The largest and most interesting of the mounds is No. 1 (Fig. 159), situated within the inclosure and directly on the bank of the river, so that the slope of the west side of the mound is continuous with the slope of the bank. It is rectangular in form, consisting first of a plat-

MOUND *b*, CARSON GROUP, COAHOMA COUNTY, MISSISSIPPI.

form 5 feet high, which forms the base, projecting as a narrow terrace on all the sides except that next the river.

Above this rises the mound proper, 20 feet high, 153 feet long at the base, and nearly 100 feet wide. The top is flat and level and on it now stands the village church, but formerly there stood on it a little conical mound 5 feet high and 25 feet in diameter, consisting as is stated almost wholly of burnt clay, charcoal, ashes, and fragments of pottery, beneath which were found a fine scallop-edged, double-eared pot and a skeleton. Every observable portion of this mound bears evidence that the mode of construction and doubtless the use made of it were the same as of those at Carson's plantation, though this group is apparently less ancient.

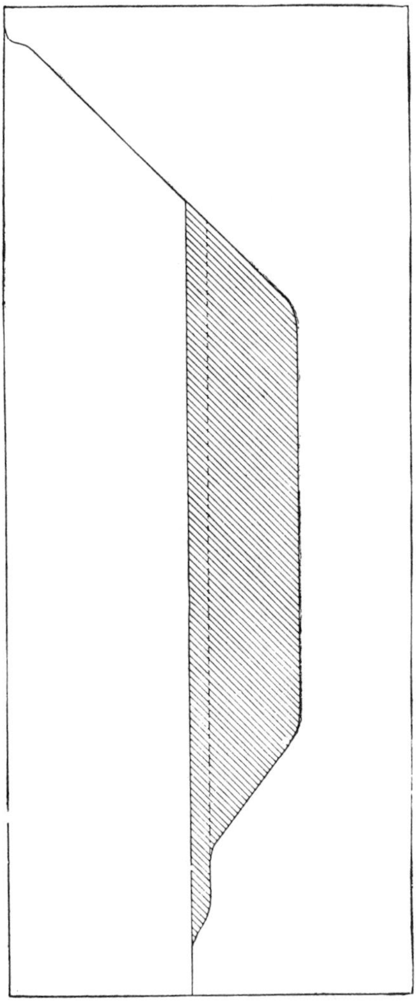

The other four mounds (2, 3, 4, and 5) are small, and of the ordinary conical form; No. 7 is but slightly elevated, and scarcely deserves to be called a mound.

No. 4, though the smallest of the group, proved to be in some respects the most interesting. It is circular, 20 feet in diameter, and 3 feet high, and little more than a heap of ashes. A trench through it showed that it consisted of ashes, charcoal, and charred animal bones, also abundant stone chips and fragments of pottery, but no entire vessels. There was still sufficient strength in the ashes to roughen the hands, affect the color of the boots, and be detected by the sense of smell; but this, though less frequent, is not unusual in the heavy fire beds of this region.

Fig. 159.—Section of mound No. 1. Clarksdale works.

Human bones having been found in grading a roadway through the low, gravelly banks of a washout at No. 6 (Fig. 158), trenches were cut in both banks. Human bones, so hard as to be cut with difficulty by the spade, were found throughout the 50 feet in length of the trench, both above and below the road (*a, a, a*), but the heaviest deposit was above the road on the north side, where they formed nearly a solid layer of skeletons scarcely a foot below the surface. So many entire skeletons were traceable that it is evident it was not a deposit of bones from scaffolds, but a burial of bodies en masse with little regard to regularity. No weapons, charcoal, ashes, or pottery were found with them, and, although tradition gives us no information in regard to them, it is probable that the burials were comparatively modern.

Mound 7, close to the burial place mentioned, was also a depository of the dead, differing from the former more in character and contents than in apparent age. The main portion of this low, dark colored mound or slightly elevated space was covered by a residence and small garden, but along a few feet of its vacant northern edge some excavations were made. The skeletons were nearly 3 feet below the surface in a single tier, lying horizontally, but without uniformity as to direction. Except the better preservation of the skeletons, the mode of burial and accompaniments and everything found in this mound were in all respects similar to the Old Town burials. But the pottery, of which only two entire vessels were obtained, like that from Dickerson's mound, is lighter colored and thinner than usual.

A coarse clay pipe, donated by Mr. John Clarke, the owner of this property, was found in an extensive line of house sites marked by patches of burnt clay at No. 8 (Fig. 158). In the excavations made among these house sites a small stone mortar, a rude celt, and two very fine ones, also many fragments of pottery, a number of fleshers and scrapers were obtained.

The largest excavation at this place is situated at the southwest corner of the inclosure. From this, in all probability, was obtained the material for building the large mound (No. 1).

During the researches made through portions of the counties of Coahoma, Bolivar, and Sunflower, for a distance of some 30 miles south of Clarksdale, a large number of ancient dwelling sites were found, having the appearance, before being disturbed, of low, flattish mounds. Many were opened and uniformly found to be mere heaps or patches of burnt clay, ashes, and the dirt accumulated during occupancy, covered by a thin layer of top soil.

SUNFLOWER COUNTY.

Not far from the shoals of Sunflower river, and in the midst of a canebrake, a mound of considerable size was discovered. The dimensions, as nearly as could be determined, are as follows: Length, 125 feet; greatest width, about 100 feet; and height to the summit of its cone, 25 feet. The apex is near the eastern end, and is surmounted by a white oak 6 feet in diameter.

Along the steep side of the eastern end was the outcropping of a bed of burnt clay in small masses or lumps, and below it some very

MOUND d, CARSON GROUP, COAHOMA COUNTY, MISSISSIPPI.

light colored fragments of pottery. Almost the first spadeful of earth revealed decaying fragments of human bones. Tracing these horizontally under the roots of the oak and under the clay bed, a skull was reached, resting on a broken platter-shaped vessel, and by the side of it a pot with a scalloped edge, a broken water bottle with female head on the top of the neck, a pottery tube, and a dipper in the form of a shell shown in Fig. 160. The portion of the platter which had been broken out to allow room for the neck of the bottle was wanting.

Another excavation was made in the top of the terrace near the middle of the mound. After cutting through a layer of brick-red chunks of burnt clay some 4 or 5 inches thick, a layer of dark colored earth something over a foot in depth was reached. Immediately beneath this

FIG. 160.—Vessel in form of a shell, Sunflower county, Mississippi.

was a medium-sized human skeleton lying horizontally on its right side. Near the skull were a broken water vessel and fragments of other vessels.

WASHINGTON COUNTY.

THE AVONDALE MOUNDS.

This group, which is shown in Fig. 161, is located on the plantation of Mrs. P. J. Sterling, 1½ miles east of Stoneville and 9 miles from Granville. The land on which they are built is a rich, level bottom, subject to overflows.

The mounds, as shown in the figure, are arranged somewhat in a semicircle. The largest, which is used as a graveyard by the whites, is 30 feet high, flat on top, and oval in form, nearly 200 feet long and about 175 broad. To the west of it is a depression of about 3 acres, from which it is probable the material was taken to build this mound. The second is 15 feet high and is covered with graves of colored people.

Numerous fragments of pottery and lumps of burnt clay, containing impressions of cane and grass, were found near the surface of the small mounds.

Cutting a trench through No. 4 (the one at the extreme left of the figure), there was reached first, a layer of sandy loam 18 inches thick, then 2 feet of burnt clay, next a layer of charcoal and ashes 18 inches thick, and thence to the base hard clay. No human bones or evidences of burial were observed.

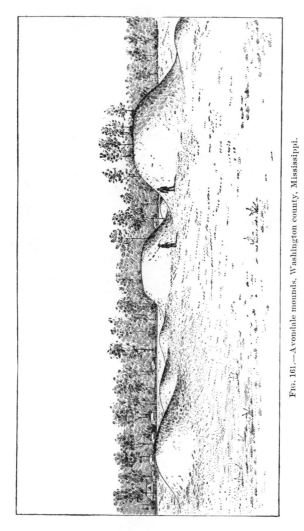

FIG. 161.—Avondale mounds, Washington county, Mississippi.

YAZOO COUNTY.

THE CHAMPLIN MOUNDS.

This group, consisting of four mounds, is situated about the center of the county, 2 miles north of Yazoo City and 2 miles east of Yazoo river. The mounds stand on low, swampy land, about half a mile from the hills, and during the flood of 1882 were surrounded by water. One of them is an irregular oval of comparatively large size, the other three are conical and smaller.

The large mound is of the form shown in Figs. 162 and 163, the first giving the contour of the base, the other a vertical section through the middle, lengthwise. The dimensions were found by careful measurements to be as follows: Length at base, from north to south, 106 feet; width of base at *a a* (Fig. 162), 50 feet; at *b b*, 36 feet; at *d d*, 38 feet; height at *a* (Fig. 163), 14 feet; at *b*, 8 feet, and at *d*, 11 feet. It was explored thoroughly down to the original surface, and found to be composed throughout of dark earth, similar to the surrounding soil of this swamp region, yet there are no excavations or depressions immediately around it from which the earth for building it could have been taken.

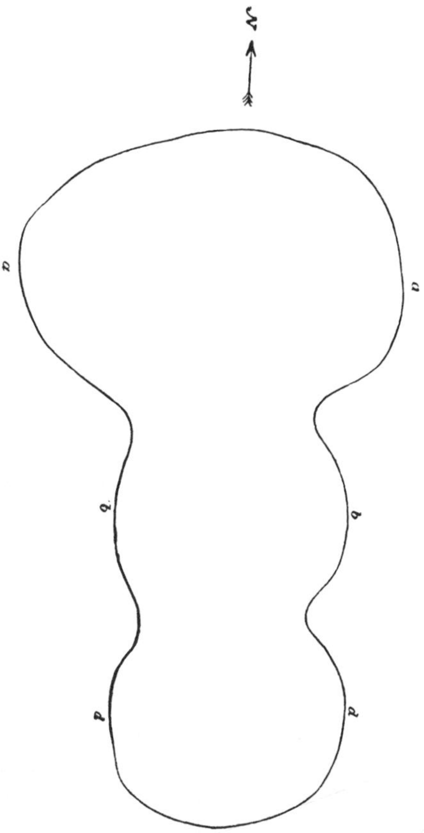

In the southern portion, at the depth of 3 feet 6 inches, were three adult skeletons about on the same level (No. 1, Fig. 163), all extended at full length. One lay with face up and head north; about the neck and wrists were a number of shell beads. Another lay also with face up, but head to the west; close by the head was a nicely polished celt. The other lay on the left side, with the head north; by the head was a polished celt and immediately in front of the face a small water bottle.

At 2, an adult skeleton lay extended on the left side, with head south. The earth immediately around it was burned hard, the bones also showing signs of fire. Mixed with this burned earth

FIG. 162.—Outline of mound No. 1, Champlin group, Yazoo county, Mississippi.

was a considerable quantity of charcoal and ashes.

At 3, same depth as 2, was the skeleton of a very young child. No relics were found with this or 2.

At the bottom of the mound, at the point marked 4, were the remains of six skeletons. These had doubtless been buried after the flesh was removed, as the bones of each had been taken apart and placed in a heap, the parts of one skeleton forming one heap. Among the rib bones of one were a few beads made of minute shells. Nothing was found with either of the other five.

Immediately under the surface of the mound at 5 was a single polished celt. At 6, 3 feet from the top, lay an adult skeleton extended on the back, head east; no relics were found with it. At 7, on the same level, was another adult skeleton lying in the same position as the last mentioned; on the breast was a polished celt. At 8 were the bones of another, separated and placed in a heap, as those previously mentioned, with a number of shell beads scattered among them. These were at the depth of 18 inches. At 9 lay the skeleton of an adult, at the depth of 3 feet, extended on the back, head west; nothing with it.

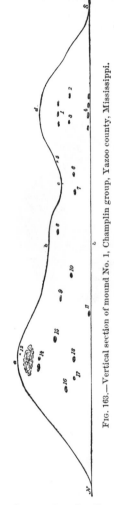

Fig. 163.—Vertical section of mound No. 1, Champlin group, Yazoo county, Mississippi.

No. 10 indicates the position of an adult skeleton at a depth of 4 feet 6 inches. This was also extended on the back, with the head east. The earth about it was unusually hard, making it impossible to get the bones out in good condition, yet the skull is sufficient to show the form, which indicates frontal pressure and backward elongation to an unusual extent.

No. 11, three adult skeletons extended, with faces up and heads east. These were lying side by side at the bottom of the mound on the natural surface of the ground, and immediately over them a covering of bark, apparently of the red oak. This consisted of a single layer of wide pieces. Nothing else was found with them.

In the northern end of the mound, immediately under the surface at the highest point, 12, was a small, red clay vessel (Fig. 164). The earth of this northern portion, to the depth of 3 feet, contained the remains of several skeletons (13), both of adults and children, which were so far decayed that their respective positions could not be determined; nor in fact was it possible to ascertain the exact number of them. Scattered among the bones were several celts, different lots of beads, and one small pot.

No. 14 indicates the position of two adult skeletons, at a depth of 4 feet, one extended on the right side, head north, the bones of the other separated and placed in a pile. Around the neck of the former were a number of shell beads.

No. 15 was the skeleton of an adult, at a depth of 9 feet, extended on the right side, head east; nothing with it.

Nos. 17 and 18, two skeletons of adults found at a depth of 10 feet; bones separated and placed in piles. No relics with them.

None of the burials in this mound were in inclosures or coffins of any kind, except the two instances where bark covering was used, as already mentioned.

All the skeletons referred to as having no relics buried with them had the heads compressed in the manner described. The others, those with ornaments or implements accompanying them, had heads of the usual type. Although this fact seems to indicate that individuals of two different tribes were buried here, it seems evident that they belonged to the same era, as there were no indications that the mound had been disturbed after it was completed.

Mound No. 2 stands 1,300 feet east of the large one and is a regular cone, 58 feet in diameter and 13 feet high. The main body was composed of dark swamp soil like that of the surrounding land, but at the bottom was a central, conical core of yellow clay, 12 feet in diameter and 3 feet high. The nearest point where the clay of which it is composed could have been obtained is half a mile away. About 3 feet beneath the apex were a few human teeth and slight traces of other bones, with which were associated a few beads made of deer horn. Immediately below the surface, on one side, an ornamented water bottle was discovered. On the top of the central clay core lay a small bed of coals and ashes some 2 or 3 feet in diameter, which contained a number of burned mussel shells.

FIG. 164.—Image vessel from Champlin mound, Mississippi.

Mound No. 3, about 700 feet from No. 2, is oval in outline, rounded on top, 35 feet long north and south, 27 feet wide, and 3 feet high. This was not explored.

No. 4, which is 275 feet due south of No. 3, is similar in form and size to the latter. It was explored and found to be composed throughout of dark, swamp soil. Nothing was discovered except a few coals.

ADAMS COUNTY.

The only mounds examined in this county are those forming the noted Selsertown group. Dr. Palmer made a hasty visit to them in 1884; subsequently, in 1887, Mr. Middleton made a careful survey of them. The description and figures here given are from Mr. Middleton's report.

These works, a general plan of which is shown in Pl. XIV, 1, consist at present of a large, circular, flat topped mound, and three others of smaller dimensions, standing upon an elevated platform, a little over 20 feet high and 5 or 6 acres in extent. They are situated in the hill country of the northern part of the county and some 6 or 7 miles from the Mississippi bottom.

The topographical features of this section are similar to those of other counties bordering on this portion of the river, consisting of the bottoms along the Mississippi and the uplands which extend back from these and form the general surface of the state. The western border of these uplands, where they join the bottoms, terminates in somewhat abrupt descents to which the term "bluffs" has been applied. In Adams county the bottoms are from 1 to 3 miles wide north of Natchez, which is the only portion of the county it is necessary to refer to. About a mile above Natchez the Mississippi river, bending eastward, strikes the foot of the bluffs, hugs them for a short distance below, and again recedes.

The general level of the uplands, some 200 or 250 feet above the bottoms, is broken by the valleys of numerous creeks and their branches, through which the water of the upper area finds its way to the Mississippi. Among the smaller streams of this immediate section is one known locally as Dunbare creek, which runs westward to the Mississippi. The country about the headwaters of this creek, where the little streams which form its branches have cut ravines, is somewhat rough and broken up into ridges, spurs, and knolls. It is here that the works mentioned are situated, about a mile northwest of the site of the old village of Selsertown, 7 miles a little west of north from Washington, and 2 miles northwest of the railroad station (Stanton).

As will be observed by reference to Pl. XIV, 1, the platform, or oblong elevation on which the mounds stand, is located on a rather narrow ridge which, starting from the higher level on the east, slopes downward gradually but irregularly toward the west, fading out in an expansion on the lower level of the creek valley a little southwest of the platform. On the north is the valley of a small creek running westward; on the south is another narrow valley or ravine in which is a small branch of Dunbare creek, running southwest. This ridge, as will be seen by reference to the figure, is quite irregular as to its surface, course, and form. Coming westward from the eastern extremity the line of highest elevation bends southward by h, terminating apparently in a spur, which was not followed out.

Following the line of the road, the descent—i to k, from the upper level h to the lower level g, of the ridge—is about 40 feet and somewhat abrupt. From k to the platform, the top of the ridge, with the exception of the rise at f, is nearly level lengthwise—that is to say, along the line of the road. The rise at f is an elongate oval knoll, from 12 to 15 feet high, and of the comparative size shown in the figure. As it is beyond all question a natural formation, no special measurement of it was made.

At the point occupied by the platform there is a sudden bend and expansion of the ridge, though the crest is near the south margin, the line running inside (north) of, but near, the southern edge of the platform.

Although the term "platform" has been used here to indicate this somewhat remarkable elevation on which the mounds are placed, Mr.

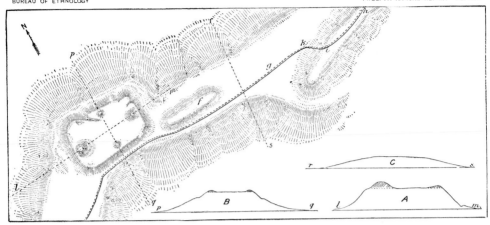

SELSERTOWN MOUND GROUP, ADAMS COUNTY, MISSISSIPPI.

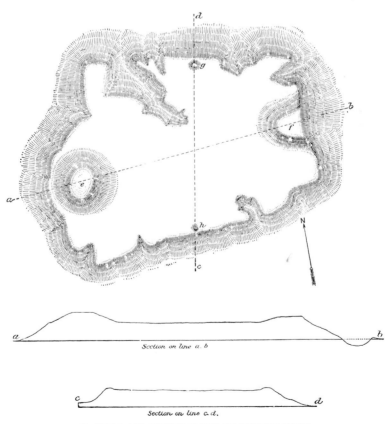

PLATFORM AND MOUNDS OF THE SELSERTOWN GROUP.

Middleton and Dr. Palmer express the opinion very confidently that it is chiefly a natural formation. This is based upon the following facts: The sudden bend and enlargement of the ridge at this point; the fact that natural knolls, or mound-like elevations, are not uncommon on the ridges of this section, as for example, the one near by at *f;* and the evidence obtained by excavating, which, so far as it was carried, sustains this view. They think it quite probable that the original form was artificially modified, so as to make the top more uniformly level and the margins more abrupt than they were formed by nature.

At the eastern end of this platform, descending northward, is an old washout or gully. The surface contour, running east and west, across the platform, the mounds, and this gully from *l* to *m* is shown in the section at *A*, and that running north and south from *p* to *q* at *B;* a section of the ridge at *r* to *s* is shown at *C*.

The shape and present condition of the platform and the mounds on it are shown in Pl. XIV, 2. The extreme length from base to base varies but slightly from 700 feet; the greatest width, which is near the west end, is about 530 feet; width at the east end, 330 feet. The extreme length of the surface area is about 590 feet; the width near the west end, 400 feet. The height varies from 21 to 45 feet, the northern and northwestern portion standing higher above the base or general slope of the ridge than the southern and eastern. The surface is comparatively level, though there are some depressions in the central portion, from which it is probable dirt was taken to be used in building the mounds.

Although the base has a somewhat regular outline, the margin of the upper surface is so cut and gashed by sharp gulleys and indentations as to give scarcely any indications of its original form.

The surface has been under cultivation for many years, but the slopes of the sides are covered with thick growths of cane, locust, sedge, and briars. The soil, which is similar to that of the surrounding area, consists of loam and red clay, mixed somewhat with sand, which, though apparently adhesive, wears away rapidly under the action of water where the surface is abraded and the vegetation removed. The two chief gullies, the one at the northwest corner and the other near the southeast corner, which have evidently been formed by washing, are probably largely due to the fact that they are the lines of drainage and are the points long used as the places of ascent and descent for persons, teams, and stock.

There are at present four mounds on this elevated area, though, according to Squier and Davis[1], there were formerly eleven. Of the four which remain, one is placed, as these authors state, about the middle of each end, that is, at the east and west margins. The other two are placed near the middle of the north and south sides. Of the other seven, no satisfactory traces were found by Mr. Middleton, but Dr. Palmer, who visited them three years before, thought he saw

[1] Anc. Mon., p. 118.

indications of other structures at points around the margin, but was inclined to the opinion that these were house sites, as fragments of pottery and pieces of burnt clay, often with fluted impressions made by split reeds, were found in abundance at such points. But neither found any traces of a central mound, and the disposition of those which remain would indicate that this central space was left unoccupied. The wearing of the mound seems also to forbid the idea of a central tumulus, as it was here the surface water seemed to collect.

The surface of the platform is strewn with fragments of pottery. On and about the smaller mounds down the northern slope, especially in the gullies or washouts, probably brought down from the top, are numerous fragments of burnt clay. This burnt clay is not in the form of bricks, nor at any point arranged in or used to form a wall. That on the slopes and in the gullies on the north side has certainly been brought down from the upper surface. It is mostly of a brick-red color and bears impressions of the split cane stamp, of which mention has heretofore been made. These have probably been taken for the impressions of fingers, an error which would have been easily corrected by observing that the curvature is outward instead of inward, as would have been the case if made by the fingers. Running through it, on what was the inner side, are the impressions of twigs and grass stems. It is in every respect similar to that observed in Arkansas, and is evidently the clay which formed the plastering of the houses, as mentioned by the French explorers, which, at the destruction of the houses by fire, was burned to the condition in which it is now found.

The largest of the four mounds, the one to which writers have generally referred, is that marked e at the western end of the platform. It is nearly circular in form, truncated but somewhat rounded on top, the slopes tolerably steep. The diameter at the base is 145 feet; the diameter of the top averages 72 feet (the upper surface being somewhat oval); height, 31 feet. It has been partially explored, but the result is not known with certainty. The last examination was made on behalf of Dr. Joseph Jones, of New Orleans, but it does not appear that he was at any time present while the excavation was going on. The depth reached was only 15 or 16 feet. This mound has, at some former time, been under cultivation, but owing, perhaps, to its steepness has been abandoned to briars and locust trees.

The next largest mound is the one marked f, at the eastern extremity of the platform. It is somewhat irregular in form but approaches in outline a semi-oval, the base resting on the margin of the platform, with which the eastern side of the mound forms a continuous slope. It is possible that cultivation of its surface and wearing away at the eastern end has somewhat changed the original form. The top is flat but irregular, the height varying from 5 to 8 feet. The diameter of the base east and west is 110 feet; the greatest diameter north and south, near the east margin, is about 3 feet less.

The other two mounds (*g* and *h*), situated near the middle of the north and south margins are circular, quite small, the one marked *g* measuring but 38 feet in diameter and 2 feet high; the other, marked *h*, 22 feet in diameter and 1½ feet high. Both have been under cultivation, which has brought to light a layer of burnt clay near the top of each, showing them to be of the same type as the low domiciliary mounds of Arkansas.

UNION COUNTY.

The group of mounds here figured (Fig. 165) is located in the southern part of Union County, Mississippi, on the SE. ¼ of Sec. 12, and NE. ¼ of Sec. 13, T. 8 S., R. 2 E.

There are fourteen mounds belonging to the group, twelve of which are together, the other two (not shown) being one east and the other west, about half a mile from the large mound, which is the most prominent of the group.

The general level of the field is about 50 feet above the creek bottoms to the north and south, which are overflowed at every hard rain.

Before the soil had been cultivated an embankment could be traced around the twelve central mounds which was about 2 feet high and 10 feet across at the base, with a ditch on the outside entirely around. The ditch was mostly and in some places entirely filled up. At present no trace of it remains and the embankment can be seen only for a few rods on the west and north sides, where it has not been plowed over. It was cut through in several places and showed no trace of wood. . This, however, is not positive evidence that no palisades existed, for it may have been washed down farther than the posts would have been sunk, the area being much worn by drains. The earth forming it is the same as the surrounding soil, and was probably thrown inward from the ditch.

Before the land was cleared timber as large as can be found in the country grew up to the ditch on the outside while inside that limit nothing grew but brush and small trees. The largest one on the embankment, cut in 1842, showed by its growth-rings that it was 52 years old. This would give a period of not more than a century in which timber has been growing on the mounds.

Dense canebrakes still exist within a few miles, which no doubt abounded in game, and in the creeks near at hand large fishes are caught in considerable numbers. The soil in this field, though now about worn out by careless tillage, was formerly very fertile.

A pond of 5 or 6 acres begins at the western line of the embankment. The earth put into the larger mound was probably taken from this point, as all the different sorts of earth used in the mounds are to be found in the field or adjacent swamps.

The line of the wall is shown as it was traced out by Mr. Parks, the first permanent settler of the country, and may not be correct, especially on the southern line. The southeast corner should be at least 100 feet farther south, or else the line should change its direction at some point as it does on the northern side. As laid down here it runs over mounds 8 and 10. From the contour of the ground it is probable that the bearing should be a little more to the south from both the

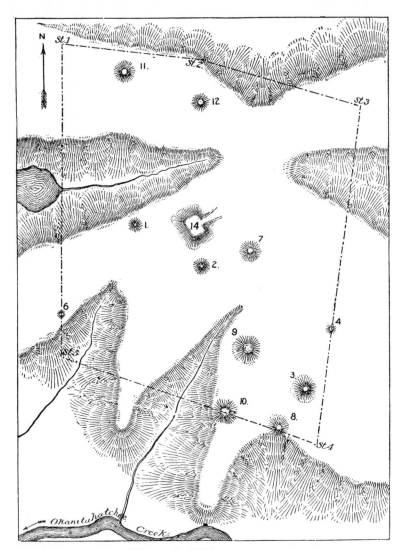

FIG. 165.—Mound group in Union county, Mississippi.

southeast and the southwest corners, and that the change in direction should take place south of mound 10.

Beginning at the northwest corner its sides measure from station to station as numbered 792, 957, 1,930, 1,505, and 1,937 feet.

In the space inclosed by mounds 3, 4, and 9 is a cemetery, as shown by the bones and numerous fragments of pottery plowed up. Some arrow-points, beads, and a number of pitted stones were found scattered about on the surface. The arrow-points are all small and chipped from water-worn pebbles of jasper, which occur in considerable quantities. With one skeleton exhumed here were found an iron pipe, some silver ornaments, copper beads, wrought nails, and a piece of glass.

The large mound is a flat-topped quadrilateral, with the longer axis nearly north and south. At the bottom, the sides, beginning with the southeast, measure 153, 210, 177 and 234 feet; on the top 87, 124, 94 and 119 feet. From these measurements it will be seen that the slope of the sides is not uniform and that they are quite difficult to ascend. On the northeast side is a graded way, 20 feet wide at the top and running out 45 feet from the base. This figure (20 feet) probably represents its original width on top along the whole length, though it is now much worn down. The height of the mound is 27 feet.

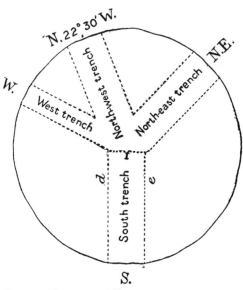

The numbers of the small mounds refer, for the first eight, to the order in which they were opened. In every case the dirt was removed down to the original soil and far enough outwardly to make it certain that the

FIG. 166.—Plan of mound No. 1, group in Union county, Mississippi.

limit of the mound was reached. Trenches, varying in width from 6 to 10 feet, were carried to the center, then run to the edge in another direction and space cleared out about the center sufficient to show that nothing of interest remained. "Surface" refers to the original soil beneath the mound, and "center" to the line directly down from the highest point. All the mounds except the first have been plowed over until they are probably 3 to 5 feet lower than when built.

Mound 1, located nearly west of the large mound, was the most prominent of the smaller ones. The first trench in this was made from the south side. (See Figs. 166, showing plan of trenches, and 167, and 168 showing sections of south trench.)

Sixteen feet from the center, resting on the surface, was a mass of loose, cloddy dirt measuring 3½ by 2 feet and extending 3½ feet up. It was such a condition as would result from a small coffin's decaying and

letting the earth above it fall in, though careful search failed to show
any traces of wood. On the bottom were found a skull, lying face
upward, some bones of the arm and neck, and the head of a femur, all

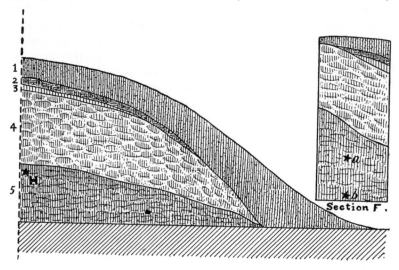

Fig. 167.—Sections along south trench, mound No. 1, Union county, Mississippi.

so badly decayed as to crumble almost at a touch. The teeth showed
that it had been a person not over middle age. Very fine particles of
galenite were adhering to the skull and to the earth in contact with it.

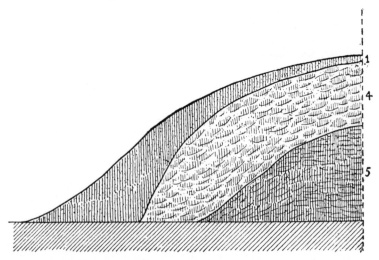

Fig. 168.—Section along south trench, mound No. 1, Union county, Mississippi.

A number of shell beads, some the entire shells of a small marine species
others cut from a large shell and drilled, lay with the skull. The frontal
bone was saved; it showed no depression at the root of the nose, and

one orbit was lower than the other, probably the result of an injury. The small size of the burial place, the position of the bones and the galenite sticking to the skull go to show that only the skeleton had been buried.

Lying west of these bones, in the hard dirt, was a scapula belonging to a larger person than the last, along with other bones too badly decayed and broken to tell what they were; also a few shell beads. At 10 feet from the center and 4 feet from the surface was a small pile of ashes with the dirt slightly burnt below, showing that a fire had been made when the mound had reached that stage and afterwards covered up before the place had been disturbed. Three feet above the surface at the center, in hard dirt, was a badly decayed skull of an old person, and one cervical vertebra. Lying on the original surface at the center were some fragments of thick, red pottery and a small amount of charcoal. Six inches above the bottom a thin seam of red clay was continuous for 3 or 4 feet around the center.

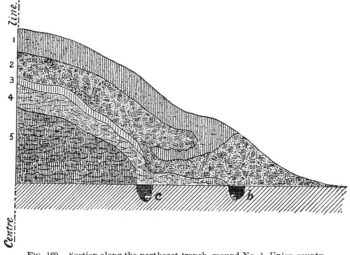

FIG. 169.—Section along the northeast trench, mound No. 1, Union county.

The next trench was run in from the northeast (see Figs. 169 and 170). Twenty-one feet from the center there was a depression of 6 inches where soil had been removed down to underlying red clay which was so hard as to be difficult to loosen with a pick. In this clay two holes, marked (*a*, Fig. 170, and *b*, Fig. 169), had been dug 6 feet apart, one north of the other. Each was a foot across and 3 feet deep, rounded at the bottom, and filled with a shiny gray ooze. In the one to the south was found a piece of skull bone, in the northern one nothing but the soft mud or slime. Fourteen feet from the center were two similar holes, one 14 inches across and 3 feet deep, the other 3 feet south of it of the same depth and 18 inches across. One is shown at *c*, Fig. 169. No traces of bones were found in these. They were filled with the same gray dirt as the first two, though it was not quite so wet. The dirt for 2 or 3 feet above all these holes was much looser than that at the sides, as if something had been placed over them which afterward gave way. Eleven feet from the center the surface rose to its natural place, making a step of 11 inches, showing that the depression was not carried on a level.

On the south side of this trench, 5 feet from the surface, were three graves, 11, 7, and 4 feet, respectively, from the center. Each was filled with loose dark dirt and surrounded by a mass of very hard clay, which showed no marks of burning, but seems rather to have been packed wet and allowed to dry before being covered over. In the first, which was 2 feet long and 18 inches across, no signs of bones appeared; in the second were the bones of the right forearm and the lower extremities, which were in their proper position and lay with the feet toward the southwest. Under the head of the right femur was a piece of rib,

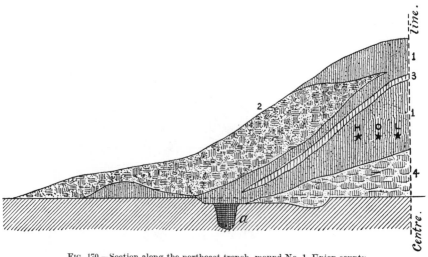

and under the middle of it the right half of a lower jaw, with the wisdom tooth just through the bone. The femur measured 17 inches and the tibia was not flattened. A few drilled shell beads, some large, others small, were found with the bones of the arm.

In the last grave were traces of wood, probably the remains of bark wrapping, which fell to dust on being touched. This grave lay toward the southeast, intersecting the second one at about 4 feet from the edge of the trench. Each was 2 feet across.

The peculiar arrangement of the dirt in this mound led the explorer to run another trench from between the north and northwest. (Figs. 171 and 172.) Eighteen feet from the center, 2 feet from the surface, were some small fragments of bones and a few human teeth. Fifteen feet from the center, on the same level, were fragments of a skull and teeth, all too decayed for handling. A foot above these were the bones of the arm and leg of another person broken up and laid in a pile. Twelve feet from the center, 4 feet from the surface, were fragments of a very thin skull with particles of galenite adhering to them. Eight feet from the center was a hole sunk a foot into the original soil and filled with loose black dirt and ashes, in which were traces of unburnt wood. From this hole a layer of unmixed ashes from 1 to 6 inches in thickness reached 6 feet to the south and west, sometimes on the surface and again several inches above it. Five feet from the center, 8½ feet from the surface, was the outer whorl of a conch shell.

A trench was next run in from the west. Eighteen feet from the center was a layer of ashes, 6 feet in diameter, 18 inches from the surface at its middle point and curved upward toward every side, or, in other words, dished. Lying on this was the lower part of the skeleton of a medium-sized man, with the feet toward the north. No bones of the

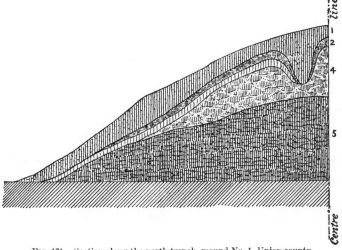

FIG. 171.—Section along the north trench, mound No. 1, Union county.

pelvis or parts above were found, although the leg bones were well preserved. Three feet above the surface the skeleton of a large, strongly-built man lay extended at full length with the face up, the head toward the east and about six feet from the center. The skull was obtained almost entire. Under it were thirteen water-worn quartz pebbles. The femur measured 18½ inches. There was no clay or hard dirt packed around the frame nor any evidence that a fire had been made where it lay, although the leg bones had fine charcoal sticking to them. The humerus was perforated near the elbow.

The arrangement of the dirt in this mound indicates that the original mound was much smaller than it is now and that the skeleton embedded in the ashes was at the center. Afterward the mound was added to on the eastern side. A glance at the sections figured makes this plain.

12 ETH——18

The lenticular masses show that the dirt had been carried in baskets or skins and thrown in without any attempt at stratification in the older part of the mound. These masses were from 12 to 18 inches across and from 4 to 6 inches thick. The lower side, as they lay in the mound, was always darker in color than the upper side. Occasionally a little charcoal or a fragment of bone or pottery occurred in the mound.

Nothing was found in mound 2 except a small piece of pottery of very neat design that had probably been dumped in with the dirt. This mound was made up of soil lying close at hand and the dirt was in layers of regular thickness, as though it had been spread when deposited. On the southeast edge was a layer of mingled dirt and charcoal, 6½ feet across, from 2 to 4 inches in thickness; a large amount of broken pottery was found scattered through it, but no ashes. This lay partly a foot below the top of the ground and partly on the surface.

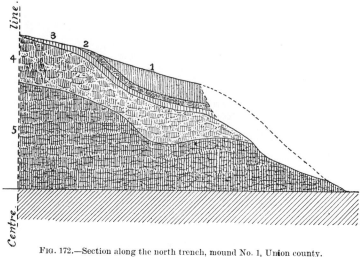

FIG. 172.—Section along the north trench, mound No. 1, Union county.

At a distance of 75 feet west of the center of mound 3 was a fireplace, on the original surface, covered with a foot of dirt that had washed down from the mound. The mingled ashes, charcoal, and dirt measured 5 feet across and 15 inches thick at the middle, running out to a thin edge and packed very hard. Along with pieces of pottery and animal bones was a piece of iron that had apparently been a brace for a saddle bow. This was 8 inches under the top of the ashes and below most of the pottery found.

Sixty feet from the center appeared a layer of gray clay, from 1 to 3 inches thick. It was continuous under as much of the mound as was removed. In the trench on the west side was found one blade of a pair of scissors. Three feet above the surface at the center was an ash bed 6 inches thick in the middle, 6 feet in diameter, curving upward or dish-shaped and running to an edge on every side. It rested directly upon dirt that had been dumped like that in the first mound, and was in very thin layers as though many successive deposits had been made and spread out. Within an inch of the bottom was a small piece of greenish glass, apparently broken from a glass bottle. Resting upon the ashes, though of less extent, was a mass 12 inches thick of charcoal, dirt, ashes, and broken pottery, in which lay an iron knife and a thin silver plate stamped with the Spanish coat of arms, Fig. 173. At the top was a thin layer of charcoal where a fire had been extinguished; this was at a lower point than had ever been reached by the plow. There was a want of conformity between this mass and the surrounding dirt, which shows it may have been of later origin; that the mound had been opened after its completion and afterward restored to its former shape; but the bed of ashes was undoubtedly as old as the mound itself, so that, although the iron knife and silver plate offer no positive proof as to age, the piece of glass is strong evidence that the mound was constructed after its builders had dealings with the whites. It may be remarked here that this group is located in the area occupied by the Chickasaws.

At about 40 feet from the center the dirt began to show the same arrangement of dumping as was seen in mound 1.

Mound 4 was made throughout of a heavy gray clay, such as forms the ground to the north of it. The embankment ran, according to local belief, directly over this mound; it was, therefore, closely examined for any signs of palisades, but without success; nor is there now the slightest indication here of either wall or ditch. A small amount of mingled dirt and charcoal appeared at what seemed to be the center of the mound, but this was evidently thrown in at the time it was built to help fill up.

FIG. 173.—Silver plate, with Spanish coat of arms; mound, Union county.

Mound 5, not shown in the figure, is outside the inclosure to the east. A wide trench through it exposed thirteen skulls with a few fragments of other bones. They were all within 10 feet of the center and arranged in three layers, the first on the surface, the second nearly 2 feet above, and the third at about the same distance above that. The skulls belonged to persons of different ages, from the child whose first teeth were beginning to appear, to the aged individual whose teeth were worn to the gums. With the oldest was a burnt clay pipe, the only relic found in the mound. The bones were put in without regard to position; a skull and a rib, for example, or a femur and a jawbone lying together. The mound was of the same dirt as the surrounding soil, except a deposit of gray clay a foot thick and 3 feet across at the center, about half of it lying below the original surface. Only one skull found here was in a condition to be preserved; all, however, were of one shape and that very like the modern Indian skull.

Mound 6, like mound 4, was on the supposed line of embankment. No trace of wood in the mound or of a ditch outside could be seen. It was formed of dirt gathered close around. Probably mounds 4 and 6 were at a break in the embankment forming a passageway through it.

Mound 7 showed at 55 feet east of the center a layer of gray clay, nowhere more than an inch in thickness, which ran 18 feet, then gave way for 9 feet to a layer of black soil, after which it reappeared and was found under all the remaining part excavated. The dirt showed the same marks of dumping as in mounds 1 and 3, and is of different colors, though all from around the mound. More charcoal and burnt dirt was found in this than in any other mound opened, but it seems to have been thrown in simply because it was convenient, being scattered here and there in small patches.

Thirty-five feet from the center and 3 feet from the surface in mingled ashes, dirt, and charcoal, with a few decayed bones, were a number of fragments of pottery, pieces of one vessel which was broken before being covered. The whole was inclosed in very hard clay. It does not seem to have been a grave, but rather a place used for cooking.

Twenty-one feet from the center and 5 feet from the surface was a tibia lying east and west; 5 feet west of it was a skull. Both were too soft to be removed. No bones were found between them, but both belonged to one individual whose body had been placed in a bed of gray sand and surrounded by ashes, charcoal, swamp mud, and burnt clay. It seems to have been an intrusive burial. Two feet southwest of the skull was a decayed femur; no other bones were with it.

All the dirt about the center of this mound was very wet and heavy, and was brought from the swamp to the northeast. The arrangement and material of the mound show that dirt had been carried in from different places at the same time. Occasionally a layer of one material could be traced 3 or 4 feet, and then be lost in some other.

Mound 8 was built partly on the slope of the ravine to the west. A layer of gray clay, averaging 4 inches in thickness, had been spread on the surface and the mound built upon it. The bottom of the mound on the western side sloped upward toward the center, following the inclination of the surface. Twenty-four feet from the center began a deposit of sticky mud from the creek bottom, which measured 2 feet in thickness at the center. The remainder of the mound was composed of about equal parts of this bottom mud and the soil near by, dumped in without any order or regularity. At the center, near the top of the mound, was a deposit of yellow sand 3 feet across in very thin curved layers, about 4 inches thick at the middle and curving to an edge at the sides. Under this was a hole a foot across and the same in depth, having a bottom of hard blue clay and filled with ashes, black dirt, and charcoal.

Near the center were some shreds of a coarse woven cloth. Six feet north of the center, in the original soil, was a hole 18 inches across and 14 inches deep, the sides burnt hard as brick, filled with charcoal and dirt. Seven feet northeast of the center was a similar but smaller hole. The gray layer at the bottom was undisturbed over both these spots, showing that the mound was built after this part of the field had been occupied.

The swamp mud ran out at 30 feet north and northeast of the center. Twenty-two feet from the center, toward the north, a deposit of gray clay, varying from a few inches to 4 feet in thickness, began and reached nearly to the edge of the mound. The dumped dirt ended at 60 feet from the center.

The field being in cultivation, none of the other mounds could be opened, except one, and there was nothing about that to indicate that it would repay investigation.

If the large mound be considered a place of residence, the most probable theory, it is not plain what use was made of the smaller ones. It is evident that those within the inclosure, with the exception of the first one opened, were not intended or used for burial purposes.

EXPLANATORY NOTES.

The courses and distances of the line of wall, as traced and located by the old settlers, are as follows, commencing at station 1, the northwest corner:

From station.	Bearing.	Distance.
		Feet.
1 to 2 ..	S. 83° E.......	792
2 to 3 ..	S. 74° E.......	957
3 to 4 ..	S. 7° 45′ W ...	1,930
4 to 5 ..	N. 77° 45′ W .	1,505
5 to 1 ..	N. 1° E	1,937

The smaller mounds were located by bearings from the center of the large mound, but the distances to all except 11 and 12 were measured from the south corner; for 11 and 12 the measurements were from the north corner. Mounds 5 and 13 are not shown on the plat.

Mound No.	Bearing.	Distance.	Diameter.	Height.
		Feet.	Feet.	Feet.
1.....	N. 88°W	352	64	14
2.....	S. 10½°E....	165	100	4
3.....	S. 34½°E.....	1056	120	6
4.....	S. 53½°E.....	891	54	2
5.....	S. 80°E......	½ mile.	50	4
6.....	S. 58°W.....	792	28	3
7.....	S. 66½°E.....	330	120	7
8.....	S. 23°E......	1,155	120	6
9.....	S. 23½°E.....	693	150	7
10.....	S. 9½°E......	990	160	8
11.....	N. 24½°W ...	891	120	4
12.....	N. 2½°E.....	561	90	3
13.....	N. 70°W....	½ mile.	Plowed level.	....

Pond, N. 75° W.   Dirt for the large mound was probably taken from the excavation which begins at the wall.

The passageway or ramp that extends from the top of the large mound to the ground is at the middle of the northeast side, beginning 79 feet from the east corner, and on the line of the base of the mound is 46 feet wide.   It is 20 feet wide at the top of the mound, and extends outward 45 feet from the base of the mound, with the corners at the bottom so rounded that they are 20 feet within the lines of the sides.

Figs. 167 (A and F) and 168 show the sides and end of the south trench; Fig. 167 A, the left or west side of the trench, and F, the north end; Fig. 168, the right or east side.   In these 1 is surface soil; 2, gray clay; 3, red clay; 4, red soil in lumps or masses; *a*, position of skull; *b*, position of pottery, and *h*, grave going a foot into the wall.

Figs. 169 and 170 show the sides of the northeast trench, same mound; Fig. 169, side toward northwest; and Fig. 170, side toward southeast. The numbers indicate the strata as follows: No. 1, red, top soil mixed with clay; 2, yellow, bluish, and gray clays and dark soil mingled in confusion; 3, gray clay from the swamp; 4, red soil in lens-shaped masses; 5, dark soil in lens-shaped masses.   *a* indicates a grave sunk in the original soil to the depth of 3 feet, filled with shining gray mud and containing part of a human skull; *b* and *c* similar pits.   H, O, L, three graves 5 feet above the original surface extending southward.

Figs. 171 and 172 represent the sections of the northwest trench, same mound; Fig. 171, east side; Fig. 172, west side.   The numbers indicate the layers as follows: 1, top soil; 2, gray clay; 3, red clay; 4, red soil in lumps or small masses; 5, black soil in lumps or small masses.

TENNESSEE.

LAUDERDALE COUNTY.

On the farm of Mr. Marley, 8 miles northwest of Ripley, are a number of small mounds, most of which had been dug over thoroughly.   Only

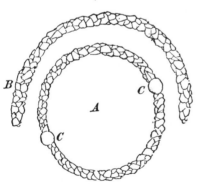

one small one remained undisturbed. In this was found an old walled fireplace, circular in form, 3 feet high and about 1 foot thick, the inside half full of ashes.   Back of this (outside) was a semicircular wall, also of burnt clay, 3 feet high and about 1 foot thick.   The annexed figure (174) gives an idea of the form and relation of these walls.   The complete circle A represents the wall around the fireplace, and B the semi-

FIG. 174.—Fireplace in mound, Lauderdale, Tenn.

circular outer wall, which was on the north side and originally may have been higher, as it reached the surface of the ground.   The little circles C C are two very smooth circular appendages or lumps of burnt clay on the wall.   Close to this fireplace were two broken dishes mixed with the burnt clay.

OBION COUNTY.

REELFOOT LAKE MOUNDS.

Around Reelfoot lake are several groups of mounds, mostly of small size. About half a mile southwest of Idlewilde four low mounds, not exceeding 2 feet in height, were examined. Below the top soil was a layer several inches thick of ashes and charcoal, in which were mussel shells, bones of birds, fishes, and quadrupeds; also, stone implements and fragments of pottery, but no burnt clay.

At the crossing, on the northwest border, another group of somewhat larger mounds was visited, but only one could be opened; it was composed entirely of clay and contained no relics.

A small group on Grassy island was also examined. One of these, circular in form and 8 feet high, was thoroughly explored, yielding a rich return for the labor spent upon it. It consisted chiefly of dark vegetable mold without any indications of layers. Fifteen skeletons were unearthed; eight of them were unaccompanied by anything except ashes and charcoal. By the others, vessels and implements were discovered as follows: By one, a stone spade and two pots; by another, two pots; by another, a drinking vessel in the form of a kneeling female, shown in Fig. 175, and two pots, one in-

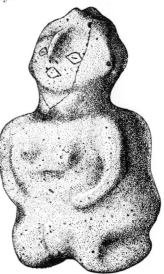

FIG. 175.—Image vessel from mound, Obion county, Tennessee.

side of the other; by the fourth, three pots; and by three others, one pot each. Another vessel was found embedded in a mass of ashes $2\frac{1}{2}$ feet thick, in which were also bird, fish, and quadruped bones, more or less charred. Several stone implements were also found scattered through the mound.

Another mound of this group, 6 feet high, was excavated and found to consist entirely of sandy loam. Nothing was discovered in it.

Two other mounds on the opposite shore of the lake, conical in form and about 7 feet high, yielded a similar result.

KENTUCKY.

While nearly all of southeastern Missouri below Cairo is level and subject to overflow during great floods, the bottoms on the Kentucky side opposite are usually narrow and the river skirted or directly flanked by bluffs, mainly of yellow clay, rising from 100 to 400 feet above it. These are cut by many creeks and rivulets, thus forming numerous headlands, easily rendered defensible, a number of which are occupied by ancient earthworks. Of the five of these visited the most interesting is in Hickman county, about 3 miles west of Oakton, and known locally as O'Byam's Fort.

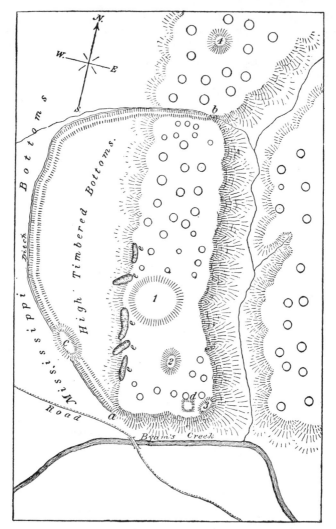

FIG. 176.—O'Byam's fort, Hickman county, Kentucky.

This work, illustrated in Fig. 176, is, as is usual in this region, upon the best position for defense in that immediate section, being located on the extreme point of a bluff some 50 feet high and almost vertical at its southern end. It consists of an inclosing wall and ditch, mounds, excavations, and hut rings.

The length of the wall and ditch from *a* around to *b*, following the irregular curve, is very nearly **600** paces, or about 1,800 feet. There is no wall along the steep bluff facing east and south. Of these outlines the southern end is so steep as to render ascent impracticable; the eastern slope is almost equally so; the northern line was well defended by embankment and ditch, and for the remainder of the circuit the embankment follows the edge of the high bottom, including in the line the isolated hillock c. Mound 3, in the extreme southeast corner, is in a fine position for observation and to prevent any attempted ascent at this corner, the most accessible point on the unwalled line of the bluffs.

The best, if not the only, ford of O'Byam's creek in this vicinity is a rock or gravel bar where the road crosses at the lower end of the bluff.

In the plan of these works (Fig. 176), 1, 2, and 3 are mounds within the inclosure and 4 a mound outside; c, a natural mound or little hillock; d, a cemetery, and e e e e e excavations. The small circles, which continue northward beyond the wall, are small saucer-shaped depressions marking the sites of ancient dwellings.

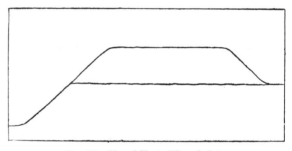

Mound No. 1, as shown upon the plan of the works, extends fully halfway across a narrow portion of

Fig. 177.—Mound No. 1, O'Byam's fort.

the bluff, and is a true flat-topped or truncated mound (Fig. 177) in all respects similar in appearance to and possibly of the same age and built by the same people as those across the Mississippi, which are now the only refuge of white men and their stock during floods. But as this and the other mounds on this side of the river are on high places, beyond the reach of the greatest flood, the object in view in building them could not have been to escape inundation.

It is very nearly a true circle 78 feet in diameter on the top and so steep on all sides that, although 23 feet high, it has a base of only 125 feet and has been covered and surrounded by a heavy growth of oak, ash, and other timber. It stands on the margin of the upper level. A number of white persons have been buried on the summit, so that entensive explorations could not be made; nevertheless enough was ascertained to prove it to be composed chiefly of yellow clay, but in successive layers and containing fire-beds of clay burnt to a brick-red color. These fire-beds differed from those usually seen, in that, while some were made of irregularly shaped little masses, approximately the size of an ordinary brick, and well burned before being laid down, each mass leaving an impression in the earth when removed, others were red upon the top only, the color gradually diminishing toward the under side as though burned by long-continued fires. The masses were probably the broken plastering of upright walls, while the other layers were parts of the hard clay floor. Charcoal, ashes, and the charred bones of animals were found with these fire-beds.

HUT RINGS.

With the exception of a small open court south of No. 1 the entire area of that portion of the inclosure or fort upon the bluff, much of the bottom, and also of the adjacent bluffs on the north and east, are literally covered by these small, circular depressions surrounded by earthen rings, indicating a considerable population.

Pits were dug in many of these, but only the usual fire-beds, charcoal, ashes, fragments of pottery, broken animal bones, and rude stone implements were found.

EXCAVATIONS.

The excavations for the mounds in this place are within the inclosure and on the side of the bluff, those near mound No. 1 being as clearly defined and as unmistakable as though but of recent date.

CEMETERY.

Mound No. 2 is said to have been once used for burial purposes, but the skeletons and accompanying relics have been removed to make place for graves of modern times. At d, near mound 3, was found a small elevation, less than 30 feet square, which had not been disturbed, and proved to be a true ancient cemetery. There was but one tier of skeletons in it, at the depth of 2 feet from the surface. Only 11 were found, lying in all directions and without any apparent system, except that they were not doubled upon each other. All seemed to be skeletons of adults. Some vessels were with them, but never more than one with a skeleton. Among the specimens discovered here was a clay rubber or muller.

Mound No. 2 is oblong, 80 by 50 feet and 5 feet high. No. 3, nearly round, 50 by 40 feet and 4 feet high, was opened, but nothing was found in it. No. 4, circular, 60 feet in diameter and 5 feet high, was opened and found to be composed of yellow clay and soil mixed; no relics or specimens in it.

On what are known as McCard's bluffs, 3 miles below O'Byam's Fort, is another group of low mounds, fire-beds, fragments of stone implements, broken pottery, and other evidences of an ancient village, but there is no inclosing wall.

PECULIAR CONICAL MOUNDS.

Here and there among the ancient works of this region are certain conical mounds, sometimes in groups or irregular lines and on the high ridges, which differ so materially from those already mentioned as to lead to the belief that they are the work of a different people. They range in size from 30 to 80 feet in diameter and from 4 to 10 feet in height, but are all true circular mounds and more than usually symmetrical in form. By excavations made in them it was ascertained that they are composed almost entirely of fine, soft, molding sand, unstratified and without any intermixture of clay or other material; nor were there any fire-beds, ashes, charcoal, or vestiges of art, or indications of burial in them, save here and there an occasional rude stone scraper.

While the material of the other mounds of this region is evidently from the earth immediately about them, these circular mounds are formed of a very fine molding sand from some unknown source.

A few mounds were observed in Ballard county about 5 miles above Cairo, but no special examination of them was made.

ALABAMA.

LAUDERDALE COUNTY.

This, the extreme northwestern county of the state, is bounded along its entire southern margin by the Tennessee river. The works described are situated on or near the north bank of this river.

STAFFORD MOUND.

This is an elongate oval mound, located a little over a mile south of Florence on the farm of Mr. S. C. Stafford, some 35 or 40 yards from the river bank. It is 8 feet high, flat on top, the length on top, north and south, 85 feet, and at the base about 125 feet; width about half the length.

A trench 10 feet wide and 15 feet long was dug in the northern end, the remainder of the upper portion having been much disturbed. When the trench had been extended southward the distance of 15 feet a layer of burnt clay was encountered at the depth of 2 feet, the 2-foot layer above it consisting of sandy soil. Immediately under the clay was a layer of ashes. Immediately under this was the much-decayed skeleton of a half-grown person lying on its side. At the back of the head was a wide-necked, bottle-shaped water vessel, tipped sidewise; by the side of it lay a stone disk which had apparently been used as a cover to the vessel. At each side of the head stood a small pot. Here the clay layer was between 4 and 5 inches thick and below this was a layer of ashes and charcoal 3 inches thick. The charcoal in this layer was burned from small sticks and brush. A few inches from the head of the skeleton mentioned was a piece of charred wood firmly fixed in the earth, apparently the remains of a post. A few inches from the skeleton at the outer edge of the burnt clay, on the east side, were pieces of pottery somewhat resembling tile. The soil being removed, it was found that the clay bed and layer of ashes gave out toward the northwest, at the end of 7½ feet in this direction. About 4 feet south of the skeleton mentioned was a hearth of burnt clay, on which was a thick layer of ashes. This hearth was in the form of an irregular square, 2½ feet in diameter and 2 inches thick; near by were a few fresh-water shells. A few inches over 7 feet south of the skeleton and at the same depth the much-decayed skeleton of a child, face down and head northward, with a pot at each side of the head. Here was another corner of the clay bed. By working westward along the edge for the distance of a little over 7 feet another skeleton was found nearly turned to dust; by it was only one pot, and near it another fireplace like the one before described. All the corners of what appeared to have been the floor of a house were worked out; then the middle of the square, which contained nothing but the top soil, the clay bed, and ash layer were removed to the sandy loam of the base. When the trench had been extended southward to a point about 32 feet from the south end a layer of burnt cane 2½ feet below the surface of the mound, but little more than an inch thick, was discovered, covering an area about 6 feet in diameter. The canes were in very small pieces. Near the middle of the mound, at the depth of 8 feet and apparently on the original surface of the ground, was a burnt-clay hearth or fireplace, about 2½ feet in diameter, circular in form, and covered with a layer of ashes. Two cylindrical pieces of charcoal about 3 inches in diameter were found in the earth just outside of the fireplace on the west side, probably the remains of posts. Twenty feet from the south end, at the depth of 6½ feet, was a layer of ashes, charred grass, and sticks, about 2 inches thick and covering a circular space about 6 feet in diameter. Scattered through the earth of the mound were fragments of pottery, animal bones, flint chips, and a few stone implements. The mound is overflowed by the greater freshets of the Tennessee river.

DOUGLASS MOUNDS.

Near lock No. 10 of the Mussel Shoals canal survey, about 12 miles east of Florence, are two mounds on the Douglass farm. They are about half a mile from the river on an elevated hill overlooking the valley. The two are about 50 feet apart, each 30 or 35 feet in diameter, 3 feet high, and composed throughout of red clay, which extends somewhat below the original surface of the ground. Here and there just below the surface of one were rude flint hoes, arrow points, and lance heads; near the surface of the other were four large rude stone implements. No skeletons, burnt clay, ashes, or charcoal were found in either.

The country immediately about the Mussel Shoals was occupied by Cherokees when the first whites settled here. This area has long been noted for the number of worked and partially worked flint implements which have been found scattered over it. As the stone from which they are manufactured is found at this place, this will doubtless account for their abundance here.

MADISON COUNTY.

Near Whitesburg, on the north bank of the Tennessee river, is a long, narrow shell heap, between 400 and 500 yards in length and about 3 or 4 feet high; at present it is only a few yards in width, but was probably wider in former times, as a portion on the river side appears to have been carried away by the freshets.

The residents of the place say that many skeletons, stone implements, and pottery vessels have been washed out of it. Three badly decayed skeletons were found at one point about 18 inches below the surface; near by were ashes and some broken stones, as though marking the site of a temporary fireplace or camp fire. A thick layer of shells covered these skeletons. Another skeleton was discovered at the depth of 3 feet, and near it ashes and broken stones, as in the other case; a third lay only 6 or 8 inches below the surface; a fourth near the river had been partly washed away; a broken pot stood by the side of it.

Numerous pieces of pottery, arrowheads, stone implements, and a copper bead were scattered among the mussel shells. Not only has this bank been disturbed by floods, but at one time large buildings stood on it, which were carried away by high water.

The fact that a portion of the shells forming this heap bear the marks of fire suggested the thought that they had been heated by the Indians to compel them to open. A great number of split, water-worn stones were scattered through the bank to the depth of 3 feet, sometimes loosely and without order, but frequently in such relation as to indicate an intentional arrangement; in this case they were accompanied by ashes, as though marking the places where fires had been built for cooking purposes.

MARSHALL COUNTY.

About 1 mile west of Guntersville is a cave known as Hampton cave. Its floor is covered to the depth of 4 feet with fragments of human bones, earth, ashes, and broken stones. This fragmentary condition of the deposits is chiefly due to the fact that they have been repeatedly turned over by treasure-hunters. Much of this deposit has been hauled away in sacks for fertilizing the land. The number of dead deposited here must have been very great, for, nothwithstanding so much has been removed, there is yet a depth of 4 feet, chiefly of broken human bones. A fine specimen of the copper, spool-shaped ornament supposed to have been worn in the ear was obtained here by Mr. James P. Whitman, who kindly presented it to the bureau.

BLOUNT COUNTY.

A cave in this county containing human remains is worthy of notice. The remains in this case were deposited in troughs, or canoe-shaped coffins, differing in this respect from any that have been mentioned. This, which is known as Cramp's cave, is 15 miles south of Blountville. In the back part is a large crevice, where it is stated the bodies were deposited in the coffins. The place is certainly well adapted for security from wild animals, as a few stones would suffice to close this room or crevice; moreover, it is much the driest portion of the cave. Persons who saw the remains at the time they were found state that they were in a good state of preservation; that the troughs were covered with matting made of bark or cane and bound around with withes or bark. Among the things found with them were wooden bowls and trays. Portions of one or two of these troughs were forwarded to and received by the Smithsonian Institution. Although the place had been thoroughly worked over the Bureau agent succeeded, after careful search, in finding part of a wooden bowl and some pieces of a trough. The troughs or coffins were evidently sections of hollow trees or had been hollowed out.

SUMTER COUNTY.

CEDAR HUMMOCK GROUP.

In Sec. 5, T. 17 N., R. 1 E., of Stephen's meridian, in what is known locally as "Cedar hummock," with a creek on the west and a slough on the east, is a group of seven mounds. The hummock land on which they stand is about 10 feet above low water. The mounds are circular, from 35 to 50 feet in diameter and from 2 to 4 feet high. The brown sand of which they are chiefly composed has been taken from the soil immediately around them, leaving depressions which are yet distinct.

In one of the three smaller mounds, at the depth of 2 feet, a small quantity of ashes was found, and with them fragments of animal bones; with these exceptions, nothing but the brown sand was observed in the smaller mounds.

In one of the four larger, at the depth of one foot, was a single skeleton, and by the thigh a stone implement; in another, at the depth of 3 feet, was a single skeleton resting on a thin layer of charcoal and ashes, and by it a few pieces of broken pottery; the third presented precisely the same particulars as the second; in the fourth, at the depth of 2 feet, lay a single skeleton.

These skeletons were invariably in the center of the mound, lying at full length, but the heads in different directions, one toward the southwest, another toward the northeast, and two toward the northwest.

ELMORE COUNTY.

Six miles north of Montgomery is Jackson lake, in which there is an island surmounted, on one side, by a mound of considerable size. This island is subject to overflow, but the top of the mound stands at all times high above the water. The length of the upper surface along the lake side is 130 feet; on this side the height, measuring down the steep slope, is 50 feet, while on the opposite side it is but 12 feet perpendicular. Growing on the upper surface are some large trees, among which are two poplars (tulip), one 3½ and the other 4½ feet in diameter, and a pine 3 feet in diameter.

A pit 8 feet square sunk in the center through sandy soil, reached, at the depth of 5 feet, a quantity of ashes, near which were four skulls; two on each side. The larger bones of the four skeletons appear to have been laid across each other very irregularly. With these remains were some shell beads, shell pins, and a piece of copper. Some fragments of pottery were scattered through the earth covering the bodies.

MOUNDS AND HOUSE REMAINS NEAR COOSA RIVER.

On the west bank of the Coosa river, about a mile above where it is joined by the Tallapoosa, are numerous evidences of a former aboriginal village. These consist of fire beds marking the location of houses or wigwams, human remains, animal bones, fragments of pottery, etc. Many of these remains have been brought to light by the falling away of the bank occasioned by the encroachment of the river.

The adjoining field not being plowed to the river bank leaves a strip of land undisturbed, in which the indications of dwellings, consisting chiefly of clay or fire-beds, usually about 5 feet across, and ashes, are most apparent.

The first one of these examined was about a foot below the surface. Here, in the earth and ashes, were numerous pieces of pottery, mostly parts of a very flat dish of unusual form, many mussel shells, animal bones, piece of a gun barrel, a glass bead, iron nails, knife blade, pieces of brass, and copper ornaments. It is evident, therefore, that this is the site of a comparatively modern Indian village.

The second was some 30 feet from the first and 18 inches below the surface. This, being at the bank, was partly washed away, only a part of a fire-bed and of a skeleton being left. On the one arm bone that remained was a brass bracelet made of drawn wire. This skeleton lay near the ashes, as usual.

A third and fourth were also examined with similar results, charred cobs and corn, pieces of pottery, animal bones, brass bracelets, etc., being found. There are no mounds here.

PARKER MOUNDS.

These are situated on the bank of the Coosa river, near its junction with the Tallapoosa.

One of them, about 50 feet in diameter and 2 feet high, which had been plowed over for years, contained two skeletons, which lay at the depth of less than a foot below the surface and about 5 feet apart, one with the head south and the other with the head west. On the breast of the smaller, which was that of a child, lay a small shell gorget; with the other were several bone implements. The mound throughout was composed of sand mixed with ashes.

The other mound, some 400 yards southwest of the first, is about 60 feet in diameter and 8 feet high. The first two feet from the top were chiefly sand, the remainder, to the bottom, clay. No ashes, coals, vestiges of art, or bones were found in it.

OLD FORT JACKSON WORKS.

These are also near the junction of the Coosa and Tallapoosa rivers and mark the site of one of the oldest Creek towns of which we have any account. It is also the site of a victory gained by Gen. Jackson over these Indians. It was here that the old French fort, Toulouse, stood. After its abandonment and decay, Fort Jackson was built on the same spot. The banks of both rivers are caving in rapidly, so that now the space between them does not exceed 300 yards; in fact, most of the site of the fort has been washed away. The mound still remains and also some of the old house sites, supposed to be the work of the Creek Indians.

The earth to the north, south, and east of the mound was found upon examination to be full of fire-beds or remains of houses, and the same was probably true of the western area, which has been washed away.

At the west end the mound is 125 feet across and nearly or quite 45 feet high; the east side is lower, and has a long slope extending about 95 feet to the base. It has been examined at various times by curiosity-hunters, and several articles of European manufacture obtained. As the owner was absent during the visit of the Bureau agent, permission to make further exploration in it was refused.

To the southeast and north is a field of three acres, which has been cultivated for many years and is thickly strewn over with fragments of pottery, charcoal, pieces of human bones, mussel shells, and fragments of burnt clay, evidently turned up from the fire beds or house remains which lie below the surface. A few, however, were discovered which lay below the reach of the plow. One of these was found undisturbed at the depth of 3 feet below the surface. Here was a much decayed skeleton lying at full length with the head toward the west; and by it stood a large earthen pot, in which were a few shell beads, and a mussel shell. A quantity of ashes also lay near the head. At another point, 2 feet below the surface, probably marking the site of another house, there was a layer of ashes 1 foot thick, in and near which were fragments of pottery, animal bones (deer and fish), and mussel shells. Another of these remains, at the depth of 3 feet, was marked by a similar pile of ashes, by which lay a skeleton with the head toward the east. Near it was a brass kettle containing glass beads, brass buckles, brass rings made from wire, and bell buttons. Another, one foot below the surface, yielded arrowheads, celts, stone disks, pottery disks, smoothing stones, fragments of clay pipes, long shell beads, and small glass beads. Among the ruins of another, 18 inches below the surface, was a single skeleton with the head west; near it, on one side, a pile of ashes, and on the other two large pots, one over the other, and in the lower one some animal bones, fragments of a turtle shell, mussel shells, and shell beads; here were also found two shell gorgets, four shell pins, some shell and glass beads mixed together, charred berries, shell spoons, charred seeds, lumps of blue coloring material, two celts, part of a brass plate, a bone punch, etc. At another point the remains presented the following series: After removing 10 inches of soil, a layer of burnt clay 5 inches thick was reached, then a clay hearth. This hearth was on a thick layer of ashes. The burnt-clay layers in these remains varied from 5 to 10 inches in thickness. In some they were entirely wanting, ashes only being present.

CLARKE COUNTY.

Four and a half miles east of Gainestown, on the north bank of the Alabama river, in Sec. 2, T. 5 N., R. 4 E. of Stephen's Meridian, is French's landing, the supposed site of old Fort Mauvilla. Not a vestige of the old fort now remains and the mound that once stood here has been carried into the river, and the so-called "burying ground" has nearly all disappeared, a strip only about 20 feet wide remaining.

At one place a foot below the surface in the break of the bank, where the wearing away is going on, were three skeletons in compact bundles, which must have been buried after the flesh had rotted off or been removed from the bones. At another point, about 30 feet distant from those mentioned, were two other similar deposits at the same depth and arranged in the same way. Fragments of pottery occurred here and there in the soil.

BARBOUR COUNTY.

The following and some of the previous notices are given simply because they may possibly aid in locating some of the old Indian villages.

At the St. Francis bend of the Chattahoochee river, 3 miles northeast of Eufaula, is an elevated bank of sandy soil on which it is said an old Creek town was once located. Although partially washed away by the river, there are sufficient remains of fire-beds, fragments of pottery, human bones, and stone implements to confirm the tradition.

MONTGOMERY COUNTY.

Nine miles southwest of the city of Montgomery and situated on the bank of the Alabama river is a group of five mounds. One of these, 8 feet high and 50 feet in diameter, was composed entirely of clay, in which, at the depth of 2 feet, lay a single skeleton; no vestiges of art with it. Another, considerably smaller, was composed wholly of brown sand, scattered through which were some fragments of pottery and broken animal bones. The third, about 60 feet in diameter and nearly 10 feet high, was covered to the depth of a foot with brown sand. The remainder was sharp, yellow, river sand; nothing was found in it. The fourth, which is slightly larger than the third, was covered with a layer of brown sand 18 inches thick, the remainder of clay to the base. In the clay, at the depth of 2 feet, lay a single skeleton. Nothing else was discovered.

TALLADEGA COUNTY.

Four miles southeast of Talladega is Cragdale, on the bank of Talladega creek, the site of a former Creek settlement. Dr. W. Taylor says that when he came to this place with his father, he being then but a boy, many of the Indian houses were still standing. He also says that it was a custom of these Indians to bury in the corners of their houses, not more than 18 inches or 2 feet below the floor; that he had frequently examined these deposits and found with the bones shell beads, carved shell ornaments, pottery, and sometimes as many as three skeletons in a place, and occasionally as many as three corners thus occupied. He also says the Creeks frequently used mussel-shells for spoons.

JEFFERSON COUNTY.

Near Jonesboro is a small group of mounds on the plantation of Mr. N. D. Talley, Sec. 8, T. 19 S., R. 4 W., of the Huntsville meridian. The valley of the small creek that flows along the northern and eastern sides of the field in which the group is located is quite wide at this point, the round, knob-like hills which form its boundary standing at quite a distance from the mounds.

The surface of the field immediately around the mounds is comparatively flat, pitching in a steep bank to the water, a few feet north of mound No. 1. (Fig. 178.) Northeast of this mound the surface has the appearance of having been dug or more probably washed out by the creek. East of mound 3 is what might be called the first bottom land, about 4 feet lower than the surface of the field. This point is above the overflow of the small creek, while farther down the valley the land is frequently inundated and had been under water a short time previous to examination.

A plat of the group is given in Fig. 178. No. 1, is an oblong mound, measuring 30 feet east and west, and about 4 feet high at the highest point. A few small pine and hackberry trees have grown on the sides since it was built. It is made of the same red, sandy soil as that found in the field in which it stands. Only a few coals and a shovelful of ashes were found in it, which had probably been thrown there at the time it was built and may have been scraped up from the surface of the field with the rest of the material for the mound, but in hunting the field over for any specimen that might have been washed out or plowed up no ash beds were seen, nor did any of the tenants of the land remember plowing through such beds.

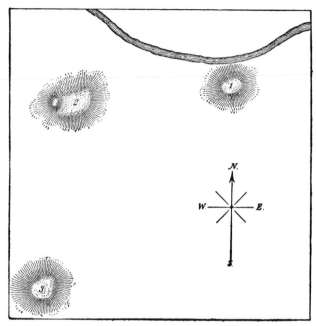

FIG. 178.—Plat of Tally mounds, Jefferson county, Alabama.

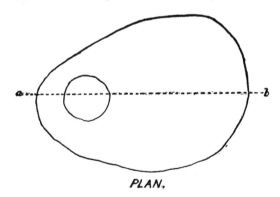

PLAN.

SECTION ON LINE a-b.

FIG. 179.—Mound No. 2, Tally group (plan and section).

No. 2 (shown in Fig. 179) has the appearance of an oval platform with a small mound on one end of it. The longer diameter of the base of the platform is about 140 feet, the greatest width 100 feet, and the height 5 feet. The height of the upper mound, which is on the smaller end of the platform, is 7 feet, the diameter of the flattened top 30 feet. Its western slope is continuous with that of the platform. The figure shows the ground plan and the section through *a b*. The upper mound has been considerably torn up by treasure hunters, but scattered over the top was a large quantity of burnt clay, much of which bore the impression of a stamp made apparently of split cane. A trench lengthwise through the platform showed that the top layer consisted of 4 feet of red, sandy soil, evidently taken from the surface of the surrounding field; the remainder, to the original surface of the ground, of pure river sand. The upper mound was composed of sandy soil down to the platform, and hence it is reasonable to conclude that it was built at the same time the upper layer was placed on the platform. No bones, ashes, charcoal, or vestiges of art were observed in any part.

No. 3 is a circular mound, about 110 feet in diameter at the base and 60 feet across the top, which is flat; height, 8 feet. A trench across it through the center showed that it was constructed of sandy soil from the surrounding field. In the central portion, about half way down, was a layer of clear river sand 3 inches thick and about 5 feet in diameter. Nothing else was found in it.

GEORGIA.

The ancient works of this state, so far as known and examined, have been so thoroughly and ably described by Col. C. C. Jones, in his "Antiquities of the Southern Indians" and in his other works, that it is unnecessary to allude to any except such as received special attention by the Bureau of Ethnology.

BARTOW COUNTY.

ETOWAH GROUP.

This deservedly celebrated group, situated close to the north bank of Etowah river, on the farm of Mr. G. H. Tumlin, 3 miles southeast of Cartersville, has been repeatedly described and figured; in fact, as I shall attempt hereafter to show, there is good reason for believing that it includes one of the mounds specially mentioned by the chroniclers of De Soto's expedition.

As the group, its several works, and the relics which have been found in and about the mounds are of great archeological interest, and possibly furnish the key to some troublesome historical questions and archeological puzzles, I will give in this connection some of the descriptions by other writers, that the reader may have all the facts before him and thus be enabled to draw his own conclusions in reference to the questions which are suggested by these remains.

The first published notice of these works (unless they are referred to by the chroniclers of De Soto's expedition) is that by Rev. Elias Cornelius,[1] and is as follows:

I have but one more article of curiosity to mention under this division. It is one of those artificial mounds which occur so frequently in the western country. I have seen many of them and read of more, but never of one of such dimension as that which I am now to describe.

It is situated in the interior of the Cherokee Nation, on the north side of the Etowee, vulgarly called the Hightower river, one of the branches of the Koosee. It stands upon a strip of alluvial land called river bottom. I visited it in company with eight Indian chiefs. The first object which excited attention was an excavation about 20 feet wide and in some parts 10 feet deep. Its course is nearly that of a semicircle, the extremities extending towards the river, which forms a small elbow. I had not time to examine it minutely. An Indian said it extended each way to the river, and had several unexcavated parts, which served for passages to the area which it incloses. To my surprise I found no enbankment on either side of it. But I did not long doubt to what place the earth had been removed; for I had scarcely proceeded 200 yards when, through the thick forest trees, a stupenduous pile met the eye, whose dimensions were in full proportion to the intrenchment. I had at the time no means of taking an accurate admeasurement. To supply my deficiency I cut a long vine, which was preserved until I had an opportunity of ascertaining its exact length. In this manner I found the distance from the margin of the summit to the base to be 111 feet. And, judging from the degree of its declivity, the perpendicular height can not be less than 75 feet. The circumference of the base, including the feet of three parapets, measured 1,114 feet. One of these parapets extends from the base to the summit, and can be ascended, though with difficulty, on horseback. The other two, after rising 30 or 40 feet, terminate in a kind of triangular platform. Its top is level and, at the time I visited it, was so completely covered with weeds, bushes, and trees of most luxuriant growth that I could not examine it as well as I wished. Its diameter, I judged, must be 150 feet. On its sides and summit are many large trees of the same description and of equal dimensions with those around it. One beech tree near the top measured 10 feet 9 inches in circumference. The earth on one side of the tree was $3\frac{1}{2}$ feet lower than on the opposite side. This fact will give a good idea of the degree of the mound's declivity. An oak, which was lying down on one of the parapets, measured at the distance of 6 feet from the butt, without the bark, 12 feet 4 inches in circumference. At a short distance to the southeast is another mound, in ascending which I took 30 steps. Its top is encircled by a breastwork 3 feet high, intersected through the middle with another elevation of a similar kind. A little farther is another mound, which I had not time to examine.

On these great works of art the Indians gazed with as much curiosity as any white man. I inquired of the oldest chief if the natives had any tradition respecting them, to which he answered in the negative. I then requested each to say what he supposed was their origin. Neither could tell, though all agreed in saying, " they were never put up by our people." It seems probable they were erected by another race who once inhabited the country. That such a race existed is now generally admitted. Who they were and what were the causes of their degeneracy or of their extermination no circumstances have yet explained. But this is no reason why we should not, as in a hundred other instances, infer that existence of the cause from its effect, without any previous knowledge of its history.

In regard to the objects which these mounds were designed to answer, it is obvious they were not always the same. Some were intended as receptacles for the dead. These are small and are distinguished by containing human bones. Some may have been designed as sites for public buildings, whether of a civil or religious kind, and others no doubt were constructed for the purposes of war. Of this last description is the Etowee mound. In proof of its suitableness for such a purpose I need only mention that the Cherokees, in their late wars with the Creeks, secured its smmmit by pickets and occupied it as a place of protection for hundreds of their women and children. Gladly would I have spent a day in examing it more minutely, but my companions, unable to appreciate my motives, grew impatient, and I was obliged to withdraw and leave a more perfect observation and description to some one else.

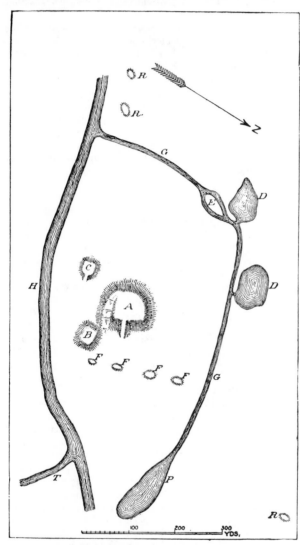

This account is particularly valuable, as it relates to the condition and appearance of these works before they were disturbed by the plow. We also find in this account some items of interest which had disappeared before the works were visited and described by the more modern observers.

The description by Col. C. C. Jones[1] is the best we find hitherto published. I therefore give it here in full, together with a reproduction of his illustration (Fig. 180):

FIG. 180.—Plat of Etowah group, copy of Jones's plat No. 1.

Viewed as a whole, this group is the most remarkable within the confines of this state. These mounds are situated in the midst of a beautiful and fertile valley. They occupy a central position in an area of some 50 acres, bounded on the south and east by the Etowah river, and on the north and west by a large ditch or artificial

---

[1] Antiquities of the Southern Indians, p. 136.

VIEW OF THE LARGE MOUND, ETOWAH GROUP.

canal, which at its lower end communicates directly with the river. This moat (G G, Pl. I), at present, varies in depth from 5 to 25 feet, and in width from 20 to 75 feet. No parapets or earth walls appear upon its edges. Along its line are two reservoirs (D D) of about an acre each, possessing an average depth of not less than 20 feet, and its upper end expands into an artificial pond (P) elliptical in form and somewhat deeper than the excavations mentioned.

Within the inclosure formed by this moat and the river are seven mounds. Three of them are preeminent in size, the one designated in the accompanying plan (Pl. I) by the letter A far surpassing the others both in its proportions and in the degree of interest which attaches to it.

To the eye of the observer, as it rests for the first time upon its towering form, it seems a monument of the past ages, venerable in its antiquity, solemn, silent, and yet not voiceless—a remarkable exhibition of the power and industry of a former race. With its erection, the modern hunter tribes, so far as our information extends, had naught to do. Composed of earth, simple, yet impressive in form, it seems calculated for an almost endless duration. The soil, gravel, and smaller stones taken from the moat and the reservoirs were expended in the construction of these tumuli. The surface of the ground, for a considerable distance around the northern bases, was then removed and placed upon their summits. Viewed from the north, the valley dips toward the mounds so that they appear to lift themselves from out a basin.

The central tumulus rises about 65 feet above the level of the valley. It is entirely artificial, consisting wholly of the earth taken from the moat and the excavations, in connection with the soil collected around its base. It has received no assistance whatever from any natural hill or elevation.

In general outline it may be regarded as quadrangular, if we disregard a slight angle to the south. That taken into account, its form is pentagonal, with summit admeasurements as follows: Length of the northern side, 150 feet; length of eastern side, 160 feet; Length of southeastern side, 100 feet; length of southern side, 90 feet, and length of western side, 100 feet. Measured east and west, its longest apex diameter is 225 feet; measured north and south it falls a little short, being about 220 feet. On its summit this tumulus is nearly level. Shorn of the luxuriant vegetation and tall forest trees, which at one time crowned it on every side, the outlines of this mound stand in bold relief. Its angles are still sharply defined. The established approach to the top is from the east. Its ascent was accomplished through the intervention of terraces rising one above the other—inclined planes leading from the one to the other. These terraces are 65 feet in width, and extend from the mound toward the southeast. Near the eastern angle, a pathway leads to the top; but it does not appear to have been intended for very general use. May it not have been designed for the priesthood alone, while assembled upon the broad terraces the worshipers gave solemn heed to the religious ceremonies performed upon the eastern summit of this ancient temple?

East of this large central mound—and so near that their flanks meet and mingle— stands a smaller mound, about 35 feet high, originally quadrangular, now nearly circular in form, and with a summit diameter of 100 feet. From its western slope is an easy and immediate communication with the terraces of the central tumulus. This mound is designated in the accompanying plate by the letter B. Two hundred and fifty feet in a westerly direction from this mound, and distant some 60 feet in a southerly direction from it, is the third (C) and the last of this immediate group. Pentagonal in form, it possesses an altitude of 23 feet. It is uniformly level at the top, and its apex diameters, measured at right angles, were, respectively, 92 and 68 feet.

East of this group, and within the inclosure, is a chain of four sepulchral mounds, (F F F F), ovoidal in shape. Little individual interest attaches to them. Nothing, aside from their location in the vicinity of these larger tumuli and their being within the area formed by the canal and the river, distinguishes them from numerous earth mounds scattered here and there through the length and breadth of the Etowah and Oostenaula valleys.

The artificial elevation E, lying northwest of the central group, is remarkable for its superficial area, and is completely surrounded by the moat which at that point divides with a view to its inclosure. The slope of the sides of these tumuli is just such as would be assumed by gradual accretions of earth successively deposited in small quantities from above.

The summits of these mounds, and the circumjacent valley for miles, have been completely denuded of the original growth which overspread them in rich profusion. The consequence is, these remarkable remains can be readily and carefully noted.

Without commenting at present upon this description, I give Col. Charles Whittlesey's account as found in the Smithsonian Report for 1881,[1] together with his illustration No. 1. (See Fig. 181.)

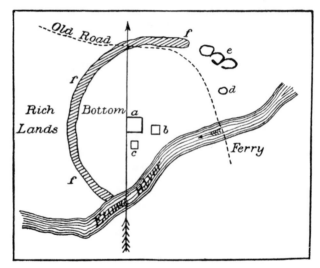

FIG. 181.—Plat of Etowah group, copy of Whittlesey's figure No. 1.

THE GREAT MOUND ON THE ETOWAH RIVER, GEORGIA.

Not having seen a detailed description of this mound I made a visit to it in behalf of the Western Reserve Historical Society, in May, 1871. It stands upon the north bank of the Etowah, about 2 miles below where it is crossed by the Chattanooga and Atlanta railway, near Cartersville. Its form, size, and elevation are singular and imposing. It occupies the easterly point or angle of a large and luxuriant river bottom, a part of which is subject to inundations. The soil is a deep, rich, black loam covering several hundred acres, which has been cultivated in corn and cotton since the Cherokees left it, about forty years since.

I was compelled, by bad weather, to make the survey in haste. The bearings were taken with a prismatic compass, the distances measured by pacing, and the elevations obtained with a pocket level. They are, therefore, subject to the corrections of future surveyors. Its base covers a space of about 3 acres, and stands at a level of 23 feet above low water in the river. In great floods the water approaches near the mound on the west, but has not been known to reach it. The body of the mound has an irregular figure, as shown in the plan. It is longest on the meridian, its diameter in

---

[1] Pp. 624-627.

that direction being about 270 feet. On the top is a nearly level area of about an acre, the average height of which is 50 feet above the base. A broad ramp or graded way (1) winds upward from the plain, around the south face of the mound, to the area on the top.

Like some of the pyramids of Egypt it has two smaller ones as tenders: one on the south, C; another to the southeast, B; each about 100 feet distant, their bases nearly square, and of nearly equal dimensions. If they were not in the shadow of the great mound they would attract attention for their size and regularity. The ground at B is 3 feet higher than at C. All of them are truncated. The mound C is not a perfectly regular figure, but approaches a square with one side broken into three lines. Its height above base is 18 feet. The bearing of its western side is north 10 degrees west, and the length on the ground 47 paces, having been somewhat spread out by plowing around the foot. On the east is a ramp, with a slope of 1 to 2 degrees, which allows of ready ascent by persons on foot.

The slopes of all the mounds are very steep and quite perfect, in some places still standing at an angle of 45 degrees. B is a regular truncated pyramid, with a square base about 106 feet on a side, two of the faces bearing 5 degrees west of the meridian. Its elevation is 22 feet. There is no ramp or place of ascent which is less steep than the general slopes. Towards the southeast corner of the surface of B is a sunken place, as though a vault had fallen in.

The proprietor has managed to cultivate the summits of all the mounds, regarding the group in the light of a continual injury by the loss of several acres of ground. Most of the material of the mounds is the rich black mold of the bottom land, with occasional lumps of red clay. The soil on their sides and summits produces corn, cotton, grass, vines, and bushes in full luxuriance. The perimeter of the base of the great mound is 534 paces. As the ground had been recently plowed and was soaked with a deluge of rain, a pace will represent little more than 2 feet. I give the circumference provisionally at 370 yards. The area on the top is like the base, oblong north and south, but its figure is more regular. Its perimeter is 231 paces.

From the center of the pyramid C a line on the magnetic meridian passes a few feet to the west of the center of the platform on the summit of A. Its sides are nowhere washed or gullied by rains. Prior to the clearing of the land, large trees flourished on the top and on the slopes. I estimate its mass to contain 117,000 cubic yards, which is about four-fifths of the Prussian earth-monument on the field of Waterloo.

At the base the ramp is 50 feet broad, growing narrower as you ascend. It curves to the right, and reaches the area on the top near its southwest corner. Twenty-five years since, before it was injured by cultivation, visitors could easily ride to the summit on horseback along the ramp. From this spot the view of the rich valley of the Etowah towards the west, and of the picturesque hills which border it on either side, is one of surpassing beauty.

About 300 yards to the north rises the second terrace of the valley, composed of red clay and gravel. Near the foot of it are the remains of a ditch, inclosing this group of mounds in an arc of a circle, at a distance of about 200 yards. The western end rests on the river, below the mounds, into which the high waters back up a considerable distance.

It has been principally filled up by cultivation. The owner of the premises says there was originally an embankment along the edge of the ditch on the side of the pyramids, but other old settlers say there was none. If the last statement is correct, a part of the earth composing the mounds can be accounted for by the ditch.

Its length is about one-fourth of a mile, and it does not extend to the river, above the mounds. Near the upper end are two oblong, irregular pits, 12 to 15 feet deep, from which a part of the earth of the mounds may have been taken. The diameter of the pits varies from 150 to 200 feet, and the breadth from 60 to 70. The ditch is reputed to have been 30 feet wide and 10 feet deep. Two hundred yards to the northeast of A are the remains of four low mounds within the ditch near the large pits. Five hundred yards to the northwest, on the edge of the second terrace, is a mound which is yet 8 feet high, although it has been industriously plowed over more than thirty years.

The place chosen by the mound-builders in this case for the location of their village is, as usual, one adapted to easy cultivation and withal one of real beauty.

The river, which reaches the base of the hills above and below, here makes a bend to the south, while the line of hills curves toward the north, leaving a broad, fertile bottom some 3 miles long east and west and a mile or more in breadth. The mounds are visible from the hills throughout the entire circuit, rendering it easy to give notice of the approach of an enemy from any quarter on this side of the river.

There is little doubt, therefore, that while one object in view in selecting this locality was to obtain land close at hand suitable for cultivation, another was, as intimated by Rev. Elias Cornelius, security and means of defense against the attacks of enemies. The general plan of the works, from an examination and survey made in person, assisted by Mr. Rogan, in 1885, is given in Fig. 182. It will be seen from this figure that the works at present consist of a broad, surrounding ditch, flanked at two points by large excavations, six included and one outside mound, though it is apparent from the descriptions of previous visitors heretofore given and what is hereafter stated that these are not all the works which formed parts of this extensive village.

The ditch, starting at *n*, on the east, 310 feet from the river and 1,140 feet from the nearest point of the large mound, runs northwest, gradually curving westward and southward so as to form an almost complete semicircle, and striking the river below at *p*, about 870 feet from the nearest point of the large mound. The distance from *m* to *p* direct is about 775 yards, and the length of the ditch from *n* to *p*, following the curve, about 1,060 yards. The greatest width of the area, that is, from the river to the margin of the large excavation *r*, is about 450 yards, the area inclosed being about 56 acres. Whether the ditch ever reached the river on the east can not be determined from present indications. There is still a slight depression, or swale, south of the termination, shown at *n*, but this does not reach the bank. Nevertheless, the plan of the works seems to require connection with the river at this point, and that this was the case may be assumed. It is probable that there was here a bridge or arrangement for crossing the ditch, and also that it was quite narrow here to prevent the too rapid influx of water from the river. A crossing point appears to have been at *w*, where the ditch enters the large reservoir or basin. The dotted lines in the plat (Fig. 182) along the break at *i* indicate the portion filled up by the present and preceding owners in order to make a crossing for a road at this point. As it approaches the large excavation *r*, it suddenly expands and increases in depth, being at the cross section 1-2, 95 feet wide

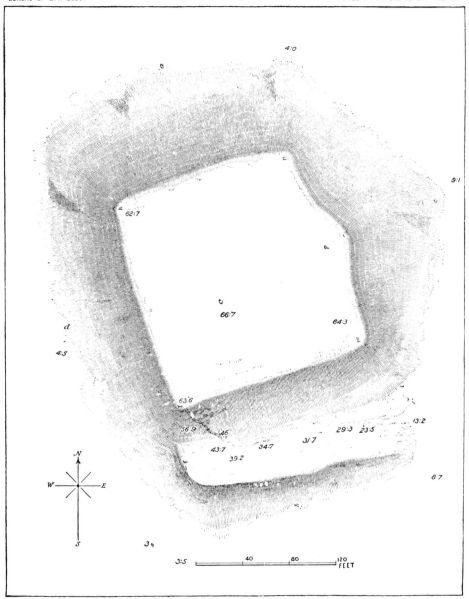

PLAN OF THE LARGE MOUND ETOWAH GROUP.

and 14 feet deep.   At the point of connection with the excavation, w, it
suddenly narrows to 12 or 14 feet, and the depth is not more than half
of what it is a few feet above.   It is evident that a dam was thrown
across at this point, as some of the stones used were still in place when
I examined it, and quite a number had fallen down into the large exca-

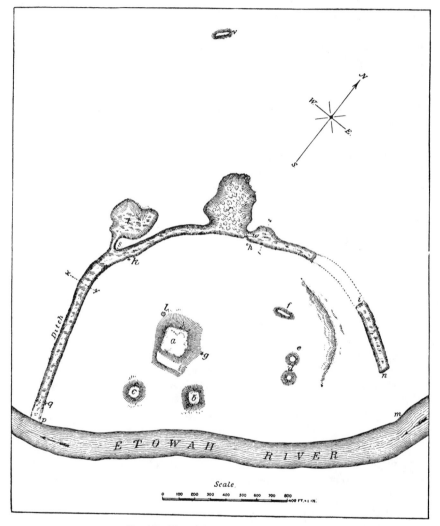

FIG. 182.—Plat of the Etowah group (original).

vation.   It is probable that this was connected with a fish-trap of some
kind, and that advantage was also taken of the near approach of the
sides to throw a wooden bridge across the ditch.

The large excavation (r) embraces an area of about 3 acres; it is not
uniform in depth; in fact, a considerable portion of the central area is

but slightly excavated and but little lower than the original surrounding surface; the remainder is about the same depth as the expanded portion of the ditch immediately above. The portion of the ditch extending from this basin to the outlet of the other, marked l, has never been plowed over and has suffered but little change from its original condition; here it is about 40 feet wide and 15 feet deep. The excavation l is correctly represented in the figure; it is over $1\frac{1}{2}$ acres in extent and is 17 feet deep at the deepest point, the eastern side, where the bank or margin is almost perpendicular, a fact which seems to forbid the idea of great antiquity. The remainder of the ditch to the river has been plowed over and hence its sides are much worn down; nevertheless the depth is some 8 or 10 feet, and the width at $x\,y$ 68 feet. The distance from s to p is 1,070 feet. Its entrance to the river has been closed by the present owner to keep out the backwater. There are no indications at any point that there ever was an embankment on either side, the material taken out having doubtless been used in building the mounds. East and north of the large mound is a considerable depression from which, in all probability, additional material was ob-

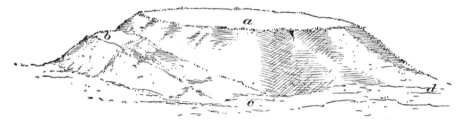

FIG. 183.—Large mound of the Etowah group.

tained. The outer margin of this depression is indicated by the shaded line. As the small mounds d, e, and f are in this depression, it is probable they were built subsequent to the construction of the larger ones.

The large mound, a.—This is truly a grand and remarkable structure, being exceeded in size in the United States, judging by the cubical contents, only by the great Cahokia mound. All the descriptions of it which I have seen fail to note the important fact that the broad roadway which ascends it on the south side does not reach the top, falling short in this respect by 20 feet perpendicular and about 30 feet slant height. This fact is apparent from the views of it given in our Fig. 183 and Pl. xv, the latter from a photograph.

A careful survey of it was made in 1884 by Mr. Victor Mindeleff for the purpose of preparing a model for the Exposition at New Orleans. A plat drawn to an exact scale, with heights, measurements, etc., is given in Pl. xvi. From this it will be seen that the highest point, c, is $66\frac{1}{2}$ feet, assuming the northwest corner, which is Mr. Mindeleff's zero, as the base. But from personal inspection and what has been discovered in regard to the other two mounds near it, I am satisfied the original surface of the ground was somewhat higher than that around it to the north and east as it now appears. The level at the southwest, which is 3 feet higher than the northwest corner, is probably very near that of the original surface of the ground. Assuming this as the base, and taking the average of the heights of the top, the true elevation is found to be 61 feet. The length of the slope a little north of the southwest corner, which is very steep, forming an angle of 45 degrees, is 86 feet; this gives within a few inches the same result as the preceding calculation. The slope here is considerably steeper than at any other point and indicates that the body of the mound is largely composed of clay, a question which could easily be determined by digging; but permission to do this has not as yet been obtained. The longest diameter, including the roadway (a to b, Pl. XVI), is 380 feet; the diameter at right angles to this (from c to d) is 330 feet, and the area of the base a little less than 3 acres. The lengths of the sides of the top, which is somewhat quadrilateral, are as follows: From k (northwest corner) to l (southwest corner), 180 feet; from l to m, 170 feet; from m to n, 176 feet; and from n to k, 164 feet; the offset at p from the line connecting m and n is about 15 feet. The area of the top is, therefore, about seven-tenths of an acre. The length of the roadway along the slope from c to b, Fig. 183), is 205 feet, the width varying from 37 to 56 feet; the height at its upper terminus (b, Fig. 183) above the base is a few inches over 40 feet. There is at the upper terminus a level space which formed the uppermost of the terraces into which this roadway was originally divided, of which some indications yet remain.

From these dimensions it is easy to calculate with approximate certainty the cubical contents of the mound, which we find to be, including the roadway, about 4,300,000 cubic feet, or 159,200 cubic yards. It therefore exceeds slightly in volume the entire wall of Fort Ancient, in Ohio,[1] and exceeds Col. Whittlesey's calculation by about 42,000 cubic yards.

The ramp, or straight, steep roadway on the east, terminating at d (Fig. 183), is not very apparent at present, though it is evident that the slope here has been lengthened intentionally, and that an addition has been made to this side for some definite purpose; but it must have been too steep for any other purpose than descent. Possibly it was an earlier roadway than that on the south, which was abandoned and partially removed when the latter was built.

Mound c.—Although this mound is described by Col. Whittlesey as somewhat square, with a roadway on the east side, I find the outline to be more rounded and but slight indications of the eastward extension. The circumference of the base is 375 feet, and the average diameter of the nearly flat top exactly 60 feet; the height, measured from the surrounding surface of the ground, is about 18 feet, but the true height

---

[1] Science, vol. 8, 1886, p. 540.

above the original surface was found, when it was excavated, to be only 15 feet.

In excavating this mound Mr. Rogan, who did this part of the work, ran a trench 6 feet wide in from the south side, going through the hard clay slope until he struck the inner circle, whence he continued widening until he had gone over the entire area within the surrounding slope, carrying the excavation down at all points to the original surface.

Continuing the excavation in this way until a complete exploration of the mound had been made, the construction was found to be as represented in Fig. 184, which shows a vertical section. The entire surrounding slope was of hard, tough, red clay, which could not have been obtained nearer than half a mile; the cylindrical core, 60 feet in diameter, and extending down to the original surface of the ground, was composed of three horizontal layers, the bottom layer, No. 1, 10 feet thick, of rich, dark, and rather loose loam; the next, No. 2, 4 feet thick, beaten (or tramped) clay, so tough and hard that it was difficult to penetrate it even with a pick; and the uppermost, No. 3, of sand and surface soil, between 1 and 2 feet thick.

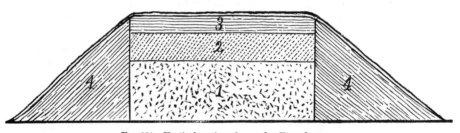

FIG. 184.—Vertical section of mound c, Etowah group.

Nothing was found in the layer of clay, No. 2, except a rude clay pipe, some small shell beads, a piece of mica, and a chunkee stone. The burials were all in the lower layer (No. 1), of dark, rich loam, and chiefly in stone cists or coffins of the usual box shape, formed of stone slabs, and distributed horizontally, as shown in Fig. 185, which is a plan of this lower bed.

Grave a, a stone sepulcher, 2½ feet wide, 8 feet long, and 2 feet deep, was formed by placing steatite slabs on edge at the sides and ends, and others across the top. The bottom consisted simply of earth hardened by fire. It contained the remains of a single skeleton, lying on its back, with the head east. The frame was heavy and about 7 feet long. The head rested on a thin copper plate ornamented with impressed figures; but the skull was crushed and the plate injured by fallen slabs. Under the copper were the remains of a skin of some kind, and under this coarse matting, apparently of split cane. The skin and matting were both so rotten that they could be secured only in fragments. At the left of the feet were two clay vessels, one a water bottle and the other a very small vase. On the right of the feet were some mussel and sea shells and immediately under the feet two conch shells (*Busycon perversum*) partially filled with small shell beads. Around each ankle was a strand of similar beads. The bones and most of the shells were so far decomposed that they could not be saved.

Grave *b*, a stone sepulcher, 4 feet long, 2 feet wide, and 1½ feet deep, differed from *a* only in size and the fact that the bottom was covered with stone slabs. The skeleton was extended on the back, head east. On the forehead was a thin plate of copper, the only article found.

Grave *c*, also a stone sepulcher, 3½ feet long, 1½ feet wide, and 1½ feet deep, the bottom being formed of burnt earth. Although extending east and west, as shown in Fig. 185, the bones had probably been disconnected and interred without regard to order, the head being found in the northeast corner with face to the wall, and the remaining portions of the skeleton in a promiscuous heap. Yet there was no indication of disturbance after burial, as the coffin was intact. Placed in the heap of bones was a thin plate of copper that had been formed by uniting and riveting together smaller sections. (See Pl. XVIII.) Some of the bones found in this grave were saved.

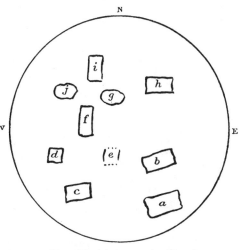

Fig. 185.—Plan of burials in mound *c*, Etowah group.

Grave *d*, a small sepulcher only 1½ feet square by 1 foot deep, contained the remains of an infant; also a few small shell beads. The slabs forming the sides and bottom of this grave bore very distinct marks of fire.

Grave *e* consisted simply of a headstone and footstone, with the skeleton of a very small child between them; head east. On the wrists were some very small shell beads. The earth on the north and south sides had been hardened in order to form the walls, a strong indication that the mound had been built up to this height and a pit dug in it.

Grave *f*, also a stone sepulcher, was 6 feet long, 3 feet wide, and 1½ feet deep, with a stone bottom. Skeleton with the head north. There were several pieces of copper about the head, which, together with the skeleton, were wrapped in a skin. The head rested on a large conch shell (*Busycon perversum*), and this on the remains of a coarse mat. Shell beads were found around the neck and also around each wrist and ankle. On the right was a small cup and on the breast an engraved shell. The copper had preserved a portion of the hair, which was saved; portions of the skin and matting were also secured. Immediately under *b* was another stone grave or coffin, 3 feet long, 1½ feet wide and deep, extending north and south. The head of the skeleton was toward the north, but the feet were doubled back under the frame in order to get it in the allotted space. The only things found with this skeleton were some beads around the neck.

FIG. 186.—Figured copper plate from mound *c* Etowah group.

At *g* the remains of a child were found without any stones about them. Some shell beads were around the neck and wrist, and an engraved shell on the breast.

Grave *h* was a stone cist 1½ feet square and 1 foot deep, stone slabs on the four sides and top, but the bottom consisted simply of earth hardened by fire. This contained only a trace of bones and presented indications of at least partial cremation, as all around the slabs, outside and inside, was a solid mass of charcoal, and the earth was burned to the depth of a foot.

Grave *i*, a stone cist 4½ feet long, 1½ feet wide and deep; bottom of earth; contained the remains of a skeleton resting on the back, head north, and feet doubled back so as to come within the coffin. On the breast was a thin plate of copper, 5 inches square, with a hole through the center. Beads were found around the wrists, and rather more than a quart about the neck.

At *j* were the remains of a small child, without stone surroundings; under the head was a piece of copper, and about the neck and wrists a number of shell beads.

These graves were not on the same level, the top of some being but 2 feet below the clay bed (No. 2), while others were from 2 to 3 feet lower. All the articles alluded to as obtained in this mound were forwarded at once to the Bureau of Ethnology, and are now in the National Museum.

FIGURED COPPER PLATE FROM MOUND *c*, ETOWAH GROUP (HUMAN FIGURE).

Examining them somewhat carefully since their reception, I find there are really more copper plates among them than at first supposed. Those which were not too much broken to determine the exact form and size are as follows:

(1) A human figure with wings, represented in Pl. XVII. This is 17 inches long and 9 inches wide. A portion of the lower part, as shown by the figure, is wanting, probably some 3 or 4 inches. There is a break across the middle, but not sufficient to interfere with tracing out the design. A crown piece of the head ornament is also wanting. This plate was found in grave *a*.

(2) Also a human figure, found in the same grave; is shown in Fig. 186. Length, 16 inches; width, 7½ inches.

(3) Figure of a bird (Pl. XVIII). This is imperfect, as part of the head and of the outer margin of the wings are wanting. Length, 13½ inches; width, 7½ inches. This plate shows indubitable evidence of having been formed of smaller pieces welded together, as the overlapping portions can be easily traced. It has also undergone repairs; a fracture, commencing on the left and running irregularly halfway across the body, has been mended by placing a strip of copper along it on the back and riveting it to the main plate; a small piece has also been riveted to the head, and the head to the body; several other pieces are attached in the same way. The rivets are small and the work neatly done. This was found in grave *c*.

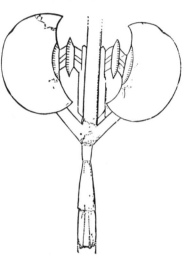

FIG. 187.—Copper badge from mound *c*, Etowah group.

(4) An ornament or badge of some kind found in grave *b* is shown in Fig. 187. The two crescent-shaped pieces are entirely plain except some slightly impressed lines on the portion connecting them with the central stem. This central stem throughout its entire length and to the width of six-tenths of an inch is raised, and cross strips placed at various points along the under side, for the purpose of inserting a strip of bone, a part of which yet remains in it and is seen in the figure where the oblique strips meet. The most important and interesting fact presented by this specimen is the evidence it furnishes that the workman who formed it made use of metallic tools, as the cutting in this case could not possibly have been done with anything except a metallic implement. A single glance at it is sufficient to satisfy any one of the truth of this assertion. Length of the stem, 9 inches; width across the crescents, 7½ inches.

12 ETH——20

(5) Part of an ornament similar to No. 4. These plates, especially No. 4, appear to be enlarged patterns of that seen behind the head in Pl. XVII.

(6) An ornament or badge, shown in Fig. 188, found under the head

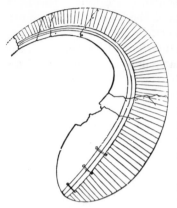

of the skeleton in grave *a*. It is imperfect, a narrow strip across the middle and a portion of the tip being missing. As shown in the figure, it measures around the outer border 19 inches, and across the broad end $3\frac{1}{2}$ inches. The six holes at the larger end, in which the remains of strings can be detected, indicate that it was, when in use, attached to some portion of the dress or fastened on a staff.

(7) A fragment from the larger end of a piece similar to the preceding. Attached to this is a piece of cloth.

FIG. 188.—Copper ornament or badge from mound *c*, Etowah group.

In addition to the foregoing there are a number of small fragments, probably broken from these plates or parts of others; but so far I have been unable to fit them to their proper places.

An examination of the supposed skin shows beyond question that it is animal matter and probably part of a tanned deer hide. The matting appears to be made of split canes.

The shell represented in Fig. 189 is the one obtained in grave *g*. The one shown in Fig. 190 is that found in grave *f*.

In one of the low mounds was subsequently found the bust shown in Fig. 191. It has been carved from a coarse marble, and shows considerable art. The face had been split off, but without injury. The length of the fragment shown in the figure is 11 inches.

I shall not attempt, at present, to speculate upon

FIG. 189.—Engraved shell, mound *c*, Etowah group.

these singular specimens of art further than to call attention to one or two facts which appear to bear upon their age and distribution.

We notice the fact, which is apparent to every one who inspects the

FIGURED COPPER PLATE FROM MOUND *c*, ETOWAH GROUP (BIRD FIGURE).

figures, that in all their leading features the designs are suggestive
of Mexican or Central American work; yet a close inspection brings
to light one or two features which are anomalies in Mexican or Central
American designs; as, for example, in Pl. XVII and Fig. 186, where the
wings are represented as rising from the back of the shoulders.
Although we can find numerous figures of winged individuals in
Mexican designs (they are unknown in Central American), they always
carry with them the idea that the individual is partly or completely
clothed in the skin of the bird. This is partly carried out in the copper plate, as is seen by the bird bill over the head; the eye being that

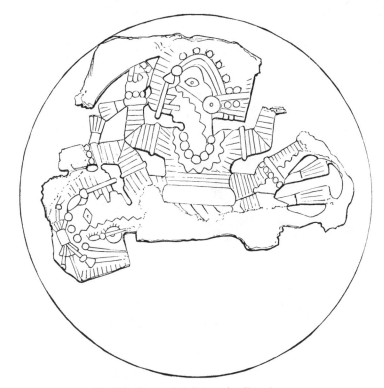

FIG. 190.—Engraved shell, mound *c*, Etowah group.

of the bird and not of the man. But when the wings are observed it
is at once seen that the artist had in mind the angel figure with wings
rising from the back of the shoulders—an idea wholly foreign to Mexican art.

Another fact worthy of note in regard to the two chief plates representing human figures is that there is a combination of Central American and Mexican designs; the graceful limbs and the ornaments of the
arms, legs, waist, and the headdress are Central American, while the
rest, with the exception possibly of what is carried in the right hand,
is Mexican.

That these plates are not wholly the work of the Indians found in- habiting the southern sections of the United States, or of their direct ancestors, is admitted. That they were not made by an aboriginal artisan of Central America or Mexico of ante-Columbian times, I think is probable if not from the designs themselves, from the apparent evi- dence that the work was done in part with hard metallic tools.

(2) Plates like those of this collection have been found, so far as I can ascertain, only in northern Georgia and northern and southern Illinois. The bird figure represented in Fig. 192, obtained by Maj. Powell, Director of the U. S. Geological Survey, from a mound near Peoria, Illinois, is introduced here for comparison with the bird figures found in the Etowah mound.

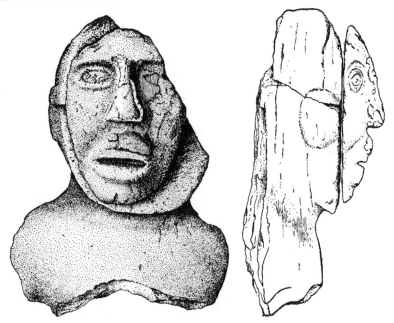

FIG. 191.—Bust from Etowah mounds.

Another was obtained from an ordinary stone grave in Union county, Illinois, by Mr. Thing, while engaged by the Bureau of Eth- nology. From a similar grave at the same place he also obtained the plate represented in Fig. 85. Fragments of another similar plate were taken by Mr. Earle from a stone grave in a mound in Alexander county, Illinois. All these specimens were received by the Bureau of Ethnol- ogy, and are now in the National Museum.

I can not enter at present into a discussion of the questions raised by the discovery of these engraved shells, nor is it necessary that I should do so, as Mr. W. H. Holmes has discussed somewhat fully these de- signs in the Second Annual Report of the Bureau of Ethnology and I have ventured in "The Story of a Mound of the Shawnees in pre-

Columbian times," to suggest a possible explanation of their presence in the interior regions. I may add that these figured copper plates and engraved shells present a problem very difficult to solve, as is evident from the following facts:

(1) A number of the designs bear too strong resemblance to those of Mexico and Central America to warrant us in supposing this similarity to be accidental. (2) The fact that some of them were found in connection with articles of European manufacture is unquestionable. (3) The indications of European workmanship are too evident to be overlooked. (4) The evidence that some of the engraved shells can be traced to the Indians is well-nigh conclusive.

Mound b.—This was examined by sinking a shaft 12 feet square in the center to the original soil, which was reached at the depth of 19 feet from the top. Nothing was found indicating burials. The top layer to the depth of 2 feet consisted chiefly of white sand; next, 9 feet of red clay; then, 2 feet more of white sand; and, lastly, 6 feet of dark sandy loam to the original surface of the ground.

About the center of the shaft were the remains of four posts, two being parallel with the other two. They were 2 feet apart one way and 6 feet the other; that is to say, they stood at the corners of a parallelogram 2 feet wide and 6 feet long, and were in a comparatively sound condition, about 6 inches in diameter and extended 4 feet below the surface of the mound. They were probably the remains of some comparatively modern structure. The plow had taken off the tops to the depth of

FIG. 192.—Copper plate with bird figure; mound near Peoria, Illinois.

several inches. In the lower sand stratum the breast bone of a turkey and several bones of a bear were discovered.

Here and there throughout the 9-foot stratum were patches of dark red clay from 18 inches to 2 feet in diameter, that had been hardened by fire. The dimensions of this mound, which is in the form of a truncated four-sided pyramid, quite regular and steep, are as follows: The longer diameter of the base 130 feet, the shorter 120 feet; the longer diameter of the level top 90 feet, the shorter 81 feet; the height in the center 19 feet, though if measured from the surrounding surface this would be increased by some 3 or 4 feet.

Subsequently a thorough examination was made of mound *g*, which stands about 450 yards north of the large mound and, as will be seen by reference to the plat (Fig. 182), outside of and some distance beyond the ditch. It is a low, conical tumulus, rounded on top, 192 feet in circumference at the base and 4½ feet high.

The construction of the mound, commencing at the bottom and going upward, is as follows: First, a layer 2 feet thick of dark red clay resting on the original surface of the ground; mixed and scattered through this layer was a considerable quantity of pure charcoal, also water-worn bowlders, all thoroughly burned; next above and lying on this a 2-inch stratum of river sand which had been burned, and, lastly, the remainder of the mound was finished up with clay of a deep red color without any admixture of ashes or charcoal, though the bottom portion, which rested immediately on the sand, presented some indications of heat. This layer was so hard that it was difficult to penetrate it.

In the 2-inch sand stratum were two small pieces of very distinctly glazed pottery and lying at the bottom of the mound, on the natural surface of the ground, a piece of unglazed, ornamented pottery and a broken clay pipe.

The bright red clay of this mound is similar to that in the land around it, while the darker variety is like that found a quarter of a mile away.

An examination was also made of the strip of land on the east side of the mounds and along the north bank of the Etowah river. This land, it is proper to remark, has been under cultivation for many years. This examination was made by sinking pits, from 5 to 7 feet square and from 2 to 4½ feet deep, at various places over the area, carrying them down in all cases to what appeared to be the second and undisturbed natural layer.

The variation in the depth of the top layer is due in part to overflows from the river, the soil in some places having been washed out and deposits made in other places by this agency. But the examination made shows this layer over the entire area, to be, in the main, one vast refuse heap, as it is composed of sandy loam, ashes, red clay, fragments of pottery, charcoal, and other refuse matter. In some places the appearance of the red clay shows that it has been dropped here in " batches" of a half bushel or less; in other places it is in a continuous mass, forming a layer; moreover, it must be borne in mind that it does not belong here, but was brought from a distance of nearly or quite half a mile, the nearest point where it could be obtained.

This made earth is literally full of mussel shells, terrapin shells, animal bones, small fragments of pottery, with patches of charcoal and ashes scattered through the mass. The pottery and animal bones were broken into minute fragments. Among the animal bones (no human bones were found here) are many of the bear and hundreds of the turkey. Waterworn bowlders were also found scattered through this deposit and in every case showed very distinctly the action of fire.

In some instances the charcoal found was in cylindrical pieces 3 or 4 inches long, but never more than 3 inches in diameter. These were evidently sections of pine saplings. In the bottom of one of the shafts were two post holes sunk into the natural soil beneath to the depth of

18 inches. These holes, which were 16 inches in diameter, had perfectly smooth sides and were filled with pure sand. The two were 12 inches apart.

At the bottom of another shaft, 4 feet below the present surface of the ground, were discovered some partially burned corncobs. These were in a little heap and completely surrounded by charcoal, which has doubtless assisted in their preservation.

This refuse layer extends some distance west of the three mounds.

Mound d.—This is located about 150 yards due east of the large mound and is one of those marked *F* in Jones's figure. It is circular in form, the diameter of the base about 50 feet, and, although it shows externally a height of only 4 feet above the surrounding ground, by excavation it was found to be in fact 9 feet high above the original surface on which it was built, the land around it having been raised by deposits from overflows and débris. The excavation was carried to the bottom, 5 feet below the present surface of the ground, there being no indication that a pit had been dug. At the depth of about 14 inches below the top of the mound a layer of partially burned clay from 2 to 3 inches thick was reached, the smooth side down. The impressions of twigs and grass could be seen running through it. This rested on a layer of packed ashes 8 inches thick, which was literally filled mith mussel shells and animal bones, but so burned and packed that it was difficult to drive a pick through the mass. Next below this was a stratum in which were pieces of charcoal, next a layer of dark red clay 2 feet thick, and lastly a bottom layer, 2 feet thick, of rich loam. This last layer was crowded with fragments of pottery and decayed animal bones, among which was noticed the head of a squirrel. Here were found one bone implement and some pieces of mica.

Mound e.—One hundred feet north of the preceding is another mound, oval in form and round topped, 60 by 80 feet in diameter and 6 feet high above the surrounding ground, but in fact 10 feet high above the original surface on which it was built. The stratification, commencing at the bottom and going upwards, was found to be as follows: First, a layer 1 foot thick of dark red clay resting on the original surface, intermixed with which was charcoal; then 1 foot of muck and charcoal; next, 2 feet of bright red clay; then 2 inches of sand; next, 1 foot of charcoal and ashes; then 3 feet of bright red clay; next, 1 foot of clay burned almost as hard as a brick; and lastly, a top layer of soil 6 inches thick. In the bottom layer were a number of fragments of pottery, and in the 1-foot layer of charcoal and ashes a piece of a polished celt and a small worked stone. The 3-foot stratum of bright red clay could not be distinguished from a natural deposit; in fact would have been taken as such but for the layer of charcoal and ashes below it. The burned clay layer was so hard that it could scarcely be broken up with a pick. The mound showed evidences of heat throughout. No traces of human or animal bones were noticed in it.

THE PARROT MOUND.

This single mound is located near the north bank of Etowah river, 3½ miles west of Cartersville, on a level bottom under cultivation. It is oval in form, rounded on top, its longest diameter (east and west), at base, being 65 feet and greatest width 48 feet; height, 8 feet. It consisted chiefly of pure yellow clay; first a top layer 5 feet thick of soft clay; then a layer from 1 to 2 inches thick of pure sand, and below this to the natural surface yellow clay. No relics or indications of fire were seen.

THE EDWARDS MOUND.

This is situated on the south side of Etowah river, directly opposite the Tumlin mounds. It is on a level bottom, 100 feet from the river, oval in form, 80 feet long at base, by 55 in width, 8 feet high, and flat on top.

An excavation of this mound showed the surrounding slope to be constructed entirely of yellow clay and distinct from the central portion, resembling in this respect mound No. 3, of the Tumlin group. The central portion was made by filling in with sand and red and yellow clay, with here and there a small batch of gravel; but wherever the gravel occurred the earth was burnt around it, and it also showed the action of fire. No human or other remains were observed.

THE LEAP MOUND.

This is 3 miles west of Cartersville and within a few feet of the Cherokee railroad, on bottom land about 35 or 40 feet above low-water mark. It is oval in form and flat on top; circumference of the base, 240 feet; longer diameter of the top, 53 feet; shorter diameter, 35 feet; height, 4½ feet. In the construction of this mound it appears that the original surface of the ground was first leveled and on this a layer, consisting of red clay, sand, and ashes, 18 inches thick, was placed; then it was finished off with yellow clay to the top.

In addition to the preceding the following mounds in this county were examined, but, presenting nothing novel or very interesting, will be very briefly noticed:

THE BEN AKERMAN MOUND.

This is situated on the farm of Mr. Benj. Akerman, 7 miles west of Cartersville, on the east side of Etowah river. It stands on the margin of a terrace overlooking the narrow valley of the river, is of the ordinary conical form, diameter 38 to 40 feet, height 4 feet, but it has been plowed over for several years. The stratification was as follows: A top layer of soil an inch or two in thickness; then, below this, a layer 3 feet thick of dark red clay, with spots here and there through it of charcoal, ashes, and burned clay and sand, or, in other words, small fire beds; below this, a foot and a half of bright red unburned clay; and last, resting on the original soil, a layer, about an inch thick, of mussel shells. In the thick layer of dark clay, near the center, was a single limestone slab standing on end; immediately over this the clay was thoroughly burned. It is perhaps worthy of notice that this clay had the appearance of having been sun-dried before being burned; from which it is inferred that a portion of the top was added sometime after the main body of the mound was built, and that the stone was planted at this time. At the bottom of this thick layer, in the center, was about a quart of charred corn (maize) and corn-cobs. Nothing else was found.

THE CONYERS MOUND.

This is situated on the farm of Mr. Conyers, in the southeastern part of the county, on Euharlee creek, is somewhat oval, the longer diameter, 98 feet, shorter 68; height, 7 feet. The stratification was as follows: First, a top layer 6 inches thick, of soil; next, a layer, 4½ feet thick, of red clay mixed with dark soil, with charcoal and ashes scattered through it. In the top of this layer, at the center, was a curious basin-shaped fire-bed, 12 inches deep at the center and 2 feet in diameter. The next layer, 6 inches thick, consisted of pure white sand, and, last, a layer, 1½ feet thick, of loam resting on the original surface of the ground. No indications of burial or articles were observed.

THE ROWLAND MOUNDS.

These are located on the south bank of Etowah river, about 3 miles southeast of Cartersville. The group consists of three mounds and a cemetery; the largest is somewhat irregular in form, the longer diameter 150 feet, the shorter 140, the whole height 20 feet, but the height of the artificial portion 15 feet, rounded on the top. One-half of this was dug away; but finding neither specimens nor skeletons, no further investigations were made, but the strata being more numerous than usual are considered of sufficient interest to be mentioned here. First, a top layer, 6 inches, of soil; then, 3½ feet of yellow clay mixed with sand; then, one foot of sand and ashes; next, 2 feet of sand; then, 1 foot of ashes; then, 3 feet of yellow clay; next, 1 foot of sand and ashes; and lastly, resting on the natural earth, a uniform level layer of red clay, 3 feet thick. The whole rested on a natural elevation about 5 feet high. This elevation probably extended, when the mound was built, over the entire bottom, but has been worn away by frequent overflows. An occasional fragment of pottery was found here and there in the different strata, but no other relics were observed. The rather heavy layers of sand and ashes indicate that the mound was built by successive additions made at widely separated periods.

The cemetery lies to the east of the mound near the bank of the river. A somewhat careful exploration of this was made, but it was found that a considerable portion of it had been washed away by the frequent overflows. This conclusion is based upon the fact that a portion of the area has been washed out to the depth of 2 to 2½ feet, leaving exposed layers of stones like those found under skeletons in the remaining graves, and numerous fragments of human bones.

At one point were three skeletons lying extended side by side on their backs, heads east. They lay at a depth of 2½ feet under the surface, and rested on a single layer of water-worn bowlders which formed the bottom of the grave. The stones had the appearance of having been heated and then dipped into cold water. At the head of the grave was a medium-sized bowl. Resting on the faces was an iron boring implement and hammer; around the neck of the middle skeleton were the remains of a strand of small shell beads. Between the skeletons were found a broken soapstone pipe, a piece of mica, and fragments of pottery.

At another point was a single skeleton, doubled up and resting on the left side. This was 2 feet below the surface, resting on a layer of stones similar to those in the other grave.

Not far distant, on the farm of Mr. Lewis Sams, three other mounds were examined, with the following results: No. 1, circular in form and round on top, circumference of base 152 feet, and height 5 feet, was found to be simply a mass of yellow sand with shells mixed through it. Part of a human upper jaw was found, but this was probably accidentally put in while building, as there were no indications of burial. At the bottom in the center was a bed of charcoal 6 inches deep and 2 feet in diameter.

No. 2, circular and flat on top; circumference of the base, 142 feet; diameter of the top, 12 feet; height, 3 feet. Built entirely of sand, without stratification, but with shells intermixed, no ashes, coals, relics, or remains in it.

No. 3, circular and round on top; circumference of base, 111 feet; height, 3 feet; composed entirely of sand.

HABERSHAM COUNTY.

But one mound in this county was examined. This is situated on the farm of Mr. Patton Jarrett, in the western part of the county, on the south bank of Tugalo river, one-fourth of a mile above the mouth of Toccoa creek. It is conical in form, the base almost exactly circular, precisely 100 feet in diameter, and a little over 14 feet high. The owner would permit no further examination than could be made by sinking one shaft. Nothing further than the stratification was ascertained, which is as follows: (1) top layer, 2½ feet of soil similar to that of the surrounding surface, but with a quantity of charcoal scattered through it; (2) a layer 1 inch thick of charcoal; (3) 6 inches of dark clay or muck; (4) 2 feet of sandy loam; (5) 6 inches of bright red, very hard, clay, apparently sun-dried; (6) 4 feet of dark, rich loam, with a little charcoal scattered through it; (7) 6 inches of dark clay or muck; (8) 6 inches of sandy loam; (9) 2 feet of dark, rich loam; and, lastly, resting on the original surface, 2 feet of river sand. In the sixth and ninth layers were a few fragments of pottery.

ELBERT COUNTY.

THE REMBERT MOUNDS.

These mounds were visited by Bartram in 1773, who thus describes them:

These wonderful labors of the ancients stand in a level plain very near the bank of the river; now 20 or 30 yards from it; they consist of conical mounts of earth and four square terraces. The great mount is in the form of a cone about 40 or 50 feet high, and the circumference of its base 200 or 300 yards, entirely composed of the loamy rich earth of the low grounds; the top or apex is flat; a spiral path or track leading from the ground up to the top is still visible, where now grows a large, beautiful spreading, red cedar. There appear four niches excavated out of the sides of this hill, at different heights from the base, fronting the four cardinal points. These niches or sentry boxes are entered into from the winding path and seem to have been meant for resting places or lookouts. The circumjacent level grounds are cleared and planted with Indian corn at present and I think the proprietor of the lands, who accompanied us to this place, said that the mount itself yielded above 100 bushels in one season.[1]

In 1848 George White (author of White's Statistics of Georgia) visited this group, in regard to which he remarks as follows:

The large mound corresponds exactly with Bartram's description of it, with this exception, that the sides and summit are covered with a growth of cane and several large trees. The smaller mounds have been almost destroyed. Capt. Rembert has excavated the smaller mounds and found human skeletons, jars, pipes, beads, breastplates, stone hammers, hatchets, arrowheads, etc. Some of these are now in our possession and are really objects of curiosity.[2]

If these descriptions were correct at the time they were made, very decided changes have taken place in the appearance of the works since then. The group, consisting of 2 mounds, is situated on the farm of Mr. Z. A. Tate, near the bank of the Savannah river, 4 miles above the mouth of Broad river. They stand on the level bottom, one 130 and the other 320 feet from the bank of the river. This bottom extends several miles north and south, and three-fourths of a mile back from the river to the hills. As will be seen by reference to Fig. 193, which shows a section, north and south, of the area, there are 2 "washouts" flanking these mounds. The one on the north (*a*), commencing at the river, extends a fourth of a mile back in a southwest direction, covering an area of 7 or 8 acres. This approaches within about 200 feet of the large mound (*b*). The one on the south (*c*) also commences at the river and extends back southeastward only a few hundred feet beyond the mounds and runs within a few feet of them. These excavations are denominated "washouts" because the present owner of the land, Mr. Tate, remembers when they were made by high water. Nevertheless,

[1] "Travels," pp. 324 to 325.　　[2] Statistics of Georgia, p. 230.

judging from present appearances, there are reasons for believing that at least a portion of the earth used in the construction of the mounds was obtained here, leaving depressions, and that, during high water, when the land was overflowed, as is frequently the case, channels were washed out from them to the river. The south margin of the southern "washout" is fully 4 feet higher than the land on which the mounds stand.

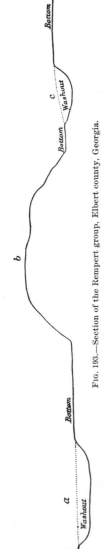

FIG. 193.—Section of the Rempert group, Elbert county, Georgia.

Mound No. 1.—This, which is much the larger of the two, stands 130 feet from the river bank, and is, exclusive of the ramp or projection, an exact circle 151 feet in diameter, nearly flat on top, and 30 feet high at the highest point (north side), but only 27 feet near the south side. The diameter of the top is about 70 feet. The plan of the ramp or rather extension, as it seems to be, is shown in Fig. 194. The vertical outline of the mound, with a section of the shaft, is presented in Fig. 195. The right or southern end of this shows the slope of the extension. This has an average width on top of 20 feet.

The mound is covered with trees such as sugarberry, walnut, hickory, and oak. One sugarberry is 6 feet in circumference (at stump height); a walnut, 5 feet; a hickory, 3½ feet; and an oak, 10 feet. The shaft was carried down to the bottom. The first foot was of soil (*a*), then 7 feet of dark sandy loam (*b*), next 1½ feet of thoroughly burned yellowish clay and sand (*c*), with a large percentage of ashes. This layer had the appearance of having been put down and packed while wet and then burned; it was so hard that it was difficult to break it. Next 3 feet of black earth, also packed (*d*); then 8½ feet of pure sand (*e*); and last, resting on the original surface, 6 feet of hard bluish muck (*f*). All of these layers, except the bottom one, had charcoal, mica, fragments of pottery, and animal bones scattered through them, but the last were so far decomposed that none of them could be saved.

As fragments of pottery and animal bones were found in spots, together with ashes and other indications of fire, it is probable these were fire beds where cooking had been done. All that portion of the shaft below the layer of burned clay was so very dry that when turned up it would crumble to dust. It is possible that the bottom layer of blue "muck" is partly the original soil, as it is much like the surrounding soil, and that a part of the surrounding surface has been washed away since the mound was built.

Mound No. 2 (not shown in the figure) stands about 40 feet west of the base of No. 1. It is oblong in form, 58 feet long north and south, 41 feet wide, and 6 feet high. A large shaft had been sunk in the middle by some previous explorer, hence investigations were confined to the eastern and western sides, which presented one or two peculiarities. With the exception of the top layer of soil, 1 foot thick, the remainder on the east side con-sisted of river sand, with particles of charcoal and vegetable matter mixed through it, while on the west it was composed of small masses of red clay and dark earth. In this, at the depth of 2½ feet, were the bones of a single adult skeleton. These were packed together in a space 2 feet square and 18 inches deep; the skull was placed face down and all the other bones piled about it. Immediately over the

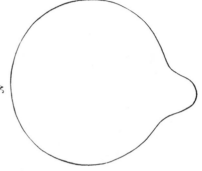

FIG. 194.—Plan of mound No. 1, Rembert group.

bones was a layer of red clay 2 inches thick, burned hard. Resting on this layer were the remains of a pretty thoroughly burned fire. A few fragments of pottery and a small clay pipe were found.

RICHMOND COUNTY.

While this report was being prepared Mr. Henry L. Reynolds, one of my assistants, was sent to certain points in Georgia and South Carolina to make examination of some works to which my attention had been called. The result of this examination is given in the following report, made by him. This includes the Hollywood mound of Richmond county, Georgia, which proved to be of unusual interest, and the McDowell mound, Kershaw county, South Carolina.

THE HOLLYWOOD MOUND.

There are two mounds situated in a bend of the Savannah river, in Richmond county, Georgia, 3 miles east from Hollywood, a small flag station on the Georgia Central railroad about 10 miles below Augusta and 5 miles above Silver bluff. This latter, which is on the South Carolina side, seems to me, after a special investigation of this question, to be the most probable site of the ancient town of Cutifachiqui, where De Soto and his army were so generously entertained.

The mounds are situated on the lowest river land, which is annually subject to inundation. The overflows of the Savannah are very destructive, particularly at this point. Cattle are drowned, the rich riparian crops are destroyed, and the farmers impoverished. At such times these mounds are the only land visible above a broad expanse of water, and it is this fact which has given rise to the tradition among the people of the vicinity that they were thrown up by some former owner of the property to serve as places of refuge for his cattle during these inundations. A quarter of a mile to the north of the mounds near the

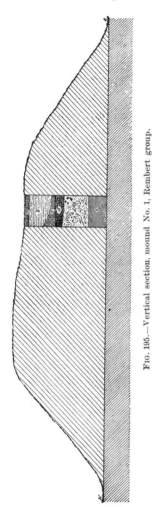

FIG. 195.—Vertical section, mound No. 1, Rembert group.

river bank is an extensive shell heap, composed chiefly of the shells of *Unio*. Upon the larger of the two mounds a simple barn has been erected. This mound appears to have been originally of the pyramidal type, but since its surface has suffered so greatly from the cattle that have been penned in upon it and the washing occasioned by floods, its original character, as well as whatever smaller physical features it may have presented, is now almost entirely lost.

Mound No. 2, the one excavated, is in an adjoining field, the property of a gentleman of Augusta, Georgia. It is 280 feet due north of No. 1, is conical in form, 10 feet high, and 70 feet in diameter. Though originally surmounted by a small log barn, which a former flood removed to a point at its base, the mound had evidently remained unmolested since that time, for several small cottonwood trees, as well as considerable underbrush, were growing upon it.

The excavation was conducted as follows: First two trenches, each 10 feet wide, were cut crosswise through the center, one north and south, the other east and west. These were carried down to the bottom, and in some places to the original pure micaceous soil that underlies the mixed loam of the surrounding field. The segments that remained were then cut down several feet beyond the radius that covered the interments found in the trenches. In this manner the

mound was thoroughly excavated and all its buried contents exposed.

The mound is stratified, or, in other words, constituted of two different kinds of soil, the upper being strictly sandy micaceous loam, 3 feet thick; the lower a hard, compact vegetable earth, taken from what is commonly called in the south " crawfish land." This rested at the bottom upon 9 inches of a very black and rich vegetable mold, permeated throughout with innumerable small pieces of burnt pottery, charcoal,

POT FROM HOLLYWOOD MOUND, GEORGIA.

shell, mica, chipped flint, and charred and decayed bones too small for identification. The surface of this black mold appeared to be the original surface upon which the mound was built.

All the interments lay within the lower division of the mound. The absence of burial in the upper division, the different character of the earth, and the presence of fragmentary pottery (N. M.[1] 135278–84) unlike that found in the subsoil, seems to indicate a subsequent addition. It also seems to indicate that the original builders or others who succeeded them were disposed to utilize these their old tombs for some purpose in connection with floods, for this additional earth seems to have been cast upon the mound to increase its elevation.

It will also be seen from the sectional diagram that there were two general series of interments which comprise the find, or rather the important contents of the mound. The lowermost of these contained specimens either resting on the black mold at the bottom or within a foot and a half above it, and the upper from a foot to 2 feet below the line separating the two strata, or from 4 to 5 feet below the surface of the mound. Fire played some part in the ceremony of burial, for hearth remains of burnt earth and ashes were seen with each series of burials. These burials were made before the subdivision was finally completed; in other words, they were not intrusive, for there was no disturbance of the soil above them.

Scattered indiscriminately throughout the soil composing the upper division of the mound were the following articles: One stone chisel (N. M. 135271), one stone celt, eight small pieces of white and blue glazed European crockery (N. M. 135279), many small fragments of Indian ware, and five pieces of old-fashioned rudely wrought iron nails much oxidized (N. M. 135280). These appeared to have been thrown up with the earth in the construction of this part of the mound.

In the subsoil the hearth A (Fig. 196, which shows a horizontal section) was first discovered almost touching the line of division. It was of reddish burnt earth, covered with pure wood ashes and a small quantity of charcoal. It was 5 feet in diameter, 2 feet thick, and rested at the bottom on fine sand. Adjoining it on the southeast lay a large culinary pot (N. M. 135205), indicated on the diagram (Fig. 196) as No. 1, the rim being 10 inches below the line dividing the lower from the upper strata and 3 feet 10 inches below the surface of the mound. Decomposed animal matter was found in the bottom mingled with scattered particles of black and white ashes. One foot and a half east from pot No. 1, on the same level, lay another pot, 2 (N. M. 135209), having inside of it another pot (N. M. 135208). In consequence of their inferior composition, badly decayed condition, and the pressure of the hard superincumbent earth, these vessels were so badly injured that they fell apart when taken out. Almost alongside of the last, on the same level, lay another, 3 (N. M. 135211), inside of which was an

---

[1] " N. M. " in this connection signifies " National Museum " number.

inverted pot (N. M. 135210). Decayed animal matter, a few bone beads, a fragment of the tooth of some animal, and some scattering charcoal cinders were found in the bottom. In the earth alongside of these pots was found a piece of iron (N. M. 135275). Directly south of pot No. 1, on the same level, 6 feet distant, lay another pot, 4 (N. M. 135212). In the earth surrounding it were found pieces of white European porcelain (N. M. 135279, Fig. 197). East of this last, 6 feet distant, lay a small pot, 5 (N. M. 135198). The rims of these two pots appeared to be about on the same level. Not far from pot No. 5 were the decayed remains of a repoussé figured copper plate (N. M. 135226) so thin and brittle that it was with difficulty that it could

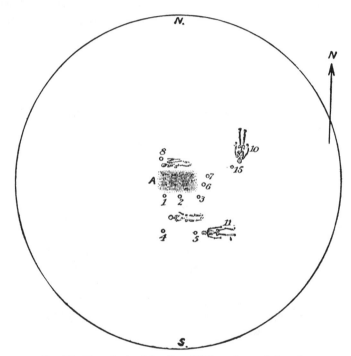

FIG. 196.—Upper horizontal section of Hollywood mound, Georgia.

be handled without breaking. Alongside were the faint indications of human burial, as seen in small pieces of decayed bone and human teeth. Between these last and those indicated by the figures 1, 2, 3 was a scant line of decayed bone, so scant and decayed that it was impossible to tell whether or not it was human. Traces of fire were seen about these bones. North of these traces of bone, and immediately under the line of pots Nos. 1, 2, 3, were three small upright timber molds, varying from 1 to 1½ feet long. No traces of the timbers remained. Apparently lying on the dividing line between the two strata, 14 feet northwest of the center, was the fragment of an old drawing knife (N. M. 135261). A rude old iron nail, very much ox-

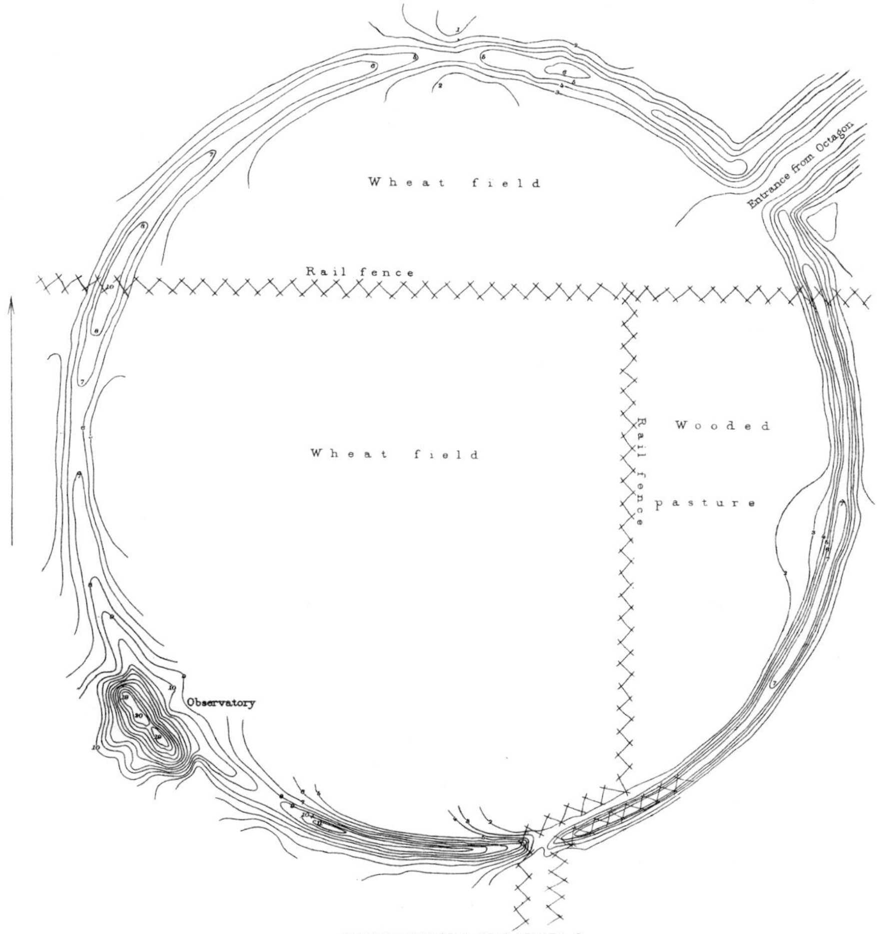

Wheat   field

Entrance from Octagon

Rail fence

Wheat   field

Rail fence

Wooded

pasture

Observatory

OBSERVATORY CIRCLE. NEAR NEWARK. O.

Scale, 150 feet to 1 inch, or 1:1800

Contour Interval 1 foot

Surveyed in 1891

dized, was found on the surface of the subsoil, 3 feet deep and 12 feet southwest of the center. Another rude though sharp-pointed ancient iron nail was found not far from the last, but 8 inches below the surface of the subsoil. A small piece of green glass was found 3 inches below the surface of the subsoil, in the southeast segment and east of the hearth. Resting on the sand that seemed to stretch over the entire area beneath these pots and the fire bed between them were the pots indicated by Nos. 6 (Pl. XIX, N. M. 135192) and 7 (N. M. 135200). A large bowl (N. M. 135199) was found inside of pot No. 6, and by the side of the two ves-sels, at the bottom, were the scanty re-

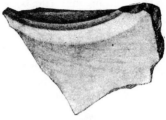

FIG. 197.—Fragment of European pottery, Hollywood mound, Georgia.

mains of some fabric. Two feet 8 inches from the surface of the mound were the remains of decayed timber, which ran down about 1½ feet to the east of the pot at 6, almost touching its eastern rim. It is not un-

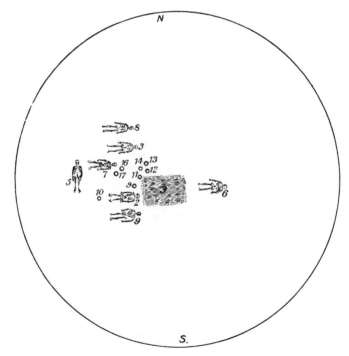

FIG. 198.—Lower horizontal section of Hollywood mound, Georgia.

likely that this was the remnant of some post planted on the surface of the mound by some of its white owners.

Alongside of the northwestern edge of the hearth A was a line of decayed bones, which, from the small pieces of skull and two or three teeth that remained, were found to be human. Though in the very last stages of decay, the remains were so remarkably meager as to give the impression that all the bones of the body could not have been buried. The soil about all the bones found in this upper layer was absolutely free from any trace of animal or vegetable matter, which leads to the opinion that the bones were buried after having been denuded of flesh. A pot, No. 8 (N. M. 135193), lay close to the skull remains thus found. Like pots 1, 6, and 8, it had a small hole in the bottom, but had another sounder pot (N. M. 135200) placed within it. Seven and a half feet to the northeast of the fire bed, on a level apparently 5 inches lower than that of the pots heretofore described, lay pot No. 15 N. M. 135213. Near it to the northeast were the remains of human bones (No. 10).

FIG. 199.—Pot from Hollywood mound, Georgia (135197).

In the lower division, as in that last described, all the articles seemed to be clustered about a hearth (B Fig. 198, which shows a lower horizontal section) and on the same general level. Here most of the human remains were found, but, like those in the upper burial, only the merest traces were observed. The conditions of this locality are very conducive to decay. Decayed and meager as they were, sufficient evidence was had in the case of each skeleton to show that it was human, such as the presence of teeth and certain identifiable bones.

The hearth B, which in some places was 10 feet in diameter, was situated wholly southwest of the center. Its composition was peculiar. It consisted of four layers of pure white ashes each one-half inch thick, separated by red burnt earth averaging an inch in thickness. Ashes

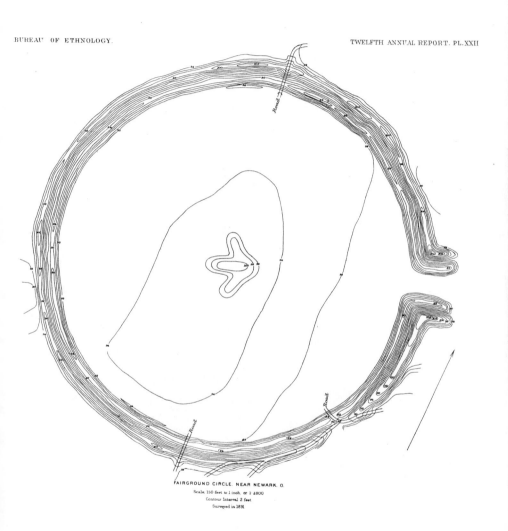

FAIRGROUND CIRCLE. NEAR NEWARK. O.

Scale, 150 feet to 1 inch, or 1 : 1800

Contour Interval 2 feet

Surveyed in 1891

formed the bottom as well as the topmost layer. The hearth rested on the curious black mold at the bottom. This black mold did not penetrate to the north and east border of the mound, but lay only over an area of which this hearth was the center.

Southwest of the hearth B and in connection with the remains of skeleton No. 2 was pot 9 (N. M. 135197), a bottle standing on a tripod of human heads, shown in Fig. 199. As traces of fire were noticed above this pot and skeleton, there seems to have been more than one ceremony attendant upon the burial of these articles. The pot 10 (N.

FIG. 200.—A painted vessel from Hollywood mound, Georgia.

M. 135194), which was found at the foot of this skeleton, seemed to have had originally a wooden cover, for in the earth taken from the top some small traces of decayed wood were noticed, and in the earth about it lay a clay pipe (N. M. 135223). Northeast of pot No. 9, and also near the fire bed, was a long-neck jar, 11 (N. M. 135295). (See Fig. 200.) At its western base lay the pipes (N. M. 135216, 135218, 135219, 135220, 135221, 135222), five typical forms of which are shown in Pl. XXIV. Pipe 3a and 3b (135216) was carved from soapstone; the remainder are of clay. Adjoining these articles on the northeast and on the same

level were pots 12, 13, and 14 (N. M. 135196, 135204, 137215), and 6
inches below the former lay a copper ax head (N. M. 135228) wrapped
in cloth and incased in bark.

FIG. 201.—Pot from Hollywood mound, Georgia.

Three or 4 feet west of these, lying against each other, were two other
pots, 16 and 17 (N. M. 135202, 135203). No. 16 (Fig. 201) was found lying
on its side upon the black mold at the bottom, and beneath it, as if the

FIG. 202.—Shell beads from Hollywood mound, Georgia.

pot were placed on top of them, were the fragments of thin and very brittle plates of copper (N. M. 135227), bearing Mexican figures in relief, some
flakes of mica, and decayed pieces of unidentified shells. The copper

FIG. 203.—Copper article from Hollywood mound, Georgia.

had been originally first wrapped in some kind of leather, then in fine,
rush matting, and the whole incased in bark. Beneath No. 17, which
was also lying on its side, was a beautiful biconcave disk of quartz

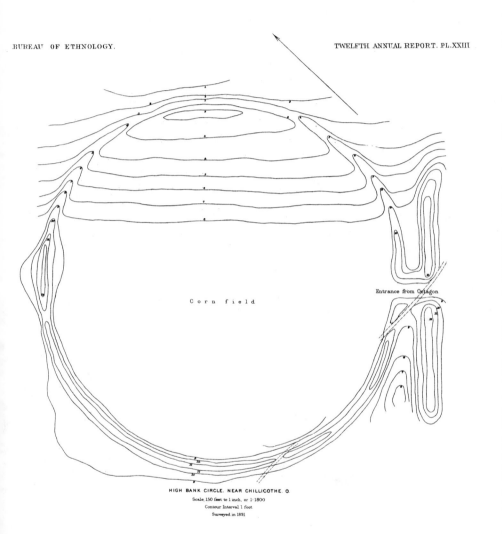

Corn field

Entrance from Octagon

HIGH BANK CIRCLE. NEAR CHILLICOTHE. O.

Scale, 150 feet to 1 inch, or 1:1800

Contour Interval 1 foot

Surveyed in 1891

(N, M. 135260).   Beneath this last, 3 or 4 inches deeper, and lying on the black mold at the bottom, were two copper celts (N. M. 135229) wrapped in cloth together and incased on both sides in bark.   Accompanying this were several large pieces of mica.   There were scarcely more than a handful of decayed bones in connection with these objects, identifiable only by the help of a few human teeth.

About the neck bones of skeleton 3, which lay 13 feet northwest of

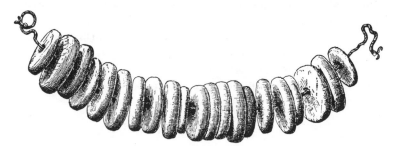

Fig. 204.—Shell beads from Hollywood mound, Georgia.

the center, were found a lot of shell beads (N. M. 135247, Fig. 202), and below these, a foot to the south, another lot of shell beads (N. M. 135242), a lot of perforated shell disks (N. M. 135248), the copper-sheathed ornament of wood (N. M. 135256) shown in Fig. 203, and a lump of galenite.

Immediately north of the remains last described, on the same level and about 15 feet northwest of the center, lay the bones and teeth of

Fig. 205.—Pipe from Hollywood mound, Georgia.

what seemed to be another skeleton (No. 8).   With it were found the lot of shell beads (N. M. 135233) shown in Fig. 204, a copper ax or celt incased in wood (N. M. 135232), the decayed remains of the colu-mella of the *Busycon perversum*, and a lump of soggy glauconite.

Nothing was found with skeleton No. 9, which lay southwest of the fire bed and near to skeleton 2 on the south, except a pipe (N. M. 135224).

Skeleton No. 5 lay about 23 feet west of the center, almost on the black mold at the bottom, and near its head were found a pipe (N. M. 135217), representing the head of an owl (Fig. 205); one decayed shell ornament, three stone celts, five discoidal stones, an anomalous stone implement, and a lump of glauconite. The apparent remains of another human burial were seen to the east of the hearth (skeleton No. 6), and near the teeth was discovered a well-shaped stone celt.

FIG. 206.—Fragment of porcelain from Hollywood mound, Georgia.

A pipe (N. M. 135225) was found in the earth two feet to the south of hearth B.

The piece of blue porcelain (N. M. 135279) shown in Fig. 206 was found 4 feet southwest of the center and 6 feet beneath the surface of the mound.

SOUTH CAROLINA.

KERSHAW DISTRICT.

McDOWELL MOUND No. 1.

The Wateree river is at present washing away the western end of a large mound situated on its left bank on the McDowell farm, 4 miles southwest from Camden, South Carolina. It is a large, oblong structure, which, after repeated plowings and floods is now reduced to 10 feet in height. Its major axis is 154 feet, and minor axis 115 feet. Three smaller mounds are yet to be seen almost adjoining it on the north and east, all of which it is said, were, formerly encircled by a low earthen wall, no trace of which, however, is now visible.

In exploring it a trench 10 to 15 feet wide and 60 feet long was run lengthwise through the mound in a northwest and southeast direction, which was connected also with a north and south trench 15 feet wide, coming from near its southern edge towards the center.

This mound was not used as a place of burial, the scattered fragments of human bones that were found being rather accidentally thrown up with the earth than remains of deliberate interments. The investigation has not succeeded in demonstrating the use for which it was constructed: possibly it was a domiciliary mound.

Some fragmentary human bones, *Unio* shells, and the bones of deer were found scattered indiscriminately here and there through the earth at a depth of from 1 to 2 feet. They manifested but little sign of decay. A foot and a half below the surface, 3 feet east of the center, were the remains of a hearth or fire-bed about 9 feet in diameter. A similar fire-bed 4 feet in diameter lay at the same depth 15 feet south of the center. In the south trench, 6 feet from the center and 3 feet deep, was a small fire-bed, alongside of which were small piles of shells and charred corncobs. The molds left by four posts which had decayed away were met with a short distance east of the center 1½ feet below the surface. The two northernmost ran down perpendicularly 4½ feet, and at the base of the southernmost, 5 feet deep, was a pile of burnt corncobs 1½ feet in diameter and 3 inches deep. Other smaller piles of these charred corncobs were found here and there through the mound at various depths, the deepest being 8 feet. No other feature of interest could be discovered in connection with them. West of the northern post hole, near its base, had been placed a small rude pot of the texture similar to the fragments found in the vicinity. It was found crushed in completely, with a few black coals and conch shells within it. Four feet to the northeast of this, on the same level, lay a pile of sixteen shells (N. M. 135763). Two small pieces of human bones were also found in the vicinity.

Twenty-five feet south of the center, at a depth of 5 feet, a large fire-bed resting on sand was encountered, directly beneath which, in vertical succession, were three others, the lowermost being 8½ feet deep. A pile of charred corncobs and a pile of shells were found adjoining these hearths on the north at the depth of 6 feet. All the shells found thus in piles in this mound were of the same kind and uniform in size. In the earth directly over these fire-beds were found a piece of perforated sheet copper (N. M. 135761) and a broken pipe (N. M. 135759). Forty-two feet east of the center, at a depth of 4 feet, four post holes were in a line north and south, but they could not be traced deeper than from a foot to a foot and a half. Immediately below the center, 9 feet deep, there was a pile of wood ashes mixed with black coals, 1½ feet in diameter. Near by lay a small pottery disk and a small piece of bone from a human arm.

MCDOWELL MOUND No. 2.

This is a small mound lying about 30 rods northeast of the one last described. It has been so materially reduced by the plow and the frequent floods of the river that it is at present only 2 feet high. A trench was carried through it north and south, 4 feet deep and 11 feet wide, but nothing was found except the remains of a perpendicular post, 1 foot in diameter, a little to the south of the center. The post was indicated by the charcoal in the mold and about 2 feet of decayed wood at the bottom. It appeared to be either of cottonwood or sassafras. Scattered promiscuously through the earth of this mound were fragments of pottery similar to that taken from mound No. 1. A small discoidal stone was found.

FLORIDA.

Some work was done in this state by Mr. Rogan, but nothing deemed worthy of notice was observed except the construction and contents of two mounds, which are briefly described as follows:

The Job Smith mound, situated in the extreme southern part of Alachua county and 1 mile north of Watcahootee, on cleared hummock land and surrounded on all sides by hummocks, was composed entirely of sand. A considerable amount of charcoal was found scattered irregularly through it, but there were no indications of stratification. It is circular in form, a little less than 3 feet high, and about 42 feet in diameter.

In the north half six skeletons were found at the bottom, all extended, heads west, and each lying on the right side. They had evidently been laid on the surface of the ground and the mound heaped over them. Around or about the head of each was a small quantity of red paint. The bones were so far decayed that they crumbled to pieces on attempting to remove them. The skeleton lying nearest the center, though not above the ordinary height, was an exceedingly stout and large-boned frame. No implements or vestiges of art of any kind were observed.

Another mound near the center of Alachua county, 3 miles southeast of Gainesville, situated on a high hummock on the land of Mrs. Peter G. Snowdon, was examined. This was composed of white sand, with small quantities of charcoal and ashes scattered here and there through it. Trees of considerable size were growing on it, one a hickory 18 inches in diameter. The mound was circular, but flat on top, 4½ feet high, and 71 feet in diameter. Close to the base, along the north side, ran a trench from which the material of which it was built was probably taken.

Exploration brought to light the fact that a level platform about 1 foot high had first been formed, on which skeletons were placed and the mound then built over them.

Thirty-seven skeletons, or rather the parts of thirty-seven skeletons, pieces of pottery, and a few decomposed conch shells (*Busycon perversum*) were discovered. The condition in which the bones were found showed that all the bodies, or possibly the skeletons after the flesh had been removed, had been buried in the following singular manner: The head was first taken off and placed in an upright position and the rest of the body or frame then disjointed and placed around and upon it. One of the skulls had a hole through it which might have been made by an ordinary rifle ball. It had entered the center of the top of the head and passed out immediately behind the right ear. The hole through which it entered was not ragged, but clean cut. The fragments of pottery were so placed as to make it clear that the vessels had been broken before burial.

ST. JOHNS AND VOLUSIA COUNTIES.

The following interesting account of some mounds in these counties has been kindly furnished the Bureau by Dr. W. H. Dall, from notes made during a trip to Florida in 1885:

MOUNDS AT SATSUMA AND ENTERPRISE.

" Having an opportunity during my absence of visiting the celebrated shell mound at Old Enterprise, on Lake Monroe, I availed myself of it

1

2

3ᵃ

3ᵇ

4

5

PIPES FROM HOLLYWOOD MOUND, GEORGIA.

in order to satisfy my curiosity in regard to certain points connected
with its construction. In this examination I developed certain facts
which seem worthy of being put on record, as they will, to some extent,
modify the inference in regard to the construction of these mounds
which might be drawn from the admirable monograph of Wyman.

"It will be understood, of course, that my remarks relate only to
the particular mounds which I have examined, though perhaps they
may prove of wider application.

"The present state of the mound at Old Enterprise is one of dilapi-
dation. It is situated on land belonging to the De Bary estate and is
fenced in, but the material is used in fertilizing orange groves and
making shell walks, and, by the owners, or with their permission,
probably two-thirds of the mound have been carted away. The work
of destruction at all events gives an excellent section of the mound
down to its very foundations, and, however deplorable it may be on
other grounds, was certainly a great help to me in determining its
structure.

"The mound is smaller than Wyman's frontispiece would lead one
to believe, a misconception which has been brought about unintention-
ally by the artist, and which might have been remedied by putting a
human figure in the foreground. Though it has extended about 150
feet along the lake shore, its width at right angles to that direction
could not have exceeded 50 feet and was probably less. The margins
were originally so steep as to be difficult to scale, except by the path
intended for ascent, but only a few yards of the original slope now
remain, and this will soon be dug away. The mound is situated just to
the eastward of the point where a considerable stream enters the lake,
forming the outlet of the beautiful Green Sulphur spring which lies a
few rods inland. North of the mound a triangular piece of swamp extends from near the stream, which its apex nearly reaches, to a little
bay 400 or 500 yards to the eastward, where the base of the triangle
may be a hundred yards in breadth or more. It is too soft to cross,
and full of saw palmetto, reeds, etc., growing in hummocks separated
by water and semifluid mud. This swamp is being cleared and drained
and will soon cease to exist, but, as the mound originally stood, must
have nearly isolated it from firm ground and formed an excellent defense
against attack from that direction. Moreover, in this swamp lived the
mollusks whose shells have been so important in the construction of
the mound.

"Westward from the mound and northwestward from the swamp lies
an orange grove and some woods; the land gradually rising from the
lake. The soil is composed of a layer 2 or 3 feet thick of beach sand,
humus, and an admixture of muddy matter derived from the swamp,
which was once more extensive in this direction. The surface of the
ground is covered with shells from the mound, which have arrived
there in three ways. Some have been carted over and spread about as
a fertilizer; much has been washed along the shore by storms and

thrown up by the waves on the banks, and some of the shells, particularly the more perfect ones, are so round and light that they have simply been blown by the wind from the sides of the mound, scattered for a mile or two over the surface near the sandy beach, but not carried inland further than open spaces would permit a brisk breeze to blow.

" Deep trenches have been dug in the orange grove to drain the ground between the rows of trees. Into these trenches a certain number of the shells from the surface have been blown or have fallen. Beside these, however, at a depth of 2 or 3 feet from the surface is a layer of mud full of shells of all sorts, and which appears to be a westward extension of the present swamp. This marl and mud appeared to be about 2 feet thick in most places and rested on a hard eolian sandstone resembling the phosphatic rock of western Florida in appearance, but much younger in age, full of recent land shells, and in which Pourtales and Wyman both found human · bones imbedded at Rock island in Lake Monroe.

"Behind the sand of the beach a little lagoon was originally formed, in which gradually accumulated the mud from decaying vegetation brought down by the streams or growing on the spot. Here flourished the *Unios*, *Viviparas*, etc., and in time formed a bed of mud and marl. Upon this the wind blew sand from the beach, and in this way the dry land has grown. The marl in position is rather soft, but when well drained it becomes very hard, almost forming a stone. The shells in it are just as they died, large and small, mostly in good condition, except the *Unios*, which are more perishable than the univalves, and always less perfect. The *Viviparas* are thin and light, but very strong, and a layer of them will sustain a weight of 150 pounds without breaking. Owing to the air they contain they are very buoyant, and a compact layer 4 inches thick spread over the soft mud of the swamp will sustain the weight of a man, a fact which I personally tested. Besides the whole shells, there is a large amount of broken and decayed shelly matter. The large *Ampullarias* are very fragile and may have been broken up, but at all events are very rare in the marl. I saw no perfect ones.

"The shore and bottom of the lake near the mound, and as far as could be observed into the deep water, are composed of clear sharp sand, affording no food or resting place for mollusks, and neither dead nor living ones are found in it, except such as may have been washed from the mound. The mound itself probably stands partly on the original sea beach and partly on the swamp.

" The way in which its materials have been scattered about prevented the attainment of certainty in the matter, but the above suggestion accords with what was observed. About two-thirds of the mound has been dug away nearly to the level of the beach. In 1848 the bluff, where the storms had washed away the lakeward slope, was 15 feet high. The summit of the mound was about 5 feet higher, and on it an

early settler built a small house, which at one time served to accommodate the occasional traveler. All traces of this are now gone and, in
fact, the part of the mound on which it stood is believed to have been
entirely dug away. The nearly vertical face from which excavations
have been made offers an excellent means of inspecting the structure
of the mound. The sides and base are buried in a talus almost exclusively composed of *Vivipara georgiana*, Lea, which have weathered out
of the general mass, and owing to their form and strength have re-
sisted decay. To the casual visitor this talus would give the idea that
the mound was composed of clear *Vivipara* shells, which would be a
very erroneous notion. After clearing away the talus it was evident
that the body of the mound is formed of mud and marl resembling
that previously described as underlying the orange grove and which I
am convinced was brought to the spot from the swamp to build the
mound. Land from the beach would be liable to be washed or blown
away at any time and the marl was but a few yards away. The main
mass, especially toward the base of the mound, is composed of this
material unstratified, and by the percolation of lime water rendered
almost as hard as stone. At about half the height of the mound slight
indications of stratification are apparent; here and there small layers
of clean shells, *Vivipara* or *Ampullaria*, are visible, an inch or two
thick and a yard or two long in section, as if the shells from a repast
had been thrown out. Bits of charcoal, occasional fish, and other
bones are more abundant as we ascend. I did not succeed in finding a
single artificial article of aboriginal origin in all the exposed area and
talus after a careful search. About 2½ feet below the surface, in the
compact material, I found one or two pieces of glass which had been
subjected to the action of fire, and which by age had become beautifully iridescent. It had been originally quite thin and of pale greenish color, like that used for cheap looking glasses, such as are used in
Indian trade. It may, however, have been a relic of the early white
settlers before referred to, though the depth to which it was buried is
adverse to this idea.

" I collected of the rough material composing the mound, about 4 feet
below the surface, enough to fill a box such as holds 100 cigars. This
weighed about 5½ pounds, and 4½ pounds of it were broken up, the contained shells were sorted and identified, with the following result, the
identifiable shells of each species being counted:

Vivipara georgiana, Lea	313
Melania etowahensis, Lea	109
Amnicola, sp. indet	1
Unio buckleyi, Lea (valves)	30
Unio (valves)	5
Ameria scalaris, Jay	4
Glandina truncata, Say	1
Helix (*Polygyra*) *auriformis*, Bld	1
Zonites minuscula, Binney	13

Zonites arborea, Say	1
Zonites (Conulus) chersina, Say	1
Pupa contracta, Say	2
Pupa rupicola, Say	14

"Total, 13 species and 495 specimens of mollusks, besides a fragment of marine shell (a *Cardium*) too small to identify, several fish scales, two pieces of fish bones, and one piece of mammalian bone unidentifiable. The shells tabulated all live in the vicinity at the present time, but are not abundant, owing to the drying up of the swamp or other causes. At suitable localities about the lake they are believed to be abundant as ever at the proper season, i. e., midsummer. Of all the above mentioned, only the *Vivipara* and *Unio* have ever been considered edible. Most of them are far too minute for food. The *Ampullarias* (*A. depressa*, Say), which, as before stated, are not disseminated through the mass, but found assembled in small patches, were therefore probably gathered elsewhere, perhaps at no great distance, and those in the mound are doubtless only relics of dinners. The assemblage is just what we might expect in a fluvial marl, and a similar assemblage would doubtless be found in a similar mass of the marl from the orange grove.

"My conclusion, therefore, is that the mound was artificially constructed as a post of observation (for which it is otherwise peculiarly well situated), a dwelling site, fortification against attack or flood, or for some other purpose requiring a dry or elevated site. That the building up, after high-water mark was passed, was intermittent, and the materials supplemented by kitchen midden matters and that the gradual elevation continued until about the time it was abandoned.

"The theory that it is solely derived from the relics of dinners, etc., seems untenable for the following reasons: (1) The character of the main mass of which it is composed as above described; (2) the original steepness of the sides, too great to have been the unintentional result of throwing out small quantities of empty shells; (3) the improbability that the builders would squat in a marsh or on a beach subject to overflow until their refuse had built them a dry site in spite of themselves; (4) the small area of the top, which renders it highly improbable that the dinner refuse of all who could sit on it could have made such a mound in many centuries; (5) and lastly, the fact that a material similar to that of which the mound is composed is close at hand and offers no difficulties to anyone desiring to get it. I should add that Mr. Le Baron, an engineer who contributed to the Smithsonian Report of 1882 an interesting list of mounds observed by him in Florida, came, on other grounds, to a similar conclusion with regard to this mound.

THE SATSUMA MOUND.

"This mound is situated on the bank of the St. Johns river, about 20 miles south of Palatka, near a small, new settlement called Satsuma.

I did not visit it, but examined a large scow load of material brought from it to Palatka for shell walks, etc. I was informed that it was about 25 feet high and 100 feet long along the bank, with a swamp behind it.

"An examination of the material showed a similar assemblage of species, many of which could not have been gathered for food or any practical use. The consolidated material was also like that at Enterprise, and I was led to suspect from these facts that the Satsuma mound might have been like the former, artificially constructed of mud from an adjacent swamp.

"The question having been recently discussed as to the use by existing residents of Florida of the fresh-water shells of the region for food and it having been incidentally stated by Wyman that the Florida "crackers" eat the *Paludina* (*Vivipara*), and *Unio*, I made careful inquiries among this class of people during my stay and found that none of them had ever heard of eating *Vivipara* and only in one case had *Unio* been tasted, and then as a matter of curiosity, which was so well satisfied that the old man said that 'if the Lord would forgive him for that one he would never try another.'

"The error appears to have arisen from the fact that both the marine and fresh-water spiral shells are called 'conchs' by these people, and the marine shells are not unfrequently used for food like 'winkles' in Great Britain; so that Wyman was led to believe that both were commonly eaten, which is certainly not the case."

NORTH CAROLINA.

CALDWELL COUNTY.

THE PATTERSON GRADING.

This work is situated near Patterson, in the northwest part of the county and close to the Yadkin river. It is a terrace or platform partly natural and partly artificial, extending out from the steep terminus of a low ridge, which here descends at an angle of about 45 degrees. The artificial portion extends out from the natural terrace about 68 feet, the height being 7 feet. A trench was cut half way across it, proving it to be composed chiefly of waterworn bowlders, and red and yellow clay, with charcoal intermingled. Here and there pieces of mica were found; at the depth of 2½ feet from the top and 6 feet from the edge was a polishing or whetstone, and at another point the fragment of a soapstone vessel with rudely carved figures on it, proving beyond question that the terrace is in part, at least, artificial.

THE T. F. NELSON MOUND.

This mound, so insignificant in appearance as scarcely to attract any notice, but hiding beneath the surface such important mementoes of the past, was located on the farm of Rev. T. F. Nelson, in the northwest part of the county, and about a mile and a half southeast of Patterson. It stood on the bottom land of the Yadkin, about 100 yards from the river, and was almost a true circle in outline, 38 feet in diameter, but not exceeding at any point 18 inches in height. The thorough excavation made, in which Mr. Rogan, the Bureau agent, was assisted by Dr. J. M. Spainhour, of Lenoir, showed that the original constructors had

Fig. 207.—T. F. Nelson mound, Caldwell county, North Carolina.

first dug a circular pit about 38 feet in diameter to the depth of 3 feet and there placed the dead, some in stone cists and others uninclosed, and afterwards covered them over, raising a slight mound above the pit. A plan of the pit, showing the stone graves and skeletons as they appeared after the removal of the dirt and before being disturbed, is given in Fig. 207.

No. 1 is a stone grave or vault standing exactly in the center of this large pit, but in a small circular pit evidently made for this special purpose, extending down 3 feet below the bottom of the larger one. This vault, built of cobblestones around a standing skeleton, was made 3 feet in diameter at the base, carried up perpendicularly for 4 feet and then narrowed so as to be covered by a single soapstone slab at the top. On the top of the head of the skeleton, which was found still standing, though much decayed, were several plates of cut mica, the only articles accompanying it.

The skeletons in Nos. 2, 3, 4, 5, 6, 7, 8, 9, and 10, though walled around in a similar manner, were in a squatting posture on the bottom of the large pit. With skeleton No. 2 was one small celt; with No. 3 a discoidal stone; with No. 6 two celts, and over No. 9, but inside the vault, a pitted stone.

Nos. 11, 12, and 13 are three skeletons found in a squatting position, with no wall around them and unaccompanied by relics of any kind. Nos. 14 and 15 were lying horizontally at full length, also uninclosed. With the former were pieces of broken pipes and with the latter one celt. No. 16 was an uninclosed "squatter" of unusually large size, not less than 7 feet high when living. Near the mouth was an entire soapstone pipe; the legs were extended in a southwest direction upon a bed of burnt earth.

The faces of all the squatting skeletons were turned away from the standing, central one.

At A was a considerable quantity of black paint in little lumps, which appear to have been molded in the hull of some nut. B indicates a cubical mass of waterworn bowlders built up solidly and symmetrically, 24 inches long, 18 inches wide, and 18 inches high, showing no indications of fire, without ashes or bones on or around it.

On the contrary, the stones built around the bodies bore more or less evidence of fire, having been blackened by smoke in places, and the earth immediately around them was considerably hardened by baking. The bones of the skeletons also showed indications of heat. Scattered throughout the mound were small pieces of pottery and charcoal.

THE T. F. NELSON TRIANGLE.

This is the name applied to an ancient triangular burying ground on the farm of Rev. T. F. Nelson, and located about 75 yards north of the mound just described.

It is simply a burial pit in the form of a triangle, the east and west sides each 48 feet long, and the southern base 32 feet, the depth varying from 2½ to 3 feet. The top was not mounded up, but level with the surrounding surface. The apex, which points directly north, extends within 3 feet of the bank of the Yadkin river, the height above the usual water level being about 12 feet. A plat of the triangle, showing the position of the burials in it, is given in Fig. 208. Nos. 1, 2, 3, 4,

5, 6, 7, 8, and 9 indicate the positions of single skeletons lying horizontally on their backs, their heads resting east or northeast. With No. 2 was a broken soapstone pipe; with Nos. 5 and 9 one small polished celt each. Nos. 10, 11, 12, 13, 14, and 15 were buried in stone vaults

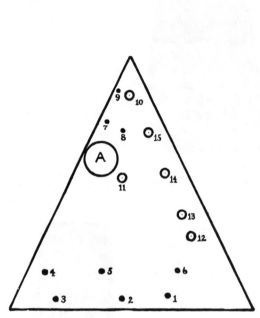

FIG. 208.—T. F. Nelson Triangle, Caldwell county, North Carolina.

FIG. 209.—Copper cylinder, Nelson triangle.

similar to those in the mound; 10, 12, 13, and 15 being in a sitting posture unaccompanied by any article. Nos. 11 and 14 indicate graves containing two skeletons each extended horizontally one above the other, the lower ones of smaller stature than those above, with the faces up,

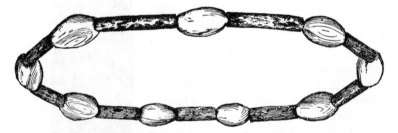

FIG. 210.—Bracelet of shell and copper beads, Nelson Triangle.

and very heavy stones placed on the extended arms and legs, fastening them down. The upper skeletons, of larger stature and face down, were resting on those below. No articles were found with them. Near No. 12 was about a peck of singular, pinkish colored earth.

In the northeast part of the triangle, at A, were ten or more bodies in one grave or group, which appeared to have been buried at one time,

FIG. 211.—Iron celt from Nelson triangle.

the chief or principal personage of the group resting horizontally on his face, with his head northeast and his feet southwest. Under his head was the large engraved shell shown in Fig. 213; around his neck were a number of large-sized shell beads; at or near his ears lay five elongate copper beads, or rather small cylinders, varying in length from $1\frac{1}{4}$ to $4\frac{1}{4}$ inches, and in diameter from one-fourth to half an inch, part of the leather thong on which they had been strung yet remaining in them. These are made of thin pieces of copper cut into strips and then rolled together so that the edges meet in a straight joint on one side. The copper looks as though it had been rolled into sheets and not hammered (Fig. 209). A piece of copper was also under his breast. His arms were bent, the hands resting about 1 foot from each side of his head. Around each wrist were the remains of a bracelet composed of copper and shell beads alternating, as shown in Fig. 210. At his right hand lay four iron implements, one of which, a roughly hammered celt or chisel, is shown in Fig. 211; another piece, some 6 or 7 inches long and about 1 inch wide, is evidently part of a sword blade or knife (Fig. 212); another, part of a punch or large awl, with a portion of the horn handle yet attached. Under his left hand was another engraved shell, the concave surface upward, and filled with shell beads of all sizes.

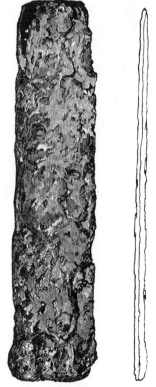

FIG. 212.—Part of iron blade, Nelson triangle.

Around and partly over this skeleton, with their heads near his, were nine others. Under the heads of two of these skeletons, lying within a foot of the head of the first, were also several engraved shells, one of which is shown in Fig. 214. Scattered over and among the bones of these ten or more skeletons were numerous polished celts, discoidal stones, copper arrow points, pieces of mica, lumps of paint, black lead, stone pipes, etc. Some of the forms of the pipes from this and the other burial places in this locality are shown in Figs. 215–220.

FIG. 213.—Engraved shell, Nelson triangle.

THE W. DAVENPORT JONES MOUND.

Two miles east of Patterson, near the north bank of the Yadkin river, running out from a low ridge to the river bank, is a natural terrace about 12 feet high, with a level area of about an acre on top, and sloping on the sides at an angle of 45 degrees, on which, according to tradition, there was formerly an Indian village. About 200 yards east of this, on the second river bottom or terrace, there was a low, circular mound 32 feet in diameter and not more than 1 foot high, on the land of Mr. W. Davenport Jones. This mound was found upon investigation to cover a circular pit of the same diameter and 3 feet deep, the margin and bottom being so well defined as to leave no doubt as to the limits of the pit; in fact the bottom, which was of clay, had been baked hard by fire to the depth of 2 or 3 inches.   The pit was filled with soil and loose yellow clay similar to the surface soil around the mound covering twenty-six skeletons and one stone heap in the relative positions shown in Fig. 221.   Some of the skeletons were inclosed in vaults formed of cobble stones.

FIG. 214.—Engraved shell, Nelson triangle.

No. 1, squatting, walled in with water-worn bowlders; the face turned to the west; no implements or ornaments.

No. 2, sitting with the face toward the center, two celts at the feet, and immediately in front of the face a cone-shaped piece of hard pottery paste.

FIG. 215.—Pipe, Caldwell county, North Carolina.

No. 3, sitting with face toward the center; several celts at the feet.
No. 4, horizontal, with the head southeast; several celts at the feet.
No. 5, horizontal, with the head toward the center; celts at the feet.
No. 6, sitting with the face toward the center; beads around the neck, a *Unio* shell on top of the head with the concave surface down, a conch

shell (*Busycon perversum*) in front of and near the face, and celts at the feet.

No. 7. Sitting facing the center; celts at the feet.

No. 8. Very large, lying on the left side, partially drawn up; walled in with bowlders; no implements.

No. 9. Horizontal, face down, head toward the center; a pot (without ears) on the head; celts and discoidal stones at the feet.

FIG. 216.—Pipe, Caldwell county, North Carolina.

No. 10. Horizontal, face up, feet towards the center; a pot with ears, over the face; stone implements at the feet.

No. 11. Horizontal, head southeast, arms extended, and a bracelet of copper and shell beads around each wrist; shell beads around the neck; face up, with food cup (without handle) at the right side of the head.

No. 12. Horizontal, lying on the back, head southeast; beads around the neck, a hook or crescent-shaped piece of copper on the breast, and

FIG. 217.—Pipe, Caldwell county, North Carolina.

a pipe near the face; one hand near each side of the head grasping conical copper ornaments (eardrops) and a bunch of hair.

No. 13. Horizontal, lying on the back, head southeast; copper and shell beads around the neck and wrists, a hook or crescent-shaped piece of copper on the breast; food cup (with handle) lying on its side with the mouth toward the face of the skeleton; a pipe near the mouth and two celts over the head.

No. 14. Horizontal, lying on the back, head northeast, arms extended, and hands resting on shells.

No. 15. Horizontal, on the back, head west, knees drawn up to the chin; stone implements at the feet.

No. 16. Too much decayed to determine the position.

No. 17. Four skeletons in one grave, horizontal, with feet toward the

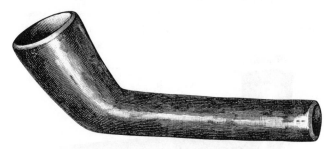

FIG. 218.—Pipe, Caldwell county, North Carolina.

west and large stones lying on the legs below the knees. No implements with them.

No. 18. Two skeletons in one grave, with heads west, faces down, knees drawn up; no implements.

No. 19. Horizontal, on the back, head east; no implements.

FIG. 219.—Pipe. Caldwell county. North Carolina.

No. 20. Sitting, walled in with bowlders, face toward the east, a large stone lying on the feet (this may have fallen from the wall); no implements.

No. 21. Sitting, walled in with bowlders. Over the head, but under the capstone of the vault, was a handful of flint arrowheads.

FIG. 220.— Pipe. Caldwell county. North Carolina.

No. 22. Doubled up, with head between the feet.

A on the diagram indicates a solid oval-shaped mass of bowlders, 32 inches long, 22 inches wide, and 24 inches high, resting on the bottom of the pit. There were no ashes, charcoal, or other sign of fire about it.

Broken pottery, mica, galena, charcoal, red and black paint, etc., were found scattered in small quantities through the earth which filled the pit. The skeletons were so badly decayed that very few bones could be saved.

R. T. LENOIR BURIAL PIT.

This is a circular burial pit, similar to those already described, but without any rounding up of the surface. It is located on the farm of Mr. Rufus T. Lenoir, about 9 miles northeast of Lenoir and nearly a mile west of Fort Defiance.

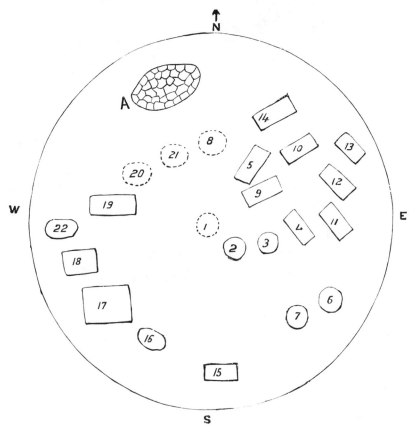

FIG. 221.—Plan of W. D. Jones mound, Caldwell county, North Carolina.

A diagram showing the relative positions of the graves or burials is given in Fig. 222.

It is on the first river terrace or bottom of Buffalo creek, and about 200 yards from this stream, which empties into the Yadkin about half a mile southwest of this point. This bottom is subject to overflow in time of high water.

The pit, which is 27 feet in diameter and about $3\frac{1}{2}$ feet deep, is almost a perfect circle and well marked, the margin, which is nearly perpendic-

ular, and the bottom being readily traced.   The dirt in this case, as in
the others, was all thrown out.

No. 1, a bed of charred or rather burnt bones occupying a space 3
feet long, 2 feet wide, and 12 inches deep, the bones so thoroughly
burned that it was impossible to determine whether they were human
or animal.   Beneath this bed the yellow sand was baked to the depth
of 1 or 2 inches.   Under the bones was a shell with two holes through it.

No. 2, a skeleton in a sitting posture, face northeast, a pipe near the
mouth and a polished celt over the head.

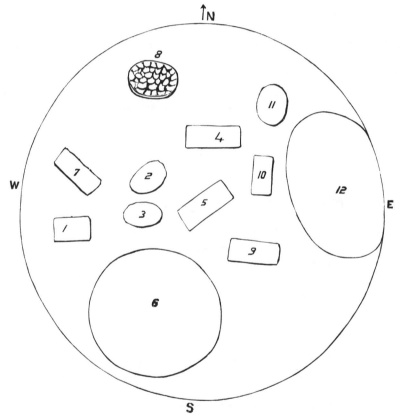

FIG. 222.—R. T. Lenoir burial pit (plan), Caldwell county, North Carolina.

No. 3, sitting skeleton, facing east, with shell beads around the neck
and also around the arms just below the shoulders.

No. 4, horizontal skeleton, lying on the back, head east and resting
on the concave surface of an engraved shell.   Conch shell (*Busycon.
perversum*) at the side of the head, and copper and shell beads around
the neck.

No. 5, horizontal, head northeast, shell beads around the neck, and
two discoidal stones and one celt at the feet.

No. 6, a communal grave containing 25 skeletons in two tiers, buried without any apparent regularity as to direction or relative position. Thirteen of the 25 were flatheads, that is, with the head artificially compressed in front. Scattered throughout this grave, between and above the skeletons, were polished celts, discoidal stones, shells, pieces of mica, galena, fragments of pottery, and one whole pot. Around the necks and wrists of some of the skeletons were also shell beads. There were a great many bones in this grave, and possibly more than 25 skeletons, but this was the number of skulls observed.

No. 8, an irregular layer of waterworn bowlders, about 4 feet square. On the top was a bed of charcoal, about 3 inches deep, on and partially imbedded in which were three skeletons, but showing no indications of having been burned. Scattered over these skeletons were discoidal stones, one saucer, shells (one of which is engraved), pipes, shell beads, and pieces of pottery.

No. 9, a grave containing three skeletons lying horizontally on their backs, two with their heads east and the one between them with the head west. They lay close together, and were unaccompanied by implements or ornaments.

No. 10, horizontal, on the right side, head north, with stone implements in front of the face.

No. 11, doubled up, top of the head south, shell beads around the neck, and celts at the feet.

No. 12, a grave containing seventeen skeletons, seven of which had compressed heads; two of the number, children. Two of the adult heads were resting on engraved shells. In this grave were four pots and two food cups, the handle of one of the latter representing an owl's head, that of the other an eagle's head. One of the small pots was inside a larger one. Scattered among the skeletons were also shell beads, polished celts, discoidal stones, paint, etc.

THE SHERRIL MOUND.

This is a small mound, 38 feet in diameter and 5 feet high, located on the farm of Sion J. Sherril, 3½ miles east of Lenoir. It was composed of yellow clay and coarse yellow sand. Nothing else except a very small quantity of charcoal was observed.

BURKE AND WILKES COUNTIES.

A conical mound 320 feet in circumference and 7 feet high, situated on the farm of Mrs. J. E. Collet, in the northern part of Burke county, was explored, but aside from the yellow sand and yellow clay of which it was chiefly composed, nothing was found in it except some remnants of charred straw and cane. These were scattered in small quantities through the mound.

On the farm of Mr. Charles Hunt in the central part of Wilkes county, is what appears to be a small, ancient cemetery, and probably the site of a camp or temporary village. It is about 3½ miles east of Wilkesboro on the second bottom or terrace of the Yadkin river and differs from the burial places just described in having no large pit, the graves being separate and independent of each other. The diagram given in Fig. 223 shows the relative positions of the graves and small pits.

No. 1, a grave or oval-shaped pit 2 feet long and 18 inches wide, the top within 8 inches of the surface of the ground, the bottom 2½ feet

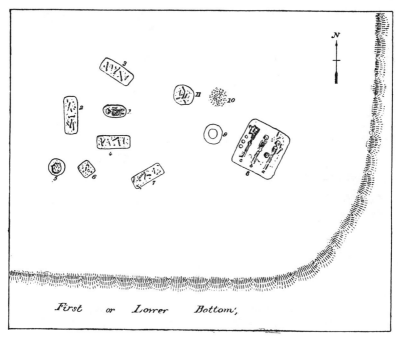

First   or   Lower   Bottom,

FIG. 223.—Ancient burial ground, Wilkes county, North Carolina.

below it. This contained the remains of a doubled skeleton, which were surrounded by charcoal; some of the bones were considerably charred. In the pit were some fragments of pottery, a few flint chips, and a decayed tortoise shell.

No. 2, a grave 2 feet wide, 6 feet long, and 5 feet deep. It contained quite a quantity of animal bones, some of them evidently those of a bear, also charcoal, mussel shells, and one bone implement, but no human skeleton.

No. 3, a grave of the same size and depth as No. 2, containing animal bones, broken pottery, and some charcoal.

No. 4, a grave, the size, depth, and contents the same as the preceding.

No. 5, a circular pit 2 feet in diameter and 2 feet deep. This contained a very large pot in which were some animal bones. It was on its side and crushed.

No. 6, a pit 2½ feet deep and 2 feet square, with a bed of charcoal in the bottom 6 inches deep. On this bed was a layer of flint chips, and on the chips a quantity of broken pottery, animal bones, a discoidal stone and a bone implement.

No, 7, a grave similar to those described.

No. 8, a large grave containing three skeletons lying at full length upon the right side, with the heads a little east of north. These are marked *a*, *b*, *c* in the diagram. Between *a* and *b*, and in front of the face of *a*, was a mass of mussel shells; at the head and back of *a* were a number of animal bones. Between *a* and *b*, opposite the pelvis, was a large broken pot. The right arm of *c* was extended forward and upward, the left arm resting across the head, a white flint chip grasped in the hand. The head of this skeleton was resting on a piece of a broken pot, and in front of the face, at the distance of a foot, was also part of a pot containing a stone fragment and some animal bones.

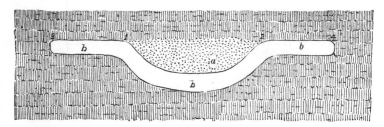

FIG. 224.—Clay hearth (or fire-bed), Wilkes county, North Carolina.

Under the legs of the three skeletons, the head extended in front of the legs of *c*, was the skeleton of a bear. In front of *c* were three broken pots containing animal bones.

No. 9, a basin-shaped fire-bed, or bed of burnt clay, 8 inches thick. A section of this bed is shown in Fig. 224, *b*, *b*, *b*, the bed of burnt clay and sand 8 inches thick, the material evidently placed here and not a part of the original soil. The basin, *a*, was filled with ashes, the depth being 12 inches, and the diameter from 1 to 2, 2 feet 3 inches; from 1 to 3, and 2 to 4, each 1 foot and 6 inches.

No. 10, a bed of mussel shells 3 inches thick and 3 feet in diameter, lying on a flat bed of burnt earth 3 inches thick.

No. 11, a pit 5 feet deep and 3 feet in diameter, filled with animal bones, mussel shells, and broken pottery.

There was no mound over any of these graves or the pit.

HAYWOOD COUNTY.

An article in the Journal of the Anthropological Institute of Great Britain and Ireland for June, 1882, in regard to some singular works of

art found in Haywood county, having excited the curiosity of our antiquarians, Mr. Emmert was sent into that region to procure, if possible,
some specimens of this singular class of articles and to ascertain
whether they were ancient or modern. After considerable difficulty he
was entirely successful in his effort. He ascertained that these articles
were made from the soapstone found in that region by some persons
who had learned how to give them the appearance of age. This is
done by placing them, after being carved, in running water which is
tinctured with iron, as most of the streams in that region are. As a
proof of the correctness of his statement Mr. Emmert had the same
parties who stated they had made some articles
for Mr. Valentine make quite a number of similar articles for the Bureau. Some of these are
represented in Figs. 225, 226, and 227 *a*, *b*.

THE BIG MOUND.

This mound, of which a section through the
length is shown in Fig. 228, is near Waynesville. It is oblong in form and flattened on
top; the length of the base, 188 feet; width,
about 70 feet; height at *a*, 12½ feet, and at *b*,
10 feet.

Pits were sunk at *a* and *b* to the original
surface, through dark earth mixed with sand,
uniform in character and showing no indications of stratification. Near the top in both
pits were found several fragments of soapstone
vessels, and at the bottom of pit 2 one celt,
one shark's tooth, and several fragments of
pottery, but no human remains or indications
of burial.

MOUND NEAR RICHLAND CREEK.

This is situated on a ridge half a mile from
Richland creek and 2 miles from Waynesville.
It is apparently double, 70 feet long, 30 feet
wide, and 3½ feet high at each end, but considerably lower in the middle. At the bottom,
under the highest point of the west end was a

FIG. 225.—Bogus article, Haywood
county, North Carolina.

bed of dark earth in which were the remains of two skeletons lying at
full length side by side. With these were found seven arrow heads,
one rude stone axe with a hole drilled through it, one polishing stone
of iron ore, two broken stone gorgets, and a small lot of mica. Under
the highest point of the east end was a similar bed of dark earth in
which were the remains of one skeleton, also stretched out at full
length. By this were three flint knives or scrapers and a clay pipe.

Some mounds in and along the borders of these two counties were explored which present some characteristics worthy of notice.

MOUND ON LYTLE'S FARM.

This mound is near Cane creek, Henderson county, in a field of bottom land owned by Mr. A. Lytle. It measured 48 feet from east to west, 38 feet from north to south, and 8 feet high. The oval shape is possibly due in part to the fact that it has long been plowed over in one direction. It was built of yellow sand throughout, showing no stratification except a single layer of coal and ashes, 3 inches thick, just above the original surface of the ground.

THE CONNER MOUND.

This mound, located on the farm of Mrs. Rebecca Conner, 1 mile from the preceding, is 6 feet high, 44 feet in diameter, round, and forms

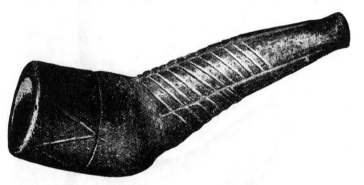

FIG. 226.—Bogus article. Haywood county. North Carolina.

a symmetrical cone. Small trees were growing on it. It was found to contain what, to all appearances, were the remains of a charcoal pit. In the center had been placed pine poles, as shown in Fig. 229, and burned to charcoal and ashes. The diameter of the base of this conical heap was 16 feet, the height nearly 6 feet, the sides sloping regularly to the apex. The interior portion consisted of ashes and small coals, mixed with earth, in which were found some burnt bones and two perforated stones.

All the mound, except the coal bed, consisted of red clay. It stood on a ridge about half a mile from the creek, on hard, gravelly soil, which bore no indications of having been disturbed before building the mound.[1]

---

[1] Attention is called here to a statement by Haywood (Nat. and Aborig. Hist. Tenn., p. 234). Speaking of the inhabitants of lower East Tennessee he says: "The former inhabitants appeared to have lived in houses which, on the outside, seemed to be the color of a blacksmith's coalpit. The houses were made by setting up poles and then digging out the dirt and covering the poles with it. They were round and generally about 10 feet in diameter."

THE ALEXANDER MOUNDS.

No. 1 is on the farm of Mr. J. B. Alexander, on the same creek, but 2 miles above the one last mentioned. It is on an elevated level one-fourth of a mile from the creek, in an old field which has been plowed over for sixty years. At the time explored it was only 2 feet high at the highest point and but 30 feet in diameter. The old settlers say it was formerly considerably higher, and that there was a ridge or raised roadway 200 feet long, running from it directly toward the creek. This is represented at present only by a line of red clay. It was entirely removed without finding any specimens or any indications of burial, but after reaching the natural surface of the ground a circu-

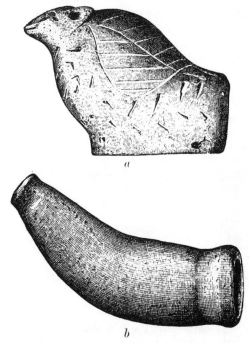

a

b

FIG. 227.—Bogus articles, Haywood county, North Carolina.

lar pit, 12 feet in diameter, was discovered, which had been dug to the depth of 4 feet in the original red clay. This was filled to the top with ashes and charcoal, but no traces of bones could be discovered, though careful search was made for them. The mound was composed entirely of red clay.

No. 2, half a mile from No. 1, diameter 52 feet, height 9 feet and hemispherical in form, was covered with trees some of which were 18 inches in diameter.

This mound was composed of three layers: a top stratum of red clay between 3 and 4 feet thick, next a layer of charcoal about 3 inches thick, running entirely across from side to side and following the curve of the surface, and last a layer of dark-colored earth extending to the original surface. In the bottom layer, lying on the original surface, were five skeletons. By the side of one of these were sixteen white quartz knives, one small stone pipe, and several arrowheads. At another point were a stone gorget, a large celt, and some arrowheads.

The sixteen white quartz implements must have been made by one individual, as they are all of the same kind of stone, of the same form, and show the same workmanship.

MOUND ON SUANANOA RIVER, BUNCOMBE COUNTY.

This mound is about 4 miles from Asheville, on the bottom land, not more than 100 yards from the river, is circular, 80 feet in diameter, and 9 feet high. A wide trench cut through it from side to side and down to the natural soil brought to light the fact that it was built partly of stone and partly of earth. The core or central portion, to the height

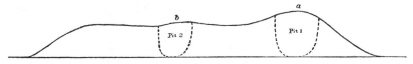

FIG. 228.—Big mound, Haywood county, North Carolina.

of 4 feet above the original surface and covering a space about 30 feet in diameter, was built of irregular blocks of stone, heaped together without order or plan. The remainder of the mound was made of dark surface soil. The top layer of earth being removed down to the

FIG. 229.—Section of Conner mound, Henderson county, North Carolina.

rock pile, the entire surface of the latter was found to be covered with charcoal and evidences that it had been burned here. Among the coal were numerous joints of charred cane. The stones were all removed, but no remains or relics, save a few arrowheads, were discovered.

THE THROSH MOUND.

This mound is on the farm of Mr. J. B. Throsh, 1½ miles from Hominy creek, Buncombe county. It is located on a ridge, is circular, 33 feet in diameter at the base, and 4 feet high. No remains or vestiges of art were found in it. Its composition was as follows: First, a top layer, 18 inches thick, of red clay similar to that around it, conforming to the curve of the mound and entirely covering the bottom layer of black earth which rested on the original soil. The latter had evidently been carried from the creek, a mile distant.

EAST TENNESSEE.

SULLIVAN COUNTY.

MOUNDS ON HOLSTON RIVER.

There are two mounds on Holston river about 10 miles east of Bristol. In Fig. 230 a plat and section of the area on which they are located are given. In the plat (A) No. 1 is the mound on the north side of the river; No. 2, the mound on the south side. At B is shown a section running northwest and southeast through the mounds (1 and 2) on the upper level, 3 the lower level or river bottom, and 4 the river.

Mound No. 1, which is on the north side of the river, was found when

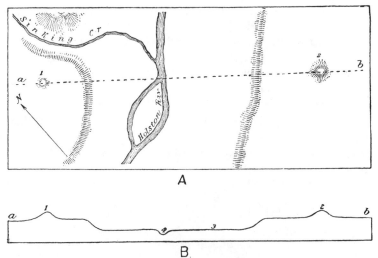

A

B

FIG. 230 —Plan of mounds on the Holston river, Sullivan county, Tennessee.

measured to be 22 feet in diameter and 4 feet high, circular in form, and composed of red clay and sand.

Resting on the original surface of the ground near the center was a stone vault shaped somewhat like a beehive. It was constructed entirely of water-worn bowlders and arched over the top by shortening and drawing in the courses. In this was a single sitting skeleton. It was evident that the body, or more likely the skeleton, had been set down in this place and the vault built around it. Lying on the head was the long copper spindle shown in Fig. 231. It is 11 inches long, one-fourth of an inch in diameter at the thickest part, and appears to have been roughly hammered out of native copper with some rude implement. Immediately under the lower jaw were two small copper drills or awls with portions of the deer-horn handles still attached to them; near the head a small pile of flint chips and by the knees a long flint knife. The bones were so decayed that most of them crumbled to pieces as soon as exposed to the air.

Mound No. 2 stood on the south side of the river opposite to No. 1 and about the same distance from the stream as the latter. It was circular in outline, rounded on top, 38 feet in diameter at the base, and 5 feet high. On the top was a pine stump 14 inches in diameter, the tree having been cut down about thirty years ago.

The excavation which was begun at the margin soon reached a wall 3 feet high and about a foot thick, built of stones taken from the bed of the river. This was followed and found to be an almost perfect circle 14 feet in diameter, in which, when the earth was cleared away, were discovered twelve small, beehive-shaped vaults built of stones of the same kind as those in the wall. One of these was exactly in the center, the other eleven being placed in a circle around it and about equally spaced, as shown in Fig. 232. The bottom of the area within the circular wall, which corresponded with the natural surface of the ground, was covered to the depth of 3 inches with charcoal and the graves or vaults were built on this layer. In each vault were the remains of a single sitting skeleton, all of adults. In the center vault a number of shell beads were found around the neck of the skeleton and near the mouth the fine stone pipe shown in Fig. 233. This pipe is made of fine-grained syenite and highly polished. No articles were found with any of the other skeletons.

Fig. 231.—Copper spindle from mound, Sullivan county, Tennessee.

Each of the two last mentioned mounds is on the bench or upper bottom and about one-fourth of a mile from the river. This locality is said to have been for a long time an Indian camping ground, which seems to be confirmed by the fact that the surface of the ground is thickly strewn with flint chips and fragments of pottery. Tradition says that the Indians once had a great battle here, and that one party buried their dead in mound No. 2 and the other party buried theirs on the opposite side of the river, where there is still a great mound of river stones.

Mound No. 3 (not shown in the plat) is also on the Holston river, 2 miles above those just described. This mound, which resembles No. 2 in several respects, was circular, 60 feet in diameter, and nearly 5 feet high. The original surface of the earth had first been covered over with charcoal to the depth of 3 inches, then the bodies or skeletons laid on it and each walled up separately with river stones; these were then covered over with a layer of black earth 18 inches thick, and on this was spread a layer of sand over a foot thick and on this was a thin layer of surface soil. On one-half of the circular layer of charcoal were six skeletons walled up separately as before stated, but so thoroughly decayed that only one skull could be saved. The other side of the mound had nothing in it except a fine stone pipe somewhat similar to that shown in Fig. 233, which was on the bed of coals some 10 or 12 feet from the nearest skeleton. Near the head of one of the skeletons were some beautiful arrow-heads, shell beads, a polished celt, and two perforated stones.

ANCIENT GRAVES NEAR KINGSPORT.

A plat showing the locality of these and some other works noticed is given in Fig. 234. In this *d* and *e* are five graves covered with piles of

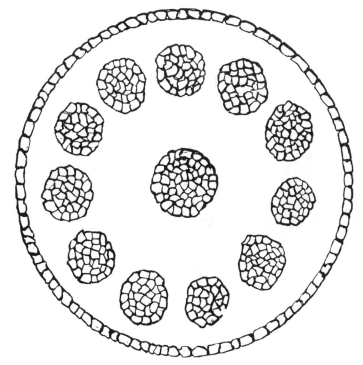

Fig. 232.—Plan of burials in mound, Sullivan county, Tennessee.

stone; *c*, the site of old Fort Patrick Henry, built in 1778; at *f*, on the opposite side of the river, is an ancient graveyard, some of the graves being covered with stones, others with earth; at *a* is a waste pit in Cherokee Island, full of broken pottery, bones, etc. The graves at *e* are on the old Birdwell farm, about a mile above the head of Long Island. They are in the top and near the break of a high bluff which here overlooks the river. The pile on each was oval in outline, measuring about 14 feet in length, 9 feet in width, and 18 inches high, composed of broken limestone. The pit of one, which for convenience is designated No. 1, appears to have been nearly equal in extent to the pile of stones over it and about 2½ feet in depth. A longitudinal section is shown in

Fig. 235. *a a* denote the surface level; 1, soil to the depth of 8 inches; 2, red clay 2 feet thick; 3, black earth, charcoal, and ashes 3 inches thick.

A longitudinal section of the other, or No. 2, shows that the layers were the same in character and about the same in thickness as those of No. 1, but the extent of the pit in this case was much less than the pile of stones over it, the length being only 8 feet and the width in proportion. No indications of burial were found in either, and had it not been for the layer of black earth, charcoal, and ashes at the bottom, and the fact that flint chips were found in this layer, we might conclude that no pit had been dug here, especially as its outline was not distinctly marked. The layer of surface soil under the piles of stone indicates that these were placed there long after the pits were filled up.

The graves at *d*, one-fourth of a mile below those at *e*, were found to be similar in covering, size, and character to the latter, except some slight peculiarities in one of them, which is designated as grave No. 3. In this the stones were not only piled over the surface, but extended down some distance into the grave, as shown in Fig. 236. These must

FIG. 233.—Stone pipe from mound, Sullivan county, Tennessee.

have been pounded in, as they were so tightly packed that it was difficult to remove them. It was limited at the sides by natural ledges of limestone, which sloped towards each other, as shown in the figure. The usual layer of dark earth, charcoal, and ashes was at the bottom. In this were found some sheets of mica, fourteen arrowheads, one stone gorget, and one small copper rod or awl about 4 inches long, some fragments of a soapstone vessel, and a lump of red paint.

Nos. 4 and 5 were precisely similar to No. 1 at *e*. Some arrowheads, flint chips, and lumps of black ore were found in the coal bed of No. 4.

As there was nothing in either of these graves or pits indicating burial, it is difficult to imagine the object in view in digging them. Other similar graves not opened are on the opposite side of the river, marked *f* on the plat.

CARTER COUNTY.

There is an ancient cemetery on the north bank of Watauga river just above the mouth of Buffalo creek. In 1886 a skeleton was found partially exposed, the river having washed away a part of the bank.

It lay at the depth of 3 feet, the head turned towards the southeast; with it were four arrowheads, several shell beads, and many small fragments of pottery; most of the latter about the head. Quite a number of skeletons were subsequently exposed by the high water and others in the process of digging a road through the grounds.

The burial ground, on which many broken stone axes, arrow points, and other stone implements have been found, but which has been pretty

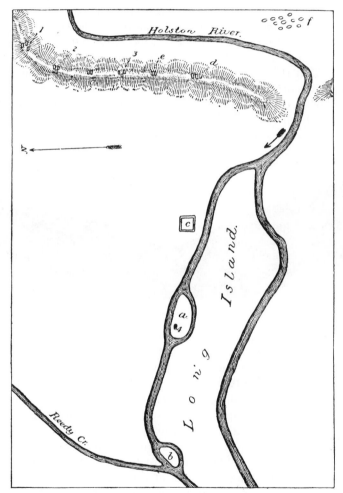

Fig. 234.—Plat showing ancient graves near Kingsport, Tennessee.

thoroughly worked over, is about one mile and a half below old Fort Watauga, mentioned by Haywood as the Watauga settlement. It is now on the farm of Mr. John S. Thomas and near the house where John Sevier and Tipton had their fight over the " State of Franklin."

On Gap creek, about 4 miles from the fort, are two caves in a rocky ridge which borders the creek on the east. One of these is comparatively small, and can be entered only by a narrow, perpendicular descent of 10 feet. Here and there are places where the floor is covered with loose earth mixed with charcoal and ashes. During a rather hasty examination the explorer found in this débris a broken stone gorget, a spearhead, and some shell beads, but no indications of burial.

COCKE COUNTY.

But one mound in this county was examined. This is on Vincent island, Pigeon river, and is about 200 feet long and varies from 4 to 6

feet in height; it was formerly about 50 feet wide, but a long strip off one side has been washed away by the river. The general appearance is that of a refuse heap.

FIG. 235.—Section of grave No. 1, near Kingsport, Tennessee.

Although the entire mound was removed, no skeletons or signs of burial were discovered; but near the center and close to bottom was a somewhat singular collection containing the following articles: Thirty-three celts, mostly polished; fragments of pottery and of soapstone vessels; four arrowheads; four stone gorgets; two discoidal stones; one broken clay pipe; two grooved stone axes; one stone pestle; four stone hammers; two large pitted stones; one unfinished stone tube; a steel-blade case knife of a peculiar pattern, and one porcelain (?) bead.

FIG. 236.—Section of grave No. 3, near Kingsport, Tennessee.

The presence of the knife and bead in this collection is difficult to account for, unless we suppose the whole to be a comparatively modern deposit, which is probably the fact.

THE RAMSEY MOUND.

On the north bank of French Broad river, immediately opposite the Franklin Railroad station, on the land of Mr. A. Ramsey, are the remains of a once large and imposing tumulus known as the Ramsey mound. It is mentioned by Haywood, who remarks in regard to it as follows:

> There is a mound on the French Broad river, 1 mile above the mouth of Nolachucky, on the east side of the French Broad, 30 feet high. There is an acre of ground on the top.[1]

At present only a small part of it remains, the rest having been washed away by the river, which has gradually encroached upon it. Mr. Ramsey, who has resided on the farm for fifty-five years, says the mound once extended to what is now the center of the river, a distance of 250 feet, and was 20 feet high, if not more. The exact dimensions

---

[1] Nat. and Aborig. Hist. Tenn., 1823, p. 146.

can not now be ascertained, but it is affirmed that the area of the level top was at least an acre and that it was cultivated as a garden. If this be correct it must have been a very large and important tumulus, probably 250 feet in length by 175 in width. What adds to the interest attaching to this work is the fact that, running around it in the form of a semicircle, and about 300 yards from it, is a series of large pits, twelve in number and somewhat evenly spaced. The dimensions can not be definitely ascertained, as they are now nearly filled up. They were probably 100 feet or more in diameter, and, according to the statement of citizens, fully 20 feet deep. Possibly they are the spots from which the material for building the mound was obtained.

JEFFERSON COUNTY.

Some explorations were made in this county, but the examinations were hasty and incomplete. The agent was, at the time of his visit, simply on a prospecting tour, expecting to return to those works which he thought worthy of special investigation.

Two mounds were discovered immediately below Taylors bend of the French Broad river, 9 miles east of Dandridge. One of these, on the north side of the river, stands on a level bottom about 300 feet from the river bank. It is circular in outline, 120 feet in diameter and 12 feet high. Trenches were cut through it, but no evidence of burial or relics of any kind were revealed. The other mound is about half a mile above the preceding, south of the river, on the farm of Mr. John B. Stakely. It stands on the level bottom about 200 feet from the river; is similar in form to the other, but smaller, the diameter being 95 feet and height a little less than 5 feet. The ground on which it stands is subject to overflow, and the mound itself has been entirely covered with water more than once. A wide trench was carried through it and down to the original soil, but neither skeletons nor relics were found; nor any indications of burial. The whole body of it was composed of dark, sandy soil like that of the ground around it. At the bottom, resting on the natural surface, was a layer of sticky yellow clay, 3 to 4 inches thick, which appeared to underlie the entire mound. The nearest place where this pipe clay is found is a ridge about a mile distant.

There is an ancient burial ground about one-fourth of a mile above, but on the opposite side of the river from the last mentioned mound.

There is a mound on the south side of French Broad river opposite Swans island, about 3 miles above Dandridge. It stands on the lower bottom which borders the river, about 200 yards from the latter. There are traces of an old "trail" leading from it across the ridges for a distance of 3 miles to some stone graves near a creek. The largest trees along the trail are marked, but the marking extends up and down the trees according to the old method of blazing routes instead of across them, as is now usual. If these marks bear any relation to the trail and graves, it is probable that all are the work of modern Cherokees.

This mound is situated on the lower end of Fain's island, in French Broad river, about 3 miles southwest of Dandridge. It stands on the extreme lower end of the island, not more than 300 feet from the water's edge. As a shaft had been sunk in the center by a previous explorer a broad trench was cut on each side. In the first or southern one sixteen skeletons were unearthed, but in the northern one nothing was found. Near the east end of the first was a series of fire beds, one below another. The uppermost, which lay near the surface of the mound, was about 3 feet in diameter, and each succeeding one was a little wider than the one above it, so that the bottom one, 3 feet below the first, measured 6 feet in diameter. All were circular and slightly basin-shaped or dished, and consisted of burnt clay, with layers of ashes between them. There were five in all. Below the last lay a mass of pure ashes, packed very hard, which extended downward some 3 feet to the bottom of the mound. The earth immediately under this bed of ashes was burned to a hard crust to the depth of 5 or 6 inches.

Fig. 237 is given to show the fire-beds (a) and the ash-bed (b) immediately below them.

The skeletons were, in most cases, lying at full length, with heads in various directions, though none toward the south. Only one or two

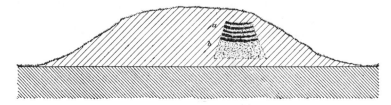

FIG. 237.—Section of mound on Fain's island, Jefferson county, Tennessee.

were folded. They were at all depths, from $2\frac{1}{2}$ to 5 feet; one lay near the bottom, at the depth of 8 feet and close to the mass of ashes under the fire beds.

With this skeleton were five celts and some shell ornaments; the skull was also obtained. The mound appeared to be composed almost entirely of dark, sandy soil, with here and there a small streak of lighter colored earth running through it.

There is an ancient burial ground on the south side of the river, opposite the mound, which has not been examined.

ROANE COUNTY.

The first works examined in this county are on Long island, in the Holston river, which is from 3 to 5 miles long and varies in width from one-fourth to 1 mile. It lies nearly east and west, the course of the river at this point being from a little south of east to a little north of west. The western portion, near the lower point is low bottom land;

the middle and upper portions are considerably higher, rising some 40
to 50 feet above low water. A plat of the island, showing the respective positions of the nineteen mounds on it, is given in Fig. 238. These,
as will be seen by the figure, are arranged in three groups, the group
a containing five mounds, being near the extreme lower or western
point on the lowest land of the island; group *b*, also containing five
mounds, near the middle; and group *c*, containing nine mounds, near the
upper or eastern end, the two latter groups being on the higher land.
The mounds are numbered from 1 to 19, though all these numbers do
not appear in the figure.

Mound 1 of group *a* (the one next the northern branch) is by far the
largest, being about 160 feet from east to west, 90 feet north and south,
and 18 feet high. It is known as the Brakebill mound, and was partially explored by Rev. E. O. Dunning on behalf of the Peabody
Museum. As Mr. Johnson, the owner, has since built a corn house on
it, permission could not be obtained to make further explorations in it.

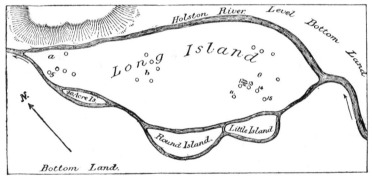

FIG. 238.—Plat of groups on Long island, Roane county, Tennessee.

Mounds 2 and 4, being covered at the time with growing corn, were
not disturbed.

Mound 3, measuring 93 feet from north to south, 105 feet east and west,
and 5 feet high, having been under cultivation for sixty years and
partially examined by a previous explorer, is considerably lower than it
originally was.

The body of the mound was composed of dark, sandy soil similar to
that of the surrounding surface of the island, with numerous small
patches of yellow clay scattered through it without any apparent order
or arrangement. In it were five skeletons near the original surface of
the ground, arranged as shown in Fig. 239. In the center, at *a*, was a
large, boat-shaped vessel of clay, 9 feet long, 4 feet wide in the middle,
but tapering to each end, and about 15 inches deep. This vessel, which
was probably only sun-dried, was watersoaked to such an extent that it
crumbled into minute fragments when an attempt was made to remove
it. It lay northwest and southeast and contained an adult skeleton

lying at full length with the head northwest. In the vessel, near the head of the skeleton, was the stone image represented in Fig. 240. This, which represents a squatting figure, is 14½ inches high and is carved out of stone. At each of the points marked *h, h, h, h*, corresponding with the cardinal points, was a sitting skeleton facing toward the center. With the one at the north was a clay pipe and two discoidal stones; lying by the feet of the one at the east was a large shell, and with the one at the south were two polished celts, one of which was broken.

Mound 5, nearest the lower point of the island and within 50 feet of the water's edge and of the ordinary conical form, measured 60 feet in diameter and 5 feet high, the highest point being toward one side.

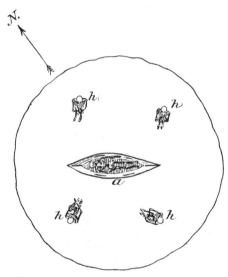

FIG 239.—Diagram of mound No. 3, Long island, Roane county, Tennessee.

One foot from the top was a layer of burnt clay from 3 to 4 inches thick, spreading horizontally over the entire area of the mound, reaching the surface all around. It did not conform to the curve of the mound, but extended horizontally. At several points on its surface, or mixed with it, were small piles or spots of charcoal and ashes. The body of the mound, both above and below this layer, consisted of dark, sandy soil.

In the central portion, close to the bottom, lay the remains of four skeletons, but so far decomposed that it was impossible to determine their positions.

Mound 11, as will be seen by reference to Fig. 238, is one of group *c*, situated on the higher ground. Diameter, 65 feet; height, a little over 7 feet. This, as proved to be the case with all those on the high ground examined, was composed entirely of very hard, compact, red clay.

About the center, at the depth of 2½ feet, was a badly decayed skeleton which must have been doubled up or bundled. There was no dark colored earth about the bones, as is usually the case, the red clay being packed about them as hard as in any other portion of the mound. Directly under this, but at the bottom of the mound, resting on the natural surface of the ground, were two other skeletons lying at full length, side by side, with heads toward the west. The bones of these were in a much better state of preservation than of the one nearer the top. With them was some red paint and near their heads one spear point and two small discoidal stones. The earth immediately surrounding these two skeletons was dark and loose, all the rest of the mound being composed of red clay, so hard that we had to use the pick to loosen it.

Mound 12, measured 52 feet in diameter and 5 feet high, and like the preceding consisted chiefly of red clay closely packed and very hard. In the center, at the depth of 3 feet, was a horizontal layer of mussel shells about 1 foot thick, covering a circular area 6 feet in diameter. The shells composing this layer were packed in dark-colored

FIG. 240.—Image from mound No. 3, Long island, Roane county, Tennessee.

earth and must have been carefully placed by hand, as they were in tiers, all with the concave side downward.[1] Underneath the layer of shells the earth was very dark and appeared to be mixed with vegetable mold to the depth of 1 foot. At the bottom of this, resting on the original surface of the ground, was a very large skeleton, lying horizontally at full length. Although very soft, the bones were sufficiently

---

[1] The same thing, as I learn from Dr. Patrick, of Belleville, Ill., was observed in a mound which formerly stood on the site of East St. Louis. These, however, as appeared from the specimen shown me, were sea shells, mostly univalves.

distinct to allow of a careful measurement before attempting to remove them. The length from the base of the skull to the bones of the toes was found to be 7 feet 3 inches. It is probable, therefore, that this individual when living was fully 7½ feet high. At the head lay some small pieces of mica and a green substance, probably the oxide of copper, though no ornament or article of copper was discovered. This was the only burial in the mound.

By reference to the plan of the group (Fig. 238), it will be observed that Nos. 12, 13, 14, and 15 form the arc of the circle. They are regularly spaced, the distance from the base of one to the base of the next being about 100 feet. No. 11 is about 200 feet from No. 12.

No. 14, 65 feet in diameter and 7 feet high, was next explored by cutting a trench 12 feet wide from side to side through the center down to the original soil. This was composed of hard, red clay, with here and there, from the depth of 1 to 3 feet, a small spot of very dark earth, which contained decayed mussel shells. At a depth of 3½ feet, near the center, lay 2 skeletons very near each other, one· with the head toward the east, the other with the head toward the west, with dark colored earth and some shells packed about them. Nothing further was discovered until near the bottom, where a bed of shells was reached. The shelfs in this bed were closely packed together in the manner of those in mound No. 12. This bed or layer was circular in outline, about 12 feet in diameter and 1 foot thick, and contained a smaller proportion of dirt than that in No. 12. The layer beneath this, resting on the original soil, consisted of dark colored earth in which, lying immediately under the center of the shell bed, were 2 skeletons. But these were so far decayed that their exact position could not be determined. Near their heads were two arrow points, two rude celts, and one discoidal stone.

Mound 15, 64 feet in diameter and 7 feet high, presented in some respects a remarkable contrast to those just described. For a depth of 5 feet it, like the others, consisted of hard, red clay; under this was a dark layer which spread over the entire area of the mound and seemed to be filled with skeletons; in fact, the entire bottom was apparently a mass of bones. All the earth above them being carefully removed, it became apparent that there was no regularity or order of burial, but that the bones were heaped together in a confused mass, it being impossible to trace out the individual skeletons. Many of the bones were broken and often three or four skulls piled together. They belonged to persons of all ages, from the young child to the aged.

The number of persons buried here was estimated at 53, as that was the number of skulls found. All must have been deposited at one time and hence after the flesh had been removed. The remains were probably gathered from other temporary depositories and brought here to be buried in one common grave.

Mound 16, 40 feet in diameter and 5 feet high, was similar to No. 15, except that in this there were only twelve skeletons.

Mound 17, similar in size and construction to No. 16, contained at the bottom 4 skeletons, much decayed; no relics with them.

Mound 18, 38 feet in diameter and 4 feet high, was composed throughout of red clay; not even a change in color was noticed until the bottom was reached. Here, in the center, was a hearth of burnt clay and ashes about 5 feet in diameter and 5 or 6 inches thick. This layer or bed of burnt clay was level on the top, and the ashes which lay on it had some pieces of charcoal scattered through them.

As already stated, all the mounds of the higher ground of the island explored were made of red clay packed very hard, and the skeletons found in them were in an advanced stage of decay, with the exception of those in mound No. 15, where, although in a confused heap, they were much better preserved. It will be observed also that the skeletons found on the low bottom land were in better condition than those found in the red clay mounds of the uplands. It is surmised from this fact that the higher land formed at first the whole island, the lower point being a subsequent addition, and that the mounds on the former portion are much older than those on the lower point.

Some 2 or 3 acres of the lower point, which was washed bare during the flood of April, 1886, is covered with fragments of pottery, broken arrowheads, flint chips, broken celts, etc. At one point the soil was all washed off down to the hard ground, exposing a floor of burnt clay about 30 feet square and 1 foot thick. In this could be distinctly seen the charred ends of posts which had been set in the ground. An examination of some of these proved them to be red cedar. They had been set into the ground through the burnt clay to the depth of about 3 feet and some of them were still comparatively sound; all were burnt off at the top. Unfortunately the explorer neglected to note at the time their respective positions.

MOUND ON THE HAGLER FARM.

This stands on the lower bottom about 100 feet from the river bank and 8 miles down the river from the preceding groups. It is immediately opposite an island on one hand and a spur which runs down from the hills on the other. A broad level bottom extends along the river above the mound for half a mile and for 2 miles below it, but is very narrow where the mound stands.

Although quite large, being 142 feet in diameter and 11 feet high, it is of the round conical type and quite symmetrical. At the depth of 2 feet was a layer of burnt clay from 6 to 8 inches thick, extending over the whole mound, not horizontally, as usual, but conforming to the curve of the upper surface. It must, therefore, have formed the upper layer of the mound when it had reached this stage of its construction.

Immediately below this skeletons began to appear and continued to be found until a depth of 5 feet was reached; below this depth there were no more indications of burial. When the bottom was reached it was seen that a ditch had been dug in the original soil 1 foot deep and 2½ feet wide, running east and west and traceable for 12 or 13 feet. At two points, as shown by the dotted lines in Fig. 241, were lateral extensions running off at right angles on each side; these could be traced only for a distance of 4 or 5 feet. Fourteen skeletons were discovered, none of which were at a greater depth than 5 feet, and all were below the layer of burned clay, which did not appear to have been disturbed. All of these skeletons were lying horizontally on their backs, at full length, and the heads of all, except that of No. 1, toward the north, as indicated in the figure, which shows the respective positions of the skeletons and the ditch below. With skeleton No. 1 were two relics, a fine spearhead and a soapstone pipe; with No. 5, a fine polished celt and two small discoidal stones; with No. 12, a singular stone tube, some small arrowheads, one discoidal stone, and a beaver's tooth.

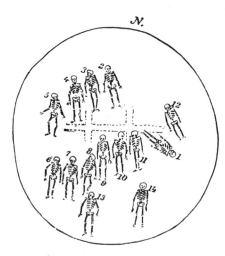

FIG. 241.—Diagram of the Hagler mound, Roane county, Tennessee.

All the specimens were found about the heads of the skeletons.

On the farm of Mr. R. H. Evans, 6 miles below Long island and 2 miles above the Hagler farm, are seven mounds, and 4 miles further down, on the lands of Mr. G. B. Johnson, five.

MOUNDS AND ANCIENT CEMETERY ON THE LEE FARM.

The farm of Mr. M. G. Lee, lying on the north side of Clinch river, about 14 miles above Kingston, contains about 1,200 acres, mostly beautiful level land, denominated here "first and second bottoms." The west side of this extensive farm is bounded in part by White Oak creek. A mile above the mouth of the creek the land is considerably higher along the river bank than it is farther back. This ridge or high ground rises somewhat as it nears the point where the creek enters the river. In times of high water the river breaks around the upper end of the high ground and flows back of it until it reaches the creek, but in April, 1886, the water rose to an unprecedented height and swept entirely over this higher ground, washing off the sandy soil in some places to the depth of several feet, exposing a number of graves and showing that here was an ancient cemetery.

The locality was visited immediately after this occurrence. The dark soil had all been washed away, leaving the hard yellow sand exposed. On the highest point of the rise could be seen a large number of skeletons, some still resting in their graves, but more washed out and scattered over the surface, or the bones drifted here and there in heaps. Several days were spent in examining this interesting spot and excavating the graves from which the skeletons had not been removed or washed out. All that could be determined was that they had been buried horizontally in comparatively shallow graves dug in the original soil for their reception. There was no regularity as to direction, some heads being east, some west, some north, and others south. The area covered was about 2 acres. Scattered over this were small broken stones, arrowheads, flint chips, fragments of pottery, etc.

Mound No. 1, about 55 feet in diameter and 3½ feet high, stood on a slight elevation about one-fourth of a mile from the river, but somewhat nearer the creek. It had been plowed over for many years, bringing to the surface human bones, some of which were lying on the top when examined.

The entire mound was removed, revealing some large flat stones near the surface. The earth about these was dark and loose, while the remainder consisted of hard red clay. Nothing further of interest was observed. It is apparent, therefore, that the skeletons which were plowed up must have been near the top of the mound, which could not have been more than 6 or 7 feet high.

Between mound No. 1 and mound No. 2, there is quite a depression, so much so that water frequently stands here. As this mound (No. 2) had never been plowed or disturbed, it retained its full proportions, being 60 feet in diameter, 10 feet high, and conical in form. At the depth of 2½ feet was a layer of rather large, flat limestone rocks, extending horizontally in all directions to the margin of the mound. Immediately beneath these stones lay twenty-five skeletons so close to them that several of the skulls and other bones were crushed by them. Some of the stones were quite large, but all of them about 4 or 5 inches thick and some with the edges nicely squared, probably by the natural fracture, as there were no traces of tool marks on them. The entire mound consisted of red clay, but that portion above the stone platform was loose and easily worked. About a foot above the bottom another bed of similar stones was reached, but this covered an area only 7 feet in diameter. Immediately under it, lying upon the original surface of the ground, were five skeletons, slightly covered with earth, over which the stones were laid. It is possible that after the first burial a small mound may have been thrown up and that a considerable interval elapsed before the second burial. That all the skeletons in a layer were deposited at one time can not be doubted. The clay between the upper and lower layers was so hard that it required the use of picks to break it up. The skeletons in the lower layer were much decayed and crushed by the weight of the stones resting on them. No order as to position appeared to have been observed in either layer. No relics save a few arrow points and discoidal stones were discovered.

Mound 3, 70 feet in diameter, 15 feet high, and conical in form, was also explored. At the depth of 3 feet were eight skeletons so far decayed that it was impossible to determine their exact positions, except that they lay at about the same level. Near the bottom, though a little above the natural surface of the ground, were three other skeletons lying about 5 or 6 feet from each other. These were in a much better state of preservation than the eight near the top. There were no stones over the skeletons as in mound 2, nor were any relics found with them nor in the mound.

Immediately below the mouth of White Oak creek is Jones island, on which it is said a mound formerly stood which has been washed away by the floods. The locality was visited, and though no traces of the mound could be seen, large quantities of broken pottery, flint chips, and other evidences of former occupancy were observed.

One mile below this place, on the south side, are two large mounds situated on the point of a ridge which runs close to the river. They are covered with heavy timber.

BLOUNT, MONROE, AND LOUDON COUNTIES.

The valley of the Little Tennessee from where it leaves the Smoky mountains, which form the boundary between North Carolina and Tennessee, to where it joins the Tennessee river in Loudon county, is undoubtedly the most interesting archeological section in the entire Appalachian district.

The numerous groups of mounds and other ancient works which are found along the valleys of the principal stream and its tributaries, appear to be intimately related to one another and are so evidently the work of one people that it is deemed unwise to arrange them by counties; moreover, this would confuse the reader, hence it is thought best to vary the usual rule in this instance and describe the groups in the order in which they follow one another, commencing with the one situated nearest the point where the river leaves the mountains, thence moving down the stream to its junction with the Holston. In order that the reader may understand the relation of these groups, a map of the area embraced is given in Pl. xxv, on which they are located. As this map is copied from one made by the geographical division of the U. S. Geological Survey from recent surveys, and the groups located by a special survey made under the Bureau of Ethnology for this purpose, it may be relied upon as being more than usually correct.

The river, after winding its way through the mountain gorges, enters a beautiful valley about half a mile wide and perfectly level to the foot of the Chilhowee mountains, to which it runs parallel for several

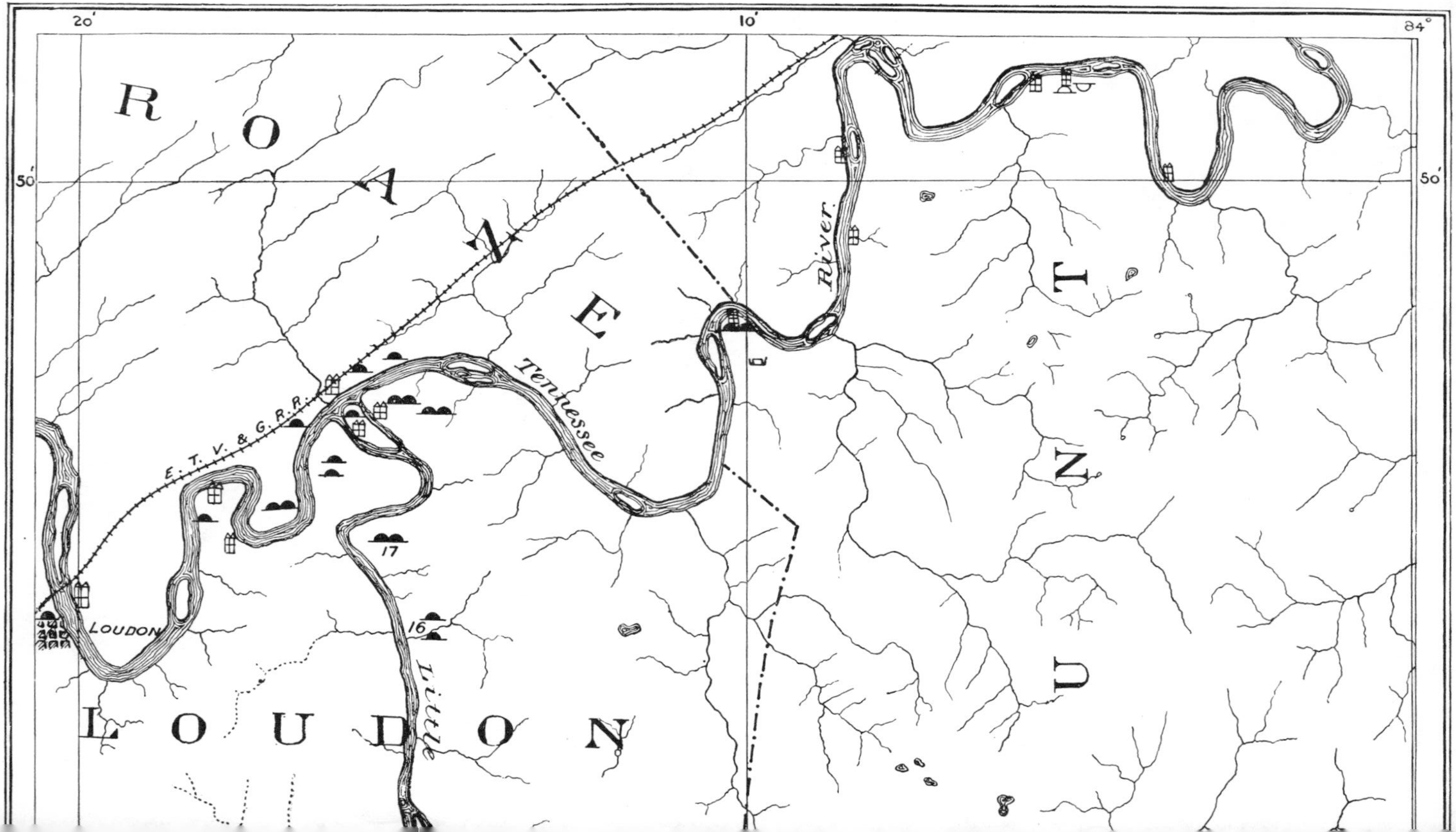

20'
10'
84°
50'
50'
ROANE
LOUDON
T
N
U
River
Tennessee
Little
E. T. V. & G. R. R.
LOUDON
17
16

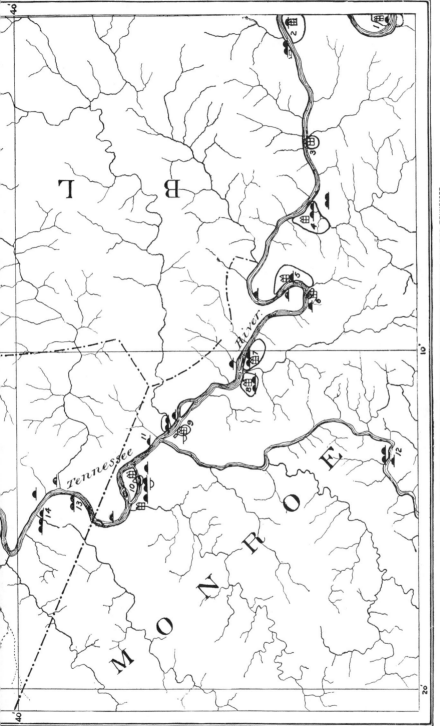

PLAT OF THE VALLEY OF THE LITTLE TENNESSEE RIVER, BLOUNT AND MONROE COUNTIES, TENNESSEE.

miles. The first bottom as we descend is known as the Hardin farm. On this is a tumulus now named the Hardin mound. This is located north of the river about 5 miles above the mouth of Abrahams creek, and nearly opposite the mouth of Tallassee creek. (No. 1, Pl. xxv.) It is of the usual conical form, measuring 120 feet in diameter and 7 feet high. In this was a single adult skeleton near the center at the depth of 2 feet, lying on its back, head east, and arms spread out as indicated at *a* in Fig. 242. Lying at the right hand were a stone pipe and a polished celt; at the left hand, a stone pipe and nine arrowheads; at the feet, a large pot broken in pieces. On the skeleton, chiefly around the neck, legs, and arms, were 1,039 beads, mostly shell; 384 of them were of large size; a few were fresh-water pearls. The bones crumbled to pieces as soon as an attempt was made to remove them. No other skeletons or indications of burial were found; but at *b, b, b, b,* resting on the natural surface of the ground, were four little piles of burnt clay, one at each of the points indicated, forming a square. These were rounded at the base, running to a sharp point at the top; di-

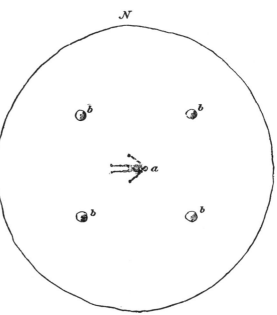

Fig. 242.—Diagram of the Hardin mound, Blount county, Tennessee.

ameter at the base, 2 feet, and height 2 feet. Some coals and ashes were about each, showing that the burning had been done after they were placed in position. There is scarcely a doubt that these remains mark the site of the old Cherokee town Tallassee. In order that the reader may understand the reason on which this assumption is based, a facsimile of Henry Timberlake's map made in 1762 is inserted here. (Pl. xxvi.) By referring to this as we proceed in our description of the groups along the Little Tennessee river, the reader will see the close correspondence in locality of the Cherokee towns with these groups.

THE M'MURRAY MOUNDS.

These mounds, four in number, are some 5 or 6 miles lower down than the preceding, the first, as we descend, being on the south side of the river, on the farm of Mr. Boyd McMurray, the others on the north side, on the farm of Mr. Samuel McMurray. (No. 2, Pl. XXV.) A plat of the area, showing the relative positions of these mounds is given in Fig. 243. The direction from the point *a* directly opposite the mouth of Abrahams creek, to mound No. 1, on the Boyd McMurray farm, is S. 86° W. and distance 1,450 feet; from mound No. 1, to the point *b*, on the north bank of the river, N. 53° W., 1,270 feet; from *b* to center of mound No. 2 on the Samuel McMurray farm, N. 76° W., 745 feet; from No. 2 to No. 3, N. 79° W., 520 feet; from No. 3 to No. 4, N. 79° W., 335 feet, the measurements always being from center to center. Mound No. 1 is 288 feet from the river bank; No. 2 is 173 feet; No. 3 is 258 feet; and No. 4 is 108 feet.

Mound 1, circular in form, 4 feet high, and with an average diameter of about 100 feet, was examined by cutting a broad trench through the center from side to side and down to the original soil. No indications of burial were observed nor was anything of interest found, except a large fire-bed. This was on the original surface of the ground exactly

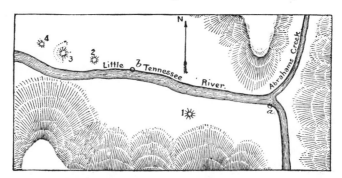

FIG. 243.—Plat of the McMurray mounds, Blount county, Tennessee.

at the center of the mound. It consisted of a layer of burnt clay between 7 and 8 feet in diameter and from 4 to 6 inches thick, and was covered with ashes; encircling the margin was a row of water-worn stones. Over this bed was a layer of clay 1 foot in thickness; the remainder of the mound was composed of dark loam like the surrounding soil.

Mound No. 2, which is circular, measured 110 feet in diameter and a few inches less than 5 feet in height. In excavating this a trench was first run in from the south side; before reaching the center a stone grave or cist was found of the usual box shape. This contained an adult skeleton, much decomposed. A trench was then carried in on the north side, and at about the same distance from the edge was another cist of the same character; also containing a single skeleton. At the center, lay four uninclosed skeletons in an extended position on the original surface; two with their feet toward the south, the other two, whose heads were nearly touching the heads of this pair, having their

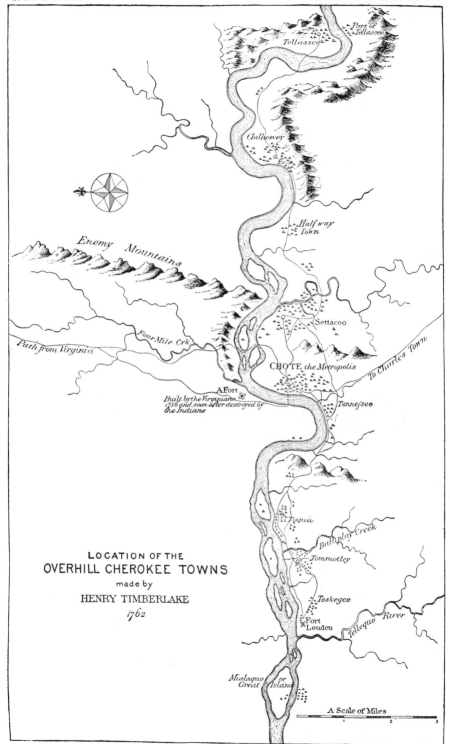

COPY OF TIMBERLAKE'S MAP OF OVERHILL CHEROKEE TOWNS.

feet toward the north. The remainder of the mound, which was composed throughout of yellow sand, except a little black earth about each skeleton, being cleared away, five other uninclosed skeletons were unearthed, which were found in the positions shown in Fig. 244. A few arrowheads, two polished celts, and some flint chips were found at different points in the mound, but none were with any of the skeletons.

It was learned from Mr. McMurray that mound No. 4 was partially explored several years ago, and that several stone graves, such as those in No. 2, were found in it. This was probably by Rev. E. O. Dunning, on behalf of the Peabody Museum. Similar graves occur in considerable numbers in the field about the mounds, especially in the vicinity of No. 3; the side stones in many cases being visible above the surface. These are indicated by the dotted line about 3

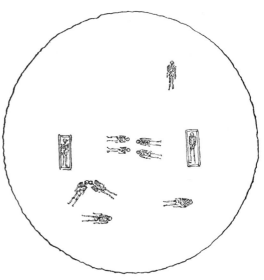

Fig. 244.—Diagram of McMurray mound. No. 2.

on the plat (Fig. 243). Several were explored but nothing found in them, except decaying skeletons.

Mound No. 3 stood on the first bottom, in a beautiful level meadow, about 250 feet from the river. Its form was an ellipse, measuring 150 by 122 feet, the longer axis being east and west; height 12 feet, but considerably reduced by the plow. A thorough excavation showed its composition, mode of construction, and contents to be as follows: The

Fig. 245.—Section of McMurray mound. No. 3.

top portion, to the depth of 5 feet (except a circular space in the center), consisted of dark, sandy soil, mixed with pieces of broken pottery, flint chippings, and charcoal. This layer, which was beneath the slight outer covering of recent vegetable mold, did not extend down the curve of the mound toward the base, but was horizontal on the under side, as shown at *b*. Fig. 245, which represents a section of the mound.

Immediately below this was a horizontal layer of charcoal (*c c*), 4 to 6 inches thick, extending horizontally over nearly the entire area of the mound at this height, except where interrupted at the center by the conical mass (*a a*). The coals composing this layer were of cane and small boughs and very closely packed. The earth next under it was very hard for a depth of several inches. From this layer (*d d*) down to the natural surface of the ground the mound was composed of dark earth similar to that in the upper layer (*b b*), and in this part were found all the skeletons hereafter mentioned, with the exception of No. 34. Extending down through the center from the top was a conical mass (*a a*)

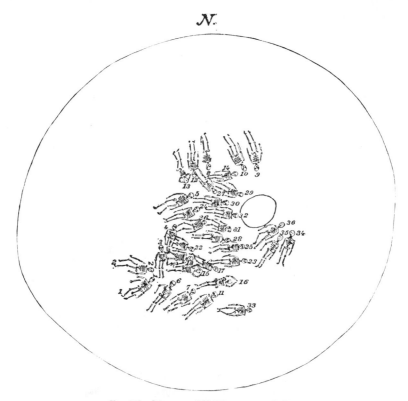

FIG. 246.—Diagram of McMurray mound, No. 3.

8 feet in diameter at the top and 4 at the bottom, composed of alternate layers of burnt clay and ashes. The clay layers were quite hard and slightly dished, and some of them a foot thick. The layers of ashes each measured 4 or 5 inches. As these beds were undoubtedly burnt in places it is plain they were made as the mound was built up. Occasional small fire-beds at various depths in the entire layer (*d d*) bear out this opinion.

In Fig. 246, which is a horizontal section or plan of the mound, are shown the skeletons in their respective positions. All these, except

No. 34—the skeleton of a child—were below the charcoal bed (*c c*) (Fig. 245) and 7 or 8 feet below the top of the mound. The area occupied by them was comparatively small, probably not more than one-fifth of that covered by the mound. They were more crowded, and more nearly on the same level than is usual in a mound of this size. In some cases they lay touching one another; for example, Nos. 18 to 22 were so close together that Nos. 19, 20, and 21 had to be omitted from the figure. They were lying face up at full length, with arms in natural position by the sides, except three (Nos. 13, 15, and 16), whose arms were turned back so as to bring the hands to the head. By referring to the figure it will be seen that nearly every one has the head to the east; five being toward the south and two or three toward the north. There were in all thirty-six, only eight of which were accompanied by any relics worth mentioning. Every pot that was found stood near the head of a skeleton; the beads and ornamented shells were about the neck or resting on the breast; the pipe, stone knife, and drilled celt were all at the head of No. 22; the celts and discoidal stones were generally found about the bones of the hands.

By reference to the diagram it will be seen that No. 32 lay near the central shaft, and fully as deep in the mound as any other skeleton; with this was an iron chisel, lying on the breast; the beads about the neck of the skeleton were so placed in relation to the chisel (which was perforated at one end) as to lead to the belief that all of them had been suspended on one cord.

The following is a list of the articles obtained from this mound:

With skeleton No. 9, one pot and two ornamented shells.

With skeleton No. 16, one pot, one ornamented shell, one discoidal stone, and beads.

With skeleton No. 18, two pots.

With skeleton No. 22, one pipe, one flint knife, one drilled celt.

With skeleton No. 26, one pipe (steatite), one celt, two discoidal stones.

With skeleton No. 27, one pipe (ornamented), two celts, one chipped flint implement.

With skeleton No. 32, one perforated iron chisel, one discoidal stone, and beads.

A cemetery, consisting chiefly of stone graves, lies immediately about this mound. Twelve of these were opened and found to be formed of slabs of slate stone, arranged in the usual box-like shape; each containing a single skeleton. The remains at this point probably mark the locality of the old Cherokee town Chilhowey, not shown on Pl. XXV.

Proceeding down the river to the mouth of Mulberry creek we find here on the south side of the river indications of a village site. These consist of fragments of pottery, broken stone implements, fire-beds, etc. But there is no mound here. This is the village site No. 3, on the plat shown in Pl. XXV, and corresponds with "Halfway-Town" of Timberlake's map. (Pl. XXVI.)

THE LATIMORE GROUP.

Moving on down the river, the next group reached is on the farm of Mr. Latimore, on the south bank, immediately above the mouth of

Citico creek.   This is the upper and outlying portion of the group numbered 4 in Pl. xxv.   A plat of the entire group is given in Fig. 247,
which includes the McSpaddin mounds just below the creek.   To show
the relation of the two groups and their immediate surroundings it may
be stated that this group consists of three mounds standing on the level
top of a spur which is about 150 feet higher than the bottom lands.

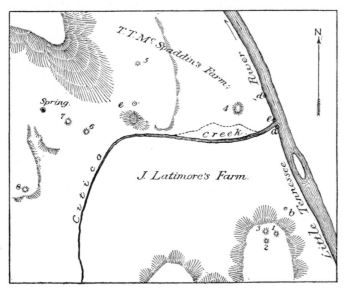

FIG. 247.—Plat of Latimore and McSpaddin mounds (Citico group), Monroe county, Tennessee.

The courses and distances between different points are as follows
(Fig. 247):

From *a*, the junction of Citico creek with the river, to *b*, at the foot of the spur,
S. 10° E., 1,476 feet.

From *b* to mound No. 1, S. 38° W., 310 feet.

From mound No. 1 to mound No. 2, S. 45° W., 143 feet.

From mound No. 2 to mound No. 3, N. 10° W., 108 feet.

From *b* directly to the river bank, 310 feet.

Measurements between the mounds are in all cases from center to center.

FIG. 248.—Vertical section, mound No. 1, Latimore group.

Mound No. 1 was slightly oval in form, 70 feet in diameter and a
little over 8 feet high.   A thorough exploration was made, bringing to
light a confused heap of human bones near the center, at a depth of
from 2 to 3 feet.   In this heap, which was as compact as it could well
be of such material, were eleven skulls, indicating that at least 11
skeletons (for the flesh must have been off when deposited) had been

buried here. All the bones were so much decayed that only one skull could be saved. Five feet farther down, near the original surface and immediately under this pile of bones, was a horizontal layer, or rather floor, of rough river stones, but no traces of coal or ashes. It was circular, with a diameter of 20 feet. (See vertical section in Fig. 248.)

Mound No. 3 was 90 feet in diameter and 8 feet high. It as well as No. 1 were composed of red clay. Two skeletons were found near the center, at a depth of less than 2 feet. Nothing else of interest was observed.

THE McSPADDIN MOUNDS.

This section of the group, but a short distance from the preceding, and on the same side of the river, is on the farm of Mr. T. T. McSpaddin, just below the mouth of Citico creek. It consists of five mounds, located as shown in Fig. 247, bearings and distances as follows:

From c, at the junction of the creek with the river, to d, on the west bank of the river, N. 22° W., 444 feet.

From d to Mound No. 4, S. 63° W., 538 feet.

From Mound No. 4 to Mound No. 5, N. 68° W., 1,896 feet; the point on this line where it crosses the rise to the second bottom is 550 feet from No. 5.

From Mound No. 5 to the point in the gap marked e, S. 24° W., 793 feet.

From e to Mound No. 6, S. 66° W., 724 feet.

From Mound No. 6 to Mound No. 7, N. 65° W., 215 feet.

From Mound No. 7 to Mound No. 8, S. 39° W., 1,270 feet.

The dotted line shows the old channel of the creek, now dry; its nearest point to Mound No. 4, is 208 feet; from the same mound to the nearest point on Citico creek as it now runs, is 480 feet. The second bottom is 10 feet higher than the first. The spur and hill, which seem to have been cut off from its point in past geological time, are of considerable height. Behind these is an area of level land on which Mounds No. 6, 7, and 8 are situated; No. 8 is at a considerable distance from the others, and beyond a ravine. The distance from No. 4 to No. 8, by way of the gap is about three-fourths of a mile.

Mound No. 4, known locally as "Citico mound," is the largest, not only of this group, but of the entire section. In shape it resembles the half of an egg divided lengthwise, being broadest and highest nearer one end, sloping thence by regular, somewhat curved lines. The length is 220 feet; greatest breadth, 184 feet; greatest height, 14 feet. It may possibly have been flat on top originally, but no satisfactory evidence of this can be had; in fact, its present form seems to be that which it has had from the beginning, so far as can be judged from an examination of its structure. As is shown in the plat, it is located on the first bottom of the Little Tennessee, and, though often surrounded by water in times of flood, was never known to be covered. For a space of 6 or 7 acres around it the soil is strewn with fragments of pottery, flint chips, broken stones, animal bones, charcoal, and other refuse. Great numbers of shell beads have been picked up here, and human skeletons have occasionally been plowed up or washed out by high water. There is a good view of the valley for 2 or 3 miles down the river from the top of the mound. On the second bottom, 600 yards northwest of this, is Mound No. 5, somewhat circular in form, 20 feet in diameter, and 2½ feet high. Immediately back of this is a high ridge terminating in a cliff almost perpendicular on the side facing the creek.

The other mounds, Nos. 6, 7, and 8, are on a high level back of the ridge. There is a deep gap, about 60 yards wide, through this ridge directly between Nos. 5 and 6, thus affording an easy passageway from one group to the other.

The first of this group explored was No. 6, which is circular in form, about 80 feet in diameter and 8 feet high, and composed entirely of red clay. The plow had thrown out 1 skeleton and penetrated to 2 others, which were found near the surface, but so badly decayed that no part of them could be preserved.

No. 5 was also composed of red clay, but no sign of burial was observed, nor were coals, ashes, or anything else of interest found in it.

The large mound, No. 4, was thoroughly overhauled to the base. At the highest point, 6 inches below the surface, was a bed of burned clay, circular in form, about 6 feet in diameter and 1 foot thick, and burned so hard as to be very difficult to break up. First, three trenches were

FIG. 249.—Vertical section of the Citico mound (McSpaddin, No. 4).

run in from the margin of the mound from the north, south, and west sides intersecting at this clay bed. In cutting these, quite a number of skeletons were unearthed, some within 2 feet of the surface, others at a depth of 9 feet, at which depth a bed of yellow sand, slightly mixed with clay and firmly packed, was reached; this lay on the original surface of the ground, and extended over the whole area covered by the mound. No skeletons were found in this lower layer or under it. By cutting the trenches in the way described the clay bed was left unbroken until its extent and relation to what lay around it had been ascertained. It was then found that, instead of there being a single clay bed, this was the top one of a series of five. The one in question was level; the others were saucer shaped, as shown at a a, Fig. 249, each extending upward and outward to the slope of the mound, each succeeding one larger than the one above it, the lowest measuring 12 feet in diameter. Alternating with them were layers of ashes; each resting on its corresponding layer of clay. About 3½ feet below these was another layer of red clay (b b) burned very hard, circular in outline, saucer-shaped, and 3 inches thick. This did not run out to the margin, though its diameter was about 20 feet.   Skeletons were found both above and below it, and some rest directly upon it.

The remainder of the mound was then removed, the result being that 91 skeletons were unearthed from the respective positions shown in Fig. 250, which is a plat of the mound showing the plan of burials. As will be seen from this figure, nearly all of the skeletons were stretched out at full length without regard to direction.   None of these were inclosed, but the earth on which each rested was very hard to the depth of 1 or 2 inches, and those lying on the clay bed, *b b*, had more or less coal and ashes about them.   Traces of rotten wood were found immediately over some of them, and with one (No. 52) was

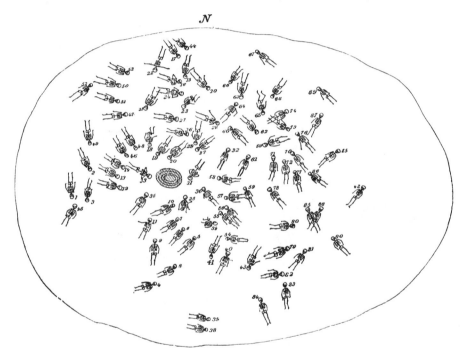

FIG. 250.—Plan of burials in the Citico mound (McSpaddin, No. 4).

a piece of solid pine a foot or more in length.   This was at a depth of 5½ feet.   Most of the articles found were lying close by the skeletons. The bones were so much decayed that but few whole skulls could be obtained.

The following list shows the depth and position of most of the skeletons and the articles found with them:

No. 4, depth 4½ feet, face downward; 2 broken pots.
No. 5, depth 7½ feet, face up; 1 broken pot.
No. 6, depth 5 feet, face down; 1 broken pot.
No. 9, depth 8½ feet, face up; 1 broken pot.
No. 10, depth 3½ feet, face up; 2 broken pots.
No. 13, depth 7 feet, face up; 1 broken pot.

No. 16, depth 7½ feet, face up, with hands resting on the breast and elbows thrust outward. By this skeleton lay 1 polished discoidal stone, 1 stone pipe, 1 broken pot, 1 rough discoidal stone, and 1 engraved shell mask. The skull was preserved.

No. 17, depth 3½ feet, face up; 1 broken pot.

No. 18, in a sitting posture; by it 2 polished celts, 5 arrowheads, and some flint nodules.

No. 21, depth 4 feet, face up, arms extended, 1 unbroken pot, and 1 polished celt.

No. 22, depth 3½ feet, face up; 1 polished celt.

No. 23, legs doubled up, but lying on its back.

No. 24, hands folded on the breast.

No. 25, squatting posture, with feet doubled under the body.

No. 26, depth 7½ feet, face up; 1 pot and 2 polished celts.

No. 31, depth 3½ feet, face up; 1 broken pot and 1 polished celt.

No. 33, depth 5½ feet, face up; by it 1 polished celt and 1 engraved shell. The skull was saved.

No. 34, depth 6 feet, sitting posture; by it 2 broken pots, 1 nicely polished stone chisel, 1 discoidal stone, and 1 stone gorget.

No. 35, depth 8 feet, face up; 2 polished celts; skull preserved.

No. 39, depth 4 feet, face up; 1 polished celt.

No. 41, 1 engraved shell.

No. 44, depth 8 feet, face up; 4 polished celts.

Fig. 251.—Moccasin-shaped pot, Citico mound.

Fig. 252.—Copper rattle or hawk's bell, Citico mound.

No. 46, depth 4½ feet, face up; 1 discoidal stone and 1 broken pot

No. 51, depth 4½ feet, face up; 1 broken pot.

No. 55, depth 3½ feet, face up; 1 polished celt.

No. 57, depth 6½ feet, face up. By this were 1 bowl, 1 shell mask, 2 shell pins, 2 bone awls or punches, and a number of shell beads.

No. 58, depth 5½ feet, face up; 3 bone implements.

No. 59, depth 7½ feet, face up. With this were 2 shell gorgets, 1 broken engraved shell, 1 shell ornament, 1 shell pin, 1 bear's tooth, and 1 discoidal stone.

No. 62, depth 5 feet, face up. With it a lump of red paint, a lot of shell beads, 4 shell pins, 1 bear's tooth, 1 discoidal stone, and 1 ornamented pot.

No. 63, depth 7 feet, face up. By it 1 broken vessel with image head.

No. 66, depth 3½ feet, face up. This was the skeleton of a child, and with it were found 1 moccasin-shaped pot (shown in Fig. 251), 4 copper sleigh-bells or rattles, 1 of which is shown in Fig. 252, and a lot of shell beads. This was buried toward the side of the mound.

No. 68, depth 8½ feet, face up. By this lay 3 shell pins and 1 ornamented pot.

No. 71, depth 6½ feet, face up. With it were 4 shell pins, a lot of shell beads, a lump of red paint, and 1 ornamented bowl.

No. 79, depth 5 feet, face up. Skeleton of a child. With it 1 shell mask or gorget, 1 engraved shell, a lot of shell beads, 2 shell pins, and a lump, apparently of lime mortar.

No. 81, depth 8 feet, face up. With it 2 perfect ornamented pots, 2 shell pins, a lot of shell beads, and a lump of red paint.

No. 89, depth 4½ feet, face up. Skeleton of a child. With it 1 pot, 1 engraved shell gorget, 13 shell pins, 1 plain shell gorget, and 846 shell beads.

No. 90, depth 2¼ feet, face up. With it the bone needle shown in Fig. 253.

FIG. 253.—Bone needle, Citico mound.

Mound No. 8.—This was almost perfectly circular, 55 feet in diameter, and between 8 and 9 feet high. It was composed entirely of red clay, and contained nothing but two skeletons, which lay at full length, side by side, on the original soil at the center of the mound.

The two clusters just described—the Latimore and McSpaddin mounds—form the group marked 4 on Pl. xxv, and correspond in location with the Cherokee town Settacoo of Timberlake's map (Pl. xxvi).

THE BACON AND M'GEE MOUNDS.

About 4 miles below the group last described, and a short distance from the little town of Mountainville, are two mounds; one on the north side of the river, on the land of J. L. Bacon, the other on the south side, nearly opposite, on the land of Mrs. Ann McGee. These belong to the group marked 5 on Pl. xxv. A plat of the area on which they are situated is given in Fig. 254. As will be seen from this, the narrow valley is bounded on both sides, at this point, by high ridges. The courses and distances between the points indicated on the plat are as follows:

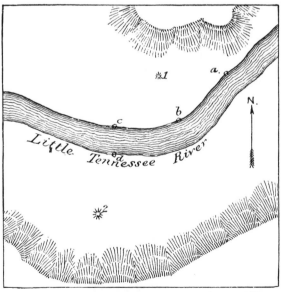

FIG. 254.—Plat of the Bacon and McGee mounds, Blount and Monroe counties, Tennessee.

From *a*, on the north bank of the river, where the bluff comes to the stream, to *b*, also on the north bank. S. 40° W. 840 feet.

From *b* to mound No. 1, N. 15° W. 428 feet.

From *b* to *c*, a point on the north bank of the river, S. 82° W. 700 feet.

From *c* to *d*, a point on the south bank, due south about 350 feet.

From *d* to mound No. 2 on the McGee farm, S. 12° W. 685 feet.

Mound No. 2 (on McGee farm).—This mound, which is an ellipse 70 by 55 feet in its two diameters and about 5 feet high, was composed throughout of red clay, which must have been brought not less than half a mile, this being the distance to the nearest point at which it could have been obtained. The soil of the surrounding area is a rich dark loam, the subsoil sandy.

The whole mound was removed, with the result indicated in Fig. 255. Thirteen whole skeletons were discovered in the positions shown, generally with their heads westward, all lying on their backs, and all, except No. 1, with their arms by their sides; No. 1 had them extended right and left.

At *c* lay twelve skulls on the same level, 3 feet below the surface of the mound, touching each other, with no other bones in connection

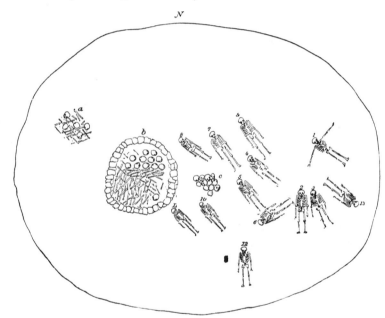

FIG. 255.—Plan of burials in McGee mound, No. 2.

with or immediately about them. At *b*, a little west of the center, and resting on the original surface, was a rough wall, about 2 feet high, built of slate stones; circular in form, inclosing a space about 9 feet in diameter. The dirt inside being cleared away, twelve skulls and a large number of long and other bones were discovered. Eleven of the skulls were lying close together on one side, as shown in the figure, the other lying alone on the opposite side, but each entirely disconnected from the other parts of the skeleton to which it belonged. The other bones were much broken and mingled together in a promiscuous mass. West of the wall and near the west end of the mound were five more skulls lying together, and amid other bones, marked *a* in the figure. The bottom of the inclosure, which corresponded with the original surface of the ground, was covered for an inch or two with coals and ashes, on which the skulls and other bones rested. But neither coal nor ashes were found outside of the wall. All the skeletons and other remains outside of the wall lay a foot or more above the original surface of the ground.

The following articles were obtained from this mound: With skeleton No. 4, 1 ornamented pot; with No. 1, 1 polished stone ornament, 1 stone pipe, 7 arrowheads, a small lot of copper beads, 1 shell gorget, 2 perforated shells, and the fragment of a bone implement. The skulls of Nos. 1 and 7 were saved.

As there are evidences about the McGee mound, on the south side of the river, of a somewhat extensive ancient village, and the locality corresponds exactly with the site of Chote, the "metropolis" and sacred

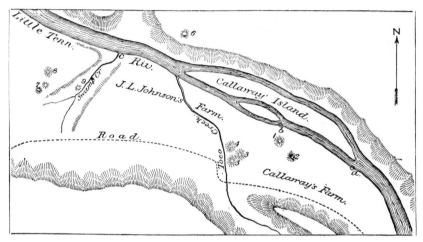

FIG. 256.—Plat of the Toco mounds, Monroe county, Tennessee.

town of the Overhill Cherokees, there can be scarcely a doubt that the remains found here pertain to that town. Mound No. 1, on the north side of the river, is near the point where Timberlake locates an old fort built by Virginians. It was not examined.

The mound and village site marked No. 6 on Pl. xxv, immediately below the preceding, are at the point where Timberlake locates the little town Tennessee, which gives a name to a great river and an important state of the Union.

THE TOCO MOUNDS.

Continuing our course down the Little Tennessee, we come next to the Toco mounds, partly on the lands of Mr. J. L. Johnson and Mr. Callaway, south of the river and just above the mouth of Toco creek and partly below the mouth of the creek. These mounds are arranged in two groups, one consisting of five mounds, situated above Toco creek, and the other consisting of three mounds, situated some distance below it, as shown in Fig. 256, which indicates the respective positions of the works. The upper one of these groups is the same as No. 7 on Pl. XXV, and corresponds with Toqua on Timberlake's map (Pl. XXVI). The lower group is No. 8 of Pl. XXV and corresponds with Tommotley of Timberlake's map (Pl. XXVI).

From *a*, a point on the south bank of the river opposite the extreme upper point of Callaway island, to *b*, a point on the south bank directly north of mound No. 1, is N. 60° W., 1,470 feet.

From *b* to mound No. 1, known as the "Big Toco mound," S., 310 feet.

From mound No. 1 to Mound No. 2, known as the "Callaway mound," S. 40° E., 320 feet.

From mound No. 1 to the three small mounds, Nos. 3, 4, and 5, which are now nearly obliterated, S. 76° W., about 800 feet.

From the Callaway mound to the foot of the ridge, S., 600 feet.

From the point *b* to the mouth of Toco creek, about 600 yards.

The north side of the river is bordered by high bluffs throughout the area shown by the diagram. No. 6 is a small mound on the top of a bluff opposite the mouth of Toco creek.

From the mouth of Toco creek to the mouth of Swamp creek, along the bank of the river, 1,050 feet.

From *c*, at the mouth of Swamp creek, to mound No. 9, S. 48° W., 850 feet.

From mound No. 9 to mound No. 8, N. 65° W., 620 feet.

From mound No. 8 to mound No. 7, S. 30° W., 327 feet.

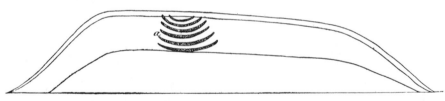

Fig. 257. — Vertical section of the Big Toco mound, Monroe county, Tennessee.

At mound No. 9 the swamp is about 250 feet wide and so wet that the mound is often surrounded by water.

Mound No. 1, which is known locally as the "Big Toco mound," is an oval, 154 by 138 feet, the longer axis being east and west. Height at west end, 24 feet; at east end, 18 feet; top flat, but sloped toward the east, the descent at this end being much more gradual than at the other. The length of the flattened top was 94 feet; greatest breadth, 78 feet. The north, west, and south slopes are very steep.

The elevation as seen from the south is shown in Fig. 257.

This mound was built chiefly of the dark sandy soil around it, which continued uniform to the depth of 9 feet. Here a layer of hard yellow earth was encountered, which continued to the original surface of the ground. Running through this upper layer of dark sandy soil were numerous streaks or thin layers of yellow sand and also of burnt clay, the latter accompanied by coals and ashes. These layers were found from within 2 feet of the top down to the depth of 9 feet. It was noticeable that many of the skeletons, all of which were discovered in this upper layer, though immediately surrounded by loose earth, had directly over them a layer of thin burnt clay, usually broken up.

A little northwest of the center of the mound, at the depth of 2 feet, commenced a series of hearths or fire-beds of burnt clay, with layers of ashes between them, placed one below another, much like those found in the large Citico mound heretofore described.   These alternate

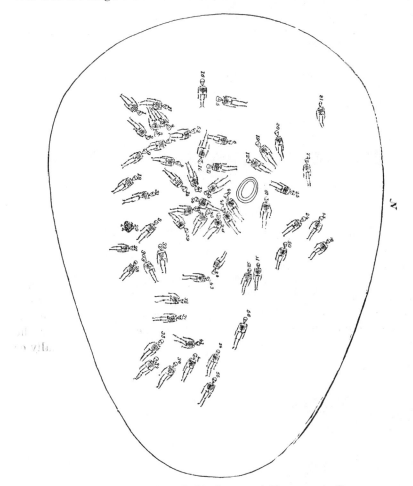

FIG. 258.—Plan of burials in the Big Toco mound, Monroe county, Tennessee.

beds continued down to the depth of 6 feet, increasing in diameter. There were no skeletons in this series of fire-beds.   (See *a*, Fig. 257.)

In several of the other layers of burnt clay (not the central series) were the remains of burnt stakes which had been driven into the surface of the mound when at these respective heights and the top portion burnt off, leaving unburnt the part in the earth.   In some cases these had rotted out, leaving only the impressions of the wood and bark;

in others, where partially charred, the remains were distinct. Some of these were observed within 3 feet of the surface; others at the depth of 6 feet, and at intermediate depths. There was always around the place where these had stood a bed of coals and ashes, and in some of them pieces of charred human bones.

Fifty-seven skeletons were discovered in this mound, the relative positions of which are shown in Fig. 258. None were nearer the top than 4 feet, and none, except No. 49, at a greater depth than 7 feet; all, except Nos. 29 and 49, lay in a horizontal position, with heads in various directions, as shown in the figure.

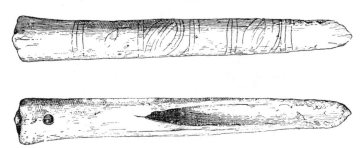

FIG. 259.—Bone implement, Big Toco mound.

Quite a number of clay vessels were discovered, mostly pots, which had crumbled to pieces; some of them seemed to be perfect while in position, but were so thoroughly soaked with water that they fell to pieces as soon as an attempt was made to remove them. Nevertheless by digging carefully around and heating those which appeared whole a few were saved unbroken. Most of the celts were near the heads of the skeletons. Sometimes, where two heads were close together, the celt or celts were placed midway between them, either intentionally or

FIG. 260.—Bone implement, Big Toco mound.

accidentally, in which case it was impossible to decide which skeleton they were buried with.

In every case where a jar or other clay vessel accompanied a skeleton it was near the head, either by the side of the skull or back of it. In most instances where beads were found they were about the neck and breast.

By reference to Fig. 258 the reader will observe that skeleton 49 is near the center of the mound; that immediately around it are eight other skeletons (Nos. 13, 14, 15, 40, 45, 46, 47, and 48), with their heads turned nearly or directly toward it. About the head of 13 were the following

specimens: A polished celt; a small discoidal stone; three bone implements, one of which is shown in Fig. 259, the other two of the form
shown in Fig. 260; a stone pipe (Fig. 261), shaped much like those in

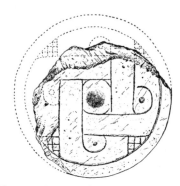

FIG. 261.—Stone pipe, Big Toco mound.   FIG. 262.—Ornamented shell, Big Toco mound.

use at the present day, and bearing evidence of long usage; and the
ornamented shell shown in Fig. 262. With No. 49, chiefly about the
head, were the following articles: Three polished celts; the stone imple-

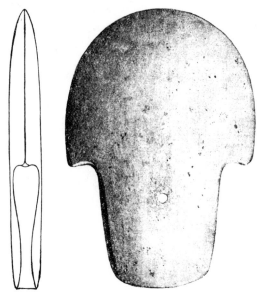

FIG. 263.—Stone implement, Big Toco mound.

ment shown in Fig. 263, finely polished; a small water bottle; a large
spearhead; a soapstone pipe (the bowl and handle had been made in
one piece, but the stem in this case was broken off and the end ground

to admit a cane stem); the pot shown in Fig. 264; an enormous shell mask, the largest, perhaps, ever found in a mound; two small ornamented shells; twenty-nine bone punches or needles, similar to that represented in Fig. 253; thirty-six arrowheads, and some very large shell beads. The bone implements were found by the right hand, which lay close to the right thigh bone; the rest of the articles were about the head, except the shell beads, which appear to have been around the body, about the hips; they were in two rows close side by side.

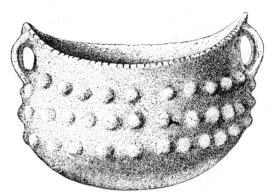

FIG. 264.—Pot, Big Toco mound.

Articles found by the other skeletons were as follows:

Skeleton 4, two polished celts and one discoidal stone.
Skeleton 5, one polished celt.
Skeleton 8, one polished celt, one soapstone pipe, one ornamented shell, and one pot.
Skeleton 9, two polished celts.
Skeleton 17, one polished celt.
Skeleton 18, two polished celts, one stone pipe, two pots, two engraved shells and one shell-ornament, and a number of shell beads.
Skeleton 22, two polished celts.
Skeleton 24, one polished celt.
Skeleton 26, two polished celts, three discoidal stones.
Skeleton 27, one polished celt.
Skeleton 28, two polished celts, one pot.
Skeleton 31, two polished celts.
Skeleton 33, two polished celts, two pots, one engraved shell, three shell ornaments, and a number of shell beads.
Skeleton 34, three polished celts.
Skeleton 36, one discoidal stone.
Skeleton 37, one polished celt, one stone pipe, one engraved shell.
Skeleton 41, one polished celt, one stone pipe, one pot, one engraved shell, one shell ornament.
Skeleton 51, one ornamented shell, one flint implement, a number of shell beads.
Skeleton 52, one ornamented shell, one shell mask, one shell gorget.

Skeleton No. 29 was buried in a perpendicular position, head downward, and rock piled on the feet, as shown in Fig. 258. The top of the head rested on the hard stratum at the depth of 9 feet from the top of the mound.

THE CALLAWAY MOUND.

Mound No. 2, known as the Callaway mound, stands on the level bottom, is conical in form, 93 feet in diameter, and 6 feet high. The soil of 8 or 10 acres around this and the Big Toco mound is very black. This seems due to a large intermixture of charcoal. Indeed, it seems almost impossible to step without treading on coals, fragments of

FIG. 265.—Vertical section of Callaway mound, Monroe county.

pottery, broken arrow-heads, shells, and flint chips. About half way between the mound and the river, the ground rises about 2 feet above the usual level, and then breaks off abruptly toward the river. On this little elevation, for a space of 50 or 60 feet in diameter, is a bed of burnt clay, the top portion broken up by the plow. It is much harder a foot or two under the surface than it is on top.

Possibly it was here the people of the village were accustomed to burn their pottery. The mound was found to be composed of loose, dark, sandy soil, similar to that around it. Lying on the surface or top, immediately under the grass, were fragments of human bones, such as pieces of the arm and leg bones, pieces of the skull, jaw bones, teeth, etc. These had doubtless been

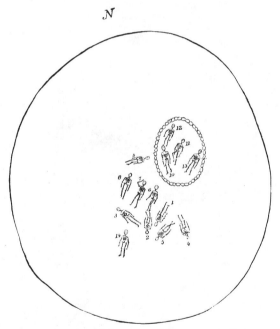

FIG. 266.—Diagram of Callaway mound, Monroe county, Tennessee.

brought up by the plow, as the mound had been cultivated for fifty years, and was considerably worn down. In the central portion, at the depth of about 18 inches, was a level bed of burnt clay and coals (1, Fig. 265), which represents a vertical section of the mound looking north (2 indicates the position of the skeletons at the bottom). This varied from 2 to 3, or more, inches in thickness, and covered an area of about 18 by 20 feet.

Fourteen skeletons were discovered in this mound, all lying extended in a horizontal position, but with their heads in different directions, as shown in Fig. 266. Some of the burials took place subsequent to the formation of the fire bed, as a few of the skeletons were above it or resting on it. Nos. 1 and 2 were lying face up, heads southwest, at a depth of 18 inches. No. 3 lay with the head to the northwest, about 20 inches below the surface of the mound; about the wrists and hands

were some small shell beads, but none about the neck, where they are usually found. No. 4 was lying on its back, head to the south; No. 5 with the head to the southwest. No. 6 was about the center of the mound and at the depth of 3 feet, head northeast. It was much better preserved than those nearer the top. A few small shell beads were lying about the neck and breast. No. 7 was lying face up, head northeast, left hand by the side, but the right arm bent upward so as to bring the hand above the head. By this hand was the water vessel shown in Figs. 267 and 268, made to represent an owl. The peculiarity of this specimen is found in the feather marks which ornament the back or portion representing the wings. The markings, instead of being like those on the Zuñi or Pueblo pottery—although the vessel is precisely of the pattern made by the Pueblo tribes—are of the strictly Mexican type. This vessel was close to the skull, and

FIG. 267.—Water vessel, Callaway mound.

almost touching the right hand. At each side of the head was a large sea shell (*Busycon perversum*), one of them 18 inches long, the circumference at the widest part 22 inches. About the neck and breast were several hundred shell beads. Skeleton No. 8 was lying in the same position and about the same depth as No. 7. Near the right hand were five somewhat singular arrow points or drills, some of which are apparently unfinished. No. 9, somewhat isolated, lay north of those last mentioned, with head directly east; depth from the surface, 3 feet. Near the northeast corner of the first pit, a stone wall, or rather a row of stone slabs set on edge, was encountered, which further investigation and a thorough removal of the dirt showed to be an oval vault (see Fig. 266) 10 feet long and 8 feet broad. This wall, composed of slabs of slate rock set on edge, was about 1 foot high, the top at the highest point 3 feet below the top of the mound. The bottom was completely covered with a layer of slate slabs, as closely fitted together as the unworked edges would admit of. Resting on this floor were four skeletons, as shown in Fig. 266 (Nos. 10, 11, 12, and 13), the heads north and northeast. With skeleton No. 11 were some fragments of copper-stained wood and some pieces of mica. Skeleton No. 14, outside of the vault, lay with the head northeast.

Mounds 7, 8, and 9 really form a separate group and probably, as above stated, mark the site of a village distinct from the one on the east of Toco creek. Nos. 7 and 8 are on a terrace some 25 feet above the water level, but No. 9, as before remarked, is in a swale drained by the little rivulet known as Swamp creek. All are of small size.

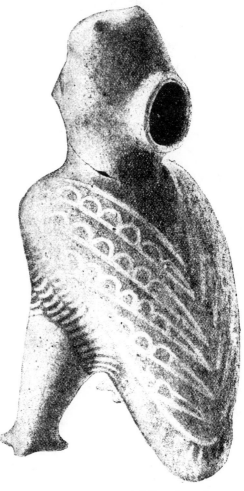

Fig. 268.—Water vessel, Callaway mound.

Nos. 7 and 8 consisted chiefly of yellowish sandy soil from the adjacent surface; for the first 2 feet from the top this was packed so hard as to require the use of a pick. In No. 8, at a depth of $2\frac{1}{2}$ feet, lay the skeleton of a child in the last stage of decay; about the head were several shell beads. Mound No. 9, similar in construction, contained four skeletons lying at a depth of $5\frac{1}{2}$ feet, and very nearly in the center of the mound. With them was a large discoidal mortar stone. Nothing else of interest was observed in any of them.

THE PATE MOUND.

On the north side of the Little Tennessee, a short distance above the mouth of Nine Mile creek, and nearly opposite Old Fort Loudon, is a single conical tumulus known locally as the Pate mound.

It is small, being only 4 feet high, with a diameter of 45 feet. Its stratification was as follows: At the top, a layer of vegetable mold about 4 inches thick; next, 3 feet of damp red clay; lastly, a layer of loose, dark clay, 8 inches thick, resting on the original soil. The lower portion of this bottom layer, to the thickness of an inch, increasing in the center to nearly 6 inches, was much darker than the other part. Six feet from the center, at a depth of three feet in the layer of red clay, lay a single folded skeleton. In the lowest layer, resting on the original surface, were three other skeletons extended horizontally, with faces up. With these were some mussel shells and a stone chisel.

The village site on the opposite (south) side of the river (No. 9, Pl. XXV) corresponds with Toskegee, of Timberlake's map, located in the immediate vicinity of Fort Loudon.

THE NILES FERRY MOUNDS.

This group, consisting of three mounds, is situated on the north side of the Little Tennessee, opposite the mouth of Tellico river and close

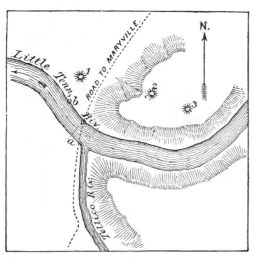

to Niles's ferry, at the crossing of the old Federal road. Fig. 269 shows their position. Nos. 2 and 3, which are comparatively small and of the usual conical type, stand on a timbered ridge which comes to the river immediately below the old blockhouse opposite Fort Loudon. No. 1 is a very large mound, standing on the second bottom, about 400 feet from the river. A single shaft was sunk part way down in it some years ago by Dr. Palmer, but it has never been thoroughly explored.

FIG. 269.—Plat of the Niles ferry mounds, Monroe county, Tennessee.

It is flat on top, 10 or 11 feet high, and about 300 feet in diameter. The Bureau agent, expecting to return to the group the following season, took no other notes than the courses and distances of the mounds from one to another and from the river.

From *a*, opposite the mouth of the Tellico river, to *b*, on the north bank of the Little Tennessee, N. 35° W., 300 feet.

From *b* to mound No. 1, N. 30° E., 410 feet.

From mound No. 1 to mound No. 2, S. 74° E., 1,200 feet (paced).

From mound No. 2 to mound No. 3, S. 75° E., 550 feet.

This group is No. 11 on the plat given in Pl. xxv.

Two miles below the preceding, on the south side of the river, is a group of three mounds, shown in Fig. 270. No. 1, conical, 53 feet in diameter and 5 feet high, and No. 3, similar but somewhat larger, were excavated and found to consist of hard, yellow clay. In the former a few fragments of human bones were found, and in the latter two skeletons. Partly on the land about the mound and partly on the island are the indications of a former village. This is the site of Timberlake's Mialaquo, and is the group marked 10 on Pl. xxv.

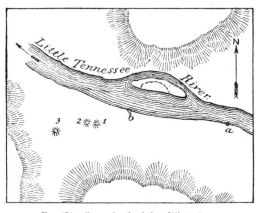

Fig. 270.—Group 2 miles below Niles's ferry.

It is necessary now to notice some other groups in Monroe county before continuing our course down the river, as the next group in this direction is in London county.

MOUNDS IN TELLICO PLAINS.

These, twelve in number, are located along the Tellico river in the extreme southern part of the county, in the little basin-like valley known as Tellico plains. Mound No. 11, on a high ridge on the east side of the river, measured 46 feet in diameter and 6 feet high. It was composed of the following strata: First, below the thin stratum of vegetable mold and decayed leaves, was a layer of red clay to the depth of 3 feet; next, a layer of dark earth varying in thickness from 6 inches to 1 foot, but conforming to the curves of the mound. In this dark earth were small deposits of sand and gravel, which were probably brought from the river, each deposit being about a load for one person. Below this dark stratum was another layer of clay, reaching to and resting upon the original surface of the ground. In this, next to the original surface, were two large lines of rotten wood, evidently the remains of two logs. These were 8 or 9 feet long, lying parallel to one another, and 6 feet apart. Between them, also resting on the original surface of the ground, was a single skeleton, lying at full length, head south and feet north, the same direction as the logs, but so far decayed that the bones crumbled to pieces when handled. There may have been a covering of bark or brush, but nothing was observed to verify such conclusion. Nothing else worthy of notice was discovered.

Nos. 8 and 9 were explored, but were found to be nothing more than heaps of yellow clay with a fire-bed near the top of each. As they were only about 40 feet in diameter and from 4 to 5 feet high, they may have been house sites.

No. 10, 6 feet high and 48 feet in diameter, was also composed of yellow clay, except a limited area, a few inches thick, next the original surface in the center. Here there was a sudden change to dark, loose earth, covering a space about 4½ feet in diameter and extending below the original surface.

This being removed, a circular pit was revealed a little over 3 feet deep, rounded at the bottom and 4½ feet in circumference. This had probably been filled with some substance which had decayed.

MOUNDS ON THE CLICK FARM.

This small group, consisting of three mounds, is situated on the Tellico river, 8 miles above its mouth, on the Click farm. Fig. 271 is a

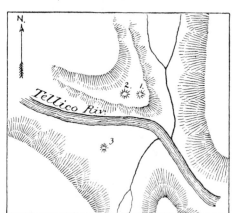

diagram showing their positions. The river runs south about 70 degrees east from a short distance above the mounds to the mouth of a small branch below, then bends to about south 30 degrees east. There is no level bottom land on either side except a few acres on which mound No. 3 stands. Nos. 1 and 2 on the north side are on the point of a high ridge. All three are hemmed in on all sides by high bluffs and ridges. From No. 1 to No. 2 the distance is 170 feet; from No. 3 to the river bank, 290 feet. All are small, Nos. 1 and 2 being about 3 feet high, and No. 3 nearly obliterated.

FIG. 271.—Plat of mounds on the Click farm, Monroe county, Tennessee.

LOUDON COUNTY.

Returning to the Little Tennessee, we continue our course down the river.

MOUNDS ABOUT MORGANTON.

Next below the group represented in Fig. 270 are some mounds on both sides of the river, in the vicinity of the little village of Morganton;

they are marked No. 13 on Pl. xxv. There are two on the north side of the river, on the Cobb farm, near Baker's creek, and three on the south side, on the Tipton farm.

Two of those on the south side were examined. They stand on the second bottom, about 200 yards from the river and 90 feet apart. In one, 64 feet in diameter and 7 feet high, composed throughout of red clay, were four badly decayed skeletons, at the bottom. The original surface of the ground on which they lay was thinly covered with coals. The other mound was similar in every respect to the first, except that it contained but two skeletons.

Another mound near Morganton (not given in the plat), but situated on Mr. Samuel Lane's farm, close to Baker creek, was examined. This, which measured 48 feet in diameter and 4 in height, stood on the bottom or lowest level of the valley, about 200 feet from the creek. The composition, commencing at the top, was as follows: First a foot of yellow clay, then a stratum of dark rich earth 8 inches thick, and last a bed of lighter colored earth extending down to and resting on the natural surface of the ground.

Below the last layer, excavated in the original soil, was an oblong pit 8 feet long, 5 feet wide, and 1 foot deep. Resting on the bottom of this pit were two adult skeletons with heads to the east. Near the head of one were eight arrow points. The bottom of the pit, previous to the deposit of the bodies in it, had been covered to the depth of 2 or 3 inches with coals and ashes. The remainder of the pit to the level of the natural surface of the ground was filled with very dark colored earth.

THE BAT CREEK MOUNDS.

Two miles below Morganton, on the west side of the Little Tennessee river, Bat creek joins this stream. Both above and below the mouth of this creek there is a pretty level valley, extending back from the river at some points half a mile to the base of the steep hills which border it. Immediately in the angle where the creek joins the river is a comparatively large mound, and on the opposite or west side of the creek are two other mounds (Nos. 2 and 3). The first is on the bottom land, the others on a level terrace some 20 or 30 feet higher than the first bottom or lowest valley level; the latter are about 100 feet distant from one another, measuring from center to center.

These (No. 14 on Pl. xxv) are on land owned by Mr. M. M. Tipton, but are different from those previously mentioned, which are about 2 miles farther up the river.

Mound 1, measuring 108 feet in diameter and 8 feet in height, was composed wholly of very dark soil, containing a great many small shells; these were in fact so abundant in places as to present the appearance of a shell heap. This condition continued to the depth of 3½ feet to a layer of hard yellow sand; under this the remainder of the mound to the original surface, except a central, circular area 2 feet in diameter, consisted of dark earth similar to that of the top layer. The central, circular core consisted of a series of burned clay beds or hearths, alternating with layers of coals and ashes. These extended downward from the layer of yellow sand to the bottom of the mound. A few charred animal bones occurred in some of the layers of ashes; nothing else of interest was observed.

On the east side of the river, directly opposite this mound, is an ancient village site where the soil is very dark and has scattered through it in abundance specimens of broken pottery, flint chips, and other evidences of occupancy. In several places little circles of burnt stones may be seen lying on beds of ashes.

On mound 2, 44 feet in diameter and 10 feet high, stood a black-oak tree 3 feet in diameter. It was composed throughout of hard red clay. At the depth of $3\frac{1}{2}$ feet was the skeleton of an adult in a horizontal position, with the head east and the arms close by the sides. The earth immediately about the bones was of a dark greenish color and about the breast were two metal buckles, one of them having a fragment of leather or hide still adhering to it. On the leg bones were still to be seen fragments of buckskin and a metal button, the latter sticking fast to the bone.

Whether or not this was an intrusive burial could not be determined, though the uniform composition of the mound and the size of the oak growing above seems to be against this supposition; nevertheless, the further discoveries made show that it was subsequent to the original burials and not in accordance with the original plan.

At a depth of a little over 4 feet, and immediately under this skeleton, the top of a stone wall was reached; this was found by further excavation to be a vault 8 feet square, built up of rough, flat limestone rocks to the height of 5 feet above the original soil on which it rested. On the inside, about half way down, were seven skeletons, numbered, for convenience, 2, 3, 4, 5, 6, 7, and 8. No. 2 was the skeleton of a child, horizontal, with the head to the east; Nos. 3 and 4 lying together with the head north, one of which was a child's skeleton, with small beads about the head; Nos. 5 and 6 were in a sitting posture in the northeast corner, and around the neck of one were many small shells and large shell beads; Nos. 7 and 8 were lying in the center with the heads close together and crushed by large flat stones which lay on them. Nothing more was found in this vault until the bottom was reached, where nine more skeletons were discovered, much decayed, and lying in all directions, seemingly thrown in without any care.

Mound 3 was of small size, measuring but 28 feet in diameter and 5 feet in height. Some large sassafras trees were standing on it, and the owner, Mr. Tipton, stated that he had cut trees from it forty years ago, and that it had been covered by a cluster of trees and grapevines as long ago as the oldest settler in the locality could recollect. At the time the excavation was made there was an old rotten stump yet on the top, the roots of which ran down to the skeletons. It was composed throughout, except about the skeletons at the bottom, of hard red clay, without any indications of stratification. Nothing of interest was discovered until the bottom was reached, where nine skeletons were found lying on the original surface of the ground, surrounded by dark colored earth. These were disposed as shown in Fig. 272. No. 1 lying at full length with the head south, and close by, parallel with it, but with the head north, was No. 2. On the same level were seven others, all lying close side by side, with heads north and in a line. All were badly decayed. No relics were found with any but No. 1, immediately under the skull and jaw bones of which were two copper bracelets, an engraved stone, a small drilled fossil, a copper bead, a bone implement, and some small pieces of polished wood. The earth about the skeletons was wet and the pieces of wood soft and colored green by contact with the copper bracelets. The bracelets had been rolled in something, probably bark, which crumbled away when they were taken out. The engraved stone lay partially under the back part of the skull and was struck by the steel prod used in prob-

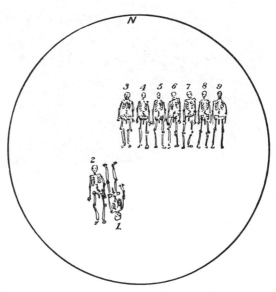

FIG. 272.—Horizontal section, Bat creek mound, No, 3, Loudon county, Tennessee.

ing. This stone is shown in Fig. 273. The engraved characters on it are beyond question letters of the Cherokee alphabet said to have been invented by George Guess (or Sequoyah), a half-breed Cherokee, about 1821.

MOUND ON A HIGH CLIFF.

On top of a high cliff overlooking the river, on the opposite side and a little above the Tipton group above mentioned, on the land of Mrs. Blankenship, is a mound 36 feet in diameter and 5 feet high, which at the time of exploration was covered with small trees. At the depth of 1 foot the top of a stone wall was encountered, which was shown by farther excavation to be an irregularly circular vault about 10 feet in diameter, which rested on the original surface of the ground. The red clay which filled this vault or small inclosure was covered by a layer of flat stones. At the bottom were six skeletons lying extended on another layer of flat stones, which covered the bottom of this vault. Four of these lay with the heads north, and two, an adult and a child, with heads east. Over this stone floor, previous to burial, had been spread a thin layer of coals and ashes.

One mile above the Tipton group mentioned, about 1 mile back from the river, on high, level upland, was found another mound 54 feet in diameter and 6 feet high. In the center of this mound, 2 feet below the top, were the bones of two skeletons lying in a pile, most of them broken and apparently buried after the flesh had been removed. A little north of the center was a straight stone wall about 10 or 12 feet

Fig. 273.—Engraved stone from Bat creek mound No. 3, Loudon county, Tennessee.

long, 2 feet high, and a foot or more in thickness. This was not on the original surface of the ground, but extended down from 2 to 4 feet below the top.

MOUNDS AT PARKS FERRY (JACKSON'S FERRY ON THE PLAT).

These are situated 10 miles east of Lenoir's at a crossing of the Little Tennessee known as Parks ferry. The group (No. 15, Pl. XXV) consists of four mounds and five stone graves. Three of the former, which may be numbered 1, 2, and 3, were on the second bottom, No. 4 being on a high terrace and in the forest.

Mound 1 measured 44 feet in diameter and 7 in height. At the depth of 18 inches, near the center, was a partially decayed skeleton in a sitting posture, without the usual dark earth about it. Continuing the excavation, the explorer passed through a layer of rather dark, hard clay to the depth of 4 feet, reaching a layer of sticky yellow clay about 3 inches thick. This, instead of conforming to the curve of the mound, was horizontal, as though it had been at one time the top, but did not reach the outer surface by about a foot and a half. Below this, to the natural surface of the ground, was a layer of lighter earth than the clay above it. A little to the north of the center of the base was a circular pit, 4 feet in diameter, which had been dug into the original soil to the depth of 4 feet. At the bottom of this were the bones of a child lying in a bed of wet ashes 4 or 5 inches thick. The rest of the pit above this bed was filled with very dark, loose earth, similar to that produced by decayed vegetable substance. Scattered through this dark earth were lumps of some green substance which crumbled to dust on exposure to the air.

Mound 2 was 32 feet in diameter and only 2 feet high, and consisted throughout of light colored earth, similar to the surrounding soil. Small bits of charcoal were scattered through it, but no indications of burial. Beneath it, at the center, was a pit in the native soil similar to that in No. 1, but only 3 feet deep. This was filled with very dark earth.

Mound 3 was similar in size and every other respect to No. 2.

Mound 4 was 35 feet in diameter and 4 feet high. Around it were depressions from which it is evident the earth was obtained to build it. Bits of charcoal were scattered all through the red clay of which it was composed. In the center, at the depth of 2 feet, was a single prostrate skeleton with the head to the northeast. Near the head were a fine steatite pipe, some flint chips, a flint drill, and a small celt. There was, as usual in this group, a circular pit in the native soil about 4 feet across and 3 feet deep, in the bottom of which lay a folded adult skeleton, surrounded by charcoal and ashes and a few fragments of steatite vessels.

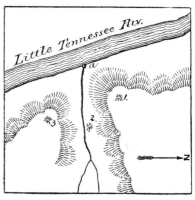

FIG. 274.—Mounds on John Jackson's farm, Loudon county, Tennessee.

A short distance from this group, at the upper end of Jackson's island, there are seven shell heaps, some of which are 60 feet in diameter, though rising but little above the general surface of the ground, yet by digging into them they were found to extend downward to the depth of from 3 to 4 feet. In these were several stone pestles, chipped flints, and other refuse material.

MOUNDS ON THE JACKSON FARM.

About the mouth of the Little Tennessee is a series of mound groups, mostly of the ordinary conical form, and of comparatively small size. The first of the series represented in Fig. 274 is on the upper end of the Jackson farm, 4 miles from Lenoir's station, and is No. 16, Pl. xxv.

The river at this point is deep and sluggish. A small creek enters it from the east side, flowing through a narrow bottom between high parallel ridges. Mound No. 2 is in the bottom, close to the creek and about half a mile from the river. It measured 60 feet in diameter and

4 feet in height, and was composed throughout of red clay, scattered through which were gravel and small stones and a few fragments of human bones.

Mounds Nos. 1 and 3 are on opposite sides of the creek, each on a high ridge. No. 1, about the same size as No. 2, had been explored. No. 3, 46 feet in diameter and 3½ feet high, was thoroughly excavated. Like

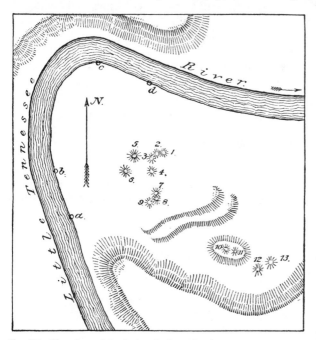

No. 2, it consisted wholly of red clay. At the depth of 1 foot was a skeleton lying with head to the south and much decayed. At the head a fine steatite pipe. Nothing else was found.

Lower down the river, near the line between Jackson's farm and the land of the Lenoir Manufacturing Company, is the group represented in Fig. 275. The following is a sum-

FIG. 275.—Mounds on John Jackson's farm, Loudon county, Tennessee.

mary of the results of the exploration made here. The letters *a, b, c, d* mark the points on the river from which courses and distances to the mounds were taken to form the plat, which is drawn to a scale, 1—18000.

No.	Diameter.	Height.	Composition.	Remarks.
	Feet.	*Feet.*		
4	60	2½	Red clay	Neither skeletons nor relics.
6	73	12	....do	Four skeletons at bottom; no relics.
7	45	3	....do	
8	45	3	....do	In each a few fragments of human bones; nothing else.
9	45	3	....do	
10	45	3	....do	
11	65	5	....do	Four skeletons at the bottom; no relics.
12	48	3½	....do	A few human bones at the bottom.

A few mounds of this group had been previously explored by other parties. This is No. 17, Pl. xxv.

The mounds at and about the point where the Little Tennessee joins
the Holston consist, as will be seen by reference to Fig. 276, of some
three or four minor groups and several single mounds.   These (with
the exception of those on the point of Lenoir's island, which are numbered separately) are numbered consecutively from 1 to 16.   Although

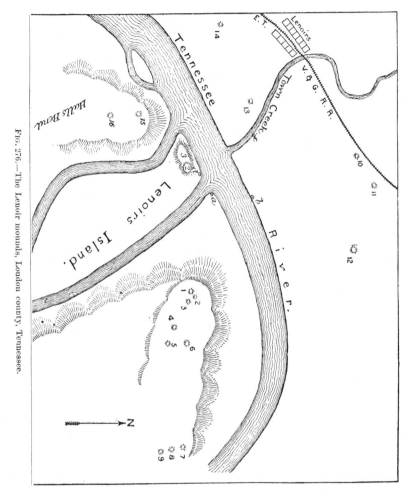

FIG. 276.—The Lenoir mounds, Loudon county, Tennessee.

these mounds are indicated on Pl. xxv, the groups are not numbered
there, as the locations compared with Fig. 276 will serve to identify
them.

The island contains about 200 acres, and its surface, which is level,
is about 15 feet above the ordinary stage of the river.   The banks are
steep and have heavy timber and much cane growing along them.   On
the northern or lower end are two mounds.   No. 1, which was found to
be very symmetrical, the base almost an exact circle 100 feet in diameter
and $6\frac{1}{2}$ feet high. was thoroughly worked over.   In it were found four-

teen skeletons, as shown in the diagram (Fig. 277). The top layer, about 18 inches thick, consisted of dark sandy soil, scattered through which were numerous fragments of pottery, shells, flint chips, and bits of charcoal. Next below this was a layer, about 4 inches thick, of yellow clay, thoroughly burnt and very hard. This conformed to the curvature of the mound, extending all around to the base, and entirely covering the nucleus which formed the original mound. Below this, and forming the nucleus, was a layer of dark, sandy soil, similar to the outer stratum, which extended nearly to the base and rested on a horizontal layer of burned clay, which covered the original surface of the ground to a depth of 4 or 5 inches. All the skeletons were found resting horizontally on, or a few inches above, this bottom layer of burnt clay or cement:

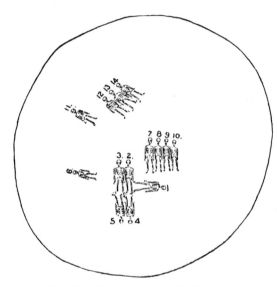

No. 1, with the head north; about the neck were several blue glass beads.

Nos. 2 and 3, lying side by side, with heads west.

Nos. 4 and 5, lying side by side, with heads east and feet close to the feet of Nos. 2 and 3.

No. 6, the skeleton of a child, lying apart from the others, with head south; about the neck were a number of beads, and around the arm bones two iron bracelets.

Nos. 7, 8, 9, and 10 were lying side by side,

Fig. 277.—Plan of burials in mound No. 1, Lenoir group.

touching one another, with heads to the west; with these were some sheets of mica and a stone knife.

No. 11 was the skeleton of a child, lying apart from the others, head southwest; there were no ornaments with it.

Nos. 12, 13, and 14 were lying side by side, with heads southwest.

Mound No. 2, like No. 1, is on the northern end of the island, but it differs in one very important respect from any other mound so far observed in this region. It has annexed to it a broad and extended terrace of the form shown in Fig. 278, A being the mound proper and B the annex or terrace. It is termed "annex," because it is evident that the mound was first completed and the terrace added afterwards, and not built up with and as a part of the mound.

The mound is circular, 108 feet in diameter, flat on top, and nearly 11 feet high. The terrace, which is level on top and 8 feet high, widens as it extends from the mound, and then gradually narrows until it comes to a point which coincides with the lower point of the island; its length is 570 and greatest breadth 380 feet.

An explanation of the plan followed in working over this mound is given, as it will illustrate the method adopted in regard to the others of which figures are given. First stakes were set on the outer margin exactly at the four cardinal points by compass. Then on a large pasteboard a line was drawn representing the outline of the base. The exploration was then made by cutting successive parallel trenches from east to west entirely across it. Whenever a skeleton was found it was carefully cleaned before an attempt to remove it was made, and its position noted as accurately as possible on the pasteboard. The result in this case is shown in Fig. 279.

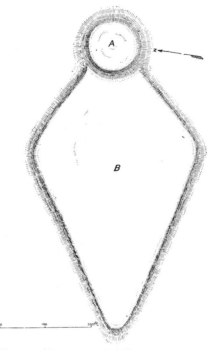

The construction of this mound was much like that of No. 1, on the Jackson farm, the chief differences being that in this case there were three layers of burnt clay instead of two, and there was a shaft extending down from top to bottom, filled with alternate layers of burnt clay and ashes, as shown in Fig. 280.

Fig. 278.—Diagram of mound No. 2, Lenoir group.

The central shaft, which was circular, 8 feet in diameter at the top and 4 at the bottom, extended from the top layer of dark soil down to the original surface of the earth. It consisted of a succession of fire beds, the clay of one layer having been placed upon the accumulated ashes and coals of the one below it.

The remains of quite a number of posts were found; these had evidently been set perpendicularly in the surface of the mound when the clay stratum d d formed the covering. Some of these were nearly or quite 18 inches in diameter, others not more than 6; they were all about on the same level. The upper ends of all were charred, showing that they had been burned off; hence no estimate of their original height could be made. The portion remaining varied from 2 to 3 feet in length, probably showing the depth to which they were inserted in the earth of the mound. The lower ends of the larger ones were cut off square, but it was not possible to decide by the marks what kind of a tool had been used. Fig. 281 shows their relative positions. At a they were placed in a circle, with a large one in the center, the circumference containing twenty-three, somewhat regularly spaced. The diameter of this circle was about 20 feet, with the door or entrance probably at 1. On the other quarter, near the central shaft (*d*), the positions of the posts around

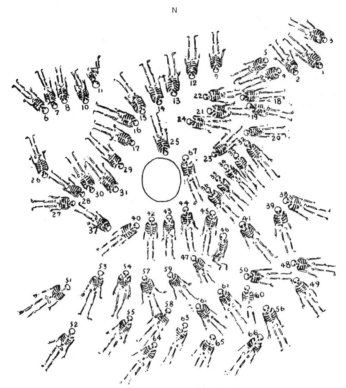

Fig. 279.—Plan of burials in mound No, 2, Lenoir group.

b indicate an irregular triangular structure of some kind. On the opposite side there seems to have been, judging by the remains of posts, a small oval structure (*e*).

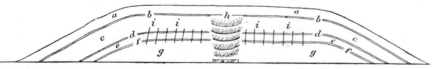

Fig. 280.—Vertical section of mound No. 2, Lenoir group.

a a, the top layer of dark sandy soil, similar to that around the mound, 1½ feet thick.
b b, a thin layer of burnt yellow clay or cement, from 3 to 4 inches thick.
c c, dark sandy soil, 2½ feet thick.
d d, a second layer of burnt clay, 3 inches.
e e, dark sandy soil, 1½ feet thick.
f f, a third layer of burnt clay, 3 inches thick.
g g, dark, mucky soil, resting on the original surface of the ground.
h, the central shaft of alternate layers of burnt clay and ashes.
i i i i, remains of upright cedar posts.

Sixty-seven skeletons were discovered, all in the lowest layer (*g*) of dark mucky earth and all except two lying horizontally at full length. Although pointing in various directions, as shown in Fig. 279, which

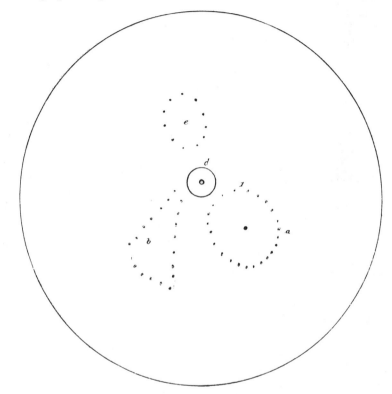

FIG. 281.—Horizontal plan of mound No. 2, Lenoir group.

represents their respective positions, it will be noticed that most of them have their heads toward the center of the mound. No. 11 was in a sitting or squatting posture, and No. 46 folded up, lying on the right side. The bones of the left leg of No. 27 were wanting.

FIG. 282.—Ornamental pot, mound No. 2, Lenoir group.

The appearance of a number of these skeletons indicated the following method of burial. The body of the deceased was covered with a layer of cane or brush; over this was spread clay or cement in a plastic state, and upon this a fire was built.

The pots were generally found at the head of the skeleton, but the fine ornamented one (Fig. 282) was lying on the breast of No. 7, while

a flint knife, some red paint, and wampum beads were about the head. The pipes were generally close to the head. In one or two cases they lay with the bones of the hand. The large shells were always on the breast or close to the neck, indicating that they had been worn attached to a cord about the neck, on which shell beads were strung. The shell ornaments (like that shown in Fig. 283) were in every case at the sides of the head, and, as not one was found with a skeleton without finding its counterpart, it is assumed that they were ear ornaments. The long-pointed shell ornaments, such as that shown in Fig. 284, were always found at the back of the head, as though they were used as hair ornaments.

FIG. 283.—Shell ornament, mound No. 2. Lenoir group.

The following is a list of specimens from this mound, showing the particular skeleton with which each was found:

Shell beads, from skeleton No. 2.

Large shell, from skeleton No. 3.

Very fine ornamented pot, flint knife, red paint, wampum beads, from skeleton No. 7.

Two fine pots, from skeleton No. 10.

Beads and shell ornament, from skeleton No. 11.

Large shell beads, three copper ornaments, from skeleton No. 12.

Pipe (Fig. 285), from skeleton No. 20.

Eleven arrowheads, from skeleton No. 24.

Large flint spearheads and wampum beads, from skeleton No. 25.

FIG. 284.—Shell ornament, mound No. 2, Lenoir group.

Large pipe and bone implements, from skeleton No. 29.

Shell ornaments, from skeleton No. 34.

Shell ornaments, from skeleton No. 35.

Shell ornaments, from skeleton No. 36.

Flint knife and broken red pipe, from skeleton No. 37.

Six polished celts, red stone implement, and two steatite pipes, from skeleton No. 39.

Bone implements, from skeleton No. 41.

Two engraved shells, from skeleton No. 43.

Two engraved shells (fine) and shell ornament, from skeleton No. 44.

Pot, from skeleton No. 45.

Fine shell, double pot, long pot, and moccasin-shaped pot, from skeleton No. 49.

Large arrowhead, from skeleton No. 50.

Fine pot, steatite pipe, shell ornaments, stone ax, clay ornaments, skull, and two discoidal stones, from skeleton No. 53.

Two discoidal stones, celt, two steatite pipes, and a pot, from skeleton No. 61.

Two spearheads and two large beads, from skeleton No. 62.

Flint knife, iron chisel, large discoidal stone and skull, from skeleton No. 63.

The terrace connected with this mound, and already described, was only partially explored, further work being prevented by high water. In a single trench, 24 feet long and 10 feet wide, cut lengthwise in the center to the original surface, 9 skeletons were discovered. The first was that of a child at a depth of 18 inches; the bones were badly decayed and unaccompanied by relics of any kind. The other 8, all adults, were found at the depth of 7 feet, close to the bottom, and in a much better state of preservation than that of the child. With them were three whole pots and a few broken beads.

FIG. 285.—Pipe, mound No. 2, Lenoir group.

The island was overflowed in 1887, the year the exploration was made, to a depth of 10 or 12 feet, the highest water, with one exception, ever known here.

Mounds 13 and 14, in the bottom between the two creeks opposite the mouth of the Little Tennessee, were explored and both found to be composed throughout of red clay. They were of the ordinary conical form, the former 54 feet in diameter and 4 feet high, the latter 46 feet in diameter and 2 feet high. In the center of the former, at the base, was a single skeleton resting on a circular layer of ashes, about 4 feet in diameter and 2 inches thick, which had been spread on the original surface of the ground. Nothing was found in No. 14.

By reference to the plat (Fig. 276) it will be seen that there are nine mounds (Nos. 1 to 9) on the point between the Holston and the Little Tennessee. They are situated on a low ridge in groups of three.

No. 4, 42 feet in diameter, 3½ feet high, was excavated, and, like all the upland mounds in this section, consisted wholly of red clay. It contained neither skeleton nor relic.

No. 1, measuring 45 feet in diameter and 2 feet high, is situated on the brow or highest point of the ridge, where it breaks off toward the Little Tennessee. The body of the mound consisted of red clay, except immediately in the center, where there was a circular bed about 6 feet in diameter, of darker colored earth, which was quite loose, the other part of the mound being very hard. This loose earth did not cease at the original surface of the ground, but continued downward to the depth of 4 feet; the pit into which it extended was circular and at the bottom were the remains of a single skeleton. With these remains were a fine steatite pipe, one large spearhead, seven arrowheads, one long polished stone, and some red and black paint.

Nos. 5 and 6 were opened and found to consist as usual of red clay with a few human bones in each.

Nos. 7, 8, and 9 had been examined previously.

Want of time prevented any further examination during this visit of this interesting group. Subsequently some other mounds not designated on the plat were examined.

One of these, lying between the Little Tennessee and Holston, near their junction and connected with a group of three, measured 38 feet in diameter and 6 feet in height. It was surrounded on the east and west by depressions from which it is probable the earth was taken to form it. Two large black-oak trees were growing on it. At the depth of 1 foot a small pile of human bones was discovered. These were all broken, and had evidently been placed here after the flesh was removed. The entire mound was composed of red clay and contained nothing of interest.

There are two mounds on top of a high bluff in what is known as Hall's bend, on the south side of the Tennessee river, opposite Lenoirs island (Nos. 15 and 16, Fig. 276). One of these, 26 feet in diameter and 3 feet high, and surrounded by a ditch about a foot in depth, was explored. A foot below the top a layer of flat stones extending over the mound was reached. Below this the remainder, to the bottom, consisted of dark soil. A circular pit 3 feet in diameter and 2 feet deep extended into the native soil; in this were two adult skeletons in a sitting posture, side by side, pressed closely one against the other in consequence of the small space. At the head of one was a fine marble pipe, and at the bottom among the leg bones of the skeletons were several rude arrow points. The earth in the pit was very dark and unctuous.

MEIGS COUNTY.

THE McANDREWS MOUNDS.

This little group, consisting of but two mounds, is on the farm of Mr. Joseph McAndrews, in the southwestern part of the county, 1 mile from Brittsville, and stands on the terrace or upland bordering the river bottom.

Mound 1, which stands a short distance from a creek, is elliptical in outline, 49 by 39 feet, the longer axis north and south, and a little over 7 feet high. A broad trench carried through it, down to the original soil, showed its construction to be as follows:

First, a top layer 12 inches thick of soil similar to that of the surface about the mound; next a layer, 18 inches thick, of red clay mixed with gravel; and lastly, a central core, 5 feet thick, of dark, rich looking earth, with much charcoal scattered through it. This core, which was conical and rounded, was but 17 feet in diameter. It contained nothing of interest except a single stone grave, built of steatite slabs. This was at one side of the center, partly in the central mass and partly in the clay. It was 4 feet long, 2 wide, and 1 deep. In it lay a single adult skeleton, folded, with head south. Although there was a top covering of steatite slabs, the cist was filled with earth and the bones were far gone into decay. A fire had been kindled on the top slabs; this had left a small bed of ashes a foot in diameter and 2 inches thick, in which were a few pieces of charred sticks and the partially calcined bones of some small animals. The bones of the inclosed skeleton showed no signs of fire. The mound, which has been plowed over for a number of years, was formerly surrounded by a ditch, traces of which are still visible; this appears to be unusual in this section.

Mound No. 2, circular, 38 feet in diameter and 8 feet high, is situated about one-fourth of a mile northeast of No. 1, on a high terrace.

A trench through the central portion brought to light nothing of importance, except the fact that it was composed of dark-red earth similar to that around it. The bones of a human skeleton were found at a depth of 3 feet. They were heaped together, in which position they may have been buried, or else they were the remains of a body that had been buried in a sitting or squatting posture. As the earth was loose above them, it may have been an intrusive burial. There were particles of charcoal scattered through the dirt.

The chief interest in this mound arises from the fact that it appears to have been a signal station. At least, it is a point well adapted to this purpose, as it commands a fine view of the opening in the ridges some 6 miles to the northwest, through which the Hiawassee flows into the Tennessee. Directly in front of this opening, in the mouth of the Hiawassee, is a large island containing between 500 and 600 acres. On the head of this is a large mound about 35 feet high. This latter locality seems to have been a place of much importance to the people who erected these structures, probably where they assembled for feasting, consultation, or ceremony. A fire signal at No. 2 could easily be seen from this place.

Two other mounds, on the farm of Mr. T. J. Watkins, in the same part of the county, were examined, but presented nothing of interest. They were both unstratified, and composed throughout of red earth like that on which they stand. One was circular, 32 feet in diameter and 4 feet high; the other oval, 40 by 20 feet, and 5 feet high.

RHEA COUNTY.

THE FRAZIER MOUNDS.

The two mounds composing this group are on the farm of Mr. Samuel Frazier, north of the Tennessee river, in the southern part of the county, 3 miles south of Washington. They are located on the second bottom, about one-fourth of a mile from the river.

Mound No. 1, circular in outline, was only 30 feet in diameter and 3 feet high. This was thoroughly worked over and found to be composed throughout of red clay, and to contain ten stone cists, placed as shown in Fig. 286. These were made of thin slabs of limestone, with bottom and covering of the same. They differed somewhat from the usual form, being from 20 to 24 inches square and from 12 to 24 inches deep. Each contained the bones of a single skeleton, in most cases of adults. In every instance, the head was at the bottom, the other bones being placed around and above it. All the space not occupied by the bones was filled with dirt. No relics were found.

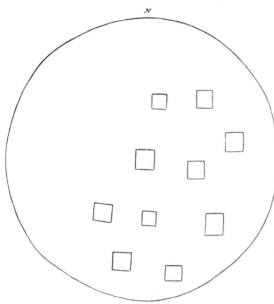

FIG. 286.—Plan of burials in mound No. 1, Frazier group, Rhea county, Tennessee.

As will be observed by reference to the figure, the graves were confined to the southeastern portion of the mound. Those nearest the center were about a foot below the surface of the mound, while the stones of those nearest the margin were partially exposed. This was probably owing to the mound's having been considerably worn down.

Mound No. 2, which stands 40 feet from No. 1, is also small, being but 27 feet in diameter and 3 feet high. It had been opened by other parties, and, according to report, found to contain stone graves similar to those in No. 1. This was verified by an examination, as the bottom and side pieces of a number of them were found still in place. These were scattered throughout the mound, and their number must have been considerable.

These small cists will probably recall to the minds of archeologists the so-called "pigmy graves" about Sparta, in the same state, which excited so much interest and surprise many years ago, when they were discovered.

WEST VIRGINIA.

FAYETTE COUNTY.

THE HUDDLESON INCLOSURE.

This work, situated on the farm of Mr. A. Huddleson, across the Kanawha river from Mount Carbon, is shown in Fig. 287. It consists of an inclosure circular in form 1,344 feet in circumference, or about 430 feet in diameter, and is located on smooth bottom land above the overflows of the river. The surrounding wall, which consists of earth like the surface soil about it and a mixture of mussel shells similar to those now found in the Kanawha river, was formerly some 3 or 4 feet high, but has been reduced by long cultivation to a mere trace.

At *a* is an ash pile 4 feet high surmounted by a long flat rock. At *b* was found a box-shaped stone cist at the depth of 1 foot below the surface. Rude stone hoes,

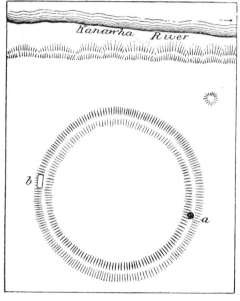

Fig. 287.—Huddleson's Circle, Fayette county, West Virginia.

flint lance and arrow heads, fish darts, and other stone implements were found scattered over the ground.

Rock etchings are numerous upon the smooth rocks near the principal fords of the river. Most of these are covered by water during the freshets. Others are found in the niches or long narrow clefts in the rocky cliffs. Although rude representations of men and animals and some probably symbolic figures are common here, none were observed superior to or essentially different from those of modern Indians

ROCK CIRCLES.

On the summits of nearly all of the prominent bluffs, spurs, and high points of this region are heaps of large angular stones. Unlike the loose cairns of the plains of the northwest and elsewhere, these appear to have been systematically constructed for some particular purpose, with a circular well-like space in the middle.

First, the earth (unless the place selected is a bare rock) is removed to the solid rock foundation and an approximately level space from 10 to 30 feet in diameter formed. Centrally on this was placed a layer of flat stones, with the best edge inward, around a circle about 3 feet in diameter. Upon the outer edge of these, others were placed with their outer edges resting upon the prepared foundation running entirely around the circle. Then another inner layer with the best edge inward and the thinner edge resting on the outer layer, the stones of one layer breaking joints with those below, as far as the size and form would admit of it. Outside of the inner row and with the edges resting on it other circles were added, until a diameter ranging from 20 to 50 feet, or even more, was attained; thus often extending upon the sloping earth not removed in forming the foundation. The last, or outer circle, usually consisted of but a single layer, over which earth was thrown, being sometimes heaped up until it equaled in contents one-half the rock pile. The height of these piles was found to vary from 4 to 8 feet, in one or two instances reaching 10 feet. But in all cases the circular space or opening in the center continued to the top the same diameter as at the bottom, somewhat resembling the so-called "wellholes" of the early western pioneers.

Many of the stones used in these heaps have evidently been obtained by rude quarrying in the stratified cliffs, often half a mile distant. Some of them measure from 4 to 6 feet in length, half as wide, and of a thickness which renders them so heavy as to require from two to four stout men to handle them. Beneath the somewhat upturned edges of many of these stones in the different layers are frequently found the decayed (and often charred) remains of human skeletons, usually horizontal, with the head or feet (generally the latter) toward the central "wellhole." With these were generally found fragments of coarse pottery, rude, but very large celts; also lance and arrow heads, and occasionally rude clay or stone pipes, but rarely, if ever, stone hoes or other agricultural implements. All the cavities of the heap not originally used for burial are filled with earth or mortar, often well baked by fire.

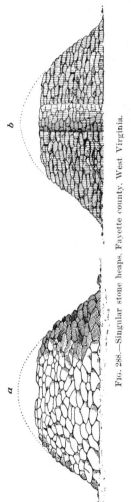

FIG. 288.—Singular stone heaps, Fayette county, West Virginia.

As typical of these heaps, Fig. 288 *a b* is given, showing one of the most perfect observed, which was thoroughly examined, carefully measured and sketched. At *a* it is shown as it appeared before being opened; at *b* is a vertical section showing the central cavity or "wellhole." This heap was found upon a rocky spur of Mount Carbon at the height of fully 1,000 feet above the river level, a point overlooking the valley of the Kanawha, and from which the latter could be distinctly seen for several miles both above and below. It measured 42 feet in diameter at the base and 6 feet 8 inches high on the inside of the well, which was in the center, and a trifle less than 3 feet in

FIG. 289.—Stone heap with two cavities, Fayette county, West Virginia.

diameter throughout. Although open at the top at the time it was examined and containing only an accumulation of decayed bones and rubbish, there were stones out of place and scattered about it sufficient in number to have finished it out and capped it over as indicated by the dotted lines in the figure. Whether they were used to complete it as indicated by these dotted lines is a matter of conjecture only.

Although rock heaps of this class generally have but one "wellhole" in them, we occasionally meet with one having two, as shown in Fig. 289. As a rule these piles are much less perfect than those shown in the figures, most of them being in a more or less disturbed condition.

FIG. 290.—Section of stone heap with triangular cavity, Fayette county, West Virginia.

A somewhat different type of these heaps from that described is occasionally observed, especially on the sharp, rocky ridges. A section of one of these is shown in Fig. 290. These, which have a triangular cavity, were undoubtedly burial places, and were not built up with the care bestowed upon the others.

ANCIENT STONE WALL UPON MOUNT CARBON.

About 1,000 feet above the town of Mount Carbon are heavy and valuable veins of coal. Some hundreds of feet above these are the remains of an ancient stone wall, the tortuous course of which can be followed along the steep face of the mountain fully a mile, then across its sharp summit and a like distance upon the other slope. It is said that it can be traced fully as much farther in such a manner as to connect the ends, and thus inclose a large area of the higher portion of the mountain. Little of this wall is now in place, it rarely being more than 1 or 2 feet in height, but the line of flat rocks strewn over a space of many feet in width, and often far down the mountain slope, indicates material largely in excess of that in an ordinary stone-wall fence. When discovered by the early white rovers of this region, something more than a century ago, many portions of it were, as affirmed both by history and tradition, intact and 5 or 6 feet wide and high, although amid timbers as large as found elsewhere upon the mountain.

ROCK CIRCLE.

On Armstrongs creek, half a mile above its junction with the Kanawha, are the remains of an interesting rock heap inside of a circle. The latter is fully 100 feet in diameter, and after the removal of material therefrom for nearly a half mile of stone fence is still 15 to 20 feet wide and 3 to 5 feet high. Central within this are the remains of what the oldest living white men and the early records and traditions of this region represent as having been a rock heap 25 or 30 feet in diameter at the base and 10 feet high, and similar to that shown in Fig. 288, except that the cap or cover was still in place when first observed. The explanation of this is supposed to be found in the fact that there was a passageway large enough to admit a man extending from the outside to the inner space.

KANAWHA COUNTY.

CLIFTON WORKS.

The Kanawha, as is usual with streams in hilly sections, meanders between bluffs, leaving a bottom now on this side and then on that. Such places have ever been the chosen haunts of the aboriginal tribes. A typical one of these bottoms is on the south side of the river, on which the present village of Clifton is located. Excavations made here for cellars, walls, and other purposes seldom fail to bring to light human bones, fragments of pottery, stone implements, and other evidences of previous occupancy. Several days were spent in making excavations here, finding marked uniformity in the earth and its contents. The sandy soil, which extends to the depth of 4 and 5 feet, was found to be literally filled with charcoal, ashes, fragments of pottery, entire and broken stone implements, etc. Although resembling in character a refuse heap, it is probably a village site or camping ground, occupied continuously, or season after season for a long time, by a band of aborigines, but so far back in the past that the entire area was overgrown with the largest timber of the valley when first visited by white men, nearly a century and a half ago. Commingled with these relics, at a depth of from 2 to 4 feet, were found several medium-sized skeletons in various stages of decay. All were lying extended on the back or side, but in no regular order in respect to each other or the points of the compass. With some of these were quite a number of large beads (probably used as rattles), made by cutting short sections of the leg bones of small animals and bones of birds. These, one bone fishhook, and several bone bodkins, found near the surface, are but slightly decayed, and are probably the work of Indians.

ROCK WALL.

Between the Kanawha river and a branch of Paint creek is a high, irregular ridge, something more than 1,000 feet above the village of Clifton. The end near the village widens out suddenly in the form of a short paddle. The comparatively level top, surrounded on all sides by steep bluffs, offered a position easily defended. The more sloping front, which was the only assailable point, was defended by a stone wall running along the brow from the eastern to the western bluff, a distance of 266 paces, or nearly 800 feet. As but little of it is now standing, its original dimensions can not be accurately determined; but judging by the quantity of flat stones still in place and strewn along the hillside below the wall, and the statements of persons who saw it when but little injured, it must have been at least 5 or 6 feet high and constructed like an ordinary stone fence. There is no trace of a gateway in it, nor are there any indications that a wall ever existed across the narrow neck behind the paddle-shaped expansion.

BROWNSTOWN WORKS.

On the site of this village, just below the point where Len's creek enters the Kanawha, are traces of an ancient earthen inclosure. Being more or less covered with dwellings and other structures and almost entirely worn away, it was impossible to trace the wall with sufficient accuracy to plat it, but it probably inclosed some 6 or 8 acres. It is said that a part of it was utilized for defense by the early white settlers. In the streets and gardens and in the washed bank of the river numerous relics have been found similar to those observed at Clifton. It is also said that certain brass ornaments have been discovered here associated with stone implements and decayed human bones, but none of these were seen.

LEN'S CREEK MOUNDS.

There are a number of mounds in the deep valley of this creek, of which one only was opened, and this because of its peculiar situation, being located where the valley is so narrow as scarcely to allow a roadway between the creek and the bluff. Although scarcely 20 feet in diameter at the base and fully 7 feet high, and otherwise peculiarly

modern in appearance, it bears on its top a beech stump 30 inches in
diameter. The material was yellow clay, evidently brought from an excavation in the hillside nearby. On the natural surface, near the center,
lying horizontally on their backs, heads south, were the skeletons of
six adults and one child. All were thoroughly charred and without any
earth intermingled with them, but covered with ashes and several
inches of charcoal and brands. It is evident that the fire was smothered
before it had fully burned out. Three coarse lance-heads and a fish
dart were found amid the bones of the adults, and at the neck of the
child three copper beads made of thick wire bent in a circular form.

ELK RIVER WORKS.

On the opposite side of Elk river and 1 mile north of Charleston there
is a circular inclosure 200 feet in diameter, the wall, after many years'
cultivation, being still from 3 to 4 feet higher than the nearly obliterated ditch which runs along the inside of it. From this ditch the surface rounds up a foot or so and continues at this height all over the
central area. The inside of the wall is quite steep, while the outside
slopes off very gradually except on the north side, which runs close to
the face of a rocky cliff. The only opening or gateway in this wall is
on the east and is guarded by a conical mound 50 feet in diameter and
5 feet high. Strewn over the top of this mound were numerous fragments of flat stones, many of which were marked with circular pits.
The removal of these only disclosed others, which were mingled with
very hard yellow clay, charcoal, ashes, stone chips, and fragments of
rude pottery. Near the center and 3 feet below the top of the mound
a decayed human skeleton was found, lying horizontally in a very rude
box-shaped stone coffin. Beneath this were other flat stones, and under
them charcoal, ashes, and baked earth, overlying the charred remains
of at least three or four other skeletons. These, judging by what
remained of them, must have been laid on the natural surface of the
ground with the heads eastward.

Four miles farther up Elk river, on the summit of a low pass, over
which ran an ancient trail, was a small conical mound 30 feet in diameter and 5 feet high. This had previously been opened to the depth of
3 feet, and, as was afterward learned, a human skeleton and fifteen or
twenty copper beads found. Carrying the excavation down to the
natural surface a single, much decayed, adult skeleton was discovered,
but nothing else.

Two miles above the preceding is a group of small conical mounds
from 2 to 3 feet high and from 20 to 30 feet in diameter. Some of these
were opened, but nothing of interest observed except that on the natural surface of the earth beneath them was always found a layer of
charcoal and ashes, among which were fragments of bones.

Midway between these and the one in the pass is a group of five
mounds. One of these, 50 feet in diameter and 4 feet high, was opened

and found to be composed of yellow clay so hard that it was difficult
to break it up with a pick. Upon the natural surface was a layer of
charcoal and ashes in which were the remains of at least two skeletons.

INCLOSURE NEAR ST. ALBIN.

Near St. Albin, in a horseshoe bend of Coal river, 2 miles above its
confluence with the Kanawha, is a bold promontory 300 feet high, belonging to the farm of Mr. B. Inman, the area of the top being some
15 or 20 acres. It is connected with the upland behind it by a long
ridge so narrow in places as scarcely to afford room on top for a wagon
track.

Here what was possibly a " graded way " was traced along and near
the outer edge of this promontory, past several small conical mounds
and rock heaps to an inclosure upon the highest part. This is near the
northern end and less than 100 feet down the rocky eastern hillside,
where there is one of the finest springs of this section. This inclosure
is circular in form and 104 feet in diameter, with a slight ditch inside
the wall, which is steep on the inside and from 3 to 4 feet high. This
wall is broken only in the northwestern part, where there is a gateway
12 feet wide. In the center of the inclosed area is a mound 20 feet in
diameter and 3 feet high.

Mr. Wilson, an old resident, affirms that when he was a boy this
work, in common with the rest of the hill, was covered with a heavy
growth of forest trees. These were long since cut down, and as the
land has never been cultivated the area is now covered with a growth
of young timber. He had partially opened the mound in his boyhood,
and the flat sandstones which he then removed from the top are still
lying at the foot. Observing a singular groove across the stones still
in place, as well as those removed, Col. Norris, the explorer, replaced
the latter and found that when properly fitted a chipped groove or
gutter 3 inches wide and nearly as deep was continuous across them
from the summit to the bottom. The object the builders of the mound
had in view in working out this channel, which must have taken a long
time with their rude tools, must be left wholly to conjecture, as there
was nothing in or about the mound to give a clue to it. The mound,
which was composed of light colored, mortar-like material, apparently
a mixture of clay and ashes, extended down 6 feet below the natural
surface. At this depth was found a single adult skeleton in the last
stages of decay, lying prostrate on its back. In the hand of the outstretched right arm was a black slate gorget.

Two hundred yards south of the inclosure, upon the slope, near the
ancient roadway, stood another mound about 50 feet in diameter and
6 feet high. This was composed of hard, tough clay to the natural
slope, and below it was a vault or pit which had been excavated before
the mound was thrown up. This was 8 feet long, 3 feet wide, and
about 3 feet deep at the upper end. In it was an adult skeleton

on its back, with head uphill (north). Upon the breast was a well formed and well finished sandstone gorget, and on it a black, leaf-shaped flint implement and a small hematite celt. No bones of the right arm were found alongside those of the body, but a careful search resulted in finding them in a line of ashes running out at right angles from the shoulder. Upon the bones of the open hand were three piles of small, black flint knives, five in each pile, all with the points turned toward the shoulder.

Two other conical mounds and one rock heap at this place were opened, but nothing of interest was found in them save fragments of bones in beds of coals and ashes on the natural surface of the ground.

The ancient roadway, which in several places upon the sloping side of the hill is truly a "graded way," seems to have been fully 20 feet wide, somewhat rounded in the middle, and rather higher than the natural surface. On the slope the lower side is graded up and sustained by a line of flat stones, and the upper side cut down precisely as a modern roadway is formed. The oldest settlers, when they first came to this region, found it covered with forest trees, as were the other ancient works. The entire length of this road was originally about half a mile, but a portion of it has been obliterated by cultivation. Possibly this is an old military road.

ANCIENT WORKS NEAR CHARLESTON.

Along the Kanawha river from 3 to 8 miles below Charleston are the most extensive and interesting ancient works to be found in the state of West Virginia. (They consist of fifty mounds, varying in diameter from 35 to 200 feet and in height from 3 to 35 feet; some eight or ten inclosures containing from less than 1 to fully 30 acres; circular, clay-lined pits from 6 to 8 feet broad and as many feet in depth, and box-shaped stone cists. All are found on the upper river terraces beyond the reach of the highest floods. A plat of the group from Mr. Middleton's survey is given in Pl. XXVII.

Upon a commanding height, overlooking alike the village of Spring Hill and all of these works, is an ancient inclosure containing about 20 acres. There are also on most of the high and jutting points of the bordering bluffs—here from 200 to 400 feet high—rock heaps 30 to 90 feet in diameter and 4 to 8 feet high.

For convenience the mounds and inclosures are numbered generally down the valley, commencing with the Criel mound (No. 1, Pl. XXVII). Those not corresponding to this order were added from a subsequent examination.

An enlarged plan of this mound and the works immediately around it is given in Fig. 291, and a section of the mound itself farther on in Fig. 292.

Inclosure a is 556 feet in circumference, with a surrounding earthen wall and interior ditch. The wall, where undisturbed by the plow, is

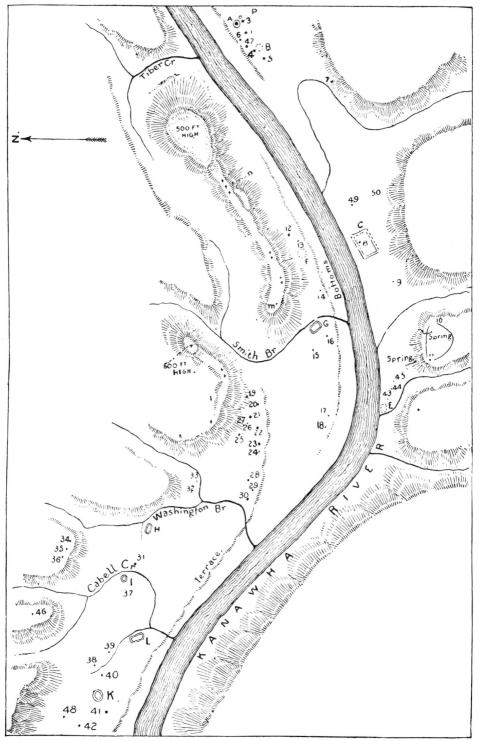

PLAT OF GROUP NEAR CHARLESTON, KANAWHA COUNTY, WEST VIRGINIA.

from 2 to 3 feet high and, as usual with the walls of inclosures, quite steep on the inside and sloping on the outside. At the south, facing mound No. 3, is a well-defined gateway. Touching it on the outside at the southeast is a circular excavation (*p*) 95 by 75 feet in diameter and 5 feet deep in the center.

In the center of the inclosure is a conical mound (No. 2) 30 feet in diameter and 3 feet high. A shaft was sunk in the center of this down to and below the natural surface. Only hard-baked earth was found and at the base a few bones, some of which were human.

Mound No. 3, which faces the southern gateway of the inclosure, is conical in form, 25 feet in diameter, and 3 feet high. This was opened by cutting a broad trench through it down to the natural surface, showing it to be a gray material, probably earth mixed with ashes and, near

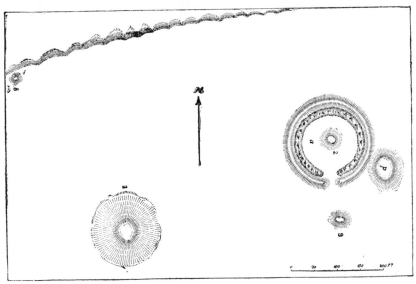

FIG. 291.—Enlarged plan of mound No. 1, and inclosure *a*. Kanawha county, West Virginia.

the bottom, well baked by fire. On this part, which covered the fragments of two human skeletons, were ashes, coals, and firebrands. The remains of the skeletons were lying extended on the natural surface, and with them were a lance head, a few fragments of pottery, and some stone chips.

Inclosure B, according to Col. Norris, situated about 600 feet southwest of A, is of the same size and form as the latter, but is so nearly obliterated by the plow that only a few faint traces remain. It seems to have had an inside ditch and a gateway opening toward the northwest, opposite which stands mound No. 4 of the plat. It is proper to state, however, that Mr. Middleton failed to find sufficient traces of this inclosure to justify giving it exact form on his plat.

Mound No. 1, locally known as the "Criel mound," is midway between the two inclosures, about 300 feet from each. The top was leveled in order to erect thereon an office and judges' stand in connection with a race course about it. It is 520 feet in circuit and 33 feet high, being, with one exception, the largest of the group; the top is 40 feet across, owing to the leveling mentioned above, to which is, perhaps, also due the fact that the center is 2 feet lower than the edge.

A shaft 12 feet across at the top, narrowing to 8 feet at the bottom, was sunk through the center to the original surface of the ground, the process being aided by lateral trenches in which were offsets (see Fig. 292, which shows a section). The material through which it passed for the first 2 feet was a light sandy loam. At the depth of 3 feet, in the center of the shaft, some human bones (*a*) were discovered, doubtless parts of a skeleton said to have been dug up before or at the time of the construction of the judges' stand. At the depth of 4 feet, in a bed of hard earth composed of mixed clay and ashes, were two skeletons (*e e*), both lying extended on their backs, heads south, and feet near the

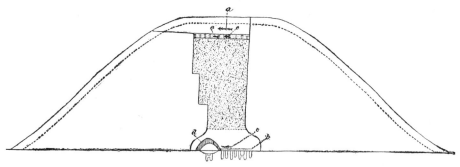

FIG. 292.—Section of mound No. 1, Kanawha county, West Virginia.

center of the shaft. Near the heads lay two celts, two stone hoes, one lance head, and two disks.

From this point downward for 20 feet farther, nearly all the material in the shaft was composed of the same apparently mixed substance, so hard as to require the constant use of the pick. At 24 feet it suddenly changed to a much softer and darker colored earth, disclosing the casts and some much decayed fragments of logs and poles from 6 to 12 inches in diameter. These, together with the fragments of bark, ashes, and animal bones which had been split lengthwise, continued to be found through a layer of about 6 feet. At the depth of 31 feet a human skeleton (*c*) was discovered lying prostrate, head north, the skull crushed, but partially preserved by contact with a sheet of copper that probably once formed part of a headdress of some kind, only fragments of which remained. By enlarging and curbing the foot of the shaft, a circular space 16 feet in diameter was uncovered, and the character and contents of the central, basal portion of the mound ascertained. First, upon the well smoothed and packed surface had been carefully spread a floor mainly of elm bark (*b*), the inner side up. Upon this was spread a layer of fine white ashes, clear of charcoal, resembling those of hickory bark, probabably 6 inches thick originally, though now not over an inch. On this the body was placed and covered with similar bark. Ten other skeletons, all buried in the same manner, were found at this point, arranged five on each side in a semicircle with the feet turned toward, but not quite touching, the one just mentioned. Owing to the crushed and decayed condition of the bones, it was impossible to decide positively as to the size and position. It is believed that all were adults of medium size and placed extended on their backs in bark wrappings. With each skeleton on the eastern side of the center, was a fine, apparently new or unused, lance head and by the side of the northern one of these five a fish dart, three arrow heads, and some decayed mussel shells. Although careful search was made, nothing was found with the five on the western side. With the central one, in addition to what has been mentioned, were six shell beads, and a flint lance head similar to those on the eastern side though larger. Near it was a hollow, conical mass or vault of very hard earth (*d*) nearly 4 feet high and fully 5 feet in diameter, the inner edge of which was in a line with and nearly touching the heads of the skeleton. This vault was partially filled with rotten wood, bark, human and other bones and a dark substance, apparently decayed matter of some kind. It was so loose as to be easily scratched out with the hands or a garden rake. The natural surface under this had been scooped out in basin shape to the depth of 2 feet and a breadth of 5 feet. In the central part of this were two circular holes each 16 inches in diameter, 4 feet deep and 6 inches from one another in an east and west line. They were lined with a kind of bluish clay and partly filled with water. About 3 feet down was a cross communication between them as shown in the figure, large enough to thrust the arm through; the hole to the east was about 4 inches deeper than the other. A flint spear head was found in each hole. Similar pairs of holes, ranging in depth from 2 to 3 feet and in diameter from 8 to 12 inches, were found beside the heads of each of the ten surrounding skeletons.

Col. Norris and Mr. Thurston, of Charleston, who assisted in excavating this mound, are of opinion that these 11 persons were buried at one time, possibly after the flesh had decayed from the bones in other depositories, or perhaps in the flesh after a battle, and that the central one was a person of importance. They seem to have been buried as above described in a timber-walled structure at least 16 feet in diameter, 6 or 8 feet high at the eaves, and conically roofed. The small central clay vault was probably a burial vault similar to those found in North Carolina mounds. It is worthy of notice in this connection that the mound in Sullivan county, Tennessee, figured on a preceding page, contained one central vault and eleven surrounding ones.

The next five mounds in order (Pl. XXVII) are circular, with dimensions as follows:

No.	Diameter.	Height.
	Feet.	*Feet.*
4	28	2½
5	21	2½
6	40	4
7	45	3½
8	112	9

The last (No. 8), known locally as the Wilson mound, is within the inclosure marked C. It was partially opened many years ago, and human bones, with several celts and lance heads, were found at the bottom, near the center. It is now used as a burial ground.

The inclosure (C) is now about obliterated; from the statements of parties familiar with it, it was nearly square, inclosing about 20 acres, the walls 5 or 6 feet high, and had an interior ditch.

Mound 9, which stands a short distance to the southwest of No. 8, is one of the oblong tumuli found in this region—diameters 75 and 40 feet and height 5 feet. A trench was dug through it, but nothing found of interest.

The wall of the ancient fort at Spring Hill (see Pl. XXVII), shown on an enlarged scale in Fig. 293, has been greatly reduced in height and partly obliterated by long cultivation. It is the only inclosure of the entire group located on a hill; is in a position allowing easy defense and supplied with living water. These facts and its large size render it probable that it was a place to which the inhabitants of the extensive village retired in times of danger. It is flanked on each side by a deep ravine and, on the northwest, fronts on a steep bluff fully 100 feet above the level of the valley. The form is somewhat that of a semicircle, the curved line being on the nearly level land above, while the straight line joining the ends of the curve is a few feet over the edge or break of the bluff. There was formerly, it is said, a ditch around the outside of the southern portion of the curve on the higher level area, but no trace of it now remains. The wall is nowhere 2 feet high or 19 feet in breadth. As near as can now be determined, the length of this circular portion from gate to gate is 2,144 feet.

The straight front wall from gate to gate is 1,132 feet long and in no place more than a foot high. There is necessarily a ditch on the inside where the wall is on the slope, as indicated in the sections shown in the figure. The area is somewhat more than 20 acres. There was apparently a gateway or entrance at each angle, the eastern one (which can not be clearly traced) being 136 feet wide, the western 123 feet. Near each gateway, inside, is a mound, Nos. 10 and 11. These were formerly of about the same shape and size, each being 8 or 9 feet high. No. 11 is now 35 by 40 feet at the base and 4 feet high. In the center, 3 feet below the surface, was a vault 8 feet long and 3 feet wide. In the bottom of this, among the decayed fragments of bark wrappings, lay a skeleton fully 7 feet long, extended at full length on the back, head west. Lying in a circle immediately above the hips were fifty-two per-

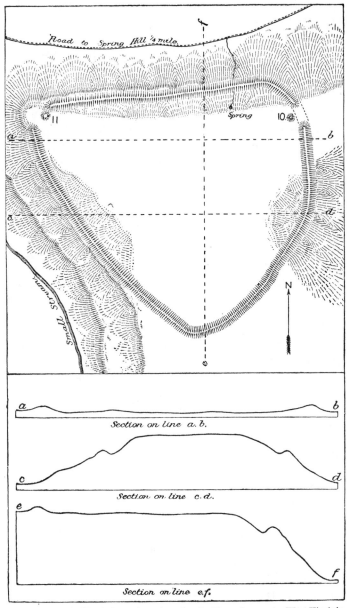

Fig. 293.—Spring Hill inclosure on enlarged scale, Kanawha county, West Virginia.

forated shell disks about an inch in diameter and one-eighth of an inch thick. The bones of the left arm were lying along the side of the body, but those of the right were stretched out horizontally at right angles to the body, the bones of the hand touching a small conical mass of earth, which proved to be a kind of vault similar to that in the Criel mound (No. 1) above described. This was formed of a mortar or cement, but the contents, which must have been animal or vegetable, were completely decayed. It was yet unbroken and barely large enough to have covered a squatting skeleton.

On the river bottom northwest of the preceding are the remains of a small inclosure, which seems to have been a square or parallelogram (E, Pl. XXVII), part of the north side having been washed away by the river. The remaining portion extends 420 feet along the river, the width being now about 100 feet. It is probable there never was a northern wall, the river forming the boundary on this side. The remaining works of the group are on the higher terrace on the opposite side of the river. Mound No. 12 is directly north of inclosure C on the opposite side. It is circular, 50 feet in diameter, and after long cultivation is now but 2 feet high, composed entirely of sandy soil.

Mound No. 13, a little southwest of No. 12, measured 35 feet in diameter and about 2 in height. Nothing of interest was found in either of these two.

Inclosure F, of which no trace now remains, was, according to the old settlers, a circle of about 65 feet diameter on the margin of a slight terrace directly opposite inclosure C. There was an inside ditch.

Moving down the river toward the southwest, we next reach a number of works which seem to be more or less connected.

The first and most important is the inclosure G, shown on an enlarged scale in Fig. 294. This is one of the best preserved and most interesting of the so-called "sacred enclosures" in the Kanawha valley. It is a parallelogram with slightly rounded corners, the longer direction being a little west of north and east of south; the length, measured from center to center of the wall, is 420 feet, width 150 feet. There is an interior ditch and the single entrance is at the south end. On the eastern side, where it has never been plowed over, the vertical distance from the bottom of the ditch to the top of the wall is from 4 to 6 feet; at other points from 2 to 3 feet. The interior area is somewhat higher than the outside surface and slightly rounded up toward the center. Close by the eastern side is a narrow ravine nearly 50 feet deep, through which runs a little rivulet known as Smith's branch.

The point marked *a* in the wall of the inclosure is the reputed site of an ancient walled well. Excavation revealed a pile of large, flat, angular stones. The water from the ditch runs through the embankment here and discharges itself over the bluff.

A number of other excavations were made in this embankment in order to ascertain its composition. At the point *b* was a cache, a circular pit about 6 feet in diameter and 7 deep, the sides plastered with clay, burned hard. This was nearly full of earth, carried in mainly by the plow. In the bottom, among what appeared to be decayed wood and corn, were numerous fragments of pottery, some of which apparently belonged to vessels broken at the time they were deposited. Six feet north of the edge of this, at *c*, was another pit, much smaller, being only 3 feet in diameter and 3 deep. In this was a mass of decomposing shells, many of them still retaining their form, but crumbling on exposure to the air. They consisted chiefly of small sea shells and

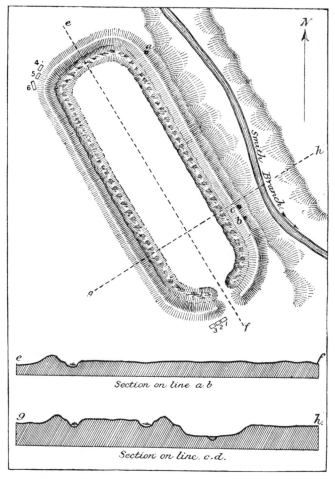

Fig. 294.—Inclosure G, Kanawha county, West Virginia.

disks, all perforated, probably shell beads placed here for security in time of danger.

At the northern and southern ends of the inclosure, outside of the walls, at the points 1 to 6, were six box-shaped stone graves, three at each end. These were formed of large, angular slabs, brought from the cliffs a fourth of a mile away. The covers of Nos. 1 and 3 had been displaced by the plow. Those at the south end, beginning with the eastern one, are numbered 1, 2, and 3; those at the north, 4, 5, and 6. The first five lay nearly east and west; No. 6 was north and south.

Grave 1, 7 feet long, 2 feet wide, and 30 inches deep at the head, contained faint traces of a human skeleton.

Grave 2: The head of this was near the foot of No. 1, in a line with it, and similar in form and size. With the decayed skeleton in this grave were two small hematite celts, four small flint knives, and one lance head.

Grave 3, with head close to and in line with No. 2, was similar to it in size and construction. Only faint traces of a skeleton.

Grave 4 was like No. 5 in size and appearance.

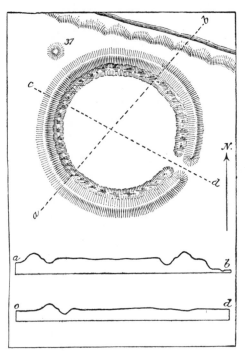

Fig. 295.—Inclosure I, Kanawha county, West Virginia.

Grave 5: A fine cist, 6½ feet long, 2½ feet wide, and 2 feet deep, having a smooth stone slab at bottom. At the eastern end of the grave, in one corner, near the head of the greatly decayed skeleton, were twenty-two entire and a number of broken flint-flake knives.

Grave 6, like No. 5 in construction, contained only traces of a small skeleton, probably a female.

In each of these six graves were two waterworn bowlders from 6 to 8 inches in diameter, placed together near the middle of the grave, always transverse to its longer axis; those in No. 6 were about 12 inches in their longest diameter.

These graves and also the caches noted appear, from their positions in reference to the inclosure, to be due to people who occupied this locality subsequent to its abandonment by the authors of the works found here.

Inclosure H, 405 feet east of the great mound No. 31, is 264 feet long and 132 feet wide, lying northwest and southeast like L, which it closely resembles in all respects. Many heavy flat rocks, probably parts of stone cists, were observed, but no complete cist was found.

Inclosure I (shown on an enlarged scale in Fig. 295) lies a little north of west from the large mound (31), is circular in form, measuring 618 feet around the top or middle of the embankment, which is much worn away, being only about 2 feet high from the ditch inside.

Inclosure L is on the Cabell farm, about 1 mile directly west of inclosure H, which it resembles in every respect, except that it is slightly larger. The form and proportions are shown in Fig. 296, from Mr. Middleton's survey, the length being 287 feet and width 150 feet, measuring from center to center of the embankment. The walls are rather less than 2 feet high and the ditch inside about 2 feet deep.

Inclosure K, shown in Fig. 297, consists of two parallel or concentric circular embankments with a ditch between them. The diameter of the outer wall, measuring from the middle on one side to the middle on the other side, is 295 feet, the diameter of the inner wall 212, the width of the walls being about 20 feet, and the width of the ditch the same. The inner wall is almost obliterated by cultivation, but the outer one is still from 1 to 2 feet high. The ditch is still about 2 feet deep. There is a broad gateway on the northwest through the outer wall and ditch, but the inner circular embankment seems to have been unbroken.

Mound 15, 540 feet west of the northern end of inclosure G, circular in form, measured 65 feet in diameter and 5 feet in height. A considerable portion had been plowed off. In the top was a basin-

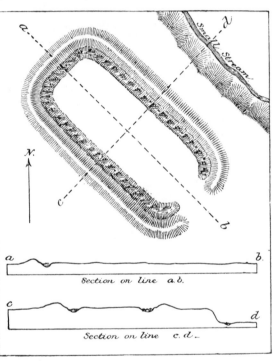

Fig. 296.—Inclosure L, Kanawha county, West Virginia.

shaped fire-bed 7 feet long, 4 feet wide, and 16 inches deep at the center. This was lined with a mixture of clay and ashes burned to a brick red on the upper surface, but the under side had a black, greasy appearance. Below this was a similar bed, on and about which were numerous small fragments of bones, too much broken and charred to show whether they were human or animal.

Mound 16, 480 feet southeast of mound 15, is conical in form, measuring 30 feet in diameter, and 2½ feet high. It was composed chiefly of hard clay. Near the center, on the original surface, were the decayed fragments of a skeleton and with them a single gorget of striped slate.

Mound 17 is 1,826 feet nearly west of mound 15. It is now only 18

inches high and 20 feet in diameter. Its surface and the surface around
it were strewn with stone chips, fragments of pottery, and lance and
arrowheads. Stone chips and arrowheads were scattered through the
hard earth of which it was composed, and a few decayed bones lay at
the bottom near the center.

Mound 18, which stands 270 feet west of mound 17, measures 65 feet
in diameter and 4½ feet high. This, like many of the other mounds,
has been worked over until the earth has been removed down to the
hard central core of brick-red clay. It is said that in plowing this
away many relics of stone, bone, and shell were found. A series of
basin-shaped fire
beds, similar to
those in mound 15,
were lying one be-
low another in the
central portion.
Below them, near
the bottom of the
mound, was a con-
siderable bed of
charcoal and ashes,
and immediately
under this, on the
original surface of
the ground, the
fragments of a
skeleton, and a
number of broken
arrow and spear
heads.

Passing north-
ward across the
railroad from this
group over a strip
of rather low
ground we reach a

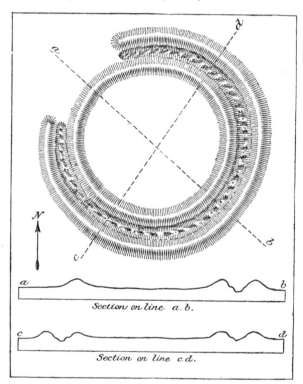

Fig. 297.—Inclosure K, Kanawha county, West Virginia.

small terrace, where there is another interesting group.

Mound 19, the one farthest to the east, is 60 feet in diameter and 5
feet high. It was found to contain a rude vault of angular stones,
some of them as much as two men could lift. This had been built on
the natural surface and was 8 feet long, 4 wide, and 3 high, but contained only the decaying fragments of a large skeleton and a few fragments of pottery.

Mound 20, a short distance southwest of the preceding and nearer
the large tumulus (Mound 21), measured 30 feet in diameter and 2½

high, and was composed throughout of a compact mass of yellow clay unlike anything immediately around it.

Mound 21, or the Great Smith mound. This, the largest of the entire series, represented on Pl. xxvii, is a somewhat regular cone 175 feet in diameter at the base and 35 feet high. A section with partial restoration is given in Fig. 298. It is a mound of two stages; the first building carried it to a height of 20 feet; after a considerable time had elapsed another stage of work carried it to its present height. The top, which was flat with a central depression, measured about 30 feet in diameter. On this were an oak stump fully 4 feet across and a black walnut of about the same size. The surface, in the depression at the top, was covered with an irregular layer of stones; beneath them were others set up edgewise around a circle 7 feet in diameter. The stones in and about this pit being removed, it was found to be 4 feet deep and paved with a floor of flat stones, upon which lay a skeleton much decayed and lacking the head. Slight traces of fire were seen, but no evidence of a coffin or covering of bark, a method of burial so common in this region. This depression resulted, as will be shown further on, from the caving in of a vault in the mound, and it is probable that the skeleton in this stone grave was an intrusive burial, placed here after the builders of the mound had abandoned it. A shaft 12 feet

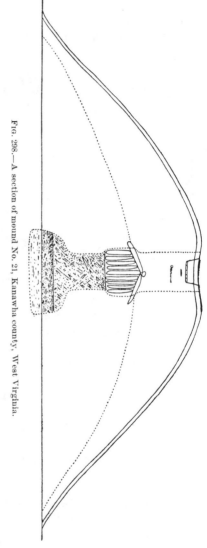

Fig. 298.—A section of mound No. 21, Kanawha county, West Virginia.

in diameter at the top was carried down to the bottom of the mound.

At the depth of 6 feet a small heap of bones was encountered, evidently those of a bundled skeleton, as some of them bore unmistakable signs of having been weathered and bleached before final burial.

At 9 feet was an entire adult skeleton of medium size, lying extended

upon the left side, head west. About it were the remains of black walnut bark, in which it had been buried. The skull showed very plainly
the flattening of the front. Below this nothing of interest was observed
nor any change of material, except some small deposits of ashes evidently carried in with dirt until the depth of 12 feet was reached,
where the fragments of a black walnut log were found; judging by the
very distinct cast, this log must have been 12 inches in diameter and
several feet in length, as it was traced into the wall of the shaft.

At the depth of 14
feet a rather large hu-
man skeleton was found,
which was in a partially
upright position with
the back against a hard
clay wall. Around it
were the remains of the
bark wrapping in which
it had been inclosed.
All the bones were badly
decayed, except those of
the left wrist, which had
been preserved by two
heavy copper bracelets.
Here was a commingled
mass of rotten timber,

FIG. 299.—Copper bracelet from mound No. 21, Kanawha county,
West Virginia.

decayed bark, and loose, dark earth. It was apparent from the indications that the shaft had entered a large vault, the timber-covered
roof of which had given away to the heavy pressure above and tumbled
in, thus accounting for the depression in the top of the mound.

Nineteen feet from the top the bottom of
this debris was reached, where, in the remains
of a bark coffin, a skeleton, measuring 7½ feet
in length and 19 inches across the shoulders,
was discovered. It lay on the bottom of the
vault stretched horizontally on the back, head
east, arms by the sides. Each wrist was encircled by six heavy copper bracelets, similar
to that shown in Fig. 299, which represents one
of the twelve. A fragment of the bark wrapping preserved by contact with the copper

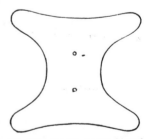

FIG. 300.—Copper gorget, Mound
No. 21, Kanawha county, W. Va.

shows that it was black walnut bark. A piece of dressed skin, which
had probably formed part of the inner wrapping, was also preserved
by the copper. From the clay with which this was connected we may
possibly infer that the body was first wrapped in a dressed skin, this
plastered over with a coating of clay (it seemed to be clay and ashes
mixed), and this surrounded by the bark. Upon the breast was a copper gorget, shown in Fig. 300; length, 3½ inches; greatest width, 3¾

inches; thickness, about one-eighth of an inch. It had been hammered into shape apparently from native copper. By each hand of this giant frame were three unused black flint lance heads; near the right hand, a small hematite celt and part of an axe of the same material, the latter bearing evidence of usage. Around the head, neck, and hips were about one hundred small perforated sea shells and thirty-two shell beads. Upon the left shoulder, one upon another, were three sheets of mica, from 8 to 10 inches long, 6 to 7 wide, and half an inch thick.

Removing the rotten timbers and bark, and loose dry earth, the size and character of the vault were ascertained. Four adult skeletons of medium size, one in each corner of the vault, were found, besides the two described. They seemed to have been wrapped in bark, and placed leaning against the sides of the vault in a nearly erect position, with faces inward. The vault was nearly square, 13 feet long and 12 wide, inside measurements.

From all the indications, the casts of posts and logs, the bark and clay lining, fallen timbers, bark of the roof, etc., it is presumed that the vault was constructed as follows: After the mound, which at this stage was 20 feet high, had been standing for an indefinite length of time, a square pit 12 by 13 feet was dug in the top to the depth of 6 feet; posts were placed along the sides and ends, the former reaching only to the surface, but the central ones, at the ends, rising 4 feet higher; on these latter was placed the ridge-pole (the walnut log first discovered).

FIG. 301.—Steatite pipe from Kanawha county. West Virginia.

The sides were plastered with a mixture of clay and ashes and possibly lined with bark; the roof was covered with poles and bark. Over all was heaped the superincumbent mound 15 feet in height. On top of this was built, perhaps at a far more recent date, the stone cairn.

With each of the four skeletons in the corners were several arrow and lance heads, 1 fish dart, and a few shell beads. Scattered through the material in the vault were several other articles. The entire list of specimens found, including those already mentioned, is as follows: 1 copper gorget (shown in Fig. 300); 16 copper bracelets (see Fig. 299); 1 steatite pipe (shown in Fig. 301); 2 stone disks, 2 hematite celts, 3 sheets of mica, 55 spear and arrow points, 1 flint knife, 1 stone pestle, 8 polished celts, 2 small hemispheres of hematite or meteoric iron; a number of perforated shells and shell beads.

After carefully curbing the opening made in tracing out the vault, work was begun again on the shaft, the material now being a hard grayish substance similar to the lining of the vault. A short distance below was a compact mass of dark clay flecked with the yellowish casts and streaks of decayed bones, some of them evidently split as in kitchen-middens. This continued to the depth of 30 feet, where the shaft entered a heavy layer of ashes, charcoal, and charred bones, some of them human, which reached nearly or quite to the natural surface, 35 feet down. The excavation was carried 2 feet farther down and considerably enlarged, but nothing more of interest was found.

It is probable that this mound pertains to three different stages, the lower part, or original mound; the upper portion (including the vault), belonging to the second period and probably contemporaneous with the celebrated Grave creek mound; and the stone cairn or vault to comparatively modern times, though it may possibly have been a sentinel station erected soon after the mound was completed.

Mound 22, a short distance southwest of mound 21, is 100 feet in diameter and 15 feet high. A trench was carried across it through the center and down to the original surface. The top layer, 2 feet thick at the top and thinning out to 1 foot on the sides, was of loose soil like the surface around. Below this was a layer of very hard, gray earth 4 feet thick; in the central portion was a bed 8 feet in diameter and 10 inches thick, of charcoal, ashes, and bones so badly broken and decayed that it was impossible to decide whether they were animal or human. In the center, at the depth of 12 feet, were the remains of an adult skeleton, horizontal, with head to the south. On the left wrist was a single slender copper bracelet much corroded, and near by were two spear heads. In the original soil, at the center, could be traced the outlines of a vault 8 feet long, 3 feet wide, and about 3 feet deep, but only slight traces of the body buried remained.

Mound 23, not far west from mound 22, is 312 feet in circumference and 25 feet high. It had never been disturbed in any way and was the most pointed and symmetrical tumulus of the group. Standing on the brow of a terrace 30 feet high, it seems much higher than it really is. It was examined by sinking a large central shaft to the bottom. From the sod at the top to the depth of 15 feet the material passed through was an exceedingly hard, gray mixture, apparently of ashes and clay. At this depth the casts of poles and timbers of various sizes began to be seen, but all were less than a foot in diameter, extending into the western and southern sides of the shaft. These casts and rotten wood and bark continued to increase in amount nearly to the natural soil, which was reached at the depth of 25 feet. The debris being removed and the bottom of the shaft enlarged until it was 14 feet in diameter, it was then found that these timbers had formed a circular or polygonal vault 12 feet across and some 8 or 10 feet high in the center. This had been built up in the form of a pen, the ends of the poles extending beyond the corners. The roof must have been sloping, as the ends of the poles used in making it extended downward beyond the walls on which they rested. On the floor of this vault, which corresponded with the original surface of the ground, were two adult skeletons, the bones of which, though but little decayed, were crushed and pressed out of position. No implement or ornament accompanied them. As the earth of this floor did not appear to be the natural soil, the shaft, to the diameter of 12 feet, was carried down 4 feet farther. This revealed the fact that previous to building the mound, a pit, the extent of which was not at first determined, had been dug to the depth of 4 feet in the original soil, and on the floor of this pit at one side, arranged in a semi-circle, had been formed six small clay vaults in the shape of beehives; they were about 3 feet in diameter at the bottom and the same in height and made of mixed clay and ashes, very hard and impervious to water. Possibly they had been allowed to dry before being covered with earth. They were partially filled with a dark, dry dust, evidently the residuum of decayed animal or vegetable matter. A few fragments of bones were found in them.

In the center of the space around which these little vaults were arranged, but only 2 feet below the floor of the large wooden vault, were two small, clay-lined cavities about the size and form of the ordinary water jars from the Arkansas mounds. Possibly they were decayed, unburnt vessels which had been deposited here at the time of burial. The bottom of this pit, which consisted of a natural deposit of yellow sand, was covered with a layer of charcoal and ashes 2 or 3 inches thick. The sand below appears to have been heated, from which it is inferred that the burning took place in the pit previous to the formation of the vaults.

Being compelled to stop work at this stage on account of extreme cold weather, Col. Norris, who was making the exploration, did not return to it until the following season, when he began by running trenches from the sides into the shaft and afterwards carried a tunnel in at the base. In one of these trenches, 9 feet from the top, was a layer of soft earth in which were numerous fragments of decayed timbers and bark; also casts of logs extending horizontally into the sides of the trench. These, it is to be presumed from what was afterwards discovered, pertained to a wooden burial vault. The tunnel carried in at the base from the south side was 10 feet wide and 8 feet high. For the distance of 20 feet it passed through the hard gray material of which the body of the mound was composed. Here it entered suddenly into a mass of soft earth of various colors that had been brought from the hillsides and bottoms near by. A short distance from this point the casts and remains of the timbers of the large central vault began to appear, but before reaching the interior the tunnel passed over a small refuse heap evidently belonging to an age preceding the date of the building of the mound. Within the area of the vault were a number of tolerably well preserved human bones, but no whole skeletons. As there were here indications of the pit before mentioned, the excavation was carried downward 4 feet, revealing five little clay vaults similar to those seen on the other side, and, like them, placed in a semicircle. About one-half of the mound was then removed and thoroughly examined. Many stone implements, some entire, but mostly broken, seemingly by the action of fire, were scattered through the hard upper layer; also a number of single valves of mussels which had been used as digging tools until they were worn from the outside entirely through.

There was a marked dissimilarity between the northern and southern sides of this mound, the former being a compact mass of variously colored soils from different points in the vicinity, in alternate horizontal layers. The separate loads of those carrying it in were plainly defined, and the different sizes of these small masses indicated that many persons, some much stronger than others, were simultaneously engaged in the work.

With the exception of the imperfect or broken specimens mentioned above, no remains of any kind were found in that portion of the mound above the fire-bed and north of the central shaft, and only two skeletons beneath it, while many interesting finds of implements were made all through the loose, ashy dirt of the southern part, and of many skeletons below it. The casts of logs and poles and the rotten wood and bark indicate the former existence of a wooden structure at least 12 feet square and 3 stories high, the posts of which extended from 2 to 4 feet below the natural surface; or, more likely, three structures, one above another. A foot above the natural surface, or 24 feet from the top of the mound, the smooth, horizontal layer of sand and ashes was continuous and uniform, except where interrupted by two heavy fire-beds, which were circular in form, 8 feet in diameter, and their inner edges about 10 feet apart on opposite sides of the center of the shaft. The earth was burned hard for 8 inches below the ashes. Below these beds, in an excavation in the original soil, were several skeletons as follows:

No. 1, a medium-sized adult, extended on the back, head south, arms by the side; 4 feet below center of the northern fire-bed. No trace of a coffin; a rude hoe and rough lance head were at the left side.

No. 2 lay 4 feet north of No. 1, at the same depth; same size and position, except that the feet were toward the center of the mound. It was inclosed in a coffin formed by leaning stone slabs together, in the form of an inverted V, over the body; another stone was set against the end of this at the head. A number of relics were with this skeleton, and on the stone over the head was a hematite celt. Two feet north of the head were the fragments of a large vessel.

No. 3, similarly placed, was 4 feet under the north edge of the other fire-bed. Some relics were found above the head, and others in a small vault near the left side.

No. 4, position like the last, head toward and 5 feet west of the center of the mound. A small vault near the head, similar to those heretofore mentioned, contained decayed material and fragments of stone.

Nos. 5 and 6 lay near together with heads south, 10 feet southeast of the center of the mound. A vault was found near the feet of the smaller skeleton.

None of these skeletons were found at the center and all were 4 feet below the natural surface of the ground on the bottom of the pit. Nine vaults, in addition to those mentioned, were disclosed; four of them on the bottom of the pit and five on the original surface of the ground.

Their average capacity was between 1 and 2 bushels, and all were partially filled with mottled dust. The interior was perfectly dry. Beneath the south edge of the southern fire bed was a vault 3 feet long, 2 feet wide, and 2 feet high; this and a smaller one a foot east of it contained mottled dust as usual. Six feet above and somewhat west of this fire-bed, in what seemed to be the remains of a bark coffin, was a streak of bright red paint, which crumbled to fragments with the bark.

Mound 24, situated west of mound 23, measuring about 100 feet in diameter and 4 feet high, was thoroughly explored and found to consist chiefly of hard gray material. Near the center, on the natural surface, was a bed of charcoal and ashes in which were charred bones, both animal and human, and with them a few spear-heads.

Mound 25, a short distance northeast of mound 23, measured 95 feet in diameter and 8 feet high. At the bottom, near the center, were the traces of a skeleton, and with it eight rather slender copper bracelets, much corroded. These were evidently made of drawn wire and indicate contact with Europeans. They had been wrapped in some kind of textile fabric, the threads of which were plainly visible. As they were of smaller size than the others found in this locality, of which mention has been made, it is presumed that they belonged to a female who was buried here.

Mound 26. This small tumulus, 35 feet in diameter and scarcely 4 feet in height, is near the northwest side of mound 21. It was composed throughout of a mingled mass of charcoal, ashes, black earth, and charred bones.

Mound 27, a short distance north of mound 21, measured 84 feet in diameter and 6 feet in height. Near the center, 1 foot from the top, a small copper bracelet was found, but a thorough excavation failed to reveal any trace of burial or anything else of interest.

Mound 28 is 300 feet in circumference and 23 feet high. Permission to explore this could not be obtained.

Mound 29, 40 feet in diameter and 4 feet high, was thoroughly explored and nothing but coals and ashes found in it.

Mound 30, 300 feet in circumference and 21 feet high, was 25 feet across the somewhat depressed top. Near the top were the remains of a stone grave containing a nearly decayed human skeleton, probably an intrusive burial. A circular shaft 12 feet in diameter was sunk to the bottom through uniformly dark, alluvial soil like that around the mound; only rotten wood and bark with casts of timbers were found. Upon the well-smoothed natural surface were evident traces of a bark floor, covered by a layer of clean, white ashes, containing traces of bones. Excavations in the natural earth revealed a circle, 12 feet in diameter, of vaults about 3 feet broad and the same in height, similar to those mentioned, placed very close together and filled with mud. This mound was not completely explored on account of the water. The rotten wood and bark, with casts of timbers, were probably the remains of a wooden vault.

The most important mounds remaining of this group are upon the Kanawha county poor farm.

Mound 31 measured 318 feet in circumference, 25 feet high, and 40 feet across its flat top. (See Fig. 302.) A 10-foot circular shaft was sunk from the top and trenches run in from the side. The top layer consisted of 2 feet of soil, immediately below which was 1 foot of mixed clay and ashes. Below this, to the bottom, the mound was composed of earth apparently largely mixed with ashes, placed in small deposits during a long period of time. Three feet below the top were two skeletons, one above the other, extended at full length, facing each other and in close contact. Above but near the heads were a pipe, celt, and some arrow or spear heads. Ten feet below these were two very large skeletons in a sitting position, facing each other, with their extended legs interlocking to the knees. Their hands, outstretched and slightly elevated, were placed in a sustaining position to a hemispherical, hollowed, coarse-grained sandstone, burned until red and brittle. This was about 2 feet across the top, and the cavity or depression was filled with white ashes containing fragments of bones burned almost to coals. Over it was placed a somewhat wider slab of limestone 3 inches

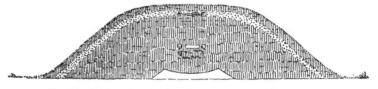

Fig. 302.—Section of mound No. 31, Kanawha county, West Virginia.

thick, which had a hemispherical or cup-shaped depression of 2 inches in diameter near the center of the under side, but this bore no trace of heat. Two copper bracelets were on the left wrist of one skeleton, a hematite celt and lancehead with the other. At a depth of 25 feet from the top the natural surface was reached, on which lay a clay bed or so-called "altar," from 6 to 18 inches thick, and covering a larger space than the 16 feet to which the shaft was here enlarged, though the altar proper was about 12 feet long by 8 feet wide. The upper portion was burned to a brick red, which gradually faded toward the bottom, which was the natural dark color of the material. The upper side had a concavity more than a foot deep. On it rested a compact layer of very fine white ashes a little less than a foot thick at the center, gradually increasing outward until fully 2 feet thick at the edges of the shaft. Scattered through it were waterworn stones from 3 to 5 inches in diameter, all bearing indications of exposure to intense heat, and fragments of bones, some of which were nearly destroyed by heat and had patches of what seemed to be melted sand adhering to them.

Mound 32 measured 50 feet in diameter and 4 feet high. At the center were two badly decayed skeletons on the natural surface, heads north; hematite celts and flint arrowheads were found with them.

Mound 33, 40 feet in diameter and 4 feet high; not opened.

Mound 34, 54 feet in diameter and 5 feet high, was thoroughly explored. A heavy fire bed was found in the center on the natural surface; south and west of it were three charred human skeletons and many fragments of flint lance and arrow heads, broken apparently by fire.

Mound 35, 62 feet in diameter and 6 feet high, was composed throughout of very hard gray earth. Nothing was found in it.

Mound 36, 34 feet at base, 3 feet high. In the natural earth beneath it was a vault 6 feet long, 2 feet wide, and 2 feet deep, which contained a small skeleton nearly decayed.

Mound 37, 60 feet at base and 7 feet high; 2 feet of soil on top, next 4 feet of hard gray earth, and at the bottom a fire-bed 1 foot thick containing charred bones.

Mound 39, 50 feet in diameter, $6\frac{1}{2}$ feet high; not opened.

Mound 40, same size as last; not opened.

Mound 41, 56 feet in diameter and 5 feet high. A broad trench through it showed it to be constructed in the same manner as mound 38.

Two circular pits or caches, which had been subjected to the action of fire, were found near mounds 17 and 18. These were opened and proved to be deep and basin-shaped, the larger about 10 feet in diameter at the top and 8 feet deep in the center. This one lay entirely beneath the surface soil, here about 1 foot thick. Judging from what was observed it is believed that after it was dug and the sides smoothed they were then plastered over with gray clay 5 or 6 inches thick, and that upon this, before it had dried, was spread a coating of bright red earth, which was then burned very hard. This might indicate that it was used as a water cistern, though the purpose for which it was dug may have been a very different one. The contents, commencing at the top, immediately below the surface soil were found to be as follows: First, a layer of fresh-water shells 2 feet thick, rounded up in the middle; next, a layer 1 foot thick of charcoal, ashes, and dark earth commingled; below this, nearly to the bottom, the material consisted of very hard earth mixed with charcoal and ashes. In this lower layer, near its upper surface, were two prostrate, extended skeletons of small size, one with the head north, face up, the other with head south. Scattered through the layer were numerous waterworn bowlders 4 to 5 inches in diameter, bearing evidence of intense heat; also, small fragments of pottery, lance heads, and fish darts, apparently broken by the action of fire. The small skeletons mentioned were badly decayed and seem to have been incased in a matrix of plastic clay.

The second pit was similar in all respects except that it was slightly smaller and contained no skeletons.

Upon all the bluffs and high points in this vicinity are found rock heaps. About forty were discovered, most of which were opened. All bear evidence of a well-hole, a few of the oblong ones having two; more than two are never found in one heap. Fig. 288, heretofore given, shows the usual form of the cavity, some being more clearly defined, others less so. Only one was found intact (marked *m* on the map, Pl. XXVII). It is on a sharp ridge some 200 feet above the river and commanding a fair view of all the works on the north side, together with those at Spring Hill and some others on the south. It was nearly covered with earth and surrounded by bushes, which had protected it from the view of relic hunters. It seems never to have exceeded 12 feet in diameter and 5 feet in height, with a well-hole $2\frac{1}{2}$ feet across and less regular than in many others noticed. Upon the removal of a flat capstone a small cavity was found; removing two additional layers, the lower of which was a mass of charcoal and ashes, the cavity was found to increase to a little more than 2 feet. At this point a stone 3 feet long, 30 inches wide, and 6 inches thick was reached, which was removed by tearing away part of the wall. Under it, in a hole 3 feet deep, was a decayed skeleton of medium size, which had been buried in a sitting or squatting position. With it were a steatite pipe, a slate gorget, a portion of the stem of another very large steatite pipe, the remainder of which had never been deposited here, and three lanceheads. From a rock heap near by some boys obtained a well preserved skull and some relics. It was probably an intrusive burial, as the capstone was not in its proper place.

Near the last described mound, and marked *n* on Pl. XXVII, is a charred bone pile on one of the finest points of observation along the entire line of bluffs; it measures 61 feet long, 37 feet at the widest part, and in some places over 2 feet high, resembling a low, oblong, oval-topped mound. Upon and around it were a great many waterworn stones of small size. Their number increased with the depth, along with charcoal, ashes, and charred bones. The bones and perhaps the flesh of hundreds of persons had been burned here; the fragments were all small and thin, indicating children or small females. It is beyond doubt that they were human bones.

The few rock shelves in the cliffs found in this region are especially rich in relics.

PUTNAM COUNTY.

INCLOSURE AND MOUNDS NEAR WINFIELD.

Upon the second terrace on the south side of the river, just below Winfield, is a circular inclosure containing about an acre, the embankment being still 2 or 3 feet high above the bottom of the interior ditch. Within and about it have been found many stone implements of various kinds. On this and the next higher terrace are a number of mounds from 4 to 10 feet high. Two near the bluff were opened.

The first was of peculiar shape, being 60 feet long, about half as wide, and 7 feet high. A wide trench was run the length of the mound, showing it to be composed mainly of hard, light colored earth, much of which seems to have been baked by heavy fires that left abundance of charcoal, ashes, and calcined bones, some of them human. Spalls and fragments of pottery were found all through the mound. At the bottom were two much decayed skeletons, prostrate, heads west. A stone and a hematite celt and some spearheads were with them.

The other mound was circular, 40 feet at base and 5 feet high. Nothing was found in it.

At the depth of 5 feet, in a mound 9 feet high, near by, were two skeletons, with two celts and some arrowheads.

Between Winfield and Buffalo are many mounds in which numerous relics of stone, bone, and copper have been found. Two miles above the latter place several acres of a high bottom are nearly covered with mussel shells, spalls, potsherds, and stone implements. Two miles below are two mounds, about 50 feet in diameter and 5 feet high, in which were found only human bones beneath a layer of charcoal and ashes.

MASON COUNTY.

On the high bottom land of Gen. John McCausland, on the south side of the river, near the Putnam County line, are five mounds, from 30 to 90 feet in diameter and 4 to 8 feet high. In one of these were found the fragments of a large pot. Like nearly all the mound pottery of this section it was composed of pounded stone and clay. The pottery from the kitchen-middens nearly always contains pulverized shells instead of stone.

ROCK HEAPS.

Two of these are found on the farm of Peter S. Couch, 3 miles below the mounds above mentioned. They are on opposite sides of a ravine, on bluffs overlooking the river. The one on the north bluff is 40 feet long north and south, 30 broad, and 4 high at its two circular well-holes; these range north and south, are 8 feet apart and 30 inches in diameter. The northern one was partially filled with loose stones and briers. Beneath these, upon the bed rock, was the skeleton of a half-grown child; with it were a badly corroded iron hatchet and some glass beads. Nothing was found in the other hole. The other heap was similar to the first, except that the holes were somewhat larger. They contained nothing of interest.

Between these bluffs and the river are five mounds, all of which were opened. The largest was 50 feet broad and 4 feet high. The portion remaining after long cultivation was composed entirely of very hard, gray clay. A fire-bed 3 by 4 feet, 3 inches thick, lay on the original surface. In another mound was a stone cist 5 feet long, and half as wide and deep, resting on the natural surface and covered with a pile of loose stones, over which the mound had been raised. Nothing was found in it. The other three were similar to the largest, but nothing of interest was discovered in them.

A mile below these, on the other side of the river, in an old culti-vated field strewn with mussel shells, are one large and several small mounds. In all those which were explored there was a layer of skele-tons on the natural surface, and two, or sometimes three, other layers above them to a height of 5 feet. The appearance of the mounds justi-fied the statement of Mr. Couch and others that at least one more layer had been removed during fifty years of steady cultivation. The skele-tons were well preserved, many of them very large, in a prostrate posi-tion, with no particular arrangement. Remains of bark coffins were apparent, barely separated by layers of dirt or ashes or both mingled; this, with the well preserved condition of the bones, gives the appear-ance of comparatively recent interment. The dirt in these mounds is not so hard as in most of the others in this section.

Three miles still farther down, on the Goshorn farm, a field on the high bottoms directly fronting the river is dotted with similar mounds, one of which is 150 feet long, 75 feet wide, and 7 feet high; all seem to be depositories of human skeletons lying horizontally, as in the Couch mounds. From these two localities, ten skulls, over five hundred beads made of the hollow bones of animals and birds, nearly two thousand small perforated seashells, many bone bodkins, bears' tusks, flint implements, fragments of pottery, stone disks, celts, and grooved axes were obtained.

A mound 50 feet in diameter and 4 feet high was composed of exceed-ingly hard, gray earth; on the natural surface were two nearly decayed skeletons.

From Kanawha falls to the mouth of the river are abundant evi-dences that the valley has been occupied by the builders of the hard-cored mounds, and subsequently by a people who accumulated kitchen-middens and buried in them or in low mounds which shovel like ashes or alluvial soil. The hard-cored, conical mounds and the large ones having vaults are invariably on the high bottoms not subject to over-flow; while the refuse heaps are upon either the first or second terrace. Though the different works are often near together, with the single exception of those on the Goshorn place they never intermingle, as though the later comers were careful not to intrude upon the grounds occupied by the more ancient works.

THE McCULLOCH MOUND.

Five miles above the mouth of the Kanawha, on the south side, on the farm of Charles E. McCulloch, is the largest mound in this sec-tion. Unlike most of the large mounds, it is not on the river bottom, but on a sloping terrace nearly a hundred feet higher, and after long cultivation is still 20 feet high and fully 300 feet in circumference. The old war trail is said to have crossed the spur upon which it stands just below it. No trace of inclosure, mound, or other work is to be found near, a peculiar circumstance when no other large mound in the entire valley stands thus isolated. A circular shaft 11 feet in diameter was sunk down through the center to the bed rock a foot below the base of the mound. A rock heap at the top had been made in a depression evidently caused by the caving in of a vault. This rock heap had been disturbed by parties who found a very large skeleton with some stone weapons. Beneath it sandstone slabs as heavy as a man could lift were scattered through the shaft, and at the bottom enough of them standing and lying at all angles to have covered the vault, and appearing to have been hurled thus by the caving in of the roof. Excepting the outside covering and 3 or 4 feet at the bottom of soil like that about it and the stones mentioned, the entire mound was composed of ashes, mostly pure, but in a few places slightly mixed with earth, all very light and easily shoveled. The somewhat sloping, natural surface had been leveled up by a layer of clay, then a bark floor laid down, and this covered with a layer of clean ashes over a space larger than the area of the vault, which must have been nearly square, about 12 feet on either side, and placed diagonally to the cardinal points. Prostrate in the ashes were the remains of at least 6 adults and some children, placed parallel, heads east. Owing to the condition of the mound at the bottom, being very wet, the bones were so decayed that it was impossible to tell how many persons had been buried here. Not a single relic of any kind was found with the remains. The casts of posts and roof timbers, from 6 to 14 inches in diameter, mainly of oak, were found, but the height of the structure could not be determined. As near as could be judged, it was probably 5 or 6 feet high and covered with heavy cross timbers, some of which extended several feet beyond the walls, and upon these had been placed a layer of flat sandstones, a huge pile of ashes being thrown over all. The stone grave at the top indicates an intrusive burial.

Numerous rock etchings were formerly to be found along this part of the Kanawha valley, but most of these have been destroyed; yet enough remain to show their rude character.

On the Miller farm, 3 miles above the mouth of the Kanawha, is a rock which has rolled down from the cliffs and lodged near the ancient trail. The face of this detached fragment, some 20 feet long by 4 wide, is covered with figures of animals, birds (one double-headed), serpents, etc. Dr. Shaw, of Point Pleasant, says the figures were much plainer fifty years ago, and that one of them represented a horse in advance of a number of horse tracks, pointing down the river, probably a record by modern Indians of the march of a party of white men.

Below the mouth of the Kanawha the caving in of the bank of the Ohio had exposed a wall of stone, on some of the slabs of which were rude totemic and other marks made by some pecking tool. Careful excavations revealed a circular inclosure about 100 feet in diameter, inside measurement. The wall was composed of angular slabs of various sizes from the hills near by and averaged 25 feet across the base by $3\frac{1}{2}$

in height. Many of the stones bore evidences of fire, the spaces between them (they were laid flat with joints broken) being filled with charcoal, ashes, and earth, separate or mixed. No gateway was found, though no doubt one exists at some point not excavated. The sediment from overflows has accumulated to the depth of about 5 feet since the wall was built, and its existence was never suspected until exposed as above stated by the falling in of the bank. This may not be aboriginal work.

On the Beal farm, 7 miles below Point Pleasant, are six inclosures and a number of small mounds, and 3 miles below these are several mounds from 6 to 20 feet high, the largest on the farm of Judge Moore. All these are very similar in appearance to the works about Charleston.

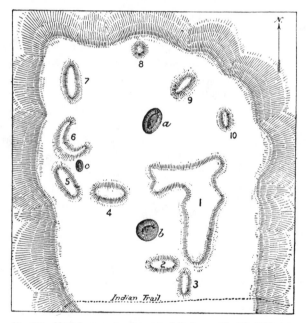

Fig. 303.—Mound group, 1 mile west of Barboursville, West Virginia.

Dwelling sites and mounds literally line the front of nearly all the bottoms along both sides of the Ohio. They are similar to those on the Couch and Goshorn farms, and, like them, are rich in skeletons and relics; many of the latter must have been obtained from the whites.

CABELL COUNTY.

For half a mile along the bank of the Ohio, just above the mouth of the Guyandotte, is an extensive deposit of refuse from a hamlet or favorite camping place, probably the latter, as the remains are found to the depth of 3 feet, showing that the site was frequently overflowed and thus built up in part by deposits from high water. Many relics, both ancient and modern, are found, the uppermost tier being a foot below the present surface. Half a mile above this is a field in which were three small mounds, two of which are now leveled. The surface for 3 or 4 acres in extent is literally covered with potsherds, shells, and fragments of stone implements. A quartz pipe with bowl formed and stem hole partially perforated was found here. The maker seems to have given up his job of boring it out after the outside had been brought to the desired form.

Midway between Guyandotte and Huntington are traces of an inclosure and hamlet site on a bottom high above the greatest floods. It was evidently long occupied, as a great number of relics have been found here. Nearly all of it has disappeared by the caving in of the banks.

About 1 mile west of Barboursville, on a hill nearly 500 feet above the Guyandotte, overlooking that stream for a long distance and offering a fine position for defense, is a group of mounds (Fig. 303) very modern in appearance; it is stated, however, that large timber covered them when the country was first settled by whites. The old war trail passes immediately south of the group, and there is a fine spring on the slope of the bluff north. The soil around is a compact yellow clay.

The following table gives their dimensions:

MOUNDS.

No.	Form.	Length.	Width.	Height.	Remarks.
		Feet.	Feet.	Feet.	
1	Irregular	150	75	6	Excavated in part.
2	Oblong	50	20	4	Excavated.
3	....do	45	15	3	Not excavated.
4	....do	54	25	4	Excavated.
5	....do	55	20	7	Do.
6	Crescent......	48	15	4	Do.
7	Oblong	60	20	6	Do.
8	Circular	20	20	4	Do.
9	Oblong	46	15	3½	Do.
10	....do	35	10	3	Not excavated.

EXCAVATIONS.

a	Oblong........	40	25	5	⎫ These have evidently been much
b	....do	35	30	4½	⎬ deeper; and there are some smaller
c	....do	20	15	3	⎭ ones near the mounds.

The trenches were run along the natural surface. All disclosed a heap of yellow clay similar to that around the mounds, and nearly all reached at one or more places in the oblong mounds the unmistakable core of older circular ones. At 6 feet from the edge of No. 7, upon the natural surface, were two skeletons in a reclining position on the side of the conical central core. At the center of this core was a partially decayed skeleton prostrate in, or rather under, a layer of charcoal and ashes. This older mound or central core was 4 feet high and 20 feet in diameter. On the north side was another skeleton placed like the first two, body reclining against the hard core and legs extended on the original surface of the ground.

In No. 9 a fire bed was found at the top; a small, hard, conical mound or core was also under this, but nothing was found in it.

At 10 feet from the south edge of No. 5 were two medium-sized skeletons, a lance head by the right side of each. These were lying at the foot of the hard, conical core, instead of reclining upon it. About 2 feet below the top of this ancient moundlet or core, and 4 feet from the top of the modern one built over it, were one very large and two ordinary sized skeletons, all having the skulls above the ribs as though buried in a sitting posture facing each other. With these bones were a fine steatite pipe, a celt, lance-head, fish dart, fragments of pottery, and mussel shells. These were probably intrusive burials. In the bottom of the old mound were fragments of a prostrate skeleton. Lying on the slope was a skeleton, well preserved, with head toward the top of the mound, and 13 feet north of it was another in like position on the slope of another small conical mound.

The other mounds were on the same plan, showing that some people had erected a mound over their dead; that subsequently the same or another people had deposited bodies on the side or at the foot of these mounds and covered them with dirt from the excavations near by, and that these later mounds had been increased in size until in some cases they had covered two or even more of the ancient ones.

OHIO.

As this state has been the field of the principal archeological investigations of Col. Whittlesey, Prof. Locke, Messrs. Squier and Davis, Rev. J. P. McLean, Dr. Hempstead, and others, and is the locality to which the Peabody Museum has chiefly directed its attention, comparatively little work was done here by the Bureau.

The explorations were chiefly by Mr. Middleton and Mr. Fowke. In the summer of 1887 a resurvey of some of the more important ancient works described and figured by Squier and Davis was made in order to determine the accuracy of the measurements and figures of these authors. The result is outlined herein, though published in full in the bulletin entitled "The Circular, Square, and Octagonal Earthworks of Ohio," issued in 1889.

KNOX COUNTY.

THE HAWN MOUND.

This is situated on the farm of Col. William H. Hawn, in Sec. 4, T. 7, R. 11, Howard township, near the bank of Owl creek. It stands on a small terrace, which is about 3 feet higher than the usual level of the

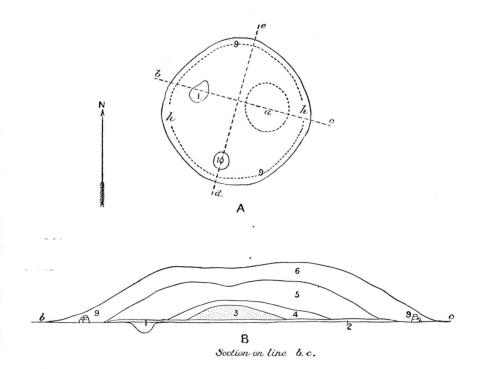

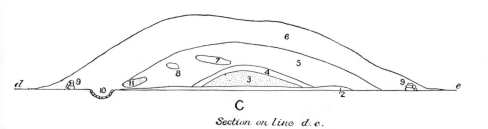

PLAN AND SECTIONS OF THE STAATS MOUND, KNOX COUNTY, OHIO.

valley near the verge. About a rod west of it is a short, deep gully that drains the fields to the north, and a few rods farther west is a deep ravine, through which flows a small, clear stream coming from the hills a short distance to the north. An iron tomahawk and many arrow heads have been plowed up around the mound. It is of the ordinary conical form, circular in outline, 45 feet in diameter, and 5 feet high at the time it was examined, though reduced fully one-half in height by thirty years' cultivation. Col. Hawn, who saw it fifty years ago, says it was then about 12 feet high, with a pointed apex, and surrounded by a log fence about 4 feet high, the bottom course being made of the trunks of trees placed end to end, the second and last courses similar, but placed across the corners. The inclosure had an opening to the east.

An east and west section is given in Fig. 304. A pit (c), in the original soil, 8 feet long, 3 feet wide, and 2 feet deep, with sloping sides, contained the skeleton of an adult, lying at full length, face up and head to the north. Over this, filling the pit and constituting the greater part of the mound, was yellow earth (h) similar to the adjacent soil. About 9 inches above the original surface of the ground was a horizontal layer (d), 9 inches thick, of muck or river mud, extending over an area about 20 feet in diameter. Above this, which showed unmistakable evidences of fire on its surface, was a mass (e) of mingled ashes and earth from a foot to 2 feet in thickness. At i there was a small fire bed. No relics of any kind were discovered except the fragment of an arrowhead made of Flint ridge stone.

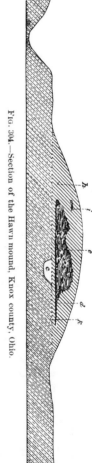

Fig. 304.—Section of the Hawn mound, Knox county, Ohio.

THE STAATS MOUND.

This mound, which is irregularly conical, with an average diameter of 52 feet, and a little over 7 feet high, is located on the farm of Jacob Staats, in Sec. 1, T. 6, R. 10, Butler township. It stands on the extreme point of a promontory that extends from the hills out into the valley of Owl creek and terminates in an abrupt descent of 90 feet. The topography of the immediate locality is shown in Fig. 305.

The base of the mound is nearly circular; in the top is a depression, as shown in sections B and C, Pl. XXVIII, but this is explained by the fact that a small pit was dug here some years ago and afterwards filled up.

Encircling the base and resting upon the original surface of the ground was a wall about a foot in height and from 2 to 3 feet thick, built chiefly of flat stones. This is shown by the dotted line 9, 9 in the ground plan (Pl. XXVIII) and at 9, 9 in the sections (B and C). It will be seen by reference to the figure (A) that an opening was left at the east and west sides (*h h*), each about 10 feet wide. The earth has

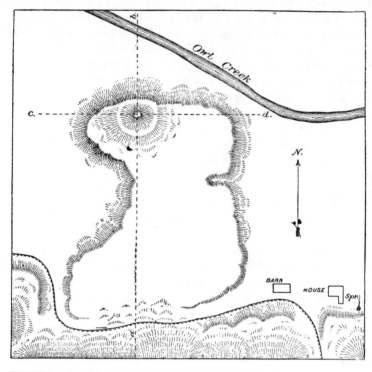

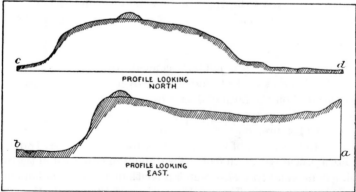

FIG. 305.—Plat and section of the area about the Staats mound, Knox county, Ohio.

washed and worn away from the upper part of the mound until it has covered the wall to the depth of a foot or more. There was nothing found to show that the wall had ever been any higher than represented. Six feet within the wall, a little north of west from the center of the mound was an oval pit (1) 8 feet long, 5 feet wide, and 2 feet deep. This had been dug in the natural soil and was filled with clean wood ashes. At its northeast corner lay a celt, and immediately east of it was a large sandstone, a good load for two men, that had been brought from the hills south of the mound. This stone bore marks of fire, lay with the weathered side up, and was covered to the depth of 3 inches by the gravel in which it was embedded. At 10 feet from the southern edge of the mound was a basin-shaped pit 3 feet in diameter and 2 feet deep. This was lined or paved with bowlders, chiefly water-worn. For a foot down from the surface the ground (indicated by the dotted circle *a*) had been burned. A layer of ashes (2, B and C) 9 inches thick had accumulated over the greater portion of the surface inclosed by the stone wall, filling and covering the pit (1) on the western side and extending to the edge of the pit (10) on the southern side. Over the central portion of this layer of ashes was a conical heap of gravel 15 feet in diameter and 18 inches thick at the center (No. 3, B and C), then a stratum of ashes 6 to 9 inches thick (4), next a layer of blue clay mixed with ashes (5) varying in thickness from 2 to 3 feet, and over the whole a covering of surface soil (6). In section C, 7 indicates a small streak of surface soil; 8, a small mass of burned clay; and 11, a small deposit of gravel. No human bones were found, except the fragment of a lower jaw.

As the position of this mound was so favorable for a beacon station and lookout, there can be little doubt that it was intended for this purpose. A beautiful valley, a mile in width and covered with a rich productive soil, extends for miles along the creek on either side. A light at this point would be visible not only to dwellers in the valley, but at all points on the surrounding hills. It is well known that the valley was a favorite spot with the Indians. The old Indian town of Minnecoosa was situated in it immediately below the promontory. Mr. Staats states that when he came here, more than fifty years ago, there was no timber on the bottoms or on the terrace, all having been cut down by the Indians "to give them a better chance to watch the game and note the movements of their enemies," and doubtless also for cultivation, as their food was partly obtained in this manner.

THE HAMMOND MOUND.

This is a small, conical mound located on the land of Mr. Hammond, in Sec. 3, T. 36, R. 10, Butler township, about a mile west of the Staats mound. It is on a terrace 20 feet higher than the bottom land of the valley and at present is 45 feet in diameter and 4 feet high, though Mr. Hammond says that when he first saw it it was fully twice as high, pointed at the top, not over 35 feet in diameter, and with two large oak trees growing on its top. The central core consisted of soil which must have been brought from the bottom land. This was covered by a foot of yellow clay, like that found on the terrace. The original surface of the ground under the northeast side had been heated for 6 or 8 inches down and was covered by an inch-thick deposit of coals and ashes. Toward the upper part of the mound was a thin horizontal layer of dark soil about 4 inches thick. In the north side, 6 feet from the center, at a depth of 2½ feet, lay some fragments of human bones, the skull not among them. Six inches above them were a few burnt bones mixed with ashes and coals, but these appear to have been brought in with the earth when the mound was built. Scattered through the earth of the central mass were two gorgets, a few flint knives, some arrow points, a pendant, spearhead, chipped celt (quartzite), and a single fragment of pottery. The top layer consisted of surface soil about 1 foot thick.

THE CEMETERY MOUND.

This mound was situated in the cemetery at Mount Vernon. A view of it is given in Pl. XXIX, from a photograph made shortly before its

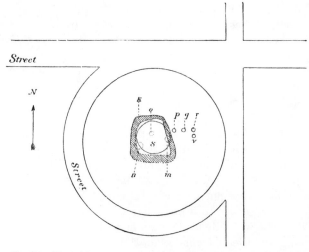

Fig. 306.— Plan of Cemetery mound, Mount Vernon, Knox county, Ohio.

removal.[1] It was conical in form, unusually symmetrical, the base being almost a circle. Diameter, 80 feet, and height, 11. The top was slightly depressed, in consequence of a pit sunk into it by a former owner, but afterward filled up. The mode of construction is shown in the plan (Fig. 306) and in the vertical section from east to west (Fig. 307).

First, a 2-inch layer (a) of surface sod, then 4 feet of fine yellow clay (b) free of stones; below this, the central core (c) reaching to the original surface, of soil, apparently from the valley to the north. The small masses or loads in which it was deposited were very distinct, as is shown in Fig. 307 (c, f, g, and i). This central mass was interrupted by a few thin seams of gray earth; first, at the depth of 6 feet from the

---

[1] This removal was made in accordance with the wishes of its owner after a lawsuit with the directors of the cemetery.

CEMETERY MOUND, MOUNT VERNON, KNOX COUNTY, OHIO.

top of the mound, a nearly horizontal layer (*d*) 2 inches thick; next, a similar layer (*e*) connecting with the former at the margins, but dipping a foot downward at the center; and thirdly, 2 feet lower, the layer (*h*).

In the central portion of the mound, resting on the original surface of the ground, was an irregularly quadrilateral stone inclosure (*k*). This was built up loosely of rough surface sandstones, all with the weathered side up. The east and west diameter varied from 10 to 13 feet, the north and south from 13 to 15. The thickness of the wall at the base was from 5 to 10 feet, the height from 1½ to 3 feet. The stones were piled up without any attempt at regularity. The dotted portion along the southern line of the wall (Fig. 306) shows where it was imperfect and in part wanting.

Within the space inclosed by the wall, and extending partly under it on the east side, was the circular pit (*s*), 12 feet in diameter and 2½ feet deep. The sides were slightly sloped, giving it a basin-like shape. It was mostly filled with dark soil in small masses, like that of the overlying mass (*i*), with which it seems to be continuous, resting on a

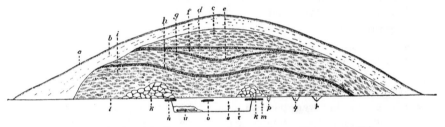

Fig. 307.—Section of the Cemetery mound, Mount Vernon, Knox county, Ohio.

white substance (*t*) an inch thick, possibly the ashes of hickory bark, which covered most of the bottom of the pit and extended over a skeleton on the west side. The portion covering the skeleton was very hard, being difficult to penetrate with a pick. The remainder of it was quite loose. The skeleton (*u*), which was badly decayed, lay at full length with the head at the west margin of the pit and the feet toward the center. Around it was a quantity of decayed vegetable matter, possibly the remains of bark wrapping. On the under jaw was a crescent-shaped piece of copper, about the hips several shell beads, along the left arm a few bear's teeth, and about the head the remains of some textile fabric.

The letters *m*, *n*, and *o* mark the position of fire-beds; *m* and *n* were on the level of the original surface, extending slightly over the pit, *n* being mostly under the wall and *m* entirely so. Each was about 6 feet in diameter, and the clay soil beneath them for a foot in depth was burned to a light brick red. The one at *o*, about the center of the pit, was comparatively small, and the clay beneath but slightly baked, indicating that but a single fire had been kindled on it. Just outside the eastern wall were four small pits or holes in the natural soil, each about a foot in depth and 9 inches in diameter, arranged as shown by *p, q, r,* and *v* (see Fig. 306). Two of them, *q* and *r*, were filled with a dark-brown "sticky substance," in which were a number of split animal bones.

A careful study of this exceedingly interesting mound leads to the conclusion that it was a work of considerable time, the various steps in its construction being about as follows:

First, the small holes *p, q, r,* and *v* were dug possibly to hold posts on which a scaffold was built to support the corpse, the split bones being cast into them after the posts were removed for burning when the final burial took place. Next, when the time came for this, the central pit (*s*) was dug, and the skeleton, the flesh being removed, was deposited in it, then the layer of ashes sprinkled over the bottom (and over the skeleton), and the pit filled up. The fire at *o* probably pertained to some superstitious burial rite, while those at *m* and *n*, which were continued for a longer time, were built by the watchers. After this a wooden covering was probably placed over the pit and the stone wall built around it. There can scarcely be a doubt, judging by the fact that the weathered sides of all the stones were uppermost, that a considerable time had elapsed before the mound was built, possibly a number of years. The mound was in all probability built in successive stages, as seems to be indicated by the seams at *d, e,* and *h.* The holes *p, q, r,* and *v* may have held posts which supported a temporary booth for the watchers instead of serving the purpose above suggested, in which case we must suppose the body was buried without first removing the flesh, and that the decay of the flesh hardened the white substance spread over it. If these suppositions be in the main correct, the individual buried here must have been an important personage in the tribe to which he belonged, and one long remembered and revered by his people.

THE SHIPLEY MOUND.

This mound is on the farm of Mr. Worthington Shipley, in Howard township. It is on the brow of a steep bluff 75 feet high, overlooking the valley of Owl creek; is circular, flattened on top, 35 feet in diameter, and 4 feet high. Under the center, extending north and south, was a pit 7 feet long, 2½ feet wide, and 2 feet deep, dug in the original soil. In this was a single skeleton, face up and head south.

HOCKING COUNTY.

ANCIENT WOKS ON THE DAVIS PLACE.

These works, consisting of two small earthern inclosures and ditches, one surrounding a large mound which covers the greater part of the included area, are situated on the SW. ¼ of Sec. 8, T. 11, R. 19, in Salt Creek township, Hocking county. They stand on the level top of a spur which

juts out from the hills bordering the valley of Salt creek.   The larger
work, which includes the mound, stands on the brink of the bluff,
which rises here to a height of 200 feet above the valley.   Fig. 308 is a
plat of the works and the ground in the immediate vicinity.   A plan
of the larger work, which, as before stated, consists of an earthern in-

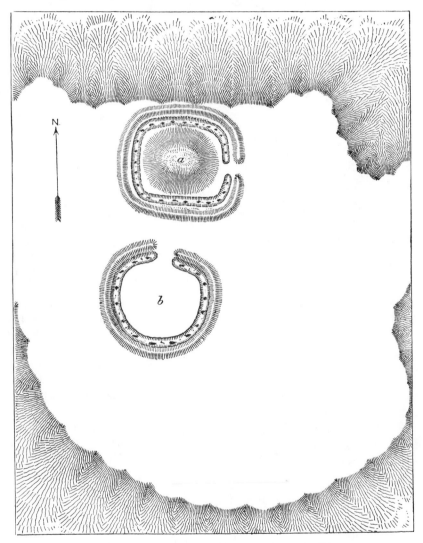

FIG. 308.—Works on the Davis place, Hocking county, Ohio.

closure, inner ditch, and included mound, is shown in Fig. 309.   It will
be seen from this that the form of both the inclosure and the mound (*a*)
is somewhat quadrilateral or oblong, the longer diameter being east
and west.   The mound, which covers the entire area, save a narrow
strip here and there, is 115 feet long and 96 wide at base, with a height

of 23 feet. At the eastern end and at the corners (which are rounded off) are strips of the original level 2 or 3 feet wide between the margin and the ditch. The top is rounded. The surrounding wall and ditch are interrupted only by the gateway at the east, which is about 30 feet wide. The ditch is 3 feet deep and varies in width from 20 to 23 feet. The wall averages 20 feet in breadth and is from 1 foot to 3 feet high. Two chestnut trees, one 6, the other 7 feet in circumference, were growing on the mound.

A partial exploration of the mound gave the following results: The first 5 feet of the top was found to consist of a layer (*a*, Fig. 309, B and C) of yellow clay similar to the surface soil of the spur; the remainder (*b*) of earth, which must have been brought from the valley below. In this latter could easily be traced the individual loads or little masses by which it had been built up, as in the case of the cemetery mound at Mount Vernon. At the base, 30 feet from the south margin, was a bed of burnt clay, on which were

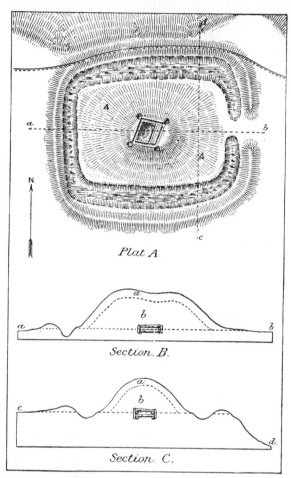

FIG. 309.—Plan of the large work, Davis place, Hocking county, Ohio.

coals and ashes. In the center, also at the base, were the remains of a square wooden vault. The logs of which it was built were completely decayed, but the molds and impressions were still very distinct, so that they could be easily traced. This was about 10 feet square, and the logs were of considerable size, most of them nearly or quite a foot in diameter. At each corner had been placed a stout upright post, and the bottom, judging by the slight remains found there, had been wholly or partially covered with poles. It had evidently been built up in the form of a pen, but neither the number of rounds nor original height could be definitely ascertained. From appearances it is probable there were not more than two or three tiers and the height not more than 2 or 3 feet. Near the center was the extended skeleton of an adult, head south, with which were enough shell beads to make a string 9 yards in length. The lower tier of logs was a foot or more down in the original soil, showing that a slight excavation had been made in the surface before the vault was built. The remains of some of the logs exhibited traces of fire, though the dirt around them showed no indications of heat. A trench was dug through the surrounding wall south of the mound. Near the middle were the remains of a post 6 inches in diameter. In another trench through the south wall, near the corner, was the burnt end of a post a foot in diameter.

A few yards south of this work is a small circular inclosure (*b*, Fig. 308) and inside ditch, the opening being toward the large inclosure. The diameter north and south is 120 feet; east and west, 124 feet. Owing to long cultivation only faint traces of them remain. The greatest height of the wall at present is not more than 15 inches.

FRANKLIN COUNTY.

ANCIENT WORKS NEAR DUBLIN.

The works represented in **Fig.** 310 are 1 mile northeast of Dublin and one-fourth of a mile east of the Scioto river. They are on a nearly level area of the higher lands of the section. Contrary to what is usual, the soil immediately around them is not nearly so fertile as that a short distance away.

At 1 is a circular embankment with an inside ditch. The diameter, measuring from the middle line of the embankment on one side to the middle on the other side, is 120 feet, the wall is about 10 feet broad and 2 feet high, and the ditch 15 feet wide and 2 feet deep, leaving a level inclosed circular area 80 feet in diameter. On the east side is a gateway 12 feet wide.

No. 2 is a rectangular inclosure with rounded corners. In measuring it, stakes were set where the middle lines of the embankment would cross if produced. The distances between these stakes were as follows: North side, 287 feet; west side, 212 feet; south side, 262 feet; east side, 220 feet. The outer line of the west wall forms a curve along its entire length; the other sides are straight. On the north, east, and west sides the wall is 25 feet across the base; on the south side, 35; its height, quite uniform throughout, is about 3 feet. It is bordered on the inside by a ditch 16 feet wide on the south side, 20 on the east and north sides, and 30 on the west side; depth about 2 feet on the east side, gradually increasing along the north from 3 to 4 feet, being widest and deepest at the southwest corner. Thus more earth was taken out along the west

12 ETH——29

line of the ditch and added to the south side of the embankment.   The
rounded outer corners of the embankment are 20 feet within the points
where the margins of the wall would intersect if carried on straight.
The corners of the inner sides of the ditch are about 10 feet within their
corresponding points.   The passageway on the eastern side is 15 feet
wide.   In all these inclosures the passage way is simply the natural surface of the ground between the ends of the ditch and wall; that is to

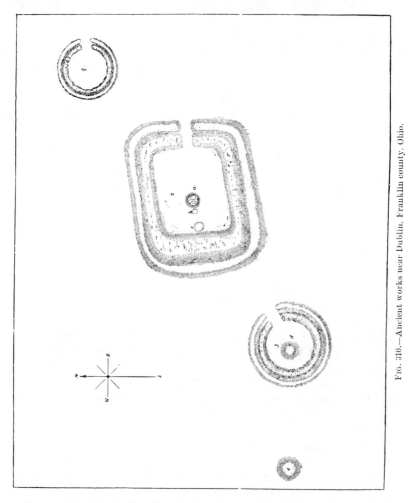

FIG. 310.—Ancient works near Dublin, Franklin county, Ohio.

say, it is not graded.   On the level space inclosed by the ditch, 100 feet
from the top of the east line of embankment, is a mound (a) 4 feet high
and 35 feet in diameter.   On the top were numerous flat stones, which
it is said had formed graves inclosing skeletons of very large size, but
nothing could be learned as to the manner in which they were buried.
Another stone grave (b), 8 feet in diameter, on the edge or bottom of
this mound on its western side, had been opened, and so torn up that

its mode of construction could not be determined. Still west, its edge extending quite up to the ditch, is another mound (c) 1 foot high and 24 feet in diameter. This has never been disturbed. From the top of the bank at the northeast corner of 2 to the nearest point on top of the embankment of inclosure 1, is 133 feet; and the line of the north edge of 2, if produced, would touch the south edge of 1.

Southwest of 2 is another circular inclosure (3) similar in construction to 1; the embankment is 18 feet across and 2 feet high; the ditch 22 feet wide and 3 feet deep in the deepest part; the level space inclosed 100 feet in diameter, making the entire diameter of the inclosure from center to center of the outer wall 162 feet. The passageway (opening directly toward 2) is 22 feet wide. In the inclosure is a mound (d) 40 feet in diameter and 3 feet high, its center being 60 feet from the inner edge of the ditch on the east. The amount of earth in this mound is hardly sufficient to account for the difference between the cubic contents of the excavation and those of the embankment.

About 500 feet west of 3 is a single mound (4) 5 feet high and 50 feet in diameter.

BROWN COUNTY.

MOUND GROUP ON HILL PLACE.

The group shown in Fig. 311 is on a high hill near the Arnheim pike, 4 miles north of Ripley, on the farm of Mr. James M. Hill, and consists of eight mounds, two of which are surrounded by a ditch and embankment.

The principal mound (1) is 72 feet in diameter and 8 feet high. Three small tumuli (2, 3, and 4), which have been plowed over for many years, are now from 1½ to 2½ feet high and from 30 to 40 feet in diameter.

No. 5 is 2½ feet high and 40 feet in diameter. This is surrounded by a circular wall and inner ditch each about 15 feet across, the diameter of the former from the middle line on one side to the middle on the other side being 151 feet, and of the ditch from center to center 119 feet. The wall is now only about 1 foot high, and the ditch scarcely more than 1 foot in depth.

No. 6 is a similar work, except that it is elliptical instead of circular, the measurements being as follows: The mound 80 feet east and west and 70 north and south; the ditch measuring from center to center 150 feet east and west and 120 feet north and south; the wall from top to top 180 by 150 feet. The mound is 5 feet high, the ditch and wall each about 15 to 18 feet wide, the height of the wall from 1 to 2 feet, and the ditch but little over a foot deep.

Westward from the latter work, one at the distance of 365 feet and the other nearly 1,200 feet, are two other mounds (7 and 8). The former of these is 3 feet high and 50 feet in diameter; the latter (8) 3½ feet high and 75 feet in diameter, is on a lower level than the other and not visible from any other mound in the whole group, yet from its position must belong with them. The relative positions are correctly indicated in the figure. The distances from center to center are as follows:

	Feet.		Feet.
From 1 to 2	120	From 1 to 5	255
From 2 to 3	120	From 1 to 6	485
From 3 to 4	155	From 6 to 7	365
From 4 to 5	180	From 7 to 8	800

Lying S. 20° W. from 1 is a large mound, about half a mile distant, in plain view. S. 50° E. about one-third of a mile is another, not visible by reason of a low intervening ridge. About 1 mile S. 30° E. was formerly an inclosure, now entirely destroyed. Nothing definite could be ascertained regarding its size or shape. It had been locally known as the Indian fort, and was on a hill overlooking the group. There is a good spring within 150 yards of 8, and another 200 yards southwest of 1. From 1 to the nearest point on Straight creek is half a mile in a northwest direction. The descent from the mounds to the creek is about 500 feet and very steep. A number of relics were found in 1 some years since. It has never been opened to the bottom. A small cache of very fine, large, leaf-shaped knives of Flint Ridge stone was exposed by the plow near by.

STONE GRAVES.

On nearly every prominent hill in the neighborhood of Ripley are stone graves, some small, apparently the burying places of a single individual, others large enough to contain a number. Nearly all of these graves have been disturbed by the persons on whose farms they are situated, either through curiosity or to utilize the stone. Very few have ever yielded any relics, and then only a celt or a few arrowheads. Over twenty different places were visited where it was claimed the graves were undisturbed before any were found intact.

Four miles east of Ripley, on a hill 500 feet high, overlooking the valley of Eagle creek and commanding an extensive view in every direction, were two that had never been opened.

The first was inclosed by a circle of large, flat limestone slabs set on edge, and measured 15 feet in diameter. The slabs fitted closely or slightly overlapped, and the space thus inclosed was on the same level as the surrounding surface; it was filled mostly with stones similar to those around the edge, with only enough dirt to fill the spaces between. The mass of earth and stone was removed to a depth of 15 inches, when large, flat rocks, lying horizontally, were reached. One of these being removed disclosed the yellow clay subsoil beneath. This was dug into about 2 feet, to make sure it was in place. There was nothing to show that the edges of the slabs had been dressed, yet they fitted so closely that only very small cracks were between them at any place and formed a floor over the whole space inclosed. Lying directly upon this rock floor, with head east, was an extended skeleton badly broken by the weight of the material above. Only a few fragments of the skull could be obtained; enough to show that it was a full half inch in thickness. With the exception of a few vertebræ, the bones of the body and upper extremities were so decayed that they could not be taken out or even uncovered sufficiently for examination, the tough, sticky soil adhering to them so that, when removed from its place, it brought fragments of the bone along with it. The femora were still solid enough to allow the dirt to be scraped away with a knife. They measured 22½ inches in length. Lying against the spinal column of the skeleton, just above the position of the pelvic bones, was a fragment, about 2 inches across, of a human skull not over one-sixteenth of an inch thick. Besides many small decayed pieces of bones, there were found one other femur of a size to correspond with those of the skeleton, and three femora of ordinary size. These last were lying close together. Why an odd number should be found is not plain. Close watch was kept, but no pieces of another were seen. The bones of the extended skeleton were in their proper position; so it would seem that a body had been buried soon after death, and at the same time portions of the skeletons of others who had died previously were placed in the grave. No two of the smaller femora were in a position such as could have corresponded with a whole skeleton placed in the grave. None of the bones were near the sides of the

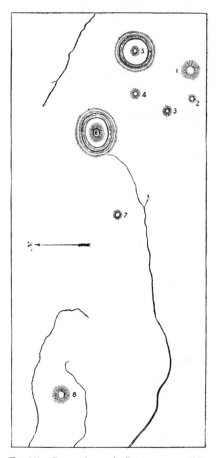

FIG. 311.—Group of mounds, Brown county, Ohio.

grave; the skeleton lay nearly across the center, and the other bones were close to its left side. The confused heaping of the stones made it impossible to discover their original method of arrangement; however, it was apparent that they were not the parts of a box grave. Possibly the remains had been covered with logs, and stones piled on the top of these. The grave was on a perfectly level spot.

Forty yards from this grave was another, on a gentle slope and at a slightly lower level than the first. This also had a circle of limestone slabs around it, some of which were perpendicular, but most of them variously inclined. The space within, measuring 19 feet across, was on a level with the surrounding surface of the ground. Beginning at the south edge, at first only dirt and small broken stones in about equal parts, were found; the yellow subsoil was 14 inches below the top, and the position of the broken stones showed they had been thrown in directly upon it. Six feet from the south side was a row of large slabs, the tops being above the ground and the bottom edges sunk into the yellow clay. Before these were disturbed the earth around them was removed and the stones and dirt within the entire circle thrown out, when it was seen that the slabs were arranged in the form of an ellipse 13 by 9½ feet, with the longer axis east and west. All the slabs of the south half of this ellipse sloped inwardly and over-lapped, the western edge of every one being placed over the eastern edge of the next one. On the north side they were so displaced by the roots of some trees that the arrangement could not be made out; pre-sumably it was the same as on the opposite side. Two feet within this ellipse (on the south side) was another row of large slabs reaching from end to end in nearly a straight line, with the tops leaning inward; on the north side were similar slabs, but the roots had moved them about so that it was impossible to say whether they corresponded with the others or not. Finally there were two rows within these just men-tioned, with the tops leaning outward (away from the center) on each side; this trough-like inclosure was 11 by 2 feet. Several large stones were lying on or partly across this, their position showing they had been laid over the top as boards are placed over a coffin. Within this box was a number of fragments of badly decayed bones. Enough were found to prove that at least one skeleton had been interred, extended with head to the east, and that it had been the frame of a strongly-built person of medium height. In addition to these there were found here some pieces of the bones of a very young child. The femora were lying in the proper position relative to each other, but so close that the heads were in contact. All the space within the larger ellipse was paved with flat stones lying on the subsoil, as in the first grave, though they were somewhat smaller in this one. No traces of bones were found outside of the box.

The accompanying Fig. 312 (A denoting the ground plan and B a vertical section north and south) is an attempt to represent as nearly as possible this unusual burial place. The letters a, b, and c indicate the same thing both in the plan and section. The outer circle (a a) is 19 feet in diameter, composed of upright stone slabs; b b is the ellipse, the diameters being 13 and 9½ feet. The stone slabs forming this ring lean inwards, as shown in the section. The roof-shaped, elliptical passage (c c) was composed of two series of stone slabs leaning toward each other and meeting at the top; d d denote the surface soil and e e the clay subsoil on which the paving stones rest.

Within a fourth of a mile of these graves, on another hill, was formerly a number of stone cists, from which nearly all the stones have been hauled away. The person who removed them said they had been set on edge, forming rectangular boxes about 8 feet by 2, large slabs laid across the top and other stones heaped on these. The position of such of the stones as were too firmly set in the ground to be easily removed, which were found still in place, showed that at least the first part of his statement was correct.

A grave 2½ miles east of Ripley, on a point giving a good view of the Ohio river and Kentucky hills, had been opened by other parties, whose statements in regard to an arch led to an examination of it. The inclosed portion, which had been pretty thoroughly cleaned out, was elliptical, 8 by 11 feet, the longer axis east and west. Like those

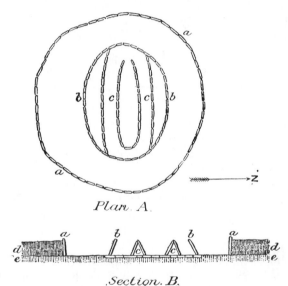

Plan A.

Section B.

FIG. 312.—Stone grave, Brown county, Ohio.

above described this had a floor of slabs resting on the yellow subsoil. The boundary of the grave was a row of slabs set on edge, inclining inward at an angle of 45 degrees, and supported underneath by a mass of small broken rocks tightly wedged in. Surrounding this were other rows similarly inclined, the whole series being about 6 feet in width entirely around the grave, and resting on the stone pavement which extended to the outside layer. Supported by these and reaching higher up, the lower edges of the stones in the upper tier being forced in between the upper edges of the ones beneath, were partial layers of another tier; and in one or two places the third tier or series could be seen, their lower edges, in turn, being between the upper edges of the second tier, each layer having a little greater inclination than the one below it. By continuing this plan an arch could have been formed clear across the space in which the body or bodies had been deposited, and, as each side would have to be drawn in only 4 feet at the widest part, the stones would have been sufficiently strong for the purpose. A section of this grave restored in part is shown in Fig. 313.

It will be seen that, although these graves differed widely in the construction of the upper part, they all agreed in having a floor or pavement of flat rocks laid upon the subsoil, upon which the body or skeleton was deposited, and that they differed materially from the box-shaped stone graves. No relics of any description were found.

Although it is going beyond the limits of the county, it may not be out of place to say here that for several miles up and down the river, on the opposite hills of Kentucky, graves similar to the above exist in great numbers; but after much search and inquiry Mr. Fowke, who examined those described, failed to find a single one which had not been torn up. There was formerly, according to the old settlers, a very large group of them in the bottom near Dover, Kentucky, 2 miles below Ripley. A milldam, a limekiln, and a long string of fence are still standing, built of stones from this cemetery, which, in addition, furnished lime to the people around for several years. Whether for mortuary or other purposes, all this stone had been carried from the neighboring hills,

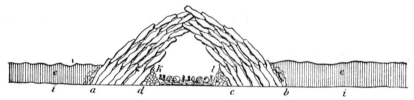

FIG. 313.—Section of a stone grave, Brown county, Ohio.

and there is no place within the fourth of a mile where it could have been obtained without carrying it up a steep bluff fully 50 feet high.

In this bottom are also several mounds, the largest 20 feet high and 120 feet in diameter. A smaller one close by, on being opened, disclosed about half a bushel of burnt limestone rocks from 2 to 4 inches through, a plate of mica, and a little charcoal. The stones were at the center, about half of them sunk into the original surface; the mica and charcoal about 5 feet west of the center. A number of large, flat stones were placed on edge, in no definite order, about the upper part of the mound. Many relics have been found on or immediately beneath the surface, within sight of Ripley. Every plowing or flood reveals them all along the banks and, in fewer numbers, on the hills and along the creeks; and though many thousand specimens have been gathered, the supply seems scarcely diminished. They are mostly celts, grooved axes, round stones, hammer-heads, arrowheads, and other flint weapons and pitted stones. Pestles and cupped stones are plentiful; nor is there a lack of pottery (always broken), perforated shells, slate ornaments, and hematites of different patterns.

At the mouth of Eagle creek, near Ripley, is the site of a former village and what has been an extensive aborginal cemetery; the latter is now nearly gone. owing to the encroachments of the creek on one side and the river on the other.

The indications are that this region was formerly occupied by a people who had villages, but lived more by hunting and fishing than by agriculture.

COSHOCTON COUNTY.

Beginning in Jefferson township, a short distance above Warsaw, and extending in a southwestern direction for 10 or 12 miles, is a series of flint deposits, the remains of what was once a continuous bed. The ground has been eroded into numerous peaks and ridges, and the flint is now found only in those hills whose tops remain above its level. At several points these deposits bear evidence of aboriginal workings, mostly along the outcrop, as the depth of earth and stone above them was too great to be removed by primitive means. Many places that have been left undisturbed are apparently no more difficult to excavate than some that have been worked. The most extensive quarrying was done on the hills immediately south of the Walhonding river, 3 miles southwest of Warsaw.

On the farm of Col. Pren Metham, southwest of his house, is a long, narrow ridge, whose top slopes downward toward the north for some distance and then gradually rises to the end. In the depression, or "saddleback," thus formed, the flint was covered only a few feet at any point. The ancient diggers began at the outcrop on one side of the ridge and worked across to' the other side, removing the flint and throwing the dirt behind them as they went. The soil is thickly covered and intermingled with spalls and fragments. There are a few pits on the ascending slope to the south of this ridge, but the thickness of the overlying soil soon becomes too great to justify its removal. The space dug over comprises about 5 acres.

Half a mile east of this, on land of Mrs. Criss, between two small ravines that intersect a short distance. to the southward, is a nearly level area of about 2 acres, rising from 6 to 12 feet above the outcrop, on which are several large pits filled with muck and water. The largest is about 100 feet across, and a high bank of earth still surrounding it shows that a large surface of the flint has been uncovered. From the hill, on one side of which this level is found, a narrow point extends for some distance to the east, and along both sides of this point the excavations or pits reach from the outcrop up the hill to a distance varying according to the thickness of the overlying stratum. At other places in the immediate vicinity are similar excavations; but those mentioned are the principal ones. Some of the pits have been cleared out by persons living near, and the method of excavating was found to be analogous to that followed at the flint quarries of Licking county.

This flint varies considerably. At the pits on Mrs. Criss's farm it is an opaque blue, with a small amount of included chalcedony and crystals.   At the point east it is white, resembling a much weathered chalcedony.   Nearer the river there is considerable chalcedony, and a clear yellowish or "honey-colored" stone, much resembling that found in Europe, though less translucent.   The greater part, however, is a dark variety, much of it being basanite.   There seems to be no regular order in its arrangement.   Sometimes the different kinds are in strata, though not always in the same relative position, while, again, three or four sorts are seen in a single large block.   There may be thin seams of shale or other rock between the flint layers, or the flint may be in a solid bed, either with one color merging into another or the line of separation sharply defined, without any change in the texture of the stone.

Just east of Col. Metham's residence, on a high point overlooking the valley for 3 or 4 miles, was a mound about 5 feet high, made of flat stones, in layers one over another, with the spaces between (where they did not fit up closely) filled with broken stone.   This had been built up over a stone box-grave containing a skeleton 7 feet long and a few relics.   On the north side of the river, northwest from this mound, running out from a hill 300 feet high, on the farm of Robert Darling, is a point whose sides at the top are perpendicular from 12 to 20 feet.   Across this point is a crescent-shaped wall of stone, convex outwardly, 3 feet high, and reaching to the bluff on each side.   It measures about 100 yards in length.

LICKING COUNTY.

With the exception of Ross, this is the most interesting county, archeologically, in the state.   From the great works at Newark, divergent mound systems reach to the Ohio at Portsmouth and Marietta.   Numerous earth mounds and inclosures occur, besides several stone inclosures and probably more stone mounds (some of great size) than in any other equal area in the Mississippi valley.

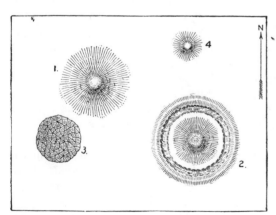

FIG. 314.—Mounds near Brownsville, Ohio.

The plat (Fig. 314) shows a group which has not been heretofore represented.   It is located 2 miles southwest of the village of Brownsville and half a mile south of the National road, on a high hill, from which the surrounding country is in view for several miles.

The most prominent mound, No. 1, is 120 feet in diameter, with a

Raccoon Creek
Area 50 Acres
Area 20 Acres
F
Parallels 2½ miles long
Road
Pond
Sandy Loam
Area 20 Acres
Area 30 Acres
E
Ohio Canal
Lock
South Fork
Newark
Sections.
500
1000 ft

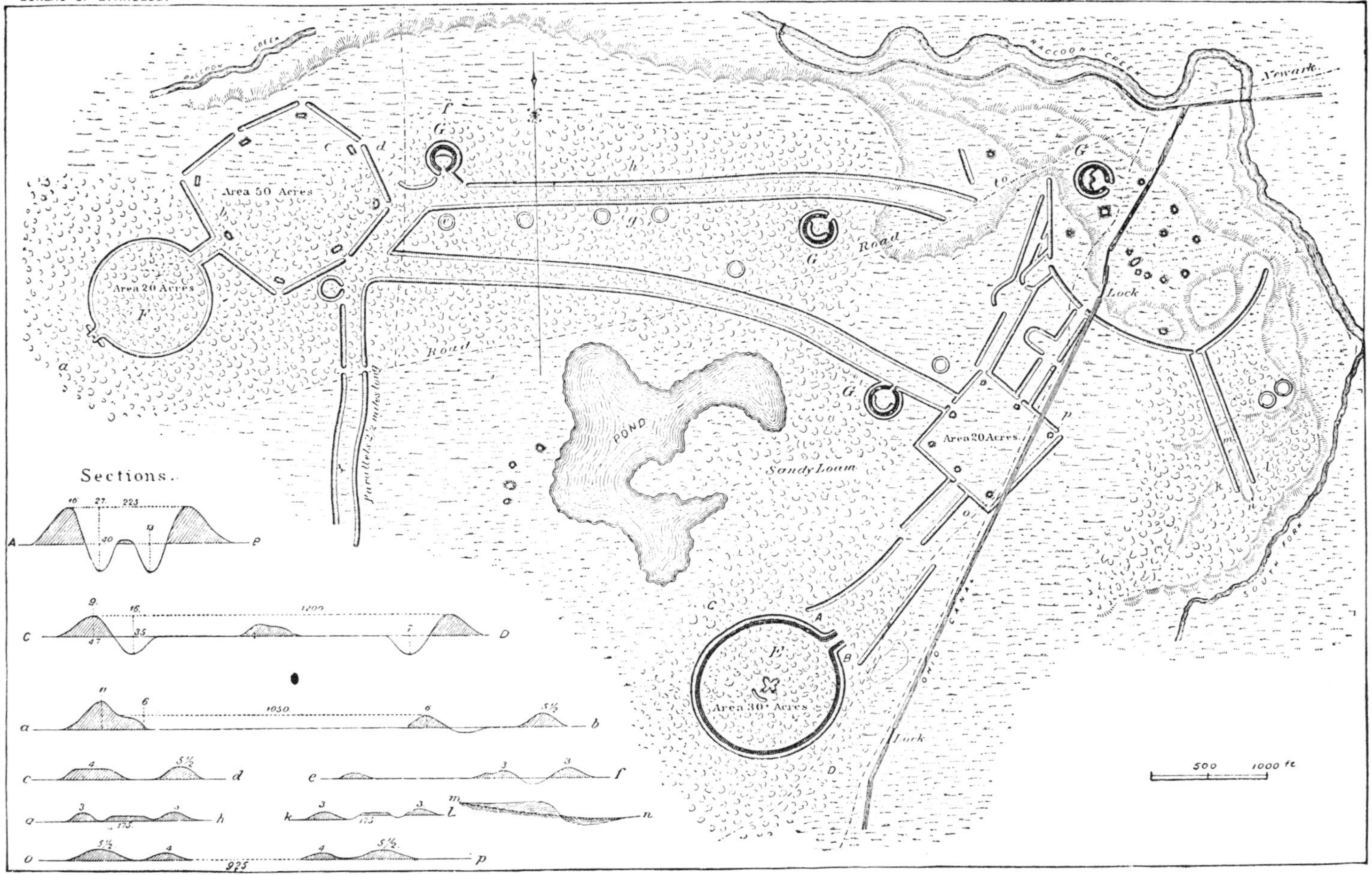

NEWARK WORKS, LICKING COUNTY, OHIO.

present height of 15 feet; it has been considerably lowered by persons digging into the top of it.

Fifteen feet southwest of this (measuring from margin to margin) is mound 3, 80 feet in circumference and about 8 feet high. Like No. 1, it has been lowered by searchers. The first 5 feet from the bottom was found to be a mingled compact mass of earth and stones; above that, stones only. Possibly the entire mound was of earth and stone at first, the former having gradually settled into the spaces between the latter. An elevation around the margin of this mound indicates an encircling wall of earth.

East of 3 is an earth mound (2) 100 feet in diameter and 5 feet high. Surrounding it is a circular ditch 1 foot deep and outside of this is a circular embankment 2 feet high.

The slope from the top of embankment to bottom of the ditch is unbroken, the plow having destroyed the original lines. From the center of the included mound to the top of the wall surrounding it is 120 feet, showing the diameter of the inclosure to be 240 feet.

Northeast of 1 is 4, an earth mound 2 feet high and 50 feet in diameter. It has also been long cultivated.

Large trees are growing on the stone mound, but not even a bush on the largest earth mound.

THE NEWARK WORKS. [1]

As the ancient works at this place have become noted the following facts, in addition to what is given by Squier and Davis in their excellent work, may be of interest to American archeologists.

The northern parallels, marked _g h_ on their plan, a copy of which is shown in our Pl. xxx, extend eastward to the brow of the upper terrace, but if they ever went down the slope and out on the next terrace, as shown in their plan, there is not now the slightest indication of it, nor does any one we were able to find in Newark remember them as so extending. Col. Whittlesey, by whom the original survey was made, is noted for his accuracy, and possibly the plan is correct in this respect, but all the evidence we could obtain is against such conclusion.

There are two large excavations immediately north of the octagon, from which it is probable the dirt was taken for the walls. There are also slight depressions along some of the walls and at a few points within and without them, from which dirt was also taken. Under the terrace, near the creek, immediately north of the opening at the northern corner of the octagon, is a strong spring of cool, limpid water.

There is considerably more space between the small circle marked G near the east end of the northern parallel, and the southern line of these parallels, than the plan of Messrs. Squier and Davis allows. This fact is worthy of notice, as within this space is the singular work shown in

---

[1] Squier and Davis, Anc. Mon., Pl. xxv.

Fig. 315. This is omitted by Squier and Davis, but is indicated in the figure of this group in McLean's Mound Builders, page 33, though the form he gives is erroneous. As will be seen by reference to the figure now given, it is an inclosure in the form of a figure 8, with an inside ditch, an opening at the east, and a wall or embankment in the form of an arc in the interior, near the middle. The entire length of the wall, following the curves from the end on one side of the gateway to the end on the other side, is 529 feet; width of gateway, 52 feet; the north and south diameters of the circles, measuring from the top of the wall, 125 feet; the length of the crescent, 107 feet; the wall and ditch are each about 9 feet wide, the one about a foot high and the other a foot deep, but quite distinct throughout.

The three mounds in a row west of the " pond " or swamp in Squier and Davis's plan are in a northwest and southeast line, and not northeast and southwest, as represented; the fourth is not to be found. Two

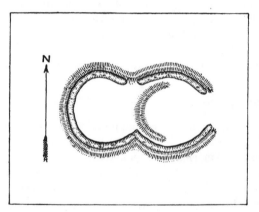

FIG. 315.—Small inclosure, Newark group, Licking county. Ohio.

are in the woods on a level, 10 feet above the swamp; the third is in a cultivated field. The north and south two are each about 33 by 63 feet, with the longer axis nearly north and south; the third, circular, 32 feet in diameter, is about midway between them. All are about 3 feet high.

The ditch within the fairground circle (E) is 5 or 6 feet lower at the entrance than at other part, and the dirt in it just such as may be found in any old ditch, being of a grayish clay color when dry, but resembling the loam around when wet. There is no evidence of the puddling which some late investigators have professed to find.

The earth for the embankments was taken in part from the ditch and in part from outside excavations plainly visible. The largest of these is marked by Squier and Davis, but there are many other places where dirt seems to have been taken up from the surface to the depth of from 1 to 2 or 3 feet. The same is true of the various works in the vicinity.

There are four distinct terraces in the bottom-lands on which these remains are situated; only the lowest one has ever been overflowed since occupation by the whites.

In order that parties desirous of doing so may have an opportunity of testing the previous surveys of the works at this place, the field notes of the survey of the " Fair ground circle," the " Observatory cir-

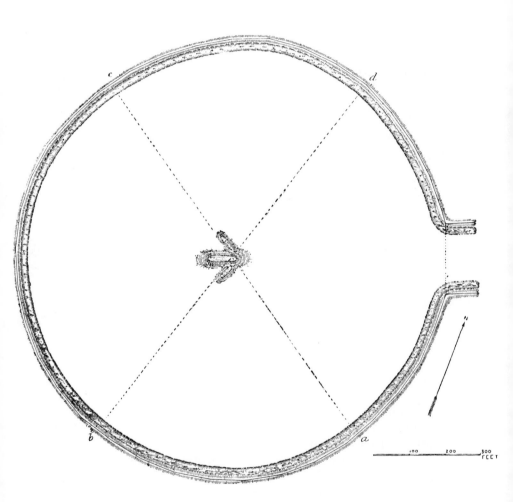

FAIR GROUND CIRCLE, NEWARK, OHIO.

cle," the " Octagon," and " Square," made by Mr. J. D. Middleton in 1888, are inserted here.

In measuring the circles chords of equal length were used, the stations being on top of the wall and always as near the middle as could be ascertained by measurement and judgment and the stakes all set before the bearings were taken. The course of each chord was taken. In measuring the Octagon, the middle lines of the wall were followed and the corners established where the lines cross each other.

FAIR GROUND CIRCLE.

This is the large circle (see Pl. XXXI) situated in the southern extremity of the group and marked E on Pl. XXV of Ancient Monuments, and has received the above name from the fact that it embraces within its circuit the fair grounds of the Licking County Agricultural Society. It is undoubtedly one of the best preserved ancient monuments of our country; it is uninjured by the plow and trees of the original forest are still standing on it. The ditch has been but slightly filled by the wash of the many years which have passed since its abandonment. The wall varies in width from 35 to 55 feet and in height from 5 to 14 feet. The ditch varies in width from 28 to 41 feet and in depth from 8 to 13 feet.

The following are the notes of the survey, commencing at station 1, in the gateway:

Stations.	Bearing.	Distance.	Width of embankment.	Width of ditch.
		Feet.	Feet.	Feet.
1 to 2	S. 20° 22′ E....	100	55	....
2 to 3	S. 1° 34′ E.....	100	45	41
3 to 4	S. 2° 55′ W....	100	57	....
4 to 5	S. 15° 17′ W...	100	44	41
5 to 6	S. 23° 32′ W...	100	40	....
6 to 7	S. 28° 59′ W...	100	44	....
7 to 8	S. 39° 50′ W...	100	45	....
8 to 9	S. 49° 25′ W...	100	42	42
9 to 10	S. 60° 37′ W...	100	47	....
10 to 11	S. 71° 25′ W...	100	44	....
11 to 12	S. 80° 31′ W..	100	43	38
12 to 13	N. 88° 50′ W ..	100	39	....
13 to 14	N. 79° 33′ W ..	100	40	....
14 to 15	N. 74° 13′ W ..	100	43	37
15 to 16	N. 59° 32′ W ..	100	33	....
16 to 17	N. 52° 32′ W ..	100	40	....
17 to 18	N. 40° 26′ W ..	100	41	....
18 to 19	N. 32° 24′ W ..	100	41	36
19 to 20	N. 24° 44′ W ..	100	43	....
20 to 21	N. 12° 20′ W ..	100	42	32
21 to 22	N. 3° 20′ W ...	100	39	....
22 to 23	N. 7° 55′ E....	100	38	....
23 to 24	N. 21° 25′ E...	100	36	....

Stations.	Bearing.	Distance.	Width of embankment.	Width of ditch.
		Feet.	Feet.	Feet.
24 to 25	N. 27° 39′ E ...	100	38	28
25 to 26	N. 36° 32′ E ...	100	35	....
26 to 27	N. 45° 04′ E ...	100	36	....
27 to 28	N. 52° 40′ E ...	100	38	35
28 to 29	N. 59° 37′ E ...	100	43	....
29 to 30	N. 68° 44′ E ...	100	46	....
30 to 31	N. 84° 15′ E ...	100	43	38
31 to 32	S. 85° 32′ E ...	100	42	....
32 to 33	S. 77° 7′ E ...	100	42	36
33 to 34	S. 63° 22′ E ...	100	38	....
34 to 35	S. 56° 1′ E ...	100	41	....
35 to 36	S. 49° 30′ E ...	100	40	34
36 to 37	S. 40° 18′ E ...	100	49	....
37 to 38	S. 38° 29′ E ...	40	53	32
38 to 1	S. 20° 22′ E ...	89	....	....
a to b	S. 23° 25′ W ...	838	....	....
a to c	S. 68° 38′ W ...	1,190	....	....
b to d	N. 20° 45′ W ...	1,186	....	....
b to c	....	839	....	....
c to d	....	837	....	....
a to d	....	834	....	....
37 to 39	N. 66° 41′ E ...	84	53	*32
2 to 50	N. 66° 27′ E ...	95	48	†33

*North wing.   †South wing.

From the plat made according to these figures we ascertain that the longest diameter, namely that running northeast and southwest, is 1,189 feet; and the shortest, southeast and northwest, is 1,163 feet; a difference of 26 feet. Although not a true circle, the difference between the longest and shortest diameters falls much short of 100 feet, the difference given by Messrs. Squier and Davis. Pl. XXXI shows the circle according to an exact scale; the dark line along the wall indicating the line of the survey.

OBSERVATORY CIRCLE.

This circle, which is marked F on Pl. XXV of "Ancient Monuments," is situated at the extreme west of the great group, and is yet very distinct, being about 3 feet high at the lowest point, the average height being between 4 and 5 feet. Most of the south half is yet in the original forest and has never been injured by the plow; but the north half has been under cultivation for a number of years and is considerably worn. The effect of this wearing is apparent not only in the decrease in height, but in the increase in width, of this portion of the wall as shown by the field notes given below. The field notes are as follows, beginning at station 0, in the middle of the gateway leading to the octagon:

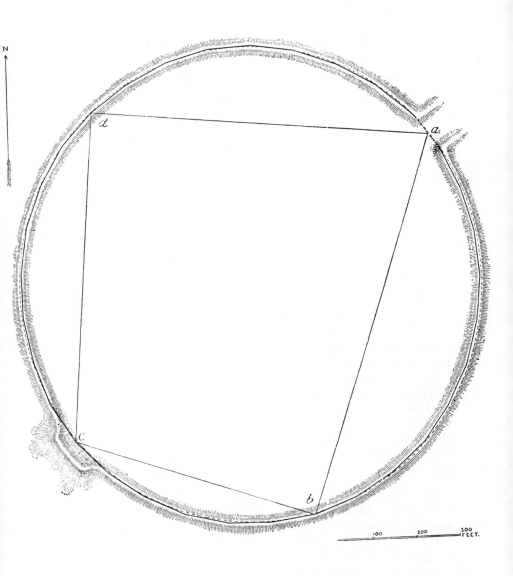

N

OBSERVATORY CIRCLE, NEWARK, OHIO.

Station.	Bearing.	Distance.	Width of wall.	Remarks.
		Feet.	Feet.	
0 to 1	S. 38° 20′ E....	42	0	Station 1 at junction of circle and south parallel.
1 to 2	S. 26° 20′ E....	100	36	
2 to 3	S. 17° 37′ E....	100	35	
3 to 4	S. 6° E........	100	38	
4 to 5	S. 5° 36′ W....	100	38	
5 to 6	S. 15° W	100	37	
6 to 7	S. 27° 45′ W...	100	36	Center of wall 2 feet east; that is, outward.
7 to 8	S. 35° 17′ W...	100	34	
8 to 9	S. 48° 40′ W...	100	37	
9 to 10	S. 58° 16′ W...	100	37	
10 to 11	S. 69° 13′ W...	100	37	
11 to 12	S. 82° W	100	35	
12 to 13	N. 89° 13′ W ..	100	41	
13 to 14	N. 76° 23′ W ..	100	37	
14 to 15	N. 66° 15′ W ..	100	(?)38	Width estimated, not measured.
15 to 16	N. 55° 56′ W ..	100	39	
16 to 17	N. 45° 10′ W..	100	....	Middle of "Observatory."
17 to 18	N. 33° 33′ W ..	100	39	
18 to 19	N. 20° 29′ W..	100	42	
19 to 20	N. 11° 22′ W..	100	43	
20 to 21	N. 1° 34′ W....	100	40	
21 to 22	N. 9° 06′ E	100	39	
22 to 23	N. 20° 54′ E ...	100	38	
23 to 24	N. 31° 12′ E ...	100	39	
24 to 25	N. 42° 32′ E ...	100	40	
25 to 26	N. 53° 43′ E ...	100	42	
26 to 27	N. 62° 43′ E ...	100	40	
27 to 28	N. 75° 07′ E ...	100	44	
28 to 29	N. 86° 23′ E ...	100	40	
29 to 30	S. 82° 17′ E....	100	44	
30 to 31	S. 72° 04′ E....	100	42	
31 to 32	S. 60° 45′ E....	100	45	
32 to 33	S. 51° 06′ E....	100	45	
33 to 34	S. 46° 29′ E....	20	....	Junction with north parallel wall.
34 to 0	S. 38° 20′ E....	42	....	Middle of gateway.
34 to 36	N. 52° 04 E....	295	....	North parallel.
1 to 37	N. 51° 53 E....	293	....	South parallel.

CHECK LINES.

0 to 11	S. 18° 28′ W..	883	....	
0 to 17	S. 51° 27′ W..	1,057	....	
0 to ½	S. 52° W	....	....	"½" indicates the half-way point in the circumference.
0 to 25	N. 85° 10′ W..	770	....	
17 to 11	S. 71° 59′ E...	570	....	
17 to 25	N. 4° 23′ E....	728	....	
25 to 11	S. 28° 03′ E....	1,024	....	

In order to bring before the eye of the reader the approximate regularity of this circular work, a figure laid off to a scale is introduced here (Pl. XXXII). The solid black line of short chords marks the line of the survey along the top of the wall, and the circular dotted line the nearest approximate circle. Great care was taken in making the survey, and the plat and calculation were found to confirm the accuracy claimed.

Measuring the various diameters, the maximum is found to be 1,059 feet and the minimum 1,050, the mean of which is 1,054.5 feet, but it is found by trial that the nearest approximate circle has a diameter of 1,054 feet. The widest divergence between the line of the survey and the circumference of the true circle is 4 feet.

The aggregate length of the chords surveyed is 3,304 feet, while the circumference of the approximate circle is 3,311 feet; adding to the sum of the chords the additional length of the arcs they subtend (0.1508 of a foot to each 100-foot chord) we have a total of 3,309 feet. It is therefore evident that the inclosure approaches, in form, very nearly an absolute circle. The area including the inner half of the wall is 20 acres, but of the interior level area it is only 18.6 acres.

"OCTAGON."

This inclosure, which is connected with the "Observatory Circle" according to resurvey, is shown in Pl. XXXIII. The southern portions, a to b, and b to c, remain almost uninjured, being still more or less covered by the original forest growth. The other lines of wall have been considerably worn by the plow, though they are still quite distinct, the height not being less at any point than $2\frac{1}{2}$ feet, as shown by the figures of the field notes. Nevertheless the wearing makes it difficult, often impossible, to determine with absolute certainty the middle line, though there is never any good reason why the survey should vary from the middle line of this, or any other of these Ohio inclosures distinctly traceable, more than 3 feet at most.

The field notes of the survey are as follows: Commencing at station No. 36 (so numbered in the survey of the Observatory Circle) at the point where the northern parallel joins the Octagon; thence to station 37, the point where the southern parallel joins the Octagon; thence to b and round to the place of beginning.

Station.	Bearing.	Distance.	Width of wall.	Height of wall.
		Feet.	Feet.	Feet.
36 to 37	S. 36° 32' E ...	82	....	....
37 to b	S. 49° 41' E....	580	40 to 43	5.7 to 4.5
b to c	N. 64° 18' E ...	624·5	37 to 48	4.3 to 4.2
c to d	N. 39° 50' E ...	625	47 to 39	5.9 to 5.8
d to e	N. 25° 28' W ..	622	41 to 50	3.4 to 3.5
e to f	N. 51° 32' W ..	621	40 to 37	2.5 to 2.6
f to g	S. 65° 40' W ...	613	47 to 43	3.8 to 4.0
g to h	S. 39° 15' W. .	621·5	45 to 47	4.3 to 4.0
to 37	S. 25° 40' E ...	581·5	43 to 41	3.8 to 3.7

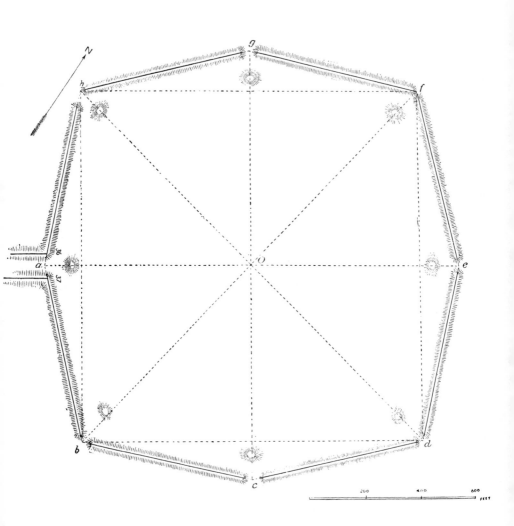

OCTAGON, NEWARK, OHIO.

The two numbers to each course, in the width and height columns, are two measurements of each wall near the ends in the direction of the survey.

The stations indicated by letters are at the intersections of the middle lines of the walls extended; station a is at the intersection of the lines of the h-36 and 37-b. The diameters as ascertained from the plat (in all cases to the intersections) are as follows:

	Feet.		Feet.
From h to b	1,218	From b to d	1,219
From d to f	1,213	From f to h	1,202
From b to f	1,708	From h to d	1,720
From a to e	1,483	From g to c	1,487

The widths of the gateways are as follows, the measurements being from base to base: At a, 46 feet; at b, 23 feet; at c, 47 feet; at d, 26 feet; at e, 37 feet; at f, 12 feet; at h, 60 feet.

The angles at the crossings of the diagonals and diameters at the center o are so nearly right angles as to be worthy of notice in this connection. For instance, the angles at crossing of the diagonals bf and dh differ but 10 minutes from true right angles, while those at the crossing of the diameters ae and cg differ but 2 minutes.

The inner angles at the intersection of the lines of the walls—that is to say, the angles of the octagon—are as follows:

At a	155° 59'	At b	113° 59'
At c	155 32	At d	114 42
At e	153 56	At f	117 12
At g	153 35	At h	115 05

THE SQUARE.

This is the smaller square inclosure on the east side of the works, and in Pl. XXV, "Ancient Monuments," is directly east of the pond. It connects with the fair-ground circle (E on the plate) by a broken line of parallels. According to Col. Whittlesey's plat it varies considerably from a true square, being distinctly narrowed on one side, but, as will be seen from the notes of the resurvey, it must have been very nearly square. As it is well nigh obliterated it was found impossible to trace the lines throughout, hence only those parts are marked in the figure (see Pl. XXXIV) which were satisfactorily determined; the untraced portions are represented by dotted lines.

The following are the field notes of the resurvey which commenced near the middle of the southeastern line of wall at 1, running thence to 2, and so on around, following the walls to station 7, whence, as the wall was visible no farther, the close was made by running directly to station 1:

12 ETH——30

Station.	Bearing.	Distance.
		Feet.
1 to 2	N. 47° 16′ E...	369·5
2 to 3	N. 41° 53′ W..	928
3 to 6	S. 47° 47′ W..	926
6 to 7	S. 41° 47′ E...	541
7 to 1	N. 82° 47′ E ..	679

Check lines.

Feet.

From 3 to 4, junction with eastern parallel 268
From 4 to 5, junction with western parallel.................... 158
From 5 to 6, western corner.................................... 500

The inner angles as ascertained by measurement on the ground are as follows:

At station 1.. 144° 30′
At station 2.. 90 51
At station 3.......... .... 89 40
At station 6... 90 26
At station 7........................ .... 124 34

Supposing the obliterated parts of the lines about the southern corner to have been straight continuations of the remaining portions, as represented in the figure, this angle would equal 89 degrees 3 minutes; and the side 6 to 8 would be 939 feet; and 8 to 2 would be 951 feet.

There are at present no indications whatever of the inner mounds represented on Col. Whittlesey's plat.

As will be seen by inspecting our figure and referring to the notes of the resurvey, this inclosure varies but slightly from a true square, the course of the opposite sides in one case differing but 31 minutes and in the other but 6 minutes. The greatest variation at the corners from a true right angle is 57 minutes.

The length of the diagonal from station 2 to 6 is 1,307 feet, ascertained from plat carefully drawn to a large scale.

Fig. 316, prepared from a survey made by Mr. Henry L. Reynolds, represents the irregularities and fall of the land between the parallel embankments of the Newark Works, Ohio, which, as will be seen in Pl. xxx, extend from the Square to the Octagon and from the Octagon eastward to Raccoon creek.

The difference in level between the entrance of the circle marked E (the Fair Ground circle) and the northwest entrance of the Square is also given.

The level of the southeast entrance of the Octagon was chosen as a datum or base from which to recken the rise or fall. This datum is indicated by the fine horizontal dotted line in Fig. 316.

Beginning at the southeast entrance of the Octagon, the course between the parallels, which ran S. 75° E. towards the Square, was well marked for 2,500 feet, for along this entire distance the embank-

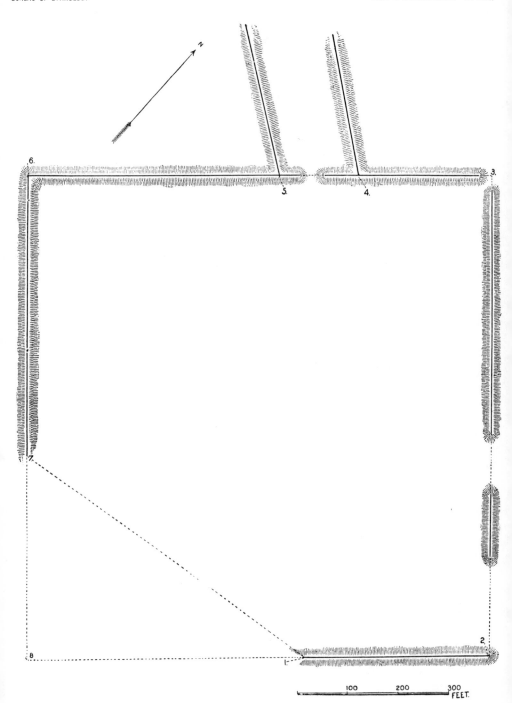

SQUARE, NEWARK, OHIO.

ments are more or less distinct. Ninety-six feet beyond this point, at Station 35 on the plat, a bend was taken to S. 70° E. in order to follow as closely as possible the original course of these embankments as marked out on the Whittlesey plat, Pl. xxx. This latter course ran 263 feet to Station 36, where another bend was taken S. 65° E. This ran 1,914 feet to Station 39. At Station 39 a bend to S. 60° E. was

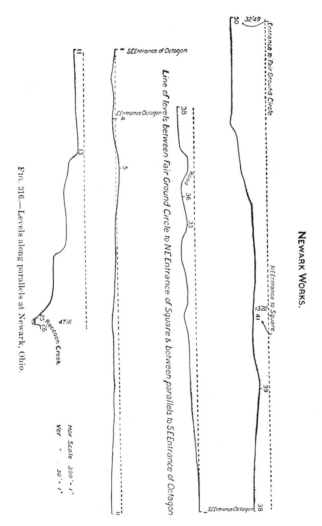

Fig. 316.—Levels along parallels at Newark, Ohio.

made, which ran 730 feet to the middle of the northwestern entrance of the Square, the parallels reappearing here this entire distance. The fall from the southeastern entrance of the Octagon to this point was thereupon determined to be 13.22 feet, over a rather undulating course, as will be seen in the plat.

Owing to the presence of a number of dwelling houses on the land just south of the Square, and the complete absence of the original parallel embankments, no defined course could be followed between the Square and Circle E. The line given on the plat ran S. 15° W. 541 feet; thence S. 10° W. 384 feet; thence S. 20° W. 842 feet; thence S. 40° W. 878 feet to connect with the middle of the entrance way of the circle. The fall from the Square to this point was ascertained to be 19.27 feet.

Before commencing the line between the parallels running eastward from the Octagon the difference in level between the southeast and the

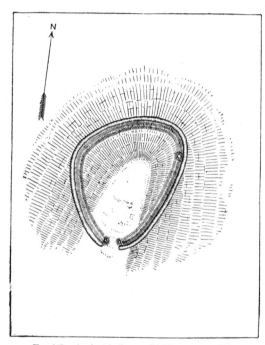

east entrances of the Octagon was determined, resulting in a fall of 3.1 feet at the latter. From this point the parallel embankments could be followed 3,970 feet. The course was found to be due east this entire distance, and continuing the direction after it could no longer be traced the creek terrace was reached, at a point Station 13, where it had evidently been artificially hollowed to produce a descent less abrupt and steep. From this point, Station 13, a continuation of the course due east to the creek would strike the thickest settled part of the town. A deflection

FIG. 317.—Ancient inclosure. Licking county, Ohio.

was therefore made here, N. 70° E. 1,503 feet, to Raccoon creek, the level of which was determined to be 47.16 feet below the level of the southeast entrance of the Octagon.

THE MOORE AND COULTER INCLOSURE.

This inclosure, shown in Fig. 317, is on the lands of Messrs. P. F. Coulter and Thomas Moore, 6½ miles southeast of Newark, on the southeast side of the road leading to Flint ridge. It is located on a hill that is cut off in every direction from the surrounding height, thus rendering the position an admirable one for defense. It is an earthen wall with the unusual feature of an outside ditch from which the dirt was taken to form the wall. The form, as shown in the figure, is an oval, with the larger end northward and a single gateway at the smaller end—southern. This entrance is on a level space and is 89 feet wide.

The wall varies in width from 16 to 20 feet; height on the inside from 1 to 2 feet and on the outside to the bottom of the ditch from 3 to 5 feet. The ditch in some places presents no outer bank, having been dug apparently only for the purpose of increasing the distance to the top of the wall, thus rendering access to the inclosure more difficult.

The entire circuit of the wall, exclusive of the gateway, is 2,176 feet, the greatest width 675 feet, and greatest length 785 feet. On every side, except in front of the gateway, the ground slopes directly from the ditch to the bottom of the hill. There are three small mounds connected with it, one at each side of the gateway and one partly on the wall near the northeastern extremity.

The three following mounds are plainly visible from the level space in front of the gateway. The large mound near the Amsterdam church, S. 48° W., distance 2½ miles; the large "Stone mound," S. 62° E., three-fourths of a mile; and another, S. 30° W., half a mile away.

STONE FORT ON FLINT RIDGE.

This inclosure, 8 miles southeast of Newark, is located on the point of an elongate level space about a mile in length. It is composed, with the exception of a short space on the east side, where it is chiefly earth, of flint blocks gathered from the out-

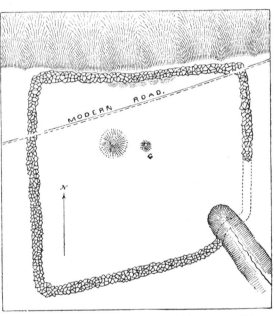

Fig. 318.—Stone fort on Flint ridge, Licking county, Ohio.

crops in the immediate vicinity, and is of the form shown in Fig. 318. The length of the north wall (the measurements in all cases being to the middle line) is 603 feet; of the eastern wall to the edge of the ravine at the southeast corner, 422 feet; of the south wall from the ravine to the southwest corner, 511 feet; of the west wall, 607 feet. Width of the wall varies from 20 to 30 feet; present height, from 1 to 2 feet.

There are two included and two exterior mounds (the latter not shown in the figure), the larger one, on the inside, being a little over 100 feet in diameter and about 15 feet high; the others, small, varying from 20 to 30 feet in diameter and from 1 to 3 feet in height. The area inclosed is about 7 acres.

This structure, shown in Fig. 319 is located partly on the SE. $\frac{1}{4}$ of section 17 and partly on the NE. $\frac{1}{4}$ of sec. 20, T. 7, R. 16, about three-quarters of a mile southeast of the town of Glenford. It stands

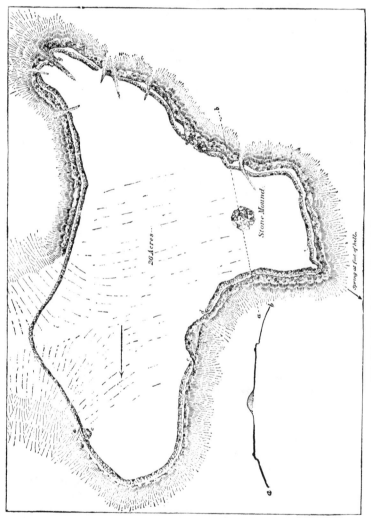

FIG. 319.—Stone fort near Glenford, Perry county, Ohio.

on a peninsular projection, or spur of a hill, about 300 feet above the creek, on the west. The wall follows the margin of the bluffs which form the three sides of the spur, and which, for some 6 to 10 feet of their upper portion, consist of rock with perpendicular face. The wall consists of rough stones laid up without order and varies in height from mere traces across the level area at the east to 5 and 6 feet, the highest portion, at the southeast and northwest. There are several breaks in it at points where it is crossed by little ravines, some of which may have been formed since it was constructed. At f a large piece of the rock across which it ran has moved out and downward several feet, and the break was repaired by filling in with stones; at c–d it passes below the margin of the bluff and over a considerable space of the descent. Why this was done, when it would have been as easily carried around the top, is a question difficult to answer. At e it crosses directly over a large bowlder. It is probable there was a gateway somewhere on the level area at the east, but the wall has been so much disturbed in this portion that it is impossible to decide this point now.

There is a well-marked gateway at the southeast corner (g). At the corner northwest of the mound the wall is much lower than on the adjacent sides. This was probably a crossing place on the way to the spring at the foot of the hill, though the descent for the first few feet is somewhat rough; yet we passed up at this point without much difficulty. The entire length of the wall, following all the curves and bends, is 6,610 feet, and the area embraced about 26 acres.

In the western portion is a stone mound slightly over 100 feet in diameter and 12 feet high. The section ($a\,b$) shown at the left passes through

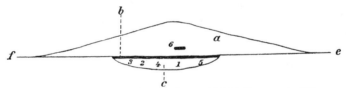

Fig. 320.—Section of the Cryder mound, near Adelphi, Ross county, Ohio.

this mound. All the stones of which the wall is built seem to have been gathered from the area within the inclosure and above the rocky margins of the bluffs. The inclosed area has been under cultivation for a number of years.

ROSS COUNTY.

THE CRYDER MOUND.

This is situated on the SE. ¼ of Sec. 1, T. 10, R. 20, on the farm of Mr. Frank Cryder, near Adelphi. It stands on a spur 60 feet above the level of the valley, is of the ordinary conical form, 32 feet in diameter and 2½ feet high, though much worn down by the plow. Mr. Cryder says it was formerly surrounded by a ditch, but without the corresponding wall like that in the Davis works. It was composed entirely of the red clay of the surrounding soil.

Previous to its erection, a circular basin-shaped excavation (c, Fig. 320) was made in the original soil, 13 feet in diameter and 2 feet deep. In this were the remains of five charred skeletons (1, 2, 3, 4, and 5) with coals and ashes about them. The skeletons (the flesh having been removed) had probably been folded or bundled before burial, the few fragments of skulls found being near the center of the piles. The entire bottom of the pit was covered 2 inches deep with coals and ashes.

Over the bones and ashes was a layer (*b*) of blue clay, which filled the pit about even with the original surface of the ground. Six inches above this, near the center of the mound, was a small quantity of burnt human bones, the remains of a single skeleton (6). These appear to have been burnt where they lay. With skeleton No. 3 in the pit were two stone gorgets and a stone tube. The letters *f e* indicate the original surface, and *a* the mass of the mound.

THE HOPETON WORKS.[1]

Neither the parallel walls nor the smaller circles can now be traced. The walls reached the bank of the terrace just over an overflowed bottom, and the river is now but a short distance away to the left. The large circle is much flattened on the eastern side. It reaches to the foot of and slightly up the slope of the terrace above. If continued with the same curve it has at the other parts, it would run up nearly to the top of the slope. Numerous low places exist about the entire work, where earth may have been removed to the depth of a foot. These may, however, be in great part natural. A considerable amount of dirt must have been taken from the bluff above, both at the points marked by Squier and Davis and at the ravine, or wash, opposite the junction of the circle and square. There would be no difficulty in getting clay at the bluffs or at the ravine to the southeast of the works. The walls of the square, so far as examined, are of the same material as the soil around—a mixture of sand, gravel, and clay. At the northwest corner of the square the opening is partly filled up, the lowest point at the end of the western wall being about a foot above the natural surface, rising and widening gradually from that place to the top of the northern wall, resembling somewhat a graded way on a small scale.

A resurvey of the circle and square was made by Mr. Middleton, on behalf of the Bureau, in 1888, the notes of which are as follows:

The only parts of this group we notice here are the large circle and the connected square.

These works are situated on the general level of the Scioto valley, designated by Squier and Davis "The Second Terrace," which here stands about 30 feet above the river level. The walls of the circle and square are yet generally distinct and, with the exception of a single break in the circle and one or two slight ones in the square, can be readily traced. In fact, the wall of the square is yet 5 feet high. The circle is more worn, the western half averaging about 2 feet high, while the eastern half is lower, fading out for a short distance near the northeast corner of the square. They are situated close to the foot of the bluff, which forms the slope to the upper level, here between 30 and 40 feet above that on which the work stands. As will be

---

[1] Squier & Davis. Anc. Mon., Pl. XVII.

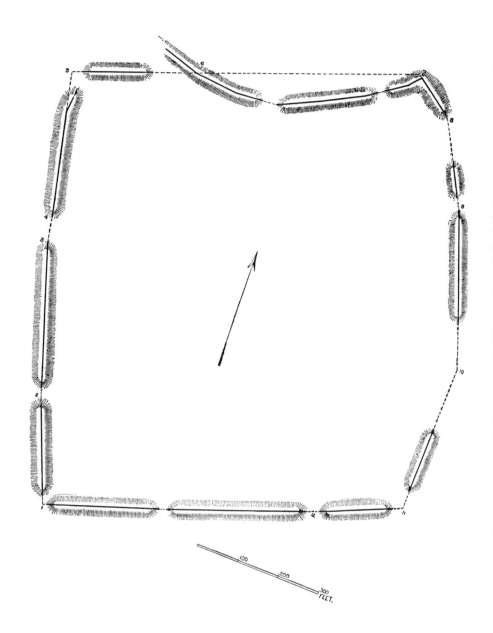

SQUARE OF HOPETON WORKS, ROSS COUNTY, OHIO.

seen by reference to the plate in Ancient Monuments, instead of a passageway between the circle and square the two are here in direct contact, part of the circular wall forming a large portion of the north line of the square.

The resurvey in this case began with station 1, at the intersection of the two adjoining lines of wall, at the southwest corner. (Pl. XXXV.)

Station.	Bearing.	Distance.	Remarks.
		Feet.	
1 to 2	N. 20° 17′ W ..	244	To center of first gateway.
2 to 3	N. 17° 10′ W ..	336·5	To end of wall at second gateway.
3 to 4	N. 8° W.......	55·5	Across the second gateway.
4 to 5	N. 12° 02′ W ..	324	To intersection at northwest corner of the square.
5 to 6	N. 70° 27′ E ...	283	To the wall of circle.
6 to 7	N. 70° 27′ E ...	508	To the intersection at northeast corner of square.
7 to 8	S. 54° E	115	To first gateway.
8 to 9	S. 27° E	207	To second gateway.
9 to 10	S. 19° E	355	To gateway of small circle.
10 to 11	S. 2° W	331	To intersection at southeast corner.
11 to 12	S. 68° W	201	To first gateway.
12 to 13	S. 71° 21′ W ...	340	To second gateway.
13 to 1	S. 72° 25′ W ...	285	To place of beginning.

Commencement on the south side, at station *a* (6 in plat of square), where the circle connects with the wall of the square. (Pl. XXXVI.)

Station 6 (a) to—	Bearing.	Distance.	Width of wall.	Remarks.
		Feet.	Feet.	
14........	N. 71° 53′ W ..	100	42	
15........	N. 63° 39′ W ..	100	38	
16........	N. 55° 29′ W ..	100	40	
17........	N. 41° W......	100	42	
18........	N. 25° 21′ W ..	100	44	
19........	N. 12° 20′ W ..	100	45	
20........	N. 0° 30′ E	100	44	
21........	N. 14° 52′ E ...	100	46	
22........	N. 22° 40′ E ...	100	42	
23........	N. 33° 28′ E ...	100	41	
24........	N. 47° 57′ E ...	100	40	}Outer half of wall obliterated.
25........	N. 55° 57′ E ...	100	43	
26........	N. 63° 45′ E ...	100	40	
27........	N. 78° 22′ E ...	100	40	
28........	S. 86° 04′ E....	100	•45	
29........	S. 81° 24′ E....	100	40	Base outlines not easily traced.
30........	S. 64° 05′ E....	100	36	Do.
31........	S. 53° 27′ E....	100	....	Outlines obliterated. Width not ascertained.

Station 31 to—	Bearing.	Distance.	Width of wall.	Remarks.
		Feet.	*Feet.*	
32........	S. 46° 20′ E....	100	36	
33........	S. 40° 15′ E....	100	....	Outlines obliterated. Width not ascertained.
34........	S. 20° 16′ E....	100	30	Outlines not easily traced.
35........	S. 5° 32′ E ...	100	30	Do.
36........	S. 4° 10′ W ..	100	38	Do.
37........	S. 16° 48′ W ..	100	39	Station on end of wall.
38........	S. 31° 56′ W ..	100	....	Wall obliterated between stations 37 and 38.
39........	S. 42° W......	100	48	18 feet from the end of wall of square.
40........	S. 57° 11′ W ..	100	41	
41........	S. 63° 35′ W ..	100	43	
42........	S. 65° 31′ W ..	100	40	Station on end of wall at gateway. Gateway 35 feet wide.
43........	S. 86° 11′ W ..	100	41	
To 6	N. 84° 32′ W ..	98	40	

CHECK LINES.

6 to 20 .	N. 38° 35′ W ..	634
6 to 28 .	N. 10° 09′ E ...	968·5
6 to 36 .	N. 57° 17′ E ...	726
20 to 28 .	N. 51° 04′ E ...	723
20 to 36 .	S. 84° 09′ E ...	1, 015
28 to 36 .	S. 38° 37′ E ...	711

These inclosures are drawn to a regular scale in Pls. XXXV and XXXVI. It is apparent from Pl. XXXV, which represents the square according to the resurvey, that the form given in Ancient Monuments, Pl. XVII, is erroneous in that it is much more regular than the facts warrant. Neither side is straight, nor is there a right angle at any point. It is not regular in any sense, but was doubtless intended for a square. Measuring the direct lines from corner to corner the lengths are as follows: That from stations 1 to 5 is 957 feet; from 5 to 7, 791 feet; from 7 to 11 is 962 feet, and from 11 to 1 is 825 feet. Messrs. Squier and Davis say it is a rectangle with a length of 950 feet and a width of 900 feet.

The circular inclosure (Pl. XXXVI) varies considerably from a true figure, the east and west diameter being 1,018 feet, while that running north and south is only 960 feet, the difference between the two being 58 feet. Nor is the curve uniform, being much sharper at some points than at others. It embraces a little less than 18 acres.

CEDAR BANK WORKS. [1]

The high bank on the river side is easy of ascent. The dirt is loose and so affords a good foothold, although the bank is as steep as the nature of the material will allow. Were the timber and brush removed, so that the looser soil could be washed off, the case might be different.

---

[1] Squier and Davis: Anc. Mon., Pl. XVIII.

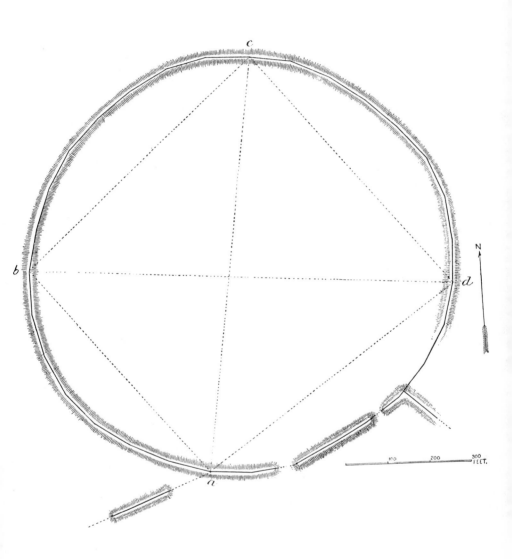

CIRCLE OF HOPETON WORKS, ROSS COUNTY, OHIO.

Below is a low bottom, subject to overflow, covered with a thick growth of small maples and sycamores, with some trees of other species. Beyond this bottom the river is reached, at a point where it forms a pool 300 feet wide with a riffle above and one below, giving several hundred yards of smooth water, seemingly a good place for fish. The river may have formed all this lower bottom since the construction of the works. There is an oak tree 5 feet in diameter growing on the south line of the embankment a short distance east of the entrance. There has been ample time in the lifetime of this tree for the river to form all the low ground.

Apparently there never was any wall along the west side, for if the river did not touch at the foot of the bluff when the work was constructed, the bluff could not have caved in to the extent indicated; and if it did touch it there would have been no necessity for a wall, as the bank would have been almost perpendicular.

The supposed "graded way" to the water is only the ravine formed by the drainage of part of the field above, and is now more difficult of ascent than any part of the steep bank. If ever used as a pathway, it had to be reworked and smoothed down after every heavy rain. There may have been a road or pathway, now obliterated, cut along one side of it, but that it is a natural ravine is beyond question.

At the bluff the south wall and ditch seem to have extended farther out than the present edge of the bank; but the small amount of wear necessary to cut the bank away to give this appearance could well result from the drainage through the ditch, as the soil here is gravelly and quite loose. The north wall stops at about 30 and the ditch at about 50 feet from the edge of the bluff.

There is no stream here known as "Dry run"; the meaning probably is "a dry run"; but the meaning is immaterial, as there is no run of any kind at the line so marked. Prairie run has a northeast trend along the level, a short distance north of the work. At the northeast corner the ditch makes a bend toward the south and extends for 90 feet to the break of the bank over the so-called "Dry run." There was no ravine on the east side when the embankment was made; the natural slope is toward the north along this line and the water running through the ditch has deepened and widened it; and being reenforced by that from the northern ditch, the combined streams overflowing near this corner have cut a channel to Prairie run. That portion of the ditch at the northeast corner, on the east, is filled up, but its course around the foot of the wall is easily seen. That a sufficient amount of water could collect to cut out such a course is shown by the height to which the drift is piled against the bushes now growing here. Still, it would require a long time for such a channel to wear, and this aids in giving an appearance of greater antiquity to this work than seems to attach to the others in this region. This eastern embankment is nearly, but not quite, straight.* The soil within this inclosure seems less fertile than at the other works; at least the growing corn is not so large or thrifty. An abundance of yellow clay is on the surface of the field to the north, close to the northeast corner of the inclosure. The north and east ditches drain several acres of ground. In the woods on the north side, the greatest elevation of the wall above the bottom of the ditch is about 8 feet.

In regard to the square, flat topped mound to the south of the inclosure, it is to be noted that the topography is not as shown in the plate. The point on which it is situated does not reach out to the terrace below, the ravines on the two sides uniting before going that far and allowing only a narrow strip of the bottom to be seen from the mound, which is lower than the ground to either side of the main ravine below; a fine view, however, of the valley and the hills beyond can be had from the south side. The point on which the mound stands is smooth and rounded, as stated by Squier and Davis, but no more so than many others similarly formed and situated, and has no indications whatever of having been artificially worked off.

HIGH BANK WORKS.[1]

Between the circle and the square, west of the level area connecting them near c d is an excavation; another is on the other side of the wall within the square.

The smaller circles and parallels are about effaced. Those farthest south can be partially traced. The wing wall from the smallest one (in the group marked A) to the bluff, has been plowed away; the larger circle, however, and its wing wall can be seen, and it is plain that the latter is only an irregularly curved embankment running out to the bluff, and was never continuous on a part of the terrace that has disappeared.

CIRCLE.

The walls of the circle and octagon are still quite prominent and are respectively 2 and 5 feet high.

This circle is very similar in size and other respects to the " observatory circle" at Newark, and, like that, is connected with an octagon, though the relative sizes of the two inclosures differ in this respect— the octagon of the Newark works is larger than the circle, while that of the High bank works is smaller than the circle. We see in this group the tendency to combine circles, octagon, and parallels as at Newark, making it probable that the works at both points are due to one people. According to Messrs. Squier and Davis, this circle is a perfect one, the diameter being 1,050 feet, which, as will be seen by what follows, agrees very closely with the result of the resurvey.

[1] Squier and Davis. Plate XVI.

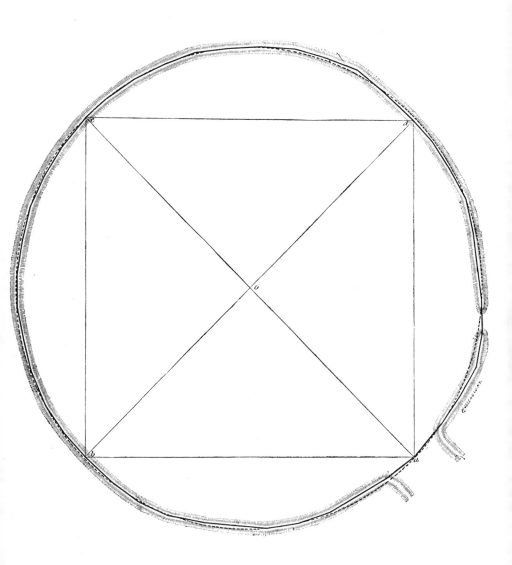

CIRCLE OF HIGH BANK WORKS, ROSS COUNTY, OHIO.

The notes of the resurvey are as follows, commencing in the center of the gateway leading to the octagon:

Stations.	Bearing.	Distance.	Width of wall.
		Feet.	*Feet.*
1 to 2	S. 62° 37′ W ..	75	30
2 to 3	S. 66° 38′ W ..	75	30
3 to 4	S. 68° W	75	32
4 to 5	S. 80° 34′ W ..	75	44
5 to 6	N. 89° 30′ W ..	75	40
6 to 7	N. 78° 18′ W ..	75	32
7 to 8	N. 75° 30′ W ..	75	33
8 to 9	N. 66° 30′ W ..	75	34
9 to 10	N. 57° 28′ W ..	75	34
10 to 11	N. 45° W	75	34
11 to 12	N. 41° W	75	39
12 to 13	N. 34° 14′ W ..	75	42
13 to 14	N. 26° 10′ W ..	75	44
14 to 15	N. 15° W	75	44
15 to 16	N. 7° 30′ W ..	75	40
16 to 17	N. 3° 36′ W ..	75	44
17 to 18	N. 8° E	75	36
18 to 19	N. 16° 35′ E...	75	40
19 to 20	N. 22° E	75	34
20 to 21	N. 34° E	75	32
21 to 22	N. 40° E	75	32
22 to 23	N. 47° 15′ E...	75	38
23 to 24	N. 58° 30′ E...	75	34
24 to 25	N. 63° 38′ E...	75	36
25 to 26	N. 75° E	75	34
26 to 27	N. 78° E	75	35
27 to 28	S. 88° E	75	32
28 to 29	S. 85° E	75	30
29 to 30	S. 77° E	75	30
30 to 31	S. 64° 39′ E...	75	32
31 to 32	S. 61° 52′ E...	75	28
32 to 33	S. 42° 48′ E...	75	32
33 to 34	S. 40° E	75	30
34 to 35	S. 35° E	75	34
35 to 36	S. 26° E	75	32
36 to 37	S. 21° 45′ E...	75	28
37 to 38	S. 4° 45′ E...	75	26
38 to 39	S. 2° E	75	32
39 to 40	S. 0° 30′ W ..	75	30
40 to 41	S. 6° 14′ W .. ·	75	26
41 to 42	S. 19° W......	75	28
42 to 43	S. 39° W......	75	30
43 to 44	S. 43° 30′ W ..	75	30
44 to 45	S. 47° 25′ W ..	75	....
45 to 1	S. 48° 49′ W ..	21.5	....

SUPPLEMENTARY.

		Feet.			*Feet.*
a to b ...	N. 81° 20′ W ..	744	b to c ...		746
a to c ...	N. 36° 28′ W ..	1,056	c to d ...		743
a to d ...	N. 8° E	741	b to d ...		1,042
a to e ...	S. 36° E.......	(*)	(*)		(*)

* Direction of entrance to Octagon.

Plotting the figure carefully from these notes, and then drawing the nearest possible coincident circle, we obtain results similar to those obtained by the survey of the Observatory circle at Newark. This is shown in Pl. XXXVII. In this plate the solid black line of short chords running along the middle of the wall marks the actual line of survey, while the dotted line is the nearest approximate circle, the center of which is at the intersection of the two designated diameters.[1] These diameters are actually surveyed lines and relate to the line of chords. The middle of that running from d to b is at the intersection, but the middle of that running from a to c is about 2 feet from the intersection toward c.

As it is impossible to show this satisfactorily in a figure on the scale given here, the attention of the reader is called to the following facts, which he can verify independently by making for himself the plat on a larger scale from the notes given above relating to the High Bank circle.

(1) The chords forming the sides of the inclosed quadrilateral subtend equal arcs of the surveyed line; that is to say, the distance along the wall from a to b is equal to that from b to c, also to that from c to d and from d to a; the distance in each case being 830.4 feet or one-fourth of the circumference according to the survey. As these chords are, respectively 744, 746, 743, and 741 feet in length, showing an extreme variation of less than 3 feet from a medium and of but 3 feet from a true quadrant, we have an evidence of the close approximation to a true circle.

(2) The extreme difference between the various diameters (except at the eccentric point at the southeast, between the gateways) does not exceed 8 feet, or a variation from the medium of 4 feet, and from that of the true circle of little more than 5 feet.

(3) A circle with a radius of 526 feet and center at the intersection of the two given diameters varies at no point from the surveyed line (except at the eccentric point in the southeast) more than 6 feet; or, in other words, both would fall on a wall only 6 feet wide.

It is evident, therefore, that we have here a very close approximation to a true circle.

OCTAGON.

The Octagon at this point (see Pl. XXXVIII) differs from that at Newark chiefly in size and closer approximation to a square. The variation from the usual form resulting from throwing the southern gateway along the wall between the angles is readily accounted for by the fact that there is here a somewhat abrupt depression which is avoided by the curve given the wall. The field notes of the resurvey are as follows, commencing at station 1 in the middle of the gateway leading to the circle:

---

[1] The actual scale on the plate (which was accidentally omitted) is 200 feet to the inch.

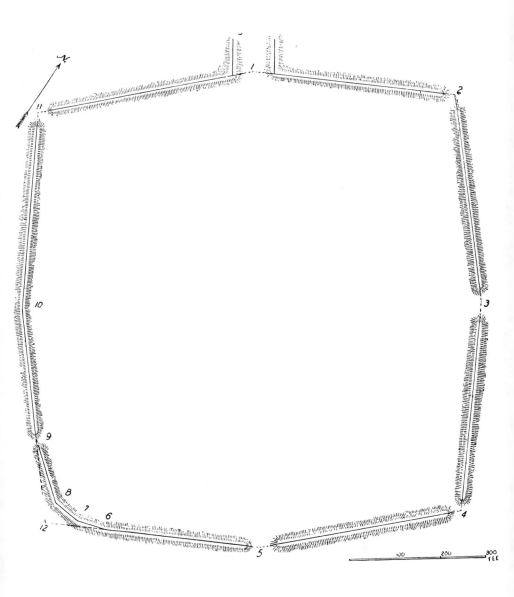

OCTAGON OF HIGH BANK WORKS, ROSS COUNTY, OHIO.

Station.	Bearing.	Distance.	Station.	Bearing.	Distance.
		Feet.			Feet.
1 to 2 ...	N. 60° 03' E ...	448	8 to 9 .	N. 53° 37' W ..	144
2 to 3 ...	S. 43° 50' E....	449	9 to 10 .	N. 42° 57' W ..	278
3 to 4 ...	S. 30° 17' E....	442	10 to 11 .	N. 31° 27 W ..	417
4 to 5 ...	S. 44° 15' W...	449	11 to 11 .	N. 43° 27' E ...	482
5 to 6 ..	S. 60° 43' W...	340	5 to 12 .	S. 60° 43' W...	470
6 to 7 ...	S. 70° 41' W...	65	12 to 10 .	N. 42° 57' W ..	453
7 to 8 ...	N. 86° 45' W ..	60			

The lengths of the sides, diameters, and diagonals, ascertained from a carefully drawn plat of large scale, are as follows:

	Feet.		Feet.
From 11 to 2	908	From 1 to 5	1,008
From 2 to 4	883	From 3 to 10	1,005
From 4 to 12	910	From 4 to 11	1,250
From 12 to 11	868	From 2 to 12	1,272

The inner angles are as follows:

At station 1	163° 24'	At station 5	163° 32'
At station 2	103 53	At station 12	103 40
At station 3	166 27	At station 10	168 30
At station 4	105 28	At station 11	105 06

It is apparent from these figures and from the plat (Pl. XXXVIII) that this inclosure is comparatively regular, the opposite angles, with one exception, differing less than half a degree and the exceptional one differing from its opposite but 2 degrees. Nevertheless the regularity is not such as would be expected from the use of instruments.

The diameter as given by Messrs. Squier and Davis is 950 feet, and the area, according to their calculation, is 18 acres. According to the resurvey the diameter in one direction (measuring to the intersections of the middle lines of the walls) is 1,008 feet and in the other 1,005. That Messrs. Squier and Davis are to be understood as counting to the middle of the walls, is to be inferred from the fact that the diameter of the circle was evidently measured in this way. Assuming they were correct in reference to the circle, it follows of necessity that their measurements of the octagon are erroneous, the diameter given being 50 feet too short and the area 2.6 acres too small; 20.6 acres being the true area.

LIBERTY TOWNSHIP WORKS.[1]

The smaller circle is not as nearly complete as shown in the plate. Instead of continuing around the head of the ravine and joining the larger circle at the right of the entrance, it comes to a stop on the bank of a ravine at a point 313 feet south of the point where it connects with the larger circle at the north or left side of the entrance. No trace of it can now be seen between these points. The entrance is still in the

[1] Squier and Davis, Pl. xx.

timber, and a fence crosses the head of the ravine between this timber and the cleared land to the south. If the circle had ever gone as far as represented it seems that it would have been preserved here, as is true of the wall on the opposite side of the gateway. Possibly the missing portion has been worn away.

The large circle is obliterated and the curved lines between the smaller circle and the square can be traced only partially.

The line indicating north and south on the plate should be changed 90 degrees, the top of the plate being east, and the directions given on the plate should be made to correspond with this change.

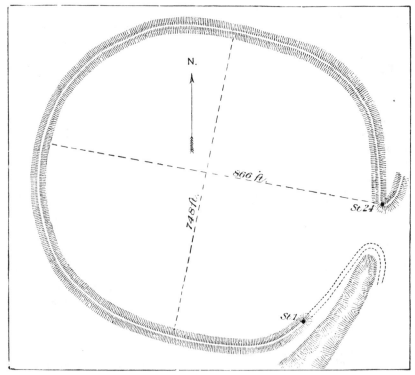

N.

866 ft.

748 ft.

St. 24

St. 1

FIG. 321.—Small circle, Liberty township works, Ross county, Ohio.

On the side next the pike the wall of the square can not be traced The opposite side and most of the other two are still plainly visible; the cross walls, however, disappear before they reach the one next to the pike. But, this portion being covered with clover and weeds, it is possible some traces were hidden; if it had been freshly plowed perhaps the lines could have been found all the way.

At the north corner (the one toward the left side of Squier and Davis's plate) the ends are worn away, and at the south corner both walls are covered with brush, so that the exact length of the northeast side could not be found. The angles at the north and east corners were obtained by taking the bearings of the three lines. These may be slightly in error, as owing to long cultivation it is impossible to tell with certainty where the center of the embankment was; but by placing the instrument as near the center as could be determined, about midway of the length, and placing the rod the same way near each end, the error will be very slight; not more than a few minutes.

Great care was taken in measuring the smaller circle, as on it Squier and Davis appear to base their claim to the mathematical accuracy of the works constructed by the "Mound-builders."

In order to prove this accuracy they present a supplementary plan on the plate, showing their method of determining the curves, and in a footnote on the following page give the lengths of the arcs and the directions. It is somewhat disappointing to find, on carefully examining this showing, that it relates wholly to a hypothetical case, and not to a circle actually surveyed. This is apparent from the following facts: The circumference of the circle, given as an illustration, is 3,600 feet and the diameter 1,146 feet, which agrees with no circle given in their entire work. Had they given an illustration from an actual survey it would have been much more satisfactory.

The courses and distances of Mr. Middleton's survey of the smaller circle of this group are inserted here, made after the plan Squier and Davis suggest, but with shorter chords; also the plat made therefrom (Fig. 321). The place of beginning is at station 1, the course southwest, westward, and so on around.

The small circle.

Stations.	Bearing.	Distance.	Differences between chords.		
		Feet.			
1 to 2	S. 60° W	100	....		
2 to 3	S. 81° 35' W ...	100	Between 1st and 2d	21°	35'
3 to 4	S. 84° 44' W ...	100	Between 2d and 3d	3	09
4 to 5	N. 74° 45' W ..	100	Between 3d and 4th	20	31
5 to 6	N. 70° W	100	Between 4th and 5th	4	45
6 to 7	N. 59° 16' W ..	100	Between 5th and 6th	10	44
7 to 8	N. 42° W	100	Between 6th and 7th	17	16
8 to 9	N. 24° 23' W ..	100	Between 7th and 8th	17	37
9 to 10	N. 12° 48' W ..	100	Between 8th and 9th	11	35
10 to 11	N. 5° 47' E	100	Between 9th and 10th	18	35
11 to 12	N. 20° 30' E ...	100	Between 10th and 11th	14	43
12 to 13	N. 34° 24' E ...	100	Between 11th and 12th	13	54
13 to 14	N. 53° 52' E ...	100	Between 12th and 13th	19	28
14 to 15	N. 67° 05' E ...	100	Between 13th and 14th	13	13
15 to 16	N. 84° 23' E ...	100	Between 14th and 15th	17	18
16 to 17	S. 81° 08' E	100	Between 15th and 16th	14	29
17 to 18	S. 73° 38' E	100	Between 16th and 17th	7	30
18 to 19	S. 71° 02' E	100	Between 17th and 18th	2	36
19 to 20	S. 65° 05' E	100	Between 18th and 19th	5	57
20 to 21	S. 39° 46' E	100	Between 19th and 20th	25	19
21 to 22	S. 20° 45' E	100	Between 20th and 21st	19	01
22 to 23	S. 7° 50' E	100	Between 21st and 22d	12	55
23 to 24	S. 0° 58' W	30	....		
24 to 1	S. 32° 20' W ...	313	....		

As will be seen by reference to these figures and the diagram, not only is the curve irregular, but the diameters differ so much in length, one being 866 feet and the other 748 feet, that the figure is much nearer an ellipse than a true circle. These evidences of error in the statements and plates of Messrs. Squier and Davis's work and manifest tokens of carelessness have a tendency to lessen somewhat our confidence in their statements as to measurements and dimensions, although the figures of the works they personally examined are generally correct as to form.

THE SQUARE.

This inclosure, shown in Pl. XXXIX, presents quite a regular figure, closely approximating a square. The notes of the survey are as follows, commencing at station *a*, the southern corner. The stations are at the intersections of the lines of the walls:

Station.	Bearing.	Distance.
		Feet.
a to *b* ...	N. 47° 14′ E ...	1, 108
b to *c* ...	N. 42° 41′ W ..	1, 106
c to *d* ...	S. 47° 06′ W ...	1, 110
d to *e* ...	S. 44° 11′ E	535
e to *a* ...	S. 41° 24′ E	568
e to *f* ...	S. 41° 24′ W ...	521
f to *g* ...	N. 84° 10′ W ..	185

A direct line from *a* to *d* runs N. 42° 52′ W. exactly 1,100 feet. The survey was, in fact, made by triangulation, the angles being as follows:

At *a* (*e a b*)	88°	38′
At *b* (*a b c*)	90	05
At *c* (*b c d*)	89	47
At *d* (*c d e*)	88	43
At *e* (*d e a*)	182	47

The angles at *a* and *d*, using the direct line between them, are as follows:

At *a* (*d a b*)	90°	06′
At *d* (*c d a*)	90	02

The following are the check lines:

	Feet.
Diagonal from *a* to *c*, N. 3° 40′ E	1, 566
Diagonal from *b* to *d*	1, 561
Diameter running northeast and southwest	1, 095
Distance between *a* and *d*	1, 102
Diameter running northwest and southeast	1, 104

The diameters are measured from the middle of the gateways in the sides.

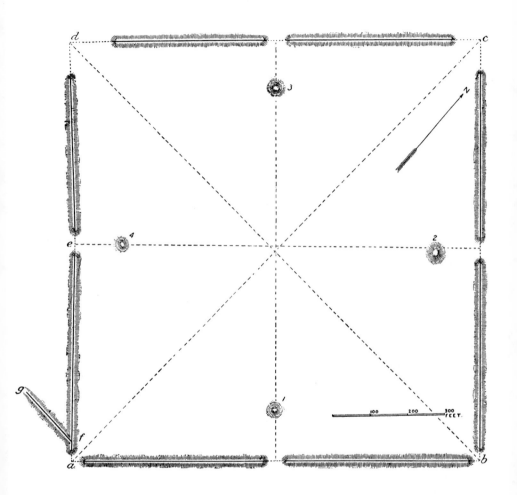

SQUARE OF LIBERTY TOWNSHIP WORKS, ROSS COUNTY, OHIO.

THE BAUM WORKS.

Although a complete resurvey of these works was made, it is not thought necessary to introduce here the notes relating to any part except the square. It may be said, however, that the resurvey of the circular portion revealed no very essential variation from the figure given in Ancient Monuments, Pl. XXI, No. 1.

The square, most of which has long been in a pasture, is rather more distinct and prominent than such remains usually are, the walls being from 2 to 4 feet high, and the gateways well marked, though no traces of the inclosed mounds remain. The circular portions of the works are much worn and two sections of considerable length are so nearly obliterated that the line can not be traced with any certainty.

Mr. Middleton's field notes relating to the square are as follows, commencing at station *a* at the western corner:

Station.	Bearing.	Distance.	Width of wall.	Whole length of sides.
		Feet.	Feet.	Feet.
a to b ...	N. 59° 17′ E ...	551	49	1,108
b to c ...	N. 59° 17′ E ...	557	56	
c to d ...	S. 30° 12′ E....	561	50	1,129
d to e ...	S. 30° 12′ E....	568	35	
e to f....	S. 59° 44′ W...	556	33	1,113
f to g ...	S. 59° 44′ W...	557	33	
g to h ...	N. 29° 56′ W ..	560	56	1,117
h to a ...	N. 29° 56′ W ..	557	57	

For the arm leading to the large circle (given only in part here) begin at station *c* at the north corner of the square and run as follows:

S. 30° 12′ E. 102 ft.; S. 81° E. 54 ft.; S. 63° 21′ E. 50 ft.; S. 52° 21′ E. 50 ft.; S. 64° E. 145 ft.

CHECK LINES.

h to d ...	N. 59° 27′ E ...	1,112
g to c ...	N. 14° 29′ E ...	1,584
b to f....	S. 30° E	1,124

The angles at the corners are—

a .... 90° 47′   e .... 90° 04′
c .... 89 20   g 89 40

It is apparent from these notes and Pl. XL, representing this inclosure, that it approximates very closely a true square. The greatest variation at the corner from a right angle is only 47 minutes. The average length of the sides is 1,117 feet, from which the extreme variation is only 12 feet, the difference between extremes being but 21 feet.

As the structure and contents of the few mounds which appear to be connected with these works may have some bearing on the question of the origin, age, and uses of the circles and squares, the description will be given here of one connected with the Baum works just mentioned, which are those figured in No. 1, Pl. XXI, Ancient Monuments. The mound referred to is that designated in this figure as a "Square pyramidal mound." It was carefully explored by my assistant, Mr. Henry L. Reynolds, whose report is as follows:

This mound is distant from the nearest gateway of the circle, N. 21° 30′ W., 1,420 feet. In the work of Messrs. Squier and Davis the height is given as 15 feet and diameter 125 feet. Its height at the time of this exploration was 12 feet above the level of the surrounding surface, and its diameter from 135 to 140 feet. This difference is due to the annual disturbance of its surface by plow and freshet. The same agencies have likewise destroyed its pyramidal form, and it resembles now an upturned wash basin. The mound was composed for the most part of clay mottled considerably with black loam and slightly in some places with patches of a grayish plastic lime. Cross trenches were run due north and south and east and west, respectively. The breadth of these at the side was from 5 to 6 feet, but as they penetrated inward they widened gradually, so that at the center the excavation became 13 feet in diameter. Considerable lateral digging was done from these trenches to uncover skeletons and other indications appearing in their sides.

Two series of upright postmolds, averaging 5 inches in diameter, equidistant 10 inches, and forming a perfect circle 36 feet in diameter, constitute a preeminent feature of this mound. Within these circular palings the mound was penetrated systematically by thin seams of fine sand sagging in the center and averaging 1 foot apart. Resting upon the natural black loam at the bottom, timbers averaging 8 inches in diameter radiated from the center, and in the south and west trenches were noticed to extend continuously to the posts. These timbers were detected, for the most part, by their burnt remains and also by the molds of dark earth in the yellow clay, produced by the decomposition of wood. Directly over these timbers was a horizontal line of decayed and burnt wood, but mostly decayed, averaging half an inch thick. The upright postmolds of the lower series were very distinct and measured 5 feet in vertical height. In one was found a small sliver of what appeared to be black walnut. Several of them contained the burnt remains of wood, and in many of these instances the black bark was clinging to the sides.

Separating this from the superstructure, as will be seen by reference to Fig. 322, was a thin, sagging streak of burnt clay. Here and there upon its surface scant traces of black wood ashes were seen, while a

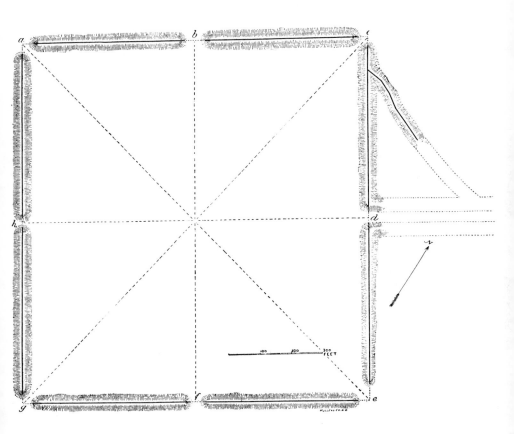

SQUARE OF THE BAUM WORKS, ROSS COUNTY, OHIO.

small quantity of white bone ashes lay scattered upon its western border. This burnt streak overlaid a thin sand seam, below which it seems it could not penetrate. The postmolds of the superstructure consisted of a double row, the outer one being uniformly directly over the lower series in a vertical line, and separated from the latter entirely around the circle by a solid line of gravel. The two rows of the upper structure averaged 18 inches apart. Both might have extended originally above the surface of the mound, since they were discovered between 1½ and 2 feet beneath the surface, which had been considerably plowed. Horizontal timber molds a little smaller in diameter, filled, in places, with charcoal, could be distinctly seen lying against the side of each line of posts at the points shown in the figure. These appear to have been cross beams or stays used for bracing pur-

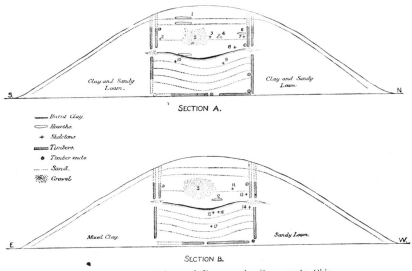

Fig. 322.—Pyramidal mound, Baum works. Ross county, Ohio.

poses. In the eastern trench a gap, 3 feet 2 inches wide, was noticed by the absence of postmolds in both upper and lower series.

All the skeletons discovered were in the area inclosed by these posts. These lay at different depths and in different positions, the favorite or predominant one, at least in the upper portion, being just inside and alongside of the inner circle of palings. The skeletons unearthed were all in a remarkably good state of preservation. None of them could have been intrusively buried, for the stratification above them was not disturbed. All excepting Nos. 15, 16, and 17 lay upon one or another of the thin seams of sand. All except No. 10 lay stretched out at full length. The latter lay partly upon the side, with knees drawn up and head crouched down upon the ribs, as though originally placed in a sitting posture. All except Nos. 13 and 16 had the arms and hands placed at the sides. The right arm of skeleton No. 13 lay bent across the stomach. The right arm of skeleton No. 16 was bent so that the hands touched the chin. From both jaws of this latter skeleton all the teeth had been extracted before interment.

With skeleton No. 1 a bone implement was found at the back of the cranium, and an incised shell and fragments of a jar at the right side of it. With No. 3, which was that of a child about 10 years old, a small clay vessel was found 5 inches behind the cranium. At the left hand of skeleton No. 8 was a shell such as is found in the sands of Paint creek. A bone implement was at the back of the cranium of No. 9. With skeleton No. 11 were found a lot of small semi-perforated shell beads, and two bone implements directly back of the cranium. By the right side of the cranium were the perfect skull and jaws of a wolf, and beneath these were two perforated ornaments of shell. In the right hand was a shell, such as is found in the creek near by, while in the left was a pipe fashioned from stone.

At the right of the feet of this skeleton was the extremity of an oblong ashpit about 4 feet long and 2 feet broad and 1 foot 10 inches in depth. It was filled with white ashes which were evidently those of human bones, since none but human bones could be identified. In these ashes and compactly filled with them was an earthen pot. It lay at the right of the feet of skeleton No. 11. It was lifted out of the ashes with great care, but the weight of its contents and its rotten condition caused it to break in pieces before it could be placed upon the ground. Numerous other pieces of pottery of a similar character were found in these ashes, and it is not improbable, from the indications, that all these ashes were originally placed in pots before interment. A perforated shell disk 2 inches in diameter and a lump of soggy sycamore wood were gathered from the ashes. Neither wood nor shell bore any signs of having been burnt. These ashes could not have been buried intrusively, since the sand layer above them was undisturbed.

Skeleton No. 15 lay 7 feet deep and a half foot below the general burnt streak. It was originally covered with a wooden structure of some kind, for the cores of two red cedar timbers were resting lengthwise upon the body and the burnt remains of probably two others could be plainly seen on each side placed parallel to those upon the body. This red cedar was still sound, but the white wood which envelopes the red cores seemed to be burnt entirely to charcoal. The indications are that these timbers were originally 1 foot above the body, for the earth to that extent over the whole length of the body was very soft. The timbers were noticed to extend slightly beyond the head and feet, while the head upon which they lay was upon its right side. The earth above them was a mixture of clay and fine sand and peculiarly moist. The length of this skeleton to the ankle bones was 6 feet and 1 inch. Two bone implements were found at its head, and at its right side near the head were two fragments of polished tubes and a hollow point of bone which appears to have been shaped with a steel knife

(Fig. 323). Three bone implements were found beneath the right elbow of skeleton No. 13. Skeleton No. 16 corresponded in level and conditions to skeleton No. 15. The timber, however, seemed to have nearly all decayed, since only a few small pieces of red cedar could be gathered and scarcely any traces of black ashes could be seen. The earth, however, for about a foot above was very soft, and two timber molds at this level were distinctly traceable, extending from the direction of the skeleton's side to a foot and a half beyond its feet. Bones of deer and bear, stag antlers, mussel shells, and many fragments of coarse pottery were found in the west trench 9½ feet beyond the postmolds.

It will be observed, if reference is had to the figure, that Nos. 2, 3, 7, and 11 are all upon the same layer, as are also Nos. 9 and 10. Nos. 14, 15, and 16 also correspond in depth, but they did not, like the others, rest upon sand. Fragmentary human bones, disturbed by the plow, were found corresponding in depth to the topmost sand streaks shown in the diagram. Black-walnut timber 4 feet long and lying 5 inches above the general burnt streak was found in a decayed and soaked condition at the point indicated in the figure. One end bore the marks of having been burnt. The soil around it was mostly a moist, dark loam mixed with patches of what has been above described as a grayish plastic lime.

FIG. 323.—Bone implement point from Baum works.

A foot and a half beneath the surface and a little to the southeast of the center a curious double fire-bed or hearth was uncovered. It was about 5 feet in diameter. Uppermost was a layer of white ashes varying from 1 to 2 inches in thickness. They were the ashes of burnt shell and bone, but no bone could be found sufficiently large to determine whether or not it was human. Beneath this was burnt clay from 4 to 5 inches thick, resting upon a layer of sand, which at this point was between 2 and 3 inches deep. The surface of this sand was quite hard. Directly beneath it came another bed of ashes of equal thickness with the one above, and of like composition, except that it contained a quantity of black wood ashes and several broken pieces of pottery. Below this appeared burnt clay again from 4 to 6 inches deep, resting, as before, upon a thin layer of sand.

A hearth somewhat similar to this, but lacking its double feature, lay almost directly beneath this last upon the general burnt streak that has been heretofore described.

This mound is situated upon the edge of the first general bottom from Paint creek, which, though protected by a huge levee, is annually inundated. In overflow times the smaller circle of the adjoining inclosure is almost entirely submerged and the summit of the mound is the only land visible above a broad expanse of water. Around the mound, upon all sides, particularly to the east, are traces of former Indian occupation. Numerous fragments of pottery similar in texture, fabrication, and ornamental features to those found in the mound bestrew the plowed ground. These were intermingled with the valves of mussel shells, pitted stones, shell disks, human bones, arrowheads, pieces of perforated stone gorgets, and a large quantity of chipped flint. Specimens of all were collected and forwarded to Washington with the relics taken from the mound.

THE SEIP WORKS.[1]

A resurvey, so far as possible, was made of the square of this group, the position of the south wall, which is now obliterated, being assumed.

Station a, or beginning point of the survey, is in the northern gateway or passageway into the circle; b is at the northeast corner; c, in the middle gateway of the eastern wall; d, at the southeast corner; e, middle point of the assumed south wall; f, the southwest corner; g, middle gateway of western wall; h, northwest corner. The center line of the walls was followed and the points where these lines crossed were taken as the corners. As the sides are straight the middle station is at the exact half-way point of each line. The result of the survey is as follows:

From—	Bearing.	Distance.
		Feet.
a to b ...	N. 79° 13′ E ...	556½
b to c ...	S. 9° 35′ E	570
c to d ...	S. 9° 35′ E	570
d to e ...	S. 79° 14′ W ...	556½
e to f....	S. 79° 14′ W ...	556½
f to g ...	N. 9° 34′ W ...	570
g to h ...	N. 9° 34′ W ...	570
h to a...	N. 79° 13′ E ...	556½

CHECK LINES.

b to f ...	S. 35° 15′ W...	1,607¼
h to d...	S. 53° 35′ E.....	....
a to e ...	S. 9° 34′ E.....	1,141
g to c ...	N. 79° 12′ E ...	1,113

It will be noticed that the eastern and western sides are 60 feet longer than given in Ancient Monuments. The southeastern and southwestern corners, which are now obliterated, were placed back to correspond with the ratio of the lines in Messrs. Squier and Davis's figure. The length of the walls from corner to corner, according to these authors, was 1,080 feet. This distance, measuring from the northern corner h and b, will throw the south line wholly in the "thoroughfare" or washout shown in their figure. This resurvey, therefore, is to be accepted as reliable only so far as it relates to the northern wall, and the eastern and western walls so far as the latter extend. Of the eastern wall there yet remains distinctly traceable 970 feet from the northeast corner *b*; and of the western wall 990 feet from the northwestern corner *h*. The walls vary in width from 40 to 44 feet.

The relation of the stations in the gateways to the ends of the walls on either side is as follows: From *a* to the end of the wall on the east, 42 feet; on the west, 48; making width of gateway 90 feet; from *h* west 46 feet, south 50 feet; from *c* north 60 feet, south 60 feet; from *g* south 40 feet, north 35 feet; from *h* south 135 feet and east 60 feet.

Part of the large circle, which is too nearly obliterated to be thoroughly traced, was surveyed in order to ascertain the curve, by commencing at station *a* in the northern gateway of the square and running thence to the nearest clearly definable point of the circle, which is numbered station 1.

From —	Bearing.	Distance.
		Feet.
a to 1	N. 19° 29′ E ...	730
1 to 2	N. 4° E	100
2 to 3	N. 1° 38′ E	100
3 to 4	N. 2° 07′ W	100
4 to 5	N. 12° 15′ W ..	100
5 to 6	N. 21° 46′ W ..	100
6 to 7	N. 24° 11′ W ..	100
7 to 8	N. 30° 53′ W ..	100
8 to 9	N. 43° 41′ W ..	100
9 to 10	N. 50° 40′ W ..	100
10 to 11	N. 56° 35′ W ..	100
11 to 12	N. 60° 35′ W ..	100
12 to 13	N. 65° 33′ W ..	100
13 to 14	N. 78° 37′ W ..	100
14 to 15	N. 79° 03′ W ..	100
15 to 16	S. 84° 11′ W ...	100
16 to 17	S. 78° 52′ W ...	100
17 to 1	S. 46° 12′ E	1.346

The square inclosure is on the first or lower bottom, the circle on the second, the difference in elevation being only 5 feet. The figure in Ancient Monuments is incorrect in that it places the square somewhat too far to the east in its relation to the circle.

PIKE COUNTY.

SEAL TOWNSHIP WORKS.[1]

These works are now in Scioto township, Seal township having been divided, and are on the lands of Mr. I N. Barnes. The large circle is about obliterated. The parallels are traceable from the square to the ravine. The south half of the square is quite distinct; the north half

---

[1] Squier and Davis. Pl. XXIV.

has been plowed away. The inclosure A is not exactly as shown; the interior level area is nearly square, but the ditch is not of the same width all around, leaving a level space between it and the embankment, as one would suppose from the sketch. When excavated the ditch was made wider at four alternate parts, so as to give a circular outline around the outside and to leave at the same time a square inclosed area with rounded corners. (See Fig. 324, made from these surveys.) A gravel pit which has been opened on the slope of the terrace west cuts off that part of the embankment almost to the ditch; but the structure of the wall is so much like that of the ground below, that a person ascending from the lower terrace would never suspect its existence until he had reached a point where it can be seen from above, there being no line of demarkation, all having the same appearance. The "wall" shown south of this work, along the edge of the terrace where it bends to the east, can no longer be traced. A ditch has been dug

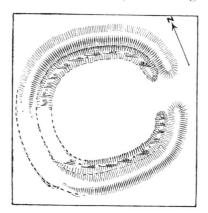

FIG. 324.—Circle *A*, Seal township works.

along near the edge, probably to get dirt for mounds or circles, and the wall, or supposed wall, was probably only the natural earth left outside of this ditch. Its top is not so high as the level just north of the ditch, as shown by Squier and Davis, in section ef, and no higher than along the brow farther east. At the point where the ditch turns north, however, the earth from it has been thrown up to form a wall along its eastern margin, meeting the circle as shown. That there has never been a wall which has been washed away by the river is proven by there being a wide fence row outside the ditch, and the ground along this fence row has been plowed. Mr. Barnes, who remembers when Squier and Davis made their survey, says it was never much higher than now, the slight reduction that has taken place being due to cultivation. He says also that he helped to clear the work having the interior ditch, and its appearance was never essentially different from what it is now.

Between the circle D and the half circle east of it is a place leading down to the next level like those at High Bank, namely, such a depression as would result from the wash of an old path. The half circle extends quite up to the edge of the bluff and the ends have fallen off, showing a section. In the circle D the interior level area is very small compared with the size of the ditch and embankment; the ground begins to slope almost at the entrance.

The work shown in supplementary plan N is a mile above the other group, close to the pike, on land belonging to T. W. Sargent's heirs.

There was a small mound near this which contained charcoal and ashes, but no bones or relics. As a means of correcting the errors made by Messrs. Squier and Davis in the measurements of this work, the result of the Bureau survey is given here.

The lengths of the sides of the square, as shown by the survey, are 854 feet east and west and 852 north and south, being an average of 53 feet greater than Messrs. Squier and Davis's measurements. The work is, however, very nearly an exact square.

According to these authors the parallels running north to the circle are 100 feet apart and 475 feet long. According to the resurvey they are 68 feet apart, measuring to the middle line of each wall, and the average length is 634 feet (the eastern 647 and western 621). The distance from the square to the break of the ravine is 427 feet for the eastern side and 400 for the western, the width of the ravine 110 feet.

THE GRADED WAY.[1]

The excavation along which the walls extend is an old watercourse. Beaver creek comes down from the hills almost directly east of this work and turns south at the foot of the hill, gradually encroaching on the terrace for a few hundred yards, when it is sharply deflected toward the hill again. At this point is an old cut-off, formed when the bed of the creek was much higher than at present, starting out toward the west and curving until it has a direction almost north. It leaves the upper terrace at the level of the second or next lower one and discharges its waters into the slough which extends along the foot of the upper terrace, or perhaps into the river when that had its course along here. This is a measure of its geologic age. It does not seem to have been at anytime a regular channel for the creek, but only a place through which a portion of its surplus water was discharged in time of freshets.

There is a secondary terrace along the west side of this cut-off for about half its length from the northern end; on the east there is a slight terrace for a few hundred feet along the last turn; the east wall, at its southern end, is built along this terrace, but rises to the main level at a short distance. In the other direction (toward the south) the terrace soon disappears.

The west wall is built its entire length on the minor terrace. It is much higher above the ground on which it stands than the eastern wall, though the absolute height of the latter is greater on account of the greater elevation of its foundation. At each end of the east wall there is a small mound. The south end of the west wall is higher and wider for about 100 feet than the other portions, being heaviest at the very end, resembling a dome-shaped mound when looked at from the level ground immediately south. Both walls have several turns or angles to correspond to the irregularities of the banks. The slopes

[1] Squier and Davis, Plate XXXI.

were dressed off smooth, or else the dirt was piled close to the edge, so that a considerable part rolled downward; at any rate there is a smooth regular slope from top to bottom.

The north end of the west wall has been so cut up by digging gravel that its form can not be determined, and it could not be learned whether there had been a mound there or not. A deep pond has been dug on the second terrace a little way out. The pond shown in the plate is a natural depression.

The east wall has been dug into lately to a limited extent on the top and sides, and a woodchuck has excavated at the bottom in one place. All these exposures show sandy soil and fine gravel, but no clay. East of the north end of the east wall there is a depression, where dirt was probably obtained for the construction of this wall; and the owner in setting out some apple trees has reached a stratum of compact yellow clay, some of which may now be seen scattered about each tree; so that, if clay had been desired by the builders of the embankments, a very little additional labor would have given it to them. They could not have been ignorant of its existence, for it shows plainly along the northern slope very close to the surface.

Both walls went down the northern slope to the level below; whether they reached any distance out on it is not apparent now. Slight traces of the wall leading southward to the mound may be detected where it crosses the lowest part of the cut-off. Beyond this cultivation has effaced it.

NOTE.—In his work entitled "Fort Ancient" Mr. Warren K. Moorehead takes occasion to criticise my estimate of the cubic contents of deposited earth in the walls of this fort as follows:

"Prof. Thomas's description of the fortification is quite accurate, but he is in error as to one thing: he says Mr. Locke's estimate as to the amount of earth in embankment is a mistake. He figures it at 154,000 cubic yards of earth. Prof. Locke falls short of the true amount and Prof. Thomas makes it still smaller. Both these gentlemen seem to forget that the wall on the ravine side is carried down 30, 40, and in some places 50 feet from the top. In some places one can plainly see that from 50 feet up the angle is very steep, being the fort wall, while from that point to the bottom the angle is much less, because it is the natural slope. When the structure was built the earth

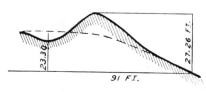

FIG. 325.—Copy of Moorehead's station 241. Pl. VI.

was thrown over and down into these ravines to make the ascent as steep as possible. We can easily trace the line of division where the artificial earth ends and the natural side of the ravine begins. In some cases this line is 40 feet from (below or lower than) the summit of the embankment. This would give the embankment an average height of 31 or 32 feet and a breadth of 69 feet. The length is one mile less than that stated by Prof. Thomas. Thus we would have a few hundred more cubic yards of earth than Prof. Locke states, and many thousands more than is given in Prof. Thomas's statement. This estimate is made after very careful consideration, and is surely not far from the correct figures" (p. 79).

The fact that Mr. Moorehead has made an egregious error is apparent to any one who has visited the fort. First, because the embankments across the level space at

THE SERPENT MOUND.

For the purpose of comparison with other published figures of the celebrated Serpent mound of Ohio, we add here a carefully drawn illustration (Fig. 326) made by Mr. W. H. Holmes while visiting this ancient

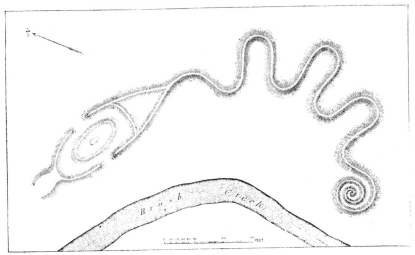

FIG. 236.—The Serpent mound, Adams county, Ohio.

work in 1888. It is given without comment, as our only object is to place on record a drawing made by a well-known artist.

the northeast part of the "New Fort" next the "Parallels," which are the highest in the entire wall measure, according to Mr. Moorehead, as shown in his section of Station 4, Plate VI, only 17 feet in height. Second, because the earth necessary to construct a wall 31 or 32 feet in height and 69 feet wide at the base would form a ditch or series of excavations of a character and dimensions of which we find at present no indications, and which, if they ever existed, would still form a marked feature. At no point is there a ditch exceeding 6 feet in depth and 30 in width.

The error in his method of estimating the contents of the wall is apparent from his calculation of the deposited earth cut up to form the wall, which is the only portion that should be included in the estimate. Take, for example, his section of station 241, plate VI, of which we insert here a copy (Fig. 325), adding only a dotted line to show the line of the original surface.

Now, instead of taking the difference between 27.26 and 23.30 feet or 3.96 feet as the height of the wall, he assumes 27.26 feet—measured perpendicularly down the outer slope 23.30 feet below the bottom of the inside ditch—as the height of the wall, and the distance from one perpendicular to the other as the width of the base. The error in this method of estimating the contents is so manifest that it needs no further illustration. A horizontal line drawn from the bottom of the ditch, that is to say from the top of the perpendicular marked 23.30 feet, would probably give about the correct height and width of the base, as the amount of the original soil above the line on the left or inner side would about equal the added earth on the outer slope above the dotted line.

PENNSYLVANIA.

VALLEY OF THE MONONGAHELA.

Throughout the valley of the Monongahela river are abundant evidences of a former population. Inclosures, village sites of all the different forms, together with numerous deposits of mussel shells, bones, pieces of pottery, and other indicia of a settled population occur frequently. From the river bottoms to the tops of the highest hills, rising more than 600 feet above the water, these remains are to be seen. At a former time the river flowed at a greater elevation than now, forming a broad terrace known as the "190-foot level," that being its height above the present bed at Pittsburg. Along this level, which for distinction will be called the "upper terrace," seemed to be the favorite place of abode of the aborigines, as remains of every kind are found more plentifully here than on either the bottoms or hill lands.

Several miles back from the river, in either direction—that is, along the water-sheds between the Ohio and Monongahela and between the latter and the Youghiogheny—many mounds are reported, but whether they really exist is a matter for future investigation.

Within a few miles of Monongahela are, or have been, a few mounds and not less than fifty stone graves. This refers to the part of the country lying immediately along the river. Of the mounds, only one was found to be composed of earth, the others being entirely of stone or of a stone interior covered with earth How the stone was arranged in them it was (with one exception, to be noted hereafter) impossible to determine. They have been repeatedly disturbed by parties who took no note of the structure and could tell nothing more than that "the rock was down at the bottom and the dirt thrown over it." It was only after several days of search and visits to all the localities of which any information could be obtained, along the entire eastern margin of Washington county, that a few could be found intact.

On the upper terrace, within the corporate limits of Monongahela city, are situated the garden and greenhouses of Mr. I. S. Crall. Two ravines on the east and west sides open directly south into Pigeon creek, and their erosion has lowered the ground until it is surrounded by higher land on every side except along the bluff next to the creek. The further side of the creek being bounded by a high hill, the view from the level land between the ravines is shut off in every direction, except through a narrow pass looking up the river; thus the tract is surrounded on every side by hills close at hand, ranging from 40 to 250 feet above its level. In excavating for foundation walls and other purposes, Mr. Crall has, at different times, unearthed skeletons, some of them of large size; the ground is strewn with mussel shells, flint chips, etc.

On the eastern side of this level, near the break of the ravine, and close to a never-failing spring, stands the largest mound above the one at McKee's rocks, measuring 9 feet in height by 60 feet in diameter. Beginning on the eastern side, a 6-foot trench was run in for 35 feet. At 17 feet from the point of beginning was found a thin layer of charcoal and burnt dirt, which at this point was between 3 and 4 feet from the original surface. This, which seems to have resulted from burning weeds and trash that had sprung up when the building was temporarily arrested at this stage, continued for 12 feet with an upward slope nearly corresponding with that of the top of the mound, showing that the latter had been built from the center upward and outward, and not by a succession of horizontal layers. This is further shown by the arrangement of the different sorts of dirt used in its construction, which show a central core or nucleus, with the successive deposits extending over it from side to side. Underlying the bottom of the mound was a tough gray clay, varying in thickness. On this the mound had been built up. At the center a hole measuring 3 feet across the top and 2 feet across the bottom had been dug down 2 feet into the original soil. In this were fragments of human bones too soft to be preserved. They indicated an adult of large size. The gray clay was unbroken over this hole. Directly over this, above the clay and resting upon it, were portions of another large skeleton, with which was found part of an unburned clay tube or pipe. About 5 feet southwest of the last mentioned skeleton, and on the same level, were a few fragments of bones, a copper gorget or breastplate, some small pieces of a gorget made apparently of stalagmite, and pieces of thin copper plate. The copper gorget was rectangular in form, 3 by 4¼ inches in size, with incurved sides, and had two holes on the longer axis. It had been doubled over along this axis until the opposite sides were in contact and then hammered down flat. These, with some traces of charcoal and woody fiber, were lying flat upon the gray clay, extending over a space 2 feet across. The layer contained only traces of wood, as though the skeleton had been covered or surrounded by thin slabs or bark, there being no indication that logs or large pieces had been used. To the large piece of copper was adhering something like wood, which was rubbed off before its nature could be determined, and some fragments of a leather or buckskin string were preserved with it. On one of the smaller pieces was some kind of fur. Four feet west of the center, a foot above the bottom, were fragments of bones and skull.

These four skeletons had either been buried in a sitting posture or doubled up on the side, or else only the bones had been interred. All the fragments were lying confusedly together. It seems probable that they were either buried in a sitting posture or doubled up, as the size of the hole at the center of the mound and the space showing traces of wood (where the copper was found) was more than would have been necessary to allow the interment of the bones alone.

Over the center of the mound, 5 feet from the bottom, were a few pieces of bone and a tooth worn down nearly to the socket. Four feet west of this was the fragment of a femur, with its axis toward the tooth; by the femur lay a small chalcedony knife. These were no doubt remains of an intrusive burial. One other skeleton had been placed at full length, about 3 feet above the bottom and 6 feet southwest from the center, with head toward the east; only the leg bones were found. This, as its depth indicates, could scarcely have been an intrusive burial; yet none of those at a greater depth were buried in the same manner.

A trench was run in from the southwestern side to intersect the first. One skeleton was found about 20 feet from the center, close to the top of the mound. The skull was completely filled with snail shells. This was very likely intrusive. Mr. Crall's workmen had previously found remains of other skeletons near this one.

A small mound northeast of this, but in the same field, was removed some years ago. Several skeletons were found in it, also a pipe, which, from the description given, must have been either quartz or calcite.

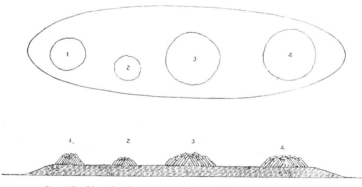

Fig. 327.—Mound and graves near Monongahela city. Pennsylvania.

In the larger mound were several flakes and chips of the flint found only in Licking or Coshocton counties, Ohio.

On the farm of Capt. William Parkinson, 2½ miles below Monongahela city, is a long, narrow point bounded on one side by the steep bluff at the foot of which flows Mingo creek, on the other by the river bottom At the level of the upper terrace is an elevation formed by throwing up the dirt on both sides toward the center, forming an elliptical mound 110 by 27 feet, 2 feet high, with the longer axis nearly east and west. On this mound were four stone graves, all on the same general plan (Fig. 327). Around the graves are bowlders from the river and flat stones, the latter set on edge, most of them with tops leaning inward; many, however, have been displaced by the roots of the trees growing above them. It seems to have been the intention of the builders to form complete circles inclosed by these stones, though, from the cause mentioned, their symmetry has been impaired. The bottom of each grave was paved with flat stones, averaging 2 inches in thickness and from 2 to 4 square feet in area. These were laid so as to fit closely together and extend to the inclosing circle. Within the circle and upon the pavement was a large mass of flat stones with the outer ones overlapping in regular order, just such an arrangement as would result from leaning a number of boards or other flat objects, one after another, against a support and then removing it. Above the stones in this position were others thrown in regardless of order or arrangement.

The grave nearest the river (No. 1) was 12 feet in diameter within the circle of upright stones. Above, in the center, had been placed an adult body, extended with head toward the north. Only a few fragments of bones were found. North of this, close to the edge of the circle, were a few fragments of a child's skull, the milk teeth still remaining in the fragments of the jaw. On the west a number of large rocks had been piled up against the outer side of the circle; the object of this was not apparent. The second grave measured 8 feet in diameter. The circle and pavement were in place, but all the upper rock had been removed. No bones remained. The third grave had been opened by other parties; so no examination of the interior was attempted. The circle, still undisturbed, was 20 feet in diameter. The fourth grave measured 24 feet across. Most of the stones in the circle were bowlders and the pavement was very irregular, owing to the displacement of the stones by the roots of trees. Small pieces of bones were found, too few and broken to tell much about their arrangement, though it appeared as if the skeleton had laid with head toward the east. Two arrow-points were found with the bones.

All the pieces of bones found had been broken and mashed flat by the weight of the overlying rock, and only such small pieces remained as were under stones which protected them from water. Yellow clay to the thickness of a foot covered the pavements and filled up the interstices of the overlying stones. All the space on top of the mound outside of the graves was covered with a pavement of rocks, the larger ones being laid flat, the smaller ones thrown in at random.

Grave No. 1 had about 2 feet of stones and clay above the pavement; grave No. 2, about 10 inches of clay only; graves No. 3 and No. 4, each about 18 inches of clay and stones.

The appearance of the whole work seems to show that, first, the mound was thrown up of dirt from its immediate neighborhood; secondly, a circle of stone was set up, a pavement laid within it, on which the bodies were placed, stones set on edge, and leaning slightly inward were placed around the body and supported in position; thirdly, clay was placed over these stones, and a lot of stones thrown over all; and, fourthly, all the space not taken up by the graves was paved with flat stones. Graves Nos. 1, 3, and 4 were in a straight line; grave No. 2 was a little to the north.

On the farm of Capt. Sparr, opposite Belle Vernon, on the upper terrace, is a level tract comprising several fields, which is bounded on one
side by the river and on the other by Maple creek, which here flows
parallel with the river for perhaps half a mile. On this tract are six
mounds or graves nearly in a straight line and bearing east of south
from the one nearest the point. This, which may be called No. 1, is 3
feet high and 25 feet across, composed entirely of stone. It has been
all torn up.

Fifty feet distant is No. 2, an earth mound 8 feet high and 50 feet in
diameter. This had a trench through it, and a number of flat stones
were scattered about over its sides, which were thrown out by the investigators; yet no one could be found who was able to tell anything about
its interior arrangement. Another 50-foot interval occurred between
this mound and the next.

No. 3 had been considerably disturbed, but not so much as to prevent its construction from being studied. A circle of bowlders and large
flat rocks, measuring 24 feet across, had been made, and the interior
paved with flagstones; next, large rocks piled above these; and earth
thrown over and around the whole. On the eastern side three rows of
the flat, up-edged stones remained. Any examination of the central
part of the mound was useless, as it had been torn up several times.

Two hundred yards from this is No. 4, a small stone grave, not over
12 feet in diameter. Sixty feet farther is a similar grave. Both of
these had been plowed around and the stones removed to such an
extent that nothing could be ascertained as to their arrangement.

Twenty-five feet from No. 5 is a stone mound, elliptical in shape, 55
feet by 125 feet in its two diameters, 3 feet high, with the longer axis
nearly north and south. This was composed almost entirely of water-
worn bowlders of various sizes, some weighing fully 200 pounds. They
were thrown in promiscuously and rested directly on the soil. For
about 8 inches from the top there was no soil, save what had accumulated from the decay of vegetable matter; below this the rocks were
packed in hard yellow clay; there was a depression on the east side of
the mounds, whence the soil had been removed and the clay thrown
on the mound obtained. Whether this had been done as the work
progressed or whether the dirt had been thrown on after the mound
was completed, is uncertain; in either case it would have settled to the
bottom, leaving the upper stones clear. The entire mound was removed,
but nothing found; it may have been modern.

It is reported that in the fields to the south and southwest of these
mounds skeletons have been found in a sitting position, under flat
stones a few inches below the surface. The statement as to the position may be considered doubtful, although the rest is quite probable.

There are two such cemeteries about 5 miles from Monongahela city,
on the farms of John Van Voorhis and Lewis Colvin. They are both

on level fields overlooking Pigeon creek and on the same elevation as the upper terrace. On Mr. Colvin's farm over one hundred of these graves have been opened, nearly all having children buried in them; not over a dozen adults have been found. In most of the graves nothing but bones has been found; in a few, some simple ornaments, such as beads, were discovered; and from two of them vessels of pottery were obtained. The general arrangement is the same in all. From 8 to 12 inches under the surface is a large flat stone; on removing this, which is always upon or just under the yellow subsoil, a hole is found varying from 12 to 24 inches in diameter and from 10 to 18 inches in depth. In this hole is found the skeleton which had been doubled up until the knees touch the skull and the feet are brought in contact with the pelvis. Such was Mr. Colvin's description, and a personal examination of three graves showed its correctness. In the first, measuring 12 inches across and 10 inches deep, covered by a stone 24 by 28 inches, were found mere traces of bone. In the second, of the same size, but covered by a stone somewhat larger, were the remains of a child not over 2 years old; with this were found five canine teeth of some carnivorous animal, pierced at the roots. In the third grave, 24 inches across and 14 inches deep, was the entire skeleton of a child about 9 years old. There was a large stone over this grave, as over the others, and in addition three smaller ones. The latter had fallen in and broken several of the bones, including the skull.

At Shire Oaks, on a point overlooking the river, are two mounds which were opened by some miners, a large one on the break of the slope and a smaller one farther back. Both resembled ordinary earth mounds, but had stone graves inside. Of the larger they could give no account, but their description of the smaller is as follows:

A quantity of dirt was thrown out and presently they found a skull; continuing to dig downward they gradually uncovered the rest of the body to the pelvis; this was at the original surface. The legs were extended at right angles to the body. The whole was inclosed by a boxlike arrangement, 6 feet in length and 3 feet in breadth at the widest part, elliptical in shape. Lying across the feet were a polished green syenite celt 7 inches long; a very symmetrical, thin, finely chipped, delicately tinted knife of chalcedony, 7¾ inches long; and a slate pipe carved to represent a catamount, with the bowl opening at the back of the neck, the stem hole near the lower end of the back and with shell rings set into deeply countersunk holes to represent the eyes.

WARREN COUNTY.

MOUNDS NEAR IRVINETON.

The mounds at this place are three in number, situated on the level bottom half a mile southeast of Irvineton and near the point where Brokenstraw creek flows into the Alleghany river, on the Irvine farm. They are of the ordinary conical type, but much worn down, having

been under cultivation for more than forty years. The spot was long
the site of a Seneca village known usually by the name of Ruccaloon.
Nothing reliable seems to be known in regard to the date of the establishment of this village, but it was destroyed by Gen. Broadhead in
1781. The Senecas were driven off, but sought refuge in the surrounding mountains and for a number of years small parties of them returned
from time to time to hunt and fish in the vicinity of their old haunt.
When the whites began to settle here in 1809 the ground was covered
with a thick growth of hazel bushes, the removal of which brought to
light abundant evidences of both habitation and cultivation. House
sites were discovered, and fragments of broken pottery, arrowheads,
and other relics were picked up from the surface or turned out by the
plow. With these were also found gun locks, hatchets, and other
weapons. The corn hills, says an eyewitness, were then as plainly discernible as though but a single year had passed since they were made.
The house sites, which were rings of earth with a central hearth or
fire-bed, were more abundant along the river about half a mile above
the creek than in the immediate locality of the mounds.

On the right bank of the river, about a mile above the mouth of the
creek, there existed at the time of the settlement spoken of a semicircular earthen wall, then about 3 feet high and including some 8 or 10 acres.

FIG. 328.—Section of Irvineton mound, Warren county, Pennsylvania.

On the same side of the river, about half a mile below the mouth of
the creek, was an ancient burying ground subsequently used by the
white settlers. In digging graves the bones of the ancient buried were
frequently unearthed. This was probably the cemetery of the Seneca
Indians, as no other for the old village has been discovered. Some
bodies, as will hereafter be noticed, had been buried in the mounds,
but these were few in number.

The smallest of the three mounds, which is on the bank just at the
mouth of the creek, was 52 feet in diameter and 3½ feet high, though
evidently much worn down and expanded by the plow. The chief features of this mound, as shown in Fig. 328, which represents a vertical
section of it, are the pit and large central stone vault (No. 1). The
former was found to be 2½ feet deep below the natural surface line
a b, and about 40 feet in diameter, the diameter probably indicating
the original extent of the mound. The upper portion of the vault had
fallen in, wedging the stones so tightly together that it was somewhat
difficult to remove them, but the original form and mode of construction could easily be made out without the aid of imagination, as the
lower portion was undisturbed. The builders had evidently miscalcu-

lated the proportions necessary for stability, as the outside diameter was 15 feet, though the walls were very thick near the base (fully 4 feet), while the height could not have exceeded 7 feet; hence, it is probable that it fell in soon after the dirt was thrown over it. The stones of which it was built were obtained in part from the bed of the neighboring stream and partly from a bluff about half a mile distant, and were of rather large size, many of them being singly a good load for two men. The bottom of the vault was formed of two layers of flat stones, separated by an intermediate layer of sand, charcoal, and remains 5 inches thick at the time it was excavated. It was apparent that these layers had not been disturbed since they were placed there, save by the pressure of the superincumbent mass. The intermediate layer was composed in great part of decomposed or finely pulverized charcoal. In this were found the teeth, decaying jaws, a single femur, and a few minute, badly decayed fragments of other bones of an adult, and with them the joint of a large reed or cane, wrapped in thin evenly hammered silver foil. The last had been wrapped in soft, spongy bark of some kind, and this coated over thickly with mud or soft clay. The weight of the stones was so great that the femur was found pressed into a flat strip and the reed split. It was not possible to determine certainly whether the burning had taken place in the mound or not. The few bones found did not appear to be charred, and the same was true of the

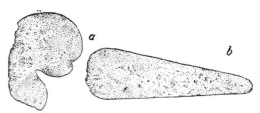

FIG. 329.—Pieces of silver from Irvineton mound.

cane joint; on the other hand, the bark, although wrapped in clay, was very distinctly charred.

A careful analysis of the metal foil has been made by Prof. F. W. Clarke, the chemist of the U. S. Geological Survey, who pronounces it comparatively pure native silver, containing no alloy. Although wrapped around the cane, a portion of it appears to have been cut into small pieces of various shapes, two of which are represented in Fig. 329, a and b. Where the margins remain uninjured, they are smoothly and evenly cut. The joint of cane, which has been taken between the nodes, is 9 inches long and must have been about an inch in diameter. A small stone gorget was obtained from the same layer.

At No. 2, on the northeast side of the pit, were a few large stones which may have formed a rude vault, but were in such a confused condition, this being the point disturbed by the first slight excavation made some twenty years ago, that it was impossible to ascertain their original arrangement. Among them were found parts of an adult skeleton. The person who dug into the pit at this point, finding human remains, stopped work and refilled the opening he had made.

Mound No. 2, situated about one-fourth of a mile northwest of No. 1, measured 63 feet in diameter and a little less than 3 feet in height. This, like the other, appears to have been built over a pit. At the depth of 2 feet the remains of four skeletons were discovered. These, so far as could be determined from what remained, had been placed horizontally at full length, with the heads west. Near the head of No. 1 were several pieces of small, brass wire in close and regular coils. At the feet of No. 4 was a copper kettle, in which were the following articles: An iron handle for a case knife, an iron lamp, and a wooden ladle; near the head were several glass beads. Somewhat to the east of the center was a pile of very small stones, apparently heaped up irregularly, extending downward to the depth of 3½ feet and measuring about 8

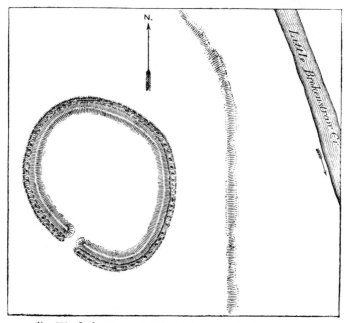

FIG. 330.—Inclosure near Pittsfield, Warren county, Pennsylvania.

feet in diameter at the bottom. Below these stones was a layer of yellowish sand about 2 inches thick, and below this a stratum of very dark earth about 10 inches thick, which showed distinct evidence of fire. The latter rested upon the bottom of the pit. The pit was not very carefully traced; hence its exact dimensions can not be given; the depth was about 2 feet. Fragments of decayed wood or bark were found near each of the skeletons, indicating burial in bark wrappings or rude wooden coffins. Near No. 4, and at the same depth, a leaden bullet was discovered.

These facts render it almost certain that the Indians who resided here or visited the locality in more recent times selected these mounds as burial places.

The accompanying sketch (Fig. 330) from a survey by Mr. Middleton represents an inclosure situated on the farm of Mr. Ransom Mead, half a mile north of Pittsfield. It consists of an embankment and exterior ditch, is somewhat oval in form, 340 feet in diameter from northwest to southeast, and 280 feet from northeast to southwest. It is on the lowest terrace, a few feet above the banks of the Little Brokenstraw creek, there being two other terraces between it and the hill. On the western side, where it has not been disturbed, the ditch is 2 feet deep and 7 feet wide, with the wall about the same dimensions; the remainder is nearly leveled by the plow. On the southwest side is an entranceway about 25 feet wide, but owing to the high grass and the leveling spoken of exact measurement was impossible. The work seems to have been a stockaded inclosure similar to those of western New York.

No other remains exist in the vicinity, though relics of various sorts have been found within and around the wall.

NEW YORK.

MADISON COUNTY.

CAZENOVIA TOWNSHIP.

Immediately east of lot 44 of Pompey township, Onondaga county, is the site of a fort mentioned by Clark,[1] as on the farm of Atwell. He gives a plan of it, representing graves within and without the inclosure, the area of which he estimates at 5 acres. The gateway is placed at the east. This fort, which has never been described, is so interesting in some respects that Rev. W. M. Beauchamp, who furnishes this description, accurately surveyed and platted it in 1886, finding the included area to be only $2\frac{3}{4}$ acres. It is remarkably narrow for nearly half its length and occupies a ridge between two ravines east of Limestone creek about a mile west of Cazenovia. No graves have been found so far as known, but some coarse relics have been exhumed. The ground has been cleared, but little of it has been plowed as yet, and the post holes, in a narrow, shallow trench, can be traced almost all the way around. They average about $2\frac{1}{2}$ feet from center to center. The east line crosses the ridge, extending nearly to the ravine on the north side, but not to that on the south, and is 225 feet long. The north line runs westwardly 320 feet to a point where the width of the fort is contracted to about 80 feet (see Fig. 331, which represents a plan of the fort); thence it pursues a slightly winding course westward 224 feet farther to the west end. This end curves southward about 100 feet. The southern side runs eastwardly, slightly curving, to the narrow point, thence a little south of east, almost in a direct line to the place of begin-

[1] Hist. of Onondaga. Vol. 2, pp. 268, 269.

ning. From this smaller end the ridge becomes very narrow, but
extends some distance farther west, coming to a point. This fort
belongs to the class generally designated prehistoric, but judging by
the relics found is so closely related to other sites near by as to lead to
the conclusion that it may have been occupied early in the seventeenth
century. The pottery found has the human faces on the angles, which
characterize that of the other Delphi forts, and the bone and horn
implements are much the same.
Some clay pipes ornamented with
human faces have been obtained,
and here was found the barbed fishhook of horn which formed the only
American example of the kind
known when Dr. Rau published his
work on "Prehistoric Fishing."
Since then, the barb of another has
been found on the Seneca river,
and Mr. Twining, of Copenhagen,
has another complete hook of the
kind found at Watertown, N. Y.
As no sea shells have been found
on the more ancient sites of Onondaga county, the presence of a scal-
lop shell, a long bead made from
Fulgur carica, and a small polished
white bead made from a univalve,
lead to the conclusion that the fort
is comparatively recent, although
no recent relics have been obtained
here.

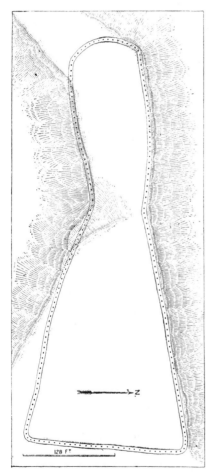

FENNER TOWNSHIP.

At a point on Nichols pond, 6
miles south of Canastota, and 3
miles east of Perryville, is a village
site of peculiar interest, as it is
claimed that here stood the Onondaga town attacked by Champlain

FIG. 331.—Ancient fort on Atwell farm, Madison
county, New York.

in 1615. A small pond bounds it
on the north, which was dry when
examined and mapped in 1882. The topography, as shown in the annexed diagram (Fig. 332), agrees very well with the historical description and the figure as given by Champlain and in The Documentary
History of New York.[1] The figure is also copied into various other
modern works. Gen. J. S. Clark, of Auburn, first drew attention to

this site. The relics found here are of horn, stone, earthenware, and shells from Oneida river and other streams.

CHAUTAUQUA COUNTY.

Very many vestiges of aboriginal occupation were found about the shores of Chautauqua lake. The first works visited were some mounds on the farm of Mr. Alonzo Felton, at Bemus point, on the north shore of the lake, situated about 100 rods from it. Mound No. 1, 6 feet high and 39 feet in diameter, was explored with the following results:

Fragments of decayed human bones, some copper beads, a fragment of a copper ornament and scraps of mica, were found at a depth of $3\frac{1}{2}$ feet. An ordinary brick similar in composition to those in the neigh-

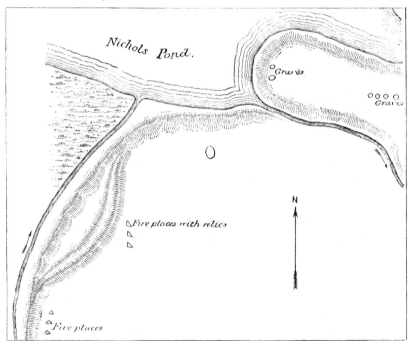

FIG. 332.—Seat of ancient Onondaga town, Madison county, New York.

borhood, but only 3 by $7\frac{1}{2}$ inches, was discovered at a depth of $4\frac{1}{2}$ feet, and below a channel made by a woodchuck. Five woodchuck holes were noticed near the apex of the mound. An arrowhead was found 2 feet below the surface; animal bones, with a piece of decayed wood, at from 2 to 3 feet. The mound was explored to the natural surface without any further results.

Mound No. 2, about 4 rods directly east of No. 1, measured 65 feet in diameter and 5 feet high. Mr. Felton states that seven or eight years ago this mound was explored, but nothing of interest found in it.

According to Mr. James Sherrard,[1] of Dunkirk, an ancient canal and

[1] Smithsonian Rept. 1881. p. 645. (The writer's name is given erroneously as Sheward.)

basin exist at Long point, 2½ miles up the eastern shore of the lake from Bemus point, but this is not artificial. Faint traces of an aboriginal embankment were noticed upon the high land back from this point overlooking the lake.

Three miles from the Chautauqua Assembly grounds, at a place called Whitneys landing, are two mounds, situated upon the Whitney farm, about 60 rods apart. The land upon which they are situated rises considerably above the level of the lake. No. 1 is 25 feet in diameter and 4 feet high. At a depth of 18 inches were four very large flat stones, placed side by side and forming a perfectly level layer. The trench was carried down to the original surface of the ground, but nothing else was found, except some fragments of human bones and the broken parts of an unbaked clay pipe.

It was afterwards ascertained from Mr. A. W. Whitney that this mound had been partially explored forty years previously, which exploration resulted in the finding of one plain stone pipe, seventeen spear-heads of the long or knife-like type, and human bones. An old pine tree, 2 feet in diameter, then stood directly on top of the mound.

The second mound measured 38 by 31 feet in diameter. It was opened at the same time as No. 1 by the same party, with no other result than that they came upon a layer of ashes at a shallow depth. A little digging was done in this mound and a biperforated stone gorget found.

A so-called "Indian pit" was dug into while making some road improvements near this place. Twenty or twenty-five bodies were uncovered which lay in rows. There were no relics of an aboriginal character.

Two mounds formerly stood upon the land of Mr. Albert Tiffany, a mile and a half from Jamestown on the Ellington road, but have been removed, and nothing reliable is known in regard to their contents. While examining the site of these mounds a stone gorget similar to that found at Whitney's landing was obtained.

The remains of an ancient earthwork near Falconer's, which followed the bank of the stream at this place, were examined. It was semicircular in form, the length, following the curve, being about 540 feet. It was utilized in the construction of a mill race (now abandoned) and was built up 3 or 4 feet higher than it was originally, and somewhat lengthened.

This was figured and described in 1860 by Mr. T. Apoleon Cheney.[1] Although the wall has, to a large extent, disappeared, yet it can be

---

[1] New York Senate Document No. 89, 1859. Pl. VI, No. 2, p. 43.

traced throughout. A diagram showing its present appearance is
given in Fig. 333. It is on the extremity of a high spur of land rising
abruptly about 100 feet above the valley, a position which commands
a magnificent view of Clear creek valley to the south and southeast.
This work, as Mr. Cheney states, is elliptical, the diameters 320 and
175 feet, but according to the remeasurements they are 270 and 170.
A north and south fence crosses the work a little east of the center.
The land on the eastern side of this has been cultivated, while that on
the other side has not. A break in the wall 6 feet wide at the south-

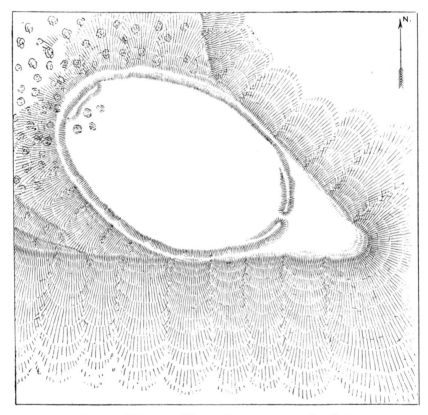

FIG. 333.—Old fort near Ellington, Chautauqua county, New York.

east may have been a gateway. The wall here was at the time of
examination 2½ feet high on the exterior and 1½ on the inside. The
area covered by the inclosure is treeless, but large trees have evidently
grown on the wall, as is shown by indications which remain, and as
averred by old citizens. The people of Ellington, as a rule, believe this
work to be of French origin, and, as they state, much digging has been
done here in search of supposed hidden treasure. The pits they have
made bear evidence of their search, but it could not be learned that
anything of interest had been found except some stone implements

and human bones. A man named Grates discovered, along with some human bones, a piece of an iron kettle. A Mr. Baldwin obtained, near the surface immediately inside of the southeast wall, what appears from examination to be an old-fashioned French ankle-cuff or manacle, with its key in the lock. Numerous arrowheads, celts, concave disks, and a stone pipe have been found in and around the work.

Mr. Baldwin says a circular embankment, 5 feet high, existed on his place fifty years ago, directly south of the above described earthwork and on the other side of the creek. It covered about 2 acres, and had small timber on it.

Mr. Cheney mentions and figures an elliptical inclosure on the south side of Clear creek, which he says was situated on the first terrace or gradual rise from the creek. He gives the longer axis as 218 feet, the shorter, 168 feet, and states that the wall had then "an altitude above the exterior surface of 9 feet, and above the surface of the interior of the work of only 5 feet; it was 32 feet in width." No traces of it now remain. It was on a farm now owned by Charles Gapleson, 2 miles east of Ellington, and situated under the shadow of his house and barn.

The site of the large parallelogram, of which Mr. Cheney speaks and which he represents on Pl. VII of his paper, was visited. This work was situated on the south side of Clear creek, on a high bluff, 2 miles above Ellington, on what is known as the old Boyd farm. It ran to the edge of the bluff, which runs about 150 feet above the creek valley, but no traces of it now remain. Mr. Isaac Stafford, who worked the ground twenty-six years ago, found about this fort bushels of stone implements, comprising arrowheads, celts, concave disks, mortars, pestles, etc. Mr. Hiram Lawrence, who also worked the land, found on the site two curiously shaped pipes, one of stone, the other of clay.

INCLOSURE ON THE FARM OF MR. FRANK LAWRENCE.

This is on the other side of the creek, in the woods, on the high land directly opposite the site of the one last mentioned. It is an embankment or earthen wall, forming an almost perfect circle, 190 feet in diameter, and now consists only of portions at the southeast and southwest, where the walls are still standing, ranging in height from $1\frac{1}{2}$ to 2 feet, measuring on the outside. It is shown in Fig. 334. The site is covered with forest trees, chiefly beech and maple, some of which, measuring from 18 inches to 2 feet in diameter, stand on the wall. This work is on the farm of Mr. Frank Lawrence. In this same field and almost adjoining this last is a portion of what may have been a similar structure. It extends across the fence into the cleared field beyond. Here the cultivation of the land has rendered it untraceable.

On the farm of Mr. N. E. G. Cowan, near Rutledge, a mound 20 feet in diameter and 6 feet high was opened some years since. Nine bodies were found buried in a sitting posture, in a circle, back to back, with feet outward. Beneath the bones was a layer of ashes. Twenty-four arrowheads, a drilled stone ornament painted red, and a celt were obtained.

A circular embankment exists on Elm creek on the farm of J. N. Metcalf. It is in the forest and comprises about 1 acre. This may be the one referred to by Larkin in "Ancient Man in America."

Mr. Thatcher, of Rutledge, an old man who lived on Clear creek when a boy, says there formerly existed two semicircular embankments 3 miles west of the village of Ellington and a mile above the two previously described. Both were situated on bluffs, and each embraced about an acre and a half. One was double-walled, with a gateway at which the walls turned outward several feet, and in front of which was a small mound.

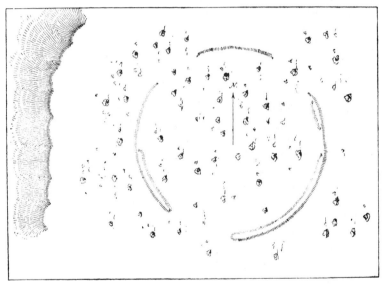

FIG. 334.—Inclosure near Ellington, Chautauqua county, New York.

INCLOSURE NEAR SINCLAIRVILLE.

This work, situated on the farm of Mr. William Scott, about a mile and a half south of Sinclairville, is oval, or, in fact, almost truly ovate in form. It stands partly on lot 30 and partly on lot 38. As the work stands mostly in the forest and has suffered but little from the plow, the wall is quite distinct throughout; but the ditch, which is outside, though traceable entirely around and mostly quite distinct, is at some points almost effaced. A large white pine stump 4 feet in diameter stands directly in the ditch on the northwest. About 400 rings of growth were counted in it. From the point where the stump stands to where the wall crosses the line between the lots, it runs along the margin of the slope to the brook on the north. At the northern extremity there is a gap which was probably a gateway leading down to the creek;

there are also at this point some indications of a graded way or pathway down the slope, but a slight ravine which has been washed out here renders it impossible to decide in regard to this with certainty. The wall in the woodland varies in height from 1½ to 3 feet, most of it being over 2 feet high. The width varies from 16 to 20 feet. In the central portion is a basin-shaped excavation or depression, 46 feet in diameter and 6 feet deep, evidently artificial. No trees are growing in it.

An inclosure formerly stood on the farm of Mr. B. F. Dennison on lot 46, Gerry township. It is stated by those who remember it that it was circular and embraced about 3 acres. There is one piece of its wall 90 feet long yet standing. It is 2 feet high on the outside, and, in form, the arc of a circle. Other works of a similar character formerly existed in the same section, but have all been effaced except two on Mr. Almy's farm.

CIRCULAR WORKS ON THE ALMY FARM, SOUTH STOCKTON.

On the farm of Mr. John Almy in South Stockton, 4 miles southwest of Sinclairville, are two circular works. They are in the woods and the walls have been worn considerably by hauling over them the heavy timber that grows here. The first measured 132 feet north and south and 1,129 feet east and west. A fence cuts off a small portion on the south, beyond which the land descends. If the embankment were a continuous circle it must have run down this slope, but no traces of a wall can now be seen here. On the western side is seen a broad, deep ditch, which must have entirely encircled the embankment. Though the bank can be traced entirely around north of the fence, perfect walls are seen only from the north to the west; they measure from 1½ to 3 feet high.

The second inclosure lies 163 feet northeast of the first. It is 184 feet north and south by 151 east and west, as near as could be determined in the absence of a wall on the eastern side. The portions of the wall standing measure from 2½ to 5½ feet high on the outside and from 6 inches to 3 feet inside. The outside ditch, therefore, is quite deep. On the east a somewhat steep declivity is seen. To continue the embankment in the line marked out by the circular wall would carry it down the declivity. It is not unlikely that this embankment, considering its circular form, was originally a continuous circle, as well as the one last described, and that the declivity by washing away in course of time encroached upon the wall and carried it away at this point. A steep declivity is also seen near the northeast part of the embankment. No relics were found here.

A circular inclosure, embracing about 2½ acres, formerly stood on the low land about 80 rods south of the above described works, on the land of Mr. S. M. Tower. This land has been cleared and plowed, and numerous stone implements and ornaments and fragments of pottery with incised ornamentation have been picked up on the site of the work. Many of these in Mr. Tower's possession were examined.

Three miles from the village of Forestville, on the Dunkirk and Forestville road, on the farm of Mr. J. G. Gould, was formerly a semicircular inclosure of 3 acres. It was nearly on the brow of a bluff above Walnut creek, back of which there is a level area that extends many miles. In the same field, on the opposite side of the road, there were formerly forty or fifty pits, only seven of which can now be seen. They average about 2 feet in diameter and from 2 to 5 feet in depth. Two of them were dug into and at the depth of 5 feet very fine gravel was reached. Nothing else was found in them.

In front of Mr. Gould's residence and 80 rods to the east a bone pit was opened several years ago. Remains of skeletons of each sex and of all ages were found; the number could not be determined. A grave had been previously opened near the above and five skeletons found in a circle with the feet outward. The position and size of the bones corresponded closely with those on Mr. Cowan's place near Rutledge.

On the high land within the village of Fredonia a mound 7 feet high was opened several years ago on the land of Mr. Levi Risley disclosing some skeletons, a pestle, a mortar, and some arrowheads.

On the road between Sheridan and Pomfret, 2 miles east of Fredonia, is what is locally known as "the Indian mound." It measures at the base 274 by 200 feet, and on top 136 by 21 feet, the maximum diameter being northeast and southwest. It is between 25 and 30 feet high and is composed of coarse gravel. There is a depression to the south as though the gravel for the mound had been obtained there. The country is perfectly level on all sides for miles, giving the mound a prominent and artificial appearance. No relics have ever been found in the vicinity. It is probably a natural formation.

About 1 mile east of Fredonia, on the road to Laona, there was formerly a circular embankment of which no trace remains. Whether it was continuous or not is unknown. The site is peculiar; it occupied, as is said, the entire area of an eminence of about an acre, rising precipitously from Canadaway creek. Directly back of this and in front of which the work must have been placed was a precipitous bluff about 25 feet in height, rendering the position in no wise suited for defense. Many arrowheads, a large number of pottery fragments with rude incisions, celts, and other Indian relics have been found on this site. There was a deep circular pit within the work, in which were some grains of charred corn and near by were found fragments of human bones very much decayed.

On the farm of Mr. Joel Button, 2 miles east of Fredonia, on the road to Forestville, was a work, now leveled, which, from Mr. Button's description, must have been almost circular and continuous, embracing 3 acres. The wall ran down a steep declivity 12 or 15 feet, making the land inclosed of different levels. If Mr. Button's description is correct the work must have inclosed a brook, now dry. An artificial depression which was originally similar in size and shape to that on the Scott farm in Gerry, though perhaps a little larger, could be seen upon the higher land within the inclosure, but nearer to the embankment than to the center. The land everywhere about here is generally flat, the same level extending to the shore of Lake Erie. A few celts, arrowheads, fragments of pottery with rude incisions (some of which were dug up with bones very much decayed), a biconcave disk, two chisels, and a highly polished celt of black stone, which had been picked up on the site, were examined.

It is stated that an old fort formerly stood on the west bank of Fay's creek, in the town of Portland, on the central part of lot 38, T. 5. The Erie road runs through what was the northern portion. It was a heavy earthwork, slightly elliptical in shape, and embraced about an acre. Clay and stone pipes and stone implements have been found within and around the walls.

There was also another, some remains of which may still be seen, on the farm of Mr. Hugh Neil, half a mile south of West Main street, in the village of Westfield.

NIAGARA COUNTY.

In Turner's History of the Holland Land Purchase reference is made to an earthwork near Lockport having a covered way leading to a spring. This was found upon the land of Mr. Sharpe, 1 mile west of Lockport. A short examination sufficed to show that it was a long natural ridge of limestone. No evidences of Indian occupation could be found. Near by, however, was the site of a small mound, dug into many years ago, which was found to consist almost entirely of small stones.

On the northern border of the Tuscarora Indian Reservation there was formerly an earthern inclosure. It was situated on the brow of the high steep bluff that constitutes the first terrace from Lake Ontario and the beautiful level country that stretches unbrokenly 10 miles to the lake. Many pieces of human bones and innumerable flint chips were observed scattered about. The embankment inclosed about an acre and a half. The bluff being a sufficient defense upon the north, no wall existed on that side. At the southeast portion is a ravine, now dry, but formerly a considerable stream flowed through it. Mount Pleasant, the Tuscarora chief, stated that inside of this work, in Revolutionary times, stood the Seneca "Refuge house," where dwelt a Seneca woman named Ge-gah'-sa-seh, or Wild Cat. This was the place of safety for criminals fleeing from the tribes, east or west. Across the ravine and two rods southwest from it was a small heap of stones where Mount Pleasant said the Tuscaroras, seventy years before, had a dance of thirty days and nights around a woman in a trance.

Upon this reservation, a little over half a mile west of the inclosure last described and about 20 rods from the edge of the same bluff, was a large bone pit. It was marked by a low conical elevation, not over a foot and a half high and 27 feet in diameter. Directly in the center was a slight depression in which lay a large flat stone with a number of similar stones under and around it. At the depth of 18 inches the bones seemed to have been disturbed. Among them was a Canadian penny. This, Mount Pleasant thought, may have been dropped in there by a missionary who, thirty years before, had found on the reservation a skull with an arrowhead sticking in it; or by some Indian, for it is, or was, an Indian custom to do this where bones have been disturbed, by way of paying for the disturbance or for some article taken from the grave. The bones seemed to have belonged to both sexes and were thrown in without order; they were, however, in a good state of preservation. Three copper rings were found near finger bones. The roots of trees that had stood above the pit made digging quite difficult; yet sixty skulls were brought to the surface, and it is quite likely that the pit contained as many as a hundred skeletons. The longest diameter of the pit was 9 feet; its depth 5 feet. There were no indications on the skulls of death from bullet wounds.

Two similar elevations, one 18 or 20 feet, the other 10 rods, directly east of this pit, were opened sufficiently to show that they were burial places of a similar character. Like the first, these contained flat stones, lying irregularly near the top. Charcoal occurred in small pieces in all. Indian implements and ornaments, and several Revolutionary relics, were found in the adjoining field.

About one-fourth of a mile directly west of the inclosure, close to the brow of the bluff overlooking the ridge road and on land adjoining the reservation on the north, are one hundred and eighteen small pits, which seem to be artificial. They extend 50 or 60 rods parallel with the edge of the bluff, which here is little more than 100 feet from the level land below. They run back 10 or 15 rods, are mostly uniform in shape and size, and are from 1 foot to $2\frac{1}{2}$ feet deep, and average 3 feet in diameter, one being 5 feet. Six of them extend in a straight line for 10 rods parallel to the edge of the bluff.

WYOMING COUNTY.

INCLOSURE ON THE DUNN FARM.

On the farm of John Dunn, on the west bank of the Genesee river, $4\frac{1}{2}$ miles above Portage, is a large embankment on the summit of a large mound-like hill 125 feet high. The embankment, shown in Fig. 335, follows the brow of the hill except on the west, where the hill forms a narrow spur, extending 57 feet beyond the inclosure on the same level, and at the northeast, where a point of the hill is cut off by the embankment. At these places the bank is higher and the ditch deeper than at other points, the former being $5\frac{1}{2}$ feet on

12 ETH——33

the outside, 3 on the inside, and 14 wide. The ditch averages 3 feet deep and runs from the western side, around the northern to the northeast corner. On the north side the hill is less steep than on the other sides. On the east it is quite steep and there is scarcely a doubt that the Genesee once washed its base; its present channel is nearly 100 rods away. The wall terminates near the northeast corner, there being no necessity for it along the east side. The south side being less precipitous has the wall extending along its edge. A passageway 6 feet wide leads through the western end to the level spur, whence the descent is easy to the land below. There is a similar opening at the northeast corner facing the easier slope at that point. The length of the work is 272 feet.

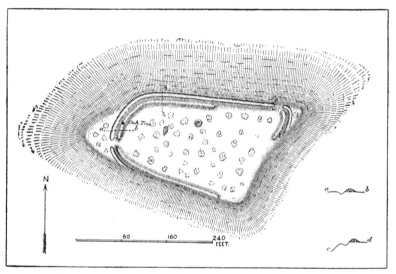

FIG. 335.—Inclosure on Dunn farm, Wyoming county, New York.

Northeast of the center is a circular pit 7 feet in diameter and 3 feet deep; it was originally much deeper and lined with cobblestones, but has been partially filled up. This was partly excavated some years ago, but without any further results than the finding of a few grains of corn, which suggest its use as a cache. No relics have been discovered in the inclosure except a couple of large stone net-sinkers.

It is stated by Mr. Dunn that a mound once stood in the low, flat meadow, 25 rods north of this hill. A pestle, a "spoon-like" stone implement, and some fragmentary human bones were found in it.

LIVINGSTON COUNTY.

An effort was made to find the work at Avon referred to by Col. W. H. Hosmer in "Yonnondio," but no one in the vicinity seemed to know anything about it. If it ever existed no trace of it remains to-day.

On Brimmer's "Sweet-Brier Farm," 2½ miles from Genesee, 60 or 70 rods south of the road leading to Jones's bridge across the Genesee river, are the remains of an ancient fortification. Two parallel ravines, the northern about 100, the southern 60 or 65 feet deep, with precipitous sides, cut through the highest portion of the land. From one to the other stretch two breastworks; the eastern one is 93 feet long, and there appears to have been a ditch on each side of it. The western one is 87 feet long, with an exterior ditch. The ravines curve in such a way as to widen the space between the walls; and the land to the west slopes gradually for about 80 rods to the bank of the Genesee. No relics have been found here.

A circular inclosure is reported to have been situated on the flats 30 rods north of the residence of the late Col. Wm. Jones, which was 2 or 3 feet high. No trace of it now remains.

On Wadsworth's "Big Tree farm," southwest of Geneseo, are two mounds; the first, 40 to 45 feet in diameter, and 4 feet high, is located just west of the dairy house. The second is half a mile to the northwest of this, and after having been under cultivation for many years, is now 40 feet in diameter and 2½ feet high. It is on the level land of the flats.

A trench was run through this from north to south. Two feet from the north end of the trench and 2 feet deep was a bed of black soil filled with charcoal 4 feet in diameter and 1 foot thick. Directly under this and lying within a radius of 2 feet, were the fragmentary remains of a human skeleton. On the west side of the pieces of skull lay a rudely made copper bead, much oxidized; on the east side, a foot distant, a similar bead. Mica was found here and there, about on a level with the bones. Four small sinkers, a flint arrowhead, fragments of some clay object, and a very small quantity of lime, were also found. The bones crumbled at a touch. Some very small bones seemed to be charred.

It is reported that a fort of some kind once stood at Bosley's mills, on Conesus lake, and that various Indian and European articles had been found in the neighborhood; whether together or not could not be ascertained.

A fort is also reported half a mile west of the village of Dansville, across Canaseragus creek and a few rods south of the Ossian road. It is said to be on a bluff overlooking the creek. To the north of it is a gorge 50 feet deep.

One mile north of Lima, knives, hatchets, and other weapons are occasionally found along with skeletons; and remains of Indians have been discovered in a sitting posture holding in their laps pots filled with corn and the bones of squirrels.

MICHIGAN.

RIFLE RIVER FORTS.

Near what is known as the Rifle river bridge on the state road lead-ing from West Branch in Ogemaw county to Lake Huron are five inclosures commonly known as Indian forts. Three are on the east side and two on the west side of the river, whose course is almost due south. Those on the east side are all in Churchill township, T. 22 N., R. 3 E.

The first one examined is on section 9, three-fourths of a mile below the bridge, 40 rods from the river and on a level piece of ground about 10 feet above the water level. The land is in heavy hemlock timber and there stands on the wall a stump 4 feet in diameter.

The heavy timber and dense underbrush made an accurate survey impossible; the notes here given are the best that could be obtained by the Bureau agent with the means at hand. The work is located at a point formed by a bend in the river and consists of an irregularly curved wall of earth and inner ditch forming an inclosure.

The following measurements were taken, beginning at the southwest entrance and going toward the south:

Stations.	Distance.	Remarks.
	Feet.	
1 to 2	45	To a sharp turn.
2 to 3	42½	Do.
3 to 4	94	To center of entrance 2.
4 to 5	100	Turn, almost a right angle.
5 to 6	135	Center of entrance 3.
6 to 7	68	Center of entrance 4.
7 to 8	86	Sharp turn.
8 to 1	34	Beginning.

The width of entrance 1 is 12 feet; of entrance 2, 12 feet; of entrance 3, 9 feet; of entrance 4, 12 feet. The bearing from entrance 1 to entrance 2 is S. 81½° E.; from entrance 1 to entrance 3, N. 40° E.; from entrance 1 to entrance 4, N. 22° E.

The wall on the inside is from 3 to 4 feet high and the average width at bottom is 8 feet.

The width of the ditch is from 16 to 17 feet. From the top of the wall to the bottom of the ditch is between 7 and 8 feet.

Entrances 3 and 4 are at points directly toward the river; and all open out on level ground, except 4, which is at a point where the wall goes along the top of a bank about 4 feet high over a bottom subject to overflow.

The next work, shown in Fig. 336, is on section 3, about a mile north of the bridge. It is about 100 rods from the river on land some 40 feet above the water level and higher than any ground in the immediate vicinity, with the exception of a narrow strip of the same hillock which gradually rises for 200 feet to the west, where it reaches a height of 10 feet above the top of the wall. At every other part the slope is away from the embankment.

The inside area is not level, being several feet higher at the south and southwest sides than at the north.

The ditch is from 3 to 4 feet deep; the wall, which is cut by five gateways, varies in height from 1 foot on each side of entrance d, to 5 feet at a, where it is about 16 feet wide; the ditch at the latter point being 12 feet wide and from 8 to 10 feet at other parts.

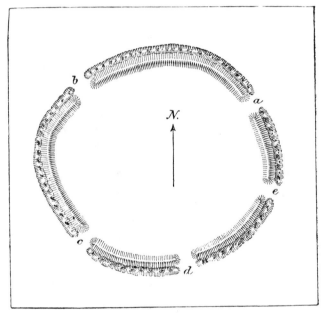

Fig. 336.—Rifle river fort No. 2, Ogemaw county, Michigan.

The circumference, measured along the top of the wall, is 920 feet, the diameter east and west 310 feet, and north and south 280 feet. The widths of the gates are as follows: a, 12 feet; b, 14 feet; c, 13 feet; d, 16 feet, and e, 11 feet.

From a point a little north of e to one a little south of it, the wall crosses a depression or shallow gully, and either from wear or because it was intentionally made so, is lighter than elsewhere; being not over a foot high on each side of the entrance, but it becomes heavier in either direction until the points designated are reached, where it acquires its ordinary size.

The third fort is on section 4, half a mile above the one last described, 20 feet above the water and directly on the river bank, the wall ending at a point where access to the water is easy.

Like the first, this was covered with a dense growth of brush. The circumference, measuring along the top of the wall, was found to be 504 feet.

The width of entrance in every case means the distance across the opening, half way between top and base of the wall.

It was not practicable to visit the works on the west side of the river.

The statement made that large mounds exist within the inclosures is an error; there are no mounds anywhere in the neighborhood.

The wall and ditch in each work are still well defined, being apparently very little altered by weather. The works are very much like those of western New York, which are attributed to the Iroquois, and it is well known that these Indians made frequent forays to this section.

Two of these works are figured and described in the Smithsonian Report for 1884, by Dr. M. L. Leach.

There are two small mounds in Bellaire, Antrim county, that have been examined. They are on a point—but not at the highest part— that slopes southward to Intermediate river, overlooking a lake on one side and a wide bottom on the other. Both are small, not over 4 feet high and 20 feet in diameter, and have a small depression or ditch around the base, as if a small amount of earth had been scooped up and thrown on the mound after it was about completed. This feature seems common to all the mounds reported in this section. In each was a skeleton in a sitting posture, the feet extended. With the largest was the outer whorl of a *Busycon* shell, probably used as a cup, the outer surface covered with incised lines crossing at right angles. At what would be the bottom if held level, it was worn nearly through from the outside. The skull was of unusually fine form and texture.

There are a great many holes on this hill, both above and below the mounds; they are from 3 to 4 feet across, nearly or quite filled with leaves, etc., and some of them have been dug into a depth of 6 feet without reaching the original bottom. They are probably old caches.

There was no one in the vicinity of the foot of Clam lake who knew anything in regard to the earthwork reported there; and the jungle about the place rendered any examination impossible. Neither could anything be learned at Rapid river of a similar earthwork. There are two mounds there, each about 6 feet high and 20 feet in diameter. An old Chippewa chief says there was a battle between that tribe and the Sioux a century ago, and that each party erected a mound over its dead. A number of skeletons was found in each.

From here to Fond du Lac, Minnesota (near Duluth), very diligent search and inquiry failed to reveal anything whatever of an aboriginal nature, except what is known to pertain to the Indians resident there within the historic period. There is a mound at Point Iroquois at the head of Ste. Marie river, another at Mille Coquin, and a third about

20 miles west of the last, which have been built by the Sioux or Chippewas.

At Little Traverse bay, Beaver islands, Mackinac straits, Sault Ste. Marie, Grand island bay, Marquette, L'Anse, Houghton, Calumet, Ontonagon, Bayfield, Ashland, and Fond du Lac, and in the neighborhood of every one of them, are still to be found traders, trappers, and hunters who have explored almost every mile of the territory, some of them having spent fifty years in such work; and the statement is unanimous that nowhere about any of these places, nor along the shores of Lake Superior generally, are any mounds to be found. A few which have been reported are either the remains of old root houses, or else due to natural causes.

It may be safely said that at none of the places where the ancient Jesuit missions were located, in any part of the country included in the above limits, are any mounds or other earthworks—using the term in its ordinary meaning and excluding those known to have been made in recent times, and of these there are but few.

Those reported at Beaver island are only the natural sand dunes or hills used occasionally like those about the foot of Lake Huron as burial places.

ARCHEOLOGICAL AREAS AND DISTRIBUTION OF TYPES.

PRIMARY ARCHEOLOGICAL SECTIONS.

Notwithstanding the numerous volumes and articles which have been published, relating wholly or in part to the ancient remains and prehistoric times of North America, we search through their pages in vain for a chapter on the distribution of the different forms and types of the works of the mound builders. We look in vain for any adequate reference to these types, or discussion of the evidence bearing upon the question of ethnic or tribal distinctions. This important branch of our archeology seems to have been entirely overlooked by these writers. This is probably due in part to the undeniable fact that the data relating to North American Archeology are in a chaotic condition, no adequate system having been adopted or satisfactory arrangement proposed by which these may be so correlated as to lead to conclusions generally acceptable to antiquarians and ethnologists. For this reason considerable attention is devoted to this subject which, as can be readily seen, has an important bearing on the problems that arise in regard to these ancient monuments. It is chiefly by the study of the distribution of the types of the works, the forms and features of the vestiges of art, and of the customs and peculiarities indicated by these, that we can hope to outline the districts occupied by the different tribes or peoples of the mound-builders. In carrying out this purpose reference has not been limited to the explorations of the Bureau, as the published results of the work of other explorers have been freely used.

Before referring to the distribution of types in the mound area under consideration, attention is called briefly to the question of primary archeological sections of North America.

No attempt has so far been made to point out and define the different primary or comprehensive archeological sections of our continent, a fact probably due to the scanty data on which to base such an attempt. Nevertheless an examination of the general works on prehistoric America will show, by the terms used, a decided tendency to arrange, or at least consider, the antiquities in a few comprehensive classes pertaining to different sections; such, for example, as "The works of the Mound-builders;" the remains of the "Cliff Dwellers," and of the "Civilized Races of Mexico and Central America."

In his work on the " Tribes of the Extreme Northwest," published as volume 1 of the " Contributions to North American Ethnology," Dr. Dall indicates three archeological sections, and suggests a fourth, as is inferred from the following language:

In our archeology, as well as in our paleontology, we must break away from received ideas and nomenclature, which fulfill their purpose in accelerating the study of the successive epochs in Europe, but which, when applied to the differing conditions of America, to a certain extent at least fetter and confuse. Even in America the conditions are by no means so uniform as to authorize a single system of nomenclature in archeology. For intelligent study we must separate at least three regions—the Mississippi valley, the Pacific slope, and the Mexican region, and perhaps to these should be added an Atlantic region, extending from the Chesapeake to Labrador.[1]

It would seem from this that he then was inclined to unite the intermontane region and the Pacific coast from California northward into one grand section. However, in his article on " Masks, Labrets," etc., published in the Third Annual Report of the Bureau, for the purpose of his treatise he arranges the west coast into the following divisions: " Central America and Mexico; New Mexico and Arizona; the region occupied by Indians from Oregon to the northern limit of the Tlinkit; the Aleutian islands; the Innuit region from Prince William sound to Point Barrow."[2]

It is not my intention to enter at this time into a general discussion of the number, extent, and boundaries of these primary sections; yet it is necessary to allude to some of them, in order that the relation archeologically of the area under consideration in this volume to the other sections may be understood. The data which have been ascertained can not be considered sufficient to justify the attempt to give exact boundaries to all, nor, in fact, to any of these more comprehensive districts; nevertheless the geographical position of the more important ones may be defined with sufficient accuracy for present purposes.

A careful examination of what has been published in regard to North American archeology, of the figures which have been made, and the specimens collected, with special reference to their bearing on the question of archeological sections, leads, in the first place, to the following conclusion: That the ancient remains belong, in a broad and comprehensive sense, to two general classes. One of these classes is limited geographically to the Atlantic slope, the other chiefly to the Pacific slope, the eastern or Rocky mountain range of the great continental mountain belt from the fifty-fifth degree of north latitude to the vicinity of the mouth of the Rio Grande where it approaches the Gulf of Mexico, forming approximately the dividing line between the two areas.

While there are manifest and marked differences in the types and character of the ancient works and remains of different areas within these two comprehensive sections, yet when those of the Pacific slope (in which are included Mexico and Central America), taken as a whole,

are compared with those of the Atlantic slope, there is a manifest dissimilarity. Commencing with Nicaragua and moving northward on the
Pacific side, we see a gradual shading of one type or series of types into
another until we reach the Alaskan region. What is particularly
worthy of notice in this survey is, that at points widely apart a characteristic which has faded out in the intermediate area reappears in a
modified form. There seems, however, to be evidence of an intrusive
element in the region of California, as the types here differ from those
north and south.

Dr. Brinton, in his late work "The American Race," arranges the
various stocks of North America into three groups, which he names
"The North Atlantic Group," "The North Pacific Group," and "The
Central Group." The primary archeological groups, however, so far as
the data enable us to judge, keeping in mind the facts above stated,
may be in part provisionally defined as follows:

1. The Isthmian section, including Costa Rica and the isthmus southward, which should be arranged with the South American groups, as
the types of its antiquities ally them with those of that continent.

2. The Mexican and Central American section, including most of
Mexico and the Central American states southward to Costa Rica.
This section is less homogeneous as regards its types of works than
the "Mound-builders" district, and in fact embraces two or more tolerably well marked subsections or rather classes of types. One is confined chiefly to Nicaragua, the others extend over the remainder of the
section, which reaches northward to Chihuahua.

3. The Pueblo or Intermontane section, embracing New Mexico, Arizona, portions of Nevada, Utah and Colorado, and the extreme northern part of Mexico; in other words, the area between the Rocky and
Sierra Nevada mountains from the latitude of Salt Lake southward
to Chihuahua. The distinguishing characteristics of this area are well
marked, and the section is, archeologically, quite homogeneous, the
types being few and not widely variant. Its closest relation is evidently with the Mexican section.

4. The California section. Our knowledge of the antiquities of the
Pacific slope north of the Pueblo section is not sufficient to indicate
the archeological districts with any degree of certainty. The most that
can be said is that the remains in the region of California present features which seem to separate them from those south as well as north,
but how far northward these peculiar features reach we have no means
of judging. That the ancient remains of Alaska form a class marking
this region as another section, may be taken for granted. I am strongly
inclined, however, to believe that when the antiquities of the region
lying between the main body of this territory and California have been
carefully examined, it will be found that there are one or two more well
marked archeological districts. The works of art, for instance, of the
region occupied by the Haida Indians and the congeneric tribes, pre-

sent marked distinctions to those of other surrounding sections, and seem to conform more nearly to the characteristics of the works of the Mexican and Central American district than to those of any other section.

5. The Mound-builders' section, embracing that part of the United States and the adjoining portion of the Dominion of Canada east of the Rocky mountains. The northern boundary is, as yet, wholly conjectural, but it is quite probable that it extends farther toward the northwest than toward the northeast. This section, though more homogeneous in its archeological features, which are well marked, than the Mexican and Central American district, is less so than the Pueblo section.

If we examine carefully the distinguishing characteristics of the ancient works of these primary sections, we shall find that they relate chiefly to the culture status or position in the scale of civilization of the peoples who occupied these different areas. But these characteristics pertain chiefly to the progress made along certain lines of culture. There are, however, other peculiar features which appear to be the outgrowth of local or ethnic influences.

When we come to study carefully the works of any one of these primary or comprehensive sections it is found that there are peculiarities limited to more restricted areas which justify us in making a further division into districts.

The present work relates only to the fifth or last of the above divisions, which is designated the "Mound-builders' section." This section is fairly well defined, except as to its northern extension, being limited on the east by the Atlantic ocean (though, as usually given, it only reaches the coast in its southern portion), on the south by the Gulf of Mexico and on the west by the Rocky mountains. The southwestern line has not been carefully defined, as but few explorations of the antiquities of Texas have as yet been made. Nevertheless enough is known to show that the statement, frequently made, that there is a continuous series of ancient works from the Gulf states, through Texas to Mexico, is erroneous and without any foundation. The western boundary line, when more carefully traced, will probably be found to bend rapidly eastward of the range as we proceed southward from the Platte valley and westward somewhat into the range north of that valley. The northern limit, on the west, has not been ascertained; it is known, however, that the section reaches to the Saskatchewan river.

In attempting to obtain a true conception of the distribution of the types of the ancient works in this section, it was soon found that the first step necessary in this branch of the subject was the preparation of a catalogue of the various localities where ancient works have been discovered, noting as far as possible the character of these various works. From this a general map was constructed showing the distribution over the whole area, also maps of certain states in which the works are most numerous. As this catalogue and the maps have been published as a bulletin by the Bureau, it is only necessary to introduce here such of the maps as may serve to illustrate the text. Pl. xx is the general map, showing by means of dots the distribution over the whole area. As each dot indicates the site of one or more, generally several, ancient works, the relative number of dots in the different areas will show approximately the relative frequency of these works in the different sections. On this, therefore, we may study the general distribution of the antiquities without reference to types.

This study reveals some important facts, but at the same time presents some features which are calculated to mislead. In the first place it shows that the ancient works, instead of being distributed uniformly over the face of the country, are found chiefly along the larger water courses and in the vicinity of the lakes. The principal apparent exceptions to this rule are seen in Wisconsin, Ohio and eastern Tennessee, but these, when examined on maps of a larger scale, are found to conform mostly to the rule and can scarcely be considered exceptions. The larger groups or masses, as the map shows, are in southern Wisconsin; along the Mississippi river from the southeast corner of Minnesota to the mouth of Red river; along the Wabash and extending from the mouth of that river across western Kentucky into middle Tennessee; along the eastern side and across the southern portion of Michigan; in southern and eastern Ohio; central and southwestern New York; in eastern Tennessee and along the eastern coast of Florida, though the antiquities in the last named section consist chiefly of shell-heaps.

While this presentation gives a substantially correct idea of the general distribution of the works, it must not be accepted as wholly correct, as it indicates to some extent the more thoroughly explored areas rather than the true proportion of the ancient works in the different sections. There is little doubt that when Mississippi, Alabama, and Georgia have been thoroughly explored many localities will be added to those indicated on the map, but it is not likely that the number will be found to equal those in the area drained by the Ohio and its affluents or in the immediate valley of the Mississippi.

One somewhat singular feature is found in the lines of former occupancy indicated by the archeological remains. The chief one is that reaching from New York through Ohio along the Ohio river and onward in the same direction to the northeastern corner of Texas; another follows the Mississippi river; another extends from the region of the Wabash to the headwaters of the Savannah river, and another across southern Michigan and southern Wisconsin. The inference, however, which might be drawn from this fact—that these lines indicate routes of migration—is not to be taken for granted. It is shown by the explorations of the Bureau, and a careful study of the different types of mounds and other works, that the generally received opinion that the lines of migration of the authors of these works were always along the principal water courses can not be accepted as entirely correct. Although the banks of the Mississippi are lined with prehistoric monuments from Lake Pepin to the mouth of Red river, showing that this was a favorite section for the ancient inhabitants, the study of these remains does not give support to the theory that this great water highway was a line of migration during the mound-building period, except for short distances. It was, no doubt, a highway for traffic and war parties, but the movements of tribes were across it rather than up and down it. This is not asserted as a mere theory or a simple deduction, but as a fact proved by the mounds themselves, whatever may be the theory in regard to their origin or uses. The longest stretch where those apparently the works of one people are found on one bank is from Dubuque, Iowa, to the mouth of Des Moines river. As we move up and down we find repeated changes from one type to another.

This fact must have a strong bearing on the study of this map with reference to the direction from which the mound-builders entered this general area and their chief movements after reaching it. The attempt, however, to follow up this thought would lead us into the domain of speculation, where we do not desire to enter at present.

In order to show this distribution more in detail, archeological maps of several of the states in which large numbers of the works are found have been prepared. On these symbols are introduced indicating the different classes of antiquities. These have been given in the Bulletin above referred to and need not be introduced here.

Examining these, we see that in New York the works are found chiefly about the lakes which have their outlet through the Oswego river; around Sackett's Harbor; along the Genesee; near the Niagara river and around Lake Chautauqua; in other words, in the drainage area of Lake Ontario, except a small section at the extreme southwest corner of the state.

In Ohio the works are chiefly in the interior and southwestern part of the state, with the exception of a number in the northeast near Lake Erie, along the Cuyahoga river, and a few groups scattered along the Ohio. These may be considered as belonging chiefly to three more limited areas and river systems, viz: First, the upper basin of the Muskingum a little east of the center of the state; second, the valley of the lower Scioto; and third, the valleys of the Great and Little Miami rivers.

Examining the maps of Indiana and Illinois, which are given together, we see that the works are confined principally to the eastern portion of the former and the western border of the latter. In the eastern part of Indiana the rule of following the streams seems to have been to a large extent abandoned; especially is this the case with the cluster in the extreme northeastern corner and the belt commencing a little north of the middle of the state and extending down the eastern border to the Ohio river. This belt, which pertains to the group in southwestern Ohio, seems to be connected with the Wabash series by lines of works along the east and west forks of White river. The group along the

Wabash is confined chiefly to the middle and lower portion of the valley. A short distance west of this, in Illinois, is a small group which appears to form almost the only archeological mark in the eastern half of this state. Turning to the western side we find a continuous belt along the Mississippi from the northern boundary to the most southern point. There is an apparent break immediately above the mouth of the Illinois river, but this stretch is known to be as well occupied by ancient works as the valley north of it. The special localities of these works had been but in part obtained at the time the map was made, but they have been added on the general map in this volume. The Illinois river formed another highway along which the moundbuilders located their villages. The groups in Knox and Sangamon counties, like that in Wayne, are somewhat isolated and probably mark the dwelling places of weak tribes or separated clans. The small group in Winnebago county at the northern boundary belongs to the effigy series of Wisconsin, which lies along the Rock river.

Turning to Wisconsin, we find that nearly all the works, a large portion of which are effigy mounds, are situated along the principal rivers or clustered about the small lakes which dot the southern half of the state. This rule has, in fact, very few exceptions in this state. The principal areas are: A belt along the Mississippi from the mouth of Black river southward to the southern boundary; another, along the Wisconsin river from the forty-fourth parallel to its mouth; a third, about the lakes which flow into Fox river.

This mapping of the mound areas is important as indicating the portions of our country occupied by the mound-builders, and also as possibly furnishing some indications, when connected with the distribution of types, of the directions whence came the people who built these works and of their migrations within the mound area.

Another question connected with the geographical distribution of these remains is that which relates to the possibility of outlining areas according to the characteristics of the works; or, in other words, of determining whether it is possible to designate the geographical range of works which appear to have been built by one tribe or people. As a matter of course, the answer to this inquiry involves the discussion of the question, Are all these remains the works of one people, or are they due to different tribes or peoples? As this question will be discussed elsewhere, only the following is added here:

Wilson, in his "Prehistoric Man," affirms that—

Assuming a community of arts and certain intimate relations in race and social conditions among the ancient people who worked the mines on Lake Superior and constructed the various earthworks that reach southward into Indiana, Ohio, and Kentucky, there is no reason to suppose that they were united as one nation. While coincidences of a remarkable kind in the construction, and still more in the dimensions, of their great earthworks point to a common knowledge of geometrical configuration and a standard of measurement,[1] no two earthworks so entirely correspond

---

[1] It is extremely doubtful whether they had any other standard than the pace and the parts of the body.

as to show absolute identity of purpose. The marked diversity between the truncated pyramidal mounds of the states on the Gulf, the geometrical inclosures of Ohio, and the symbolic earthworks of Wisconsin indicate varied usages of distinct communities. * * * The Scioto and Ohio valleys, it may be presumed, were the seats of separate states.[1]

MacLean, who has studied the Ohio works and has had the advantage of living in the midst of them, declares it as his opinion that "there could not have been a central government, but there must have been separate, although cognate, nations. * * * If the mounds of Wisconsin belong to the same era as those of Ohio we have another distinct nation."[2]

The idea of one great nation is very fascinating, but the facts and reason are against it. If allowed to have their due weight on our minds they must lead us to the more prosaic conclusion that the mound-builders were divided into different tribes and peoples, which, though occupying much the same position in the culture scale, and hence resembling each other in many of their habits, customs, and modes of life, were as widely separated in regard to their ethnic relations and languages as the Indian tribes when first encountered by the white races. The extent alone of the area over which the ancient works are distributed ought to lead to this conclusion. It is scarcely possible that there could have been a nation of pre-Columbian times without beasts of burden or domestic animals, not yet sufficiently advanced in the arts to build houses of brick or stone, and evidently not above the Pueblo Indians in their culture status, yet with a central, controlling power, governing villages and communities so widely separated as Wisconsin and Florida, New York and Louisiana. Even if due allowance be made for all the changes and migrations which occurred during the mound-building period, and for the differences in the ages of the works, it will not do away with this difficulty.

We are, therefore, forced to the conclusion that the mound-builders belonged to several different tribes or nations. Analogy also leads to the same conclusion. History, linguistics, and archeology make it evident that the area of the section above mentioned as the "Mexican and Central American" was occupied not only by various tribes, but by several distinct ethnic stocks or families. The ruins of Nicaragua and Oaxaca present marked differences to those of Yucatan and Anahuac, while the latter offer dissimilarities sufficient without other evidence to justify us in attributing them to different peoples. In addition to these broad distinguishing features there are minor variances which we must attribute to tribal peculiarities or local influences. If there be just grounds for assigning the works of the section, where culture had reached its highest grade on the continent, to different tribes and peoples, is it reasonable to suppose that the antiquities scattered over the broad extent of the mound area are attributable to a single nation?

[1] Edition 1876, vol. 1. p. 320.   [2] Mound-Builders, p. 140.

ARCHEOLOGICAL DISTRICTS OF THE MOUND AREA.

Any attempt to mark out and define archeological districts must be based upon two assumptions: First, that the mound builders pertained to various tribes differing in customs, habits, arts, and beliefs to a sufficient extent to be manifest in their enduring works, and, second, that these tribes had fixed seats and were comparatively sedentary, occupying their respective areas for periods of considerable length. In other words, it would be scarcely possible to ascertain and mark out such districts if the aboriginal population which left behind these monuments was constantly shifting. The number and magnitude of the monuments afford in themselves ample proof that the builders were sedentary and long occupied their respective seats. It is because of this fact that so many writers have rejected the idea that the Indians could have been the authors, judging the character of the latter erroneously by their life after they had been disturbed by the European settlements.

That the people who built the mounds belonged to different tribes is being generally admitted by archeologists of the present day, and that these tribes were sedentary is conceded by all. Nevertheless, the conclusions upon these points, to be entirely satisfactory, must be reached by a careful study of the monuments. If they afford data by which archeological districts can be satisfactorily outlined the just inference is that the people who left behind them these monuments were substantially sedentary and belonged to different stocks.

Although this be true in a general way it does not follow as a necessary conclusion that these districts correspond in all cases with the areas occupied by different tribes, families of cognate tribes of the different linguistic stocks. The study of art in its relation to ethnology has shown too clearly for anyone to doubt the conclusion that lines of art are not governed wholly by ethnic or racial identity. There are numerous agencies equally potent with racial peculiarities and ethnic characteristics, in directing and influencing these lines; such, for example, as necessity, environment, materials, vicinage, etc. The mind and requirements of man being substantially the same everywhere and in all ages, the primitive works of art which relate to supplying these requirements will be substantially the same where the conditions are alike. Hence we see the stone arrow-point, the stone celt, and the clay vessel common to most uncivilized peoples throughout the world. Nevertheless, racial, tribal, and even more restricted peculiarities will manifest themselves to a certain extent in the structures, burials, and works of art of all peoples in a savage, barbarous, or even semicivilized state. There are minor differences, dependent upon traditional usages or tribal customs, which in most cases manifest themselves in some way upon the works of the most savage and barbarous peoples. These may be discovered by close and careful study.

THE NORTHERN SECTION.

The ancient monuments of the Northern states and the minor vestiges of art found in them, considered in the aggregate, differ so materially from those of most of the Southern states that it will be best to consider them geographically in two sections, the one to be called the Northern Section and the other the Southern Section, each to be subdivided into archeological districts, determined by the characteristics of the works and the indications of differences in customs. Of course the boundaries of these districts can not be definitely given until the ancient works have been thoroughly explored and all the data obtainable carefully studied, hence all we can do at present is to indicate these areas in general terms and give provisionally their geographical boundaries.

The dividing line between the two sections as fixed provisionally runs from the vicinity of Kansas City to the confluence of the Missouri and the Mississippi; thence southeast so as to leave the greater part of Illinois, most of Kentucky, all of Tennessee, except the western third, all of North Carolina and, of course, all the States north of these in the Northern Section; all south of the line to the Gulf of Mexico forming the Southern Section. A number of the works, however, of Kentucky, Tennessee, and Southern Illinois appear to be more closely allied to those south than to those north. There is, as might be expected, a mingling of the two classes of types along this dividing line. The reader must understand that, although considered in the aggregate, the distinctions between the works of the two sections are quite manifest, they are not so marked as the differences between the divisions of the Mexican and Central American Section, heretofore referred to.

The subdivision into districts is of more importance, as this is based upon differences between the antiquities of different areas, presumed to have resulted from varied customs and to have some relation to tribal or ethnic peculiarities. These districts will be noticed and provisionally outlined as we proceed in our review of the various types of works, reference being made first to those of the Northern Section.

THE DAKOTAN DISTRICT.

This includes North Dakota, South Dakota, Minnesota, Wisconsin, the adjoining portions of Manitoba, the extreme northeastern corner of Iowa, and a narrow strip along the northern boundary of Illinois.

The distinguishing features of this district are the singular earthworks made to resemble various animals, to which the name "effigy mounds" or simply "effigies" is usually applied[1]; the long narrow

[1] Naidallac in "L'Amérique Prehistorique," p. 127, says: "These are found in Iowa, Ohio, Illinois, Missouri, Indiana, and in general, in all the states comprised in the Far West; but the principal center of these singular structures appears to have been in Wisconsin, where they may be counted by thousands." This statement is erroneous so far as it refers to any other section than what is included in this district and Ohio. No such works have been found in Nebraska, Missouri, Indiana, or Michigan.

earthen embankments known as " elongate " or " wall-like mounds ;" the connected series of low conical mounds; lines or rows of conical mounds, and the various modes of burial.

The earthen effigies are confined almost exclusively to the eastern portion of the district and constitute the most noted and chief distinguishing feature of the ancient works of that area. Minnesota, except the extreme southeastern corner, is devoid of works of this type; but in the Dakotas, especially South Dakota, they are replaced by the "bowlder mosaics" or surface figures formed of bowlders. Notwithstanding the fact that the effigies are considered the distinguishing archeologic feature of this area, yet the peculiar oblong or wall-like mounds to be noticed more particularly farther on, the connected series of low conical tumuli, and the arrangement in rows, are features confined almost exclusively to this district. The peculiarity of the effigy mounds, as all readers of archeological literature are aware, is that they are made intentionally to resemble the forms of various animals known to the builders and apparently, in a few cases, to resemble inanimate objects. The supposed " man mounds " are most likely poor representations of swallow-tailed birds. The animals indicated by these peculiar works, so far as they can be identified with reasonable certainty, pertain to the modern fauna of the district. The supposed exception to this rule—the so-called " elephant mound "—as proven by the evidence presented in the report of field work, was probably intended to represent a bear.

The portion of the district over which mounds of this type extend may be designated by the following boundary line: Starting on the shore of Lake Michigan a little south of the line between Wisconsin and Illinois, it runs westward to the vicinity of Rock river, where it makes a sudden curve southward to include an extension down the valley of that river a short distance into Illinois. Bending northwest, it strikes the Mississippi very near the extreme southwest corner of Wisconsin. Passing a short distance westward into Iowa, it bends northward, including about two counties in this state and the extreme southeastern county of Minnesota. Thence, recrossing the Mississippi a little north of La-crosse, it continues in a nearly direct line to the head of Green bay; thence south along the shore of Lake Michigan to the starting point. It is possible the boundary will be extended farther northward when that portion of the state has been more thoroughly explored. Nevertheless, the indications are that comparatively few effigies will be found outside of the line given; in fact, when we pass north of Fox river on t_ e eastern slope, and the latitude of Adams county in the Wisconsin valley, works of this class are rare.

An examination of their distribution leads to the inference that here the leading water courses have, to a large extent, determined the lines and areas of settlement. Much the larger portion of them are found along the main streams or leading branches of the Wisconsin, Fox, and Rock rivers, and along the east side of the Mississippi from Grant to Lacrosse counties.

There appears to have been no rule in reference to the character of the ground by which the builders were governed in selecting the localities for their imitative works, as they are found on the level shore of Lake Michigan in the vicinity of Milwaukee, on the gentle slopes that border the lakes about Madison, while at and around Prairie du Chien they are found from the bottoms subject to occasional overflow, up to the crests of the sharpest ridges which divide the drainage areas of the streams of that region. Nor is a level spot oftener selected than one that slopes to a greater or less degree. They occasionally occur on quite steep hillsides and on sharp crested spurs where the summit is so narrow as to necessitate lapping over from one side to the other. The preference of the builders, however, seems to have been for the highlands, especially those bordering upon the rivers and lakes. Even the summits of the high bluffs which flank the Mississippi were selected as the sites of the most complicated groups of effigies. As a general rule they are in groups or connected with groups, few being found wholly isolated; and even the groups of a given section, as Rev. S. D. Peet concludes, appear to have been arranged or located with reference to a village or tribal system of some kind.

The various forms which these works were made to assume have been displayed so graphically and, for the greater part, so correctly by Dr. Lapham in his justly celebrated work, "The Antiquities of Wisconsin," that but little is left for the archeologist of the present day to do in this direction, except to multiply examples of the forms there given. No one who has examined these works will hesitate to acknowledge that it was the intention of the builders to imitate the forms of particular animals. Although it is true that in the majority of cases there may be some doubt as to the particular species intended, yet in very many instances careful inspection will leave but little uncertainty in the mind of the observer in this respect. Even the untrained and careless eye will distinguish the characteristics which mark one as a bird, another as a quadruped, and another as a reptile. But the careful student will soon learn to detect the features which mark the more characteristic species. Rev. S. D. Peet, who has devoted much time to the study of these peculiar works, is decidedly of the opinion that he can determine in most cases the species represented where the mounds are uninjured. Even the shape and proportions of the body are often so well imitated as to justify a decision.

One of the most remarkable things in reference to these works, which has not heretofore been particularly noticed, is the truly imitative curving and rounding of the body of the animal. Standing at the extremity and looking over one which has suffered but little wearing, it is difficult to exclude the idea that the builders had the animal lying before them when they built the mound.

Of course they vary greatly in size and the relative proportions they bear to the animals represented, but this variation is greater when the similar effigies of different sections are compared than when those of one locality are compared with each other. Take for illustration the following measurements of the spread of the birds' wings, that is, from tip to tip. Six in Crawford County, Wisconsin, are as follows (two of the measurements being duplicated): 280, 228, 230, and 253 feet, while in other sections they are found varying thus: 133, 150, 189, 32, 360, 412, and 325 feet. The sizes of the effigies of quadrupeds are indicated by the following lengths of the body in feet: 110, 60, 115, 83, 50, 80, 98, 70, etc. The elevation varies from a few inches to 4 or 5 feet, though very few exceed 4 feet.

It is a somewhat singular fact, and one that should be taken into consideration in the study of these anomalous works, that, as a general rule, the heads point southward, especially in the vicinity of rivers running in this direction. In several instances entire series of these effigies, which have been termed not inaptly "droves," are observed pointing southward or down stream. This general direction of these structures is mentioned more than once by Lapham and is to some extent observable in his plates.

Rev. S. D. Peet remarks [1]:

It is singular that the emblematic mounds should be so strictly confined to the geographical limits of this single state. The imaginary line known as the southern limit of Wisconsin certainly forms no geographical or physical barrier which should make a separating boundary between the ancient races. The barriers of nature, which are presented by Lake Michigan on one side and by the Mississippi river on the other, might have separated the prehistoric inhabitants and to a degree isolated those dwelling in Wisconsin from those to either side, but to the southward scarcely a shadow of difference can be discovered. The same soil and scenery extend in this direction far beyond the limits of the state, and the geographical characteristics are nearly the same throughout the several states surrounding.

This fact, therefore, we may presume is owing to some cause which has disappeared, and what more likely, we may ask, than that in this southern direction were other tribes which prevented further extension into the prairie region of Illinois? The occurrence of a few of the unmistakable elongate, wall like mounds as far south as the region of Spoon river in the latitude of Peoria, indicates an attempt on the part of the effigy builders to push out in this direction, either when entering their more northern home or after they had established themselves there.

The comparatively few excavations which have been made in these works indicate that they were not intended for burial purposes, nor has anything yet been observed which would lead to the belief that they were thrown up for dwelling sites. Several theories have been advanced as to the use and object for which they were built, but these will be referred to elsewhere.

If the following, by an unknown writer whose article appeared in the

New York Sun of August 2, 1885, is to be relied upon, the western portion of the district is not devoid of effigy mounds:

Among the Bad lands of Dakota there are several effigy mounds resembling animals and fishes. Along the Little Missouri river, commencing at its head water, are 30 or 40 mounds, most beautifully arranged on terraces one above the other. These are made to resemble birds, fishes, and beasts. Some of the fishes have fins plainly marked, while in many cases the birds have their wings spread as if about to fly. On one terrace there are about 50 small round mounds scattered promiscuously in every direction. On another just above it is the effigy, probably, of a frog that measures nearly 100 feet in length. The next terrace has 16 ordinary mounds, square and oblong, while the next one has a pair of beavers side by side that measure 54 feet from tip to tail. On the summit of one of the buttes is a reddened circle of earth which has been cut down by the continual washing of the rains, thus exposing some partially burned brick dust or clay. The mound was opened some years ago by a party of buffalo hunters passing through the Bad lands, and from all that could be learned from an inspection of the mound it seemed to have been either an aboriginal crematory or else a place of torture. A mass of human skeletons was found inside and all the bones were partially burned.

The account given by A. Barrandt in the Smithsonian Report for 1870[1] of some ancient works on the Yellowstone seems to lend color to the above article. He mentions not only groups of mounds, some of comparatively large size, but alludes specially to "elongate mounds," which indicate that the authors pertained to the effigy-building tribes.

BOWLDER MOSAICS.

From the emblematic mounds we pass naturally to the surface bowlder figures, or, as they are aptly named by Prof. Todd, "bowlder mosaics," of Dakota. According to Mr. T. H. Lewis, antiquities of this type are found " from western Iowa and Nebraska to Manitoba and from western Minnesota through Dakota to Montana;" they appear, however, to be more frequent in South Dakota than in any other region.

These curious remains consist of animal, human, and other figures outlined with granite bowlders (occasionally with buffalo bones) upon the surface of the ground, usually upon elevated positions, and sometimes upon the summits of the highest buttes. The human form, the turtle, and the serpent are the usual and, in fact, almost the only figures found. They are generally accompanied by numerous stone circles, which are known to be old tepee or wigwam sites. In some instances long lines of bowlders or buffalo bones and small stone cairns are also associated with them or found in the same neighborhood. Like the bowlder circles they are more or less imbedded in the ground, but this fact does not necessarily indicate any great antiquity. It should also be observed that, as a general rule, they appear to bear some relation to the tepee circles, since the latter occupy the most prominent sites and best positions, while the figures are placed in the midst of them in an area apparently left open for the purpose. the tepees having been previously located. There are, however, exceptions to this rule. Whether their significance be mythical, religious, or totemic is a question which yet remains to be determined. Although of much smaller dimensions than the massive effigies of Wisconsin, yet there can be scarcely a doubt that they represent in this more western area the others in the eastern section, and that they are the latest and comparatively modern indications of a long maintained custom abandoned only when the influence of European civilization began to be felt. This seems to be proved beyond any reasonable doubt by their association with other remains which are explained by historical evidence and by the fact that a few are formed of bones.

ELONGATE MOUNDS.

The elongate or wall-like mounds form another feature peculiar to this district; in fact, they may properly be called the peculiar feature, as the effigies, though more striking and attracting most attention, are not confined exclusively to this district, a few, as before stated, being found elsewhere, while true elongate mounds, so far as I am aware, have not been observed in any other district except those in northern Illinois referred to and one or two in northeastern Missouri.

Tumuli of this class appear more like sections of earthen walls than true mounds in the limited sense and are quite different in appearance from the oblong or elongate oval mounds. They vary in length from 50 to 900 feet, though the usual length is from 75 to 200 feet, the width from 15 to 35 feet, and the height from a few inches to 4 feet. They are usually straight, terminating abruptly at the ends; yet in a few instances they are bent abruptly or are slightly curved, and are occasionally tapered to a point at one end. Examples of the different forms may be seen by referring to the plates of Dr. Lapham's "Antiquities of Wisconsin," especially Pls. 11, 26, 42, 43, 47, 48, and 49; and also to that part of the preceding "Field Report" relating to Crawford county, Wisconsin. They are usually connected with groups containing other forms. Although there is seldom exact uniformity in their relation to each other in a group, as to direction, that is to say, they are not always placed parallel to one another, or at right angles, yet there is a general trend in one direction in each group; the direction may be quite different in one group from what it is in another but a short distance away. They are not confined to level ground, as some are found running directly, or obliquely, up and down quite steep slopes, as, for example, those represented in Dr. Lapham's plate 26, where the slope is nearly 40 degrees.

The area over which works of this type extend is somewhat broader than that to which the effigies are limited (omitting from consideration the few of the latter in distant districts), as they are found as far south in Illinois as the latitude of Peoria, northward along the Souris river, and westward. if we rightly interpret Mr. Barrandt's statement, as far as the valley of the Yellowstone. Yet there are broad areas within these bounds where neither effigies nor elongate mounds have as yet been discovered.

The use of these elongate embankments is a mystery yet remaining to be satisfactorily solved. That they were not intended as burial places is proved by excavations, the finding of human remains in them being of very rare occurrence, and these, in some, if not most instances, being evidently intrusive or subsequent burials. Rev. S. D. Peet expresses the opinion that they were chiefly used as game drives. He thinks it possible that a wooden or brush screen of some kind extended along the top as a means of forcing the animals in the desired direction, while hunters hidden behind the earthen ridges could shoot into the herd as it passed along within the lines. However, the necessity in such arrangement for the embankment is not obvious.

A somewhat unique variety of this class of mounds occurs along the Souris river in southern Manitoba and the adjoining portion of North Dakota. These, some of which are shown in Figs. 1 and 2, differ from the ordinary elongate tumuli only in the fact that they have a mound-like enlargement at each end. The only example given by Lapham is found on his Pl. 13. As these terminal expansions do not appear to have been intended for burial purposes they may be considered as intermediate forms between the preceding type and that which follows.

Another class of works which appears to be peculiar to this district consists of series or rows of low, conical mounds connected by low, wall-like embankments. Examples of this class may be seen in Lapham's Pl. 48, and in some of the figures of the preceding Field Report, relating to Crawford county, Wisconsin. The walls of Fort Aztalan [1] are composed chiefly of connected series of this type, a fact worthy of special notice, as it justifies us in attributing this remarkable group of works to the authors of the elongate and effigy mounds. The intimate relation between the elongate and effigy mounds convinces everyone that the two classes are attributable to the same people. The transition from the simple, elongate form to the connected series is too evident to be overlooked.

Excavations have been made in quite a number of these connected tumuli by the Bureau agents, but generally without any other result than finding them to be simple heaps of dirt with occasional indications of fire. In one opened by Lapham at Aztalan were found the remains of two skeletons which he supposed had been buried in a sitting posture, though it is quite as likely they were bundled. In the mounds of this fort were burnt clay and charred grass, from which it seems probable that they were dwelling sites. In fact the only reasonable sugges-

---

[1] Antiq. Wis., Pl. 34.

tion which can be offered in regard to the use of these low, connected tumuli is that they were wigwam or house sites. The burnt clay mixed with charred grass at Aztalan indicates that, in some instances, they were plastered, probably dome-shaped, or at least earth-walled, as were many of the residences of Indians in former times. If this supposition, which is strongly supported by the data, be accepted, we must conclude that in the northwest some change of custom had taken place, as here we find but two mounds in a series, connected by embankments from 50 to 150 yards in length.

As will be noticed a little further on, there are a few conical (usually burial) mounds which have narrow, ridge-like embankments extending from them to a greater or less distance.

ROWS OR LINES OF CONICAL MOUNDS.

We come now to another feature which appears to be confined almost exclusively to the works of this district. This is found in the arrangement of the ordinary conical mounds of the groups in rows, usually in a single series. That this custom prevailed among the mound-builders of the eastern portion of the district will be seen by referring to the plates of Dr. Lapham's work and the figures of groups in the preceding field report. In several instances this seems to be due to the topography of the locality, such as the margin of a lake or bluff; but there are numerous other cases where the level, open, and expanded area occupied permitted any arrangement of the mounds and other structures agreeable to the fancy of the builders. Hence we conclude that lines or rows of mounds in such localities furnish evidence of some peculiar custom of the people who erected them. That they are attributable to the authors of the effigy and elongate mounds is proved by several facts. One, which seems to settle the question, is their intimate association with these types. As illustrations of this statement the reader is referred to Lapham's plate 48 and the plat of the Vilas group, Crawford county, Wisconsin, in this volume. In both cases we see lines of works formed of the three types, elongate, connected and separate mounds accompanied by effigies, and this on level, open areas, where there is ample room for any desired arrangement. The intimate relation between these forms and the propriety of attributing them to one people must, therefore, be conceded.

Another conclusion which seems to be justified by a study of these works and which has an important bearing upon their comparative ages, is that there has been a gradual transition during the mound-building age from one form to another. Apparently this change has been from the more complicated and massive forms to the simple, conical tumuli, ending with groups of this type, showing no decided tendency to any specific arrangement, as in this last type we find evidences of the most recent construction. The indications of such change were noticed by Dr. Lapham, who remarks:

Another curious circumstance that may be noticed by inspection of the figures of mounds accompanying this work is the gradual transition, as it were, or change of one form into another. Examples can be found of all forms from a true circle [circular mound], through the oval and elongate-oval, to the oblong mounds and long ridges. Again there is a succession of mounds, from the simple ridge of considerable size at one end and gradually diminishing to a point at the other [this form is, however, rare] through the intermediate forms having one, two, three, or four projections to the "turtle form." In this way, also, we may trace a gradual development (so to speak) of nearly all the more complicated forms.

It is not pretended that this was the order in which the mounds were erected, or that the aborigines gradually acquired the art by successive essays or lessons. Indeed we are led to believe that the more complicated forms are the most ancient.

The relative ages of the different works in Wisconsin, so far as they can be ascertained from the facts now before us, are probably about as follows:

First and oldest. The animal forms and the great works at Aztalan.

Second. The conical mounds built for sepulchral purposes, which come down to a very recent period.

Third. The indication of garden beds planted in regular, geometrical figures or straight lines.

Fourth. The plantations of the present tribes, who plant without system or regularity.

Thus the taste for regular forms and arrangements and the habits of construction with earthy materials seem to have been gradually lost, until all traces of them disappear in our modern, degenerate red men.

The animal-shaped mounds and accompanying oblongs and ridges, constituting the first of the above series, are composed of whitish clay or the subsoil of the country. The mounds of the second series, or burial mounds, are usually composed of black mold or loam, promiscuously intermixed with the lighter-colored subsoil.[1]

BURIAL MOUNDS.

As a general rule the burial mounds of this district are comparatively small, seldom exceeding 10 feet in height and usually ranging from 3 to 6. They are in nearly all cases of the simple conical form. There is, however, one peculiarity in regard to form, which occasionally occurs, that is worthy of notice. This peculiarity consists of one or more ridges or long, narrow embankments which extend from the mound directly outward. These have been noticed in Wisconsin by Lapham[2] and by the present writer in North Dakota. What these appendages signify is unknown; nevertheless it is probable that they are a result of the custom of building embankments with a mound at each end as seen in North Dakota and Manitoba.

It seems to have been a custom prevailing to a greater or less extent over the entire district and to some extent in other northern sections to first dig a shallow, basin-shaped pit in the original soil, bury the dead in this, and heap the mound over them. In other cases the bodies or skeletons were deposited on the original surface. In many instances, where there are no indications of intrusive burial, they were placed at different depths in the mound; and what is strange, this frequently occurs where the mounds are unstratified.

---

[1] Antiq. Wis., pp. 91. 92.   [2] Ibid., pp. 25. 51. 57.

The methods of placing the bodies were various; sometimes they were placed horizontally without regard to the relation of one to the other, but occasionally they were laid regularly side by side. Very often the skeletons were " bundled;" that is to say, the bones were dislocated and formed into a bundle, the skull being placed on the top or at the end. Sometimes they were folded as completely as possible by drawing up the knees to the chin. In other cases the bones are found in a confused heap. It is evident that in the latter case, and where bundled, the burial took place after the flesh had been removed by exposure on scaffolds, previous burial, or otherwise. The very common opinion that these confused heaps have resulted from hasty burial after a battle is erroneous, as it is absurd to suppose that bones would have become wholly detached from the skeletons to which they pertained and become mixed in a confused manner in the mass by the mere process of decay.

Instances occur where the skeletons are found in a sitting posture, sometimes in a circle, with the faces inward. It is probable that some of the cases of sitting posture reported are inferred from finding the bones in a heap, with the skull on top, when in fact they were originally bundled. It is due to Mr. James D. Middleton to state that it was by his study of the methods of burial while exploring mounds in Wisconsin that special attention was called to this mode of bundling.

In the western or Dakota area, which includes the immediately adjoining portion of Manitoba, only three modes of burial appear to have prevailed: The excavated pit, in which bundled skeletons were deposited; burial in a horizontal position on the original surface or in strata, the mounds in the latter case always being stratified, and the upper burials being apparently much more recent than the lower ones; and burial of bones in confused masses. The mounds in this portion of the district frequently yield evidences of contact with the whites by the presence in them of glass beads and other articles of European manufacture.

The burial mounds of central and southern Minnesota have not been sufficiently explored to justify a discussion of their relation to the works of the other portions of the district; however, some of them are of comparatively recent date, as articles of European manufacture, which can not be attributed to intrusive burial, have been found in them.

In the eastern or Wisconsin portion of the district there is greater variety in the modes of burial and construction of burial mounds. In the northwestern part of the state, especially in Barron county, the burial mounds, which are small, usually consist of two or three layers, the bottom one, or central core, consisting chiefly of very hard clay. Lying on the original surface or in an excavation in the original soil are usually from one to four bundled skeletons. Intrusive burials, which frequently occur, are usually above this central core, though occasionally it has been penetrated to a slight depth.

In the southern or effigy belt the excavated pit is of very common occurrence, but as a rule the mounds, especially the small ones, are unstratified. The skeletons, however, are deposited in all the methods known to the district—horizontally, bundled, folded, sitting, and in confused heaps. Here, as in the western area, indications of a wooden covering over the skeletons are occasionally found; and in the larger mounds, usually stratified, slight stone walls appear to have been built in some cases around the skeletons. Charcoal, ashes, and other indications of fire have been frequently observed in the mounds of Crawford and Grant counties, but to a less extent elsewhere.

Vestiges of art are comparatively rare in the burial mounds of this district, yet here and there are found an arrowpoint, a chipped flint scraper, or celt (in some instances remarkably fine specimens), a few copper gorgets, copper beads, copper spindles, etc.; but pottery is rare, though some specimens have been discovered.

Intrusive burials are common, some of which can very readily be distinguished from the original burial, but this is by no means true of all, as in some of the unstratified mounds skeletons are found at all depths, the upper ones in some instances showing unmistakable evidence of having been inclosed in plank coffins.

THE HURON-IROQUOIS DISTRICT.[1]

Throughout the district here termed Huron-Iroquois (see Fig. 337) are works of a simple kind, many of which are apparently defensive. These may be banks of earth, sometimes of a rectangular outline, but oftener of an irregularly circular form, which has an outer ditch, in most cases, and forms a walled inclosure. Others are simply defensive walls across points of land, as bluffs, or ridges between ravines. Often the stockade takes the place of the bank of earth, the interior signs of habitation remaining unchanged. Besides these are camp and village sites which show no traces of defensive works, though their other remains may not always differ from those found in inclosures. Burial mounds and ossuaries occur, as well as simpler cemeteries.

DISTRIBUTION.

These monuments are often in groups, in which one or more forms may be prominent, while a general family likeness may be seen through all.

In Canada walled inclosures prevail in a section of country lying north of the west half of Lake Erie, but they do not extend far inland. Near the west end of Lake Ontario, and also about Lake Simcoe and the southeast part of the Georgian Bay, the stockade and ossuary are as marked features, yet with distinctions which allow of local classification. Along the bay of Quintic, in Prince Edward county, is a series of burial mounds of a somewhat peculiar type, some of which have been reported farther north, along the river Trent. They occur in pairs of equal size, and are lined with stones. The St. Lawrence river also has mounds, mostly on islands. From the Thousand islands eastward, defensive walls, earth inclosures, and undefended villages occasionally occur on both sides, but usually at some distance from the river. The

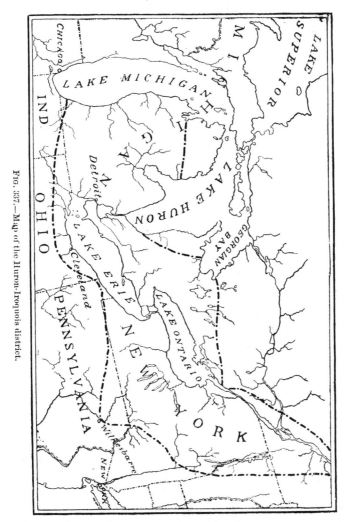

FIG. 337.—Map of the Huron-Iroquois district.

general features of the site commonly called Hochelaga, at Montreal, indicate a stockade, but no certain traces of this remain.

In New York the Mohawk valley is almost limited to the stockade in its defensive works. The solitary exception, mentioned by Squier in his Antiquities of New York and the West,[1] as being a little west of Fort Plain, is closely connected, by its other remains, with the palisaded

---

[1] Edition 1851, pp. 82, 83.

towns of that vicinity, some of the historic examples of which may have used postholes. The valley is also without burial mounds or bone pits, unless, possibly, at its extreme western end.

Westward of this valley to Canandaigua lake, stockades, earthen walls, and inclosures are found single or in small groups, but mounds and ossuaries are rare. The monuments of the Susquehanna valley, reaching south to Wilkesbarre, are connected with these, but are fewer in number. The detached group about Black river and Sandy creek, in Jefferson county, New York, with its numerous earthworks, has also plain relations to the monuments of central New York, but small ossuaries are more frequent. The ditch and bank are the rule in its defensive works. The low, circular mounds, found near Perch lake, are now considered hut-rings.

West of Canandaigua lake, inclosures maintain much of the same character, occurring singly, in clusters, or in lines, but burial mounds and ossuaries are much more numerous and inclosures often larger. The stockade is not rare east of the Genesee river, but earthworks form the rule thence to the western border of the state. Allusion is made, of course, to those which have been obliterated in recent times, as well as those of which traces remain.

West of New York there are few traces of sedentary occupation near Lake Erie until the valley of the Cuyahoga river is reached, on both sides of which works occur. Mounds and inclosures of earth extend south into Summit and Ashland counties and thence westward; most of the works of Ashland county, however, pertain to the district south of this. A few monuments, apparently of this district, are found in northeastern Indiana. They closely resemble those of New York.

Similar works occur in Michigan, mostly on the eastern side of that state. The north line of Ogemaw county and thence northwestward may be taken as a provisional northern line, though indications of sedentary occupation, such as characterize the district, have been reported from Alpena and Antrim counties. In the extreme northern part of the lower peninsular nothing has been found excepting the ossuary described by Schoolcraft.[1] This was on Isle Ronde, at the west end of Lake Huron. The rock region about Lake Superior is destitute of mounds and defensive works on all sides.

In all this large district the mounds seem almost exclusively intended for burial purposes, and in a large part of those opened remains of several persons have been found. Stockades, earthen walls, and inclosures vary in their outlines according to their situation; cutting off points of land, following the contour of hills or ridges, or taking more regular forms where the surface allowed it. Some differences in design occasionally appear, but their general uniformity makes it unnecessary to give examples from all parts. Indications of agricultural pursuits are everywhere found.

[1] In No. 7 of his "Letters on the Antiquities of the Western Country," written in 1843.

BURIAL MOUNDS.

These are found over nearly the whole district, though rare in some parts. If the term be applied to slight elevations over graves, they may have been once common, but have been overlooked or obliterated. In many instances, as in Michigan, sand dunes have been mistaken for artificial mounds, especially where they have been chosen for burial. In New York a similar error may often be found, where gravel and sand have taken the form of the tumulus, through purely natural causes. None of the mounds are of great size, and the form is usually a low and broad round topped cone.

An exceptional example of the burial mound was described by Mr. T. A. Cheney.[1] It was in Conewango township, Cattaraugus county, and on the brow of a hill. The account is not perfectly clear, but is here given in Mr. Cheney's own words:

The form of the tumulus is of intermediate character between the ellipse and the parallelogram; the interior mound, at its base, has a major axis of 65 feet, while the minor axis is 61 feet, with an altitude above the first platform or embankment of 10 feet, or an entire elevation of some 13 feet. This embankment, with an entrance or gateway upon the east side 30 feet in width, has an entire circumference of 170 feet. * * * In making an excavation, eight skeletons, buried in a sitting posture and at regular intervals of space, so as to form a circle within the mound, were disinterred. Some slight appearance yet existed to show that framework had inclosed the dead at time of interment. These osteological remains were of very large size, but were so much decomposed that they mostly crumbled to dust. The relics of art here disclosed were also of a peculiar and interesting character—amulets, chisels, etc., of elaborate workmanship, resembling the Mexican and Peruvian antiquities.

There is an evident error in the above outside measurement, which may have been either 370 or 470 feet. Mr. Cheney's observations were usually accurate; and this work, which consisted of an inclosure and interior mound, may be considered intrusive in this section if exactly described. No other like it has been found in the district.[2]

Mounds within large defensive inclosures are rare. One near Caryville, Genesee county, New York, was of so marked a character as to give the inclosure the name of the "Bone fort." It was noted by the Rev. Samuel Kirkland in his journal as an immense mass of bones slightly covered with earth. Other small elevations elsewhere seem to have been simple heaps of refuse, left within the walls for convenience, as in a work in Augusta, Canada, near the St. Lawrence. Some small interior mounds reported in Michigan, if more than this, may have been dwelling sites.

Many of these burial mounds are but piles of human bones covered with earth, a common type in western New York. Others show careful arrangement. One, which Squier examined,[3] differed internally from others known. It was on Tonawanda island, Niagara river, and

[1] "Ancient Monuments in western New York," 13th Ann. Rept. Reg. Univ. N. Y., 1860. p. 40. pl. 3.
[2] This mound is now obliterated.   [3] Antiq. of New York, p. 97.

was originally about 15 feet in height. At the base appeared to
have been a circle of stones perhaps 10 feet in diameter, within which
were several small heaps of bones, each comprising three or four skeletons. The bones are of individuals of all ages and had evidently been
deposited after the removal of the flesh. Traces of fire were to be discovered upon the stones. Some chippings of flint and broken arrow
points, as also some fragments of deer's horns which appeared to have
been worked into form, were found among the bones.

Traces of fire are frequent, and were quite marked in the mound at
Greene, Chenango county, New York, which has been so often described.
In this there was an intrusive burial, but the lower deposits of bones
unarranged are said to have been burned. In a mound recently removed, on a ridge near the outlet of Onondaga lake, New York, several
skeletons lay side by side in the southwest part. These were much
decayed, some crumbling, and others hardening on exposure to the air.
There were no traces of fire upon them when the mound was destroyed
in 1884, and stone implements and ornaments were found with them.
In opening the center of the mound in 1880 these were not disturbed,
and nothing of importance was then found. There were fragments of
flint, broken earthenware, burned human bones, and stones showing
the marks of fire. As the material was taken from the ridge and as
this had been occupied, it would not follow that the fire had any direct
relation to the mound. This was elliptical, about 4 feet high in 1880,
and must have been built over a natural or artificial depression, as the
original surface was reached at that time at a depth of 7 feet. The
most remarkable mounds in this district are those described by Mr. T.
C. Wallbridge.[1] They are mostly on the southern shore of the bay of
Quinté, Ontario, Canada, in the township of Ameliasburg, and there
form a group of one hundred or more distinct tumuli. Generally they
occur in pairs of uniform size, and are truncated cones 30 to 50 feet in
diameter and about 12 feet high. A shallow basin is found at the top,
which may be due to the sinking of the interior. Few were found
which had not been opened. Internally there were many large stones,
and those in the best condition seemed examples of stone burial cists,
with a few human remains. The articles found were mostly of bone.

STONE MOUNDS OR HEAPS.

Since the colonizing of New York the practice of casting stones upon
heaps was continued by some of the Indian tribes in the eastern part
of that state. In the Livingston Manor Patent, New York Documentary History,[2] mention is made of "heaps of stones which the Indians
throw upon one another as they pass by, from an ancient custom
amongst them." In 1753 the Rev. Gideon Hawley saw this act by his
Mohawk guide, in the Schoharie valley, and thought it one of supersti-
tion. Other stone heaps have been found within inclosures, and are

[1] Canadian Journal, new series, 1860, vol. v., pp. 409-417.   [2] Vol. 3. p. 693.

recognized as defensive ammunition. In other cases they marked places of burial. Two such instances occurred near Baldwinsville, N. Y., where skeletons were found beneath the heaps, and they have been noted elsewhere. Some have been supposed to mark treaties, but they are nowhere large in this district.

HUT RINGS.

The best examples of these occur about Perch lake, Jefferson county, New York. They were at first described as circular mounds, but recent investigation has proved them to have been the floors of lodges, gradually raised. They are depressed in the center, and the outer, circular edge is from 2 to 5 feet high, composed of burnt stone and camp refuse. No earthenware is found in them, but plenty of flint chips. The diameter ranges from 20 to 30 feet. A few examples in Onondaga county, New York, differ from these in their lower outlines, and in the presence of pottery. In the same county, J. V. H. Clark[1] described, in Pompey, "numerous circular elevations made of stones, some 12 or 14 feet in diameter and about 18 inches high. They were arranged in regular rows, some 2 or 3 rods apart, and were probably the foundations of cabins or wigwams."

OSSUARIES.

One mode of burial, known as the ossuary, is most common about Lake Simcoe and a part of the Georgian bay, and about the shores of the western end of Lake Ontario, in Canada. In this the bodies, the skeletons, or the bundles of large bones were placed in a common grave below the surface, which soon regained much of its customary appearance. Mr. A. F. Hunter, of Barrie, Ontario, who has thoroughly studied Simcoe county, reports over 150 of these, of all sizes, mostly mapped and described by him. Early accounts of interment in these are well known and need not be repeated. Ossuaries near Lake Simcoe are usually circular, but at Beverley, near Lake Ontario, they are quite long and of considerable width. In the former case there is often a perceptible ring around the edge. This would depend on the amount of perishable material buried, and the filling in of the pit. They vary greatly in size, ranging from a few skeletons to many hundreds. Mr. Hunter estimated the average number at 300. The copper kettles often found in these pits usually have a hole in the bottom, revealing a fear that these graves might be robbed.

An ossuary was opened in Beverley, in 1886, by Mr. David Boyle, which was 25 feet long by 12 feet broad. This is about one-fifth of the superficial area of the one in the same town described by Mr. School-craft in 1843. Except in outline they do not differ from those of Simcoe county. A rude pit of this kind at Ottawa, opened in 1843, is the

---

[1] Onondaga, vol. 2, p. 261.

northernmost known in Canada, east of the Great lakes, but their occurrence would not be surprising farther north in the valley of the St. Lawrence. The New York ossuaries, or bone pits, present no unusual features, but are usually reported as instances of "promiscuous" or confused burial. By this is intended interment without respect to the age of the person or position of the bones, as though these had been gathered without care and thrown into a common mass. This may have been done in some cases, but the practice of arranging the bones in bundles would give the impression of confusion to the casual observer. In these the long bones were placed together, with the skull at one end, and some of the smaller bones were often lacking. If the bundles were buried singly, they might be taken for sitting or crouching figures.

In some graves recently opened near Cayuga lake, New York, successive tiers of skeletons were found, arranged horizontally, the layers being separated by a thin stratum of earth. In one pit there were four tiers, with twenty skeletons. The others had less. This was near Union Springs. Such careful arrangement seems rare. Relics were found in every pit, but not with each skeleton, and it may be added that articles in New York aboriginal graves are usually perfect.

Some ossuaries may be due to hasty burial, as after a severe battle. A case in point is recorded in the second Esopus war of 1663.[1] The Dutch "came to the fort of the Esopus Indians * * * and there found five large pits into which they had cast their dead. The wolves had rooted up and devoured some of them. Lower down on the hill were four other pits, full of dead Indians." The frequent practice of giving final burial only when the flesh was removed from the bones may have originated in guarding against wild beasts.

Usually skeletons in these pits lie horizontally. Mr. T. A. Cheney[2] describes three pits, or ossuaries, in Terry township, Chautauqua county, in which a different arrangement was found. Within and about an elliptical inclosure skeletons were found buried in a horizontal position. Fifty rods away were three rectangular pits 9 feet in diameter and slightly depressed. In these were many skeletons in a sitting posture. In an ossuary at the village of Barrie, Simcoe county, Ontario, many skulls had arrows in the forehead, and were buried face downward.

There seems, therefore, to have been no settled plan of burial of this kind, and taste, convenience, or time produced many variations in the internal arrangement. In most cases there are no remaining signs of protection, but in one described by Turner[3] piles of sandstone were placed over the bones. Another instance occurred in Jefferson county, New York, and is described by Squier.[4] Both of these seem intermediate between the ossuary and the stone heap or mound.

---

[1] N. Y. Doc. Hist., vol. 4, p. 80.
[2] Thirteenth Ann. Rep. of the Regents of the University of the State of New York, 1860, p. 45.
[3] Holland Purchase, p. 27.
[4] Antiquities of the state of New York, p. 29.

GRAVES AND CEMETERIES.

In single graves and cemeteries burial is by no means uniform. The sitting or crouching posture is frequent and the horizontal almost as much so. Articles may be found with the dead or not. Besides implements and ornaments, vessels containing food were often placed in the tomb. Graves are often marked by depressions in cemeteries in New York, and without mentioning this, Mr. Clark alludes to its cause[1] in speaking of an early burial place: "The skeletons were universally found buried in a sitting posture facing the east, with some domestic utensil or weapon of war between the thigh bones. They are usually found 2 or 3 feet below the surface. The skull and bones of the body are uniformly sunk to a level with the legs. From appearances, the bodies, after being placed in their graves, were covered with brush previous to casting the earth upon them."

A Dutch account, written in 1632,[2] says that a dying person was placed in this position, which was retained after death. Another account in 1671,[3] adds that when the body was thus placed in the ground they " stow wood all around, which they cover with planks; on the planks, which are covered with earth and stones, palisades are fastened in such a manner that the tomb resembles a little house, to which they pay divine reverence."

Occasional examples of stone graves are found, and one such was reported at East Syracuse, New York, in 1879. As described at the time, flat stones set on edge formed a carefully made vault, but with no mortar. As the other graves opened were of the ordinary type, this may be doubtful. In opening the West Shore railroad through the Mohawk valley occasional graves were found reported as covered with large flat stones, and others have been described in Chenango county, New York, as having layers of cobblestones above and below the bodies.[4]

The most remarkable example of this kind in New York was described by Mr. S. L. Frey in the American Naturalist.[5] A group of graves was opened which contained some curious tubes and other remarkable relics, still retained at Canajoharie and Palatine bridge. The spot was on the hillside, a little east of the latter place. The graves had been lined with flat stones and varied from 3 to 4 feet in depth, bowlders being placed above the bodies when buried. The position was not the same in all, and in one case two skeletons were found in one grave. The peculiar tubes and reddish earth connect this with graves in Swanton, Vermont.

INCLOSURES.

Stockades and earthworks both occur, but the latter have naturally attracted the most attention. If the bank was partly intended to sup-

---

[1] Onondaga, vol. 2, p. 257.   [3] Ibid., vol. 4, p. 127.   [5] Vol. 13, 1879, pp. 637–644.
[2] N. Y. Doc. Hist., vol. 3. p. 46.   [4] Historical Magazine, 1873, p. 13.

port palisades, it yet was high enough for a breastwork, and probably served as such. A single gateway sufficed for some small inclosures, but there were usually more. These works vary greatly in size, some having an area of large dimensions. Quite rarely they present no marks of occupation. While often on commanding spots, they are frequently overlooked by some near eminence, and are occasionally found on low lands or in swamps. If the situation has natural defenses, as steep banks, either of ravines or streams, these parts may be left apparently open.

Stockades and embankments have been found near together, and palisades may have had supports of earth, piles of wood, or cross timbers, such as the Hurons and Iroquois commonly used when first known. The first would remain, the last two would leave no trace. There is little direct evidence that palisades surmounted the earthworks, and reasons can be given for this. Besides cross timbers, other supports were sometimes used, suggestive of the bank of earth. The Seneca village visited by La Salle in 1669 had "palisades 12 or 13 feet high, bound together at the top and supported at the base behind the palisades by large masses of wood of the height of a man."

A well-preserved trace of an oblong stockade near Cazenovia, New York was recently examined by the writer. The line of the palisade was a trench a foot wide and deep, in which the posts were set at intervals of about 30 inches from center to center. No holes were dug, but the space between was refilled. By the settling of the ground and the decay of the posts the trench became distinct again. With so slight a hold the need of binders at the top and cross timbers at the sides becomes evident. With these appliances there may sometimes have been no digging at all.

As a rule gateways show no signs of defense, though some there must have been. In a few instances these are found. The double walled inclosure in Shelby, Orleans county, New York, has not its inner and outer gateways opposite, but the inner gateway is protected by the outer wall. A large earthwork, nearly a parallelogram, described by Mr. T. A. Cheney,[1] had a wide gateway, "with elevated mounds upon each side, to guard the entrance." These formed really an outer and inner wall. An overlapping wall, forming a gateway, occurred in Macomb county, Michigan, but a simple inside barrier of wood may have been the usual defense, protecting the approaches within.

The outside ditch is rarely lacking in earthworks, and rarely found with stockades, if at all. In one instance, in Michigan, the trench appears partly within and partly without, as though a matter of indifference, and convenience may commonly have governed its position more than considerations of defense, being simply the places where earth for the wall was most easily procured.

---

[1] Anc. Mon. in western New York, p. 44, Pl. VII.

UNINCLOSED VILLAGES AND CAMPS.

Many places which were inhabited show no signs of inclosures, and yet may have had simple defenses of wood. They are known by indications of occupation, as the blackened earth, collections of burnt stones, and articles found in the ground. Many minor distinctions may be founded on these, but they are most frequent along lakes and streams, especially at fords and fishing places. They range from single lodges to considerable villages, and sometimes show indications of successive occupation. Many yield articles not found within inclosures.

CACHES.

The use of caches is well understood, but those of New York and Canada are among the proofs of the agricultural pursuits of the early inhabitants. Large quantities of corn are found in them, with occasional remains of other vegetable productions. They are not peculiar to this district. They appear to have been usually lined with bark.

FISH WEIRS AND POUNDS.

Very few bone fishhooks occur, but the bone harpoon or spear is more common. Flat net sinkers are abundant in New York, but have escaped notice in Canada. Stone fish weirs yet remain in some New York streams, though many have been destroyed. In the Vanderkemp letters of 1792,[1] published by the Buffalo Historical Society, is an account of a voyage down the Oneida river.

" We passed," says the writer, " sometimes, through our unexpertness, large rifts with difficulty. It was said here was an ancient Indian eel-weir, by which this natural obstruction in the bed of the river had been increased."

Another large one yet exists on the Seneca river, a dozen miles or more from this. In low water it is partly visible, and what remains was measured by the writer a few years since. Towards the north bank it has been removed to allow the passage of large boats. Commencing on the south shore, a stone wall runs down the stream at a moderate angle with the bank for 210 feet; then up the river at a similar angle with the current for 340 feet; then down stream 145 feet, returning 160 feet. This point is about 100 feet from the north bank, to which another may have extended. If 350 feet were added for this, there would be a total length of 1,200 feet by 2 feet deep. There are others on the same river, also well made of field stones of considerable size.

Fish pounds of stakes, although used in both New York and Canada, have proved more perishable. The best known example is at "The Narrows," Orillia, Canada, which was described at an early day, and was once called " Hurdle lake." The stakes forming the pound were of tamarac.

---

[1] P. 85.

Many of the garden beds of Michigan fall within this district, but these low mounds extend also into other states. They are mainly distinguished from the large cornfields farther east by their symmetrical arrangement and accuracy of outline, forms possibly due to differences of natural surface. No relics have been found to prove a connection, and the question of their origin may be deferred.

In several parts of New York very large corn hills remained until a recent date, and have been described by Schoolcraft, Clark, and others. They were much larger than those made by the whites, a small mound being raised sufficient to contain several hills, and this was used for many years. These mounds were arranged in rows, but did not form a continuous plat, as in the garden beds.

THE ANCIENT INHABITANTS OF THE DISTRICT.

In this brief summary no attempt has been made to distinguish the tribes which may have dwelt in the district or to point out when they did so. It is sufficient now to say that the constant progress of colonization in New York and Canada produced a gradual change in the arts of savage life, so that primitive implements, ornaments, and utensils are found on the same village sites and in the same graves with those derived from the white man. Those who received European articles are well known in history, but they had in this district arts like those found in its graves and inclosures. Its builders of simple walls and mounds, in such ways, are directly connected with the historic red man, and the latter transition stages can be fully traced.

THE ILLINOIS DISTRICT.

The limits of this district east and west have not as yet been satisfactorily determined; hence it can only be defined as including the middle and eastern portions of Iowa, northeastern and possibly central Missouri, Illinois as far south as the mouth of the Illinois river, and the western half of Indiana. Nor are the type characters by any means so well marked as those of most of the other districts. The differences in the features and types of the works and relics indicate the presence in the area embraced of different tribes, some of which must have occupied in succession the same sections. Especially does this appear to be true of the eastern portion of Iowa and the western part of Illinois. There are certain types of this last-mentioned region which bear such strong resemblance to some of the works and remains of southeastern Indiana and southern Ohio as to justify the belief that there was some relation between the mound-builders of the two areas. On the other hand, however, there are works in eastern Illinois and western Indiana which seem to justify the belief that they are attributable to other tribes than the authors of those last mentioned. The antiquities of northeastern Missouri and some of those of Calhoun county, Illinois, present marked peculiarities not found in other portions of the district, yet do not seem to be connected with those of the regions immediately south. The district has therefore been designated rather because of the want of conformity in types with the works of surrounding areas than on account of indications that they are to be attributed to a single family or a number of cognate tribes.

As will be seen by reference to the map showing the distribution of ancient works, they are found in this district chiefly along the larger watercourses, three-fourths of all those noted being situated along the Mississippi, Illinois, and Wabash rivers. There are, however, a few interior clusters in Illinois, as the one in and about Knox county, another in Sangamon county, and another in the southeastern part of the state. Along the Mississippi and Illinois rivers they are found upon the uplands, ridges, and bluffs as well as on the bottoms which border the streams. In Calhoun county, Illinois, and northeastern Missouri, which are more broken than other parts of the district, the groups generally consist of single lines of tumuli along the narrow crests. As a general, though not universal, rule the larger mounds are found on the lowlands or valley levels.

Contrasting the works of this district with the types of the Dakotan district, it is sufficient to state that (except along the northern border where there has been an overlapping and intermingling of types) we do not find here the imitations of animal forms, the elongate, wall-like tumuli, nor the series of connected mounds. Nor does it appear to have been a custom of the mound builders of this district to arrange the small tumuli in lines. It is true, however, that series and irregular lines are found along the margins of the bluffs and on the crests of ridges in western Illinois, especially in Calhoun county, and also in northeastern Missouri, but the arrangement appears to have resulted from the topographical features rather than from design. Messrs. Hardy and Scheetz,[1] who made some important explorations in the latter section, were however inclined to believe from their observations that there was a tendency here to place the mounds in rows even on the level areas.

The works of this district are distinguished from the archeologic remains immediately south chiefly by the absence of pyramidal mounds—less perhaps than half a score being found within the designated boundary; by the marked differences in the pottery and other minor vestiges of art, especially the pipes, and by the differences in the burial customs. The frequent occurrence here of the "monitor" or broad, curved base pipe, which is found neither north nor south, is a marked feature.

BURIAL MOUNDS.

As the chief variations in types observed within the district are found in the burial mounds, attention is called to them first. It is necessary

---

to state here, lest an erroneous impression be conveyed to the reader who may be acquainted with the works of the northern part of the district, that one class of mounds found in the northeastern part of Iowa and northwestern part of Illinois, although within the limits assigned to the district, is omitted from consideration, as the modes of construction and burial show this class to belong unquestionably to the Dakotan types. On the Iowa side these appear to fade out going south by the time the Maquoketa river is reached, but continue on the Illinois side into Rock Island and Stark counties.

Excluding these we notice the following types as those which appear to be most characteristic, some of which seem to be limited to particular sections of the district and to indicate the locations of different tribes.

In the region of Scott, Muscatine, and Louisa counties, Iowa, on the west side of the Mississippi but extending as far south as Calhoun county, Illinois, on the east side, certain types both of mounds and specimens of art are found which resemble so closely some of the antiquities of the Ohio and Appalachian districts (hereafter described) as to indicate some relationship between the mound builders of these different sections. For example, we find at the bottom of some of the mounds of the section indicated the basin-shaped clay mass, or more correctly clay mass with basin-shaped depression in the middle, reminding us of the so-called "altars" of the Ohio mounds. These are usually the larger mounds of this region, and are generally, though not always, found on the low lands. They are also in some cases burial mounds, which is seldom true of the type in Ohio. A description of one is given here in order that the reader may see upon what evidence this claim of resemblance is based. A full description will be found in the account of the field work, and also in Science. [1]

This mound, which forms one of a group of five located on the spur of a bluff about 150 feet high, overlooking the Illinois river, stood on the very brink of a precipice. Roundly conical in form, it measured 95 feet in diameter at the base and about 17 feet in height. From the top to the depth of 14 feet it consisted chiefly of yellow clay obtained from the surrounding surface of the bluff. In this, at the depth of 4 feet, was a horizontal layer of hard, gray earth 8 inches thick and 20 feet in diameter. Three feet lower was a layer of burnt clay about the same thickness and extent. Although particles of charcoal were mixed through it, no ashes were observed on or about it (see Fig. 65).

At the depth of 14 feet was reached what seemed to be a nucleus or original mound over which the heavy mass of clay had been thrown. Over this lay a thin covering of whitish material, apparently light ashes, not more than 2 inches thick and extending entirely over the upper surface of this nucleus, which was nearly circular in outline, about 40 feet in diameter, and rounded up to a height of a little over 3 feet in the middle. Under the layer of ashes was a single layer of stones extending over the central portion but not reaching the outer margin. When these were removed it was ascertained that a basin-shaped depression, oval in outline, 10 by 13 feet and nearly 3 feet deep in the middle, had been made in this central mass. This was lined throughout with a layer of stone and was filled with the yellow surface soil of the ridge, but immediately over the stones was a thin layer of white ashes mixed with charred leaves and grass. Under the stones, resting on the natural surface of the ridge, was a thin layer of decayed vegetable matter. Under the center of this, in a slight excavation in the original soil, was a single skeleton lying at full length on its back—but, strange to say, the head was wanting. Not a tooth nor any other part of it could be found, though careful search was made. As the other bones were comparatively well preserved it is presumed that the head was removed before burial. It is worthy of note that the stones bore evidence of having remained in position exposed to the air for a considerable length of time before being covered. The similarity of this structure to the so-called "altars" of the Ohio mounds is so apparent that it is only necessary to call attention to it.

In other mounds of the section under consideration cubical piles of stones occur similar to those observed in some of the mounds of western North Carolina. In one instance a beehive-shaped vault of hardened clay covering a skeleton was observed, reminding us of similar clay vaults in some two or three mounds of Kanawha valley, West Virginia, and the little stone vaults in the mounds of western North Carolina and eastern Tennessee. In addition to these resemblances is the well-known fact that in the section now referred to the curved base or monitor pipe, so characteristic of the typical mounds of Ohio, is found in large numbers.

There are, however, other features of the mounds of this region worthy of notice, some of which indicate the presence of other tribes than the builders of the mounds alluded to. It is assumed that, as a rule, the presence of the monitor pipe in a mound may be taken as evidence that the builders, notwithstanding the differences in the construction of the mounds and mode of burial, were related to the authors of those referred to or had adopted some of their peculiar customs from long, intimate association. It is often the case that different modes of construction and burial dependent upon station, condition in life, calling, achievements, etc., are found in the mounds apparently constructed by the people of a single tribe or even a single village. For example, the mounds of the Cook farm group, Scott county, Iowa, from which the well known engraved tablets of the Davenport Academy of Sciences were taken, presented the following different features: Some were stratified, others not; in some the skeletons were placed horizontally on the ground, in others they were in a sitting posture, while in others they were dismembered and in a confused heap; in some there were cubical piles of stone which were wanting in others; in some the skeletons were covered with a hard layer or mortar-like coating which was wanting in most of them; and lastly there were evidences in one or two of the use of fire in the burial ceremonies, though not found in the others. Most of the mounds, though not all, covered a burial pit or slight excavation in the original soil.

Several instances have been noticed where the mounds examined were found to contain stone vaults of various forms. In some two or three cases these vaults were square, or oblong inclosures consisting of a surrounding wall built up of unhewn stone to the height of 2 or 3 feet. Within these were found a number of skeletons supposed, from the position in which the bones were found, to have been buried in a sitting posture. In one case the vault, which was divided by cross partitions, was covered with timbers from which the bark had been removed. Another was without a covering, the dirt having been thrown in on the bodies to fill the vault and piled up over it to form the mound. These vaults vary in size from 7 to 12 feet on a side, and have been observed in Jo Daviess and Cass counties, Illinois, and Clay county, Missouri. Similar shaped vaults, sunk in the natural soil and not covered by mounds, have been discovered in Pike and Montgomery counties, Missouri.

In some instances dome-shaped stone vaults have been observed. In these cases it would seem that the bodies or skeletons had been placed on the natural surface in a sitting posture, then inclosed by a circular wall of rough stones contracted toward the top and covered with a single flat stone. It must be borne in mind, however, that mounds of these particular types are usually accompanied by others presenting quite different modes of burial. For example, we are informed by Dr. J. F. Snyder,[1] who has made a somewhat careful study of the antiquities of Cass county, Illinois, where mounds of the last mentioned type occur, that there are three kinds of burial mounds. First, those with dome-shaped vaults, as described; second, those with oblong or square cists formed by setting up stone slabs on edge and covering with similar slabs—apparently the box-shaped stone graves; and third, small mounds, usually in rows along the crests of ridges, each containing the bones of several individuals uninclosed. In some of these the skeletons are folded or sitting up with the feet drawn under the hips; in some the bones are in confused masses. A few have basin-shaped excavations beneath them.

The mounds of northeastern Missouri present some peculiarities worthy of notice. As to composition they are made wholly of earth, of earth and stones, or wholly of stones. In the latter two the bodies buried in them are covered by stones thrown over them, or are inclosed in stone receptacles of various forms. In a few cases these receptacles are box-shaped stone cists similar to those so common in southern Illi-

THOMAS.]   THE ILLINOIS DISTRICT.   555

nois and middle Tennessee. There are, however, peculiarities in the
modes of burial which seem to indicate that different peoples were the
authors of the works of the different sections. It seems that the mound-
builders of northeastern Missouri often burned the bodies, then gathered up the charred bones and ashes and mixed them into a mass with
clay. Where the bodies were buried without being thus treated, a flat
stone was sometimes laid on the head.

In the eastern portion of the district, which includes western Indiana, the mounds occur principally upon the small streams emptying
into Lake Michigan and upon the lower waters of the Wabash river,
few, if any, being found in the intermediate area.

The mounds of northwestern Indiana are found chiefly in Laporte
county. Some of them are of medium or comparatively large size,
ranging from 10 to 20 feet in height. All are composed of earth and
are generally burial tumuli. Quite a number of copper articles, such
as celts and awls, some vessels of pottery, and an occasional carved
pipe, have been obtained from them. In some the skeletons seem to
have been placed in a sitting posture, while in others they were placed
horizontally. In some cases there is evidence that after the bodies
were deposited on the natural surface and covered with earth a fire
was kindled on this and the mound heaped over it. A number of the
mounds from 2 to 3 feet high contained no indications of having been
used for burial purposes, but, judging from the fire-beds and refuse
material found in them, were built as dwelling sites.

In the valley of the lower Wabash mounds occur in considerable
numbers and of various types. Near Merom, on the Indiana side, is
an extensive group partially surrounded by an earthen wall. This
consists largely of hut rings, reminding us of similar groups in southern Illinois and southeastern Missouri; as in the latter, there is one
chief mound and a few smaller ones. The former was a burial mound.
Another extensive group is found near Hutsonville, on the Illinois side.
There are, however, no indications that this was surrounded by an
embankment, though some of the large tumuli present the rather uncommon feature in this section of being surrounded by a circular
embankment or ridge. Most of the small mounds, as well as some of
the larger ones, appear to have been only dwelling sites, as they contained no indications of having been used for burial purposes. "The
absence of human remains and all refuse in the shape of kitchen heaps,
as well as implements," led the explorers to the conclusion that the
place was not inhabited for any great length of time, and that it may
have been simply a place of resort at special seasons for some particular purpose.

Numerous "earthworks" are reported in the vicinity of Merom, but,
no description being furnished nor any examination made by the
Bureau agents, we are unable to judge of their character or type. Mr.
Collett, the state geologist of Indiana, who makes the statement, adds

that they are "of such an extent as to require for their construction time and the persistent labor of many people. Situated on the river bluffs, their location combines picturesque scenery, susceptibility for defense and convenience to transportation, water, and productive lands." He also states that there is evidence here that conical knolls of the loess have been artificially rounded and used for sepulchral purposes.

Other mounds on the Indiana side of the lower Wabash, especially in Knox county, are of comparatively large size and appear in some instances to have been truncated, earthen pyramids. Very little evidence of burial has been found in them; it is, therefore, to be presumed that they were built for other than burial purposes. They contain traces of fire, the prevailing feature being the presence of one or more strata of ashes in which are found fragments of bones. On the Illinois side of this part of the valley and in the region of Sangamon river in the central part of the state, the mounds, which occur in considerable number, are comparatively small, unstratified, and used only for burial purposes. Some of them at least are comparatively recent, as articles showing contact with the whites are found in them where there are no indications of intrusive burial. The same is true also of a class of small mounds found in northwestern Illinois. It is frequently the case that the skeletons found in mounds of this type are in a sitting posture; occasionally the bones are in a confused heap; however, the horizontal position is probably more common than any other. As a rule, but few implements or ornaments are found in mounds of this class.

In reference to this north and south belt of the district, extending from the northwest part of Indiana southward and including the Wabash valley, it may be stated with considerable confidence that its archeological features indicate the presence here of several different tribes. It may also be affirmed that these tribes were small ones, or portions of large ones which remained for a comparatively short period in this section.

There is a group of mounds in Vanderburg county, Indiana, that seems out of place in the region where it is found.

These mounds, as will be seen by reference to our "Catalogue of Prehistoric Works East of the Rocky Mountains," were first noticed by Mr. John Collett[1] and subsequently briefly described by Floyd Stinson, in the Smithsonian Report for 1881. Recently I have examined the group and had a survey made of it. As the description is not included in the report of the field work, it is given here.

This group, commonly known as the "Angel mounds," is situated about 8 miles southeast of Evansville, in Vanderburg county, near the Warwick county line, close to the Ohio river. At this point of its course the Ohio sends off a branch or bayou which cuts off the "Three Mile island." It is on the margin of this bayou opposite the lower end of

---

the island that the group, consisting of six mounds and an earthen wall, is located. A plat of the group is given in Pl. XLI.

Starting from the bank of the bayou and moving northward we first cross a strip of low land several rods wide which borders the stream and is subject to annual overflows. We then come to a low bluff some 8 to 12 feet high which forms the break or edge of the terrace or general level, and which is undoubtedly the old bank of the Ohio. Ascending this and moving north by the mound marked D and turning our face to the east, we have a full and clear view of the large mound (A) which is the prominent feature of the group as shown in Fig. 338, which represents the elevation as seen from the west. A plat of it is given in Fig. 339. It is a flat-topped mound, oblong in form, capped at one end by a conical mound, and furnished at the same end with an apron-like extension. The height at the northern end (A) is 27 feet, but this increases as we approach the lower end (D) to 30 feet. The height of the apron varies from 6 to 10 feet. The entire length of the base from north to south is about 520 feet, the width varying from 130 to 150 feet. The length of the top of the upper level on the west side is 236 feet; of the apron, about 150 feet. The width of the top of the upper level varies from 93 to 110 feet.

The conical portion at the southeast corner of the main structure rises to the height of 20 feet above the upper level, the circumference at this level being 290 feet, giving a diameter of 93 feet. This is, more correctly speaking, an addition to the original structure and not simply a superimposed mound, for the slope on the southeast portion extends down to the original surface of the ground and beyond the base of the main structure. This feature, though rare, has been observed in some two or three other cases, as, for example, in one of the mounds of the Seip works, in Ross county, Ohio, and one of the Linn mounds, Union county, Illinois.

The structure marked B, Pl. XLI, is a low, conical mound about 100 feet in diameter, much worn by the plow, so that at present it is only some 3 or 4 feet high. It is 665 feet N. 54° E. of A (measuring from the point d on the top of the latter). Near by is a small excavation from which part of the earth used in building the mound was probably taken. The surface of the ground between these two mounds is strewn with fragments of pottery, broken mussel-shells, flint chips, etc.

Mound C is situated 650 feet N. 86° W. of the large mound. It is a low, conical tumulus, the north and south diameter being 102 feet, and

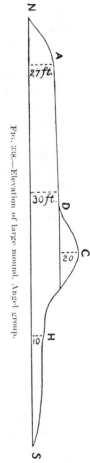

FIG. 338.—Elevation of large mound. Angel group.

the east and west 108 feet.   It has been explored by Mr. Charles Artes, who has made a study of the archeology of this region.   He found it to be composed throughout of sandy soil, with no relics or burials except one stone cist near the southern edge, in which nothing was discovered.

Mound D (the smallest of the group) lies 425 feet S. 40° W. of A, is 75 feet in diameter and similar in form and construction to B and C. It has also been explored by Mr. Artes, who found near the center a stone cist 3 feet square containing thirteen skulls.   Twelve of these were arranged in a circle near the sides of the cist, while the other was lying in the center with two thigh bones resting by it.   No other bones were found.

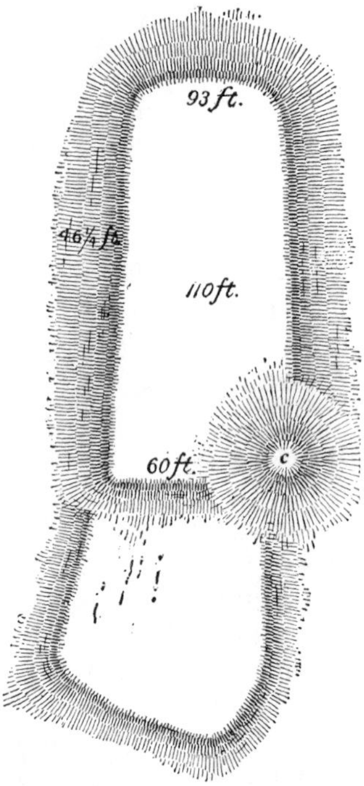

Nine hundred and sixty-five feet N. 52° W. of the large mound is a flat-topped circular mound (E), 338 feet in circumference at the base.   The diameters across the level top north and south and east and west are respectively 61 and 52 feet. It is about 12 feet high.

Undoubtedly the finest mound of the group (F) is situated 1,480 feet S. 56° W. of A.   It is a flat-topped circular structure about 15 feet high and very symmetrical.   The slope is nearly the same on all sides.   The circumference at the base is 550 feet, while the diameters of the top are 98 feet north and south and 100 feet east and west.   On the southwest there is a depression in the slope of the side, resembling an indented or depressed graded way, but whether it was originally so or is of modern origin can not well be ascertained.   The top of the mound has been used as a cemetery by the whites who have owned it.   On the southern side stands an oak tree 4 feet 3 inches in diameter.   The field surrounding this mound is subject to overflow during very high water.

FIG. 339.—Plat of large mound, Angel group.

An inclosing embankment or surrounding wall may be traced from mound C in a circular direction around to the eastern extremity of the bluff skirting the field in which mounds A, B, C, and D are situated. This, as will be seen by reference to the figure, includes A, B, and D, but does not inclose mounds E and F.   In width it varies from 15 to 25 feet.   Its height, in places where least disturbed, is from 3 to 5 feet on the west and north and from 4 to 8 feet on the east.   The length of the entire wall is 2,600 feet.   At a distance of 1,400 feet from mound C, following the line of the embankment, and 900 feet northeast of the

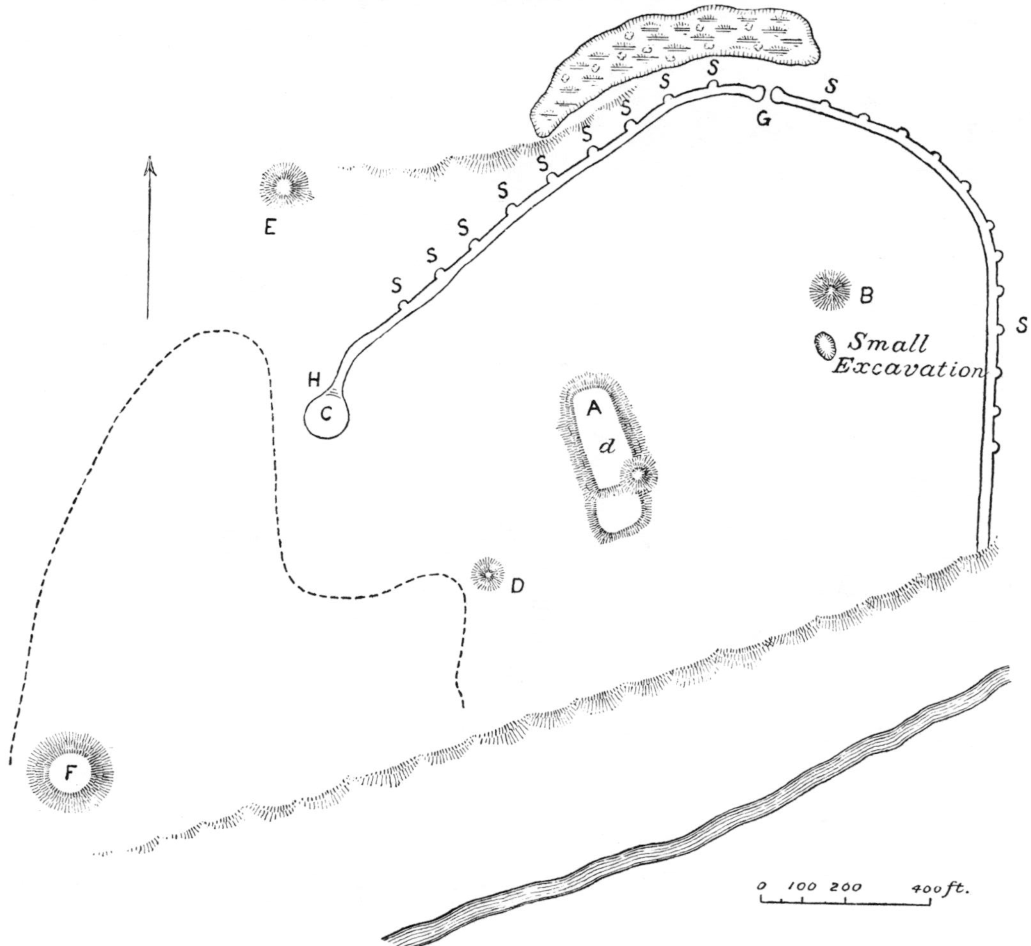

PLAT OF THE "ANGEL MOUNDS," NEAR EVANSVILLE, INDIANA.

F

E

H
C

D

A
a

B
Small
Excavation

G

S S S S S S S S S S S S S S S

0 100 200 400 ft.

large tumulus A, is a gateway (G), the original width of which, judging from present appearances, was 20 feet. The drainage of a portion of the field is at present through this gateway. Along the line of the embankment, where not effaced by the plow, are buttress-like enlargements (S), projecting outwards from 20 to 30 feet. The distance between these enlargements varies, increasing from east to west. Two measured on the east were 97 feet apart, two on the north 107, and two on the west 120 feet. Standing on the outer edge of one of these enlargements a person commands a clear view along the line for some distance. The eastern portion of the embankment rises 6 to 8 feet above the level of the adjoining field and the top is nearly level with the general surface of the field containing mounds A and B.

Careful search was made for an embankment extending to the bluff on the west, but no indications of such could be discovered. There is a ridge (shown by hachured lines on Pl. XLI) somewhat resembling the earthwork already mentioned, which was found to extend east and west for a short distance north of the regular embankment. It is wider than the other and was traced to the edge of the woods, where all signs of it were lost, nor could it be found beyond mound E. It is probably a natural swell of the surface rather than an artificial structure. No ditches were found near either of the earth walls, if the latter may be so called.

There is an excavation of considerable extent, in which large forest trees are growing, a short distance north of the inclosure. It is from this excavation that the earth composing the large mound was in all probability taken, as on the side towards this the slope is very gradual.

Mounds A and B are situated on the farm of Charles Grimm, C, D, and E on Silas Angel's farm, and mound F on Edward Collins's farm.

The distances between the mounds, measuring from center to center, are as follows:

	Feet.		Feet.
A to B	665	C to E	500
A to C	650	C to F	1,080
A to D	425	D to E	1,050
A to E	965	D to F	1,030
A to F	1,480	E to F	1,556
C to D	500		

In a few instances both in the eastern and western parts of the district mounds have been explored containing stone graves of the regular box-shaped type. Also some instances occur of earth-mounds covered over with a layer of stones, as mounds in southeastern Indiana and in the Kanawha valley in West Virginia are found occasionally to be.

A number of ordinary small burial mounds found on the bluffs and higher grounds of Pike and Brown counties, Illinois, opened by the Bureau agent, were constructed in the usual method in this portion of the district—that is, with a layer of hard mortar-like substance, or clay and ashes mixed, covering the skeletons or bottom layer. The positions of the skeletons found were various and the number of intrusive burials unusually large. The peculiarity observed was that in a number where there were intrusive burials near the surface no skeletons, or but the slightest fragments of bones of the original burial below the hard, undisturbed layer, could be found, although there were clear indications that the mounds were built and had apparently been used for general interment.

As yet but comparatively few cemeteries, or burials not in mounds, have been discovered, although they are quite common in southern Illinois, which, for reasons hereafter given, is included in the Tennessee district. In the latter, however, the bodies are usually inclosed in stone graves, which is very rarely the case with those in the northern part of the state. In some graves discovered on the gravelly point of a ridge in Lasalle county, among the relics found were rude stone pipes, shell beads, and a clay vessel made to represent a squatting human figure. Image pottery of this type is quite common in southern Illinois and southeastern Missouri, but is exceedingly rare in the northern part of the state, or in fact in any part of the district.

Although as a general rule the conical mounds of this district are burial tumuli, yet there is a class found in considerable numbers at certain points which appear to have been intended simply as dwelling sites. Some of these have already been noticed. Others are found along the Mississippi in its course between Iowa and Illinois. They are small, varying from 15 to 50 feet in diameter and from 1 to 3 or 4 feet in height, flattish on top. They are always in groups, occasionally of considerable extent. Excavations have revealed beds of burnt clay and ashes and a few burnt stones. It must be remarked, however, that the tumuli of this type found in northern Illinois appear in several cases, judging by the accompanying works, to be attributable to the authors of the effigy mounds. Those last mentioned are found chiefly in Mercer, Whitesides, and Rock Island counties.

In this district are found also hut-rings or lodge sites marking the locations of ancient villages. These however are not in so great numbers as in the district immediately south, yet they are discovered occasionally from western Iowa to eastern Indiana, thus extending over an area that must have been occupied in prehistoric times by several different tribes.

True pyramidal mounds are of rare occurrence in the district; besides those mentioned, two or three have been observed in western Illinois, one in Iowa, and one or two in the central part of Missouri, though it is doubtful whether the last mentioned should be included in this district.

There are but few inclosures, the most important being those in Allamakee county, Iowa, described in the preceding part of this volume, and also in the Fifth Annual Report of the Bureau. On the banks of Fox river, in La Salle county, Illinois, there is an irregularly semicircular wall forming an inclosure of comparatively small size. There are, at one point in Louisa county, Iowa, two parallel walls across a bluff point. As each has a ditch on the side of approach it is evident they were thrown up as defensive works. There are a few inclosures in western and middle Indiana. In addition to those alluded to, one in Orange county is worthy of passing notice. It consists of a double wall and an intervening ditch; on the inclosed area are twelve small mounds supposed from the slight exploration made to be dwelling sites.

There have been discovered in Cass and Whitesides counties, Illinois, some rather singular antiquities in the form of stone floors or pavements; some in mounds but others under the surface with no mound above them. These are described as composed of flat stones fitted as closely together as possible without dressing, usually over a space about 12 by 8 feet and depressed in the middle to the depth of 10 inches. Some of these floors consist of only one layer of stones, others of two. The stones are found reddened and cracked by long exposure to heat, and in one instance were covered with a mass of ashes and coals a foot thick in the center. Scattered through this mass were the charred human bones of at least three skeletons, but there were indications that more bodies than these had been burned here. This mass, however, had evidently been covered with dirt while yet smouldering. Stone floors, so far as I am aware, have as yet been discovered at but three or four other points—one in southern Illinois, another at Fort Ancient, Ohio, and another in western Pennsylvania. Those, however, of Cass and Whitesides counties, if we may judge by the description, which is not very clear, seem to bear a closer resemblance to the basin-shaped clay beds of the mounds in Little Tennessee valley than to any other remains yet observed.

Several caches of flint implements have been found in the valley of the Illinois river. In some cases those found in a single cache amounted to several hundred. In one instance, where the number hidden away amounted to some hundreds, a pit had been dug and the implements deposited in regular layers with alternate layers of sand between. This seems to justify the conclusion reached by some archeologists that the object was to render them more easily worked to the desired finish.

THE OHIO DISTRICT.

This includes, as at present defined, the eastern part of Indiana, all of Ohio, except the northern belt along the lake border belonging to the Huron-Iroquois district, and the southwestern portion of West Virginia. The eastern and western limits are not well marked and no attempt is made here to give definite boundaries in these directions. On the south, the Ohio river appears to form a pretty well defined limit, the peculiar features of the opposite districts showing themselves but seldom on the northern side.

As the principal works of this district have been often described and are well known, a brief mention of the distinguishing features and notice of some types not so well known is all that is deemed necessary here.

INCLOSURES.

The works of this kind found in the district are generally and justly considered its distinguishing archeological feature. These may, in a general sense, be treated under three heads: First, the hill forts; second, the geometrical inclosures; and third, the defensive walls forming partial inclosures.

The first class, which corresponds with Squier and Davis's " works of defense," includes those works built unquestionably for defense on elevated and naturally strong positions. The localities selected are usually bluff headlands, isolated hills, and elevated points defended on either hand by deep ravines, leaving only a narrow neck connecting the upper level with the level of the high plateau. The sides of these elevations are generally steep and difficult of access, in some cases precipitous and apparently inaccessible to any attacking party.

If we examine the works figured on Pls. IV, V, VI, VII, VIII (Nos. 1, 3, and 4), Pl. IX (Nos. 1 and 2), and (No. 3) Pl. XII of "Ancient Monuments," we find evidence of deliberate and thoughtful attempts to fortify positions naturally very strong. In nearly all of these instances the positions chosen are elevated, isolated, or nearly isolated, areas with precipitous descents on two or more sides. Along the margin of the descent, usually following the windings and indentations of the bluff, a wall of stone, of stones and earth, or earth alone, has been thrown up, a ditch running along the inner side furnishing the earthy material. In some cases where the commencement of the descent from the upper area is not abrupt the wall is carried along the slope a short distance below the upper level, as, for example, at "Fortified Hill," in Butler county, Ohio.[1]

It is true, as the authors of " Ancient Monuments" state, that works of this particular type " are never commanded from neighboring positions," a fact no doubt of some significance when we come to compare these works with other inclosures which seem to have been intended for a similar purpose, that of defense. This, however, will be referred to hereafter.

Some of these works present indications of growth or change subsequent to their erection. For example, the smaller area of Fort Ancient, occupying the point of the bluff, appears to be somewhat older than the remaining portion, a theory advanced by the author in an article in " Science," in 1886,[2] and adopted by Mr. Moorehead in his " Fort Ancient," in which he repeatedly uses the terms "Old Fort" and " New Fort" for the two parts, and in the sense here indicated. The in-

---

[1] Anc. Mon., Pl. VI.   [2] Vol. 8, Dec. 10, 1886, p. 538.

closure shown in No. 3, Pl. XI, "Ancient Monuments," where there are two walls some distance apart, is probably an instance where the inclosed area was contracted subsequent to its first occupancy. This is inferred from the fact that the inner wall passes over a mound (probably natural) which it seems would have been avoided in the original plan when the line might have been fixed wherever desired. It is also probable that some of the short walls about the chief gateway of "Fortified Hill," Butler county, shown in Pl. VI, "Ancient Monuments," are additions to the original plan. The reasons for this supposition become more apparent upon a personal examination of the topographical features of the locality. The easy approach at this gateway renders it the weak point of the fort.

The work with the double wall above mentioned and some others in central and southwestern Ohio, similar in character, except that they usually consist of a single wall and ditch, belong to a slightly different type than the "hill forts" referred to, and constitute the third class above mentioned. They occupy peninsulas formed by the bends of the rivers or larger streams, and the headlands at the junctions of deep ravines or uniting streams, and consist of a curved or irregular line of wall and ditch across the isthmus, or running from one bank to the other, the precipitous descents at the sides and around the point forming the defenses at these points of the area. Some of these works bear a strong resemblance to the works in the northern part of Ohio, which we have ascribed to the tribes of the Huron-Iroquois district, and, possibly, may be due in part to some tribes of this family. It is to be observed that a few of the same type occur in Kentucky. They may have been erected by the people who built the more elaborate hill forts, yet I am rather inclined to doubt this. However, as they are simple in character and are found at widely separate points in the mound area, it is unsafe to consider them of ethnic significance without further proof. We will probably be justified in assuming that they can not be ascribed to the builders of the geometrical works which constitute our second class of inclosures.

The works of this second class are usually more or less regular in form and are located on level areas, generally in the river valleys. The leading types of this class are the well known circles, squares, and octagons, or, as they are collectively termed, " geometrical works," found chiefly in the Scioto valley and about Newark, Ohio. Others which may be included in the class, though varying from the typical forms, are found in the Kanawha valley, West Virginia. Most of those of southern and central Ohio are figured with comparative accuracy by Messrs. Squier and Davis in "Ancient Monuments." But when deductions are to be drawn depending upon accurate measurements, it will be necessary to take into consideration certain errors in their work pointed out by the present author in a bulletin entitled "The Circular, Square, and Octagonal Earthworks of Ohio," published by the Bureau in 1889. This precaution is necessary because important inferences in regard to the origin and authors of these works have been drawn from the measurements given in "Ancient Monuments" and the assuring statement of the authors that these were made by them in person with great care. Notwithstanding this and the undeniable fact that a few of the circles and squares approximate very closely to true geometrical figures, and that some three or four are found to correspond pretty closely in size and form, yet the apparent errors in this respect manifest in their work and shown by a resurvey of some of the groups, render it necessary in making close comparison to have recourse to a more exact survey. The Bureau has endeavored to have this done, the result of which is shown in the bulletin referred to and in the preceding part of this volume.

The statement by the above named authors in regard to the general character of the works of this type, condensed as follows, may be accepted as correct:

They are mostly regular in their structure and occupy the broad and level river bottoms, seldom occurring upon the tablelands or where the surface of the ground is undulating or broken. They are usually square or circular in form; sometimes they are slightly elliptical. Sometimes we find them isolated, but more frequently in groups. The greater number of the circles are of comparatively small size, varying in diameter from 150 to 400 feet, and having the ditch, when present (as is usually the case), interior to the wall. They have, as an almost universal rule, a single gateway. Apart from these, numerous little circles 30 to 50 feet in diameter are observed in the vicinity of large works. [These hut-rings, for such undoubtedly they were, have nearly all been obliterated, scarcely a single one remaining at this time.] The larger circles are oftenest found in combination with rectangular works connected with them directly or by avenues. Some of these circles are of great extent, embracing 50 or more acres, though generally from 15 to 25. They seldom have a ditch, but whenever it occurs it is interior to the wall. The connected square or rectangular works never have ditches exterior or interior. The walls of these inclosures are composed of earth taken up evenly from the surface or from large shallow pits near by. They vary in height (with one or two exceptions), where not worn down by the plow, from 3 to 7 feet, and in width at base from 25 to 45 feet. The "Fair-Ground Circle" E at Newark, however, has a wall which, at some points, reaches a height of from 15 to 17 feet above the ground level. In one or two instances the circles are formed by two walls with a ditch between them, as the one at Circleville described by Atwater.

These authors express the belief that the works of this type were not erected for defensive purposes, but were designed for sacred or religious uses and as places for performing superstitious rites. This theory has been accepted by a large portion of subsequent writers upon this subject, among whom we may name as prominent Dr. Daniel Wilson. There are, however, exceptions worthy of notice. Baldwin, in his Ancient America, expresses no decided opinion on the question, but suggests "that a portion of them, it may be, encircled villages or towns." Foster (Prehistoric Races), although a decided opponent to the theory of the Indian origin of the mounds, objects to the suggestion that these valley inclosures were built for religious purposes, basing his opinion largely upon his knowledge of the Indian modes of defense. His remarks on this point have so much force in them that we quote the following paragraph:

Those works in northern Ohio and Western New York, which exhibit the trenches on the outside of the parapet, are also classed as defensive, while those which occupy level plateaux in the valley of the Ohio, with the trench inside, which are by far the most numerous [?] are classed as sacred inclosures. I do not recognize the importance of this distinction. Many writers, who have speculated upon this feature, seem to have adopted the idea that the enemy, whoever he may have been, settled down before these works, as did the Greeks under the walls of Troy, and engaged in a protracted siege. Now, every one acquainted with Indian warfare knows that it consists in surprises. A blow is struck, a massacre ensues, and a retreat follows. Savages have not the means of subduing a fortification by regular approaches, nor the accumulated provisions to sustain them while awaiting the result. A company of infantry on the plains, protected by an enclosure of palisades, trunks of trees set upright and sharpened to a point, may defy the combined power of the Indians indefinitely, or until their supplies give out. The mound-builders, if their enemies were like modern Indians, had only to guard against sudden attacks, and a row of pickets, without reference to whether the trench were inside or outside, would be effectual. Catlin has shown that the Mandans, in fortifying their villages, constructed the ditch inside, the warriors using the embankment as a shelter while they shot their arrows through the interstices of the pickets.[1]

Short[2] carefully avoids any discussion of the question, which fact may be accepted as a clear indication that he did not feel inclined to give his assent to the view advanced by the authors of "Ancient Monuments." Nadaillac,[3] on the other hand, is disposed to adopt it in a modified sense. But in the American edition, the following words introduced by the editor, Prof. Dall, express an entirely opposite view: "It is more reasonable to suppose them to have been fortified villages, according to a usage met with in various parts of the Mississippi valley by the first explorers."[4]

Lewis H. Morgan[5] remarks that "with respect to the large circular inclosures adjacent to and communicating with the squares, it is not necessary that we should know their object. The one attached to the High Bank Pueblo contains 20 acres of land, and doubtless subserved some useful purpose in their plan of life. The first suggestion which presents itself is, that as a substitute for a fence it surrounded the garden of the village in which they cultivated their maize, beans, squashes, and tobacco. At the Minnitare village a similar inclosure may now be seen by the side of the village surrounding their cultivated land, consisting partly of hedge and partly of stakes." This is the most likely explanation of these works that has yet been presented. Whether these dirt walls were mere supports to stockades is a question not yet settled; nevertheless, as they were intended as a protection not only against wild beasts, but also against human foes, it is probable that they

[1] Letters and notes * * * on the N. A. Indians, London, 1844. vol. I. p. 81. Prehistoric races 1881. pp. 174-175.
[2] North Americans of Antiquity.
[3] L'Amérique Préhistorique.
[4] P 101.
[5] Houses and House Life of the American Aboriginese.

were surmounted by stakes or supported a wooden fence or screen of some kind. The fact that the ditch, when present, is on the inside, is not an important factor in reaching a conclusion, as this is quite consistent with the Indian mode of warfare, as suggested by Foster.

In addition to the types of inclosures and defensive walls mentioned, there are some other varieties that deserve a passing notice. The lines of parallel walls, as those at Newark and Portsmouth, Ohio, are well known examples of one peculiar type. Some of the singular works described and figured in Ancient Monuments and elsewhere are to a large extent imaginary. Of these we may name Nos. 1 and 2, Pl. XXXIV of that work. The wing to No. 1 is not only imaginary, but, according to the Bureau assistant who visited the locality, was made impossible by the topography.

In the Kanawha valley the forms seem to be related to the regular works of Ohio, though much changed. We see hill forts here as there, and circular inclosures with a single gateway; but, instead of the combined circle and square, we see here elongate figures with parallel sides and semicircular ends. But it must be remembered that here the space is much contracted, rendering the construction of such extensive and elaborate works as those of the Scioto valley impossible. Moreover, these mountain valleys could only have been temporary retreats for large tribes or only for those devoted to hunting.

NEWARK AND HIGH BANK CIRCLES.

We insert here figures of the "Observatory" (Pl. XXI) and "Fair Ground" (Pl. XXII) circles at Newark (Pls. XXXI and XL), and of the "High Bank" circle (Pl. XXIII) near Chillicothe from a recent survey made by Mr. Henry Gannett, Geographer of the U. S. Geological Survey, in person, with use of plane table, in order to show the form of the walls. The dimensions and form as found by this survey are in such close agreement with that made by Mr. Middleton that they may be considered practically the same.

BURIAL MOUNDS.

The peculiarity of the mounds of this region which has been most frequently referred to as a marked characteristic is the presence in those of comparatively large size of a basin-shaped mass of clay at the bottom, to which the term "altar" has been applied; but as this is limited to a particular class, a more general description is necessary in order to throw light upon the customs of the mound-builders of this district. We therefore refer first to the burial mounds.

The conclusion reached by the authors of Ancient Monuments in regard to the burial tumuli of this region is given in general terms as follows:

Mounds of this class are very numerous. They are generally of considerable size, varying from 6 to 80 feet in height, but having an average altitude of from 15 to 20 or 25 feet. They stand without the walls of inclosures at a distance more or less remote from them. Many are isolated, with no other monuments near them; but they frequently occur in groups, sometimes in close connection with each other and exhibiting a dependence which was not without its meaning. They are destitute of altars, nor do they possess the regularity which characterizes the "temple mounds." Their usual form is that of a simple cone; sometimes they are elliptical or pear-shaped.

These mounds invariably cover a skeleton (in very rare instances more than one, as in the case of the Grave creek mound), which at the time of interment was enveloped in bark or coarse matting, or inclosed in a rude sarcophagus of timber, the traces and, in some instances, the very casts of which remain. Occasionally the chamber of the dead is built of stone, rudely laid up without cement of any kind. Burial by fire seems to have been frequently practiced by the mound-builders. Urn burial also appears to have prevailed to a considerable extent in the Southern States. With the skeletons in these mounds are found various remains of art, comprising ornaments, utensils, and weapons.[1]

These conclusions can not be accepted as generally applicable even in the region now being considered. Instead of the average altitude being from 15 to 25 feet, it is less than 10 feet. Nor is the statement that they very rarely cover more than one skeleton to be taken as a general rule, but as applicable only to those examined by these authors.

The mounds of this class in this district (which, as before stated, includes West Virginia) present the following types:

(1) Those containing a vault or sarcophagus constructed of timber, in which the body or bodies were interred. This is in most cases at the bottom of the mound, resting on the original surface of the ground, though it is occasionally at some distance up in the mound, and a few instances occur where it is sunk in the original soil. The bodies interred in these were usually wrapped in bark. These vaults are either round or quadrangular, the latter sometimes built up of logs laid lengthwise, but in other cases, as are the former, of posts placed perpendicularly side by side. In a few instances those in which the logs are laid horizontally are strengthened by upright posts at the corners, and in one or two instances one circular vault stood immediately above another.

Some of these differences are slight, but important from the fact that they are not common and, so far as known, found in no other district, being limited to a comparatively few mounds; but most of these are important ones. They also form connecting links which indicate some relation between the builders of the works of Ohio and West Virginia.

In some cases fire-beds occur within the larger vaults, while in cases of some smaller ones there are indications that fire was kindled on top of the vault after being completed. Prof. E. B. Andrews describes one of the latter, which he opened in Athens county, as follows:

This is a low mound, about 6 feet high, with a broad base, perhaps 40 feet in diameter. It has for years been plowed over and its original height has been considerably reduced. My attention was drawn to this mound by the burnt clay on its top. A trench 5 feet wide was dug through the center. On the east side much burnt yellow clay was found, while on the west end of the trench considerable black earth appeared, which I took to be kitchen refuse. About 5 feet below the

_____
[1] P. 161.

top we came upon large quantities of charcoal, especially on the western side. Underneath the charcoal was found a skeleton with the head to the east. The body had evidently been inclosed in some wooden structure. First, there was a platform of wood placed upon the ground on the original level of the plain. On this wooden floor timbers or logs were placed on each side of the body longitudinally, and over these timbers there were laid other pieces of wood, forming an inclosed box or coffin. A part of this wood was only charred; the rest was burnt to ashes. The middle part of the body was in the hottest fire, and many of the vertebræ, ribs, and other bones were burnt to a black cinder, and at this point the inclosing timbers were burnt to ashes. The timbers inclosing the lower extremities were only charred.

I am led to think that before any fire was kindled a layer of dirt was thrown over the wooden structure, making a sort of burial. On this dirt a fire was built, but by some misplacement of the dirt the fire reached the timbers below, and at such points as the air could penetrate there was an active combustion, but at others, where the dirt still remained, there was only a smothered fire, like that in a charcoal pit. It is difficult to explain the existence of the charred timbers in any other way. There must have been other fires than that immediately around and above the body, and many of them, because on one side of the mound the clay is burned even to the top of the mound. In one place, 3 feet above the body, the clay is vitrified.

It is possible that fires were built at different levels and that most of the ashes were blown away by winds which often sweep over the plain. I have stated that there was first laid down a sort of floor of wood, on which the body was placed. On the same floor were placed about 500 copper beads, forming a line almost around the body.[1]

(2) Mounds containing structures of stones. These structures are of two or three different types, which are apparently of ethnic significance.

The two principal varieties are the box-shaped cist and the dome-shaped vault. The latter are seldom found of the usual form in this district; some in the extreme southern portion of Ohio which seem to be of ethnic significance and to belong to a small separate district, mostly in Kentucky, are made of angular stones arranged in successive series from the base to the top. In a few cases these cover other little vaults of various forms made by setting stone slabs on edge or leaning them together so as to form a roof-shaped structure.

Stone vaults and cists are usually found in earthen mounds, yet they occasionally occur in those of stone. Atwater says:[2]

I saw one of these stone tumuli which had been piled on the surface of the earth, on the spot where three skeletons had been buried in stone coffins, beneath the surface. * * * The graves appear to have been dug to about the depth of ours in the present time. After the bottoms and sides were lined with thin, flat stones, the corpses were placed in these graves.

In some cases a low stone wall, a foot or so in height, is built around the outer margin of the mound, but so as to be within the outer line and covered by the earth of the mound. But these do not appear to be in all cases burial mounds.

In one or two instances the floor of the mound has been found covered with stones placed in from one to three regular layers. A stone layer in the body of the mound or over the burials, in other words a

[1] Tenth Rep. Peabody Mus., Vol. II, pp. 59-60.   [2] Trans. Amer. Antiq. Soc., Vol. I (1820), p. 184.

stone stratum, is not rare, but floors of the kind mentioned are exceedingly uncommon.

A somewhat singular type occurs sparingly in the Indiana and West Virginia portions of the district. In this variety, instead of the stones being inside, they form a covering over the outside, usually in the form of a single layer.

(3) Mounds in which the skeletons are inclosed neither in wooden nor in stone vaults, nor in pits in the original soil. As the characteristics of this class are negative, a few examples will convey a better idea of them than any attempt to give a general description.

Messrs. Squier and Davis[1] describe a mound 65 or 70 feet in diameter, 15 feet high, unstratified, and composed of earth taken from the surrounding plain. Nothing worthy of remark was found until the base was reached. Here a single skeleton was discovered, lying horizontally, which had been simply enveloped in bark. The burial in this case they supposed to have been as follows:

The surface of the ground was first carefully leveled and packed over an area perhaps 10 or 15 feet square. This area was then covered with sheets of bark, on which, in the center, the body of the dead was deposited, with a few articles of stone at its side, and a few small ornaments near the head. It was then covered over with another layer of bark and the mound heaped above.

A mound in the Kanawha valley, West Virginia, opened by Col. Norris, and described in the preceding part of this volume, presented precisely similar features.

Atwater, speaking of a mound at Chillicothe, says:[2]

Its perpendicular height was about 15 feet and the diameter of its base about 60. It was composed of sand and contained human bones belonging to skeletons which were buried in different parts of it. It was not until this pile of earth was carefully removed and the original surface exposed to view that a probable conjecture of its original design could be formed. About 20 feet square of the surface had been leveled and covered with bark. On the center of this lay a human skeleton, over which had been spread a mat manufactured either from weeds [reeds?] or bark.

Other mounds of this class show no preparation of the original surface nor indications of bark wrappings, the bodies having been simply laid upon the surface of the ground and covered with earth. In other cases the bones, partially charred, are found in ashes, the earth beneath and about them burned. In a few instances the bones are in a confused heap, more or less charred, and ashes are about them, but no other indications of heat, the burning having been done before depositing. In some cases of burial on the original surface and in excavations in the original soil, some of the skeletons are folded, though this method of arranging the body does not appear to have been practiced to any considerable extent in this district.

(4) Mounds wholly or partly of stone. Some rather singular mounds have been described as found in different parts of Ohio, but unfortunately they have nearly all been removed and the descriptions are based

---

largely on memory and second-hand statements and hence do not have that stamp of accuracy and authenticity desirable. For example, a large stone mound, which formerly stood a short distance from Newark, is described[1] as circular in form, 182 feet in diameter and some 40 or 50 feet high, composed of stones. These, when removed, were found to cover some fifteen or sixteen small earth mounds. In one of these were human bones and river shells; in another was a layer of hard, white, fire clay, and 2 or 3 feet below this was a wooden trough covered with a layer of small logs, in which was a skeleton that appeared to have been wrapped in some kind of coarse cloth. With it were fifteen copper rings and a breastplate (gorget) of the same metal. The clay above it being impervious to water, the wood and bones were well preserved. The wood bore what appeared to be the marks of some hard, metallic tool. Another of these earth tumuli contained a large number of human bones.

A mound near Madisonville opened on behalf of the Peabody Museum was found to cover a stone heap 5 feet high and 90 feet in diameter. In this the remains of 71 skeletons were found. "In addition to the outer stones of the mound, each body had been surrounded with stones at the time of burial," some set on edges, others simply piled around the bodies. A small mound in the Kanawha valley, covered with a layer of stones, was found to be composed of stones and clay mixed. In the center was a single skeleton in a cist formed of stone slabs. Simple stone cairns, some of which cover human remains, and others that show no indications of having been used for burial purposes, although not common, are found at various points in this district.

A singular variety of stone mounds, though not generally used for burial purposes, has been observed in Kanawha valley. These are usually sharply conical, built up generally by placing layer after layer of stones shingle fashion around a central space, so that when complete a well-like hole is left in the center. In a few instances two of these holes are found in one mound.

Of the tumuli supposed to have been erected for other than burial purposes the most noted are those which Messrs. Squier and Davis have designated "sacrificial mounds," but are more commonly known at the present time as "altar mounds." They are usually comparatively large in size and conical in form, often having a top layer of gravel and pebbles. At the bottom, on the original surface of the ground, is usually a regularly shaped mass of burned clay, with a basin-like depression in the middle, to which the authors above named have applied the term "altar," supposing it to have been used as a place to offer up propitiatory sacrifices. This mass of clay is circular, square, or oblong in form, varying in diameter or length from 4 or 5 to 50 feet and in height from 1 to 2 feet. The basin-shaped depression in the top is always circu-

---

[1] Smithson. Rep., 1866, p. 359.

lar and the outer margins of the mass are usually much sloped. Between the top layer of gravel and the clay structure at the bottom there are generally from one to four thin layers of sand. This type is confined almost exclusively to the southern half of Ohio, the exceptions, so far as known, being in Illinois and West Virginia.

Some of the mounds of this type, as has been shown by the explorations of the Bureau agents and others, were certainly used by the builders as places for depositing the dead.

Other mounds not used for burial purposes are quite generally supposed to have been erected as signal stations. While many of them are undoubtedly well situated for this purpose and no other explanation can now be given for their use, yet I must confess to considerable doubt of the correctness of this conclusion. Of all those seen by the writer the one best situated for this purpose is found in Knox county, Ohio, and described in the preceding volume as the Staats mound. It was opened by Mr. Middleton, of the Bureau, and found to contain a large amount of ashes, but no indications of burial. The outer border was surrounded by a low stone wall. From this, which is located upon a high bluff point that projects into the valley, the opposite range of hills and the valley, in which we may suppose the aboriginal village to have been situated and where an Indian village was actually located in early pioneer days, may be clearly seen for some miles both above and below. It is more than probable that the point where the mound is situated was selected as a signal station, and that the mound was in some way connected therewith; nevertheless the idea that mounds on such elevated points were built to add to the height, to extend the view, seems to the writer preposterous.

PYRAMIDAL MOUNDS.

Structures of this class, though not common in this district, are not entirely wanting. As examples we may refer to those forming part of the Marietta group so frequently described and figured in works relating to American archeology. Besides these we notice mounds of this class in connection with the Cedar Bank works and one with the Baum works, a description of which is given in the preceding part of this report. The exploration of the latter proves that in some cases mounds of this class were used as depositories for the dead.

STONE GRAVES.

The fact that these are occasionally found in mounds has incidentally been noticed. Others, however, of the box-shaped type not in mounds, have been discovered in limited numbers in various parts of the district. These have perhaps been observed in the greatest number in Ashland county, Ohio, at points where old Delaware villages were located. Others occur in eastern Indiana, especially in Franklin county; in the Kanawha valley, West Virginia, and elsewhere.

A somewhat remarkable cemetery, in connection with which are numerous ash pits, has been discovered by the agents of the Peabody museum in the vicinity of Madisonville, Ohio. This cemetery extends over an area of 15 acres. It seems to consist of bodies simply buried in the earth to the depth of 2 or 3 feet below the surface. Under the leaf mold, scattered among the graves and almost as abundant, are small, well-like pits from 3 to 4 feet in diameter and from 4 to 7 feet deep. From the fact that most of them contain ashes they have been designated "ash pits." The ashes found in them are generally mixed with kitchen refuse or the remains of cached material, such as maize. In some of them corn, sometimes yet on the cob, has been found, and, in a few, human bones.

It is said that the hilltops bordering the Mad river valley "are literally sown with the dead." In these cases "a pit has been dug and the remains interred below the surface," but the surface indications are obliterated. "The bodies occur singly, or in graves grouped together, or crowded promiscuously into large trenches, and are in almost every position, prostrate and sitting." Sometimes the parts of the skeletons are separated, having been thrown in without order or arrangement.

An instance was observed in Butler county, Ohio, in which a number of bodies buried in a natural mound had been placed in a circle with the heads toward the center, a mode of burial noticed in middle Tennessee.

Shell and refuse heaps are rare. One, however, of considerable size, has been discovered on Blennerhasset island, containing shells and refuse materials. A small refuse heap was found beneath a mound in West Virginia.

Some remarkable inscriptions or sculptured figures occur on rocks in the vicinity of Barnesville, Belmont county, Ohio. These consist of footprints, serpent figures, face outlines, and various other forms. Other inscriptions have been found in Cuyahoga county, near Newark, in Licking county, and elsewhere.

Burial caves are of rare occurrence in this district, two or three only having been discovered.

The most extensive series of ancient flint quarries in the United States is found in the central part of Ohio, along what is known as "Flint ridge," extending across the southern part of Licking and western part of Muskingum counties. "Its most western point is on the road leading from Newark to Zanesville, about 8 miles from the former place and half a mile from the eastern line of Franklin township. From here it extends eastward across Hopewell township and about 2 miles into Muskingum county, making its entire length very nearly 8 miles, counting by section lines, and fully 10 miles following the turns of the road. At about 2 miles from its western end, north of the village of

Brownsville, it reaches its greatest breadth, 2½ miles."[1] Pits are found in great numbers over this area. At one point 10 or 12 acres have been dug over, at another 6, at another 2, and so on. In some places the pits extend in continuous lines for half a mile or more. Ancient "work-shops" are abundant here. Of these Mr. Smith distinguishes two classes or varieties, the "blocking-out shops" and the "finishing shops." "At the first kind, which are always near the pits, it seems the flint blocks were brought to a size and shape convenient for dressing into such implements as were desired. In them are always found the largest hammers, though smaller ones are sometimes picked up as well. * * * These finishing shops are characterized by the smaller fragments, thin flakes, and broken or unfinished implements, very seldom found in the blocking-out shops. The hammers found in them are generally of small size."[2]

The peculiar features of the district are to be found in the form, size, and regularity of the lowland inclosures, the size and character of the hill forts, the so-called "altars" in the typical mounds, some certain forms of vaults, the presence in large numbers of monitor pipes, and certain ornamental lines and figures of pottery. Yet these features apply more particularly to the central and southern portions of Ohio than to the whole district. Nevertheless they are so intimately related to what seem to be but modifications of these types in eastern Indiana and West Virginia that there can be but little doubt that they are attributable to the same people. There are, however, clear indications of the presence of three or four different tribes of mound-builders or different waves of population in this district.

THE APPALACHIAN DISTRICT.

This district includes east Tennessee, or that part of the state east of the Cumberland mountains; the western part of North Carolina; the extreme southwestern part of Virginia and a strip along the northern part of Georgia. The portion of Georgia mentioned is also included in the "Tennessee district," and perhaps should also be included in the Gulf district, as there appears to be an intermingling here of the types of the three districts.

The ancient works of this district present some marked peculiarities in the construction of the mounds, the modes of burial, and the forms of the pipes. As these peculiarities have been brought to light through the explorations carried on by the Bureau of Ethnology, the descriptions of the mounds will be found in the preceding part of this volume and hence need only be referred to here. They are also partly described and contents noted in the paper by the present writer entitled "Burial Mounds of the Northern Section," in the Fifth Annual Report of the Bureau of Ethnology, and in a work entitled "The Cherokees in pre-Columbian Times."

[1] C. M. Smith, Smithson. Rep., 1884, p. 853.   [2] Ibid., pp. 864–865.

As the most characteristic archeologic features of the district are found in the form of the burial mounds, their contents and the modes of burial, reference is made to the mounds of this class first.

They are of several different types, but apparently the work of one people.

A type confined chiefly to Caldwell county, North Carolina, presents some peculiar and interesting features. In this a pit, usually circular, but in one case triangular, is dug in the original soil 30 to 40 feet in diameter and to the depth of 2 to 3 feet. On the level bottom of this pit the bodies (or skeletons) are placed, generally separately, some sitting and covered over by little beehive-shaped vaults of cobble stone, others without any such covering. Some of these skeletons are in a sitting posture, others lying horizontally on the back or side. Over the whole, dirt is thrown to fill up the pit and raise a slight mound. In some cases a number of skeletons are found together in one part of the pit. Buried with these skeletons are numerous stone pipes, polished celts, engraved shells, copper beads, and small, rude discoidal stones. Another feature worthy of notice is the presence, in some of these mounds, of altar-shaped piles of stones.

In one instance in east Tennessee, instead of a pit there was a circular stone wall some 2 or 3 feet high, the little vaults being in this and the mound built over all.

Some of the burial mounds along the Little Tennessee river are of comparatively large size, each usually marking the site of an ancient village. In most of these was found a series of basin-shaped fire-beds placed one above another. Scattered through the mound, except in the lower stratum of from 2 to 6 feet, were numerous skeletons placed horizontally in various directions. In some cases as many as ninety skeletons have been found in one mound.

Of other types we may mention the following as occasionally occurring: Comparatively small mounds in which the skeletons are lying on or near the original surface, side by side, with heads in one direction, or in two series, the heads of the two series in different directions. In some cases a mound contains a rude stone vault built up to the height of 1 or 2 feet in a square or circular form in which are the remains of one or more individuals. A most singular type has been observed in western North Carolina, though it can not be stated positively that it was erected for burial purposes. One of these, which will illustrate the type, was a mound about 45 feet in diameter and 6 feet high. In the center of this, resting on the original surface of the ground, was a conical mass of charcoal and ashes, 16 feet in diameter at the base and 5 feet high. The outer portion of this mass consisted of charcoal, evidently the remains of pine poles, which had been placed in several layers sloping toward the apex; the inner portion consisted of ashes and coals mixed with earth, in which were found some burnt human bones, and a few accompanying articles, among which were two stones with holes drilled through them. Fragments of bones and some relics were at the base, in the center.

Another type, which is found also in other districts, is the simple burial mound heaped over bodies laid upon the original surface. In this section they are generally stratified; the bodies, however, in these mounds are often placed with evident reference to relative position, contrasting in this respect with burials in the large mounds, where skeletons are found with heads in various directions.

An important fact regarding the large mounds of this region, most of which appear to have been used for burial purposes, though some but incidentally and not as the primary object of their construction, is the frequent occurrence of the remains of upright posts. These are so placed as to leave no doubt that they formed parts of buildings erected on the mounds. In some cases they are in sufficient numbers to indicate the form of the structure, which is generally circular, though occasionally rectangular.

STONE GRAVES.

Stone graves of the regular box shape are found in the valley of the Little Tennessee and in the mountains through which it passes, as well as in certain portions of northeastern Georgia. The last mentioned, however, are embraced in the Tennessee district, that and the present district overlapping at this point. The graves of this type in the valley of the Little Tennessee river are probably due, as will be shown hereafter, to an intrusive element which temporarily obtained a foothold in this part of the district. A single stone-grave mound has been discovered in the district; this was also in the valley of the Little Tennessee. One of the cists in this tumulus, the only one described, presented the unusual feature of a roof-shaped covering.

ARTICLES FOUND.

The most characteristic articles found in the mounds of this district are shell masks; engraved shells, usually bearing the conventional serpent symbol; conical copper ear pendants; cylindrical copper beads; stone pipes, usually with stems; polished celts; discoidal stones and shell beads. A few articles indicating contact with European civilization, such as fragments of iron implements, hawk bells, and glass beads, have also been discovered in mounds of this section.

THE CENTRAL OR TENNESSEE DISTRICT.

This district, which is irregular in form, is governed in its limits, except perhaps at its eastern extremity, by no geographical or topographical features; commencing on the west at or near the Mississippi between the mouths of the Missouri and the Ohio, it extends southeast to the headwaters of the Savannah. It includes that part of Illinois south of the

mouth of the Illinois river; all of Kentucky except the extreme northeastern portion; all of middle and most of west Tennessee and a strip
across the northern part of Georgia; and probably that portion of northern Alabama lying north of the Tennessee river.

There is strong evidence of an intrusive element, or, as appears
more likely, a preceding and independent element, in the northern portion of Kentucky and the extreme southern portion of Ohio, which area
should perhaps constitute a separate district, were it not for the overlapping and intermingling of types characteristic of the adjoining portions of the neighboring districts.

The characteristics which distinguish the antiquities of this district
as a whole from those of most of the southern districts as well as from
those of the more northern areas are the following: The general distribution and large number of stone graves herein designated the "box-
shaped" type, showing that this was the usual mode of burial practiced
by the aborigines of this area, and the occurrence of certain types of
copper articles and engraved shells. These may be considered as the
peculiar features. The other characteristics, which also prevail to a
greater or less extent in one or more adjoining districts are the forms,
character, and comparative abundance of pottery, the long-necked water jar being a typical variety—southeastern Missouri and eastern Arkansas being the only rivals in this respect; the occurrence of hut rings
found in equal abundance only in southeastern Missouri; the engraved
shells and shell masks of certain varieties, which seem to be confined
chiefly to this and the Appalachian districts, and the scarcity of carved
stone pipes, which is true also as to some southern sections. As serving further to mark the district it may be added that here we find a
much larger proportion of pyramidal mounds than in either of the other
northern districts, though not so many as in Arkansas; also numerous
inclosures. Stone walls, stone inclosures, and burial caves are perhaps
more frequent here than in any other area except West Virginia.

The boundary of the district can not be well defined geographically,
as there is in some parts such an intermingling of forms and types,
and in others such gradual changes from one variety to another, as to
leave the investigator in doubt whether to include certain areas of considerable extent. Especially is this true in regard to the western extension. Therefore I have been governed in my decision chiefly by the
limits of the stone-grave area and the occurrence of certain varieties of
monuments which appear usually to accompany them and certain classes
of articles found in them.

INCLOSURES.

Inclosures or embankments of earth abound in the central counties
of Tennessee, and while not confined exclusively to this portion of the
state, are of more frequent occurrence here than elsewhere in the limits of the region denominated "The Central or Tennessee district."

Located on a map, they form a series extending in a northeast and southwest direction through the central portions of Kentucky and Tennessee. They occur most frequently, however, along the Big Harpeth river and its branches, but are scattered in an irregular line through the eastern and southern counties surrounding Davidson and Williamson, with a few outlying posts to the northwest and southwest, reaching in the former direction as far as Union county in Illinois and in the latter to the southern border of Tennessee. Though aboriginal remains, as mounds, stone graves, hut rings, cemeteries, etc., are probably more abundant in Davidson county in and around Nashville than in any other section of the district, there is a noticeable absence of anything like fortifications in that immediate vicinity. Dr. Joseph Jones mentions traces of an ancient earthwork in connection with stone graves and hut rings on a hill 9 miles to the north of Nashville, and remains of a similar character about the same distance to the south of that city, near Brentwood, in Williamson county.

The works of this kind bear a general resemblance to each other, though there are some minor points of difference and a few strongly marked exceptions to the usual type. The inclosures are generally more or less circular or semicircular in form, and situated on a bluff or steep bank of a stream or river. In many instances this bluff, where very steep, forms the protection for one side of the inclosure, the ends of the wall terminating on the edge of the bluff. They are almost invariably accompanied by stone graves, hut rings, and ditches, the latter generally inside, following the line of the inclosing wall. The mounds are mostly of the conical type, but each inclosure contains one and sometimes two that are decidedly larger than the others, and usually pyramidal and flat-topped, though not generally symmetrical in form, most of them being oblong. Occasionally a round one is found, but as a general rule they are truncated. The smaller mounds and hut rings are scattered irregularly over the inclosed area, and not infrequently are found outside the wall. The works near Sandersville, in Sumner county, those near Lebanon in Wilson county, the De Graffenried works near Franklin, in Williamson county, and others on the Big and West Harpeth rivers, are good types of this class of works. In Jackson county near Floyd's lick, and in Henry county in the vicinity of Paris, similar inclosures have been discovered. There are a few instances, as in the northern districts, where the embankment is merely a straight or slightly curving wall thrown across a spur or ridge of land at the junction of two streams where the banks are of sufficient height to prevent surprise from that quarter, and the wall is thrown across to guard the landward or more easily accessible side. A work of this kind was found about 12 miles below Carthage, on the Cumberland river, in Smith county. The wall was accompanied by an interior ditch, and had an entrance way, opposite which, and about 6 feet from it, on the inside, were the remains of a wall so placed as to form a rear guard.

A similar work is reported in Hickman county at the intersection of Duck and Piney rivers, near Centerville, and another in La Rue county, Kentucky. An embankment of earth and stone in the fork of Duck river, in Coffee county, near Manchester, though much more elaborate, really belongs to the latter class, the wall having been thrown from bluff to bluff across one end of a narrow strip of land between the east and west branches of Duck river. Across the other end is a similar wall; beginning where the bluffs terminate on each side of the strip of land, and diverging from the streams, it forms an angle about midway between the two. This work also has a guarded entrance, a short wall extending inward on each side of the main entrance forming a parallelogram. The right wall, extending a little beyond the other, bends at a right angle across the end of the space thus inclosed, leaving room for an inside gateway between it and the end of the left wall. Two stone mounds, some 3 feet higher than the general wall, guard the main entrance from the outside. This work is an exception to the general rule, as no mounds, graves, hut rings, or other remains of archeologic interest are found in or about it, except a single large mound, elliptical in form, and built of earth and loose stones, which stands about half a mile from the main entrance.

It is not unusual to find along these walls slight elevations or projections, supposed by some to have been the foundations for towers or some such works for observation or defense. The inclosure near Sandersville, in Sumner county, before mentioned, furnishes an example of this kind; also that in Wilson county, near Lebanon, which is a circular earthwork having an interior ditch. Slight elevations occur at regular intervals along the inside of this wall. They are somewhat higher than the embankment and slope to the bottom of the ditch. This slope is divided into two parts by a level bench nearly 3 feet wide. Another inclosure in Williamson county, on the West Harpeth river, is of this type, the irregularly circular embankment being wider at intervals as if some tower or defensive structure had occupied each of these points.

The most remarkable examples of this class of works, however, are found in Hardin county, in the neighborhood of Savannah. On the east side of the Tennessee river, on the high grounds adjoining the town, are extensive earthworks inclosing a group of mounds. The embankment is five-sided, the ends terminating on the high bluff of the river. At intervals of 80 yards along this wall are the remains of bastions which extend about 20 yards to the front along the main line and 30 yards at the main angles. About 55 yards in advance of this line, and parallel to it, is a similar but less elevated embankment, now partly obliterated, but still traceable. The bastions of this latter line project 40 feet in front and alternate with those of the main line. Three miles below Savannah, in the same county, a similar system of earthworks is found at the foot of a bluff which rises 50 feet above the bottom lands of the Tennessee river. There is in this instance, however, only a single line of wall with the bastions projecting to the front. In the construction of the walls these works bear a remarkable resemblance to those of "Aztalan" in Jefferson county, Wisconsin. The work in Vanderburg county, Indiana, in the group known as "the Angel mounds," heretofore described, evidently belongs to this type and was probably built by the same people.

"Covered ways," or passages, protected by embankments leading down to an adjacent stream or spring, are found in some of the inclosures of Tennessee, and open gateways through the walls, as well as raised passageways over them, afford the common means of entrance.

A few inclosures in Kentucky may be noticed as being within the limits of this district. In Fayette county, on a slight hill near North Elkhorn creek, is a circular inclosure, consisting of a ditch from which the earth was thrown up to form an embankment. Near this is another work of similar construction, but differing slightly from the usual type. The circular platform defined by the ditch is on a level with the top of the outside wall, and seems to have been raised above the natural surface of the ridge. A raised pathway on a level with the platform interrupts the ditch on the northwest side. In a hollow between the two last-mentioned works is a shallow ditch inclosing an area of about 82 feet in diameter. An inclosure in the form of an irregular polygon, resembling closely those in western New York, is mentioned in Collins's History of Kentucky as existing in this county. In Montgomery county, in what is denominated the "Old Fort Woods," there are three circular inclosures, each having the inner space excavated.

MOUNDS.

Pyramidal mounds, with which are classed all rectangular and truncated tumuli, are to be found in most of the inclosures, the usual arrangement being as follows: A large truncated mound around which is a space clear of other remains, while scattered through other portions of the inclosed area are smaller conical mounds, stone graves, hut rings, and sometimes pits or excavations. There are occasionally two or three mounds of a larger size in each group or system of earthworks, but there is, as before stated, almost always one that exceeds all the others in its dimensions, and that often contains beds of ashes and hearths of hard-burned earth, indicating that it had been used as a residence site rather than as a burial mound. Isolated groups of mounds, or groups not connected with embankments or any system of works, are of frequent occurrence. A group of this kind, containing between 40 and 50 mounds, is noticed near the mouth of Lost creek, opposite Wabash island, in Union county, Kentucky. Three such groups occur near Uniontown, in the same county. Some of the latter were burial mounds; others were without human remains, but contained other relics. About 2 miles from the ferry landing, opposite Shawnee-town, is a remarkable group of mounds, consisting of three subgroups, each of which has its principal mound superior in size to others of its group.

The large truncated mound, though a leading feature of almost every group of mounds or system of earthworks, is not always of the regularly square or even of the rectangular form, being sometimes pear-shaped and sometimes oval. These are most numerous in the middle and southwestern portions of Tennessee, though those at Mount Sterling, Kentucky; one in Vanderburg county, Indiana; the great Cahokia mound, in Madison county, Illinois; the Linn mound, in Union county, of the same state, and the celebrated Etowah mound, in Bartow county, Georgia, all included in this district, show a distribution of this type over a considerable area. The true pyramidal mound is found most frequently in Davidson, Williamson, and some adjacent counties.

There are a few cases where roadways have been found leading to the top of some of these large mounds. A mound connected with the peculiar embankment a few miles from Savannah, in Hardin county, Tennessee, had three arms running out from it, apparently pathways, affording means of easy ascent to the top. A mound in Montgomery county, Kentucky, has an inclined way leading to the top; the roadway to the Etowah mound is peculiar in winding up the side instead of approaching at right angles.

Stone-grave mounds are found in connection with most of the ancient works in the valleys of the Cumberland and Tennessee rivers and along many of their tributaries, also in some of the southern counties of Illinois and in northwestern Kentucky. One or two have been found in northern Georgia and also in southern Indiana.

There seems to be no particular rule observed in depositing the dead in these mounds. Sometimes the graves are placed irregularly through the mound, no systematic arrangement being observed; sometimes they are found in tiers, one above another. A group of five mounds in Davidson county, Tennessee, about $4\frac{1}{2}$ miles southwest from Nashville, presents this latter arrangement. The mounds contained the bodies of from 600 to 800 people arranged in regular layers or tiers. Fragments of pottery, stone implements, and other articles were found on the covering stones and beside the graves. On the original soil beneath the graves were several beds of ashes. One mound of this group, conical in form, had apparently been built up by the accumulation of stone graves, placed in five tiers, the one above having fewer in number than the one beneath it. No regularity was observed in placing the bodies. One body was buried here without the stone cist.

A stone grave mound about 10 miles from Nashville near Brentwood presents a good example of this arrangement, being one of the most perfect in its construction. The stone graves, especially toward the center of the mound, were placed one upon another, forming in the

central and highest part of the mound three or four ranges. The oldest and lowest graves were of the small square variety similar to the
well known type found near Sparta, thought at first to be pigmy graves,
and like them containing detached bones or bundled skeletons, while
those on or near the summit were of the natural length and width of
the inclosed skeleton. The lids of the upper stone cists were so placed
as to form a uniformly rounded sloping rock surface. In one of the
graves of this mound was an inner compartment containing the bones
of a child.

A mound inside the inclosure near Lebanon, in Wilson county, Tennessee, presented a different mode of construction, the graves being
arranged about the outer portion of the mound in the form of a hollow
square in two or three irregular rows and in three tiers. In this mound,
as in the one near Nashville before mentioned, one body was found
buried without a coffin. Pottery, relics of copper and stone, and pieces
of mica were found in these graves.

Another method of arranging the stone coffins was by placing them
with the heads to the center, the feet extending toward the circumference of the mound like the radii of a circle. Stone graves disposed in
this manner have been found in a mound in Davidson county, Tennessee, on the bank of the Cumberland river, opposite Nashville. In the
center of the mound, the point from which the sarcophagi radiated,
was a large vase or basin-shaped vessel composed of clay and pulverized river shells. It still retained the impression of the basket or cloth
in which it was molded. The rim was a true circle and was covered
an inch thick with ashes from some incinerated matter. There were
two rows of stone coffins ranged around this central basin, the circle
of graves being constructed with great care and all the bodies ornamented with beads of bone and shell.

A mound in Williamson county, Tennessee, on the West Harpeth
river, and another in Sumner county presented the same arrangement
of stone graves like the spokes of a wheel.

A number of mounds discovered in Union county, Kentucky, show
a remarkable blending of different modes of sepulture which is worthy
of notice. For instance, in one mound of the Lost creek group, opposite Wabash island, some of the earlier burials were without stone coffins and unaccompanied by relics of any kind, while others were covered by stone slabs set up "roof shaped" over the bodies. In the later
burials the bodies were arranged in the form of a wheel, with the heads
to the center and accompanied by clay vases or pots. With one body
were found two copper bells. In this mound, at a depth of 6 feet from
the summit, was a circular pavement of limestone, and a foot above
this a layer of clay. Bones were found in all parts of the mound.

Another mound in the same county contained a number of stone
graves and two layers of bodies without the stone coffins, but having
pots buried with them. The stone grave burials appeared to be more

recent than others and the latter were much disturbed by them. Where not disturbed these earlier burials presented the wheel-like arrangements before noticed. Two stone pipes and a few burial urns with seven ears were found in the disturbed portion of this mound.

In the Lindsay mound, near Raleigh in the same county, the bodies were arranged in a circle on their backs with heads to the center, faces turned to the left side, and feet toward the margin of the mound. The circle was extended toward the circumference by an additional row of bodies. On the west side the bodies were five layers deep. The regularity in placing the bodies was somewhat broken toward the margin on the east side. In the earlier burials, or those at the bottom of the mound, the bodies were laid on the surface of the ground, which had been scraped clear of vegetable matter. No relics were deposited with these. With the later burials were found burial urns or pots. In this mound were two or three deep pits or excavations filled with mixed or discolored earth, at the bottom of which were human remains. One of these, in which only a few animal bones were found, was shaped like an inverted cone. Some of these pits reached into the original surface. Thus there were three different modes of burial in this mound: Those where the bodies were laid on the surface without the accompaniment of vases or other works of art, and covered with yellow sandy loam; those of a later date, with which burial urns had been deposited, three or four tiers of which were covered with clay; and those of the deep pits or excavations. Another mound in the vicinity of Raleigh, explored many years ago, displayed an unusually systematic arrangement in its internal construction. In all cases, without exception, the bodies were laid on the left side with heads turned to a common center. At the head of each was an earthen vessel, and these were graded in size according to the age or size of the individual. The bodies were laid on the original surface of the ground, and on the foreheads of some was placed a single valve of a *Unio* shell. The heads of some of them were artificially compressed. This mound contained no stone cists, though there were many in the neighborhood, of the short, square variety, lined with black bituminous shale and containing folded or bundled skeletons.

In some of the tumuli classed as "stone-grave mounds" the graves are not of the regular box-shaped type, being sometimes, as in the one in Union county, Kentucky, "tent" or "roof shaped," that is, the stones are set up on their edges on each side of the body and slanted so as to meet above it, thus forming a triangular covering.

Another variety was found in a mound in Allen county, Kentucky, which consisted of a vault 10 feet deep and 8 feet in diameter, round, and walled up with stones like a well. The bottom was made of stones laid edgewise and keyed in with smaller stones. At every 2 feet in this well was a layer of large flat rocks, and between these layers were human remains. Stone graves of the roof-shaped variety were found in the vicinity, varying in length from 2½ to 8 feet. Occasionally a mound is found the internal construction of which differs so materially from the usual type as to be worthy of notice. One of these anomalies is a small, double mound within the inclosure at Savannah, Hardin county, Tennessee. This contained three furnaces or trenches, with rude arches thrown over them of irregular masses of hardened clay. From these a number of small flues 8 or 10 inches in diameter went up, some of them directly toward the surface of the mound, others twisting and winding about through it in all directions. Large logs completely charred, in both upright and horizontal positions, the ends burned off by fire, human bones, and ashes were found in it.

Another type is the stratified mound built up of layers of different materials, as sand, clay, ashes, stones, etc. Examples of this kind are found in several localities in the central portions of Tennessee and occasionally in Kentucky. One in Union county, Kentucky, was constructed in a peculiar manner, having a hard central core of sand, over which the mound was built by depositing loads of earth of about half a bushel each; these were distinctly marked in sections in the mottled layers. A few stone cairns or rock piles are noticed throughout this region, some of them covering ashes and charred bones.

Sometimes the remains of wooden posts are found in the mounds in such a position as to indicate that they upheld or formed part of a building or structure of some kind, as those in one mound of the Lebanon group, and remains of wooden vaults have also been discovered, though they are rare. A mound already mentioned in Union county, Kentucky, near Raleigh, appeared to contain a vault or chamber of some kind, from the presence of the remains of charred logs, both in an upright and a horizontal position. A wooden structure was found in the earth in the vicinity of an aboriginal cemetery in Williamson county, Tennessee. It was traced about 10 feet in length and 5 in width, but no graves were found in or under it.

BURIAL CAVES.

Cave burials occur in this district in the following counties: In Grayson, Hart, Edmonson, Barren, Warren, and Fayette counties, Kentucky; Smith, White, Warren, Giles, Marion, and Fentress counties, Tennessee, and Bartow county, Georgia. These localities lie mostly in a belt extending in a north and south direction through the center of the district.

In most of these caves, both in Kentucky and Tennessee, the bodies appear to have been laid on the floor of the cave, sometimes in beds of ashes, sometimes on a pavement of flat stones. There are, however, some instances in which the bodies have been found incased in stone slabs, and afterwards imbedded in clay or ashes. In Smith and Warren counties, Tennessee, and in Warren and Fayette counties, Kentucky, the flesh of the bodies was preserved and the hair was yellow and of fine texture. In some cases the bodies were enveloped in several thicknesses of coarse cloth with an outer wrapping of deer skin. Some of the bodies were wrapped in a kind of cloth made of bark fiber, into which feathers were woven in such a manner as to form a smooth surface. In two cases the bodies, placed in a sitting or squatting posture, were incased in baskets. In one of the caves in Smith county the body of a female is said to have been found, having about the waist a silver girdle, with marks resembling letters.

A cave was discovered in Giles county which had several rooms and was entered by a concealed passage. A flat stone partly closed the entrance and other stones were rolled in to fill up the mouth. In Bartow county, Georgia, a human skeleton was found in a cave in a limestone bluff walled in, in a similar manner.

In some localities, as in Fentress, Grayson, and Marion counties, caves have been discovered which, in the great quantities of ashes, the numerous fragments of pottery, animal bones, implements, and ornaments of various kinds, bear evidence of having been used as dwelling places.

These cave burials are found along the rivers and streams in the vicinity of fertile valleys and cool springs.

STONE GRAVES.

The stone grave cemeteries are found on the hill slopes and in the valleys, along the rivers, and scattered over the richest and most fertile lands of Tennessee and Kentucky. They occur in connection with nearly every system of earthworks, but are not confined to them, as large cemeteries exist where there are no mounds or embankments in the vicinity. When connected with fortifications they are usually within the embankments, though sometimes a few are scattered outside. The rectangular, box-shaped stone cist is the prevailing type, both in the cemeteries and in the stone grave mounds. These often vary in size from the small square grave 2 feet in length and the same in width to 7 feet in length and 3 in width. There are, however, a few variations from this type which merit description. The roof-shaped grave has already been alluded to. These are made by setting large pieces or slabs of rock on edge and slanting them toward each other until they meet above the body, forming a covering like the roof of a house. Graves of this type are found in widely separated localities both in Kentucky and Tennessee and are met with in mounds as well as in cemeteries. They are not always of a uniform size, but vary in length from 2½ to 8 feet.

On a bluff near Newport in Campbell county, Kentucky, were two graves which were formed by placing a curbing of regular fragments of stone of considerable size so as to form a circle of 10 feet in diameter, from which flat stones were inclined outward shingled one over the other so as to form a band 6 feet wide. Bones were found beneath the stones of this band. It has been suggested that these graves were more recent than the box-shaped cists, but this is doubtful. Others somewhat similar have been observed in southern Ohio.

Graves of a peculiar character have been discovered on the brow of a hill near Pageville, in Barren county, Kentucky. These were circular in form, between 4 and 5 feet in diameter and 3 feet deep. Slabs of limestone about 3 feet long and from 1 to 2 feet wide, brought from some distance, had been placed on end around this pit and the bottom covered with thin shale brought from the creek a quarter of a mile away. Bodies of adults were placed in a sitting posture against the upright slabs. Earth had been thrown over all and a few flat stones placed on the top. A few bones of children were also found, but their position could not be determined. The bodies were evidently all placed in this grave at the same time. There were about thirty graves of this kind at this point.

Besides these variations there are a few minor differences, such as graves lined with large pieces of broken pottery neatly fitted together; a pottery burial case made in two sections, or a case with a cover; rectangular cists large enough to contain several bodies, etc.

HUT RINGS.

Hut rings are frequent adjuncts of mound groups, and are often found inside the inclosures and also scattered about outside the earthen walls. Floors of hard-burned earth are sometimes found in the center of these rings, underneath which are human bones and sometimes stone graves.

RELICS.

Of the relics found in the mounds and graves of this district, the most characteristic is the pottery, which is found in greater abundance here than in any other section of the United States, except southeastern Missouri and Arkansas. Like that of the last-mentioned two areas, which it resembles very closely, the chief types are the narrow-necked water bottles and the image pottery. Another distinguishing feature is found in the engraved shells, some of which are peculiar to this district, while other types are found elsewhere only in the Appalachian section. Engraved or stamped copper plates of a peculiar type have also been found in limited numbers. These are important, not only because of the figures they bear, but also because they appear to be limited exclusively to the stone grave area.

Other articles not confined exclusively to the district, but occurring more frequently here than elsewhere, are the copper spool supposed to have been worn in the ear, and wooden ornaments probably used as ear pendants, covered with thin plates of copper. The latter, however, are comparatively rare, having been found only in southern Illinois and in the vicinity of Nashville. A few stone idols have also been found in this district, and, what is strange, they have been discovered at the extreme eastern and western ends of it—in northern Georgia and southern Illinois.

THE SOUTHERN SECTION.

This section is limited, as at present arranged, to the Arkansas and Gulf districts, though it is probable that future investigations will show that it should be further subdivided.

THE ARKANSAS DISTRICT.

This district includes the southeastern counties of Missouri, the state of Arkansas, and the northern part of Louisiana. The ancient works, however, are confined chiefly to the eastern portion of the area included in these bounds. Although embraced in the district, a large portion of the groups of works and types of pottery of southeastern Missouri resemble those of southern Illinois and the Cumberland valley so closely as to leave no definite marks of distinction between the two classes. This strong resemblance between the works of these sections, which has been repeatedly noticed, possibly indicates the presence for a time in this region of some of the same people who occupied the Tennessee district, though the important characteristic of the latter—the box-shaped stone grave—is wanting here.

The chief distinction between the archeology of southeastern Missouri and the rest of the district is found in the numerous groups of hut rings marking village sites, often surrounded by earthen walls, usually forming quadrangular inclosures.

The distinguishing features of the district as a whole, especially when compared with the archeology of the northern areas, are the large, oblong, terraced, pyramidal mounds, and the low, flattish, domiciliary mounds or house sites, which seem to take the place in Arkansas of the hut-rings in southeastern Missouri. Other characteristics are the occasional remains or marks of rectangular dwellings, the forms and ornamentation of the pottery, and the forms of the few pipes which have been discovered.

A brief notice of the leading types, based almost exclusively on the results of the explorations carried on by the Bureau of Ethnology, the details of which have been given in the preceding part of this volume, is presented here that the reader may judge of the propriety of considering this a separate district.

HOUSE SITES.

The remains of this type consist of low, flattish mounds, from 1 to 5 feet high and from 15 to 100 feet in diameter. In opening them the strata are usually found to occur in the following order: First, a top layer of surface soil from 1 to 2 feet thick; next, a layer of burned clay, varying from 4 to 12 inches (though usually from 4 to 8 inches thick), and broken into lumps, seldom in a uniform unbroken layer; immediately below this is a layer of ashes and charcoal, in which are usually found fragments of pottery and occasionally whole vessels, stone chips, broken bones of animals, and other refuse material; immediately below this is sometimes a layer of hardened muck or dark clay; at this depth there is often found, in the eastern part of the state, a skeleton, or sometimes two.

The burnt clay often contains impressions of grass or small twigs, and sometimes is ornamented on one side by being stamped apparently with an implement made of split reeds of large size. Hard-burned fragments of this clay have given origin to the statement often made that brick is found in southern mounds.

That this clay is plaster from the houses of the mound-builders is shown by the fact that remains of the upright posts and of the cane lathing forming the walls of the building have been found, and from other facts mentioned hereafter.

These remains of the houses of the mound-builders of Arkansas are not confined to the small mounds of the type mentioned, as they frequently occur in the larger mounds, both of the pyramidal and conical form. Sometimes the repeated building, burning, and covering on the same spot results in forming a mound of considerable size, as, for example, the one in Butler county, southeast Missouri, explored by Col. Norris and heretofore described in this volume. So far as the explorations which have been made indicate, these small, domiciliary mounds appear to be confined chiefly to the low alluvial sections of Arkansas, and seem to have resulted from the following customs: First, that of forming an earthern platform a foot or two in height on which was placed a dwelling, and, second, that of burying the dead in the floor, then burning the house over them and covering the ruins with earth. Examples illustrating these statements will be found in the first part of this report.

Remains of ancient houses, apparently of the mound-building age, and connected with or pertaining to mound groups, but not in mounds, were discovered in a few localities. These were some 2 or 3 feet beneath the surface of the ground with the usual mass of burned clay plastering, remains of the posts of the walls, etc. In the two or three cases observed, the buildings consisted of two or three rooms, each about 10 or 12 feet square.

The ordinary conical burial mounds of Arkansas and also of Mississippi present marked differences from those of southern Missouri. These are fully illustrated by the examples given in the reports of the Bureau assistants. The chief variations were found in the condition of the skeletons; in some groups nearly or quite all were closely folded up, though seldom in a sitting posture: in other localities they were found chiefly lying at full length. In a few instances promiscuous masses, like those of the northern section heretofore described, were found, but these appear to be comparatively rare in the south. In some cases, especially in the graves. remains of the bark wrapping (apparently elm) were observed. Stone graves seem to be entirely unknown in this section.

The eastern portion of Arkansas is noted for the number and size of its pyramidal mounds, many of which are terraced and very regular in form, as may be seen by reference to the figures in this volume, part 1. Others, precisely of the same form, are found in all of the Gulf states, but not so numerous as here, unless possibly in the central part of Alabama, a region that has been but partially explored. The oblong is the prevailing form, the square pyramid being comparatively rare.

In addition to the oblong and square truncated pyramids, there are found here and there truncated mounds of several different forms. For example, the "Rogers mound," Phillips county, Arkansas, figured in the first part of this volume, which is oval in outline, the longer diameter at the base 247 feet, the shorter nearly 200 feet, height 20 feet. On top of this is a small hemispherical mound 50 feet in diameter and 5 feet high. Excavating the small tumulus, Col. Norris found near the surface a very heavy fire-bed. Other similar beds were found at various points near the surface of the terrace or main mound.

Another found near Osceola, Mississippi county, same state, is of the form shown in Fig. 132.[1] The dimensions of this somewhat unusual, though not unique, structure are as follows: "Altitude of the first terrace 11 feet, width 129 feet, length 158 feet; altitude of the second terrace 3 feet 7 inches, width 60 feet, length 93 feet; altitude of the third terrace 6 feet, width 63 feet, length 78 feet." As the writer makes the whole length 375 feet, it is probable the measurements given apply to the upper levels. Excavations brought to light, near the surface, a layer of burnt clay, broken, as usual, into fragments, which Mr. Evans denominates brick. At the depth of 8 feet some human bones were found in an advanced state of decay, but no skulls were observed.

Messrs. Squier and Davis [2] make the statement that the principal mound of the group at the junction of the Washita, Tenzas, and Catahoula rivers (now Troyville), Louisiana, has a spiral pathway winding around it from bottom to top. An examination of it was made by a Bureau assistant in 1883, at which time no indication of such a pathway was visible. It is true much of the top had been removed and the mound much defaced during the late war, but sufficient remained to indicate such a pathway if it existed. A description and figure of these works will be found in the preceding part of this volume. They also state, in a note on the page of their work above referred to, that "mounds with spiral pathways are frequent at the south and are occasionally found at the north." Later investigations have failed to confirm this assertion; in fact, they prove it to be entirely erroneous, as not one such has been discovered.

There is no intention of entering at this point into a discussion of the object and uses of these pyramidal and truncated mounds, yet we

---

[1] S. B. Evans, in Chicago Times, April 9, 1881.　　[2] Anc. Mon. p. 117.

venture the assertion, which is borne out by history and explorations, that in the south as a general rule they were the sites of council houses, residences of the chiefs, and possibly of temples.

INCLOSURES.

Though not numerous in the district, inclosures are by no mean wanting. They occur, however, in the largest proportion in south-eastern Missouri. The latter, as heretofore remarked, are usually quadrangular and inclose groups of hut-rings, with an occasional mound. These, I am inclined to believe, should be considered a distinct type, due probably to one or more tribes different from the authors of the Arkansas works. The few inclosures found in Arkansas and Louisiana and two or three in southeastern Missouri are usually irregularly semicircular, abutting on water courses or swamps. As a general rule they inclose one, rarely two, large and from two or three to several smaller mounds. It is to be remarked that the large mound is seldom if ever a regular pyramid. This fact, though seemingly of slight importance, may prove of value in studying the archeology of this region, as the same fact is found to be true of some groups in southern Illinois, southern Indiana, and middle Tennessee. It is scarcely necessary to state that the walls as well as the mounds are in all cases built wholly of earth. In or immediately adjoining some of the inclosures are irregular excavations, a few of which are of considerable size, whether for other purposes than obtaining earth for the mounds is a question yet undecided.

GRADED WAYS AND RAMPS.

These occur in connection with a few of the large mounds of Louisiana and southeastern Missouri, but very few are found in Arkansas. The best examples of these appendages are seen in a group in Stoddard county, Missouri, known as the " Rich Woods mounds," figured in the first part of this volume, and the Moorehouse group of Louisiana, figured in " Ancient Monuments." The former is, in some respects, one of the most remarkable groups in the entire district. The very large number of mounds it contains, the fact that three different series of these are united by ramps, the various forms presented (one of which is unique), and the large area over which the group extends, render it exceedingly interesting and worthy of more careful study. The only true crescent-shaped mound observed during the explorations carried on by the Bureau, is found here.

The pottery, which is found in great abundance, affords one of the chief archeological features of the district. As has been repeatedly remarked, the pottery of southeastern Missouri—the necked jar or water bottle, and vessels ornamented with bird, animal, or human heads, being prominent types—resembles so closely that found about Cahokia, Illinois, and in the vicinity of Nashville, Tennessee, as to be generally indistinguishable from it. But as we pass southward into Arkansas and approach the mouth of the Arkansas river we observe a change in the quality and color of the ware, it being of a finer grade and lighter color; it is also more highly ornamented, with colored or incised lines and figures. New and peculiar types are also found here; in fact, the finest collections of ancient pottery of the mound region have been made in Arkansas. It is here alone that full-faced globular jars, or ollas, have been obtained, which may be supposed to be genuine attempts to portray features. As these and other characteristic specimens are shown by Mr. Holmes in his various papers, further mention here is unnecessary.

One thing which appears somewhat remarkable is the very small number of pipes which have been found in this district. It is true that some three or four of the finest specimens of stone pipes yet discovered have been obtained here, but these are large and evidently those used only on ceremonial occasions. On the other hand, those for individual use are comparatively rare, usually of clay and rudely made.

THE GULF DISTRICT.

This district, as at present defined, includes the Gulf states east of the Mississippi (except a narrow strip along the northern boundary of Alabama and Georgia) and South Carolina. It is probable, however, that more thorough explorations will lead to the separation both of South Carolina and peninsular Florida each as a separate archeological division.

As the archeology of this southern area has been admirably and somewhat fully written by Mr. C. C. Jones in his work on the Antiquities of the Southern Indians, it will be unnecessary for us to present at this point more than a very brief outline of some of the leading types.

The works of this district are distinguished from those of the northern section chiefly by the large proportion of truncated pyramidal mounds, the occurrence of extensive ditches and canals, and the large number of shell heaps, the last being confined to the coasts of Florida and Alabama.

PYRAMIDAL MOUNDS.

All varieties of this type are represented, though the simple four-sided structure is the most common, those of other forms being of rare occurrence. One or two pentagonal and hexagonal pyramids have been noticed, but these are of such rare occurrence that they can not be considered as types. A few truncated cones, which are included under this head, have also been observed. Pyramidal mounds with terraces occur here and there, but are far less frequent than in Arkansas. They also differ from the latter in having frequently one or more graded ways or ramps. Few mounds with these appendages have been observed in this or in the Arkansas district, the "Rich Woods" group in southeastern Missouri being exceptional. In one instance (as is true also of the Rich Woods group) a series, consisting in this case of five pyramidal mounds, is formed by connecting ramps or graded ways. The graded ways leading up to the summit of mounds usually proceed from a point opposite a side, directly toward the center of the mound or middle of the side, the only instance known of one winding up the side being that of the large mound of the Etowah group, Bartow county, Georgia, which, though not included in this district, was probably built by the ancient inhabitants of it. Mention is made by several authors of winding ways up mounds, but so far the Bureau explorations have failed to confirm these statements.

Explorations in mounds of this type have been carried on only to a limited extent and have revealed but little of interest, though the negative evidence furnished on one point is valuable, to wit: That they were not built for burial purposes, though there are a few instances in which human remains have been found in them. In some instances layers of burnt clay, charcoal, and ashes have been observed. In other cases burnt clay in fragments, showing the marks of twigs or grass, and pieces of charred wood, most likely the remains of plastered wooden structures, have been observed. In short, the evidence obtained, though scanty, points to the correctness of the generally received opinion that these structures were erected as sites for the public buildings of the tribe or village and for the dwellings of the chiefs or leading personages.

Some two or three mounds of peculiar form have been discovered in Mississippi and the Arkansas district that have not been observed elsewhere in the mound area. These may be described as earthen platforms surmounted by a conical mound or a conical mound surrounded by a terrace. Sometimes the conical mound is small in proportion to the platform and is not central, in which case the first definition best describes the work; in other cases the platform appears only as a narrow terrace running around the mound. These, however, are very rare, only three or four being known. A double mound of this type, or mound with two apices, has been observed in western Mississippi, which is described and figured in the previous part of this volume.

BURIAL MOUNDS AND MODES OF BURIAL.

One distinguishing feature between the modes of burial in this district and those immediately north is the absence of stone graves and wooden vaults. Of the former none have been noticed, so far as known, in the entire district, except where it is overlapped by the Tennessee district in northern Georgia. Of the latter very few, if any, examples have been observed. Sometimes indications of a bark wrapping or wrapping made of cane matting are noticed. It is also the case that remains of leather are found in such relation to the skeleton as to show that the body had been wrapped in buckskin and this surrounded by cane matting.

The skeletons as a usual thing are found in a horizontal position, but generally without any rule in regard to direction. Exceptional cases occur in which all the bodies in a mound, or most of them, are placed with the head in one direction or in a circle. For example, in a mound of western Florida there were three groups of skeletons, from 7 to 14 in a group, those of each group forming a circle, the heads being toward the center. This would indicate that the burial had taken place after the flesh had been removed, or, in other words, that they were brought here at a general burial from other depositories. Examples of bundled skeletons sometimes occur, but these are confined principally to the Florida peninsula. One mound in which the burials were of this type has been observed in Alabama. Burials in a sitting posture are comparatively rare, the only examples known being those mentioned by Jones in his Antiquities of the Southern Indians. Burials in confused masses or ossuaries are also comparatively rare. The somewhat singular fact was noticed in Yazoo county, Mississippi, of extended and bundled skeletons and round heads and compressed heads in the same mound, which was of comparatively large size. Indications of fire are found in a large portion of the burial mounds of this district.

An ancient cemetery has been discovered here and there, but the explorers have failed to give sufficient details by which to make comparisons with the graves of other sections. So far as observed they are mostly in the vicinity of mounds; in some, undoubted indications of contact with the whites have been found, showing them to be of comparatively recent date.

BURIAL CAVES.

Some burial caves have been discovered in northern Alabama. In one of these the bodies appear to have been laid in wooden troughs and covered with matting and these placed in crevices of the rock. In the same cave were several wooden bowls and trays. The floor of another cave was covered to the depth of 4 feet with fragments of human bones, earth, ashes, and stone chips. From this débris two or three spool-shaped, copper ear ornaments were obtained. Around the middle of one of these was a portion of the string with which they were probably wound when in use.

INCLOSURES AND WALLS.

Notwithstanding the frequent mention by the early writers of walled villages in this district, the number of inclosures is much less in proportion to the other works than in Ohio. Nor is there sufficient uniformity to indicate any particular form as the prevailing type; yet we can say confidently that there is nothing in the form or size of these structures to indicate relation to those of the more northern districts.

Stone walls, which Col. Jones thinks were made for defense, are found on Stone mountain, Mount Yona, and other peaks of northern Georgia. These, however, are in the area overlapped by other districts, and hence can not be attributed with certainty to the authors of the works of the district now under consideration. They are, however, of much interest as indicating a state of bitter warfare, as this only will explain the necessity of retiring to these mountain fastnesses and fortifying them. There is, however, one of these fortified hills on the line between Bibb and Twigs counties, same state, which must be included geographically in this district.

Of the earthen inclosures some are semicircular, resting on the banks of streams; some are circular, but these are of comparatively small size, and a few are irregularly quadrangular. The regular forms both of inclosures and mounds of the southern states figured by Squier and Davis chiefly from Rafinesque's MSS. are to a large extent works of imagination. The groups, it is true, exist or did exist, but so far as they remain correspond in few respects with the figures or descriptions.

CANALS OR DITCHES.

In addition to the ditches which usually line the walls of inclosures, a few instances occur where the surrounding defense consisted of a ditch only. This is true in regard to the celebrated Etowah group, and some two or three other groups in Georgia.

Canals of considerable extent which are considered prehistoric are found at several points. One of these is said to be 14 miles in length.

POTTERY AND OTHER MINOR VESTIGES OF ART.

The prehistoric remains of this kind found in this district have been so thoroughly described by C. C. Jones, that it is unnecessary to do more here than refer to a few prominent types. The chief variations from the more northern and trans-Mississippi types are found in the forms of the pipes and the forms and ornamentation of the pottery. Pipes, however, are not abundant among the archeological collections from this district, and a large portion of them approach in form the modern type, or type in use subsequent to European colonization. One peculiar type of pottery is the large vase with conical bottom. These are found chiefly in Georgia and South Carolina. Another form peculiar to this region is the more elongate vessel with rounded bottom, to which the name "burial urn" has been applied, because in a few instances human bones have been found in them; these, however, are comparatively rare, as urn burial was a mode of disposing of the dead but seldom practiced in any part of the mound region.

The finest specimens of polished discoidal stones, supposed to have been used in the game of " chunkee," have been found in this district, chiefly in Georgia.

THE MOUND-BUILDERS.

GENERAL OBSERVATIONS.

Having given the results of the mound explorations carried on by the Bureau, and a review of the types of the works with reference to their geographical distribution, we propose to discuss under the above title some of the questions relating to the authors and uses of these works. The chief object in view, however, is to determine if possible whether or not the Indians were the authors. The reasons for this course can be stated in a few words.

If the explorations of the ancient monuments of the mound area under consideration should prove that the authors were Indians, the investigations in regard to the objects and uses of these works will be greatly limited; will in fact, be merged into the study of the habits, customs, arts, etc., of the Indians as they were before being modified by contact with European civilization. If, on the other hand, the opposite conclusion should be reached, the field of investigation will nevertheless be much restricted, as one very important factor will be eliminated, and the attention of students will be turned in a different direction.

There is, however, the possibility, as maintained by some authorities, that an intermediate result may be reached; that is to say, that part of these works are attributable to the Indians, while the remainder must be attributed to another or other races.

Even should this conclusion be reached after careful examination of all the data obtained, the result will tend to limit greatly the field of investigation. For it will be impossible to reach such conclusion without having determined the characteristics which distinguish these classes of works from one another. This, as will be admitted, will be a very important step toward the solution of the chief problems presented by these remains.

Such being the case, a discussion of the question "Who were the mound-builders?" or, as we prefer to put it, "Were the mound-builders Indians?" should not be considered out of place in this connection, particularly as this is the pivot on which the conclusions in reference to all the other problems relating to these works must turn.

Doubt has been expressed by some archeologists as to the sufficiency of the data so far obtained to justify a conclusion on this subject. This is owing, in part at least, to the fact that the wealth of material obtained by the Bureau of Ethnology bearing upon this question had not, at the time this doubt was expressed, become generally known. It is probable that the evidence presented in the preceding part of this report, together with the reports of recent explorations made by others, will serve, to some extent, to dispel such doubt. In any case the propriety of undertaking the discussion of the question at this time will be determined by the result.

As different conclusions are often reached because of the different senses in which the principal terms used are understood, it may be well to define at the outset the sense in which they are here used. In the present case the terms that need to be most clearly defined are "Indians," as referring to the former inhabitants, and "mound area," as referring to the geographical district alluded to.

As already stated, the term "mound area," as herein used, is limited to that portion of the United States east of the Rocky mountains, and the adjoining sections of the Dominion of Canada. The name "Indians," although generally used in a much broader sense and as embracing the entire American race, is, in this discussion, limited to the aboriginal tribes found occupying the above described area when first visited by Europeans, and to their immediate ancestors. This restriction is, of course, an arbitrary one, but is adopted here to avoid confusion.

Within these limitations the first and chief question to be considered may be stated briefly as follows:

Were all the mounds and other ancient works of the mound area as above defined, constructed by the Indians, in the restricted sense above mentioned, or are they wholly, or in part, to be attributed to other and more highly cultured races, as the Nahuatal tribes, the Mayas, the Pueblo tribes, or some lost race of which there is no historical mention?

No one believes it possible to ascertain the history of the construction of each mound and earthwork; the utmost that can be hoped for is that we may be able to determine with reasonable certainty that works of a particular class or locality were built by a known tribe or people; or negatively, that works of a given type can not be attributed to any people of whom we possess historical information.

One step, therefore, in the investigation, and a very important one, too, is to reach the general conclusion whether all classes of these remains in the region designated may be justly attributed to the Indians, in the sense stated above, or whether there are some types which must be ascribed to a different race; to a people who had attained a higher position in the scale of civilization than the Indians. This the author believes is possible, although we may not be able to determine conclusively what tribe or people erected any given work. Nevertheless, the conclusion will be strengthened by every proof that the works of particular sections, or certain types, are to be ascribed to particular tribes or stocks.

The author's position in regard to the question, as above stated, will appear further on.

DIFFERENT OPINIONS.

Before entering upon the discussion of the question propounded, it will be best to present a brief review of the different opinions which have so far been published to the world.

It was not until about the close of the eighteenth century that the scientific men of the eastern states became fully impressed with the fact that remarkable antiquities were to be found in our country.

About this time President Stiles, of New Haven, Dr. Franklin, Dr. Barton, and a few other leading minds of that day, becoming thoroughly convinced of the existence of these antiquities, and having received descriptions of a number of them, began to advance theories as to their origin. Bartram had come to the conclusion, from personal observations and from the statements of the Indians, that they knew nothing of the origin of certain monuments; that these belonged to the most distant antiquity.[1] Nevertheless, it is an error to infer from this, as some have done, that he attributed these works to a highly civilized people who had become extinct, or, in fact, to any other than the Indian race. Schoolcraft remarked truly:[2] "Bartram, a writer and traveler of eminent merit as a naturalist, and close observer of the Indian arts and society, who, in 1773, passed through their territories from Florida to the Mississippi, speaks often of the 'Indian mounts or tumuli and terraces, monuments of the ancients,' terms applied by him to Indian nations who had preceded the then existing stocks. Tradition among them had denoted such prior occupants, with manners and customs like themselves, whom they had displaced. The great Muscoge or Muscogulgee confederacy was then at its height. The Natchez had fallen forty years before. The Utches had been conquered, and, with the Coosidas and Alabamas, had become a part of 'The Nation,' a term commonly applied to them in the South. He had observed some works of this ancient race of tribes, and particularly a stone sepulchre at Keowe, of which tradition ascribed the origin to these 'ancients.' Yet he closes his travels with this observation: 'Concerning the monuments of Americans, I deem it necessary to observe, as my opinion, that none of them that I have seen, discover the least signs of the arts, sciences, or architecture of the Europeans, or other inhabitants of the old world; yet evidently betray every mark of the most distant antiquity.'"

He might have added also that in speaking of the works at "Apalachucla, old town," he says: "Those Indians have a tradition that these remains are the ruins of an ancient Indian town and fortress."[3]

Dr. Franklin in reply to the inquiry of President Stiles suggested that the works in Ohio might have been constructed by De Soto in his wanderings. This suggestion was followed up by Noah Webster with

[1] "Travels (1791)," pp. 367 and 390.   [2] Hist. Indian Tribes (1856), Vol. 5. p. 115.   [3] "Travels," p. 522.

an attempt to sustain it,[1] but subsequently this able lexicographer entirely abandoned this position and attributed these works to the aboriginal Indians. Capt. Heart, in reply to the inquiries addressed to him by Dr. Barton, gives his opinion that the works could not have been constructed by De Soto and his followers, but belonged to an age preceding the discovery of America by Columbus; that they were not due to the Indians or their predecessors, but to a people not altogether in an uncultivated state, as they must have been under the subordination of law and a well governed police.[2]

This is probably the first clear and distinct expression of a view which has subsequently obtained the assent of so many of the leading writers on American archeology.

About the commencement of the nineteenth century two new and important characters appear on the stage of American archeology. These are Bishop Madison, of Virginia, and Rev. Thaddeus M. Harris, of Massachusetts. " These two gentlemen," as remarked by Dr. Haven,[3] * * * " are among the first who, uniting opportunities of personal observation to the advantage of scientific culture, imparted to the public their impressions of western antiquities. They represent the two classes of observers whose opposite views still divide the sentiment of the country; one class seeing no evidence of art beyond what might be expected of existing tribes, with the simple difference of a more numerous population and consequently better defined and more permanent habitations; the others finding proofs of skill and refinement, to be explained, as they believe, only on the supposition that a superior native race, or more probably a people of foreign and higher civilization once occupied the soil."

Bishop Madison was the representative of the first class. Dr. Harris represented that section of the second class maintaining the opinion that the mound-builders were Toltecs, who, after residing for a time in this region, moved south into Mexico.

As the principal theories which are held at the present day on this subject are substantially set forth in these authorities, it is unnecessary to follow up the history of the controversy except so far as is required in order to notice the various modifications of the two leading views.

Those holding the opinion that the Indians were not the authors of these works, although agreeing on this point, and hence included in one class, differ widely among themselves as to the people to whom they are to be ascribed; one section, of which Dr. Harris may be considered the pioneer, holding that they were built by the Toltecs, who occupied the Mississippi valley previous to their appearance in the vale of Anahuac.[4]

[1] American Magazine Dec., 1787, Jan. and Feb., 1788. Am. Museum. Also referred to by Haven, Smithson. Contri., vol. VIII, pp. 24, 25.
[2] Trans. Am. Phil. Soc. vol. III, 1793, pp. 217–218.
[3] Archeology of the United States, Smithson. Contri. vol. VIII, p. 31.
[4] In alluding here and elsewhere to the Toltecs, we do not intend to assert thereby a belief in the reality of such a people, nor do we wish to be understood by this note as denying their existence, as this is a question that does not enter into the present discussion.

Among the more recent advocates of this view may be classed the following authors: Messrs. Squier and Davis in their "Ancient Monuments of the Mississippi Valley" (though Mr. Squier subsequently changed his opinion so far as it related to the antiquities of New York, which he became convinced should be attributed to the Iroquois tribes); Mr. John T. Short in his " North Americans of Antiquity;" Dr. Dawson in his " Fossil Man," who identifies the Tallegwi with the Toltecs; Rev. J. P. McLean in his " Mound Builders, " and Dr. Joseph Jones in his "Antiquities of Tennessee."

Wilson, in his " Prehistoric Man," modifies this view somewhat, looking to the region south of Mexico for the original home of the Toltecs and deriving the Aztecs from the mound-builders.

Another section of this class includes those who, although rejecting the idea of an Indian origin, are satisfied with simply designating the authors of these works a "lost race," without following the inquiry into the more uncertain field of racial or ethnical relations. To this type belong most of the authors of recent short articles and brief reports on American archeology, and quite a number of diligent workers in this field whose names are not before the world as authors.

J. D. Baldwin, in his " Ancient America," expresses the belief that the mound-builders were Toltecs, but thinks they came originally from Mexico, or further south, and after occupying the Ohio valley and the Gulf states, probably for centuries, were at last driven southward by an influx of barbarous hordes from the northern region, and appeared again in Mexico.[1] Bradford, thirty years previous to this, had suggested Mexico as their original home.[2] Lewis H. Morgan, on the other hand, supposes that the authors of these remains came from the Pueblo tribes of New Mexico.[3] Dr. Foster[4] agrees substantially with Baldwin. In this general class may also be included a number of extravagant hypotheses, such as those advanced by Rafinesque, George Jones, Delafield, and others.

The class maintaining the view that these monuments are the work of Indians found inhabiting the country at the time of its discovery or their ancestors, numbered, up to a recent date, but comparatively few leading authorities among its advocates; in other words, the followers of Bishop Madison are, or at least were until recently, far less numerous than the followers of Dr. Harris. The differences between the advocates of this view are of minor importance and only appear when the investigation is carried one step further back, and the attempt made to designate the particular tribe, nation, people, or ethnic family to which they pertained.

The tradition of the Delawares, as given by Heckwelder, having brought upon the stage the Tallegwi, they are made to play a most important part in the speculations of those inclined to the theory of an

---

[1] Ancient America, pp. 70-75.

[2] American Antiquities, p. 71.

[3] Beach, Indian Miscellany, p. 176. Also, North American Review, October, 1888.

[4] Prehistoric Races, pp. 339-342.

Indian origin. And as this tradition agrees very well with a number of facts brought to light by antiquarian and philological researches, it has had considerable influence in shaping the conclusion even of those who are not professed believers in it.

One of the ablest early advocates of the Indian origin of these works was Dr. McCulloh; and his conclusions based, as they were, on the comparatively slender data then obtainable, are remarkable, not only for the clearness with which they are stated and the distinctness with which they are defined, but as being more in accordance with all the facts ascertained than perhaps those of any contemporary.

Samuel G. Drake, Henry Schoolcraft, Dr. Haven, and Sir John Lubbock are also disposed to ascribe these ancient works to the Indians. Among the recent advocates of this theory are the following, who have made known their position in regard to the question by their writings or addresses:

Judge C. C. Baldwin, in a paper read before the State Archeological Society of Ohio, expresses the belief that the mound-builders of Ohio were village Indians. Col. F. M. Force expresses a similar opinion in his paper entitled "The Mound-Builders," read before the Cincinnati Literary Club. Dr. D. G. Brinton brings forward, in an article published in the October number, 1881, of the American Antiquarian, considerable historical evidence tending to the conclusion that the Indians were the authors of these ancient works.[1] Dr. P. R. Hoy, in a paper entitled "Who built the Mounds?" published in the Transactions of the Wisconsin Academy of Science,[2] brings forward a number of facts to sustain the same view. Mr. Lucien Carr, of Cambridge, Mass., in a paper entitled "The Mounds of the Mississippi Valley, historically considered" (contained in the memoirs of the Kentucky Geological Survey), has presented a very strong array of historical evidence, going to show not only that the Indians east of the Mississippi, at the time they were first discovered by Europeans, were sedentary and agricultural, but also that several of the tribes were in the habit of building mounds. Several articles and two small volumes have also been published by the author of this volume, taking the same view. The articles will be found in the "American Antiquarian," "Magazine of American History," "Science," "American Anthropologist," and elsewhere. The two small works are "The Cherokees in pre-Columbian Times," and "The Shawnees in pre-Columbian Times."

These recent papers may justly be considered the commencement of a rediscussion of this question, in which the Indian, after a long exclusion, will be readmitted as a possible factor in the problem.

Prof. Dall has likewise taken an advanced step in this direction in the excellent American edition of Marquis de Nadaillac's "Prehistoric America," boldly accepting the results of later investigations; and the same is true in regard to Prof. N. S. Shaler's "Kentucky."

---

[1] Compare Hist. Mag., Feb., 1866. p. 35, Am. Antiq., 1881, vol. 4, p. 9 and American Race, p. 88.
[2] Vol. VI, 1881–'83, p. 84.

One reason why so little progress has been made in unraveling this riddle of the American Sphinx is that most of the authors who have written upon the subject of American archeology have proceeded upon certain assumptions which virtually closed the door against a free and unbiased investigation.

Even the most intelligent writers on this subject commence or interlard their discussions with such expressions as the following:

An ancient and unknown people left remains of settled life and of a certain degree of civilization in the valleys of the Mississippi and its tributaries.[1]

Among those nations who are without recognized descendants are the Mound-builders, who lived east of the Mississippi.[2]

The evidences of the former existence of a prehistoric race known as the Mound-builders, who at one time occupied the principal affluents of the Mississippi, the Gulf coast, and the region of the Great Lakes, are too conclusive to admit of doubt. These evidences consist of tumuli symmetrically raised and often enclosed in mathematical figures, such as the square, the octagon, and circle, with long lines of circumvallation; of pits in the solid rock, and rubbish heaps formed in the prosecution of their mining operations; and of a variety of utensils wrought in stone or copper, or molded in clay, *which evince a knowledge of art and methodical labor foreign to the red man.*[3]

An ancient race entirely distinct from the Indian, possessing a certain degree of civilization, once inhabited the central portion of the United States.[4]

The monuments described *are not the work of the Indian tribes found in the country, nor of any tribe resembling them in institutions.*[5]

The only evidence we have of the existence of a people conventionally called the Mound-builders, *preceding the modern Indians* in the occupancy of this continent, consist of material relics.[6]

The professor [alluding to Dr. Joseph Jones, author of The Antiquities of Tennessee] has clearly shown that *the Mound-builder people and the Indians were distinct,* and has set at rest a question upon which some doubts were still entertained by a certain school of archeologists which has really never been very strong.[7]

And so on in the same strain through most of the works relating to this subject, thus virtually deciding the question before, or without, properly discussing it. A few have ventured the suggestion that possibly these ancient works were due to the Indian race found in possession of the country at the time of its discovery by the Europeans. But this suggestion, instead of receiving serious attention and being properly and thoroughly investigated, has generally been thrust aside as unworthy of consideration. For example, one writer dismisses it with the remark:

I am not aware that the opinion that the red men were the authors of the most extensive works, though maintained by some scholars of high repute, is held by any who have given them personal and thorough examination.[8]

Another unfortunate and unwarranted assumption which has been a serious stumbling block in the way of the solution of this problem is, that there is such a general similarity in these ancient monuments as

[1] Baldwin. Ancient America, p. 14.
[2] Lewis H. Morgan, Beach's Indian Miscellany. p. 243.
[3] Foster's Prehistoric Races, p. 97.
[4] McLean. Mound Builders. p. 13.
[5] Bancroft. Native Races, IV, p. 787.
[6] Farquharson, in Proc. Davenport Acad. Sci., Vol, II, p. 103.
[7] Short. North Americans of Antiquity, p. 65.
[8] Conant. Footprints of a Vanished Race. p. IV (preface).

to justify the conclusion that they are the works of one people, of one great nation. Scattered through the large majority of works where allusion is made to this subject are to be found such expressions as the following:

The differences which have already been pointed out between the monuments of the several portions of the valley, of the northern, central, and southern divisions, are not sufficiently marked to authorize the belief that they were the works of separate nations. The features common to all are elementary and *identify them as appertaining to a single grand system.*[1]

While the character of these structures, as traced over wide areas, differs in minor particulars still there is a general uniformity *which stamps the authors as one people, the subjects of one controlling government.*[2]

This ancient people, whose remains indicate unity and civilization, *must have been organized as a nation with a central administration which all recognized.*[3]

They [the mound-builders] were probably *one people;* that is, composed of tribes living under similar laws, religion, and other institutions. Such variations as are observed in the monuments are only those that would naturally occur between central and frontier regions, although the animal mounds of the northwest present some difficulties.[4]

Short, in his " North Americans of Antiquity," proceeds upon the same theory as, in fact, do the large majority of those who have written upon the subject. Yet, as will soon become apparent to any one who will study the different forms of these works with any care, the only similarity between the extremes of form and construction is the fact that they are built of earth. Between these extremes, if the earthworks of the world were classified, would fall much the larger portion of both hemispheres. The conical tumuli bear a far more striking resemblance in form to the mounds of Japan, Siberia, and northern Europe, and some of the burrows of the British isles than they do to the effigy mounds of Wisconsin, the circles and squares of Ohio, or the pyramidal and truncated tumuli of the Southern States. It is probably not going too far to say that if the most skillful engineer of the present day were to undertake the task of building as many different forms of earthworks as his skill could devise, it would be difficult for him to exceed the variety now found. So varied are they that it has been found impossible to classify them according to form, except in a very loose and general way.

Almost every animal their builders were acquainted with has served as a model, and almost every geometrical form from a spiral to a pyramid has been imitated. Examining their internal structure, they are found to be equally varied.

That there are certain types in form and construction which prevail in certain sections is true, but the claim that there is throughout a general similarity which stamps their authors as one people, unless this term is used as denoting one race, is wholly without foundation.

It is admitted that these works and the minor vestiges of art found

[1] Squier and Davis, Anc. Mon., p. 301.	[3] Baldwin, Ancient America, p. 57.
[2] Foster, Prehistoric Races, p. 97.	[4] Bancroft, Native Races, IV, 785.

in them indicate that their authors belonged to one race, and differed but little from each other in regard to the position reached in the grade of culture; but the inference to be drawn from the expressions and statements referred to, and in most cases intended to be conveyed by them, is that the mound-builders belonged to one great nation, one people connected together by one system of government. Even where these writers are most guarded their speculations in reference to these monuments are based upon this theory, and their expressions are constantly revealing the fact that their minds are pervaded with this idea.

The thought that once a mighty nation occupied the valley of the Mississippi with its frontier settlements resting on the lake shores and gulf coast, nestling in the valleys of the Appalachian range and skirting the broad plains of the west; a nation with its systems of government and religion, but which has disappeared, leaving behind it no evidences of its glory, power, and extent, save these silent, forest-covered remains, has something so fascinating and attractive in it, that once it has taken possession of the mind it warps and biases all its investigations and conclusions.

There seems to pervade the minds of many explorers, and in fact of some American archeologists, no doubt under the spur of this enchanting thought, the hope and expectation that some great and astounding find will yet be made which will confirm this theory.

One reason why this view has so generally prevailed is, that the conclusions of later authors have been based mainly on the descriptions and characteristics of the Ohio mounds. For instance, the work entitled "The Mound-Builders" by the Rev. J. P. McLean, is—with the exception of the appendix—based almost wholly on the statements of Squier and Davis, although the author resided in the very heart of the mound area, and, as his "Archeology of Butler County" shows, was familiar with the works of this region.

Yet in the face of all this is the undeniable fact that, wherever these remains are found we see, as is well known even to the writers who express these views, evidences of warfare, of precautions against attack and surprise, of attempts at defense; not along the borders alone of the mound area, but in every section of it; proving beyond any reasonable doubt a condition of tribal warfare, and hence of tribal divisions.

It is strange that these writers should so press this idea of a single nation, when in the same work they speak of numerous fortifications scattered over the mound regions, of signal mounds and lookout stations on numberless hills, and of other indications of warfare. To suppose that all these could be accounted for on the idea that they were constructed as a defense against incoming hordes of savages by a people whose "settlements were widespread as the extent of their (the Mound-builders) remains indicate."[1] is preposterous, for they

---

[1] Short: North Americans of Antiquity, p. 97.

accompany, to a greater or less extent, almost every village site throughout the vast area embraced.

A third serious hindrance to legitimate progress is found in the nomenclature which has come into use, a number of the terms commonly employed being nothing more nor less than theories crystallized into names; such, for example, as "Sacred Enclosures," "Temple Mounds," "Altar Mounds," "Sacrificial Mounds," etc. So deeply have these become embedded in the minds of most writers on American archeology, that in alluding to our ancient earthworks they are used as though no question could arise as to their correctness. In fact, many writers on this subject seem to proceed upon the theory that the mound-builders devoted most of their time to religious ceremonies. A charred bone or an ash bed in a tumulus suggests to them sacrifice, a mound-covered stone heap or hard mass of clay is at once construed into a sacrificial altar, and in every truncated mound they behold the site of a temple, where the people, led by their priests, assembled to perform their religious rites and ceremonies. Even the plates of mica, found so frequently in these structures, are supposed by some to have been used by the priests as reflectors to concentrate the rays of the sun for the purpose of igniting the fuel on the altar, thus causing the people to believe they had called down sacred fire from the sun, their supreme divinity.

Take, for example, the expression of a no less able and conscientious writer than Dr. Lapham. Speaking of the masses of burnt clay and other evidences of fire found in the walls of the earthworks at Aztalan, Wisconsin, he remarks: "From all the facts observed it is likely that the clay was mixed with the straw and made into some coarse kind of envelope or covering for sacrifices about to be consumed. The whole was probably then placed on the wall of earth, mixed with the requisite fuel, and burned. The promiscuous mixture of charcoal, burned clay, charred bones, blackened pottery, etc., can only in this way be accounted for." [1]

Examining the facts as given in his most excellent work on the Antiquities of Wisconsin, we are astonished to find how small a basis he had upon which to build such a theory.

The Aztalan remains consist in part of surrounding walls, which have mound-like enlargements:

Whether these walls are only a series of ordinary mounds, such as are found all over the western country, differing only in being united to one another, it may, perhaps, be difficult to decide. They may, possibly, have been designed for the same and for other purposes. On opening the walls near the top it is occasionally found that the earth has been burned. Irregular masses of hard, reddish clay, full of cavities, bear distinct impressions of straw, or rather wild hay, with which they had been mixed before burning. These places are of no very considerable extent, nor are they more than 6 inches in depth. Fragments of the same kind are found scattered about, and they have been observed in other localities at a great distance

---

[1] Antiquities of Wisconsin, p. 44.

from these ancient ruins. *   *   *   As indicating the origin of this burned clay, it is important to state that it is usually mixed with pieces of charcoal, partially burned bones, etc. Fragments of pottery are also found in the same connection.[1]

If these embankments are true walls, the places selected for cremating bodies would seem to be very unusual and wholly inappropriate. Moreover, we find on the next page of his work proof that burial was practiced by the occupants. At the bottom of one of the mound-like enlargements were found the remains of two bodies which he judged had been buried in a sitting posture. Near the surface of the same mound were found fragments of pottery, charcoal, half-burned human bones, and masses of burned clay. If the theory advanced be correct, we would have here evidence in the same mound of two methods of disposing of the dead. If the object were to consume the body, it would be very strange that it should be first inclosed in a mass of clay and the burned remains afterward left uncared-for.

It is much more probable that the clay mixed with wild grass was used as plastering for winter houses which were built on these enlargements or mounds, or for wooden palisades. The presence of partially burned human bones may be easily accounted for without resorting to the theory of human sacrifice or intentional cremation, as will hereafter be shown.

I am inclined, from personal examination, to accept Dr. Lapham's suggestion that these supposed walls are only a series of mounds united by embankments. Similar series are found in Crawford county, in the same State.

In the latter case they seem to have been used only as house sites.

Dr. Lapham was, beyond question, one of the most careful and conscientious students of our antiquities, yet this idea of the predominance of religious ceremonies in the customs of the mound-builders had taken such strong hold on his mind that the evidence of fire, even in the inclosing walls, was sufficient to bring sacrifice forward as an explanation of the condition observed, notwithstanding that he was inclined to the opinion that the mound-builders and Indians belonged to the same race.

Messrs. Squier and Davis in the explanation of their reasons for designating certain works "sacred inclosures" remark [2] as follows:

Thus, when we find an inclosure containing a number of mounds, all of which it is capable of demonstration were religious in their purposes, or in some way connected with the superstitions of the people who built them, the conclusion is irresistible that the inclosure itself was also deemed sacred.

How are we to demonstrate that a mound was intended for religious purposes? The answer given by these authors is to be gathered from their chapter on "altar or sacrificial mounds," and is in substance as follows: If it has a (so-called) "altar" in it and is stratified, it has been built for religious purposes, though the altar alone would doubt-

[1] Lapham. Antiquities of Wisconsin, p. 43.   [2] Anc. Mon., p. 47.

less have sufficed with them to place a mound in this category. Even the character of the sacrifices is supposed to be clearly indicated, as they remark that—

The inference that human sacrifices were made here and the remains afterwards thus collected and deposited, or that a system of burial of this extraordinary character was practiced in certain cases, seems to follow legitimately from the facts and circumstances here presented.[1]

According to Short, "Prof. E. B. Andrews has shown that the supposed uniformity of stratification in altar mounds is a fallacy. In many instances the earth has been dumped together indiscriminately."[2] The Bureau explorations also tend to throw doubt upon the theory of the authors of "Ancient Monuments" in this respect, and also on the supposition that "altar mounds" are never used for burial purposes.

Although there will be occasion hereafter to allude to this subject, it will not be amiss to notice here some reasons for protesting against the use of terms implying sacrifice.

It is evident that the use of the terms "sacred inclosures" and "sacrificial mounds" by Messrs Squier and Davis hinges upon the object and use of the so-called "altars." If they are in error in this respect their whole theory falls to the ground and the use of these terms is unwarranted and misleading.

If these altars were used for sacrificial purposes in a religious sense, or in any true sense of the term, as these authors evidently imply, and, moreover, for human sacrifice, it is remarkable that so many of them (some ten or twelve) should be found in the single inclosure denominated "Mound city;" that a single village should have nearly a dozen different places of offering sacrifices. It is very strange that true sacrificial altars used by the same people, by the inhabitants of a single village, should have varied so greatly that while some were circular and some elliptical, others were squares or parallelograms; some but 2 feet across, while others were 50 feet or more in length, by 12 to 15 in breadth. A basin-shaped mass of clay 45 or 50 feet long, 12 feet wide, and not more than 18 inches high, with broad, sloping margins, would be an unusual altar.

Passing by these serious objections, let us examine the evidence upon which Messrs. Squier and Davis base their conclusions respecting these structures. It appears that they examined some forty or fifty of these altar-containing tumuli: their statement is, "of one hundred mounds examined, sixty were altar or temple mounds."[3] Allowing ten of this number for temple mounds, the number belonging to the other class would be fifty. Of these, they describe and figure as types ten or eleven, seven of which were on the restricted and inclosed area of 13 acres, designated "Mound city."

The altar basin of one was filled to the brim with fine dry ashes, intermixed with which were some fragments of ornamented pottery

---

[1] Anc. Mon., p. 159.   [2] North Americans of Antiquity. p. 83, note.   [3] Anc. Mon., p. 142.

and a few copper disks, and opaque mica in sheets so laid as to over-lap one another. Resting on these were some charred human bones, probably those of a single skeleton.

There certainly is nothing in this to indicate that there had been a sacrifice. The facts might warrant the conclusion that cremation had been attempted; but to base the theory of sacrifice on these facts is unjustifiable. It was apparent that the mica and bones were care-fully placed there after the fire had died out, and with the evident intention of sepulture. Moreover, as the authors inform us, "the lay-ers of mica and calcined bones * * * were peculiar to this indi-vidual mound, and were not found in any other of the class."

In the basin of another was "a deposit of fine ashes, intermixed with charcoal, 3 inches thick." In these ashes were some fragments of pottery and a few shell and pearl beads. The basin of another con-tained nothing more than a mass, 4 or 5 inches thick, of something like lime mortar, apparently made from calcined shells, fragments of the shells being intermixed. It will scarcely be claimed that these contain any indications of sacrifice.

The basin of another of large size was filled with relics, chiefly articles of stone and copper, and fragments of pottery mixed with coal and ashes. A single fragment of a partially calcined bone was found on the altar; it was the patella of a human skeleton.

In the basin of mound No. 8 was found the collection of articles which has become so noted in works relating to American archeology. This deposit, we are informed, consisted of "not far from 200 pipes carved in stone; many pearl and shell beads; numerous disks, tubes, etc., of copper, and a number of other ornaments of copper covered with silver, etc.," intermixed with much ashes.

The altar of mound 18 "contained no relics, but was thinly covered with a carbonaceous deposit resembling burned leaves."

The altar of mound 7 was nothing more than "a smooth, level floor of clay slightly burned, which was covered with a thin layer of sand an inch in thickness. A small portion of one side was covered with a layer of mica, the rounded pieces overlapping as the scales of a fish."

The basin of a small altar in another mound was rich in relics con-taining "several instruments of obsidian;" "several scrolls tastefully cut from thin sheets of mica;" traces of cloth made of doubled and twisted thread; a number of bone implements; a quantity of pearl beads, and some fragments of copper in thin, narrow slips.

The altar of one was simply a mound-shaped mass covered with stones; that of another consisted of sand with a median stratum of charcoal, and a dished surface paved with small cobblestones.

These are all the examples of the type designated "sacrificial mounds" which these authors describe, and they furnish the evidence upon which archeologists are expected to accept the theory that these structures were built and used for sacrificial purposes. If this be sufficient to warrant such a theory, what is to be the conclusion in reference to the hundreds of burned clay beds of the mounds described in the preceding descriptive part of this report? Are we to suppose that all were intended for sacrificial purposes? Is it not far more probable that the inhabitants of the little village in the inclosure made use of fire for some other purpose than for human sacrifices, which seems to be virtually implied by the theory advanced? Nor is this said in jest, for every evidence of fire mentioned as being found in this inclosure is supposed to have been connected with religious ceremonies. Even a deposit of chipped flints is supposed to be a religious or sacrificial offering. Speaking of this deposit or cache, these authors say:

> If they were thus placed as an offering we can form some estimate, in view of the facts that they must have been brought from a great distance and fashioned with great toil, of the devotional fervor which induced the sacrifice, or the magnitude of the calamity which that sacrifice was intended to divert. * * * There is little doubt that the deposit was final, and was made in compliance with some religious requirements.

As caches of stone implements have been discovered in different localities, sometimes where no mound has been raised over them, it is more likely that in this case the workman adopted this plan of concealing his treasure to prevent its being disturbed.

Sir John Lubbock[1] remarks as follows in regard to the opinion expressed by Messrs. Squier and Davis respecting these constructions:

> This conclusion does not seem to us altogether satisfactory, and although these altar-containing mounds differ in so many respects from the above described tumuli, we still feel disposed to regard them as sepulchral rather than sacrificial. Not having, however, had the advantage of examining them for ourselves, we throw this out as a suggestion rather than express it as an opinion. We confess that we feel much difficulty in understanding why altars should be covered up in this manner. We call to mind no analogous case.

Had this author been aware of the fact that there are hundreds of mounds stratified much after the manner of those described by Messrs. Squier and Davis that are true burial mounds; many others which have no altar and yet are not burial mounds; and others that have been explored as widely apart as Iowa and North Carolina which contained true, altar-shaped masses built of cobblestones, some of which showed no indications whatever of fire, while others were covered with layers of charcoal and ashes in which were imbedded skeletons or human bones bearing no marks of heat, he would probably have expressed a still more decided dissent.

It may not be possible, at the present day, to decide with certainty as to the object and use of those so-called altars, but the theory that they were used for sacrificial purposes seems to be wholly gratuitous and without the shadow of evidence in its favor. There are some grounds, as will appear further on, for believing that some of these clay beds were used as places for torturing prisoners of war, the chief sacrifice the Indians were accustomed to make.

---

[1] Smithson. Rept. 1862, p. 328. Also Prehistoric Times, 4th edn., 1878, p. 276.

There are perhaps sufficient data on which to base a theory of cremation, as has been done by Dorman,[1] whose remarks on the subject are appropriate in this place:

It is extremely doubtful whether a great error has not been made by many able American archeologists in denominating a class of artificial mounds "altar mounds." Many things have tended to lead them into this error. The burial customs of the aboriginal Americans have not been thoroughly investigated. A supposed great antiquity has been ascribed to them, and a special race of moundbuilders has been created to furnish builders for the great monuments of what has been called an extinct race. Whence they came and where they have gone has puzzled the brain of many an antiquarian. This imaginary people, with an elaborate ritual of sacrifice offered on the altars so carefully covered with an abundance of earth to protect them from the sacrilegious hands of barbarian intruders, will, however, eventually be resolved into a very primitive people and their sacrificial altars turned into cremation pyres,.where the bodies of the dead were burned with their worldly effects and a tumulus erected over their remains. Upon most of these supposed altars human bones have been found;[2] in a few, however, their absence is noted by explorers. They may have been reduced to ashes, but it is not necessary to account for their absence in this way alone, for the custom, as we have seen, was very prevalent of preserving the bones after cremation and removing them, and among many of the tribes they were reduced to a powder, which was used in some liquid as a drinking potion for the relatives. The altar-mound theorists have had to account for the presence of human bones by the horrible rite of human sacrifice. The conclusion that the mounds of this class were devoted to this superstitious rite does not appear to be satisfactory. They rather appear to indicate that cremation was practiced. The sacrificial origin of these mounds has been inferred from the fact that articles of only one class occur in them. This would only indicate that a division of labor was established, because with their belief in a future life and a continuance of all the employments of the present life many of the products of any skillful person and material for new labor would be deposited with such a person. On this subject of sacrifice, running as it does through all their ceremonial life, I would refer the reader to that part of this work devoted to that subject. Evidences have been found of cremation in Florida mounds.

Notwithstanding the opinion in regard to cremation so confidently expressed in this quotation, there are some strong reasons for doubting its correctness, as will hereafter be shown.

The term "mound-builders," although adopted from necessity, is an unfortunate one, as its constant use has accustomed the mind to look upon the authors of these ancient works as one people, thus fixing in the mind an unproven theory and checking to some extent that investigation of the subject which is necessary to a correct conclusion.

It is not asserted, nor does the author wish to be understood as now maintaining, that all these expressed and implied theories are incorrect. Whether the mound-builders devoted much of their time to religious ceremonies, whether they were accustomed to make religious sacrifices, whether there were sacred inclosures, sacrificial and temple mounds,.etc., are questions to be settled, if possible, by careful investigations and legitimate deductions. The protest expressed is against the method which has been so generally followed of taking them for granted, and then, without any proof of their correctness, proceeding

---

[1] Origin of Primitive Superstitions, p. 187.   [2] This is an error.—C. T.

to build up theories and arrive at conclusions based upon them; and also against the pernicious practice of grafting into our archeological nomenclature terms which involve these assumptions.

For example, it has been assumed that the mound-builders were sun worshippers, and this theory is given such prominence and influence that legitimate conclusions from material data are set aside because they seem to contradict it. So strong is the hold that these assumptions have taken upon the minds of many students of American archeology that it is well nigh impossible to persuade them to examine carefully a theory which seems to contravene them.

OBJECTIONS ANSWERED.

As it is necessary to a proper and legitimate discussion of the question before us to free ourselves, as far as possible, from the unwarranted assumptions mentioned in the previous pages, it may be well to examine briefly a few of the more important ones—which are presented as objections to the theory that the authors of the mounds were Indians—before entering upon the direct discussion.

It is proper to state at this point, however, that the author believes the theory which attributes these works to the Indians (using this term in the limited sense heretofore explained) to be the correct one. Excluding such remains as pertain to civilized European races of a date subsequent to the discovery of America by Columbus, he attributes all the ancient artificial works found in the Mississippi valley and Gulf states, or in that part of the United States east of the Rocky mountains, to the Indian tribes found in possession of this region at the time of its discovery, and their ancestors. This limitation excludes from consideration the cultured tribes of Mexico and Central America, and also the Pueblo Indians of New Mexico and Arizona. That there may have been intercourse between some of the tribes who occupied this region and the people of Mexico and Central America and the Pueblo tribes of the southwest is not only possible, but very probable. It is to be understood, therefore, while the position the author takes on this question does not exclude the idea of such intercourse, it does exclude the supposition that these works are due in whole or in part to the more cultivated people of Mexico or Central America, as well as all theories which attribute them to any other people than the Indians in the limited sense heretofore mentioned. That some of the tribes may have become extinct or merged into others in the past is more than probable, but this in no way affects the proposition.

One reason why the Indian has been so generally, so persistently, and so unceremoniously refused admission as a possible factor in this problem is because of the opinion, which seems to be almost universally held, that when first encountered on our continent by the European explorers he was the same restless, roving, unsettled, unhoused, and unagricultural savage, wherever found, as we have learned to consider him in more modern times.

As it is conceded that the mound-builders, judging by the extent and magnitude of their works, must have been to some extent a sedentary people, having fixed villages and depending very largely for subsistence upon the products of the soil, it is assumed as a necessary inference that they could not have been Indians, as these were nomads depending for subsistence almost wholly upon the chase, spurning the restraints of settled life and agricultural pursuits.

Although this idea had been advanced previous to his time, yet Gallatin may be considered the father of the theory, as he was the first to clearly formulate it, and it is largely through the influence his writings exerted upon the scientific world that it has taken such hold on the minds of subsequent writers.

It is apparent that Messrs. Squier and Davis took the work of this author as their chief guide in forming their theories, so far as they relate to the points on which he touched. As most authors of general works on American archæology, written since the publication of the " Ancient Monuments," have taken therefrom the larger portion of their material as well as their conclusions in regard thereto, so far as these relate to the region under consideration, Gallatin may be considered the father of the theory to which we have alluded. Even in one of the latest works on American archeology—Nadaillac's " Prehistoric America "—this statement occurs: [1]

Between 1845 and 1847 more than two hundred mounds were excavated by them [Squier and Davies], and the description they give, published by the Smithsonian Institution, is still our best guide with regard to these remains.

Attention is therefore called for a moment to Gallatin's reasons for concluding that the Indians could not have been the mound-builders, as these are based almost wholly on the theory above mentioned.

I quote the following from the general observations in the " Introductory Essay" to his justly celebrated " Synopsis of the Indian Tribes of North America." [2]

But we know that north of the latitude of the Rio Gila there is nothing west of the Rio Colorado but a sandy desert, nothing between that river and the Rio Norte, but accumulated ridges of mountains; nothing east of the last river but the buffalo plains. In fact we find in no part of the country, whether east or north, adjacent to the northern civilized provinces of Mexico, any trace or any probability of the former existence of an agricultural people. But we may easily understand that the civilization of Mexico gradually extended its influence, as from a common center, northwardly as well as southwardly; that the northerly tribes, as far north as the thirtieth degree of latitude, and perhaps the Rio Gila, without having made the same progress in arts or attained the same degree of wealth as the ancient inhabitants of Mexico, may have been gradually converted into an agricultural people, and that, like the German nations in Europe, they may ultimately have conquered their less warlike southern neighbors.

---

[1] Am. Ed. 1884, p. 81.   [2] Trans. Am. Antiq. Soc. (1838) Vol. 2, pp. 146–151.

The next and more immediate subject of inquiry is, how we shall account for those ancient tumuli, fortifications, and the remnants, both east and west of the Mississippi, the origin of which is entirely unknown to the Indians, who in the seventeenth century were the sole inhabitants, and still continue to occupy a part of that country.

On this, as on many other subjects relative to our Indians, we are still in want of facts. We are not yet sufficiently acquainted with the extent of the country over which the monuments are spread, or how far they differ in character, extent, or number in the different sections of the country. They only appear to have been more numerous and of greater importance in the vicinity of the Mississippi and the valley of the Ohio. There is nothing in their construction or the remnants which they contain indicative of a much more advanced state of civilization than that of the present inhabitants. But it may be inferred from their number and size that they were the work of a more populous nation than any now existing; and if the inference is correct it would necessarily imply a state of society in which greater progress had been made in agriculture. For wherever satisfactory evidence of a greater population is found this could not have existed without adequate means of subsistence, greater than can be supplied by the chase alone.

Those monuments seem, in two respects, to differ from any erections that can be ascribed to the Indians, such as they were first found by the first French or English settlers. Some are of a character apparently different from those purely intended for defense. It may be doubted whether those extensive mounds, so regularly shaped and with a rectangular basis, such as that near the Mississippi on which the refugee monks of La Trappe had built their convent, 100 feet in height, facing the four cardinal points and with those platforms designated by the name of *apron*, are entirely the work of man, or whether they may not have been natural hills artificially shaped by his hands. But, if they have been correctly described, they have a strong family likeness to the Mexican pyramids. as they are called, and were probably connected with the worship of the nation. Of these, for there appears to be at least two more, and of other inclosures or works which can not be accounted for by a reference to military purposes only, we want full and precise descriptions.

But, if considered only as fortifications, ramparts of earth in a forest country strike us as a singular mode of defense against savage enemies and Indian weapons. All the defensive works, without exception, that were used by the Indians east of the Mississippi, from the time they were first known to us, were of a uniform character. The descriptions of Mauville, at the time of De Soto's expedition, and of Hochelaga, by Cartier, agree entirely with the Indian forts within our own knowledge, with that of the Five Nations in the siege of which Champlain was engaged in 1615, and of which he has left a correct drawing, and with every other description given by the early writers. They all consisted of wooden palisades strongly secured, with an internal gallery, from which the besieged party might under cover repel the assailants with missile weapons. And they were also of a moderate size, and such as could be defended by the population of an Indian village. Wood affords the natural means of fortification against a savage enemy, where the material is abundant. It can not indeed be understood how these works could have been properly defended, unless they were surrounded not only by the rampart but also by a palisade. And it is, on any supposition, extremely difficult to account for works containing 500 acres, such as that on the banks of the Missouri, which was correctly measured by Lewis and Clarke.

The only conjecture I can form, and it is but a conjecture, is that the people who erected those works came from the west, and that it was during their residence in the prairie country that they were compelled to resort to that species of defensive works. They may, as is often the case, have persisted in the habit when there was no longer occasion for it. From the Colorado on the Rio Norte, the way to the Mississippi was easy by the river Platte or the Arkansas. The conjecture is entitled to consideration only in case further investigation should show a probable connection between the monuments of the valley of the Mississippi and those of Mexico. The extensive tract of alluvial land along the Mississippi opposite St. Louis, now called the American Bottom, is the place in which are found the strongest indications of a concentrated population.

Although he admits that "there is nothing in the construction of these [ancient] works or the character of the articles found in them indicative of a much higher civilization than that of the Indians," yet he ascribes them to a different people. The process of reasoning by which he reaches this conclusion need not be quoted, as it can be briefly summarized as follows: The number and magnitude of ancient works indicate a dense population, hence a people depending to a large extent upon agriculture for subsistence—ergo, they could not have been Indians, as Indians relied but little upon agriculture for subsistence.

Although admitting that agriculture was practiced to a limited extent by Indians, he insists that the population was scattered and sparse because the food supply derived from the chase had not reached its maximum limit at the time they became known to Europeans. This may have been true in regard to the buffalo region of the Northwest, but can not be correctly affirmed of the southern section, as will hereafter be shown. Moreover his own statements, found elsewhere in the paper referred to, refute his argument, so far as it relates to the south and some other sections.

Compare, for example, the following:

Whatever opinion may be entertained of the respective population of the four great southern nations three hundred and one hundred and fifty years ago, it appears certain that their habits and social state had not, during that interval, undergone any material alteration. They were probably as ferocious, but less addicted to war than the northern Indians. Those of New England, the Iroquois tribes, the Sauks and Foxes, had perhaps made equal progress in agriculture; but, generally speaking the southern depended more on the cultivation of the soil and less on hunting than the Algonkin Lenape tribes. We find the Spaniards under De Soto feeding almost exclusively on maize and complaining of the want of meat. Two hundred years later, Bernard Romans says, that near one-half of the Choctaws have never killed a deer during their lives, and that, whilst in their country, he had but two or three opportunities of eating venison in as many months. Those southern tribes have also remained respectively united together as one nation. The Choctaws and Chicasaws are the only exception of any importance; and the Muskhogees, as has been seen, incorporated, instead of exterminating subordinate tribes." [1]

It is evident from this and abundant proof which can be adduced, not only that the maximum supply from the chase had been reached in the southern sections, but had long since ceased to afford even a moiety of the food necessary for subsistence. He adds, that the Indians "of New England, the Iroquois tribes, the Sauks and Foxes had perhaps made equal progress in agriculture." That the entire argument is without foundation will appear further on.

But this is not the only inconsistency into which this able author

---

[1] Trans. Am. Ant. Soc., Vol. 2, pp. 107, 108.

runs in consequence of his position in regard to the mound-builders. His statement in the quotation made from his paper, that "we find in no part of the country, whether east or north adjacent to the northern civilized provinces of Mexico, any trace or any probability of the former existence of an agricultural people," is not only incorrect as shown by subsequent explorations and even by earlier historical evidence, but is inconsistent with his supposition in regard to the former home of the mound-builders. For, as will be seen by reference to the extract from his "synopsis"—it is from this same desert, barren western country which he pronounces void of any indications of former cultivation that he derives the agricultural mound-builders. In this he agrees with Lewis H. Morgan, who looks to this area as their former home because, as he says, "the evidence of Indian occupation and cultivation throughout the greater part of this area is sufficient to suggest the hypothesis that the Indian here first attained to the condition of the middle status of barbarism and sent forth the migrating bands who carried this advanced culture to the Mississippi valley, to Mexico, and Central America and not unlikely to South America as well."[1]

Turning to the more recent authorities we take the following as specimens of the usual method of disposing of this question:

A broad chasm is to be spanne l before we can link the mound-builders to the North American Indians. They were essentially different in their form of government, their habits, and their daily pursuits.

The latter, since known to the white man, has spurned the restraints of a sedentary life which attach to agriculture, and whose requirements, in his view, are ignoble. He was never known to erect structures which would survive the lapse of a gener-ation. His lodges consist of a few poles, one end planted in the ground and the other secured with withes at the top, and over which were stretched plaits of matting, or of birch bark, or of the skin of the buffalo.[2]

The proofs hereafter presented will show how far this is from being correct, and that this writer, though of acknowledged ability, was ignorant of the evidence bearing on this subject, or, carried away by a pre-conceived theory, wholly disregarded it.

As a single item, we give here a statement from the account of "the first voyage of Raleigh (1584) to Virginia:"[3]

After they had been divers times aboard our ships myself with seven more went 20 miles into the river that runneth toward the city of Skicoak, which river they call Ocam, and the evening following we came to an island which they call Roanoke, distant from the harbor which we entered seven leagues; and at the north end thereof was a village of nine houses built of cedar and fortified round about with sharp trees to keep out their enemies, and the entrance into it made like a turnpike very artificially. When we came toward it, standing near to the water side, the wife of Granganimo, the king's brother, came running out to meet us very cheerfully and friendly. * * * When we were come into the outer room, having five rooms in her house, she caused us to sit down by a great fire, and after took off our clothes and washed them and dried them again; some of the women plucked off our stockings,

[1] Contrib. N. A. Ethn., Vol. 4, p. 192; also Beach's Indian Miscellany. pp. 235.

[2] Foster: Prehistoric Races, p. 347.

[3] Hakluyt's Voyages. London Ed., 1600, Vol. 3, p. 304.

washed them, some washed our feet in warm water, and she herself took great pains to see all things ordered in the best manner she could, making great haste to dress some meat for us to eat. * * * Their vessels are earthen pots, very large, white, and sweet; their dishes are wooden platters of sweet timber.

Yet the writer above quoted adds:

To suppose that such a race threw up the strong lines of circumvallation and the symmetrical mounds which crown so many of our river terraces is as preposterous almost as to suppose that they built the pyramids of Egypt.

Another says:

There is no trace or probability of any direct relationship whatever between the mound-builders and the barbarous Indians found in the country. The wild Indians of this continent have never known such a condition as that of the mound-builders. They had nothing in common with it. In Africa, Asia, and elsewhere among the more uncivilized families of the human race there is not as much really original barbarisms as some anthropologists are inclined to assume, but there can be no serious doubt that the wild Indians of North America were original barbarians born of a stock which had never at any time been either civilized or closely associated with the influence of civilization. * * * It is absurd to suppose a relationship or a connection of any kind between the original barbarism of these Indians and the civilization of the mound-builders.[1]

Why this opinion has prevailed in the minds of the masses who have learned it from the history and tradition of Indian life and Indian warfare since the establishment of European colonies in this country, can easily be understood, but why writers should so speak of them who had access to the older records, giving accounts of the habits and customs of the Indian tribes when first observed by European navigators and explorers, is difficult to conceive, when the records, almost without exception, notice the fact that although addicted to war, much devoted to the chase, and often base and treacherous, they were generally found from the Mississippi to the Atlantic dwelling in settled villages and cultivating the soil.

In fact, when first visited by Europeans there was scarcely a tribe from the Atlantic to the borders of the western plains but that had its fixed seat, its local habitation, and subsisted to a very large extent upon the products of agriculture.

De Soto found all the tribes he visited, from the Florida peninsula to the western part of Arkansas, cultivating maize and various vegetables. The early voyagers along the Atlantic shore found the same thing true from Florida to Massachusetts. Capt. John Smith and his colony, and in fact all the early colonies, depended very largely for subsistence upon this fact. Jacques Cartier found the inhabitants of old Hochelaga cultivating maize. Champlain testifies to the same thing's being true of the Iroquois. La Salle and his companions observed the Indians of Illinois, and from thence southward along the Mississippi, cultivating and to a large extent subsisting upon maize.

The truth of these statements has been so thoroughly demonstrated by Mr. Lucien Carr in his " Mounds of the Mississippi Valley Histori-

[1] Baldwin, Ancient America, pp. 60, 61.

cally Considered," that but little is left for others to offer on this subject. Nevertheless a somewhat fuller presentation of some of the statements of the early authorities bearing on the subject is given here.

Thomas Hariot, a very intelligent and reliable observer, gives the following notes in regard to the method of cultivating maize and other vegetables by the Indians of the Virginia coast:

Pagatowr, a kind of grain so called by the inhabitants; the same in the West Indies is called Mayze, Englishmen call it Guiny-wheat or Turkey-wheat, according to the names of the countries from whence the like hath been brought. The grain is about the bigness of our ordinary English peas and not much different in form and shape; but of divers colors, some white, some red, some yellow and some blue. All of these yield a very white and sweet flour, being used according to his kind, it maketh a very good bread. We made of the same in the country some malt whereof was brewed as good ale as was to be desired. So likewise by the help of hops thereof may be made as good beer.   *   *   *

Okindgier, called by us beans, because in greatness and partly in shape they are like the beans in England, saving that they are flatter.   *   *   *

Wickonzowr, called by us pease, in respect of the beans for distinctions sake, because they are much less although in form they little differ.   *   *   *

Macoqwer, according to their several forms, called by us Pompions, Melons, and Gourds because they are of like forms as those kinds in England.

All the aforesaid commodities for victual are set or sowed, sometimes in grounds apart and severally by themselves, but for the most part together in one ground mixtly: the manner thereof with the dressing and preparing of the ground, because I will note unto you the fertility of the soil, I think good briefly to describe.

The ground they never fatten with muck, dung or anything, neither plow nor dig it as we in England, but only prepare it in sort as followeth: A few days before they sow or set, the men with wooden instruments made almost in the form of mattocks or hoes with long handles, the women with short peckers or parers, because they use them sitting, of a foot long, and about five inches in breadth, do only break the upper part of the ground to raise up the weeds, grass, and old stubs of cornstalks with their roots. The which after a day or two days drying in the sun, being scraped up into many small heaps, to save them labor for carrying them away, they burn to ashes. And whereas some may think that they use the ashes for to better the ground, I say that then they would either disperse the ashes abroad, which we observe they do not, except the heaps be too great, or else would take special care to set their corn where the ashes lie, which also we find they are careless of. And this is all the husbanding of their ground that they use.

Then their setting or sowing is after this manner. First, for their corn, beginning in one corner of the plot with a pecker they make a hole wherein they put out four grains, with care that they touch not one another, (about an inch asunder) and cover them with the mould again; and so throughout the whole plot, making such holes and using them after such manner, but with this regard, that they be made in ranks, every rank differing from the other half a fathom or a yard, and the holes also in every rank. By this means there is a yard of spare ground between every hole; where, according to discretion here and there, they set as many beans and pease; in divers places also among the seeds of Macocqwer, Melden and Planta Solis.   *   *   * There is an herb which is sowed apart by itself, and it is called by the inhabitants Uppowoc; in the West Indies it has divers names according to the several places and countries where it groweth and is used; the Spaniards generally call it tobacco, the leaves thereof being dried and brought into powder they use to take the fume or smoke thereof by sucking it through pipes made of clay, into their stomach and head, from whence it purgeth superfluous fleame and other gross humors, and openeth all the pores and passages of the body; by which means the use thereof not only preserveth the body from obstruction, but also (if any be so that they have not been of too long continuance) in short time breaketh them: whereby their bodies are notably preserved in health, and know not many grievous diseases, wherewithal we in England are oftentimes afflicted.[1]

This, we must bear in mind, was written in 1587, nearly twenty years before the first permanent European settlement in Virginia. Another point worthy of notice as indicative of considerable experience in cultivation is that there were in use in the section visited by Mr. Hariot four varieties of maize.

Beverly, in his History of Virginia,[2] says:

Besides all these, our natives had originally amongst them, Indian corn, Peas, Beans, Potatoes (Sweet Potatoes) and Tobacco.

This Indian Corn was the staff of food upon which the Indians did ever depend; for when sickness, bad weather, war or any other accident kept them from hunting, fishing and fowling, this, with the addition of some Peas, Beans and such other fruits of the Earth, as were then in season, was the family's dependence and the support of their women and children.

There are four sorts of Indian Corn, two of which are early ripe, and two late ripe, all growing in the same manner. Every single grain of this when planted produces a tall up-right Stalk which has several ears hanging on the sides of it, from six to ten inches long. * * * The late ripe corn is diversify'ed by the shape of the grain only, without respect to the accidental differences in colour, some being blue, some red, some yellow, some white and some streak'd. That therefore which makes the distinction is the plumpness or shrivelling of the grain; the one looks as smooth and as full as the early ripe corn and this they call flint corn: the other has a larger grain and looks shrivell'd with a dent on the back of the grain as if it had never come to perfection, and this they call *she-corn*.

All these sorts are planted alike in rows, three, four or five grains in a hill, the larger sort at four or five foot distance, the lesser sort nearer. The Indians used to give it one or two weedings and make a hill about it, and so the labor was done. They likewise plant a bean in the same hill with the corn, upon whose stalk it sustains itself.

The Indians sow'd peas sometimes in the intervals of the rows of corn, but more generally in a patch of ground by themselves. * * *

Their potatoes are either red or white, about as long as a boy's leg, and sometimes as long and big as both the leg and thigh of a young child, and very much resembling it in shape.

How the Indians order'd their tobacco I am not certain, they now depending chiefly upon the English for what they smoak.

This long extract from Beverly has been given, as it furnishes additional evidence of the long cultivation of maize, the varieties being the same now chiefly in use in the South.

Marquette, speaking of the Illinois Indians as seen by him on his first visit,[3] remarks:

They live by game, which is abundant in this country, and on Indian corn (bled d'inde), of which they always gather a good crop, so that they have never suffered by famine. They also sow beans and melons, which are excellent, especially those with a red seed. Their squashes are not of the best; they dry them in the sun to eat in the winter and spring.

---

[1] Hariot (Thomas)—"A Brief & True Report," etc., of Virginia, Reprint, N. Y., 1872, pp. 13–16.
[2] Second edn., London, 1722, pp. 125–128.
[3] Voyages and Discov., English trans. Hist. Coll. La., 1852, vol. IV, p. 33. Original French, p. 246.

In the "Relation," by Vimont,[1] twenty-nine tribes living south of the lakes are mentioned as sedentary and cultivators of the soil. Le Clercq says[2] that "The Algomquins, Iroquois, Hurons, Nipsiriniens, Neuters, and Five Nations were indeed sedentary."

Du Pratz says:

"All the nations I have known, and who inhabit from the sea as far as the Illinois, and even farther, which is a space of about 1,500 miles, carefully cultivate the maize corn, which they make their principal subsistence."[3]

According to Jacques Cartier, who visited Canada as early as 1535, and was, so far as known, the first European explorer who passed up the St. Lawrence, the Indians of Hochelaga (now Montreal) "had good and large fields full of corn, * * * which they preserve in garets at the tops of their houses."[4]

Champlain,[5] A. D. 1610, speaking of the Indians immediately around Lakes Erie and Ontario, says that most of them cultivated corn, which was their principal article of food, and which they also exchanged for skins with the hunter tribes living to the north. They stored it in the tops of their houses, and cultivated it in quantities so that they might have on hand a supply large enough to last three or four years in case of failure of the crop.[6]

The wheat (Indian corn) being thus sown in the manner that we do beans, of a grain obtained only from a stalk or cane, the cane bears two or three spikes, and each spike yields a hundred, two hundred, sometimes 400 grains, and some yield even more. The cane grows to the height of a man and more, and is very large (it does not grow so well or so high, nor the spike as large nor the grain so good in Canada nor in France, as there) in the Huron country.

The grain ripens in four months and in some places in three. After this they gather it and bind it by the leaves turned up at the top and arrange it in sheaves, which they hang all along the length of the cabin from top to bottom on poles, which they arrange in the form of a rack (rattelier) descending to the front edge of the bench. All this is so nicely done that it seems like tapestry hung the whole length of the cabins. The grain being well dried and suitable to press (or pound), the women and girls take out the grains, clean them, and put them in their large tubs or tuns made for this purpose, and placed in their porch or in one corner of the cabin.[7]

The amount of corn of the Iroquois destroyed by Denonville in 1687 is estimated at more than a million bushels.[8] According to Tonty, who took part in the expedition, they were seven days engaged in cutting up the corn of four villages.[9]

It is unnecessary to allude to the testimony given by Mr. Carr in

[1] Jesuit Relations for 1640 (Reprint 1858) vol. I, p. 35.
[2] Estab. of the Faith. Shea's transl. (1881), vol. I, p. 110.
[3] Du Pratz, Hist. La., vol. II, p. 239 (London, 1763.) French ed., Paris, 1758. vol. III, p. 8.
[4] Hakluyt's Voyages (London, 1810), vol. III, p. 272.
[5] Voyages de Champlain, liv. IV, cap. 8, Paris, 1632.
[6] Voyages de Champlain, p. 301. Sagard, Voyagess du pays des Hurons, Paris, 1632. p. 134. Edn. 1865, part 1, p. 92.
[7] Sagard, Voyages des Hurons (edn. 1865), pt. 1, p. 93.
[8] Charlevoix, Hist. Nouv. France, Paris 1744, v. II, p. 355. Doc. Hist. N. Y. 1st series, 1849, p. 238.
[9] Hist. Coll. La., vol. I. p. 70.

regard to agriculture among the Algonquin tribes east of the Hudson river, as this is a part of the history of the early Pilgrim settlement, and is too well known to need repeating here. Had it not been for the corn furnished this settlement in its early days by the Indians willingly or through force, there would be few if any descendants of the Pilgrim fathers to write their history or sing their praises.

So far as history tells us anything in regard to the Indians of Pennsylvania and New Jersey in reference to this subject, it shows them to have been cultivators of the soil.

The evidence in regard to the agriculture of the Virginia Indians has been given in part, to which may be added the fact that the Jamestown colony depended entirely on the natives for corn during the first few years of its existence.

The evidence that the tribes of North and South Carolina were largely dependent upon agriculture for subsistence is found in Lawson's "Carolina" and Adair's "History of the American Indians." From the former we learn that the tribes toward the coast cultivated many kinds of "pulse" (by which term he means chiefly corn), part of which they ate green in summer, keeping great quantities for their winter supply.[1]

It is from the southern Indians that the farmers of to-day derive the method of constructing cribs on posts to secure their corn against vermin, as is evident from the following passage in Lawson's History.

These Santee Indians * * * make themselves cribs after a very curious manner, wherein they secure their corn from vermin, which are more frequent in these warm climates than countries more distant from the sun. These pretty fabrics are commonly supported with eight feet or posts about 7 feet from the ground, well daubed within and without upon laths with loam or clay, which makes them tight and fit to keep out the smallest insect, there being a small door at the gable end, which is made of the same composition.[2]

In regard to the Gulf States east of the Mississippi and also Arkansas, the evidence on the point under consideration is so abundant that we can not give space here for more than a mere summary. Corn was grown everywhere in great abundance. De Soto and his Spanish followers, amounting at the outset to more than 600 men, 200 horses, and a drove of hogs, subsisted during the four years they were traversing the country almost wholly upon the products of the natives' fields. The amount of game taken during this time would scarcely have sufficed them for a single month.

Such expressions as the following are abundant in the narratives of the chroniclers of this ill-starred expedition:

"In the barns and in the fields great store of maize. * * * Many sown fields which reached from one town to the other."[3] "The maize that was in the other towns was brought hither; and in all, it was

---

[1] London ed. 1718, p. 207.
[2] Raleigh ed. 1860, p. 35.
[3] Gentleman of Elvas, Hist. Coll. La., vol. II, p. 152.

esteemed to be six thousand hanegs [fanegas]."[1] "As soon as they came to Cale the governor commanded them to gather all the maize that was ripe in the field, which was sufficient for three months."[2] When we remember that this was sufficient for 600 men, 200 horses, and a hundred or more hogs, and that it was taken from the field of a single Indian town, we can more readily appreciate the fact that these natives were agriculturists, notwithstanding the statements of modern archeologists to the contrary.

It is stated in Barnard de la Harpe's "Journal"[3] that M. le Sueur "sent two Canadians to invite the Avavois and the Octotatas to settle near the fort because they were good farmers and he wished to employ them in cultivating the land and working the mines."

M. Thaumer de la Source,[4] speaking of the Tounicas, says they live "entirely on Indian corn; they do not hunt like other Indians."

It is unnecessary to add further testimony, as Mr. Carr's summary of evidence which applies to the entire mound area, unless it be the Dakotan region, leaves no ground on which the doubter can find a foothold.

Such is the testimony of the older authorities and of those who have studied the history of the discoveries of our continent and the early European intercourse with its aborigines.

Marquis de Nadaillac, reviewing Mr. Carr's work, admits that "at numerous points in North America the Indians were much more advanced than their numerous descendants,"[5] but he contends that the evidence dates from the sixteenth, seventeenth, and eighteenth centuries, and hence leaves a break unclosed and the chain incomplete. Such an objection is, to say the least, out of place in the writings of so able an author. The evidence reaches back to the first contact of Europeans with the natives of the different sections, and shows their habits and customs before being affected by European civilization, and, as the reader will observe, it applies generally and almost without exception to the tribes living east of the Mississippi.

In the American edition of his "Prehistoric America," edited by Dr. Dall, the position taken by the author on the question now under consideration appears to be abandoned, but this is probably due to the editor of this edition.

The evidence adduced seems conclusive that, excepting a few unimportant cases, the tribes from the Atlantic to the prairies of the west and from the lakes to the gulf were cultivators of the soil, which is sufficient proof, if other evidence were wanting, which is not the case, that they must have been sedentary, or at least had fixed villages and determinate localities.

That from time to time, as was the case with the more civilized

[1] Gentleman of Elvas, Hist. Coll. La., vol. II, p. 203.
[2] Ibid., p. 130.
[3] Hist. Coll. La., vol. III, p. 26.
[4] Shea's Early Voyages up and down the Mississippi, p. 81.
[5] Revue d'Anthropologie, Jan. 15, 1885.

nations of Mexico and Central America, the fortunes of war may have
compelled a tribe to change its location is undoubtedly true, but this
does not warrant the belief so generally entertained that they were
nothing more than wandering hordes of savages without any fixed

FIG. 340.—The village of Secotan.

abodes. It is also true that the dwellings of some of the tribes were of
a primitive and very simple character, easily destroyed and easily re-
built, but in most cases each prominent village had its public house or
houses, such as a council house, temple, and barracoa or grain house,

indicating permanency. In the southern region, and even in some northern sections, the buildings, although of perishable materials and primitive architecture, were more substantial; and, as will be shown further on, fortified villages were not uncommon in both sections.

A few references to the statements of early explorers and travelers will be sufficient to substantiate the above conclusions in regard to the houses of the aborigines.

We present first a figure from De Bry,[1] drawn by Le Moyne de Morgues, the artist of Laudonniere's expeditions to the coast of Florida. (See Pl. XLII.)

This, which represents a scene on the Florida or South Carolina coast about 1585, was drawn by the artist to show one phase of the burial ceremonies of a deceased chief. In one part we observe a few of the houses of the native village.

We also give a second sketch (Fig. 340), drawn by John Wyth, an artist who accompanied Sir Richard Grenville's expedition in 1585. We copy this also from De Bry: "Some of their towns," says the artist,[2] "are not inclosed with a palisade, and are much more pleasant; Seco- tan, for example, here drawn from nature. The houses are more scat- tered, and a greater degree of comfort and cultivation is observed, with gardens in which tobacco (E) is cultivated, woods filled with deer, and field of corn. In the fields they erect a stage (F) in which a sentry is sta- tioned to guard against the depredations of birds and thieves. Their corn they plant in rows (H), for it grows so large, with thick stalk and broad leaves, that one plant would stint the other and it would never arrive at maturity. They have also a curious place (C) where they con- vene with their neighbors at their feasts, * * * and from which they go to the feast (D). On the opposite side is their place of prayer (B), and near to it the sepulcher of their chiefs (A). * * * They have gardens for melons (I) and a place (K) where they build their sacred fires. At a little distance from the town is the pond (L) from which they obtain water."

Although the artists may have brought together what were observed at different times, there is no reason to question the reality of what is pictured. If so, no one who looks at these pictures can doubt that the people whose homes are represented were sedentary and cultivators of the soil.

In order to show the interior of an Indian house we present this cut (Fig. 341) from Capt. John Smith's "History of Virginia."[3] Morgan, speaking of this figure, says:[4]

The engraving is probably an improvement upon the original house in the sym- metry of the structure, but it is doubtless a truthful representation of its mechanism. It seems likely that a double set of upright poles were used, one upon the outside

---

[1] Brevis Narratio (1591) Tab. XI.

[2] Contributions to North Am. Eth.   Vol. IV, p. 117.

[3] Richmond ed., 1819, p. 130.

[4] Houses and House Life of the American Aborigines.   Contributions to North American Ethn. Vol. 4, pp. 117, 118.

and one on the inside, between which the mattings of canes or willows were secured, as the houses at Pomeiock and Secotan are ribbed externally at intervals of about eight feet, showing four, five, and six sections.

As the writer last mentioned made a careful study of all the evidence relating to the Iroquois houses, his conclusion in regard to their size, form, and mode of construction is given rather than extracts from the original authorities:

The "long house" of the Iroquois   *   *   *   was from fifty to eighty and sometimes one hundred feet long. It consisted of a strong frame of upright poles set in the

FIG. 341.—Interior of house of Virginia Indians. From Smith's History,

ground, which were strengthened with horizontal poles attached with withes, and surmounted with a triangular, and in some cases with a round roof. It was covered over both sides and roof with large strips of elm bark tied to the frame with strings or splints. An external frame of poles for the sides and of rafters for the roof were then adjusted to hold the bark shingles between them, the two frames being tied together. The interior of the house was comparted at intervals of six or eight feet, leaving each chamber entirely open like a stall upon the passageway which passed through the center of the house from end to end. At each end was a doorway covered with suspended skins.

The following from Sagard's "Voyages des Hurons"[1] relates to the dwellings of the Hurons:

These twenty-five cities and villages are inhabited by two or three thousand men of war, at the most, without including the entire population, which numbers perhaps thirty or forty thousand souls in all. The principal town had formerly two hundred large cabins, each one containing a number of households. * * * Their cabins, called by them "Ganonchia," are built, as I have said, in the shape of arbors or garden bowers, covered with the bark of trees, of the length of 25 to 30 toises [50 to 60 yards] more or less, for they are not all of the same length, and six [12 yards] in width, leaving in the center a hall ten or twelve feet wide extending from one end to the other. On each side there is a sort of bench or platform four or five feet high.

Among the "tracts and other papers relating to the origin, settlement, and progress of the colonies in North America, collected by Peter Force," is "A Relation by William Hitton of a discovery made on the Coast of Florida." In this[2] is the following statement:

That which we noted there was a fair house, round, two hundred feet at least, completely covered with palmetto leaves, the wall plate being twelve feet high or thereabouts, and within, lodging rooms and forms. Two pillars at the entrance and a high seat above all the rest.

This was probably a council house, but at that early day little was known of the Indian customs.

Marquette, speaking of the Illinois Indians, says:

Their cabins are very large; they are lined and floored with rush-mats.[3]

Gravier, who passed down the Mississippi in 1700, speaks as follows of the customs and cabins of the Arkansas Indians living near the mouth of the Arkansas river:[4]

The men do here what the peasants do in France; they cultivate and dig the earth, plant and harvest the crops, cut the wood and bring it to the cabin, dress the deer and buffalo skins when they have any. They dress them the best of all Indians that I have seen. The women do only indoor work, make the earthen pots and their clothes. Their cabins are round and vaulted. They are lathed with canes and plastered with mud from bottom to top, within and without, with a good covering of straw. * * * Their bed is of round canes raised on four posts three feet high, and a cane mat serves as a mattress. Nothing is neater than their cabins. * * * Their granaries are near their cabins, made like dove-cotes, built on four large posts, 15 or 16 feet high, well put together and well polished, so that mice can not climb up, and in this way they protect their corn and squashes, which are still better than those of the Illinois.

As reference will be made hereafter to the Indian forts and fortifications, it is unnecessary to mention them here. Nevertheless we give the following quotation from Jacques Cartier's account of his second voyage up the St. Lawrence:

We went along and about a mile and a half farther we began to finde goodly and large fields, full of such corne as the countrie yieldeth. It is even as the Millet of

[1] Paris ed., 1865, pp. 80, 81.
[2] Page 5.
[3] Relation of Voyages and Discoveries of Marquette, by Dablon, Hist. Coll. La, vol. 4, p. 33.
[4] Journal of the Voyage of Father Gravier in 1700, Shea's Early Voyages up and down the Mississippi, p. 134.

Brasil as great and somewhat bigger than small peason wherewith they live even as we doe with ours. In the midst of the fieldes is the citie of Hochelaga [site of Montreal] placed neere and as it were joined to a great mountain that is tilled round about very fertill, on the top of which you may see very farre, we named it Mount Roiall. The citie of Hochelaga is round, compassed about with timber with three courses of rampires, one within another, framed like a sharpe spire but laide acrosse above. The middle most of them is made and built as a direct line, but perpendicular. The rampires are framed and fashioned with peeces of timber, layed along on the ground, very well and cunningly joined together after their fashion. This enclosure is in height about two rods. It hath but one gate or entree thereat which is shut with piles, stakes and barres. Over it, and also in many places of the wall, there be places to runne along and ladders to get up, all full of stones for the defence of it. There are in the towne about fiftie houses about fiftie paces long and twelve or fifteene broad, built all of wood covered over with the barke of the wood as broad as any boord, very finely and cunning joined together. Within the said houses there are many roomes lodgings and chambers. In the middle of every one there is a great court in the middle whereof they make their fire. * * * They have also on the top of their houses certaine garrets within which they keep their corn to make their bread withall.[1]

Further reference to the houses of the Indians will be made when we come to speak of the dwellings of the mound-builders.

It is evident, therefore, from the abundant evidence relating thereto, that the statement in regard to the habits and customs of the Indians, found in most works on the archeology of the United States, and on which the objection to the theory that the people of this race were the mound-builders is founded, are incorrect and not justified by the facts. That most of the tribes were savage and cruel in some of their customs and practices must be admitted; but this is equally true of the more civilized people of Mexico and Central America.

OTHER OBJECTIONS ANSWERED.

Another objection which was formerly urged, but is now giving way before the light of more recent investigation, is the supposed great antiquity of the mounds and other ancient works, as indicated by the assumed fact that they are always found, when near streams, on the upper or older river terraces. This assumption, which has been followed by most writers on the subject of our antiquities down to a very recent date, was first clearly stated by Squier and Davis in the closing paragraph of their oft-quoted and standard work on the "Ancient Monuments of the Mississippi Valley," but was hinted at by Atwater as early as 1820.[1] The theory, as given by Squier and Davis, is as follows:

The fact that none of the ancient monuments occur upon the latest formed terraces of the river valleys of Ohio, is one of much importance in its bearings upon this question (the antiquity of these works). If, as we are amply warranted in believing, these terraces mark the degrees of subsidence of the streams, one of the four which may be traced has been formed since those streams have followed their present

---

[1] Hakluyt, vol. 3 (London ed., 1810), p. 272.   [1] Trans. Amer. Antiq. Soc., vol. 1. p. 219.

courses. There is no good reason for supposing that the mound-builders would have avoided building upon that terrace while they erected their works promiscuously upon all the others.

While it may be true that few (for there are some) ancient works occur on the last formed river terrace in Ohio, for the very good reason that the builders had learned, probably by sad experience, that this lower terrace was subject to repeated overflows, it is well known that in other sections, as, for example, along the southern and middle Mississippi, where this arrangement of successive terraces is not found, the mounds as a rule are on what is known as the "bottom" or flat valley which borders the river throughout most of its course. In fact, they are so common on levels subject to overflow as to lead many who are cognizant of this to believe they were built for the purpose of raising the dwellings of the inhabitants above the floods. Nor is this belief without some foundation if credence is given to the following statement of Garcilasso de la Vega.[1] Speaking of the inundation which occurred when Moscoso was preparing to go down the Mississippi, he says:

During similar inundations or risings in the great river, the Indians contrive to live on any high or lofty ground or hills, and if there are none they build them with their own hands, principally for the dwellings of the caciques; they are 3 or 4 "estados" high from the ground, built on heavy timber firmly fixed in the ground, with stakes intervening, and on top of these they place other timber, all of which is roofed over and divided into four parts to contain their provisions, their valuables, etc.

This description, which is somewhat confused, appears to apply to the mound and dwelling on it, or a kind of scaffolding. Throughout eastern Arkansas, and at some points in southeast Missouri, the mounds are often the only retreat for cattle and other stock in time of high water. One great hindrance to the mound explorations carried on in this region by the United States Bureau of Ethnology has been the unwillingness of the owners of mounds, on this account, to have them opened.

A foolish idea has prevailed in the minds of many persons that the Indians and mound-builders were wiser in this respect than the people of the present day, and would never plant their villages where they were subject to overflow. In addition to the evidence already given it happens that in one of the old authorities there is mentioned an incident bearing on this question which concerns both mound-builders and Indians, if the two people be distinct.

Herrera, who generally follows Garcilasso, but who certainly had access to other data which are not now extant, states [2] that when Moscoso, who was placed in command of the Spanish expedition after De Soto's death, returned to an Indian town named Amenoya, situated on

[1] Hist. Fla., p. 231. Edition before mentioned.
[2] Decade IV. Bk. X. Chap. II, vol. VI, p. 18, Stevens's Eng. transl. (1726); Decade VII. Bk. VII. Chap. V, p. 136, of orig. Sp.

the banks of the Mississippi, probably not far distant from Helena in
Arkansas, and there prepared for his descent of the Mississippi, "An
old Indian woman who could not make her escape with the rest[1] asked
them why they staid there, since that river overflowed every fourteen
years, and that was the year when it would happen." The prediction
proved true, as "the river began to rise on the 10th of March and
increased so much that on the 18th the water broke in at the gates of
the town so that there was no going along the streets two days after
without canoes. This inundation was forty days in rising to the height—
that is, to the 20th of April—the river extending itself above 20 leagues
on each side, so that nothing was to be seen in all the country about
but the tops of the highest trees, the people going about everywhere
in canoes."

The expression "broke in at the gates" shows that this town was
surrounded by an earthen wall, and the fact that the people could go
from house to house in canoes perhaps shows that they were on mounds.
We have, moreover, the statement in the same work that in a town on
the same side of the river, a short distance below, some of the houses
were on mounds.

Notwithstanding the fact that the opinion on this point advanced by
Squier and Davis, Baldwin, and others, seems to have been generally
abandoned, it is repeated in Bancroft's "Native Races"[2] and Maclean's
"Mound Builders."[3]

Another argument used to support the theory of the great antiquity
of these works, and hence that which holds that the Indians were not
the authors of them, is drawn from the supposed great age of trees often
found growing on them. It is stated that from one in Ohio a tree was
cut (species not given) which presented eight hundred consecutive rings
of growth, indicating that at least eight hundred years had elapsed
since this work was abandoned. That on another, a chestnut, 23 feet
in circumference and having about six hundred rings, was observed.

From these and numerous other similar cases which might be mentioned, though but one or two others have been found equal to these in
girth and number of rings, it is taken for granted as beyond controversy that the mounds of the region mentioned must have been abandoned at least seven or eight centuries ago, and as several generations
of trees must have preceded these giants of the forest, the reasonable
inference is that they were abandoned one or possibly two thousand
years ago.

Recent investigations have served to destroy confidence in this
hitherto supposed certain test of age, as it is found that even within
the latitude of the northern half of the United States from one to three
rings are formed each year; and that there is no certainty in this respect,
even with the same species in the same latitude.

---

[1] Herrera speaks of this person as a man, but Garcilasso says expressly "a woman."
[2] Vol. IV. p. 789.   [3] Page 135.

Nor will size furnish a sure and satisfactory indication. We are therefore at sea, as yet, on this question, and must be until botanists take hold of the subject and work out some better rule for determining the age of trees than has heretofore been given. Dr. Lapham undertook a few years ago to reach a conclusion on the point at issue by an investigation of the trees of Wisconsin. The result as given by Dr. Foster [1] is as follows:

By placing the edge of a sheet of paper across a newly felled tree in the direction of the radius, one may with a sharp pencil mark the thickness of the several rings of growth, and by measuring a number of such rings we may find the average increase of wood each year. It was thus that the items were collected for the following table, showing the number of rings measured, their aggregate width, the average annual growth thus found, and the number of years required for an increase of 1 foot in diameter of a number of our common forest trees:

Growth of native forest trees of Wisconsin.

	Number of rings measured.	Width in inches.	Growth in one year, in inches.	Number of years for 1 foot of growth.
Basswood (Tilia Americana)...........	94	5.70	.1212	99
Sugar maple (Acer saccharinum)	83	2.45	.1166	103
Wild cherry (Prunus serotina)	44	2.03	.0922	130
Elm (Ulmus Americana)...............	179	9.45	.1056	114
White ash (Fraxinus Americana)	172	10.09	.1172	102
White oak (Quercus alba)	160	9.00	.1124	107
Burr oak (Quercus macrocarpa)	12	.60	.1000	120
Red oak (Quercus rubra)	62	6.90	.2226	54
Beech (Fagus ferruginea)	160	9.45	.1180	102
Yellow birch (Betula excelsa)	20	1.28	.1280	94
White pine (Pinus strobus)..........	60	5.40	.1800	67
Hemlock (Abies Canadensis)	42	3.72	.1770	68
Tamarack (Larix Americana)	192	12.95	.1344	89
White cedar (Thuja occidentalis).....	82	4.00	.0976	123
Mean				98

A more thorough and systematic investigation of the annual growth of trees would lead to results of greater certainty; but the measurements already made and embodied in this table are sufficient to show that there can not be any great age assigned to the average trees of our present forests.

It will be seen that it requires the lapse of from fifty-four to one hundred and thirty years for trees to increase their diameter 1 foot, and with the average of the trees measured the time is less than one hundred years.

Three or four feet diameter is a large tree; few exceed that size; and hence we may infer that few of the trees now growing in Wisconsin can antedate the discovery of this continent by Columbus. An occasional tree exceeds these dimensions, but they are exceedingly rare.

Perhaps the largest and oldest tree in the state is the one noted by the government surveyor near Manitowoc, a white cedar 22 feet in circumference. By this table it will be seen that this tree is one of the slowest growth, requiring one hundred and twenty-three years to add 1 foot to its diameter.

---

[1] Prehistoric Races. pp. 373–375 note and table.

Seven times this quantity, or eight hundred and sixty years, is therefore the age of this exceptionally large tree.

Further south, where trees attain a larger size, they have had, at the same time, owing to the more genial climate and more fertile soil, a much more rapid growth, so that they probably do not exceed the trees of Wisconsin in age.

There can be no means of determining how many successive forests may have preceded the present, and occupied the soil since any given epoch, as that of the Mound-builders, all traces of the former trees having been long since effaced. A few years suffice to convert a fallen trunk into humus that can not be distinguished from the other portions of the accumulating soil.

This result, as will be seen, is based entirely on the theory of one ring per year. It is somewhat strange that the number of years for one foot of growth given in his table is, as a rule, about double that given by English botanists. The following is given here as possibly throwing some light on this subject in reference to the growth of trees of one kind in the latitude of southern Illinois.

Old Fort Chartres, of Monroe county, Illinois, situated on bottom land, was finally abandoned in 1772.[1] In 1802 it was visited by Governor Reynolds, who states that, at that time, " Large trees were growing in the houses which once contained the elegant and accomplished French officers and soldiers."[2] Maj. Stoddard visited it in 1804, when, according to his statement, "the enclosure was covered with trees from 7 to 12 inches in diameter."[3] This was but thirty-two years after its abandonment, hence the rate of growth of the largest trees must have been 1 foot in thirty-two years, or 0.375 inch per year. As the species of tree is not mentioned, this leaves the matter somewhat indefinite. But there is another witness who is more explicit. In 1820 Mr. Beck, the publisher of the " Illinois and Missouri Gazette," not only visited the ruins, but made a careful survey of them.

He states that at that time he found " in the hall of one of the houses an oak growing, 18 inches in diameter."[1] As this was forty-eight years after the abandonment, the rate of growth of this tree was 1 foot in thirty-two years, or 0.375 inch per year, precisely the same as the largest tree mentioned by Maj. Stoddard. As the tree measured by Mr. Beck was growing in the hall of one of the houses, it must have sprung from the acorn after the premises were abandoned.

This probably affords one of the best tests for the latitude indicated that has been, so far, placed on record. Supposing the growth of the large chestnut, 23 feet in circumference, heretofore mentioned as standing on one of the Ohio works, to have been at the same rate, its age was 233 years, instead of 600, as the rings indicated. This, it is admitted, is little better than mere guessing, but taking for granted, as recent investigations show, that the rings of growth cannot be relied

[1] E. G. Mason. "Old Fort Chartres" in Fergus' Hist. Series. No. 12. "Illinois in the 18th Century." p. 42. (Paper read before Chicago Hist. Soc., June 16, 1884.)

[2] Hist. Illinois. ed. 1879, p. 26.

[3] E. G. Mason. loc. cit.

[1] Beck's Gazetteer of Illinois and Missouri. Albany. 1823. pp. 109–110.

on as a sure indication of age, the conclusion reached is as likely to be correct as that based upon any other data we now possess.

Dr. Hoy, whose testimony will be accepted without question, states in a little pamphlet, entitled "Who built the mounds?"[2] that white elms planted in the streets of Racine, Wis., in 1847 and 1848, measured in 1882 from 6 to 8 feet in circumference, 2 feet from the ground. Maples planted at the same time measured from 4 to 5 feet in circumference; black and golden willows, 8 feet; poplars, 8½ to 9 feet. He also makes the following statement:

At the time Dr. Lapham and I surveyed the large group of mounds near Racine, in September, 1850, there was a pin oak sapling growing on the center of a small mound situated near the house of William Bull. That sapling is now (1882) 56 inches in diameter, although that species of tree is ordinarily not a rapid grower.[1]

As will be seen from this statement, the time required for the growth of one foot in this case was less than one-fourth that given by Dr. Lapham.

We may suppose that generation after generation of trees have grown to maturity on the mounds, and crumbled to dust before those now found on them began their existence. Such a supposition, however, is wholly gratuitous, unless based upon some evidence. But no such evidence has been found during the explorations carried on by the Bureau, nor has any been adduced by any other explorers. On the contrary, there are some reasons for believing the reverse of this supposition to be true. The roots of oaks and some other trees found growing on mounds will often penetrate to a great depth in search of moisture. One instance was observed in southeastern Missouri, where the roots of an oak ran down more than 10 feet, most of the distance through a solid mass of clay so hard that it had to be cut with an ax.

These roots, after the tree is dead, will, as a matter of course, decay; but they will often leave traces of their existence, especially where they pass through clay or earth of any other color than that into which they are converted.

It is not likely that several generations of trees would have grown to maturity on the mounds without some of them being blown down and leaving the little mound and depression so often seen in forests from this cause. Had this occurred, it is not probable that the indications would have been obliterated much sooner than the little depressions and rings marking the ancient dwelling sites.

These facts, alone, it is admitted, would not furnish a satisfactory test of age, yet they have some bearing on the question and are worthy of consideration. Notwithstanding the opinion of botanists, we are justified in the conclusion that the age of trees has been much overrated, especially as there is much error in counting rings by those not thoroughly acquainted with the subject, the number given often being double the true count, and that the one with 800 rings was more likely under than over 400 years old. Botanists apparently neglect the only satisfactory test, which is, to examine the rings and measure the growth of trees of different species whose age is known. No other test can be accepted by the other branches of science.

It is also contended that the magnitude of some of the earthworks indicates a much higher culture and a more systematic government and centralized power than have been found in Indian history. That there must have been sufficient intelligence to plan the works is evident; that there must have been some means of bringing into harmony the views of the people and of combining their forces is also apparent. But the fact that at the discovery of the country several of the tribes were accustomed (as will hereafter be shown) to build villages, surround them with palisades and moats, and in some cases to erect just such mounds as we now find, shows, beyond contradiction, that they had the necessary intelligence to plan such works and the means of combining forces to build them.

The supposition of a lost race, or of a migration from the more cultured people of Central America, aids but little in explaining the means by which they were built, as it does not supply them with beasts of burden nor metallic implements to assist them. There is nothing found in these monuments or elsewhere to indicate that the mound-builders had any other implements or any other means of conveying earth or of building these works than the Indians possessed.

It is rather strange that most writers who claim for these remains such high antiquity contend at the same time for a much more advanced culture than that attained by the Indians. It is true that when we stand at the base of the great Cahokia mound and study its vast proportions, we can scarcely bring ourselves to believe it was built without some other means of collecting and conveying material than that possessed by the Indians. But what other means could a lost race have had? The Indians had wooden spades, baskets, skins of animals, wooden and clay vessels, and textile fabrics; they also had stone implements. Moreover, the fact should be borne in mind that this great mound is unique in respect to size, being more than treble in contents that of any other true mound in the United States. Nor has it yet been ascertained with satisfactory certainty that it is entirely artificial. The very large mounds are the exceptions, there being but four or five of them in the entire area under consideration, the contents of the largest, save of the single exception noticed, being less than 5,000,000 cubic feet. In fact, when they are measured accurately the height is found in some cases to diminish to half that usually given, as in the case of the one near New Madrid, Missouri; and as a general rule the labor necessary to build them could not have exceeded that which has often been performed by Indians. It is also more than likely that all the people of a tribe, both men and women, aided in the work, and that

the large works were built by additions made during successive generations. But the best evidence that they could build such structures is
the fact that they did build them, that in truth they made every form
of ancient works known to exist in the bounds of our country, even to
the large canals of which there are yet traces. Nor should this astonish
us, since it is known that the cyclopean works of the old world, the dol-
mens, great stone circles, etc., were built by the earliest inhabitants of
these countries, who had not advanced beyond the stage of barbarism.[1]

INSCRIBED TABLETS.

Another objection to the Indian origin of these ancient monuments
is based upon certain inscribed tablets bearing supposed letters or
hieroglyphs, which are claimed to have been found in mounds. For
example, the "tablet of the Grave creek mound," over which Schoolcraft exercised all his linguistic knowledge, and after corresponding
with Prof. Page, of Copenhagen, and M. Jomard, of Paris, arrived at
the conclusion that, though mainly Celtiberic, the twenty-two alphabetic characters include four corresponding with ancient Greek letters,
four with Etruscan, five with old northern runes, six with ancient
Gaelic, seven with the old Erse, ten with the Phœnician, fourteen with
the Anglo-Saxon, and sixteen with the Celtiberic. Prof. Jomard, after
a laborious investigation, pronounced the inscription Lybian, and Mr.
W. B. Hodgson, Numidian.

The folly of relying upon such relics as this Grave creek tablet as
evidence of a written language is apparent from the above conclusions.
That Schoolcraft and the other savants mentioned could have believed
the inscription to be alphabetic, and a genuine mound-builder's relic,
and yet made up of several alphabets, would be inconceivable but for
the undeniable evidence. This simple fact ought to be sufficient to
cast it aside as unworthy of consideration. However, it may be added
that since Dr. Daniel Wilson's sharp criticism,[2] and Prof. Read's critical
examination of the evidence,[3] this relic is discarded by most archeologists.

Other tablets have been accepted by some of our archeologists and
linguists as conclusive evidence that the mound-builders had a written
language, one author even going so far as to give to the world a (supposed) translation of an entire inscription.[4]

If the marks upon these tablets are true letters or alphabetic signs,
and are the work of the veritable mound-builders, it must be admitted
that those who made them were not Indians, but a people much further

---

[1] This, being the point at issue, must of course be maintained with satisfactory evidence, which
will be attempted further on.

[2] Prehistoric Man, 3d ed. (1876), vol. II, pp. 100–102.

[3] Am. Antiq., vol. I, pp. 139–149.

[4] Ibid., vol. IV, 1882, pp. 145–153.

advanced in the arts of civilized life than most of the known aborigines of the continent.

As the decision on this point appears to hinge almost entirely on the conclusion reached in regard to the inscribed plates known as "the Davenport tablets," our report would be incomplete and unsatisfactory to archeologists without some expression of opinion in regard to the claims of these relics to genuineness and antiquity. These tablets, which are deposited in the Museum of the Davenport Academy of Natural Sciences, Davenport, Iowa, have become so well known to the world through the publications of that society that it is unnecessary to give here the history of their discovery, as it is given in full in these publications.

There are three of them, two of shale found in one mound, known as No. 3 of the Cook farm group, and one of limestone from mound No. 11 of the same group.

In order that some references made herein may be understood, we must refer the reader to Pls. I, II, III, and VII of the second volume of the Proceedings of the Davenport Academy of Sciences. In speaking of these, the inscription on the shale tablet showing the arcs and persons dancing around the fire (Pl. I) is designated, as the finders term it, "the cremation scene;" that on the reverse (Pl. II), "the hunting scene;" the smaller tablet (Pl. III), "the calendar;" the other (Pl. VII), "the limestone tablet."

The two shale tablets, being found in the same grave of mound No. 3, and side by side, must of necessity stand in the same category. Whatever conclusion is reached in regard to the antiquity, authenticity, and origin of one must apply to the other. Is the limestone tablet so intimately related to these that it must also be placed in the some category? It was found in a mound of the same group, which presented no characteristics different from the rest; in fact, it was an almost exact copy in every detail of mound No. 10, which is described and figured by Mr. Gass.[1]

Examining the excellent albertypes (Pls. I and VII, Proceedings, Vol. 2—"the cremation scene"), the reader will observe that there are three Arabic 8's on the former, one of which is so much like that on the latter as almost to lead to the belief that the two were made by one hand. Moreover, there are, as stated by the finder of the latter, four other characters on it identical with characters in the "cremation scene." It is also stated in the proceedings that the bird figures on the limestone tablet " have each a bit of quartz crystal set in for an eye like the eyes of the animal figure from mound No. 3, * * * and, like those, they are held in place by white cement of some kind."

While this fact is calculated to excite surprise, it renders it almost impossible to avoid the conclusion that all these tablets belong to the same category and to the same age and that what is true in regard to

[1] Proceedings. vol. II. p. 141.

the authenticity of one is true of all. We shall therefore proceed upon this basis.

At the outset, doubts of their authenticity are raised in the mind by their anomalous character; nothing in any respect like them having been found which has stood the test of criticism for a moment save, perhaps, the Grave creek tablet, and even this, since the examination by Whittlesey and the scathing criticism by Dr. Wilson, heretofore alluded to, can no longer be considered an accepted antiquity. This doubt is somewhat intensified by the fact that the discoveries are made in one locality, in quick succession, and through the same instrumentality which brought to light other anomalous relics. This feeling of doubt and uncertainty seems to have been entertained at first by members of the Academy, if we may judge by the language of one of their leading and ablest scientists, Dr. Farquharson,[1] who says:

It is objected, and seriously, too, that this discovery comes too apropos, too pat, in fact, and so partakes in the mind of some too much of the nature of a stage trick, a *Deus ex machina*. However, if it is a true, a bona fide discovery, some one else among the great army of searchers, in the course of time and from the very necessity of the case, must have made the same or a like one; nor need we fear that our find, remarkable as it is, will long remain unique and solitary, for, as Mr. Haven truly says, "Science and civilization do not leave solitary monuments."

But it is proper to remark that, notwithstanding these seeming doubts at the outset, Dr. Farquharson and all the other members of the society (with possibly one exception), after examination and discussion, settled down into the firm belief in the authenticity and genuineness of the tablets as veritable mound relics, and as entitled to acceptance on the part of archeologists.

The characters on these tablets render it absolutely certain that they can not be ascribed to any American tribe or people of ante-Columbian time of whose work and art we possess any knowledge. A few of the inscribed characters and several of the figures can be found in the inscriptions and rock carvings by Indians, but there are others which can not be attributed to them unless after long intercourse with European civilization. It will doubtless be admitted by all that, if genuine relics of the mound-builders of pre-Columbian times, they must be attributed to a lost race or people of whom we possess no knowledge, or that they are waifs from the eastern continent.

A still more serious objection to their acceptance as genuine is the fact that the characters on the " cremation scene," if true letters, must belong to not less than half a dozen alphabets.

Dr. Seyffarth, in his attempt at an explanation, published in volume 3 of the Proceedings, was forced to go to at least half a dozen different alphabets to find the letters given in this single short inscription. The remarks of Dr. Wilson in regard to the Grave creek tablet[2] are so applicable here that we can not refrain from quoting them:

---

[1] Proc. Dav. Acad. Nat. Sci., vol. II. p. 103.
[2] Preh. Man. 3d ed., vol. II. p. 100.

It thus appears that this ingenious little stone is even more accommodating than the Dighton rock in adapting itself to all conceivable theories of ante-Columbian colonization, and, in fact, constitutes an epitome of the prehistoric literature of the new world. Had Sir Henry Rawlinson dug up such a medley of languages at one of the corners of the tower of Babel it might have less surprised us. This curious analysis, so contrary to all previous philological experience, does not seem to have staggered the faith of the elucidator.

Nor does the same fact appear to have staggered Dr. Seyffarth, undoubtedly an excellent linguist, who made an analysis of the characters, or the Rev. J. Campbell, who presented a translation of the Davenport tablets.

Taking them up one by one, let us examine them somewhat critically. In doing so, the excellent albertypes prepared by Bierstadt and published in volume 2 of the Proceedings, which are all that could be desired in this respect, will be taken as the basis.

We will consider first the limestone tablet found in mound No. 11.

It will be seen that this plate has carved upon it, too plainly to be misunderstood, figures of two "Monitor" pipes. This is admitted by Mr. Harrison in his description,[1] as he says: "At each of the upper corners is cut a complete figure of a bird pipe, such as are found carved of stone in these mounds, and nearly of full size." In addition to this there is cut, immediately over the head of the personage represented, a figure in the usual form of the copper "axes" found in the mounds, or of the ordinary axes of the present day. There is, therefore, no escape from the conclusion either that this is a genuine relic of the mound-building age, or that it was made since the explorations of recent times have brought these axes and pipes to light.

The representation of the sun with a face and rays is an anomaly in mound-builders' art. The circle with denticuli, probably intended to represent the sun, is found occasionally, carved on shells, and stone disks somewhat of the same form have been found. Shell and even stone masks with the human face outlined are not uncommon, but it is believed that nothing like the figure on this stone is to be found elsewhere on mound relics of this country. Nevertheless, as it is somewhat common among barbarous and civilized people, and is occasionally found among the rock etchings of the Indians,[2] it would not excite surprise at being represented here, were it not for the connection in which it is found. But it is impossible to avoid surprise at finding to the left of the "ax" a regularly formed Arabic 8, made as is customary with writers of the present day, and near the upper right-hand corner the Roman numeral VIII or VI and II, the middle space being slightly wider than between the other strokes. These, be it remembered, are not museum marks, but parts of the original inscription on the stone when found.

Comparing the Arabic 8 on this stone with that on the cremation scene

[1] Proc. Davenport Acad. Sci., vol. II, p. 225.   [2] First Ann. Rept. Bureau Ethn., p. 371.

near the upper right-hand corner of the plate, the resemblance is found to be so strong as to indicate that both were made by one hand. As they were found in mounds of the same group and apparently of the same age, it is not improbable that this is the case.

The facts as to the finding, given by the members of the Academy and published in the proceedings, are not calculated to strengthen belief in its genuineness. In the first place, although situated in the immediate vicinity of, and in the triangle formed by, Nos. 1, 9, and 10, this mound seems to have escaped notice until the latter part of 1877. In the second place, although constructed like some of the other mounds of the group, it seems to have been the only one not used as a place of sepulture. No. 10, which it resembles in almost every particular, contained comparatively few human bones, though enough to show that one individual had been buried there.

Yet in this case the whole object in view in digging the pit, building the stone heap, and throwing up the tumulus seems to have been to make a resting or hiding place for this tablet. Still, this is not im-

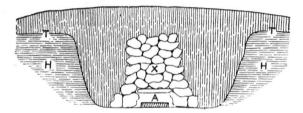

Fig. 342.—Section of mound 11. Cook farm group, Iowa.

possible, as one of the Ohio mounds mentioned by Messrs. Squier and Davis seems to have been intended simply as a cache for flint implements.

In the third place, the condition of the tablet and immediate surroundings, when found, seems so contrary to all experience in reference to ancient mounds as to lead to the belief that it was recently made or recently meddled with.

The account by Mr. Harrison[1] is accompanied by a cut, Fig. 17, of which our Fig. 342 is an exact copy. By reference to this, it will be seen that there was an excavation in the original earth, T T indicating the line of the original surface and H H the original earth forming the sides of the pit.

This pit, as we are informed by Mr. Harrison, extended down to the clay, the floor being a level and very compact stratum of yellow clay, such as has been frequently noticed and described in reference to other mounds of this group. In this excavation, resting on the floor, was the stone pile X, over which the mound of earth was thrown. This earth, after passing through the frozen crust, was, as we are told, "easy to

---

[1] Proc. Dav. Acad. Nat. Sci., pp. 221-223.

handle, being composed of dark soil with some admixture of clay;" moreover, there appears to have been no indication of stratification. At the bottom, and just under the stone pile, was a miniature vault, A, 5 inches in depth and a "little larger than the tablet," probably about 13 or 14 by 8 or 9 inches, the bottom of the excavation forming the bottom of the vault.

This vault appears to have been walled around by the outer lower stones of the pile and covered by a single flat slab. In the bottom of it, immediately under A, lay the tablet, an inch and a half thick, on which were four arrow points, a little quartz crystal, and a *Unio* shell. With the exception of these, which occupied considerably less than half the space, this little vault was empty; for it is stated in the published account that, " on raising the flat stone, an irregularly rectangular engraved tablet was suddenly exposed to view as it lay face up in a walled vault evidently built for its reception."

But, in order to be certain as to this inference, the following inquiry was addressed to Mr. W. H. Pratt, the curator of the museum of the academy, who was familiar with all the facts: " Was the cavity A, Fig. 17, Proc. Dav. Acad. Sci., p. 222, Vol. 2, filled with dirt when first discovered ?"—to which he kindly returned this answer: " Mr. C. E. Harrison, who assisted in the work, states that the cavity in which the limestone tablet was found contained scarcely any dirt when the flat stone with which it was covered was raised, exposing it to view."

That there should have been an unfilled space in the base of a pile of loose or " uncemented" stones, standing in an excavation beneath a heap of comparatively loose dirt which had stood there for centuries, is certainly most extraordinary. The excavation in which the pile was placed would necessarily gather about it the water that percolated through the earth above and the layer of compact clay below would have prevented its rapid escape downwards.

The interior of mounds has frequently been found comparatively dry when there was opportunity for drainage and the body was composed of hard, compact, mortarlike material. A stone grave has occasionally been found only partially filled with earth where well covered, and standing high enough in a mound to shed the water. But here the conditions are entirely different. The mound was so low that for three years it had escaped the trained eyes of eager searchers, was composed of comparatively loose earth, and had been plowed over for years; beneath it was a pit which acted as a reservoir into which the water gathered, and at the bottom was compact clay to prevent its ready escape. The stone slab over the little vault and loose unmortared stones at the sides would not prevent the water from entering at the sides. Moreover it must also be borne in mind that there was no side drainage except as the water soaked into the earth. It follows, therefore, that all the sediment carried down by the water would have been deposited in this little vault and the excavation around it.

In a letter written in 1882 by Mr. A. S. Tiffany to Col. Norris, and subsequently, in a letter to the present author, avowed by him, before the academy, to be genuine, is the following statement:

The limestone tablet I am certain is a fraud. Mr. Gass was assisted in digging it out by Mr. Harrison and Mr. Hume. Mr. Hume informs me that there was a wall of small bowlders around the tablet. On the tablet there were some arrow points, a quartz crystal and a *Unio* shell filled with red paint, the whole being covered with a rough limestone slab, the space between it and the tablet not filled with earth, and the paint bright and clean.

Mr. Tiffany was one of the founders of the academy and, as appears from the proceedings, was long one of its most prominent, active, and trusted members and was still a member at the time the letters referred to were written. It is proper to state that he accepts the shale tablets as genuine, but stands by the above statement in regard to the limestone tablet, and did so in a meeting of the academy in presence of all the members.

If these statements concerning the conditions under which this tablet was found be correct, which we have no reason to doubt, as they are made by the parties concerned, there are strong reasons for suspecting that it was a "plant" made probably by some unknown person, to deceive the members of the academy. The simple fact that the little vault under the pile of rough, uncemented stones was empty, save for the relics, appears absolutely to forbid the idea of age; for under such conditions as in this case it would, unless hermetically sealed, have been filled, in the length of time, with earth from the sides, carried in by the infiltrating water.

THE SHALE TABLETS.

As the evidence in regard to the limestone tablet seems not only to preclude the idea of any great age, but also to indicate that it was a "plant" made to deceive the members of the Davenport Academy, we are led to inquire whether the authenticity of the shale tablets rests on any better foundation.

If the conclusion in regard to the former be correct, and the reasons given for considering them all as belonging to the same category be deemed conclusive, the question is settled and requires no further discussion. But the object at present is not merely to make a point in argument, but to arrive at truth; therefore the following suggestions in regard to the latter are presented. As the two were found in the same grave, they will be considered together, conclusions reached in regard to the age of one necessarily applying to the other.

Some blunders made by the society and its members in bringing before the public the facts in reference to these relics and their discovery, though readily accounted for, excite a fear in the mind that proper care was not taken at the time to verify statements and guard against imposition. Compare, for example, Fig. 3, Pl. II, Proceedings, Vol. I, with Fig. 8, p. 92, Proceedings, Vol. II. both purporting to be figures of mound 3, Cook farm group, in which these relics were found. The former, it is true, was made when only the southern part of the mound containing the grave, or pit, *a*, had been examined. It shows neither the layers of shells nor the pit in which the skeletons were found, and only one skeleton is indicated in the supplemental plan. As the complete exploration of this part was made in 1874, these facts must have been known at that time, and Mr. Gass, the explorer, was at hand to refer to at any time; yet, here is a figure presented to the public, which is evidently to a large extent, if not wholly, imaginary, but still purporting to be given to a scale. Moreover, attention appears to have been called at the time to the possibility of error, as Dr. Farquharson says:[1] " Of this [mound 3] the Rev. Mr. Gass (the explorer) says ' *the outer and inner arrangements were quite similar to the first.*' But his further description shows that it was not, no layers of stones or of shells being mentioned." The italics are his own. In the subsequent description of the whole mound, by Gass, the portion relating to the south half is based entirely on the first exploration made in 1874, and not only are the shell-beds and the pits mentioned, but he goes on to say:

The fact that the bottom of this grave sloped upward and outward, in all directions, confirmed our opinion that all the contents of this mound had been discovered, and a further search would be useless. Messrs. Farquharson, Tiffany, and Pratt, to whom full permission was given to prosecute a further research, concurred in this opinion, and did not think it advisable to avail themselves of the opportunity. The work on this mound was therefore discontinued.[2]

Notwithstanding all these facts, a figure is presented in the Proceedings vol. I, Pl. II, purporting to represent a section of this mound, which is erroneous in every particular, in fact is purely imaginary. What are we to infer from this in regard to the figures of other mounds, on the same plate? As a rule, the illustrations by the Academy appear to be not only correct, but very well done: but we feel constrained to express a fear that those on Pls. II and III of Vol. I have been made without proper care. We feel it a duty to express this fear, because, relying upon their correctness, not having carefully studied their history, we copied them into a preceding work and based conclusions on what they show.

The description by Mr. Gass leaves the impression that the layers of shells over the two graves were undisturbed, though he does not positively assert this to be the case. Nevertheless, the following facts which he mentions are somewhat difficult to account for on this supposition. Scattered throug the soil above the first layer of shells over grave B, in which the tablets were found, were a number of human bones, but no entire skeleton, while in the corresponding position over A were two entire skeletons. Stones were also found here, correspond-

[1] Proc. Davenport Acad. Nat. Sci., Vol. I, p. 119.   [2] Op. cit., p. 959.

ing with those found in connection with the skeletons. "Associated with these bones," says Mr. Gass, "which, like those on the other side of the mound, were doubtless of modern times, we found a few glass beads and fragments of a brass ring." Below the second layer of shells and within the pit or grave B "was a stratum of loose, black soil or vegetable mold of 18 or 20 inches. * * * In this soil were discovered fragments of human bones and small pieces of coal slate or bituminous shale."

In this grave there was no entire skeleton, but "south of the tablets, i. e., in the southwest corner of the grave, were found a few pieces of skull bones, one piece of which was saturated with the green carbonate of copper. Also, several pieces of human cervical vertebræ. * * * In this grave were a great number of bones of the body, and also in the northeast corner, as in the southwest corner above mentioned, some pieces of skull and bones of the neck. It seems probable that here had been two skeletons, lying one with the head to the west and the other to the east, but this can not positively be determined."

It is difficult to account for this condition of affairs on the supposition that there had been no disturbance subsequent to burial, more especially as it contrasts so strongly with the condition of grave A. The copper ax found in B bore no indication of having been wrapped in cloth; here were also crystals of " dog-tooth spar." In all parts of the grave were many pieces of rotten wood.

The tablets were not discovered until " about 5 o'clock in the afternoon" (January 10). " *They were covered on both sides with clay, on removal of which the markings were for the first time discovered.*" Yet we are informed which side of each lay upward. Possibly this may have been determined in the case of the one by the spade mark; but how it could have been ascertained in reference to the other is an enigma.

Attention is called to these things because they indicate a want of proper care in the observation, or an unintentional weaving of theory into the description, and, though doubtless made in good faith, tend to lessen in the opinion of archeologists the value of the statements of the discoverers.

An inspection of the albertypes of the "Calendar tablet" (Pl. III, Vol. II) is sufficient to satisfy anyone that it is based upon the idea of dividing the year into twelve parts or months and the four seasons. This is admitted by Dr. Farquharson, who says:

If, again, we consider it as zodiacal, the signs in the outer circle being symbols of the constellations along the sun's path, then, though the signs are different, yet the resemblance to the common zodiac is so great as to suggest contact with one of the many nations or races which have adopted that very ancient delineation of the sun's pathway through the heavens.[1]

Dr. S. Seyffarth, who seems to have full faith in it, has no hesitancy in expressing the same opinion. " This," he says, " is, no doubt, the most

[1] Proc. Davenport Acad. Nat. Sci., vol. II. p. 109.

interesting and most important tablet ever discovered in North America, for it represents a planetary configuration, the twelve signs of the zodiac, known to all nations of old, and the seven planets, conjoined with six different signs."[1]

It must, therefore, be post-Columbian or have been obtained in some ancient time through contact with people of the eastern hemisphere, as it corresponds with no native American system of which we have any knowledge. The fact that the diameter of the inner circle is exactly 2 inches, of the next $3\frac{1}{2}$ inches, and the next to the outer one 5 inches, "certainly has a modern look," as Dr. Farquharson readily admits. The circles have every appearance of having been made with compasses or dividers of some kind, though the hole made at the center by the stationary point has been erased by grinding out a broader depression, seemingly for this very purpose.

Turning next to the large tablet on which are found the "Cremation" and "Hunting" scenes (Pls. I and II, Vol. II, of the Proceedings), it is impossible to avoid surprise, mingled with strong suspicion of a trick, at the incongruities of the inscriptions, especially when taken in connection with the "Calendar." As a whole, except the lettering, the two scenes remind us at the first glance of the rock etchings of the Indians, and have what may be termed "an Indian look." Probably this is mainly due to the form of the dancing figures and sun figure in the cremation scene and the squatting figures in the hunting scene. But the letter inscription (for that they are intended for letters can not be doubted) dispels any such idea. Nor could it long be entertained, even without this, for, inspecting them closely, we notice that the large tree on the one side and the smoke on the other side are not like the usual representation of these things in Indian pictography, but more like the rude efforts of a civilized life.

There can be little doubt that the animal figure under the large tree was intended for an elephant; hence it must have been drawn either long ages ago or else since this animal has been brought to America in modern times, or the tablet must be a waif from the Eastern continent. The two figures facing each other near the upper right-hand corner, same scene, bear a better likeness to pigs than to any thing else, and the middle one at the top is more like a cow than like a buffalo. It may be said these variations are too minute to be worthy of notice. Alone perhaps they are, but, when they constantly vary in the direction of animals known at the present day and are taken in connection with the numerous other causes for suspicion, they become valuable in making up a verdict. The interrupted bar across this scene appears to be a stream or waterway, as the animals in it are aquatic, one of them being a seal or possibly a manatee.

It may not be out of place to call attention to the fact that nearly

---

[1] Proc. Davenport. Acad. Nat. Sci., vol. III. p. 77.

all the letter characters of the "cremation scene," as represented on the albertype, may be found on page 1766 of Webster's Unabridged Dictionary, edition of 1872, where the letters of the ancient alphabets of the Old World are figured. A few, it is true, are reversed, and in some instances the form is slightly varied but the resemblance in most cases is very apparent. The reader can make the comparison for himself, but special notice may be taken that in the upper of the two transverse curved lines, near the right-hand end, the two forms of the "Gallic O" appear together just as given on the page referred to. He will also observe that in some instances a number of characters in close relation on the tablet are found near together in the dictionary. Here also we find the "8" so often repeated on the tablet. A photograph or the albertype must be used for this comparison.

It is true that on this page of the dictionary may be found letters of almost every form; but this comparison not only confirms the statement heretofore made, that the inscription must have been made up of letters pertaining to half a dozen different alphabets, but tends to strengthen the suspicion that these tablets were prepared and "planted" in order to deceive the members of the academy.

The theory that the mounds were the work of a lost race of comparatively civilized people who occupied this country in the far distant past, had taken hold of a large portion of our archeologists. There have long been a hope and belief that at some time discoveries would be made to confirm this. It was also further believed that the mammoth or American elephant was still in existence when this civilized race inhabited the country, but satisfactory evidence on these points was wanting.

The objects and uses of the so-called "altars" found chiefly in the Ohio mounds were unsettled questions.

Suddenly the archeological world is surprised at finding itself in possession of proof on all these points. A tablet is taken from a mound under the very shadow of one of our leading scientific academies on which is an inscription of sufficient length to silence all doubt as to its being alphabetic, and immediately under it is the altar with the smoking sacrifice or burning body on it. Nay, more, on the reverse is the figure of the elephant. Nor is this all: In the same mound is another tablet with markings for the zodiacal signs, a calendar in fact. But good fortune, not satisfied with this generosity, throws into the hands of the same individual two elephant pipes, so distinct that there can be no doubt as to the animal intended. To clinch this evidence and show that it relates to the true mound-builders, the fairy goddess leads the same hands to a mound which contains a tablet bearing figures of the veritable mound-builders' pipes and copper axe, some of the letters of the other tablet and the sun symbol. Thanks to the energy of one person the evidence on all these questions is furnished, which, if accepted as credible, must forever settle them.

A consideration of all the facts leads us, inevitably, to the conclusion that these relics are frauds: that is, they are modern productions made to deceive. It is by no means a pleasant task to present this subject to the public in what we believe to be its true light. It is proper, however, to add that the members of the Davenport Academy are, with the single exception named, so far as known, firm believers in the genuineness and authenticity of these finds.

Mr. Gass, the finder, we understand, has always, in the sections where he has lived, been considered a man of honesty and truthfulness. If these have ever been questioned, it has been in regard to his archeological transactions. Nor is there any reason to doubt that these tablets were taken from the mounds substantially in the manner recorded. Admitting this to be true (and it is the evidence on which members of the Academy seem to hang their faith), it falls far short of proving them to be genuine mound-builder relics.

Such remains should therefore be put aside as not entitled to any other consideration than as simple curiosities, unless supported hereafter by other and well authenticated finds of a similar character. Whether found as stated or not, they ought not to have any weight in determining the status of the mound-builders unless more like them are discovered. There is an immense mass of undoubted data to be studied, upon which our conclusions may be safely based.

OTHER TESTIMONY.

Another objection to the theory that the mound-builders were Indians is based upon the oft-repeated statement of the Indians that they know nothing of the origin of these works; that when they first entered the territory they found them already built and abandoned. This objection has already been sufficiently answered by others, by calling attention to the fact that these same Indians have not the faintest tradition of some of the most important events in their own history dating back less than two centuries. For example, De Soto's expedition, although it must have been the most remarkable event in the past history of the southern tribes, seems to have been forgotten by them when the French adventurers, one hundred and thirty years later, appeared on the scene. It is proper, however, to state that Thomas S. Woodward, in his "Reminiscences of the Creek or Muscogee Indians," asserts that the Indians of this tribe did have a traditionary remembrance of this expedition. Other similar instances have been referred to by recent authorities and need not be repeated here. However, as will be shown hereafter, the Indians were not wholly without traditions in regard to the mounds. It is apparent, therefore, that when the real facts are ascertained most of these objections will disappear as being without foundation.

The historical evidence is clear and undisputed that when the region under consideration was discovered by Europeans it was inhabited by Indians only, of whose previous history nothing is known except what is given in vague and uncertain traditions and what has been gleaned by a study of their languages, customs, folklore, and beliefs.

On the other hand, there is no historical or other evidence, unless it be derived from the antiquities themselves, that any other race or people than the Indians ever occupied this region or any part of it previous to its discovery by Europeans, at the close of the fifteenth century. The discovery in the eleventh century by the Northmen is not denied, but, as this left no permanent result, it can have no bearing upon the question, and hence is not taken into consideration.

We enter the discussion, therefore, with at least a presumption in favor of the view that these works were built by the Indians, a presumption which has not received the consideration it is entitled to, as every fact ascertained by the exploration of these works which indicates a similarity between the "mound-builders" and Indians in customs, arts, religion, government, or mode of life is an argument in favor of the theory of an Indian origin. In fact, the presumption is so strong, that it can be overcome only by showing that these works, or the specimens of art found in them, which are unquestionably the work of the builders, are beyond the capacity of the Indians before their habits, customs, etc., were modified by contact with Europeans. Even should a few specimens of art of undoubted ante-Columbian origin be found in them, which are evidently beyond the capacity of any of the tribes known to have inhabited this section, this will not be sufficient to establish the theory that these works, or any of them, were built by a "lost race," or by the cultured races of Central America or Mexico, as they may have been obtained by intercourse with these cultured races, or may be relics wafted by winds and waves, in wrecked vessels, from the eastern continent.

Suppose, for example, that a mound is found in Tennessee, which in appearance, construction, and contents—with a single exception—is in every respect precisely like those attributed to the so-called "veritable mound-builders," and that this single exception is an ordinary, old-fashioned, steel-bladed "case knife" with a bone handle, found at the bottom of the tumulus, where it could not reasonably be attributed to an intrusive burial, must we conclude that the "veritable mound-builders" manufactured knives of this class? Yet a case precisely of this kind in every particular occurred during the investigations carried on by the Bureau of Ethnology in 1884.

Unless there should be corroboratory proof to connect them with the mound-builders, and other evidence indicating a corresponding advance in art, these anomalous waifs, such as the tablets with letters engraved upon them, even if genuine, are of no value in the question now under discussion. The whole of the testimony furnished by an examination of these ancient works and the specimens of art contained in them must be taken into consideration and must decide the question.

THE HISTORICAL EVIDENCE.

One serious objection urged against the theory that the Indians were the authors of the ancient works is that the great number of them, the magnitude of some of them, and the art displayed in their construction, indicate a centralized and systematic form of government and a skill foreign to and entirely above the culture status of the Indians.[1]

This opinion is based largely upon the statements made in regard to these works and their contents, which a more careful examination has shewn to be in many cases erroneous and overdrawn.

For example, the estimates as to size, where given without careful measurements, are, as a very general rule, largely in excess of the true dimensions. The statement so often made that many of these monuments have been constructed with such mathematical accuracy as to indicate not only a unit of measure, but also the use of instruments, is found upon a reexamination to be without any basis, unless the near approach of some three or four circles and as many squares of Ohio to mathematical correctness be sufficient to warrant this opinion. As a very general, and in fact almost universal, rule the figures are more or less irregular, and indicate nothing higher in art than an Indian could form with his eye and by pacing. Circles and squares are simple figures known to all savage tribes and easily formed; hence the fact that a few, and a very few, approach mathematical accuracy is not sufficient to counterbalance the vast amount of evidence on the other side.

The size of a few of the mounds and extent of some of the works are therefore the only difficulties to be explained in attributing these monuments to the Indians, unless the specimens of art or remains found in them are incompatible with such a conclusion.

If it can be shown that any of the tribes found occupying that part of the country where these works are located did, at the time they were first visited, occupy and use mounds of the same kind as those now seen, as though accustomed to them, and also did in many instances build them, we shall be justified in ascribing all these structures to the same race. At least this will be a fair and reasonable inference until some fact is presented which is irreconcilable with such conclusion, or some certain proof is brought forward showing that other races have, at some time in the past, occupied this region.

As has been justly remarked by Mr. Lucien Carr,[2] "In pursuing this branch of our inquiry the only method open to us is to proceed by comparison." Should evidence be produced showing that Indians did erect

---

[1] Squier and Davis, Ancient Monuments. pp. 45 and 301; Foster Prehistoric Races, pp. 97 and 300; Baldwin Anc. America. p. 34; McLean, Mound Builders. pp. 88, 89; Conant, Footprints of a Vanished Race, p. 14; Bancroft Native Races, vol. IV, p. 786; Nadaillac, Revue de Anthrop.

[2] Mounds of the Mississippi Valley. p. 57.

such structures, it is not likely that it will be possible, except in a few cases, to identify the particular works alluded to by this evidence, nor to fix upon the precise time when they were erected. The utmost that can be hoped for in this direction is that by a more careful and thorough study of the remains it may be found possible in some cases to determine the peculiar characteristics which mark them as the work of certain tribes. If this can be done the mound problem will be solved, and it will be possible with this basis to commence the reconstruction of the history of the mound-builders and the mound-building age.

Let us, then, turn to the historical evidence bearing on this question, and compare the monuments which have come down to the present time with the statements found in this evidence.

Commencing with the history and monuments of the southern section of our country, the well known narratives of the expedition of the unfortunate Adelantado, Hernando De Soto, are the first authorities to which reference is here made.

It is probable that six original chronicles of this famous expedition were written,[1] only three of which are now in existence. These are, first, a brief narration by Luis Hernandez de Biedma; second, a more lengthy relation by a "Fidalgo of Elvas," a Portuguese;[2] and, third, a second-hand account by Garcilasso de La Vega, made up from the manuscript of Alonzo de Carmona, and information furnished by John Cole and other survivors of the expedition. The first and second narratives are by eye-witnesses of the events they describe. In each of these are frequent mentions of mounds and other works similar to those now found scattered over this section.

Biedma, in his "Narrative," states that "The caciques of this country make a custom of raising near their dwellings very high hills, on which they sometimes build their houses. On one of these we planted the cross."[3]

The descriptions of mounds given by Garcilasso are so exact, and correspond so perfectly with the remains found in the southern states, that, although his work is looked upon by many as a semi-romance, we

[1] In addition to the three named in the text there was, as we learn from Garcilasso, a "Relacion" by "Alonzo de Carmona," of which he made use when preparing his "Florida." According to Buckingham Smith (Bradford Club Series, Vol. v., p. XXVIII), an account was written by Roderigo Rangel, the private secretary of the Adelantado, "which afforded the material for the chapters, now incomplete, of Oviedo." Also, that another account was composed by a captain who remained in America, "for which pictures in colors, of the battle scenes with the Indians of Florida, were at one time in the cabinet of Philip II." Smith also affirms that the last named was the source from which Herrera drew supplies. It may be true that this was one of the sources from which he drew, but it is certain that Garcilasso's "Florida" was his chief reliance. There were several individuals named Alonzo who returned from the expedition, but it is probable the one alluded to by Garcilasso is the Alonzo mentioned in the list of the survivors as from Seville.

[2] Buckingham Smith is inclined to believe this Fidalgo was Alvaro Fernandez, but for reasons not necessary to be presented here I take this author to be Antonio Martinez Segurado. But it is possible the Alonzo de Carmona of Garcilasso is the author, as one of the returned Portuguese bore the name of Alonzo Gutierrez, which name, strange to say, is repeated three times in the list of survivors.

[3] English Transl. in French's Histor. Coll. La. II. p. 105. Bradford Club series, v. 5, p. 251.

are forced to the conclusion that his information was derived from parties who had seen them. Take for example the following passage:

The town and the houses of the cacique Ossachile are like those of other caciques in Florida. * * * The Indians try to place their villages on elevated sites; but inasmuch as in Florida there are not many sites of this kind where they can conveniently build, they erect elevations themselves in the following manner: They select the spot and carry there a quantity of earth, which they form into a kind of platform two or three pikes in height, the summit of which is large enough to give room for twelve, fifteen, or twenty houses, to lodge the cacique and his attendants. At the foot of this elevation they mark out a square place, according to the size of the village, around which the leading men have their houses.[1] * * * To ascend the elevation they have a straight passageway from bottom to top, 15 or 20 feet wide. Here steps are made by massive beams, and others are planted firmly in the ground to serve as walls. On all other sides of the platform the sides are cut steep.[2]

The gentleman of Elvas, speaking of the town of Ucita, where De Soto first landed in Florida, which was undoubtedly some point on Tampa bay, says[3] "The town was of seven or eight houses. The lord's house stood near the beach upon a very high mount made by hand for strength." It is quite probable that tradition is correct in fixing the final landing place at Phillippi's point, near the head of what is known as "Old Tampa bay," as it is stated by the authority last quoted that after the horsemen had been landed "the seamen only remained on board, who going up every day a little with the tide, the end of eight days brought them near to the town."[4]

Now it so happens that, at this point of De Soto's fruitless expedition, which can be determined with greater certainty than any other, the shore is lined with mounds and shell heaps; for full description and plats of which the reader is referred to the report of Mr. S. T. Walker.[5] Speaking of a mound at Phillippi's point, he says:

This is one of the largest mounds on Tampa bay, and it is unfortunate that there are impediments in the way of exploration. The structure is nearly half an acre in extent and four different men claim an interest in it, a land corner being located on it; besides this, it supports an orange grove. The location is beautiful, the land fertile, and fresh water abundant. Some years ago a storm drove the waters of the bay against it, carrying away a portion of the eastern base and exposing its internal structure. It is built of sand and shell in alternate layers. It is said that many bones were washed out of it at the time; but its structure and general appearance indicate that it was designed as a domiciliary mound like others of its class."[6]

Mr. Walker found on opening another mound, 8 miles south of the one just mentioned, a mass of human bones disposed in three strata or layers:

In the lower stratum I found no ornaments and but little pottery, but in the middle and top layers, especially the latter, nearly every cranium was encircled by

[1] The open area or square here spoken of is still very frequently observed in the village sites of the mound-builders, as noticed several times on the preceding field report.
[2] Historia de la Florida. Edition 1723, Lib. I. Pt. I, cap. XXX, p. 69.
[3] Bradford Club Series. Vol. 5, p. 23. Hist. Coll. La. vol. 2, p. 123.
[4] Op. cit. p. 23, Hist. Coll. La., vol. 2, p. 123.
[5] Smithsonian Report, 1879, pp. 392-422.
[6] Op. cit., pp. 410-411.

strings of colored beads, brass and copper ornaments, trinkets, etc. Among other curious objects were a pair of scissors and a fragment of looking-glass. By using patience and care I obtained many strings of beads in the order they were worn by their owners. In two cases fragments of string remained in the beads, preserved by the copper. The beads, many of them being of cut glass and of various colors, were very beautiful.[1]

These facts form a chain of evidence relating to the authors of these works so complete as to leave no doubt regarding the conclusion to be drawn. Some at least of these mounds were there when De Soto landed and were then occupied by the Indians who evidently informed the Spaniards that they had built them.

In one low mound but 3 feet high are found three tiers of skeletons, the mode of burial alike in all and similar to that in other neighboring mounds, but during the time that elapsed between the deposition of the lower and middle tiers the Europeans had appeared on the peninsula and brought with them the implements and ornaments of civilized life.

Turning again to the chronicles, let us examine what further is said in them in reference to mounds.

It is quite probable that where Biedma says, speaking of what was seen at Cutifachiqui, " the governor opened a large temple built in the woods, in which were buried the chiefs of the country, and took from it a quantity of pearls amounting to six or seven arrobes, which were spoiled by being buried in the ground,"[2] he really alludes to a burial mound opened by the Spaniards. The Gentleman of Elvas, mentioning the same transaction, states that[3] " the lady [of Cutifachiqui], perceiving that the Christians esteemed the pearls, advised the governor to send to search certain graves that were in the town, and that he would find many; and that if he would send to the dispeopled towns he might load all his horses." These two statements together probably justify the conclusion that burial mounds are alluded to.

The extravagant and probably somewhat imaginative description, given by John Cole to Garcilasso, of the temple at Tolomeco (the adjacent " dispeopled town " mentioned by the Gentleman of Elvas) doubtless relates to what the Fidalgo calls the " barbacoas," in which he says " were large quantities of clothing, shawls of thread made from the bark of trees, and others of feathers, white, gray, vermillion, and yellow, rich and proper for winter; * * * also many well-dressed deerskins, of colors drawn over with designs, of which had been made shoes, stockings, and hose."[4] There is, however, one statement in this fancy sketch worthy of notice in this connection. " It [Tolomeco] is

[1] Loc. cit.
[2] Hist. Coll. La., II, p. 101. Buckingham Smith's translation varies slightly from that given here. He uses the word "mosque" instead of "temple," and adds after "burial in the ground." the words "and in the adipose substance of the dead."
[3] Hist. Coll. Louisana, II, 144; Bradford Club Ser. 5, p. 63.
[4] Bradford Club Series, 5, p. 63.

situated on the high land above the banks of the river. * * * At a distance were seen the dwellings of the chiefs situated on an eminence, and were conspicuous for their size and the work which had been bestowed upon them."[1]

That the pearls here alluded to were in part at least nothing more than shell beads may be assumed without any doubt. Had they been genuine pearls it is not likely De Soto would have left them there so willingly. Moreover, nothing is heard afterwards, when other adventurers visited this region, of its wealth in pearls. Shell beads are common in southern mounds, often occurring in great numbers, while pearls are comparatively rare.

This Portuguese gentleman (Gentleman of Elvas) also frequently mentions towns surrounded by "walls" and "palisades."[2] These he describes as follows:[3]

The wall, as well of that [town] as of others which afterwards we saw, was of great posts thrust deep into the ground and very rough, and many long rails as big as one's arm laid across between them, and the wall was about the height of a lance, and it was daubed within and without with clay and had loop-holes.

He speaks of another town "where the cacique used to reside, which was very great, walled, and beset with towers, and many loopholes were in the towers and walls. * * * Within a league and half a league were great towns all walled. Where the governor was lodged was a great lake that came near unto the wall, and it entered into a ditch that went round about the town, wanting but little to environ it round."[4]

If the reader will compare this description with the works on Etowah river, Georgia, figured by C. C. Jones,[5] and also from a resurvey in the preceding part of this volume, with the works of Moorhouse parish, Louisiana, figured by Squier and Davis,[6] the works at the Knapp place near Little Rock, Arkansas, and those in Catahoula parish, Louisiana, figured in this volume, he can not fail to observe the close correspondence between the narrator's statement and these remains.

Speaking of the arrival of De Soto at the province of Guaxule, evidently in the northern part of Georgia, and probably on the headwaters of the Coosa river, Garcilasso says:

The chief, whose name was also Guaxule, came out with 500 men to meet him and took him in the village [pueblo] in which were 300 houses, and lodged him in his own. This house stood on a high mound [cerro] similar to others we have already mentioned. Round about was a roadway sufficiently broad for six men to walk abreast.[7]

There are good reasons, as will hereafter be shown, for believing that this refers to the celebrated Etowah mound near Cartersville.

The town of Talisse is described as "strong in the extreme, for,

[1] Hist. Florida, Lib. 3, cap. XIV, p. 130.
[2] Hist. Coll. La., II, pp. 153, 158. 159, 162, 165, 172, 186. and 203.
[3] P. 153.
[4] P. 72.
[5] Antiquities Southern Indians, pl. 1.
[6] Ancient monuments, pl. XXXVIII, fig. 4.
[7] Hist. Florida, ed. 1723, lib. III, cap. XX. p. 139.

besides the inclosure of timber and earth, it was nearly surrounded by a great river."[1]

He describes the Indian fortress called Alibamo as being "quadrangular, the four fronts of equal length, built of jointed timbers, each front being 400 paces. On the inside there were two other palisades from side to side. The front wall had three small gates, quite too low for a horseman to enter. One door or gate was in the center of the front and two others at the sides, next to the corners. On the right [rear] of those three gates each front has three other walls, so that if the Spaniards should gain the first the second would be defended, and so with the third and fourth. The gates of the posterior front (or face) opened upon a river which flows by the rear of the fort. This river though narrow is very deep, and the banks very high and difficult to ascend."[2] It will be observed that this fort, between 1,000 and 1,200 feet square, corresponds very well with the average size of the moundbuilders' inclosures. The method of strengthening the main entrance by inner walls was also followed in some instances by the mound-builders, as is shown in some of the Ohio works, as, for example, "Fortified Hill," Butler county. Other quotations of a similar tenor to those already given might be made from this book, but these will suffice.

Herrera's account of De Soto's wanderings is taken chiefly from Garcilasso's work, which he says he consulted, still, as it is possible, in fact certain, that he had access to documents not now obtainable, the following quotations are given from Stevens's English translation:

Some made their escape to the Lord's house, which stood on a ridge to which there was no way up but by stairs.[3] * * * The frontier town to Casquin was fortified with a Ditch * * * full of water, conveyed to it through a canal from the great River, being the distance of three leagues. The Ditch enclosed three parts of the town, the fourth being secured with high and thick Palisades.[4]

Having entered the province of Amilco they traveled 30 leagues through it to a town of 400 houses, and a large square, where the Cacique's house stood upon a mount made by art on the bank of the river.[5]

Entered upon a woody desert, and came into the province of Guachacoya; the first town they came to being the capital thereof, seated on hillocks by the great river's side, on one of which was the Lord's house.[6]

As heretofore stated the town which Moscoso and his companions occupied on their return to the Mississippi, which was 17 leagues above Guachacoya and in the province of Aminoya, must have consisted of houses placed on mounds and surrounded by an earthen wall as it is stated that "when they were at the procession of Palm Sunday * * * the water broke in at the gates of the town so that there was no going along the streets two days after without canoes."[7]

The next evidence is found on a plate by Le Moyne, in the Brevis Narratio.[8] Here a small mound is figured in the scene which is repre-

[1] Lib. III, cap. XXIII, p. 144.
[2] Lib. IV, cap. I, p. 173.
[3] Vol. v, p. 324. Orig. Sp., Vol. IV, Dec. VII, p. 31.
[4] Vol. v, p. 336. Orig. Sp., Vol. IV, Dec. VII, p. 33.
[5] Vol VI, p. 5. Orig. Sp., Vol. IV, Dec. VII. p. 132.
[6] Vol. VI, p. 6. Orig. Sp., Vol. IV. Dec. VII, p. 132.
[7] Vol. VI, p. 18.
[8] Pars. I. Tab. XI.

sented (in our Pl. XLII); on top is placed a single univalve shell and around the base of the mound there is a circle of arrows thrust into the ground. The accompanying note states that this represents the sepulture of a chief or ruler of a province, and that the cup from which he was accustomed to drink was placed on the "tumulus," and that many arrows were planted about the "tumulus." It is true the mound appears so small that it is scarcely worthy of the name. But it is possible this is the core on which additional layers are to be placed, as is often found to be the case with mounds. It is not an unusual thing to find large univalve shells, especially *Busycon perversum* in southern mounds, and occasionally one of very large size converted into a drinking cup is found, as for example that represented in Fig. 133.

Another important fact observable in this picture is that the large building, which was undoubtedly the dwelling of the deceased chief, and others, which probably belonged to the members of his family, are on fire. As is well known, it was a custom among some tribes to burn the houses of those who died. As no mention of this is made in the accompanying note, we have proof in this fact that the artist has tried to represent faithfully what he saw.

We have taken for granted that the interested reader will make the comparison, as we proceed with these extracts, between the customs of the Indians mentioned in them and those of the mound-builders as revealed by the exploration and study of the mounds. Still it may not be amiss for us to call attention from time to time to some facts which have special bearing upon the question under consideration.

The frequent statements in the chronicles of De Soto's expedition that houses stood on "mounts made by art," or hand, the positive assertion that the natives were in the habit of building mounds, and the total absence in these chronicles of any word or hint referring them to any former inhabitants or other people, leave no doubt that De Soto and his followers understood clearly and beyond question that the people they found occupying the country were the builders of these mounds.

The resemblances in many respects of the fortifications and other works of the Indians mentioned by these chroniclers to the works of the mound-builders, are so many arguments in favor of the theory of the identity of the two peoples. That such resemblances do not necessarily imply relationship is admitted. But in this discussion we must constantly bear in mind the fact that the only people known to history as inhabitants of the region under consideration, other than those derived from the eastern continent in post-Columbian times, are Indians in the limited sense heretofore noted. It follows, therefore, that each of these resemblances is a fact that must be explained away by those who deny the Indian origin of the mounds.

After the termination of De Soto's fruitless expedition, but few and slight glimpses are obtained of this southern region until the French adventurers began to appear upon the scene one hundred and thirty years afterwards, in the latter part of the seventeenth century. The numerous narratives and accounts of their voyages which have been left furnish comparatively few notices of these mounds and earthworks, so few, as has been supposed, that modern investigators have expressed astonishment at the fact, as it is evident that in many instances they were upon the spots where these works are now found; as, for example, the Cahokia group; those near the mouth of the Arkansas, those in the Chickasaw country and in northern Mississippi, and elsewhere. But a more careful examination of the records brings to light a number of corroborative items.

Joutel, in his account of the return journey of his party after the death of La Salle, speaking of their halt among the Arkansas Indians at the mouth of the Arkansas river, says:

> The house we were then in was built of pieces of cedar laid one upon another and rounded away at the corners. It is seated on a small eminence half a musket shot from the village in a country abounding in all things.[1]

The French as given by Margry [2] is as follows: " Celuy (village' dans lequel nous estions, estoit sur une petite hauteur où la dite rivière ne desborde point. La maison est postée, à une demi portée de pistolet du village, sur un lieu un peu élevé." It is true that this may have been a natural elevation, and there is nothing in the statement to warrant the positive conclusion that it was not, but the generally level area of the locality in which it was situated, the manner in which it is alluded to, and the fact that mounds are found there, lead to the belief that it was an artificial mound.

Father Gravier, in the account of his voyage down the Mississippi, notes the following fact, which probably refers to the earthworks that mark the sites of abandoned towns. Speaking of the Akansea he says: " We went out and cabined a league lower down, half a league from the old village of the Akansea, where they formerly received the late Father Marquette and which is discernible now only by the old outworks, there being no cabins left." [3] As there were no cabins left what were the " old outworks" to which he alludes? Speaking of the " Tounikas" he says: "They have only one small temple, raised on a mound of earth." [4]

M. Thaumer de la Source, in a letter included by St. Cosme in the account of his voyage, alluding to the manners and customs of the same people (the Tounicas) says that " their houses are made of palisades and earth and are very large: they make fire in them only twice a day and do their cookery outside in earthen pots," and that they " have a temple on a little hill." [5]

M. de la Harpe, speaking of the Indians located along the Yazoo

[1] Journal in Hist. Coll. La., 1, p. 176.
[2] Découvertes, Vol. 3, p. 442.
[3] Shea's Trans. in Early French Voyages on the Mississippi, p. 126.
[4] Ibid. p. 136.
[5] Shea's Early French Voyages on the Mississippi, pp. 80-81.

COPY OF PLATE XL. "BREVIS NARRATIO."

river at the commencement of the eighteenth century, says: "The cabins of the Yasous, Courois, Offagoula, and Ouspie are dispersed over the country upon mounds of earth made with their own hands, from which it is inferred that these nations are very ancient and were formerly very numerous, although at the present time they hardly num- ber two hundred and fifty persons.[1]

This language would seem to imply that at this time there were numerous mounds unoccupied, otherwise there could be no grounds for the inference drawn by this author.

Dumont[2] notes the fact that in one of the Natchez villages the house of the chief was placed on a mound.

La Petit remarks that " the temple of the Natchez in shape resembles an earthen oven 100 feet in circumference," and " to enable them better to converse together they raise a mount of artificial soil on which they build his [the chief's] cabin, which is of the same construction as the temple, * * * and when the great chief dies they demolish his cabin and then raise a new mound, on which they build the cabin of him who is to replace him in this dignity, for he never lodges in that of his predecessor."[3] This will account in part for the seemingly large number of mounds compared with the supposed Indian population.

Le Page Du Pratz, who visited the Natchez nation in 1720, has given the following notice of the mound on which their temple was placed:

As I was an intimate friend of the sovereign of the Natchez he showed me their temple, which is about thirty feet square, and stands on an artificial mount about eight feet high, by the side of a small river. The mound slopes insensibly from the main front, which is northwards, but on the other sides it is somewhat steeper.[4]

He also states that the house of the Great Sun, " not less than thirty feet on each face and about twenty feet high, is like that of the temple, upon a mound of earth about eight feet high and sixty feet across."[5] The size given here and elsewhere of the mounds should not be overlooked, as they correspond closely with those now found in the same sections.

He also mentions the following mode of defense, which may serve to explain the origin of some of the isolated circular walls occasionally met with:

When a nation is too weak to defend itself in the field they endeavor to protect themselves by a fort. This fort is built circularly of two rows of large logs of wood, the logs of the inner row being opposite the joining of the outer row. These logs are about fifteen feet long, five feet of which are sunk in the ground. The outer logs are about two feet thick and the inner about half as much. At every forty paces along the wall a circular tower juts out, and at the entrance of the fort, which is always next the river, the two ends of the wall pass each other and leave a side opening."[6]

[1] Historical Journ. in Hist. Coll. La., III, p. 106.
[2] Memoires Historique de la Louisiana, Tome II, p. 109.
[3] Hist. Coll. La., III, 141-2 (note); also Lettres Edifiantes et Curieuses, Tome I, p. 260-1.
[4] Hist. of La., Eng. Trans., new ed., 1774, p. 353; ed. of 1763, vol. II, p. 211. Original ed., 1758, vol. III, p. 16.
[5] Op. cit., ed. 1758, vol. II, p. 361.
[6] Ed. 1774, p. 375.

If this description be compared with the figure of the inclosure near Evansville, given in the second part of this volume, the strong resemblance will be seen at once.

Adair, in his "History of the American Indians," says the Indians daub their houses with "tough mortar mixed with dry grass;" that they build winter or hot houses after the manner of Dutch ovens, covered with clay mixed with grass, and, as "they usually build on *rising ground*, the floor is often a yard lower than the earth, which serves them as a breastwork against an enemy, and a small peeping window is level with the surface of the outside ground to enable them to rake any lurking invaders in case of an attack." In reference to the town house he says: "The only difference between it and the winter house, or stove, is in its dimensions and application. It is usually built *on the top of a hill.*" [1]

There is scarcely any reason to doubt that he refers, by the expressions italicized, at least the last one, to artificial mounds. Further reference will hereafter be made to some of his statements in this connection, as they give at least a hint as to the explanation of some things found in the mounds.

Following up the recorded accounts of these works in the order of time, we next refer to the notices found in William Bartram's notes of a journey through the southern states made in 1773. In this work frequent mention is made of mounds, but notice will be taken of those only which appear to connect them in some way with the Indians then occupying that region, or that indicate their recent desertion.

He makes the following remarks in regard to a mound on Lake George:

At about fifty yards distance from the landing place stands a magnificent Indian mount. About fifteen years ago I visited this place, at which time there were no settlements of white people, but all appeared wild and savage; yet in that uncultivated state it possessed an almost inexpressible air of grandeur which was now entirely changed.

At that time there was a very considerable *extent of old fields* round about the mount; there was also a large orange grove, together with palms and live oaks, extending from near the mount along the banks downwards. * * * But what greatly contributed towards completing the magnificence of the scene was a noble Indian highway which led from the great mount on a straight line, three-quarters of a mile, first through a point or wing of the orange grove and continuing thence through an awful forest of live oaks, it was terminated by palms and laurel magnolias on the verge of an oblong artificial lake, which was on the edge of an extensive, green, level savanna. This grand highway was about fifty yards wide, sunk a little below the common level, and the earth thrown up on each side, making a bank of about two feet high.[2]

The condition observed here certainly does not warrant the belief that the place had been abandoned for centuries before this intelligent traveler visited it. Yet the historical records relating to the region reach back two centuries and a half previous to that visit. Had any people of superior culture to that of the Indians inhabited the region in that time or within a century previous thereto, some notice of the fact would be found in the somewhat abundant literature relating to the

---

[1] Pp. 417–421.　　　　[2] Bartram's Travels, p. 99.

section. As all the facts are easily explained upon the very natural and reasonable supposition that the Indians were the authors of these works, it is incumbent upon those who hold a different theory to give a satisfactory explanation thereof in accordance with such theory.

At another point he found the ground covered with small tumuli, which marked the burial places " of the Yamassees who were here slain by the Creeks in the last decisive battle, the Creeks having driven them into this point between the doubling of the river, where few of them escaped the fury of the conquerors. These graves occupied the whole grove, consisting of 2 or 3 acres of ground; there were near thirty of these cemeteries of the dead, nearly of an equal size and form; they were oblong, 20 feet in length, 10 or 12 feet in width and 3 or 4 feet high, now overgrown with orange trees, live oaks, laurel magnolias, red bays, and other trees and shrubs."[1]

In the midst of his poetical description of the Cherokee country about the sources of the Tennessee river, he pauses to record the following observation (the italics are ours):

On these towering hills appeared the ruins of the ancient famous town of Sticoe. Here was a vast *Indian mount or tumulus* and great terrace *on which stood the council house*, with banks encompassing their circus; here were also old peach and plum orchards.[2]

The council house of the Cherokees at Cowe he describes as a "large rotunda, capable of accommodating several hundred people; it stands on the top of an ancient *artificial mount of earth*, of about twenty feet perpendicular, and the rotunda on the top of it being above thirty feet more gives the whole fabric an elevation of about sixty feet from the common surface of the ground. But it may be proper to observe that this mount on which the rotunda stands is of a much ancienter date than the building, and perhaps was raised for another purpose. The Cherokees themselves are as ignorant as we are by what people or for what purpose these artificial hills were raised."[3]

He describes the ancient town of Apalachucla as follows:

It had been situated on a peninsula formed by a doubling of the river, and indeed appears to have been a very famous capital by the artificial mounds or terraces, and a very populous settlement from its extent and expansive old fields stretching beyond the scope of the sight along the low grounds of the river. We viewed the mounds or terraces on which formerly stood their town house or rotunda and square or areopagus, and a little back of this on a level height or natural step above the low grounds is a vast artificial terrace or four square mound, now seven or eight feet higher than the common surface of the ground; in front of one square or side of this mound adjoins a very extensive oblong square yard or artificial level plain, sunk a little below the common surface, and surrounded with a bank or narrow terrace formed with the earth thrown out of this yard at the time of its formation.[4]

In the following quotation he states expressly that the Choctaws were in the habit of raising mounds over their communal graves:

As soon as a person is dead they erect a scaffold eighteen or twenty feet high, in a grove adjacent to the town, where they lay the corpse, lightly covered with a

---

mantle; here it is suffered to remain, visited and protected by the friends and relations, until the flesh becomes putrid, so as easily to part from the bones, then undertakers, who make it their business, carefully strip the flesh from the bones, wash and cleanse them, and when dry and purified by the air, having provided a curiously wrought chest or coffin fabricated of bones[1] and splints, they place all the bones therein, which is deposited in the bone-house, a building erected for that purpose in every town. And when this house is full a general solemn funeral takes place. When the nearest kindred or friends of the deceased, on a day appointed, repair to the bone-house, take up the respective coffins, and following one another in order of seniority, the nearest relations and connections attending their respective corpse and the multitude following after them, all as one family, with united voice of alternate allelujah and lamentation, slowly proceeding to the place of general interment, where they place the coffins in order, forming a pyramid, and lastly cover all over with earth, which raises a conical hill or mount. When they return to town in order of solemn procession, concluding the day with a festival, which is called the feast of the dead."[2]

Remains of coffins or wrappings of cane matting have frequently been found in southern mounds.

The description of the walls connected with the chunk yards as given in the Bartram MS.[3] is familiar and need not be repeated here.

These statements, mostly mere incidental mentions in works of travelers and explorers, whose minds and thoughts were intent on things more directly appertaining to practical life than archeological researches, made without regard to their bearing on the questions relating to the origin of these works, are entitled to credit; and, although they do not prove positively that all ancient monuments of the mound region are to be attributed to the Indians, they do prove beyond contradiction that some of them were built by Indians and that at the first advent of the white man they were in common use among this people in the southern section. In other words, this evidence makes out a prima facie case, which must be rebutted by facts which are, or appear to be inconsistent with this conclusion.

How soon are things familiar to a preceding generation relegated to the domain of antiquity! A century after the close of the foregoing testimony these remains, long forsaken and forgotten, begin to be discovered one by one, and are looked upon by the new generation tion which has arisen, as strange and mysterious mementos of a "long lost" and "unknown race," and are classed, according to modern archeological nomenclature, as "prehistoric remains." Where the plow has not invaded them the oak, walnut, and beech, taking root in the rich, rank soil, have grown to full stature, and their size and numerous rings of growth are taken as indications of the vast antiquity of these strange works. The imagination, having once obtained the rein, runs back over the ages until it is lost in the haze of the past. Is it strange that the "untutored savage," without writings or records, should in a few—a very few—generations lose sight of the past when our own civilized race forgets in the same time?

---

[1] Bones is evidently a misprint for "canes."
[2] Ibid., p. 516.

[3] Squier & Davis, Anc. Mon., p. 12, and Squier Aborig. Mon. of New York, p. 135.

Turning to the older records relating to the northern section of the country, we are surprised at finding in them so few references to the artificial mounds of this region. I have succeeded in finding, after a somewhat laborious and careful examination, but one mention or indication of them in the Jesuit Relations and none in the writings of the Recollects (though there are several mentions of southern mounds). Yet one of the missionaries must have passed a good portion of the winter of 1700 in the very midst of the Cahokia group, as Father Gravier says: "Une de nos missionaires les doit visiter durant tout l'hyver de 2 et 2 jours, et en autant aux Kaowikia qui ont pris leur quartier d'hyver a 4 lieues plus haut que le village." [1]

One of the early notices of mounds in this section is by Cadwallader Colden, in his "History of the Five Nations," in which he notes the fact that "a round hill" was sometimes raised over the grave in which a corpse had been deposited.[2]

Carver noticed ancient earthworks on the Mississippi near Lake Pepin, but knew nothing of their origin.[3]

Heckwelder observed some of these works near Detroit, of which Dr. Steiner published an account in a Philadelphia periodical in 1789 or 1790. This description was afterwards given briefly in his history of the "Manners and Customs of the Indian Nations," and is quoted in other papers.

Although so little relating to mounds is to be gleaned from the older records, they do mention some facts which afford a reasonable explanation of some of the ancient monuments found in the northern section of our country.

As, for example, the communal or tribal burials, where the bones and remains of all the dead of a village, region, or tribe who had died subsequent to the preceding general burial (usually eight or ten years) were collected together and deposited in one common grave. This method, which, as we have seen, was also followed by some of the southern tribes, has been frequently described; among others, by William Bartram in the quotation already given; by Dumont,[4] and by Barnard Romans.[5] But the fullest and most vivid description is that by Jean de Breboeuf, in his account "*Des Ceremonies qu'ils (les Hurons) gardent en leur sepulture et de leur deuil,*" and "*De la Feste solemnelle des morts.*" [6]

Although it is stated in reference to these burials by the southern tribes that they closed by heaping a mound over the grave, so far no statement has been found that such was the case in regard to those in

[1] Rel. ou Journ. du Voyage, by Jaques Gravier, orig. Fr., p. 8.

[2] Introduction, p. 16, London, 1747.

[3] Travels, ed. 1796, Phila., pp. 35, 36; ed. 1779, London, p. 57.

[4] Memoires. Hist. La., T. 1, p. 246.

[5] Adair, quoted by Dr. Brinton and C. C. Jones, "Antiq. Southern Indians," p. 190, does not describe or mention at the place referred to, or elsewhere, that I can find, the communal burial.

[6] Jesuit Relations for 1636, pp. 129–139, translation 5th Ann. Rept. Bureau Ethn., pp. 110–119. See also Lafitau, "Moeurs des Sauvages," II, pp. 447–455.

the northern section. That this method prevailed can only be inferred from the southern custom and from what is found in the mounds of the northern region, which will be noticed hereafter.

Another item under this heading furnished by history is the well attested fact that it was a very common custom among the northern as well as the southern tribes to erect palisades around their villages for defense against attack. As there will be occasion to speak of these again, further reference to them at present is omitted.

Although there are so few references to mound building by the northern tribes in the older authorities, we are not without evidence on this point, as is shown by the following statements made by comparatively modern writers:

Lewis C. Beck, in his Gazetteer of the States of Illinois and Missouri, affirms that "one of the largest mounds in this country has been thrown up on this stream (the Osage of Missouri) within the last thirty or forty years by the Osages near the great Osage village in honor of one of their deceased chiefs."[1] It is probable that this is the mound referred to by Maj. Sibley in his statement to Featherstonehaugh, in which he says that "an ancient chief of the Osage Indians informed him whilst he was among them that a large conical mound, which he (Maj. Sibley) "was in the habit of seeing every day whilst he resided amongst them, was constructed while he was a boy. That a chief of his nation unexpectedly died while all the men of his tribe were hunting in a distant country; his friends buried him in the usual manner, with his weapons, his earthen pot, and the usual accompaniments, and raised a small mound over his remains. When the nation returned from the hunt this mound was enlarged at intervals, every man assisting to carry materials, and thus the accumulation of earth went on for a long period, until it reached its present height, when they dressed it off at the top in a conical form. The old chief said he had been informed and believed that all the mounds had a similar origin."[2]

Lewis and Clark, as is well known, mention not only the erection of a mound over a modern chief, but also numerous earthworks, including mounds, which were known to be the work of modern Indians.[3]

Gen. L. V. Bierce, in his "Historical Reminiscences of Summit County" (Ohio), states that when Nickasaw, an old Wyandot Indian of that county, was killed, "the Indians buried him on the ground where he fell, and according to their custom raised a mound over him to commemorate the place and circumstances of his death. His grave is yet to be seen."[4]

The author of the History of Wisconsin states that "it is related by intelligent Indian traders that a custom once prevailed among certain

[1] P. 308.

[2] Excursion through the Slave States, p. 70. It is proper to state that Mr. Collet, of St. Louis, says he made a search for this mound, but was unable to find it.

[3] Travels, Dublin ed., 1817, pp. 30, 31, 55, 67, 115, 117, 118, 122, etc.

[4] P. 128.

tribes, on the burial of a chief or brave of distinction, to consider his grave as entitled to the tribute of a portion of earth from each passer-by, which the traveler sedulously carried with him on his journey. Hence the first grave formed a nucleus around which, in the accumulation of the accustomed tributes of respect thus paid, a mound was soon formed."[1]

According to the same author[2] the tumulus at the Great Butte des Morts ("great hill of the dead") was raised over the bones of Outagamie (Fox Indian) warriors slain in battle with the French in 1706.

In 1706 an expedition, under Capt. Morand, was sent from Michilimackinack against them, and in the attack upon them by surprise at this their stronghold more than 1,000 of their warriors perished, and the "great hill of the dead" was raised over their bones by the survivors, who, a few years afterwards, left this part of the country and removed further to the west. Other accounts differ in regard to the time when the great battle was fought which nearly destroyed the tribe and caused their removal; but all agree that the mound was raised and received its significant name from such an event.

There is given in the first report of the Wisconsin Historical Society[3] a Winnebago tradition, in which it is stated that mounds of certain localities in the state were built by Winnebagoes and others by the Sacs and Foxes.

There is also an Indian tradition, apparently founded on fact, that the Essex mounds, Clinton county, Michigan, are the burying places of the dead killed in a battle between the Chippewas and Pottawatomies, which occurred not many generations ago.[4]

Other instances of Indians, both of the northern and southern sections, erecting mounds over their dead in modern times might be referred to, but the evidence adduced is sufficient to show that history bears out the assertion that the Indians found inhabiting this country were in the habit of building mounds.

A COMPARISON OF THE WORKS OF THE MOUND-BUILDERS WITH THOSE OF THE INDIANS.

The historical evidence adduced is apparently sufficient to prove beyond a reasonable doubt that some Indian tribes inhabiting the southern portion of the country at the time it was first visited did erect mounds and construct walls for defense. Nevertheless, as this evidence does not appear to be wholly satisfactory to a number of archeologists, and applies almost exclusively to one section, it is necessary, in order to clear the question of doubt, to present such other proofs as the subject will admit of. From the character of the subject these proofs must consist, to a great extent, of comparisons.

As has already been stated, every similarity shown between the works, art, customs, etc., of the mound-builders and the Indians is an

[1] Smith's History of Wisconsin, vol. III. pp. 245, 246.
[2] Loc. cit., III. p. 262.
[3] Pp. 88, 89.
[4] Smithson. Rep., 1884, p. 848

evidence in support of the view here maintained, a fact which the reader should constantly keep in mind as he proceeds. Every comparison and every fact which tends to eliminate from consideration, as the possible authors of these monuments, the Mexican and Central American peoples, is, to this extent at least, an argument in favor of the theory that they are due to Indians in the sense in which this term is here used.

ARCHITECTURE OF THE MOUND-BUILDERS.

One of the first things which strikes the mind of the archeologist who carefully studies these works, as being very significant, is the entire absence in them of any evidence of architectural knowledge and skill approaching that exhibited by the ruins of Mexico and Central America, or of that exhibited by the structures of the Pueblo Indians.

It is true that truncated, pyramidal mounds of large size and somewhat regular proportions are found in the region designated; and that some of these have ramps or roadways leading up to them. But when compared with the teocalli or pyramids of Mexico and Yucatan the differences in the manifestations of architectural skill are so great and so fundamental, and the resemblances so faint and few, as to furnish no grounds whatever for attributing the two classes of works to the same people. The fact that the works of the one people consist chiefly of wrought stone, and that such materials as worked stones are wholly unknown to the other, forbids the idea of relationship.

Mexico, Central America, and Peru are dotted with the ruins of stone edifices, but in all the mound-building area of the United States not the slightest vestige of one attributable to the people who left these earthen structures, is to be found. The utmost they attained to in this direction was the construction of stone cairns, rude stone walls and stone vaults of cobblestones and undressed blocks. This fact is too significant to be overlooked in this comparison and should have its weight in forming a conclusion, especially when it is backed by numerous other corresponding differences.

If, as some authorities maintain, the mound-builders came from Mexico or the Pueblo region, where the custom was to use stone in their structures, it is remarkably strange that they should so suddenly and completely abandon the use of this material as to leave not a single edifice to bear testimony to their knowledge of its use. If, on the other hand, as maintained by others, the mound-builders, after abandoning the Mississippi valley passed into Mexico and Central America, it is strange that they should have so suddenly become proficient masons without leaving in their original home or marking their line of march with some indications of their budding architectural proclivities. It is true that the same question may be raised in regard to other customs which seem to have developed, flourished, and died out in particular areas. But the change in this case is so radical that it would seem we ought to find some remains of their earlier and ruder efforts; and if we accept the generally received opinion of the migration of the Nahuas from the Northwest, so strongly and, as I believe, successfully argued by numerous authors on linguistic, traditional, and other grounds, we should find some examples of their earlier efforts. Attention is called to an article by Becker, which seems to have been generally overlooked.[1]

Though hundreds of groups of mounds, marking the sites of ancient villages, are to be seen scattered over the Mississippi valley and Gulf states, yet in none of all these is there a single house remaining. The inference is, therefore, irresistible, that the houses of the mound-builders were constructed of perishable materials; that the people who made the mounds were not yet sufficiently advanced in art to use brick or stone in building; or that they lived a roving, restless life that would not justify the time and trouble necessary to erect such permanent structures. As the latter supposition is at variance with the evidence furnished by the magnitude and extent of many groups of these remains, we are forced to the conclusion that the former is the true explanation of the fact observed. One chief objection to the Indian origin of these works is, as already stated, that their builders must have been sedentary, depending largely upon agriculture for subsistence. It is evident, therefore, that they had dwellings of some kind, and as remains of neither stone nor brick structures are found, which could have been used for this purpose, they must have been constructed of perishable materials, such as was supplied in abundance by the forests of the region in which they dwelt.

It is apparent, therefore, that in this one respect, at least, the dwellings of the mound-builders were similar to those of the Indians. But this is not all that can be said in reference to the houses of the former, for there still remain indications of their form and character, although no complete examples are left for inspection. In various places, especially in Tennessee, Illinois, and southeast Missouri, the sites of thousands of them are yet distinctly marked by little circular depressions with rings of earth around them. These remains give the shape and size of one class of dwellings common in the regions named. Excavations in the center usually bring to light the ashes and hearth that mark the place where the fire was built, and occasionally unearth fragments of the vessels used in cooking, the bones of animals on whose flesh the inmates fed, and other articles pertaining to domestic use.

The form and size of these rings and the relics found in them would seem to be sufficient to justify the inference that they are the remains of the houses of the authors of the ancient works with which they are connected; and such was the conclusion reached by Prof. Putnam, who

---

[1] Cong. Intern. Americanistes. Luxembourg, 1877, pp. 325–350.

found many of these hut rings or lodge sites during his explorations in Tennessee. He writes as follows concerning them:

Scattered irregularly within the inclosure [the earthen wall which inclosed the area] are nearly one hundred more or less defined circular ridges of earth which are from a few inches to a little over three feet in height, and of diameters varying from ten to fifty feet.   *   *   *   An examination of these numerous low mounds or rather earth rings, as there could generally be traced a central depression, soon convinced me that I had before me the remains of the dwellings of the people who had erected the large mound, made the earthen embankment, buried their dead in the stone graves, and lived in this fortified town, as I now feel I have a right to designate it.[1]

The force of this conviction can be felt only by those who carefully examine these ancient works in person; words can not convey the impression, in this respect, that is carried to the mind through the eye.

Further testimony as to the meaning of the circular remains of this kind is found in the fact that they are seldom, if ever, met with except on the site of an ancient village, and often one that was defended by an incl)sure. For examples of this class the reader is referred to the illustrations and descriptions given in the previous part of this volume of works in Tennessee, southern Illinois, and southeastern Missouri. For proof that these are similar to Indian villages at the time the latter were first known to the whites, see the preceding historical evidence. Some of the villages described by the early travelers and explorers would have left precisely such remains as some of those herein described and figured. The want of regularity in the arrangement of these hut-rings, their size and circular form; the central fire, and the perishable materials of which they were made furnish evidences of customs and modes of life too strongly resembling those of the Indians in the earlier historical days to be overlooked.

But the testimony in regard to the dwellings of the mound-builders is not yet exhausted, meager as it has generally been supposed to be. During the progress of explorations by assistants of the Bureau of Ethnology in southeast Missouri, Arkansas, and Mississippi, especially in Arkansas, in numerous instances, probably hundreds, beds of hard-burned clay, containing impressions of grass and cane, were observed. These were generally found 1 or 2 feet below the surface of low flat mounds, from 1 to 5 feet high, and from 15 to 50 feet in diameter, though by no means confined to tumuli of this character, as they were also observed near the surface of the large flat-topped and conical mounds. So common were these burnt clay beds in the low flat mounds and so evidently the remains of former houses that the explorers generally speak of them in their reports as "house sites."

As a general rule, in opening them, the strata are found to occur in this order: first, a top layer of soil from 1 to 2 feet thick; then a layer of burnt clay from 4 inches to a foot thick (though usually varying from 4 to 8 inches) which formed the plastering of the walls. This was

---

[1] Eleventh Rept. Peabody Mus., vol. 2. pp. 347–348.

always broken into lumps, never in a uniform unbroken layer, showing that it had fallen and was not originally placed where found; immediately below this is a thin layer of hardened muck or dark clay, though this does not always seem to be distinct; at this depth, in the mounds of the eastern part of Arkansas are usually found one and sometimes two skeletons.

Take for example the following statement by Dr. Palmer[1] in reference to these beds. Speaking of the slight elevations which here are not rings, as farther north, but low, flat mounds, he says:

As an almost universal rule, after removing a foot or two of top soil a layer of burnt clay in a broken or fragmentary condition would be found, sometimes with impressions of grass or twigs which easily crumbled, but was often hard and stamped apparently with an implement made of split reeds of comparatively large size. This layer was in places a foot thick and frequently burned to a brick red or even to clinkers. Below this, at a depth of 3 to 5 feet from the surface, were more or less ashes, and often 6 inches of charred grass immediately covering skeletons. The latter were found lying in all directions, some with the face up, others with it down, and others on the side. With these were vessels of clay; in some cases one sometimes more.

At another place, in a broad platform-like elevation not more than 3 feet high, he found and traced, by the burnt clay, the outlines of three rectangular houses. The edges of the upright walls were very apparent in this case, as also the clay which must have fallen from them, and which raised the outer marginal lines considerably higher than the inner area. "The fire," Dr. Palmer remarks, "must have been very fierce, and the clay around the edges was evidently at some height above the floor, as I judge from the irregular way in which it is scattered around the margins."

Excavations in the areas showed that they were covered with a layer of burnt clay, uneven and broken; immediately below this a layer of ashes 6 inches thick, and below this black loam. On these areas were growing some large trees, one a poplar (tulip tree) 3 feet in diameter.

Below one of these floors were found a skeleton, some pottery, and a pipe. A large oak formerly stood at this point, but has been blown down. Close by these dwelling sites is a large mound, 10 feet high, in the form of a truncated pyramid. A plan of these houses is shown in Fig. 136. Subsequently the remains of another dwelling of precisely the same form—that is, two square rooms joined and a third of the same size immediately behind these two—was found in the same region by Col. Norris. In this case the remains of the upright posts and reed lathing forming the walls were found, also the clay plastering. The sides of the room varied in length from 11½ to something over 12 feet. These are represented in figs. 117, 118. Numerous cases, similar in character, differing only in details, will be found in the preceding part of this volume, but it will be necessary to refer particularly only to two others.

---

[1] Ante p. 227.

Mr. Thing, digging into the summit of a medium-sized mound in southeastern Missouri, where there was a slight circular depression in the top, found at the depth of 2 feet a layer of burnt clay similar to those already mentioned, which he describes as follows: "In the top of the mound, in a small, circular depression, I dug down about two feet, when I came to a sort of platform of burnt clay. It seemed to be made of irregularly shaped pieces, one side being smooth and the other rough; and, what was peculiar, the smooth side was down." It is easy to account for this on the supposition that it had been the plastering of an upright wall, which, when the wooden support gave way before the flames, had fallen over in a broad sheet, thus carrying the smooth outer side downward. In confirmation of this view we may state that down the slope, on one side, were also found loose fragments of the burnt clay which had evidently broken loose from the mass and rolled down the side.

Our next illustration is from the report of Col. Norris; the locality, Butler county, Mo.; the group consisting of an inclosure and ditch, two large outer excavations, and four mounds inside. The largest of these four mounds measured about 150 feet in length, 120 in width, and 20 feet high at the highest point. A longitudinal section is shown in the figure.

The description by Col. Norris, made on the ground, leaves but little doubt that the poles and burnt clay which he describes were the remains of houses, the fire having been smothered by dirt thrown over the burning heap before the timber portion was entirely consumed.

Prof. Swallow describes a room formed by poles, lathed with split cane, plastered with clay both inside and out, forming a solid mass, which he found in a mound in southeastern Missouri. This plastering was, as he says, left rough on the outside but smooth on the inside, and some of it was burned as red and hard as brick, while other parts were only sun dried. Some of the rafters and cane laths were found decayed, some burnt to coal, and others all rotted but the bark. The inner plastering was found flat on the floor of the room as it had *fallen in, and under it* were the bones and pots.[1]

The discoveries made by Prof. Swallow, Col. Norris, Mr. Thing, and Dr. Palmer all harmonize and show beyond a reasonable doubt that the layers of burned clay so frequently found in southern mounds are, in part at least, the plastering of houses which have been destroyed by fire. The numerous instances of this kind which have now been brought to light, and the presence of skeletons under the ashes and clay, render it probable that the houses were abandoned at the death of a member or members of the family, burned over them after they had been

[1] Eighth Rep. Peabody Mus. pp. 17–18. I may as well add here that I have examined in person one of these clay beds found near the surface of a large mound, and that specimens of those found by three Bureau assistants are now in the National Museum, also specimens of the charred grass or straw of which Dr. Palmer speaks.

buried or covered with earth (for the bones are very rarely charred), and that immediately a mound was thrown over the ruins. The mode of burial in houses was common among the Muskoki or Creeks[1] and the Chickasaws.[2]

C. C. Jones says that the Indians of Georgia "often interred beneath the floor of the cabin and then burnt the hut of the deceased over his head."[3] In Pl. XLII, copied from De Bry, the houses of the deceased, as before stated, are being burned, although the burial appears to be taking place outside the village inclosure. It also appears that in some cases the mound so made was afterwards used as a dwelling site by the same or some other people, as it is not unusual to find two, and even three, beds at different depths.

That the houses of the Indians occupying this region, when first visited by whites, were very similar to those of the mound-builders is evident from the statements of the early writers, a few of which are given here.

La Harpe, speaking of the tribes in some parts of Arkansas, says: "The Indians build their huts dome-fashion out of clay and reeds." Schoolcraft says the Pawnees formerly built similar houses. In Iberville's Journal[4] it is stated that the cabins of the Bayagoulas were round, about 30 feet in diameter and plastered with clay to the height of a man. Adair says "They are lathed with cane and plastered with mud from bottom to top, within and without, with a good covering of straw."

Henri de Tonty, the real hero of the French discoveries on the Mississippi, says the cabins of the Tensas were square, with the roof dome-shaped; that the walls were plastered with clay to the height of 12 feet and were 2 feet thick.[5]

A description of the Indian square houses of this southern section by Du Pratz[6] is so exactly in point that I insert a translation of the whole passage:

The cabins of the natives are all perfectly square, none of them are less than fifteen feet in extent in every direction, but there are some which are more than thirty. The following is their manner of building them: The natives go into the new forest to seek the trunks of young walnut trees of four inches in diameter and from eighteen to twenty feet long; they plant the largest ones at four corners to form the breadth and the dome; but before fixing the others they prepare the scaffolding; it consists of four poles fastened together at the top, the lower ends corresponding to the four corners; on these four poles others are fastened crosswise at a distance of a foot apart; this makes a ladder with four sides, or four ladders joined together. This done, they fix the other poles in the ground in a straight line between those of the

[1] Bartram's Travels, 1791, p. 515.

[2] Barnard Romans, "A Concise Nat. His. of East and West Florida," II, p. 71.

[3] Antiq. Southern Indians, p. 203.

[4] Relation in Margry, Découvertes, 4th part, p. 170.

[5] Relation of Henry de Tonty in Margry, Découvertes, vol. I, p. 600. "L'on nous fit d'abord entrer dans une cabane de 40 pieds de face; les murailles en sont de bouzillage, éspaisses de deux pieds et hautes de douze. La couverture est faite en dome, de nattes de cannes, si bien travaillées que la pluye ne perce point à travers."

[6] Hist. La. II, p. 173, (French ed.) English ed. 1764, p. 359.

corners; when they are thus planted they are lightly bound to a pole which crosses them on the inside of each side (of the house). For this purpose large splints of stalks are used to tie them, at the height of five or six feet, according to the size of the cabin, which forms the walls; these upright poles are not more than about fifteen inches apart from each other; a young man then mounts to the end of one of the corner poles with a cord in his teeth, fastens the cord to the pole, and as he mounts within, the pole bends because those who are below draw the cord to bend the pole as much as is necessary; at the same time another young man fixes the pole of the opposite corner in the same way; the two poles being thus bent at a suitable height, they are fastened strongly and evenly. The same is done with the poles of the other two corners as they are joined at the point, which make altogether the figure of a bower or a summer house, such as we have in France. After this work they fasten sticks on the lower sides or walls at a distance of about eight inches across, as high as the pole of which I have spoken, which forms the length of the wall.

These sticks being thus fastened, they make mud walls of clay in which they put a sufficient amount of Spanish moss. These walls are not more than 4 inches thick. They leave no opening but the door, which is only 2 feet in width by 4 in height. There are some much smaller. They then cover the frame work, which I have just described, with mats of reeds, putting the smoothest on the inside of the cabin, taking care to fasten them together so that they are well joined. After this they make large bundles of grass of the tallest that can be found in the low lands, and which is 4 or 5 feet long; this is put on in the same way as straw, which is used to cover thatched houses. The grass is fastened with large canes and splints also of canes. When the cabin is covered with grass they cover all with a matting of canes well bound together, and at the bottom they make a ring of "bind weeds" (lianes) all around the cabin; then they turn the grass evenly, and with this defense, however great the wind may be, it can do nothing against the cabin. These coverings last twenty years without being repaired.

Numerous other quotations to the same effect might be given, but these are sufficient to show that the remains found in the mounds of the south are precisely what would result from the destruction by fire of the houses in use by the Indians when first encountered by Europeans. Combining the testimony furnished by the mounds with the historical evidence, which the close agreement between the two certainly justifies, it is evident that the houses of the mound-builders were built of wooden materials or wood and clay combined, and were of at least two forms, circular and rectangular; that the fire was usually placed in the center and the smoke allowed to escape through an opening at the top; that in the southern sections they were usually plastered with clay and thatched with straw or grass, and that the plastering was often ornamented by stamping it with a stamp made of split cane, and, in some cases, was painted red. Prof. Swallow noticed this color on the plastering of the burned room he discovered. A coat of paint has also been detected on some of the pieces which we have obtained in our explorations. This testimony would seem to be well-nigh conclusive that Indians were the builders of the houses, traces of which are found in the Arkansas mounds, and, if so, of the mounds also.

FORTIFICATIONS, ETC.

Mr. Squier, who carefully studied the antiquities of Ohio and arrived at the conclusion that they are to be attributed to a people occupying a much higher culture-status than the Indians, subsequently entered upon the investigation of those of New York, little doubting that he would arrive at a similar conclusion in reference to their origin. The result of this examination is best given in his own words:

In full view of the facts before presented, I am driven to a conclusion little anticipated when I started upon my trip of exploration, that the earthworks of western New York were erected by the Iroquois or their western neighbors, and do not possess an antiquity going very far back of the discovery. Their general occurrence upon a line parallel to and not far distant from the lakes favors the hypothesis that they were built by frontier tribes, an hypothesis entirely conformable to aboriginal traditions. Here, according to these traditions, every foot of ground was contested between the Iroquois and Gah-kwahs, and other western tribes; and here, as a consequence, where most exposed to attack, were permanent defenses most necessary.[1]

The facts presented by this author are sufficient to satisfy anyone not wedded to a preconceived opinion of the correctness of his conclusion as to the authors of these works. Here we find earthen embankments and inclosures often, with accompanying ditches, which this author has satisfactorily proven mark the sites of palisaded inclosures similar to those observed by Champlain during his voyages of discovery. (See also the evidence presented in the preceding part of this volume relating to the antiquities of New York.)

As similar earthworks are found in Ohio, in the Southern states, and elsewhere, and, as we know from what is stated by the narrators of De Soto's expedition and by other authorities, that Indians in different parts of the country when first encountered by Europeans were in the habit of fortifying their towns with palisades, there is good reason for believing that many of these remains had a similar origin to those of New York. That some may owe their existence to different customs, of which no notice has been preserved, is true, but, the correctness of Mr. Squier's conclusion being admitted, we certainly have a satisfactory explanation of the origin of a large portion of them.

The Gentleman of Elvas, as already quoted, states that "The wall, as well of that town as of others which we afterwards saw, was of great posts thrust deep into the ground, and very rough and many long rails as big as one's arm laid across between them, and the wall was about the height of a lance, and it was daubed within and without with clay, and had loopholes."[2] The decay of a work like this would leave a circular wall of earth like those seen in various sections of the country.

Caleb Atwater states that the wall of an inclosure at Circleville, Ohio, showed evidences of having supported a palisade or wooden

[1] Aboriginal Monuments of New York, p. 83.   [2] French's Hist. Coll. La., vol. II, p. 153.

stockade: "The round fort was picketed in, if we are to judge from the appearance of the ground on and about the walls. Halfway up the outside of the inner wall is a place distinctly to be seen, where a row of pickets once stood and where it was placed when this work of defense was originally erected."[1]

The town of Talisse was fortified by an inclosure of timber and earth.[2] Garcilasso's description of the fortress of Alibamo heretofore given is also important in this connection, as in this case the figure was quadrangular and had gates, behind which were three parallel short walls to defend the place against an attempted entrance by an attacking party. An almost exact parallel is seen in the defenses to the chief gateway of the work in Butler county, Ohio, known as Fortified Hill, figured in Ancient Monuments, Pl. 6.

The reader is also referred to Du Pratz's description of Indian forts heretofore given.

Strong defensive forts were common in the north as well as in the south. Charlevoix represents the villages of the Canadian Indians as defended by double, and frequently triple rows of palisades, interwoven with branches of trees. Jacques Cartier found the town of Hochelaga (now Montreal) thus defended in 1535. (See his description heretofore given; *ante*, p. 624.)

Another early writer, speaking of one branch of the Hurons, remarks as follows:

In this extent of country there are about twenty-five cities and villages, some of which are not inclosed or protected, but the others are fortified with strong palisades of wood in three rows, interlaced together and redoubled inside by large and strong pieces of bark to the height of 8 or 9 feet. Beneath, there are large trees placed lengthwise on strong, short forks of tree trunks. Then on the top of these palisades there are galleries or watch towers which they furnish with stones in time of war, to cast upon the enemy, and also water with which to extinguish the fire if applied to their palisades.[3]

The villages of the Pequots in New England were similarly protected. Champlain found the villages of Iroquois defended by strong walls, forming forts, apparently impregnable to any mode of attack with which they were acquainted. In fact, one withstood all his attempts to capture it.

De Bry,[4] John Smith and Beverly,[5] and Lafitau,[6] note the fact that many of the Indian villages were surrounded by palisaded walls, the gate or entrance being formed by one end of the wall overlapping or passing by the other which according to the last named author was the usual method. (See Fig. 343 from De Bry's Brevis Narratio.) Attention is called to the ancient work in Allamakee county, Iowa, heretofore described and figured. The resemblance in this case to those described by the above named authors is so striking, that we can scarcely doubt that this work marks the line of a former palisade.

[1] Trans. Am. Antq. Soc. (1820), vol. 1, p. 145.
[2] Garcilasso Hist. Florida, Lib. 3, cap. 23, p. 144.
[3] Sagard, "Le grand Voyage du pays des Hurons," ed. 1865, p. 79.
[4] Brevis Narratio, etc.
[5] History of Virginia.
[6] Moeurs des Sauvages.

Many other examples might be given; but these will suffice to show that the Indians were accustomed to construct fortifications similar in form and size to the inclosure, now attributed to the mound-builders, which, if burned down or allowed to decay, would in all probability leave just such walls as form these inclosures. The only objection to this explanation is the fact that in some of the sections where the Indian towns are known to have been surrounded by palisades no such circular earthern walls have been discovered. This may be accounted for on the supposition, which is in fact confirmed by abundant evidence, that in some sections the walls were braced by earthen embankments or heavily plastered with clay, while in other sections they were not. The former would leave the earthen rings, while the latter would not.

The inclosing and other walls of the Ohio works usually have a very distinct layer of clay. Some of the lines of Fortified Hill, in Butler county, can now be traced only by this layer of clay, when turned up by the plow, as I observed during a visit to it in 1884.

Intimately connected with this evidence, and tending to strengthen the conclusion arrived at, is the fact that in some instances these defensive works were surrounded by ditches or canals. For example, in the quotations already made we learn that near one town "was a great

Fig. 343.—Village of Pomeiock, from Brevis Narratio.

lake that came into the wall; and it entered into a ditch that went round about the town, wanting but little to environ it round; from the lake to the great river was made a weir by which fish came into it;"[1] that "the frontier town to Casquin was fortified with a ditch 40 fathoms wide and 10 in depth, full of water" ("fathoms" here is doubtless an error, and should be "cubits"). Biedma states that in one place they "reached a village in the midst of a plain surrounded by walls and a ditch filled with water, which had been made by the Indians."[2]

Although the examples given are not numerous, still they are sufficient to show that the Indians did in some cases surround their villages and fortifications with ditches and canals similar to those found in several instances surrounding groups of ancient works in the South,

[1] Hist. Coll. La., vol. 2, p. 172.   [2] Ibid., vol. 2, p. 105.

as, for example, the Etowah group already referred to (see Pl. I, p. 136, Jones's "Southern Indians," and our Fig. 182 in the preceding part of this volume). Another example, found in Hancock county, Georgia, is shown in Pl. II, p. 144, same work; also another in Pl. III. Others are also figured in Squier and Davis's "Ancient Monuments" and elsewhere.

We are therefore compelled, unless we discard the only authorities we have on the habits, customs, arts, character, and condition of the Indian tribes when first encountered by Europeans, to admit that they did construct just such mounds, walls, ditches, and canals as are now found in various parts of our country, especially the southern sections, which have been generally attributed to a "lost race," or to a people more highly civilized than the Indians.

Rev. S. D. Peet, in a series of articles relating to "Ancient Village Architecture," published in vol. V, of the American Antiquarian[1], writes as follows:

We give these pictures [of villages from De Bry] and call attention to the description furnished by travelers, since they by their very uniformity afford us a clue to the village life of those races which are not so well known. We may, in fact, take these descriptions and study the works of the mound-builders, and in them perhaps find an explanation of those very structures which have so long puzzled archeologists. * * * We now call attention, in the second place, to the village architecture of the mound-builders. There are several ways in which the villages of the mound-builders may be identified. First, the descriptions given by the early explorers. It is a remarkable fact that the earthworks in the Southern states were, when discovered, occupied as village sites. A large number of these villages have been described, and, although the sites have not been identified in later times, yet the descriptions indicate that the very mounds which are now being studied as objects of so great interest were then used as residences for the various tribes. Ferdinand (?) de Soto and his army were the first to discover the mounds. Mention is frequently made of them by the historians of the expedition. This mention is incidental, and so connected with the account of the people and the various incidents of the expedition as to escape notice, yet the descriptions correspond closely with the works as they are now found. Some of the villages were surrounded by stockades, and were so situated as to be used for defenses or for fortifications, but a large number of them are also described as having elevated mounds, which were used by the caciques for their residences and as observatories from which they could overlook the villages. It is not unlikely that some of the more prominent of these mounds may be identified. There are many such mounds described in the narratives. One such is mentioned in Georgia, one in Alabama, and one in Mississippi. One mound is described around which there was a terrace wide enough to accommodate twelve horsemen. On another mound the platform was large enough to accommodate twelve or thirteen large houses, which were used for the residence of the family and the tenants of the cacique. This was not far from New Madrid, in Missouri. It was upon the terrace of one of these mounds that De Soto stood when he uttered his reproaches against his followers, having found out the dissatisfaction and revolt which had arisen among them. This was after he had passed the Mississippi river and about the time when he became discouraged in his fruitless expedition. The narrative shows that these prominent earthworks were associated universally with village life. Sometimes the dwelling of the cacique would be on the high mound which served as a fortress, the only ascent to it being by ladders. At other times mention is made of the fact that from the summit of these mounds extensive prospects could

[1] Vol. V. 1883, pp. 49–50.

be had and many native villages could be brought to view. The villages are described as seated " in a plain betwixt two streams, as nearly encircled by a deep moat fifty paces in breadth, and where the moat did not extend was defended by a strong wall of timber near a wide and rapid river. The largest they discovered in Florida." This was the Mississippi: "On a high artificial mound on one side of the village stood the dwelling of the cacique, which served as a fortress." Thus throughout this whole region, from the seacoast at Tampa bay, in the states of Florida, South Carolina, Georgia, Alabama, Mississippi, Arkansas, these ancient villages appeared occupied by the various tribes, such as Creeks, Catawbas, Cherokees, Choctaws, Chickasaws, Quapaws, Kansas, and possibly Shawnees.

At another point in the same series he remarks:

> We now turn to the mound-builders' works. The same system of erecting military inclosures and connecting them by lookout stations seems to have prevailed among them that existed among the later Indians.[1]

Thus it is seen that, when the architectural works of the mound-builders are compared with those of the Indians, there is such a general similarity as to render it unnecessary to look further for the authors.

The mound-builders erected mounds, fortified their villages with wooden palisades and ditches, dwelt in houses made of perishable materials, many of which were plastered with clay. The Indians erected similar mounds, surrounded their villages with wooden palisades and ditches, and dwelt in houses made of perishable materials, which in many cases were plastered with clay.

It is true that, when Cortez invaded Mexico, he found some of the villages fortified by wooden palisades[2] much like those built by the Indians of the Atlantic and Gulf states, even to the overlapping of the ends. But the similarity holds good no further, as the usual Mexican method was to protect with stone walls.[3] Their pyramids or mounds were of stone in whole or in part and their houses, of which traces remain, were chiefly of the same material. There is in fact nothing to be found in the remains of the mound-builders which can, even by a reasonable stretch of the imagination, be considered Mexican or Central American architecture in embryo.

SIMILARITY IN BURIAL CUSTOMS.

There are perhaps no other remains of a barbarous or unenlightened people which give us so clear a conception of their superstitions and religious beliefs as those which relate to the disposal of their dead. By the modes adopted for such disposal and relics found in the receptacles of the dead, we are enabled, not only to understand something of their superstitions and religious beliefs, but also to judge of their culture status and to gain some knowledge of their customs, modes of life, and art.

---

[1] July, 1883, p. 238.
[2] Herrera, Hist. Gen., Dec. 11, Book II, Chap. IV, Stevens's Trans.
[3] Cortez, Cartas de Relacion, pp. 59 to 60.

The mortuary customs of the mound-builders, as gleaned from an examination of their burial mounds, ancient cemeteries, and other depositories of their dead, present so many striking resemblances to those of the Indians when first encountered by the whites, as to leave but little room for doubt regarding the identity of the two peoples. Nor is this similarity limited to the customs in the broad and general sense, but it is carried down to the more minute and striking peculiarities.

Among the general features in which resemblances are noted are the following:

The mound-builders, even within the comparatively limited area to which the present discussion refers, as shown in the preceding part of this volume, were accustomed to dispose of their dead in many different ways; their modes of sepulture were also quite varied, indicating tribal distinctions among them. The same statement will apply with equal force to the Indians.

"The commonest mode of burial among North American Indians," we are informed by Dr. Yarrow,[1] "has been that of interment in the ground, and this has taken place in a number of ways." The different ways he mentions are "in pits, graves, or holes in the ground, stone graves or cists, in mounds, beneath or in cabins, wigwams, houses or lodges, and in caves."

The most common method of burial among the mound-builders was by inhumation also, and all the different ways mentioned by Dr. Yarrow, as practiced by the Indians, were in vogue among the former. It was for a long time supposed that their chief and almost only place of depositing their dead was in the burial mounds, but more thorough explorations have revealed the fact that near many—and as may hereafter be found most—mound villages, are cemeteries, often of considerable extent.

The chief value of this fact in this connection is that it forms one item of evidence against the theory held by some antiquarians that the mound-builders were Mexicans, as the usual mode of disposing of the dead by the latter was cremation.[2] According to Brasseur de Bourbourg, the Toltecs also practiced cremation.[3] Attention is therefore called to this fact as it is one of a number having a similar bearing which will appear in the course of this discussion.

Turning now to the particular resemblances between the mortuary customs of the mound-builders and those of the Indians, we notice the following:

(1) *The custom of removing the flesh of the dead before depositing them in their final resting places.*—This custom, which has been incidentally mentioned in the preceding references to the burial mounds of the different sections, appears to have been more or less common among the

[1] 1st. Rep. Bureau Ethnology, p. 93.
[2] Clavigero. Hist. Mex., Cullen's transl., vol. 1, p. 325; Torquemada, Monarq. Ind., vol. 1, p. 60. etc.
[3] Bancroft, Native Races. vol. 11, p. 609.

mound-builders and Indians. The proof that it was followed to considerable extent by the former in various sections, is evident from the following facts:

The confused masses of human bones frequently found in mounds, which show by their relation to each other that they must have been gathered together after the flesh had been removed, as this condition could not possibly have been assumed by decay if the bodies had been buried in their natural state. Instances of this kind are so numerous and well known that it is scarcely necessary to produce any evidence in regard to them. The well-known example referred to by Jefferson in his Notes on Virginia[1] is in point. Concerning this he says: "Appearances certainly indicate that it [the barrow] has derived both origin and growth from the accustomary collection of bones and deposition of them together."

See notices of similar deposits as follows: In Wisconsin, mentioned by Mr. Armstrong[2]; in Florida, mentioned by James Bell[3] and Mr. Walker[4]; in Cass county, Illinois, mentioned by Mr. Snyder;[5] in Georgia, by Jones.[6]

Similar deposits are mentioned, by the explorers of the Bureau of Ethnology, as being found in Wisconsin, Illinois, northeastern Missouri, North Carolina, and Arkansas.

Another proof of this custom was observed by the Bureau assistants, Mr. Middleton and Col. Norris, in Wisconsin, Illinois, and northeast Missouri. In numerous mounds the skeletons were found closely packed side by side immediately beneath a layer of hard, mortar-like substance. The fact that this mortar had completely filled the interstices, and in many cases the skulls, showed that it had been placed over them while in a plastic condition, and as it must soon have hardened and assumed the condition in which it was found, it is evident the skeletons had been buried after the removal of the flesh.

As another evidence, we may mention the fact that the bones of full-grown individuals are sometimes found in stone graves (some of these graves in mounds) which are so small that the body of an adult could not by any possible means have been pressed into them. Instances of this kind have occurred in southern Illinois, Missouri, and Tennessee. In some cases the bones of a full-grown individual have been found in graves of this kind less than 2 feet long and scarcely a foot wide. In some instances, where the tomb has not been disturbed, the parts of the skeleton are so displaced as to make it evident they were deposited after the flesh was removed. The "bundled" skeletons so common in the northern mounds are all cases in point, as there can be no question that the bones had been arranged after the flesh had been removed or rotted away.

---

[1] 4th American edition, 1801, p. 146.
[2] Smithson. Rep., 1879, p. 337.
[3] Ibid., 1881, p. 636.
[4] Ibid., 1879, p. 398.
[5] Ibid., 1881, p. 563.
[6] Antiq. Southern Indians, p. 193.

From personal examination I conclude that some, if not most, of the "folded" skeletons [1] found in mounds were buried after the flesh had been removed, as the folding, to the extent noticed, could not have been done with the flesh on; and the positions in most cases were such as could not possibly have been assumed in consequence of the decay of the body and the settling of the mound. The partial calcining of the bones in vaults and under layers of clay, where the evidence shows that fire was applied to the outside of the vault or above the clay layers, can be accounted for only on the supposition that the flesh had been removed before burial. Other proofs that this custom prevailed among the mound-builders, in various sections of the country might be adduced, but this is unnecessary, as it will doubtless be conceded.

That it was the custom of a number of tribes of Indians when first visited by the whites, and even down to a comparatively modern date, to bury the skeletons after the flesh had been removed or rotted away, is well known to all students of Indian customs and habits.

Heckwelder says, "The Nanticokes had the singular custom of removing the bones of their deceased from the old burial place to a place of deposit in the country they now dwell in." [2] The account of the communal burial among the Hurons by Breboeuf has already been noticed. The same custom is alluded to by Lafitau,[3] and Bartram observed it among the Choctaws.[4] It is also mentioned by Bossu,[5] by Adair,[6] and others. For a general account of the modes of burial among the Indian tribes the reader is referred to Dr. Yarrow's paper in the First Annual Report of the Bureau of Ethnology.

It is foreign to the present purpose to enter into a comparison of the burial customs of the various aboriginal nations of the continent. Moreover, the data bearing upon the subject are so numerous that a volume would be required for this purpose. But it is worthy of notice in this connection that the custom of removing the flesh before burial does not appear to have been practiced to any considerable extent, if at all, by the Mexican or Central American nations, nor by the New Mexican tribes or Indians farther west.

(2) *Burials beneath or in dwellings.*—The evidence brought to light by the agents of the Bureau of Ethnology of a custom among the mound-builders of Arkansas and Mississippi of burying in or under their dwellings has already been alluded to. That such was also the custom of some of the southern Indian tribes is a well attested historical fact. Bartram [7] affirms it to have been in vogue among the "Muscogulgees" or Creeks, and Barnard Romans [8] says it was practiced by the Chicka-

---

[1] A distinction is made here between "bundled" and "folded." The former refers to those which have been disarticulated and placed in a compact bundle, the skull usually placed on top or at the end, the latter where the knees are brought up against the breast, and the heels against the pelvis.

[2] Hist. Indian Nations, p. 75.

[3] Mœurs des Sauvages.

[4] Travels, p. 516.

[5] Travels through Louisiana, vol. i. p. 298

[6] Hist. Amer. Indians, p. 183.

[7] Travels, p. 515.

[8] Concise Nat. Hist. of East and West Florida, p. 71.

saws. C. C. Jones[1] says that " the Indians (of Georgia) often interred beneath the floor of the cabin and then burned the hut of the deceased over his head." Dr. Brinton says, " The burial of the priests was like that of the chiefs, except that the spot chosen was in their own houses, and the whole burned over them, resembling in this a practice universal among the Caribs and reappearing among the Natchez, Cherokees, and Arkansas."[2] This furnishes a complete explanation of the fact observed by the Bureau explorers.

(3) *Burials in a sitting or squatting posture.*—It was a very common practice to bury some of the dead in a sitting or squatting posture. The examples of this kind are too numerous and too well known to justify burdening these pages with the proofs. It is enough to add that the descriptions in the reports of the assistants in the previous part of this volume and the published accounts of other explorers show that this custom prevailed to a certain extent in Wisconsin, Iowa, Illinois, northeastern Missouri, Ohio, West Virginia, and North Carolina. Instances have also been observed elsewhere.[3] That the same custom was followed by several of the Indian tribes is attested by the following authorities: La Hontan, Bossu,[4] Lawson,[5] Bartram,[6] Adair,[7] etc.

(4) *The use of fire in burial ceremonies.*—Another respect in which the burial customs of the mound-builders corresponded with those of the Indians, was the use of fire in the funeral ceremonies. As heretofore remarked, the inference has been very generally drawn from the evidences of fire found in the mounds that the people who erected these monuments offered human sacrifices to their deities. It is true that charred and even almost wholly consumed human bones are often found, showing that bodies or skeletons were sometimes burned, but it does not necessarily follow from this fact that they were offered as sacrifices. Moreover, judging from all the data in our possession, I think the weight of evidence is decidedly against such conclusion.

The presence of charred bones in these works might readily be accounted for on the supposition that cremation was adopted by some of the tribes as a means of disposing of the dead, and such is the opinion of Dorman, who remarks:[8] " Cremation appears to have been the usual method of disposing of the dead among most of these northern tribes." The same view is also held by Wilson.[9] Still, I am not disposed, as will hereafter be seen, to accept this as the true explanation of the facts alluded to, though cremation was possibly practiced to a limited extent by the mound-builders.

In assuming that Indians were the mound-builders, very little, if anything, can be found to support the theory of human sacrifice in the

[1] Antiq. Southern Indians. p. 203.
Floridian Peninsula. p. 183. See also Hakluyt's Voyages. vol. III. p. 37.
[3] Georgia and Florida. Jones' Antiq. Southern Indians. pp. 183-185.
[4] Travels through Louisiana. vol. II. p. 251.
[5] Hist. Carolina. p. 182.
[6] Travels. p. 515.
[7] Hist. American Indians. p. 182.
[8] Origin Prim. Superst., p. 171.
[9] Prehistoric Man. II. third ed., 1876. p. 211.

method supposed to be indicated by these remains. Dorman says: "Human sacrifices never prevailed to any extent among the barbarous tribes of the north. Very few cases of compulsory human sacrifice are found."[1]

This author quotes several authorities showing that human sacrifice was practiced by Indian tribes in that part of the United States now under consideration, but a careful examination of these shows that they do not sustain the allegation. For example, he says,[2] "Human sacrifice was practiced among the Miamis, for we are told by Mr. Drake that Little Turtle, the famous Miami chief, did more than any other to abolish human sacrifice among his people." An examination of Drake's remark shows that it was quoted from Schoolcraft, and that it refers not to true sacrifice, but to the torture of prisoners by the use of fire.

He also refers to Haywood's statement that "there are many evidences of the practice of human sacrifice among those tribes living on the Ohio, Cumberland, and Tennessee rivers,"[3] when reference to that author's work shows that it is only an opinion based upon what is found in the mounds of these regions.

The other quotations, except those relating to the Natches Indians and the nations of Mexico, Central America, and Peru, furnish nothing to sustain the theory that the mound-builders were in the habit of offering human sacrifices, in the true sense of the word. There is some evidence that they were in the habit of torturing prisoners with fire. By referring to the description of ancient works in Union county, Illinois, given in the first part of this volume, the reader will find an account of a stone pavement which was probably a place where prisoners were burned. This was found at the depth of 1 foot below the surface of the ground, was nearly circular, and about 9 feet in diameter. It was formed of flat stones so closely joined together that it was almost impossible to run an iron prod down between them. Scattered through the earth resting on it were the charred fragments of human bones, ashes, and charcoal.

In several of the mounds opened by Mr. Emmert in Monroe county, east Tennessee, circular beds of burnt clay were discovered. In the middle of more than one of these were the remains of a burnt stake, around which were ashes, charcoal, and charred human bones.

Haywood[4] and Dr. Ramsey[5] say that a Mrs. Bean, who was captured by the Cherokees, was taken to a mound in this section to be burnt, but was saved by one of the Indian women. It is a fair inference, therefore, that these beds of burnt clay and charred remains mark the places where prisoners were burnt.

I have expressed my doubts as to their resorting to cremation as a means of disposing of their dead, but since the discussion of this ques-

[1] Origin Prim. Superst., p. 209.
[2] P. 209.
[3] Loc. cit.
[4] Nat. and Ab. Hist. of Tennessee, p. 278.
[5] Annals of Tennessee, p. 157.

tion is not necessary to the object at present in view, will mention very briefly some reasons for this opinion.

It is true Dorman, Wilson and many others believe that cremation was a common practice with the mound-builders, but this theory is founded, as before stated, almost wholly upon the presence of burned bones and the evidences of fire in the mounds. Reference is made, by those holding this theory, to the Indians who, it is affirmed in many cases, followed this method of disposing of the dead, but after a somewhat thorough investigation I fail to find the data upon which to base this affirmation, except so far as the tribes of the Pacific slope and of Mexico and southward are concerned. Dr. Yarrow, in his able paper on the "Burial Customs of our Indians,"[1] evidently leans to the same view, but it is apparent from the cautious manner in which he refers to it that the proof is not entirely satisfactory.

Du Pratz[2] says: "There is no nation of Louisiana which follows the custom of burning the body." Louisiana, as used by its author, included all the Mississippi valley south of the Ohio, and all the Gulf states except Florida. In this statement he agrees with Romans and other early authors who mention the modes of burial and of disposing of the dead. Pickett[3] says the Choctaws were in the habit of killing and cutting up their prisoners of war, after which the parts were burned. The same writer says:[4] "From all we have read and heard of the Choctaws we are satisfied that it was their custom to take from the bone house the skeletons, with which they repaired in funeral procession to the suburbs of the town, where they placed them on the ground in one heap, together with the property of the dead, such as pots, bows, arrows, ornaments, curious-shaped stones for dressing deerskins, and a variety of other things. *Over this heap they first threw charcoal and ashes*, probably to preserve the bones, and the next operation was to cover all with earth. This left a mound several feet high." This corresponds so well with what has been found in some southern mounds that it seems to furnish a satisfactory explanation of the presence of coal and ashes in some of the tumuli.

By referring to the description of the North Carolina mounds heretofore given the reader will find that, in one of them, three skeletons were imbedded in ashes and coal on an altar-shaped structure, yet none of the bones were burned or even charred. Fire had also been applied to the outside of some of the little beehive-shaped stone vaults to such an extent as to show, in some cases, the effect of the heat on the bones of the inclosed skeletons, the burial having evidently taken place after the flesh was removed. In the mound opened in Sullivan county, eastern Tennessee, which is heretofore described and figured, the floor was covered with charcoal and ashes, yet no evidence whatever of any burning of bodies or bones was found.

[1] First Annual Report Bureau Ethn.
[2] Hist. Louisiana, 1758, vol. III, p. 24.
[3] Hist. Alabama, 3d ed., vol. I. p. 140.
[4] Ibid., vol. I. p. 142.

In several mounds opened by Col. Norris and Mr. Middleton in southwestern Wisconsin and the adjoining sections of Iowa and Illinois, there were abundant evidences that after the body or bodies had been buried and a layer, usually of a mortar-like substance, spread over them, a fire was kindled on this layer. Sometimes this was so fierce and the layer so thin and defective that the bones beneath were more or less charred. Hundreds of similar cases have been observed, showing that while fire was connected in some way with the burial ceremonies, there is very little evidence to be found indicating that there was an intentional cremation. A few instances possibly have been found to warrant this conclusion, but in the great majority of cases where charred or partially consumed human bones have been found, the explanation is easily given without recourse to the theory of cremation or sacrifice.

The following account of an Indian burial by Mr. Robert H. Poynter of De Sha county, Arkansas, as given in the Smithsonian report for 1882, page 828, is exactly in point in this connection. He says that Wal-ka-ma-tu-ba, an old Indian, was buried in 1834 in the following manner:

The house in which the family lived was built of round logs, covered with bark, and daubed with mud. In the middle of the house a board was driven about 3 feet into the ground, and the old man was lashed to this with thongs, in a sitting posture, with his knees drawn up in front of his chin and his hands crossed and fastened under his knees. The body was then entirely incased in mud, built up like a round mound, and smoothed over. A fire was kindled over the pile and the clay burnt to a crisp. Six months afterward the family were moved away and the mound opened. The body was well preserved.

The following statement by Prof. E. B. Andrews[1] in regard to a mound opened by him in Athens county, Ohio, may throw some light on this subject:

A trench 5 feet wide was dug through the center. On the east side much burnt yellow clay was found, while on the west end of the trench considerable black earth appeared, which I took to be kitchen refuse. About 5 feet below the top we came upon large quantities of charcoal, especially on the western side. Underneath the charcoal was found a skeleton with the head to the east. The body had evidently been inclosed in some wooden structure. First there was a platform of wood placed upon the ground, on the original level of the plain. On this wooden floor timbers or logs were placed on each side of the body longitudinally, and over these timbers there were laid other pieces of wood, forming an inclosed box or coffin. A part of this wood was only charred; the rest was burnt to ashes. The middle part of the body was in the hottest fire, and many of the vertebræ, ribs, and other bones were burnt to a black cinder, and at this point the inclosing timbers were burnt to ashes. The timbers inclosing the lower extremities were only charred.

I am led to think that before any fire was kindled a layer of dirt was thrown over the wooden structure, making a sort of burial. On this dirt a fire was built, but by some misplacement of the dirt the fire reached the timbers below, and at such points as the air could penetrate there was an active combustion, but at others where the dirt still remained there was only a smothered fire like that in a charcoal pit. It is difficult to explain the existence of the charred timbers in any other way. There must have been other fires than that immediately around and above the body, and many of them, because on one side of the mound the clay is burned even to the top of the mound. In one place 3 feet above the body the clay is vitrified. It is possible that fires were built at different levels—open fires—and that most of the ashes were blown away by the winds which often sweep over the plain. I have stated that there was first laid down a sort of floor of wood, on which the body was placed. On the same floor were placed about 500 copper beads, forming a line almost around the body. Of course the string (in another mound in the neighborhood copper beads were found strung on a buckskin string) was burned and the beads were more or less separated by the movement of the timbers and earth. Sometimes several were found in contact in proper order. Several beads were completely rusted away. Where the timbers were not burned to ashes but only charred, the beads were found lying upon the lowest layer of charred wood with another layer resting upon them. From the small diameter of the concentric or growth rings in the charcoal in the bottom layer I infer that there was nothing more elaborate than a platform of poles for the resting place of the body. Where the wood was burned to ashes the beads were found in the ashes.

(5) *Resemblances in other respects.*—That it was the custom of some of the mound-building people to bury their dead in box-shaped stone cists is now well known. That a few Indian tribes followed the same custom is attested by history and fully proved by other evidence, as will hereafter be shown.

According to Lawson[1] it was not uncommon among the Indians of Carolina to wrap the body of the deceased at the time of burial in mats made of rushes or cane. Remains of rush or cane matting have frequently been found about human remains in southern mounds.

It was also a custom with several Indian tribes to place bark beneath and often above the body. Numerous evidences of a similar mode of burial have been found in the mounds. Whether or not aerial or scaffold burial was resorted to by any of the mound-builders is not, as a matter of course, susceptible at this date of direct proof, yet the fact that communal or bone burial was practiced by the mound-builders in the same sections where this mode of preliminary sepulture was customary with the Indians of historic times, indicates that it was also a custom of the former.

In some cases it has been observed by the Bureau assistants while exploring in the northwestern sections that some of the bones in these buried masses bore what seemed certain evidence of exposure to the elements previous to burial.

[1] Hist. Carolina, p. 81.

GENERAL RESEMBLANCES IN HABITS, CUSTOMS, ART, ETC.

In addition to the special points of resemblance between the burial customs of the Indians and mound-builders alluded to, the facts warrant the assertion that in all respects, so far as they can be traced correctly, there are to be found strong resemblances between the habits, customs, and art of the mound-builders and those of the Indians previous to change under the influence of contact with the Europeans. Both made use of stone implements, and so precisely similar are the articles of this class, that it is impossible to distinguish those made by the one people from those made by the other. In fact, they are brought together in most collections and attributed to the one people or to the other according to the fancy or opinion of the collector or curator.

We find even Dr. Rau, whose long and careful study of articles of this class, both of Europe and America, would certainly enable him, if anyone, to decide in this case, thus frankly stating his opinion:

In North America chipped as well as ground stone implements are abundant, yet they occur promiscuously, and thus far can not be respectively referred to certain epochs in the development of the aborigines of the country. [1]

Instead of burdening these pages with proofs of these statements by specific references to finds and authorities, an allusion to the work of Dr. C. C. Abbott on the handiwork in stone, bone, and clay of the native races of the Northern Atlantic seaboard of America, entitled "Primitive Industry," will suffice. As the area embraced in this work, as remarked by the author, does not "include any territory known to have been permanently occupied by the so-called mound-builders," the articles found here must be ascribed to the Indians, unless, as suggested by the author, some of a more primitive type found in the Trenton gravel are to be attributed to a preceding and ruder people. Examining those of the first class, which are ascribed to the Indians, and to which much the larger portion of the work is devoted, we find almost every type of stone article found in the mound area, not only the rudely chipped scrapers, hoes, celts, knives, spear and arrow heads, but also polished or ground celts, axes, hammers, chisels, and gouges. Here are also found drills, awls, and perforators, slickstones and dressers, mortars, pestles and pitted stones, pipes of various forms and finish, discoidal stones, and net-sinkers, butterfly stones and other supposed ceremonial objects, masks or face figures and bird-shaped stones, gorgets, totems, pendants, trinkets, etc. Nor does the resemblance stop with types, but is carried down to specific forms and finish, leaving absolutely no possible line of demarcation between them and the similar articles attributed to the mound-builders. So persistently true is this, that had we these stone articles alone to refer to, it is probable

---

[1] Smithsonian Arch. Coll., p. 7.

we would be forced to the conclusion, as held by some writers, that the former inhabitants of that portion of the United States east of the Mississippi pertained to one nation, unless the prevalence of certain of the forms or more elaborate types in particular sections should afford some ground for districting.

The full force of this evidence, which is considered valuable in this connection, can only be clearly understood and appreciated by an examination of the work alluded to. If every form and type of stone implement and ornament found in connection with the works of the mound-builders were also in use among the Indians, it is, of course, unnecessary to look further for their origin.

The bone and shell articles found in the mounds do not present any type or finish, except such as can be traced to the Indians. Some of the figures on the engraved shells are difficult to account for and appear to be derived from some other source, but in every case these have been found in mounds or graves, which there are strong and satisfactory reasons for believing are the work of Indians; this will be shown hereafter.

Mound and Indian pottery compared.—The pottery of the mound-builders has often been referred to as proof of a higher culture-status than, and an advance in art beyond that attained by the Indians. It appears probable that some writers have been led to this conclusion by an examination of the figures, drawings, and photographs, without a personal inspection of the articles.

That all mound pottery is comparatively rude and primitive in type, manufacture, and material must be admitted. It is true that specimens are frequently found which give evidence of considerable skill and advance in art as compared with the pottery of other barbarous people, but there is nothing to remind us of the better ware of Peru, Mexico, or Central America, and, so far as my examination extends, I have not seen a single piece that is equal in the character of the ware to some of the old Pueblo pottery. The finest quality of mound ware I have seen is a broken specimen which was found with an intrusive burial in a Wisconsin mound, and, strange to say, the figures on it, which are rather unusual, are almost exactly like those on pottery found in mounds of Early county, Georgia.

The vase with a bird figure, found by Squier and Davis in an Ohio mound, is presented in most works on American archeology as an evidence of the advanced stage of ceramic art among the mound-builders, but Dr. Rau, who examined the collection of these authors, says:

Having seen the best specimens of mound pottery obtained during the survey of Messrs. Squier and Davis, I do not hesitate to assert that the clay vessels fabricated at the Cahokia creek were in every respect equal to those exhumed from the mounds of the Mississippi valley, and Dr. Davis himself, who examined my specimens from the first named locality, expressed the same opinion.[1]

[1] Smithsonian Rep., 1866, p. 349.

The Cahokia pottery, which he found along the creek of that name, he ascribes to Indians, as he remarks:

The question now arises, Who were the makers of these manufactures of clay? I simply ascribe them to the Cahokia Indians, who dwelt, until a comparatively recent period, on the banks of the creek that still bears the name of their tribe. Concerning the antiquity of the manufactures described on the preceding pages, I am not prepared to give an estimate. Only a hundred years may have elapsed since they were made, yet it is also possible that they are much older. The appearance of the fragments rather indicates a modern origin.[1]

Those who are aware of the extreme caution of this distinguished archeologist in expressing an opinion of this kind, will be fully assured that he had carefully studied all the facts bearing upon the subject before giving it publicity.

Most of the mound pottery, as the reader is probably aware, is mixed with pulverized shells, which is also true of most Indian pottery.[2]

Dumont describes the method of preparing the materials and manufacturing the pottery as follows:

The industry of these native women and girls is admirable. I have already spoken of the skill with which, with their fingers alone and without a wheel, they make all sorts of pottery. The manner in which they proceed to do it is as follows: After having collected the earth necessary for this work, and cleaned it well, they take shells and pound them up to a very fine and delicate powder. This they mix thoroughly with the earth which has been provided, and moistening the whole with a little water they knead it with their hands and feet into a paste. This they make into long rolls from 6 to 7 feet in length and of the thickness desired. If they wish to form a basin or vase they take one of these rolls by one end; and marking with the left thumb, on this mass, the center of the article to be made, they whirl it (the roll) about this center with wonderful swiftness and dexterity, describing a spiral. From time to time they dip their fingers in the water which they are always careful to have at hand, and with the right hand they smooth the outside and inside of the vessel which they intend to form, which without this care would be undulating. By this process they make all sorts of earthen utensils, as dishes, plates, basins, pots, and ewers, some of which contain 40 to 50 pints. The baking of this pottery does not require any great preparation. After it is dried in the shade a great fire is lighted; and when they think there are coals enough they clear a space in the center and arrange their vessels there and cover them with coals. In this manner the pottery receives the necessary baking; after this they can be put on the fire and are as firm as ours. There is no doubt that their firmness is to be attributed to the mixture which the women make of the powdered shells with the earth.

Du Pratz says: "The [Natchez] women make pots of an extraordinary size, cruses with a medium-sized opening, jars, bottles with long necks, holding 2 pints, and pots or cruses for holding bear's oil."[3] Also that they colored them a beautiful red by using ocher, which becomes red after burning. As heretofore remarked, the bottle-shaped vase with a long neck is the typical form of clay vessels found in the mounds of

[1] Smithsonian Rep., 1886, p. 350.
[2] Dumont. Mem. Hist. La., II, p. 271 (1753); Adair, Hist. Am. Ind., p. 424; Loskiel., Gesch. der Miss., p. 70, etc.
[3] Hist. La. (1758), Vol. II, p. 179.

Arkansas and southeastern Missouri, and is also common to the mounds and stone graves of middle Tennessee. Those colored or ornamented with red are also often found in the mounds of this section. The long-necked bottles and colored pottery form very important items of evidence in the present discussion, for the description given by Du Pratz of these vessels and Dumont's account of the method of manufacture leave but scant room for doubt that those found in the mounds were made by the same people that made those of which the above named authors speak.

It is also worthy of notice in this connection that the two localities, near St. Genevieve, Missouri, and near Shawneetown, Illlinois, where so many fragments of large clay vessels supposed by many to have been used in " making salt " have been found, were occupied for a considerable length of time by the Shawnees. Nor should the fact be overlooked that that they are marked with those impressions, so common in mound pottery, which are usually attributed to basketwork in which the vessels are supposed to have been placed while drying previous to burning, though in reality in these instances they are due to a textile fabric or pattern-markers.

The statements so often made that the mound pottery, especially that of Ohio, far excels anything made by the Indians is a mistake and is not justified by the facts. Wilson, carried away with this supposed superiority of the Ohio mound pottery, goes so far in his comparison with other mound pottery as to ascribe the ornamented ware found in the mounds of Mississippi to the " red Indian," yet asserts in the same paragraph that it suggests " no analogy to the finer ware of the Ohio mounds."[1] On the other hand, Nadaillac affirms that the pottery of Missouri (that found in the southeastern part of the state) " is superior to that of Ohio."[2]

So far as I can ascertain, the supposed superiority of the Ohio mound pottery, maintained by so many writers, is based on the description of two vessels by Squier and Davis, and, as we have seen from what is stated by Dr. Rau, a competent witness, is not supported by evidence.

Mound-builders and Indians cultivated maize.—A resemblance between the customs of the mound-builders and Indians is to be found in the fact that both cultivated and relied, to a certain extent, upon maize or Indian corn for subsistence. As proofs have already been presented showing that this statement is true in regard to the latter, it s only necessary to add here the evidence that it is also true as to the former. That the mound-builders must have relied greatly upon agricultural products for subsistence is maintained, as heretofore shown, by those who contend they were not Indians, and is admitted by all. It is also generally admitted that maize was their chief food product, but this is not left to inference alone, as there are proofs of it from the mounds. Not only are there prints of the cobs on many clay vessels, but lumps of clay bearing the impress of the ears; also charred cobs, ears, and

[1] Preh. Man., II. p. 23. [2] L'Amérique Préhistorique, p. 141.

grains have been repeatedly found in mounds and in pits or caches which appear to be the work of the " veritable mound-builders."

Another fact may also be mentioned in this connection, which, though negative in character, appears to point to the same conclusion. Although metates are, and from time immemorial have been, in common use among the Central Americans, Mexicans, and Pueblo Indians of New Mexico and Arizona, not one has been found in connection with the ancient works east of the plains; and so far as ascertained only two or three have been found in this entire area. These were dug or plowed up in Missouri not far from the Missouri river, but without any indications of having pertained to the mound-builders. Probably these may have been brought here by the plain tribes which shifted back and forth from side to side or by the Spaniards who visited Missouri at an early day to form an alliance with the Osages.[1]

The mound-builders used stone mortars for grinding paint and for other purposes, but none adapted to, or that we can suppose were ordinarily used for grinding maize have been observed. It is therefore more than probable that they made use of the wooden hominy mortar just as the Indians were accustomed to do.

The marked absence of this useful implement from all the works of the mound-builders east of the Rocky mountains is a very important fact in this connection. As it appears to have been used not only by the cultured but also by most of the wild tribes from New Mexico to the isthmus, and was unknown to the mound-builders of the Mississippi valley, we have in this fact an indication that the people of the two regions were widely distinct from each other. It affords an argument against the theory which connects the mound-builders and Pueblo tribes, and also against those which connect the former and the Mexican nations. At least it renders doubtful the theory which derives the former from the latter. Coming into a forest-covered region would doubtless cause some change in customs, but this change would not be so sudden as to leave no traces of them. Passing from a forest to a woodless region would of course account for a change of custom in this respect.

Articles of shell.—There are some marked resemblances in the customs of the two peoples in regard to the various articles made by them from shells. Several species of large, univalve, marine shells were used by the Indians as drinking cups. These were usually prepared for this purpose by removing the columella. Proof of this custom is found in the statements of several of the early writers. The manner in which they were used is shown in the Brevis Narratio of De Bry, Pls. XIX and XL. and described by Haywood.[2] The statement of the latter author is as follows:

Our southern Indians, at the annual feast of harvest, send to those who are sick at home or unable to come out one of the old consecrated shells full of the sancti-

[1] Du Pratz Hist. Louisiana, English Transl., p. 320   [2] Nat. and Aboriginal Hist. Tenn., p. 156.

lied bitter *cassena*. The Creeks used it in 1778 in one of their evening entertainments at Altassa, where, after the assembly were seated in the council, illuminated by their mystical cane fire in the center, two middle-aged men came together, each having a very large conch shell full of black drink, advancing with slow, uniform, and steady steps, their eyes and countenances lifted up, and singing very low, but sweetly, till they came within 6 or 8 steps of the king's and white people's seats, when they stopped, and each rested his shell upon a little table; but soon taking it up again advanced, and each presented his shell, one to the king and the other to the chief of the white people.

The shells used for this purpose appear to have been chiefly *Busycon perrersum* and *Cassis flammea.*

Specimens of these species, prepared for use as drinking cups, have been found in mounds and ancient graves in most of the Southern states and also as far north as Wisconsin. Clay vessels made in imitation of them have also been found.[1]

A fact worth noticing in this connection is that a specimen of *Busycon perversum* obtained from a mound in Arkansas (see Fig. 133) has an elaborate ornamental design engraved on the outer surface. As it is evident that this particular species was used by the Indians for sacred drinking cups, and, as will hereafter be shown, there are the best of reasons for believing the mounds of that part of Arkansas where this specimen was found were built by Indians, we connect the most advanced art of the mound builders with the Indians.

I call special attention to these little details, as they are illustrative of a multitude of minute threads which seem to bind these two peoples together. It is in the details we are to find the strong proofs of the theory we are contending for.

The shell beads form another of these threads of evidence. The manufacture and use of shell beads is common among unenlightened peoples, and hence the fact that both mound-builders and Indians made use of them is nothing in point. But when we come to note the particular forms and find that there are characteristics by which the prehistoric specimens of the Mississippi valley and Gulf states can, as a general rule, be distinguished from those of all other sections of North America, we touch another of those threads of evidence just alluded to. This is further strengthened by the fact that many and probably most of the forms found in the mounds can be traced to the Indians of the same region.

A number of these forms are mentioned by the old writers, notably Beverly in his History and Present State of Virginia,[2] and Lawson in his History of Carolina.[3] Biedma also notes the fact that among the riches of the Indians of Pacaha (Quapaws?) " were beads made of sea snails," thousands of which have been found in the mounds.

Shell spoons and scrapers were used by the Indians and hundreds have been found in the mounds.

[1] See Art in Shell, by Mr. Holmes, pp. 194–198, 2d Rept. Bur. Ethn.

[2] P. 58. London, 1705. Also ed. 1722, pp. 195–196.

[3] P. 315. Raleigh reprint. (1860.)

The shell gorgets appear to furnish, by their peculiar form and ornamentation, a very evident connecting link between the two peoples. The various forms taken from the mounds will be found figured in Mr. Holmes's paper in the second report of the Bureau of Ethnology. Some of these are also given in our figures in the previous part of this volume. Beverly,[1] speaking of shell ornaments made by the Indians, remarks: " Of this shell [which he calls the cunk shell] they also make round tablets of about 4 inches diameter, which they polish as smooth as the other, and sometimes they *etch or grave thereon* circles, stars, a half moon, or any other figure suitable to their fancy. These they wear instead of medals before or behind their neck."

Lawson's[1] testimony corresponds with this: " They oftentimes make of this shell a sort of gorge, which they wear about their neck in a string, so it hangs on their collar, whereon sometimes is graven a cross or some odd sort of figure which comes next in their fancy."

We have only to examine Fig. 3, Pl. LII, 2d Ann. Rep. Bur. Ethn., and our Fig. 213 to find Beverly's circles and half moon, although the chief engraved figure is intended to represent a serpent. On the shell represented in the former of these figures we see Lawson's cross. Moreover, we see in all the two holes through which to pass the string for suspending them. As some of the shells have been found in typical mounds, and with the original and lowest burials, and also in stone graves, they form a connecting link between the true moundbuilders and historic Indians which seems to identify the two as one people, at least in the region where these relics are found. Further reference will hereafter be made to them for the purpose of identifying certain tribes as mound-builders.

Dumont remarks that—

There are still to be seen on the seashore beautiful shells made by snails (or limaçon), which are called burgaux; they are very useful for making handsome tobacco boxes, for they bear their mother-of-pearl with them. It is of these burgaux that the native women make their ear rings. For this purpose they take the end of it which they rub a long time on hard stones, and thus give it the form of a nail furnished with a head, in order that when they place them in their ears they will be held by this kind of pivot. For these savages have much larger holes in their ears than our Frenchmen; the thumb could be passed through them, however large it might be. The savages also wear around the neck plates made of pieces of these shells, which are shaped in the same manner on stones, and which they form into round or oval pieces of about 3 or 4 inches in diameter. They are then pierced near the edge by means of fire and used as ornaments.[2]

The nail-shaped pieces and circular ornaments alluded to are very common in mounds. Examples of these types are shown by Mr. Holmes in his article entitled "Art in Shell of the Ancient Americans," Second Annual Report of the Bureau of Ethnology, and in our figures 283 and 284.[3]

---

[1] Lawson, Hist. of Carolina, p. 315, Raleigh reprint. (1860.)

[2] Mem. Hist. La. (Paris, 1753), vol. 1, p. 94.

[3] Pls. XXX and XLVI.

Pipes and tobacco.—That the mound-builders were great smokers is proven by the very large number of pipes which have been found in their mounds and graves. So numerous are these and so widely distributed over the mound area east of the Rocky mountains that pipe-making and pipe-smoking may be taken as a marked characteristic of this ancient people. Moreover the fact that smoking the pipe prevailed to a greater or less extent over this entire area indicates that the mound-building age was continuous.

That the pipe was an essential to Indian happiness is too well known to need any proof here. We have therefore in the evidence of the very general use of the pipe among the mound-builders one proof that they were Indians in the limited sense mentioned. At any rate it furnishes one reason for concluding that they were not directly connected with the Nahua tribes of Mexico or the Maya-Quiche tribes of Central America. The pipe was not an article in general use among either the Nahua or Maya nations; not a single one appears to be represented in their ancient manuscripts or paintings or their carved inscriptions; the cigar is represented, but no pipe. According to Bancroft, "The habit of smoking did not possess among the Nahuas the peculiar character attached to it by the North American natives, as an indispensable accessory to treaties, the cementing of friendship, and so forth, but was indulged in chiefly by the sick as a pastime, and for its stimulating effect." "Tobacco," he adds, "was generally smoked after dinner, in the form of paper, reed, or maize-leaf cigarettes, called *pocyetl*, 'smoking tobacco,' or *acayetl*, 'tobacco-reed,' 'the leaf being mixed in a paste,' says Veytia, 'with *xochiocotzotl*, liquidambar, aromatic herbs, and pulverized charcoal, so as to keep smoldering when once lighted and shed a perfume.'"[1]

This appears, so far as my examinations have extended, to correspond with what is stated by the older authorities, or, perhaps, it would be more correct to say, with what they do not state, as but very little is said upon the subject which is corroborative, for, had the pipe been in use among the Nahuas and Mayas, as it was among the Indians and mound-builders, it would have had a prominent place in their paintings, manuscripts, and sculpture, and the old Spanish authors would have had much to say in regard to it. The museum at Mexico does not contain above half a dozen pipes with bowls.

This fact is certainly one argument against the theory that the mound-builders of the Mississippi valley were Aztecs or Mayas, and what strengthens it is that the ancient stone pipes of the Pacific slope, especially of southern California, are of an entirely different type from those of the mounds east of the Rocky mountains, the prevailing form being a flattened tube, as may be seen by reference to Vol. VII of Lieut. Wheeler's Survey.

---

[1] Native Races, II, 287.

LINKS CONNECTING THE INDIANS DIRECTLY WITH THE MOUND-BUILDERS.

THE ETOWAH MOUND—STONE GRAVES.

In this class of proofs properly belongs the historical evidence; but, as this has been given in a previous chapter, reference is made here only to certain facts which seem to bridge over the supposed gap separating the Indians of historic times from the mound-builders, and to identify certain tribes as pertaining to the latter.

THE LARGE ETOWAH MOUND.

As the historical evidence adduced shows beyond contradiction that the Indians of the southern portion of the country at the time they were first encountered by Europeans did erect mounds, construct walls of defense, and dig canals, the question of their ability to plan and to combine and control force for the construction of such works must be conceded. Yet there are probably some long wedded to the theory of a "lost race" or Toltec migration, who will still maintain that only the tumuli and other works of inferior dimensions and simple designs, and the ruder works of art are to be attributed to the Indians, but that the larger and more extensive remains are due to a different race.

If De Soto's route could be traced minutely and with absolute certainty, it would be possible, no doubt, to identify, so far as they remain, the mounds and other works of which the chroniclers of his expedition speak; but unfortunately this can not be done. Still, there are some parts of it that can be determined within reasonable limits. For example, scarcely a doubt remains that he passed through the northern part of Georgia, striking the head waters of the Coosa river. Now it so happens that while in this region he stopped at an Indian town (Guaxule) in which the house of the cacique was situated on a mound of sufficient size to attract the attention of those of his followers who were Garcilasso's informants. This, there are reasons for believing, was the celebrated Etowah mound near Cartersville. It is true Dr. C. C. Jones, the leading authority on the antiquities of the southern States, locates Guaxule in the southeast corner of Murray county,[1] but in this instance I think he is certainly in error, as no mound has been found there which will in any respect answer the description given.

Garcilasso says: "La casa estava en un cerro alto, como de otras semejantes hemas dicho. Tenio toda ella al derredor un paseadero que podian pasearse por èl seis hombres juntos." "The house stood on a high hill (mound) *similar to others we have already mentioned.* It had round about it a roadway on which six men might march abreast."[2]

---

[1] Hernando De Soto, p. 35.
[2] History of Florida. Ed. 1723, Lib. III, Cap. XX, p. 139, and Ed. of 1605.

This language is peculiar, and, so far as I am aware, can apply to no other mound in Georgia than the large one near Cartersville, Georgia. Nor is this a mere supposition, for my assistants have made careful search throughout northern Georgia, the immediately adjoining portions of South Carolina, and eastern Tennessee, without finding any other mound that can possibly answer this description. The words "similar to others we have mentioned" are evidently intended to signify that it was artificial, and this is conceded by all who have noticed the passage: "alto" (high) in the mouths of the explorers indicates something more elevated than ordinary mounds. The roadway or passage-way round about it is peculiar and is the only mention of the kind by any of the three chroniclers. How is it to be explained?

Col. C. C. Jones says that this "roadway" was a terrace, but it is scarcely possible that any terrace at the end or side of a mound forming an apron-like extension (the only form which has been found in the South), could have been so described as to convey the idea of a roadway, which the mode of estimating the width shows was intended.

As Garcilasso wrote from information and not from personal observation, he often failed to catch from his informant a correct notion of the things described to him. In this case it seems that he understood there was a terrace running entirely around the mound or a roadway winding around from the bottom to the top. The broad way winding up the side of the Etowah mound (see Fig. 183) appears to answer the description better than what is seen in any other ancient structure in Georgia. It is broad and ascends at a gentle slope, giving to the observer the idea of a roadway, for which it was evidently intended. It is a large mound, quite high, and one that would doubtless arrest the attention of the Spanish soldiers. Its dimensions indicate that the tribe by which it was built was strong in numbers and might send forth "500 warriors" to greet the Spanish adventurers. The locality is also within the limits of De Soto's route as given by the best authorities; and, lastly, there is no other mound within the possible limits of his route which will in any respect answer the description. As Garcilasso must have learned of this mound from his informants and described it according to the impression conveyed to his mind, we are justified in accepting the statement as substantially correct. The agreement between the statement and the fact that a mound of the peculiar kind described is found in the limited region referred to, would be a remarkable coincidence if the former were not based on the personal observations of the informants. We are therefore fully justified in believing that the work alluded to by the old Spanish author is none other than the great mound on the Etowah river, near Cartersville, Georgia, and that here we can point to one of the Indian villages mentioned by the chroniclers of the Adelantado's unfortunate expedition.

If this conclusion be correct, there is no good reason for doubting that the Indians were the authors of this, one of the largest mounds found in the country, its solid contents being not less than 4,000,000 cubic feet. This is corroborated, as will hereafter be shown, by the fact that one of the three prominent mounds of the group was found, when excavated, to contain burials in box-shaped stone cists of the form so common in middle Tennessee.

As stone cists or graves have been mentioned, it may be as well to direct attention at this point to this class of works which form a connecting link between the prehistoric and historic times.

STONE GRAVES.

In order that the reader may understand clearly the argument based upon these works it is necessary to give here a brief explanation.

There are several forms and varieties of stone graves, or cists, found in the mound area embraced in this discussion, some being of cobble-stone, others of slabs, some round, others polygonal, some roof-shaped, others square, and others box-shaped, or parallelograms. The reference at present is only to the last mentioned—the box-shaped type, made of stone slabs, as heretofore described. If the evidence shows that this variety is found only in certain districts, pertains to a certain class of works, and is usually accompanied by certain types of art, we are warranted in using it as an ethnic characteristic, or as indicating the presence of particular tribes. If it can be further shown that graves of this form are found in mounds attributed to the so-called mound-builders, and that certain tribes of Indians of historic times were also accustomed to bury in them, we are warranted in assuming a continuity of custom from the mound-building age to historic times, or, in other words, that those graves found in the mounds are attributable to the same people (or allied tribes) found using them at a later date. This conclusion will be strengthened by finding that certain peculiar types of art are limited to the regions where these graves exist, and are found almost exclusively in connection with them.

This will indicate the line of argument proposed and the character of the proofs to be presented. If the result prove satisfactory it is evident that we will have an index pointing to particular tribes known to historic times, who were mound-builders in the mound-building age. It is scarcely possible that any tribe was so isolated as to leave no marks of connection with others, hence it is more than likely that having identified one we shall obtain clews to another. We should also observe that while our evidence is pointing in one direction, it is at the same time eliminating the supposed possibilities in another.

These graves, as is well known, are formed of rough unhewn slabs or flat pieces of stone, thus: First—in a pit some 2 or 3 feet deep, and of the desired dimensions, dug for the purpose—a layer is placed to form the floor; next, similar pieces are set on edge for the sides and ends, over which other slabs are laid flat, forming the covering, the whole, when finished, making a rude, box-shaped coffin or sepulcher.

Sometimes one or more of the six faces are wanting; occasionally the bottom consists of a layer of waterworn bowlders; sometimes the top is not a single layer, but other pieces are laid over the joints, and sometimes they are placed shingle fashion. They vary in length from 14 inches to 8 feet, and in width from 9 inches to 3 feet. It is not an unusual thing to find a mound containing a number of these cists arranged in two, three, or more tiers. As a general rule those not in mounds are near the surface of the ground, and in some instances even projecting above it. It is probable that no one who has examined them has failed to note their strong resemblance to the European mode of burial. Even Dr. Joseph Jones, who attributes them to some "ancient race," was forcibly reminded of this resemblance, as he remarks: "In looking at the rude, stone coffins of Tennessee, I have again and again been impressed with the idea that in some former age this ancient race must have come in contact with Europeans and derived this mode of burial from them."[1]

After a somewhat lengthy review of the various modes of burial practiced by the aborigines of America he arrives at the following conclusion: "We have now carefully examined at the modes of burial practiced by the American aborigines, in extenso, and it is evident that the ancient race of Tennessee is distinguished from all others by their peculiar method of interment in rude, stone coffins. Whilst the custom of burying the dead in the sitting posture was almost universal with the various tribes and nations of North and South America, the ancient inhabitants of Tennessee and Kentucky buried most commonly in long, stone graves, with the body resting at length, as among civilized nations of the present day in Europe and America."[2]

Since the publication of Dr. Jones's paper much additional information in regard to these graves has been obtained, and the area in which they occur has been greatly extended, but the result has been, as will be seen in the sequel, rather to confirm than to disprove the opinion here expressed. Graves of the same character have been observed in northern Georgia, in the lower portions of eastern Tennessee, in the valley of the Delaware river, at various points in Ohio and in southern Illinois. Yet, strange as it may seem, all these places were at one time or another occupied by the same people who formerly dwelt in the Cumberland valley, or by closely allied tribes.

It appears from these facts that this is an ethnic characteristic, though depending upon the presence of the proper materials. Our next step is to prove that the same mode of burial was adopted by one or more of the Indian tribes of historic times.

Dr. Jones, although believing in the great antiquity of these works, was, as already noticed, so strongly impressed with the resemblance to the European mode of burial that he expresses the belief that "in some former age this ancient race must have come in contact with

---

[1] Aboriginal Remains, Tenn., pp. 35; Sm. Cont., Vol. XXII.   [2] Ibid., p. 34.

Europeans and derived this mode of burial from them. This view," he continues, "is sustained not only by the presence of copper crosses and of vases with crosses and scalloped circles painted around them, and of bones evidently diseased by syphilis, in the stone graves, but also by certain traditions formerly preserved by the surrounding Indian tribes."[1]

Dr. Jones may have been mistaken in some of his conclusions; this language is therefore given here as much because it indicates the impression made upon a well informed mind by the careful study of these works, as for the statements in it. Attention, however, is called to the copper crosses mentioned, as they are an indication of contact with Europeans. Not that the presence of a cross is necessarily an indication of contact with European civilization—for many are found which must have been in existence long before the discovery by Columbus—but because of the peculiar form of some of those alluded to.

But the position assumed does not rest on such vague and uncertain proof as it is stated positively by Loskiel that the Delawares were accustomed to bury their dead in this wise; his words are as follows:

They buried their dead by digging a grave of the required size and about one or two feet deep; they put flat stones at the bottom and set others at each end and each side on the edge; then laid the body in, generally on the back at full length, covered the grave with the same kind of stone laid as closely together as *practicable, without cement, sometimes laying smaller stones over* the joints or cracks to keep the earth from falling into the grave. Then they covered the grave with earth, not generally more than two or three feet high.[2]

Barber states that—

Several tribes were accustomed to incase their dead in stone boxes or tombs. Among these were the Lenni-Lenape, or Delawares, of Pennsylvania, although the graves already opened show an antiquity of probably not more than one hundred and fifty or two hundred years, because the native contents, consisting of fragments of rude pottery and ornaments, are associated usually with articles of European manufacture, such as glass beads, iron or copper implements, and portions of firearms. A number of graves have been examined in the vicinity of the Delaware Watergap. The tumuli were scarcely distinguishable, but were surrounded by traces of shallow trenches. The skeletons lay at a depth of about three feet, and were in almost every instance inclosed in rude stone coffins. In one case the body had been placed in a slight excavation, facing the east, and above it a low mound had been built.[3]

This evidence is not only conclusive as to the fact that some Indians of historic times did bury in cists of this form, but it at the same time specifies the tribes—the Delawares and, by inference, the Shawnees—for as, at the time indicated a part of the latter, as is well known, were living with or in the vicinity of the former, the two tribes being ethnically related. This introduces a new factor into the argument and limits its scope, as it directs the inquiry along a particular line. The fact of the

---

[1] Aboriginal Remains. Tenn., p. 35; Sm. Cont., Vol. xxii.
[2] Hist. Miss. United Brethren, p. 120.
[3] American Naturalist, Vol. xi. 1877, p. 199.

removal of a portion of the Shawnees from the south to the valley of the Delaware, is too well known to require the proof to be given here.

Returning now to the Cumberland valley and regions of middle Tennessee, already referred to, we find here, beyond any reasonable doubt, if the number of graves be any indication, the chief home of the people who buried in stone graves of the peculiar form mentioned. That we can not attribute any of these graves south of the Ohio to the Delawares will be conceded. The natural inference, therefore, is, if they are to be considered as an ethnic characteristic, that they are due to the Shawnees. There is undoubted historical evidence that this people resided in the region of the Cumberland from the earliest notice we have of them until their final departure therefrom at a comparatively recent date. Col. Force correctly remarks, " We first find the Shawano in actual history about the year 1660 and living along the Cumberland river, or the Cumberland and Tennessee."[1]

There existed formerly a tradition that this nation extended settlements as far to the southeast as the banks of the Savannah river, and the name of this river is yet supposed by some to have been derived from the presence of this tribe. Although the latter supposition is founded on a slender and very doubtful basis, and much error has crept into the explanations of the tradition which has led to its rejection by some of our best investigators of the present day, there are good reasons for accepting it as true when restricted to its more exact and limited form. This is found in Milfort,[2] who places them in upper Georgia, in the Tugelo region, and on the headwaters of the large Georgia rivers. If this be correct we have some foundation for the tradition which places them on the Savannah, as the Tugelo river is one of its upper branches. With this limitation, and the caution as to accepting Milfort's date, which is evidently very far wrong, the tradition given by Gen. Robertson found in Haywood's Natural and Aboriginal History of Tennessee,[3] may be considered as corroborative:

In 1772 the Little Corn Planter, an intelligent Cherokee chief, who was then supposed to be 90 years of age, stated, in giving a history of his own nation, that the Savannechers, which was the name universally given by the Indians to those whom the English call Shawanese, removed from Savannah river, *between Georgia and South Carolina, by permission of the Cherokees, to Cumberland*, they having been fallen upon and almost ruined by a combination of several of the neighboring tribes of Indians. That many years afterwards a difference took place between the two nations, and the Cherokees, unexpectedly to the Shawnees, marched in a large body to the frontiers of the latter. There, dividing into several small parties, they treacherously, as he expressed himself, fell upon them and put to death a great number. The Shawanese then forted themselves and maintained a long war in defense of their possession of the country, even after the Chickasaws had joined the Cherokees. He observed that when he was a small boy, which must have been about 1689, he remembered to have heard his father, who was a great chief, say he once took a large party against the Shawanese, etc.

---

[1] Early Notices of the Indians of Ohio, p. 40. See also Marquette's statements in Jes. Rel., 1670, p. 91, and in his Journal, p. 32. Paris Reprint, 1845, etc.
[2] Memoire (1802), p. 9.   [3] P. 222.

The map of North America, by John Senex, 1710, indicates villages of the Chaouanons on the headwaters of the Savannah. On the De L'Isle map of 1700 the Ontouagannha (Shawnees) are placed on the headwaters of the great rivers of South Carolina. It is evident, therefore, that it was the understanding and belief at an early day that Shawnees had at some time dwelt in the region of the upper Savannah; also that this name and its synonyms were used to designate a particular people. In confirmation of the theory advanced, stone graves of the particular type we are now considering have been found in the upper part of Nacoochee valley, which is in the Tugelo region.[1] Others, as shown in Part I, have been found by the Bureau assistants on Etowah river, farther west in northern Georgia.

The tradition given by Robertson helps to explain a puzzling fact discovered by the Bureau explorers, to wit, that quite a number of these graves have been found along the Little Tennessee river, in the vicinity of the site of some of the Cherokee "Overhill towns." As the evidence derived from history and the mounds, as will be hereafter shown, indicated the occupancy of this region from time immemorial by the Cherokees, who are known to have been long the deadly enemies of the Shawnees, the presence of these graves seemed to conflict with the theory herein advanced. But the tradition given by Robertson indicates a previous friendly relation between the two tribes which will serve, in a measure at least, to explain this riddle.

There is also another item of evidence on this point. By referring to Schoolcraft's History of the Indian Tribes, the reader will find the following statement:

A discontented portion of the Shawnee tribe from Virginia broke off from the nation, which removed to the Scioto country, in Ohio, about the year 1730, and formed a town known by the name of Lulbegrud, in what is now Clark county [Kentucky], about 30 miles east of this place [Lexington]. This tribe left this country about 1750, and went to east Tennessee, to the Cherokee Nation.[2]

The following remark in Haywood's "Civil and Political History of Tennessee"[3] is worthy of note here:

A nation of Indians called the Cheavanoes is laid down [on an old map] as settled below the Cherokees in the county adjacent to where Fort Deposit now stands, on the Tennessee and southwardly of it, which is supposed to be the people now called the Shawnees, who may have settled there under the auspices of their old friends and allies the Cherokees, after the expulsion of the Shawnees from the Savannah river. This conjecture is fortified by the circumstance that the French in ancient times called what is now the Cumberland by the name Shauvanon, on which the Shawnees were for many years settled.

The Cherokees had another tradition, that when they first crossed the Alleghanies to the west, that is, from North Carolina into eastern Tennessee, they found the Shawnees at war with the Creeks.[4] This would indicate that the Cherokees had penetrated into North Carolina before they had into the valley of the upper Tennessee or Hogohega.

[1] Jones's Southern Indians, p. 214.   [3] P. 27.
[2] Hist. of the Indians. Vol. I, p. 301.   [4] Ramsey's Annals of Tenn., p. 84.

Some years ago Mr. George E. Sellers discovered near the salt spring in Gallatin county, Illinois, on Saline river, fragments of clay vessels of unusually large size, which excited much interest in the minds of antiquarians, not only because of the size of the vessels indicated by the fragments, but also because of the fact that they appeared to have been used by some prehistoric people in the manufacture of salt and because they bore impressions made by some textile fabric. In the same immediate locality were also discovered a large number of box-shaped stone graves. That the latter were the work of the people who made the pottery Mr. Sellers demonstrated by finding that many of the graves were lined at the bottom with fragments of these large clay "salt pans." [1]

It is worthy of notice that mention of this pottery had been made long previously by J. M. Peck in the Gazetteer of Illinois.[2] He remarks that "about the Gallatin and Big Muddy[3] salines large fragments of earthenware are very frequently found under the surface of the earth. They appear to have been portions of large kettles used, probably, by the natives for obtaining salt."

The settlement of the Shawnees at Shawneetown on the Ohio river in this (Gallatin) county in comparatively modern times is attested, not only by history, but also by the name by which the town is still known. But there is some evidence that an older Shawnee village was at one time located at the very point where this "salt-kettle" pottery and these stone graves are found. In the American State Papers[4] is a communication by the Illinois and Wabash Land Company to the Senate and House of Representatives in which occurs the following statements:

On the 5th of July, 1773, the bargain was completed by which these Indians (Illinois) for a large and valuable consideration agreed to sell to Murray and his associates two tracts of land which are thus bounded: the first begins on the east side of the Mississippi river at the mouth of Heron creek, called by the French 'the river of Mary,' being about a league below the mouth of the Kaskaskias river. From thence the line runs a straight course northward of east about eight leagues, be it more or less, to the hilly plains; thence the same course in a direct line to a remarkable place known by the name of the Buffalo Hoofs, seventeen leagues or thereabouts, be it more or less; thence the same course in a direct line to the *Salt Lick creek*, about seven leagues, be it more or less; thence *crossing the creek* about one league below *the ancient Shawnese town*, in an easterly, or a little to the north of east course, in a direct line to the Ohio river, about four leagues, be it more or less; thence down the Ohio by its several courses until it empties into the Mississippi," etc.

A copy of the deed is also given dated July 20, 1773,[5] containing the same boundaries, and with it the proof of record in the office at Kaskaskia the 2d of September, 1773.

Although the claim was rightly rejected by Congress and the directions given are slightly erroneous, as the geography of the west was not

[1] Popular Science Monthly, Vol. XI. pp. 573-584.
[2] 1834, p. 52.
[3] I know from personal observation that this is true in regard to the latter locality.
[4] Public Lands, class VIII, vol. 2. p. 108. Gales and Seaton edition, 1834.
[5] P. 117.

well understood at that time, we are justified in believing that the localities are correctly named, as it is not likely such a vast claim would have
been based on boundaries determined by imaginary places.   These
were real and given as correctly as the information then obtainable
would admit of.   The location of the "ancient Shawanese town" is
pretty definitely fixed, as it is on Saline river, above where the line
crosses, and about four leagues from the Ohio, and was at that time,
1773, known as the Ancient Shawnese town.   The Shawnee village of
modern times was on the banks of the Ohio where the city named after
them now stands, nor was it ancient at the making of the aforesaid
deed, as it was in its prime in 1806, when visited by Ashe.[1]   It is also
worthy of notice that the old town was not included in the bounds
given, while the land on which the latter stood was.

The next point is to show that the Shawnees were in the habit of
making salt. Collins, in his History of Kentucky,[2] gives an account
of the capture and adventures of Mrs. Mary Ingals, the first white
woman known to have visited Kentucky.   In this narrative occurs the
following statement:

The first white woman in Kentucky was Mrs. Mary Ingals, née Draper, who in
1756 with her two little boys, her sister-in-law, Mrs. Draper, and others, was taken
prisoner by the Shawanee Indians from her home on the top of the great Allegheny
ridge, in Montgomery county, West Virginia.   The captives were taken down the
Kanawha to the salt region and, after a few days spent in making salt, to the Indian
village at the mouth of the Scioto river.

By the treaty of Fort Wayne, June 7, 1803, proclaimed December 26,
1803, between the Delawares, Shawnees and other tribes, and the United
States, it was agreed that in consideration of the relinquishment of title
to "the great salt spring upon the saline creek which falls into the
Ohio below the mouth of the Wabash, with a quantity of land surrounding it, not exceeding 4 miles square, the United States * * *
hereby engage to deliver yearly and every year, for the use of said Indians, a quantity of salt not exceeding 150 bushels.[3]

Another very significant fact in this connection is that fragments of
large earthen vessels similar in character to those found in Gallatin
county, Illinois, have also been found in connection with the stone
graves of Cumberland valley, the impressions made by the textile
fabrics showing the same stitches as the former.   Another place where
pottery of the same kind has been found is about the salt lick near St.
Genevieve, Mo., a section inhabited for a time by Shawnees and Delawares.[4]

Some graves of this type have been found in Washington county,
Maryland.[5] History informs us that there were two Shawnee settlements in this region, one in the adjoining county of Maryland (Alleghany) and another in the neighborhood of Winchester, Virginia.[6]

[1] Travels in America, 1808, p. 269.
[2] Vol. II (1874), p. 53.
[3] Treaties of U. S. with Indian Tribes, ed. 1873, p. 370.
[4] Royce in American Antiq., Vol. III, pp. 188-9.
[5] Smithsonian Rep., 1882, p. 797.
[6] Royce in American Antiq., Vol. III, p. 186; Virginia State Papers, 1, p. 63.

Mr. Taylor mentions, in the Smithsonian report for 1877,[1] some stone graves of the type under consideration found on the Mahoning river, Pennsylvania. An important fact in this connection is that these graves were in a mound. He describes the mound as 35 feet in diameter and 5 feet high, having on one side a projection 35 feet long of the same height as the mound. Near by a cache was discovered containing twenty-one iron implements, such as axes, hatchets, tomahawks, hoes, and wedges. He adds the significant fact that near the mound once stood the Indian (Delaware) village of Keesh-kushkee.

Graves of the same type have been discovered in Lee county, Virginia, one of which is noticed in the Eleventh Report of the Peabody Museum.[2] I have also noticed some in a mound on the Tennessee side near the southern boundary of Scott county, Virginia. Allusion has already been made to the occasional presence of the Shawnees in this region. In the map of North America by John Senex, Chouanon villages are indicated in this particular section.

The presence of these graves in any part of Ohio can easily be accounted for on the theory advanced by the well known fact that both Shawnees and Delawares were located at various points in it and were, during the wars in which they were engaged, moving about from point to point, but the mention of a few coincidences may not be out of place. In the American Antiquarian for July, 1881, is the description of one of these cists found in a mound in the eastern part of Montgomery county. Mr. Royce's article, already referred to, states that there was a Shawnee village three miles north of Xenia in the adjoining county, also on Mad river, which opens into the Miami a short distance above the location of the mound.

Stone graves have been found in large numbers at various points along the Ohio, from Portsmouth to Ripley, a region known to have been occupied at various times by the Shawnees.

Similar graves have also been discovered in Ashland county, of which mention is made in the Smithsonian Report for 1881.[3] These were, as will be seen by reference to the same report, precisely in the locality of former Delaware villages.

Without stopping to give other proofs, the evidence is now deemed sufficient to assume that the Shawnees and Delawares were accustomed to bury in stone graves of the type under consideration and that the graves found south of the Ohio are to be attributed to the former Indians and those north to the two tribes.

As graves of this kind are common over the West side of southern Illinois, from the mouth of the Illinois river to the junction of the Ohio and Mississippi, we call attention to some evidence bearing on their origin.

Hunter, whose travels were in the West, states that some of the Indians he met with during his captivity buried in graves of this kind.

---

[1] P. 307.   [2] P. 208.   [3] P. 598.

According to a statement by Dr. Rau, furnished Mr. C. C. Jones and repeated to me personally, "it is a fact well remembered by many persons in this neighborhood (Monroe county, Illinois) that the Indians who inhabited this region during the early part of the present century (probably Kickapoos) buried their dead in stone coffins."[1]

Dr. Shoemaker, who resided on a farm near Columbia in 1861, showed Dr. Rau, in one of his fields, an empty stone grave of an Indian who had been killed by one of his own tribe and there interred within the recollection of some of the farmers of Monroe county.

It is doubtful whether Dr. Rau is correct in ascribing these graves to the Kickapoos, as their most southern locality appears to have been in the region of Sangamon county.[2] It is more probable they were made by the Kaskaskias, Tamaroas, and Cahokias. Be this as it may, it is evident that they are due to some of the tribes of this section known as Illinois Indians, pertaining to the same branch of the Algonkin family as the Shawnees and Delawares. An old lady of Jackson county, who the writer knew was accounted one of the first settlers of that county, informed one of the Bureau assistants that she had seen a Kaskaskia Indian buried in a certain stone grave which she pointed out to him. The evidence that many of those in southern Illinois are comparatively recent is shown by Mr. Middleton's account of those he explored in that region.

That the stone graves of southern Illinois were made by the same people who built those of the Cumberland valley, or closely allied tribes, is indicated not only by the graves themselves, but by other resemblances, as, for example, the similarity of works in Union and Alexander counties, Illinois, to those examined by Prof. Putman near Nashville, Tennessee.

On the Linn place, in Union county, as shown in the field report, there is a wall inclosing an area of some 25 or more acres. Within this inclosure are several mounds, one of considerable size, also a number of small excavations or depressions, which evidently mark the sites of circular dwellings. The large mound, about 140 feet in diameter and 13 feet high, was, as shown by the excavation made in it, built for some other purpose than that of burial. First, there had been a fire built apparently on the surface of the ground, and over the ashes a mound of comparatively small size raised; this was coated over with clay and hardened by a fire made by burning straw and brush on it. Over this, probably while burning, a layer of clay and sand was made and also burned, then more earth, and probably a third layer of clay mixed with sand.

Not far away, only a few miles, was a mound (one on Mill creek examined by Mr. Earle) literally crowded with stone graves, and at various points in the intermediate region similar graves over which no

---

[1] Antiq. So. Indians, p. 220.   [2] Reynolds' Hist. Illinois, p. 20.

mound had been raised. Turning now to Prof. Putnam's account of his exploration of the mounds and graves near Nashville, we find this statement:

The examination of the mounds at Greenwood near Lebanon, which were inside an earth embankment inclosing an area of several acres, proves conclusively that in this case (and by inference in all similar earthworks, of which several have been described in the State) the earthwork with its ditch was the remnant of a protecting wall about a village, inside which the houses of the people were built and their dead buried; also that the large mounds similar to the one in this inclosure (which is 15 feet high by about 150 feet in diameter) were for some purpose, other than that of burial, possibly connected with the religious rites or superstitions of the people, or the erection of a particular building, as shown by the fact that before this large mound was erected a very extensive fire had been built upon the surface over which the mound was raised, while the remains of burnt bones and other evidences of a feast were apparent; also from the remains of a stake of red cedar. Again, after the mounds had been erected to the height of seven feet, another similar and extensive fire had existed, leaving the same evidences of burnt bones, etc., with the addition of burnt corncobs. The mound had then been completed and my removal of probably about one-third of it did not reveal any evidence of its having been used for burial or for an ordinary dwelling, though it is very likely to have been the location of some important building, and the extensive fires, which had twice nearly covered its whole area might have been owing to the destruction of such a building by fire.

The houses of the people were circular in outline, from fifteen to forty feet in diameter, and probably made entirely of poles covered with mud, mats, or skins, as their decay has left simply a ring of rich black earth, mixed with refuse consisting of bones, broken pottery, etc.[1]

The close resemblance between the works in the two places, even down to details, seems to leave no doubt that they were made by one and the same people.

But the resemblance does not stop here. Near the center of the large mound on the Linn place, at the depth of about 3 feet, I found a broad, flat rock about 20 inches long by 12 wide. Prof. Putnam also found three similar slabs at a like depth in the large mound he opened.[2] In the stone grave mound he also found "an ornament of very thin copper, which was originally circular and with a corrugated surface."[3] Mr. Earle also found fragments of very thin copper with a corrugated surface, or, as he correctly describes them, "raised lines," in the mound on Mill creek.

Lest it be said that there is no proof that the mounds on the Linn place had any connection with the graves in the Mill creek mound, as the two were some 4 miles apart, attention is called to Mr. Perrine's statement in the Smithsonian Report for the year 1872.[4] Although our measurements differ materially, his figures being simply estimates, yet I know from his own statement to me, from personal examination and the description he gives, that he refers to the works on the Linn place. In one of the mounds of this group (the one outside of the inclosure) he

[1] Eleventh Report Peabody Museum, vol. II. p. 205. [2] Ibid., 341. [3] Ibid., 343. [4] Pp. 418–419.

found a large number of skeletons which "were carefully inclosed with flat stones, each skeleton being separate." These were evidently stone graves. The resemblance, therefore, between the two groups is complete, and leads to the conclusion that the works on the Linn place in Illinois are to be attributed to the same people who built those in Tennessee described by Prof. Putnam. In other words, it affords some grounds for believing that the Shawnees were in Illinois previous to their return thither in more modern times from the Cumberland valley.

Taking all these corroborating facts together, there are reasonable grounds for concluding that graves of the type now under consideration, although found in widely separated localities, are attributable to the Shawnee Indians and their congeners, the Delawares and Illinois, and that those south of the Ohio are due entirely to the first named tribe. That they are the work of Indians must be admitted by all who are willing to be convinced by evidence, and this is the only point at present insisted upon.

That the authors of these graves were mound-builders is proved beyond question by the fact that in most cases the graves are connected with mounds, and in numerous cases in the various sections where found (except when due to the Delawares, who were never mound-builders) are in mounds sometimes in two, three, and even four tiers.

The importance and bearing of this evidence does not stop with what has been stated, for it is so interlocked with other facts relating to the works of the "veritable mound-builders" as to leave no hiatus into which the theory of a "lost race" or "Toltec occupation" can possibly be thrust. It forms an unbroken chain, connecting the mound-builders and historical Indians, which no sophistry or reasoning can break. Not only are these graves found in mounds of considerable size, but they are also connected with one of the most noted groups in the United States.

The group alluded to is the one on Col. Tumlin's place, near Cartersville, Ga., known as the Etowah mounds, of which a full description will be found in this volume, and of which mention is made a few pages back.

In the smallest of the three large mounds were found stone graves precisely of the type attributable, when found south of the Ohio, to the Shawnees; not in a situation where they could be ascribed to intrusive burials, but in the bottom layer of a comparatively large mound, with a thick and undisturbed layer of hard packed clay above them. It is also worthy of notice that the locality is intermediate between the principal seat of the Shawnees in the Cumberland valley and their eastern outposts in northeastern Georgia, where both tradition and stone graves indicate a settlement. The tradition regarding this settlement has already been given.

In these graves were found the remarkable figured copper plates and certain engraved shells elsewhere described and illustrated.

It is apparent to every one who will inspect the figures that in all their leading characters the designs are suggestive of Mexican or Central American origin. In fact there can be no doubt that they were derived in some way from these more civilized countries either directly or, as is more probable, indirectly. While there is nothing to be found in the designs or workmanship of the shells suggestive of European influence, the same can not be said of the copper plates. First, the wings arise from the back as angel wings, and do not replace the arms, as in Mexican designs; second, the stamping seems to have been done with a harder metal than the aborigines were acquainted with. But the decision of this question is not essential to the point at present under discussion. What bears more directly on this point, and is corroborative of the theory here advanced, is that the only other copper articles similar to those described which have been obtained, were found at the following points:

Fragments in a stone grave at Lebanon, in middle Tennessee, by Prof. Putnam;[1] fragments in a stone grave in a mound at Mill creek, southern Illinois, by Mr. Earle; in a stone grave in Jackson county, Illinois, by Mr. Thing; in a mound of Madison county, Illinois, by Mr. H. R. Howland; and in a small mound at Peoria, Illinois, by Maj. J. W. Powell. All except the specimens found by Prof. Putnam and Mr. H. R. Howland were obtained by the Bureau of Ethnology and are now in the National Museum.

There can be but little doubt that the specimens obtained from the simple stone graves by Prof. Putnam and Mr. Thing are to be attributed to Indian burials, but surely not to Indian manufacture. We have therefore two unbroken chains connecting the Indians of historic times with the " veritable mound-builders," and the facts which form the links of these chains throw some additional light on the history of that somewhat mysterious people, the Shawnees. The engraved shells also form another link which not only connects the mound-builders with historic times, as heretofore intimated, but tends to corroborate what has been advanced in regard to the Shawnees.

ENGRAVED SHELLS, STONE PIPES, COPPER ARTICLES, STONE IMAGES.

ENGRAVED SHELLS.

These form another link connecting the Indians of historic times with the mound-builders, and, what is of still more importance, their presence in a given locality appears to be an almost certain indication that that particular locality was occupied at some time by one of two tribes. There are probably some exceptions to this rule, but it is believed they are few.

The following list of localities where specimens have been found,

---

[1] Fifteenth Rep. Peabody Mus., 1882, Fig. 13, p. 102.

although including only a portion of those which have been discovered, will indicate correctly the area over which they have been carried:

Lick creek .... East Tennessee ... from mound.
Near Knoxville .... East Tennessee ... from mound.
Near Nashville .... Tennessee .... from mound.
Near Nashville .... Tennessee .... from stone grave.
Old Town .... Tennessee .... from mound.
Franklin .... Tennessee .... from mound.
Sevierville .... Tennessee .... from mound.
Bartow county .... Georgia .... from stone grave in mound.
Monroe county .... East Tennessee ... from mounds.
Lee county .... Virginia .... from mounds.
Virginia [county not known] .... from grave.
Caldwell county .... North Carolina ... from mound.
Near Mussel-Shoals .... Alabama .... from cave.
New Madrid ......, ... Missouri .... from mound.
Union county .... Illinois .... from mound.
St. Clair county .... Illinois .... from stone grave.

One in the National Museum is marked " Mississippi," but the locality given is more than doubtful.

In other words, they are found in all parts of Tennessee, except the extreme western portion, in western North Carolina, in northern Georgia, the extreme northern part of Alabama, southeastern Missouri, southern Illinois, and in Virginia, particularly the extreme southwestern part; but western North Carolina, eastern and middle Tennessee, especially the Cumberland valley, are the places where they have been found in the greatest numbers.

Although having a somewhat extensive range, they do not appear to be found, except in isolated cases, beyond the possible haunts of the Cherokees and Shawnees. At least, with the exception of those found in western North Carolina and eastern Tennessee, they pertain to the works of the authors of the stone graves. It is worthy of note in this connection that the " bird head " so common on one class of engraved shells (found almost exclusively in the stone graves of middle Tennessee) appears also, and in the same type, both on stone and bone implements in New Jersey.[1] In regard to the former Dr. Abbott remarks as follows: " Here we see a reference apparently to just such disks, and the interest in the reproduction of the same figures on other objects found in New Jersey lies in the probable indication that there is in the latter a trace at least of tribal relationship with the southern Indians. Did we not learn from the writings of Heckwelder that the Lenape had " the turkey totem," we might suppose that this drawing of such bird heads originated with intrusive southern Shawnees, who at one time occupied lands in the Delaware valley and who are supposed by some writers to have been closely related to the earliest inhabitants of the southern and southwestern states. Inasmuch as we shall find that,

---

[1] Abbott's Primitive Industry. pp. 71 and 207.

not only on this slate knife, but on a bone implement also, similar heads of birds are engraved, it is probable that the identity of the design is not a mere coincidence, but that it must be explained either in accordance with the statements of Heckwelder or be considered as the work of southern Shawnees after their arrival in New Jersey. In the latter event the theory that these (shell) disks are the work of a people different from and anterior to the Indians found in the Cumberland valley at the time of the discovery of that region by the whites, is apparently not sustained by the facts." [1]

That engraved shell gorgets were in use among the Indians, both of North Carolina and Virginia, is already established by the historical references given, and that they were common among the people who buried in stone graves and built mounds is known to and admitted by all recent authorities on American archeology and proved beyond question by the evidence furnished in the preceding field report. The only reasonable explanation of these facts is that the Indians were the authors of these stone graves and the builders of the mounds associated therewith. If this be admitted, the conclusion is inevitable that the Cherokees and Shawnees were mound-builders and thus as investigation proceeds step by step the vision of a "lost race" and a Toltec occupation gradually fades from view.

The chief difficulty which arises in connection with these shells is the fact that a few of them bear undoubted Mexican designs which pertain to pre-Columbian times. Take, for example, those found in the "Big Toco mound," described and figured in the preceding part of this volume. The Mexican origin of the designs is admitted by every one who sees them, yet the proof that this mound was built and used by the Cherokees is so strong as scarcely to admit of a doubt. How these two facts are to be reconciled is a problem not easily solved. As this has no special bearing on the particular point now under discussion, its consideration is unnecessary at present.

PIPES.

The ancient works of Ohio, with their "altar mounds," "sacred inclosures," and their "mathematically accurate," but mysterious circles and squares, are still pointed to as impregnable to the attacks of this Indian theory. That the rays of light falling upon their origin are few and dim is admitted; still we are not left wholly in the dark on this point.

If the proof is satisfactory that the mounds of the southern half of the United States and a large portion of those of the upper Mississippi valley are of Indian origin, in the sense heretofore defined, there should be very strong evidence in the opposite direction in regard to these to lead to the belief that they pertain to a different race. Even should the evidence fail to indicate the tribe or tribes by whom they were

---

built, this will not justify the assertion that they are not of Indian origin.

If the evidence relating to these works has in it nothing decidedly opposed to the theory, then the presumption must, for the reasons heretofore given, be in favor of the view that the authors were Indians. The *onus probandi* is on those who deny this and not on those who advocate it.

It is legitimate, therefore, to assume that the Ohio works were made by Indians until evidence to the contrary is produced.

The geographical position of the defensive works connected with these remains indicate, as has been often remarked by writers on this subject, a pressure by northern hordes which finally resulted in driving the inhabitants of the fertile valleys of the Miami, Scioto, and Muskingum southward, possibly into the Gulf states, where they became incorporated with the tribes of that section.[1] If this is assumed as correct it only tends to confirm the theory of an Indian origin. But the decision is not left to mere assumption and the indications mentioned, as there are other and more direct evidences bearing upon this point to be found in the works of art and modes of burial of this region.

That the mound-builders of Ohio made and used the pipe is proved by the large number of pipes found in the mounds, and that they cultivated tobacco may reasonably be inferred from this fact. Attention has already been called to the very general use of the pipe among the mound-builders as an evidence of their relation to the Indians; also to the fact that in this respect and the forms of the pipes they differed widely from the Nahua, Maya, and Pueblo tribes. The object in referring to them at this point is to show that the monuments of Ohio, which have so long been represented as the typical works of the mound-builders, were built by Indians.

Although varied indefinitely by the addition of animal and other figures, the typical or simple form of the pipe of the Ohio mound-builders appears to have been that represented by Squier and Davis in their Fig. 68.[2] The peculiar feature is the broad, flat, and slightly curved base or stem which projects beyond the bowl to an extent usually equal to the perforated end.

Now, if it can be shown that any known tribe of Indians used pipes of this form, this will furnish another link connecting the Indians and mound-builders. It has, however, been asserted positively that no such proof can be adduced, one writer, speaking of this question, remarking: " I do not care to argue the question at present, but it would be well to bear in mind one fact, viz, no people have ever yet been found, so far as reported, who ever made or used or who knew of any people who did make or use the mound pipe, such as is found in our Mississippi mounds, which is quite a distinct type. 'Platform,' 'curved base,' 'mon-

---

[1] Force. Some early notices of the Indians of Ohio, p. 74, etc.
[2] Anc. Monuments, p. 179.

itor' pipes they are called and used without a stem. The bowl is always central, whether having some animal carved around it or not."[1]

If this writer had referred to Adair's History of the American Indians, page 423, he would have found this statement: "They [Indians] make beautiful stone pipes; and the Cheerake, the best of any of the Indians; for their mountainous country contains many different sorts and colors of soils proper for such uses. They easily form them with their tomahawks and afterwards finish them in any form with their knives, the pipes being of a very soft quality till they are smoked with and used in the fire, when they become quite hard. They are often a full span long and the bowls are about half as large again as those of our English pipes. The fore part of each commonly runs out with a sharp peak two or three fingers broad and a quarter of an inch thick;" and he adds further, as if intending to describe the typical form of the Ohio pipe, "on both sides of the bowl lengthwise." This addition is important, as it leaves no doubt in the mind as to the particular form of pipe intended. As this statement was made over a century ago, it must have been from seeing them in use and not from having discovered them in mounds.

E. A. Barber[2] says: "The earliest stone pipes from the mounds were 'always carved from a single piece and consist of a flat curved base of variable length and width, with the bowl rising from the center of the convex side' (Anc. Mon., 228). * The typical mound pipe is the 'Monitor' form, as it may be termed, possessing a short, cylindrical, urn- or spool-shaped bowl rising from the center of a flat and slightly curved base."

According to this statement the "Monitor" type is considered the oldest form of the mound-builder's pipe and yet we not only have the evidence that it was in use among the Indians of this region, but it is easy to trace in the mound specimens the modifications which brought into use the simple form of the modern Indian pipe. For example there is one of the form shown in Fig. 301 from Hamilton County, Ohio; another from a large mound in Kanawha valley, West Virginia; several taken from Indian graves in Essex county, Mass.;[3] another found in the grave of a Seneca Indian in the valley of the Genessee;[4] and others found by the assistants of the Bureau of Ethnology in the mounds of western North Carolina and east Tennessee.

So far the modification consists in simply shortening the forward projection of the stem or base, the bowl remaining perpendicular. The next modification is shown in Fig. 344, which represents a type less common than the preceding, but found in several localities, as, for example, in Hamilton county, Ohio; mounds in Sullivan county, eastern Tennessee (by the Bureau assistants); and in Virginia.[5] In these, although

---

1 The Young Mineralogist and Antiquarian, April, 1885, p. 79.

2 Amer. Nat., vol. 16 (1882), pp. 265–266.

3 Abbott, Primitive Industry. Fig. 313, p. 319; Bulletin Essex Institute, vol. 3, p. 123.

4 Morgan, League of the Iroquois, p. 356.

5 Rau, Arch. Coll., Smithsonian Inst., p. 50, Fig. 190.

retaining the broad or winged stem, we see the bowl assuming the forward slope and in some instances (as some of those found in the mounds of east Tennessee) the projection of the stem is reduced to a simple rim or is entirely wanting. (See Figs. 233 and 285.)

FIG. 344.—Pipe from Virginia.

The next step brings us to what may be considered the typical form of the modern pipe as shown in Figs. 217, 218, and 219. This pattern, according to Dr. Abbott,[1] is seldom found in New England or the Middle States, "except of a much smaller size and made of clay." He figures one from Isle of Wight county, Virginia, "made of compact steatite." A large number of this form were found in the North Carolina mounds, some with stems almost or quite a foot in length.

It is hardly necessary to add that among the specimens obtained from the various localities can be found every possible gradation, from the ancient Ohio type to the modern form last mentioned. There is, therefore, in this peculiar line of art and custom an unbroken chain connecting the mound-builders of Ohio with the Indian of historic times, and, what strengthens the argument, in the same fact is evidence that disconnects the makers from the Mexican and Central American peoples.

EVIDENCE OF TRIBAL DIVISIONS—SUBSEQUENT USE OF MOUNDS BY INDIANS.

Allusion was made in the introduction to some reasons for believing that the mound-builders consisted of various tribes; but one or two additional facts bearing on the same point may be mentioned here.

That one tribe often occupied works which had been built by other tribes is undoubtedly true, as the fact is attested both by history and by the works themselves.

For example, the relics found in and about the Etowah group in northern Georgia, so often mentioned, indicate that it was the scene of many a sharp conflict between contending tribes. It was also the scene of a severe contest between the Cherokees and Creeks in their long and bloody war, one of the group being occupied by the former and its summit surrounded by pickets as a place for the protection of hundreds of their women and children,[2] probably in the same manner as the cacique, who occupied it when De Soto passed through, rendered it secure. At the time of the Rev. E. Cornelius's visit in 1817, the top of the mound, second in size, was encircled by a breastwork 3 feet high, intersected through the middle with another elevation of a

---

[1] Primitive Industry, p. 320.   [2] E. Cornelius. Am. Jour. Sci. (Silliman's), 7th Ser., vol. 1, p. 324.

similar kind.[1] He does not state whether these breastworks were those left by the Cherokees or were of an older date, and, although Squier and Davis[2] and Jones appear to take for granted that it was this lower mound the Cherokees occupied and that these "breastworks" were the remains of their defenses, I think it doubtful, as they would most probably have chosen the larger mound as more easily defended and more secure than the lower one, so near the large one overlooking it. Possibly they occupied both.

It is also well known that in the northern sections it was a very common custom among the Indians, at a comparatively recent date, to use the mounds as depositories for their dead.

One very marked example of subsequent occupancy for a long period, shown by the works themselves, is that of the group in Allamakee county, Iowa, examined by Col. P. W. Norris in 1882, of which an account has been given.

Another point worthy of notice in this connection is that we have here one evidence, at least, that the mound-builders consisted of different tribes, as many, if not most, of the burial mounds of the group are evidently the work of the last occupants. Moreover, there are some reasons for believing that these last occupants belonged to or were closely related to the effigy mound-building tribes of Wisconsin.

Dr. Lapham, who made a long and careful study of the ancient works of Wisconsin, and left behind a monument of his industry in this direction in his well-known "Antiquities of Wisconsin," published in the "Contributions of the Smithsonian Institution," gave it as his deliberate conclusion that the custom of erecting circular or conical tumuli over the dead was followed by the Indians of that region down to a comparatively modern date.

The explorations made by the agents of the Bureau of Ethnology, heretofore described, have given results coinciding exactly with those obtained by Drs. Lapham and Hoy and tending to the same conclusions. As a general rule the conical tumuli, which, as we have seen, are usually of comparatively small size, were all found to be burial mounds, mostly unstratified and of the same character as those opened by Dr. Lapham and others.[3]

One fact observed by these agents to which attention has not heretofore been called, but which must have had its influence on Dr. Lapham's mind, is, that there appears to be no marked distinction between the intrusive burials by modern Indians in a large portion of these mounds and the original burials for which the tumuli were constructed. In both there are from one to many skeletons in a place; in both they are found stretched out horizontally and also folded; in both there are

---

[1] These had all disappeared by the time of our next notice, about 1880, and when I examined the works in 1883 no sign of these fortifications could be seen, unless the remains of four posts, found a few feet below the surface, formed a part of them.

[2] Ancient Monuments, p. 109.

[3] Lapham's Antiquities of Wisconsin. p. 9.

frequent evidences of fire and partially consumed bones; in both we find instances where the mortar-like covering, common in this district, has been used; and in both we occasionally meet with those confused masses of bones which seem to have been gathered from temporary depositories and brought here as a final resting place. Moreover, the transition from one to the other is so gradual as to leave nothing, save the position in the mound and the presence of articles of civilized life, to distinguish the former from the latter.

A large number of these mounds, as already stated, are unstratified, each single mound having been thrown up and completed at one time, as suggested by Dr. Hoy,[1] and not by successive additions; yet in some of these, as observed by the Bureau agents, skeletons were found at various depths, some stretched out at full length and others folded up in the same tumulus. In some cases the bones of all were so much decayed that none could be preserved. Several instances of this kind were observed; in some cases those skeletons and accompanying articles near the surface or top of the mound indicated burial after contact with the whites.

It is apparent from these facts that although some of the burial mounds of this district must be attributed to the so-called "veritable mound-builders," others were undoubtedly built by the Indians found inhabiting it at the advent of the whites. There can scarcely be a doubt that some of the small unstratified tumuli are the work of Indians. If this is conceded there would seem to be no halting place short of attributing all of this class to the same race. The fact stated by Dr. Hoy and verified by the Bureau agents, that in some cases there is evidence that the bodies had been "covered by a bark or log roofing,"[2] is in exact accord with a well-known burial custom of some of the tribes of the Northwest.[3]

These facts fully justify Dr. Lapham's conclusion that they are to be attributed to the Indians. Some, which varied from this type, he was inclined to ascribe to tribes which had migrated, been driven off by or incorporated into other tribes previous to the advent of the white race. But he maintained, and, as the evidence shows, with good reason, that the subsequent tribes, or those found by the Europeans, occupying the country, "continued the practice of mound-building so far as to erect a circular or conical tumulus over the dead." He also adds significantly: "This practice appears to be a remnant of ancient customs that connects the mound-builders with the present tribes."[4]

If it be conceded that the unstratified mounds are the work of Indians, there would seem to be no escape from the conclusion that most of the burial mounds of the same section are to be ascribed to them, for although

---

[1] Lapham's Antiquities of Wisconsin, p. 10.
[2] Loc. cit.
[3] Dr. Yarrow's Mortuary Customs, 1st Ann. Rep. Bureau Ethn., pp. 94 and 141. Schoolcraft's Hist. Ind. Tribes, Vol. III, p. 193.
[4] Ibid., p. 89.

there are some two or three types, yet the gradation from one to the other is so complete as to leave no line of distinction, and Dr. Lapham is fully justified in the assertion that the evidence connects the "mound-builders" with the modern tribes. The stratified mounds in which the hard clay or mortar-like covering over the remains is found, which is also common in Illinois and Iowa mounds, may be the work of different tribes from those which constructed the small, unstratified tumuli of Wisconsin, but the distinctions between the two classes are not such as to justify the belief that they are to be attributed to a different race, or a people occupying a higher or widely different culture-status. The differences are, in fact, not more marked than has occasionally been found in a single group.

Having reached this conclusion, it is impossible to pause here. We are compelled to take one step further in the same direction and ascribe the singular structures known as "effigy mounds" to the same people. The two classes are too intimately connected to admit of the supposition that the effigy mounds were built by one race or people and the conical tumuli by another. It would be as reasonable to assume that the inclosures of Ohio were the work of one people, but the mounds accompanying them of another. That the works of different tribes or nations may frequently be found intermingled on areas over which successive waves of population have passed, must be admitted, but that one part of what is clearly a system is to be attributed to one people and the other part to another is absurd and unworthy of serious consideration. The only possible explanations of the origin, object, or meaning of these singular structures are based, whether confessedly so or not, on the theory that they are of Indian origin; for their illustrations and explanations are drawn from Indian customs, arts and beliefs. Remove the Indian factor from the problem and we are left without the shadow of a hypothesis.

The fact that the effigy mounds were not generally used as places of sepulture and that no cemeteries, save the burial mounds, are found in connection with them, is almost conclusive proof that the two, as a rule, must be attributed to the same people, that they belong to the same system.

To what particular tribes the ancient works of this northwestern section are to be attributed is of course a question which must be answered chiefly by conjecture. Nevertheless, there are some good reasons for believing that the effigy mounds and those works belonging to the same system are attributable to one or more tribes of the Siouan stock. As has been shown in the preceding part of the volume, the custom of placing the small tumuli in lines connected and disconnected to form the long wall-like mounds seems to have been peculiar to the builders of the effigies. Following up this hint and tracing the transitions in form from what appears to be the more ancient to the more recent types, we are led to the comparatively modern surface figures of the Siouan tribes. As this evidence is given in the preceding part of this volume, it is unnecessary to repeat it here.

It is not only possible but apparently evident that there are many mounds in the northwestern section of which we are now speaking that were built by other tribes, but there is no longer any substantial reason for denying that the effigies and other works pertaining thereto are due to the Siouan tribes.

EVIDENCES OF CONTACT WITH MODERN EUROPEAN CIVILIZATION FOUND IN THE MOUNDS.

It has been customary whenever an article indicating contact with Europeans was discovered in a mound to attribute it to an intrusive burial, or where this was incompatible with the conditions, the mound was placed in the category of modern Indian mounds, as distinguished from the works of the true "mound-builders." The more careful investigations of the past few years show that these distinctions fail to account for all the finds of this character, as many of the articles of European manufacture, or those showing evidence of contact with Europeans, are often found so connected with undoubted works of the mound-builders as to forbid both these explanations.

COPPER ARTICLES.

For example, a careful examination of the copper articles found in the mounds should lead anyone, not swayed by some preconceived notion, to the conclusion that many of them were made of copper brought over to America by Europeans, which would as a matter of course indicate (if they do not pertain to intrusive burials) that the mounds in which such specimens are found were erected subsequent to the discovery by Columbus.

The copper articles found in the mounds and ancient graves belong, as may be readily seen by those who will inspect them, to two usually very distinct classes; those of the one class evidently hammered out with rude stone implements; those of the other class showing as plainly that they have been made from quite thin, smooth, and even sheets. If we examine, for instance, the bracelets, of which there are numerous specimens in the various museums and collections of our country, this difference will be found very apparent. Those of the one class are solid, usually about the thickness of the larger end of a large porcupine quill, and roughly hammered out. A figure of this type may be seen on page 97 of the Fifteenth Report of the Peabody Museum, and others in Schoolcraft's History of American Indians, also our Fig. 299. Those of the other class are made of sheet copper by first forming a cylinder of the required size, then bending it to the proper shape. These are usually found in Indian graves and intrusive burials; but occasionally they are obtained from mounds also; for example, one of the eight found in the large mound in Kanawha valley, near Charleston, West Virginia, was of this type. A bracelet of the same type, now in the Peabody Museum, was found in one of the mounds of Little Miami valley.

Cylinders and cylindrical beads made from sheet copper have also frequently been found in mounds and graves. See, for example, the one from a North Carolina mound shown in Fig. 209. One obtained from an Indian grave near Newport, Rhode Island, is figured by Dr. Rau;[1] others, of various sizes, and also conical ear-bobs of sheet copper were found in the North Carolina mounds. The copper bands figured by Prof. Putnam in the Fifteenth Report of the Peabody Museum, as obtained from the Ohio mounds, appear to be of the same character. Speaking of the implement figured on page 61, Tenth Report Peabody Museum, Prof. Andrews, who unearthed it from a mound in Perry county, Ohio, remarks as follows: "It was made from a single piece of copper, the outline of which is indicated in the figure. The copper was hammered out into so smooth and even a sheet that no traces of the hammer are visible. It would be taken indeed for rolled sheet copper." And yet the professor, who has given us one of the best descriptions of Ohio mounds published, seems, by his remarks on the preceding page, to discredit his own eyes.

As a reference to all the articles made of sheet copper found in mounds and graves would be a tedious recital, and would require a personal inspection of all mentioned in order to determine the classes to which they severally belong, it must suffice to repeat what has been stated, that, as a general rule, the distinctive characteristics which determine the class to which they belong may be readily seen.

As a matter of course no one denies that the mound-builders made implements and ornaments of native copper, and frequently hammered this copper into thin sheets with the rude implements of which they were possessed. What is here affirmed, and what, it is believed, can be successfully maintained by reference to and inspection of the articles, is, that many of them, found in mounds as well as ancient graves, have been made from sheets of copper so uniform and even as to forbid the belief that they were hammered out with the rude implements possessed by the mound-builders of pre-Columbian times. A careful chemical and microscopical examination of the various specimens might possibly settle the point; however, as this has not been done, we must for the present rely upon inspection.

The amount of copper traded and given to the Indians along the Atlantic coast was much greater than anyone would imagine who has not taken the trouble to look into the matter. It is necessary to refer to the accounts of early voyages and to the early histories to prove the truth of this statement. On almost every page of Smith's History

---

[1] Smithsonian Archeological Coll., p. 61, Fig. 234.

of Virginia is found mention of copper traded to the Indians for food or pelts. So abundant was the supply, as learned from this author, that in a short time goods "could not be had for a pound of copper which before was sold us for an ounce." [1] Strachey, notwithstanding what he previously stated in regard to minerals of this country, and among them copper, remarks as follows:

It hath been Powhatan's great care to keep us by all means from the acquaintance of those nations that border and confront him, for besides his knowledge how easily and willingly his enemies will be drawn upon him by the least countenance and encouragement from us, he doth, by keeping us from trading with them, monopolize all the copper brought into Virginia by the English. And whereas the English are now content to receive in exchange a few measures of corn for a great deal of that mettell (valuing yt according to the extreme price yt bears with them, not to the estymacion yt hath with us), Powhatan doth again vend some small quantity thereof to his neighbor nations for one hundred tyme the value, reserving, notwithstanding, for himself a plentiful quantity to leavy men withal when he shall find cause to use them against us, for the before-remembered weroance of Paspahegh did once wage fourteen or fifteen weroances to assist him in the attempt upon the fort of James-towne, for one copper plate promised to each weroance. [2]

But European copper found its way into the country along the Atlantic coast long before the settlement in Virginia. The various voyagers who sailed along the shore, and there were many of whom no account is on record, all left more or less of this metal in the hands of the Indians. Much also was doubtless obtained from shipwrecked vessels. Hawkins, who touched the coasts of Florida in 1564–'65, says that when the French first arrived in that region gold and silver were obtained in considerable amount from the Indians, but the supply ere long gave out.

How they came by this gold and silver the Frenchman knew not as yet, but by guess, who having traveled to the southwest of the cape, having found the same dangerous, by means of sundry banks, as we have also found the same; and there finding masts which were wrecks of Spaniards coming from Mexico, judged that they had gotten treasure by them. For it is most true that divers wrecks have been made of Spaniards having much treasure, for the Frenchmen having traveled cape-ward an hundred and fifty miles did find two Spaniards with the Floridians, which they brought afterwards to their fort, whereof one was in a caraval coming from the Indies which was cast away fourteen years ago, and the other twelve years; of whose fellows some escaped, other some were slain by the inhabitants. It seemeth they had estimation of their gold and silver, for it is wrought flat and graven, which they wear about their necks, other some round like a pancake with a hole in the midst to bolster up their breasts withal. [3]

We seem also to have proof in the preceding statement that the Indians engraved figures on metallic articles, which is a very important item in this connection, if true.

Laudonniere asserts that it was gotten out of the ships that were lost upon the coast. [4]

Relics of the unfortunate expedition of Ayllon were dug up by De Soto's followers from a grave or mound at Cutifachiqui, an Indian town

[1] Smith's History of Virginia, Richmond reprint, 1819, vol. I. p. 166.
[2] His. of Travels into Va. Cap. VIII, p. 103, London. 1849.
[3] Hakluyt, III. p. 615.   [4] Hakluyt, III. p. 369.

probably located on the Savannah river above Augusta.[1] Accounts of other wrecked vessels were also given, but it is more than likely that of much the larger number no record was ever made.

The rapidity with which articles obtained by barter on the coast or taken from wrecks found their way into the interior and the distance to which they afterwards traveled do not appear to be fully appreciated by antiquarians.

OTHER METALS.

Smith states that he found hatchets, knives, pieces of iron and brass in the hands of the Indians at the head of Chesapeake bay which he learned were from the French on the St. Lawrence (or " river of Canada," as he names it),[2] and yet but a short time had elapsed since the entrance of the latter into that region. Cabeza de Vaca found a hawk-bell in the hands of the natives of Texas (or Louisiana), which may have been carried from hand to hand and tribe to tribe from Mexico, though more likely obtained from some vessel wrecked on the coast. Father Marquette, in his voyage down the Mississippi says he found guns, axes, hoes, knives, beads, and glass bottles in the hands of some Indians below the mouth of the Ohio, probably Chickasaws.[3]

These (if his statement is to be believed) must have come, as he supposes, from the "eastern side," that is to say, the English settlements on the Atlantic coast.

From these and similar examples which might be mentioned, it is apparent that articles of European manufacture found their way rapidly into the interior, passing from hand to hand in the course of trade and traffic between the tribes or by capture in war. Nor is this to be wondered at when seashells, such as *Busycon perversum* and others, are found in the mounds of Illinois and Wisconsin and articles of native copper probably from northwestern Michigan occur in the mounds of Ohio and West Virginia and at even more eastern points.

Most authors writing on this subject also fail to appreciate properly the fact that traders, trappers, hunters, adventurers, and coureurs de bois were traversing the wilds of the new continent in advance of any notice we have of such adventures. It is apparent from some statements in the Ensayo Cronologico that Spanish adventurers had found their way to the Coza region, probably in northern Georgia, a few years after the return of the remnant of De Soto's followers. These rovers must have carried with them some articles of European manufacture which, finding their way into the hands of the chief men of the tribes, would be interred with them.

Here we may also appropriately refer to a fact which seems to be generally overlooked by writers on North American archeology, to wit, the very early date at which the manufacture of articles similar to those in use among the Indians for the purpose of traffic commenced. Biedma alludes in his Relation of De Soto's Expedition to this subject,

[1] French's Hist. Coll. La. II. pp. 101 and 144.　Pub. Hakluyt Soc. vol. IX, pp. 57 and 181.
[2] Hist. Virginia. Vol. I. p. 182-183.　　　　[3] Hist. Coll. La.. IV. p. 44.

as he speaks of "small pearls similar to those which are brought from Spain to barter with the Indians."[1] These I think we may safely assume to be shell beads, as it is not likely the Spaniards brought true pearls to barter to the Indians for furs and pelts. Moreover, very few pearls have been discovered in the mounds of that southern section which have been opened, while on the contrary shell beads have been found in great abundance.

In one of the mounds of east Tennessee three small copper sleigh bells were found by the skeleton of a child, in a large mound containing many other skeletons. These are perhaps what the early writers call "hawk bells," but have precisely the form of the sleigh bell. The mound in which they were found, as will be seen by referring to the preceding field report, was of considerable size, and there was no reason for supposing there were any intrusive burials. In fact, intrusive burials in mounds seldom, if ever, occur in eastern Tennesse; no positive instance has been brought to light by the extensive explorations of the Bureau of Ethnology in this section.

In another mound in the same section, on which a small pine tree was growing and which presented no indications whatever of having been disturbed, was found a steel-bladed, bone-handled case-knife. This was of the old style, having the end of the blade curved upward. The mound in which it was found had never been plowed, was of comparatively small size, and about 6 feet high. The knife was found near the bottom; there was no intrusive burial in the mound, and if not deposited at the time the mound was thrown up it must have fallen in at a subsequent excavation, though the clayey soil of which it was formed presented no indication of such disturbance.

Mention is made in the preceding part of this volume of a stone having engraved upon it letters of the Cherokee alphabet, which was found in a mound near the locality of the old Cherokee settlements in the valley of the Little Tennessee. The strange circumstance in this case, which presents a puzzle difficult to solve, is that the evidence seems positive that the mound was at least a hundred years old, and that it was known that it had not been disturbed in sixty years.

A small mound in Bartow county, Georgia, on being excavated was found to be composed wholly of clay and to contain no indications of burial. This had not been disturbed since it was built, as was evident from the undisturbed strata, yet at the bottom, among other fragments, was a small piece of glazed pottery, which Mr. Holmes pronounces of Spanish origin.

A mound situated on the bank of the Savannah river at Hollywood was recently opened by Mr. H. L. Reynolds, one of the Bureau assistants, which contained undoubted evidence of contact with European civilization. This is situated in the section where most authorities agree in locating the Indian town of Cutifachiqui, visited by De Soto in his famous expedition, and is heretofore mentioned.

---

[1] Hakluyt Soc. Pub., vol. IX, p. 189.

Mention has already been made of finds by Mr. Walker in some mounds near Tampa Bay, Florida, and therefore need not be repeated here.

While excavating that part of the Ohio canal running through Benton township, Cuyahoga county, it became necessary to remove part of a small mound. In this, says Mr. W. H. Price, under whose direction the work was done, were the remains of one or more skeletons, a gunbarrel, and perhaps some of the mountings of the stock.[1]

With one of the burials in the works of Union county, Mississippi, Mr. Fowke, the Bureau assistant, found a piece of silver stamped with the Spanish coat of arms, a figure of which has been given, also the irons of a saddle-tree. As this locality is in the territory occupied by the Chickasaws, a people visted by De Soto in his expedition, it is possible these articles are mementoes of the trials and hardships suffered here by that unfortunate expedition.

In the rubbish thrown out of one of the stone graves of the Hale mound, Alexander county, Illinois, heretofore described and figured, was found a small brass Catholic medal, which we know from the saints' names stamped on it can not be older than the year 1700.

In one of the Arkansas mounds excavated by one of the Bureau agents was an earthen bottle modeled after the old French decanters. In another was discovered a tooth which Prof. Baird pronounced that of a hog.

A circular mound of the group at Hazen Corners, Crawford county, Wisconsin, which consists of effigies and elongate mounds, was opened by one of the Bureau assistants. There were no indications of burial, but at the bottom, in the center, was a small pile of stone implements, among which was a regularly shaped, genuine gun-flint. In some of the mounds of this section the Bureau assistants found a copper kettle, silver bracelets with Roman letters stamped upon them, silver brooches and crosses; but these pertained to intrusive burials and hence are not introduced into this list of cases as bearing upon the point now referred to.

From mounds in Le Sueur county, Minnesota, about 4 miles north of St. Peter, Mr. Blackiston obtained the following articles: A silver wristlet with "Montreal" and "B. C." stamped upon it; tubular copper ear-pendants; a string of thirty white china beads, a large brown glass bead, four common pins, a needle, a small pearl ornament, and a quartz arrow point.[2]

From the Ninth Annual Report of the Geological Survey of Minnesota, above referred to,[3] we learn that a "blue-glass bead" was obtained by Prof. Winchell in one of the mounds at Big Stone lake.

The fragments of iron implements obtained from a mound in Caldwell county, North Carolina, showing undoubted evidence of contact

---

[1] Anc. Mon., p. 146.   [3] P. 162.
[2] Geol. and Nat. Hist. Surv. Minn., vol. i (1872–'82), p. 647.   Ninth Ann. Geol. Rep. Minn., 1880, p. 164.

with European civilization, have already been referred to in a previous
publication by the Bureau. Articles of iron were also found by the
Bureau agents in some two or three mounds in east Tennessee, of
which mention is made in the preceding report of field works.

It is possible that Prof. Putnam is correct in assuming that what Dr.
Hildreth found in the Marietta mound did not warrant his conclusion
that a sword had been buried there. But there are very strong reasons
for believing that the corrugated silver band which Dr. Hildreth
believed to be part of a sword scabbard was a band for the hair made
by white men (some we know were traded to the Indians) or of material furnished by them.[1] The brief manner, however, in which he
disposes of Atwater's statement in regard to the articles found by him
in the mound at Circleville, Ohio, is by no means satisfactory to archeologists. He says:

> The reference to iron in the mound at Circleville by Mr. Atwater would not be
> worthy of consideration were it not for the widespread belief that he found a steel
> sword and piece of cast iron. He simply found a piece of antler, in one end of which
> a hole had been bored and around this part was a band of silver. This he called "the
> handle of either a small sword or a large knife," and he distinctly states that "no
> iron was found, but an oxide remained of similar shape and size." This is evidently
> purely a case of imagination and misconception. Similar pieces cut from antlers
> have since proved to be common and are generally believed to be handles for small
> drills and knives made of stone or copper.[2]

Notwithstanding this curt dismissal of the subject it is a fact that
can not be disputed that the Bureau agent found in one of the North
Carolina mounds a similar piece of an antler in which still remained a
part of the iron implement of which it formed the handle. It is also
true that chemical analysis showed that this was not meteoric iron.
Prof. Putnam's assumption is therefore wholly gratuitous.

In reference to "plate of iron," he remarks:

> In these days, when only the most careful and critical work is of any value, some-
> thing more definite than this statement is required before it can be claimed that cast
> iron has been found in Ohio mounds.

Mr. Atwater says he was present when the mound was removed and
"carefully examined the contents." In speaking of the horn handle he
says, "The handle either of a small sword or a large knife, made of
elk's horn; around the end where the blade had been inserted in a
ferule, yet no iron was found, but an oxide of similar shape and size."[3] As
the minuteness of details as to size and relative positions, of articles in
the mound indicate that he took notes at the time, his statements of facts
as to what he saw should not be rejected because they do not agree
with a preconceived theory—especially as he was the best qualified and
most careful observer of his day in this line. The silver ferule and
hole in the handle are sufficient in themselves to raise a presumption
that there was a blade of some kind and to suggest contact with the

[1] Proc. Am. Antiq. Soc., New Series, vol. 2. 1882–'83, pp. 349–363.
[2] Loc. cit.. p. 350.   [3] Trans. Am. Antiq. Soc., vol. 1. p. 178.

whites. Add to this the further statement that "an oxide remained of a similar shape and size," and the evidence is too strong to be set aside by a mere opinion. Moreover, his statement that "no iron was found" shows careful observation and a desire to state precisely what he saw. As hunting knives with deer-horn handles and silver ferules were common in the days of the first settlement of the country, there would be no hesitancy in accepting the statement where there is a willingness to admit that the mound was built after the advent of the whites.

It is a very bold assumption that a man of Atwater's attainments and experience as an antiquarian would take iron-colored clay for a plate of oxidized iron. He does not say that it was cast iron, but, that before being disturbed by the spade it "resembled a plate of cast iron." We therefore feel fully justified in giving this mound as one example where evidence of contact with European civilization was found.

The following examples are taken from Dr. P. R. Hoy's paper entitled "Who built the Mounds?" [1]

James Mathew, a brother of Rev. Father Mathew, of Racine, settled on Zumbro river in Olmstead county, Minnesota, in 1860. When he first plowed the land there was a mound 6 feet high and 20 feet in breadth, and so situated that it was in the way of properly cultivating the land, so he made an attempt to plow it down. He sank the plow to the beam repeatedly, but succeeded in reducing the height only about 2 feet. The next year he procured a scraper and went to work systematically to remove the entire mound. After scraping down the eminence to within about 2 feet of the base he came to some rotten wood. On carefully removing the top he discovered a kind of cage built of large stakes driven into the ground, as close together as possible, and covered with a split log, finished by plastering the outside thickly with clay, this forming a rude lodge which was about 3 feet long and a little less in breadth. In this pen he found one skeleton of an adult in a good state of preservation, and with the bones were found two iron hatchets, a dozen flint arrow heads, a copper ring 2 inches in diameter, a lot of shell beads, and a red stone pipe of rather large size and ingeniously ornamented with lead. Father Mathew visited his brother a few days after this find. On his return he brought the entire lot of implements home with him.

From Mr. West, an intelligent and reliable gentleman of Racine, Wisconsin, Dr. Hoy received an accurate description of a mound opened. From this it appears that the mound was small, being only about 10 feet in diameter and 2½ feet high. The much decayed skeleton was in a pit in the original soil under the mound, and near the center was a copper kettle. "This kettle was about 6 inches across, with straight sides; it had ears and no bale, and, in one place on its side where there had been a hole, there was a rivet inserted, made of copper."

He mentions other mounds situated near the junction of White and Fox rivers, in one of which had been buried on the original surface of the ground four persons, two adults and two children. "Each was covered," continues the account, "with a thick stratum of compact

[1] Read before the Montreal meeting (1882) of the Amer. Assoc. Adv. Sci., but published in pamphlet form.

clay, thus forming a rude kind of sarcophagus.   On breaking open these
clay cases we found human bones partly decayed, and three copper
kettles, one of which had some nuts in it, perhaps pecans; another had
what are supposed to be bones of a rabbit; also there were many silver
earrings, breast pins, and one beautiful, double-armed, ringed, silver
cross, with R. C. in Roman capitals engraved in the center of the upper
arm of the cross, also a large quantity of blue glass beads." In the
other was found one copper kettle of rather large size " and a small
fur-covered, brass-nailed trunk, 10 by 12 inches and 8 inches in height.
In this trunk were discovered a lot of cheap silver trinkets."

THE MUSKOKI TRIBES.

As I have in two small works, one entitled " The Cherokees in pre-
Columbian Times," [1] the other "The story of a mound, or the Shawnees
in pre-Columbian Times," [2] discussed the probability that the tribes
named were mound-builders, there is no necessity for repeating the
discussion here.

By reference to these works it will be seen that I arrived at the conclusion that both the Cherokees and Shawnees were mound-builders,
the evidence leading to this conviction, some of which has been given
in preceding chapters, being apparently so strong as to dispel all doubt
on the subject.

I would, however, call attention to the very strong evidence that the
Cherokees were mound-builders, presented in the preceding report of
field work.   By referring to the plat of the Little Tennessee valley,
Pl. xxv, and Timberlake's Map, Pl. xxvi, showing the locality of the
Cherokee " Overhill towns" and locations of the mound groups, it will
be seen that each of the former is marked by one of the latter.

Mr. Gallatin, Dr. Brinton, and Mr. Gatschet (especially the latter in
his excellent work on the " Migration legend of the Creeks") have
demonstrated from the aboriginal names of persons, places, and things
mentioned by the narrators of De Soto's expedition, that the tribes
then inhabiting the southern states through which the wanderers
passed, were the same as those subsequently found occupying this
region.   It follows, therefore, that the theory advanced by some
writers,[3] that the Creeks or Muskoki (Muscogee or Muscogulgee) tribes
migrated to this region from some point west of the Mississippi, subsequent to the date of De Soto's expedition, is erroneous, and may be
dismissed from further consideration.

From the narratives of the Adelantado's march and a few faint
glimpses we catch from other sources, we are justified in concluding

[1] First published in the American Anthropologist, then in book form by Judd & Detweiler, Washington, D. C., 1891.
[2] First published in Science, then in book form by N. D. Hodges, New York, 1890.
[3] Milfort " Memoire," etc.   Pickett " History of Alabama," Vol. 1, p. 74, et seq.

that the southern tribes east of the Mississippi were in a comparatively quiet and settled condition, and that most of them were at the time settled in villages and building and using mounds and defensive works in the manner they had been accustomed to from an unknown period in the past. That this was true of the Creeks, Choctaws, Chickasaws, and other tribes of the Muskoki family and also of the Natchez, may be assumed with little fear of being in error.

Although the ancient works of these states have not been explored sufficiently to enable us to speak positively on this point, still the data so far obtained indicate that the condition observed by De Soto and his followers had been maintained without any radical and general modification for a period of considerable length previous thereto. In other words, there is nothing in the character of the works or of the vestiges of art found in them indicating extensive and general movements, or successive waves of population materially differing in culture or customs. But this general statement must be considered as here applied only to the Gulf states, for when we reach the northern limits of Georgia and enter Tennessee we find in the ancient works undoubted evidences of the presence of different tribes or peoples.

From the geographical distribution of the works of this southern district east of the Mississippi river and the lines along which certain types of art are found, it is safe to assume that the general movement has been from the west toward the east or the reverse. This inference is drawn chiefly from the fact that there appears to be no continuous series of similar works, or those belonging to the same general type, along the lines of the larger rivers (except the Mississippi). In other words, the direction of the movement does not appear to have been governed here by the water courses. The works are scattered along the same parallels of latitude, their lines of distribution crossing the main streams at right angles. As this transverse belt ceases towards the east before reaching the Atlantic coast, and its southern border lies mostly at a considerable distance from the Gulf, the most reasonable and natural explanation is that the migration was from the west.

There are but few, if any, indications in the works themselves of the date of this movement, which, in all probability, consisted of successive waves. That it preceded the discovery by Columbus at least by one or more centuries is indicated by the works and their contents, and the conditions observed by De Soto, but on the other hand its antiquity appears to be limited, if we suppose mound-building to have commenced soon after arrival, by the fact that we find in the works no evidences of any marked progress in art during occupancy.

The chief seats of power east of the Mississippi appear to have been (judging from the works and history) at Cutifachiqui, the exact locality of which has not been ascertained, but was probably on the Savannah river a short distance above Augusta; the site of the Etowah mounds near Cartersville, Georgia, probably the Guaxule of De Soto's chronicles; the locality in Early county, Georgia, marked by the Messier mounds; the "old town" of Apalachucla, mentioned by Bartram, which could not have been far distant and pertained to the same limited tribe; the site of the Prince mounds near Carthage, Alabama; the Mauvilla of De Soto's day; Chisca or Chicasa, in northern Mississippi, doubtless the chief village of the Chickasaws; and the vicinity of Natchez. These localities, so far as known, are marked by mounds and the remains of other works. Even where we are unable now to determine them we have historical evidence that they were marked by mounds or other earthworks. I may remark in passing that the power of the Chickasaw tribe does not appear to have reached its zenith, in the section in which they were then found, until after the date of De Soto's visit. There are, in fact, some reasons for believing they had not then occupied this locality for any great length of time. Judging by the testimony of the mounds and the narrative of De Soto's march, I am not inclined to believe the statement of the Natchez Indians regarding their former great numerical strength, controlling power, and extensive sway, even after making due allowance for the usual exaggeration, unless we can identify them with the builders and former occupants of the great Cahokia group, which is very improbable.

Judging by the progress made in the ceramic art, I should think one of the most polished tribes of this region was located during the mound-building age in that portion of the country extending from Early county, Georgia, to the valley of the Ochlochonee river. The ornamentation and form of the pottery is somewhat peculiar, and judging from the latter I am inclined to believe the makers had seen some vessels manufactured by the whites. Are we to ascribe these to the Lower Creeks or shall we attribute them to the Yuchi (Uches)? The latter, as we learn from Hawkins, were more "civil, orderly, and industrious than their neighbors, the Lower Creeks."[1]

When we reach the northern portion of Georgia we find indisputable evidences of being in the marches, the debatable ground between contending powers or hostile tribes. The site of the Etowah groups so often mentioned must have been a place of some importance in mound-building times. Here we find evidences of culture and art equal to that obtained from the mounds of any other locality in that portion of the United States included in the scope of this work, not even excepting the far-famed works of the Ohio. The locality was well chosen when we consider the means of security and defense adopted and the necessity of relying largely upon the products of agriculture for subsistence, yet the silent ruins, when compelled to yield up their hidden treasures, give unmistakeable evidences of the ravages of war and of occupancy by different peoples. The fragments of stone images found here are of such a character as to lead any one who examines them to

[1] For a discussion of the localities occupied by this tribe, the reader is referred to Mr. Gatschet's work, before mentioned, vol. I, pp. 17–24.

the conclusion that they must have been maliciously and intentionally broken.

Some of the pottery, which, unfortunately, has been discovered only in fragments, bears a strong resemblance to that found in Early county, indicating occupancy for a time by the Creeks or Uchees. On the other hand, the mode of sepulture and articles found in the small mound connect the builders, as heretofore stated, with that people who made the stone graves and built the mounds of the Cumberland valley, who, as we have shown, we are warranted in assuming were Shawnees; and, finally, we are justified by articles taken from graves discovered here and from history in asserting that it was for a time occupied by the Cherokees, though none of the works except some neighboring graves can be ascribed to them; but I think it quite probable the fragmentary condition of the stone images is due to their savage hatred of all pertaining to a hereditary foe. In an article published in the Magazine of American History,[1] I was inclined to attribute these works entirely to the "Creeks," using this term in the broad sense, believing they were occupied at the time of De Soto's visit by people under the sway of the cacique of Cutifachiqui; but the explorations made since that article was written have introduced a new factor into the problem and materially modified the opinion there expressed. From the language of the Gentleman of Elvas, as follows: "In that journey (from Xualla to Guazule) the lady of Cutifachiqui (whom the governor carried with him, as is aforesaid, with purpose to carry her to Guazule because her territory reached thither), going on with the bond women which led her," etc., I was led to believe that Guazule was then included in the dominion of the cacique; but referring since to what is said by Garcilasso on this point, I find he states very particularly, even repeating it, that this town was beyond the limits of the territory of the cacique, and governed by a cacique belonging to another tribe, though, to assist the Spaniards, she sent ambassadors thither to solicit the aid of the inhabitants in their behalf.

Mr. Gatschet[2] refers to a tradition that the Shawnees once resided in upper Georgia around Tugelo (in the region of Habersham county) and on the headwaters of the large Georgia rivers, but thinks it requires further examination. We have, as already shown, satisfactory evidences that this tribe not only held possession for a time of the locality on Etowah river, but were probably also the builders of one, at least, of the mounds there; we also have the testimony of C. C. Jones[3] that stone graves have been found in Habersham county, which fact indicates their presence in that region. In addition to this we have the statement of Milfort[4] that lands were obtained here from the "Savanogues, savages."

---

[1] May number, 1884.
[2] Op. cit., Vol. I, p. 23.
[3] Antiq Southern Indians. p. 214.
[4] Memoire, p. 9.

GENERAL OBSERVATIONS.

The hope of ultimately solving the great problems of the pre-Columbian times of our continent is perhaps as lively to-day as in former years. But, with the vast increase of knowledge in recent years in reference to the data bearing on these questions, a modification of the hope entertained has taken place. While no thought any longer exists of ascertaining the exact date of or any definite particulars in regard to the migration by which the western continent received its first settlers; yet there is an expectation that the advance in scientific knowledge and methods of investigation, together with the long and careful study of all the data, will result in determining in a general sense the age in which this first introduction of population took place, and in deciding what race or races contributed to this population.

This expectation includes the determination with reasonable certainty of the route or routes of this migration. The method of treating the subject has also been changed from that of mere theorizing to scientific deduction. The literary world is now and then amused at the revival of some old, exploded theory or the presentation of some new one equally absurd; but allusion is made here only to those efforts which appear to be based on some legitimate data.

The tendency at present appears to be to base the tentative efforts in this direction on the linguistic evidence, leaving out of view the important aid to be derived from a careful study of the archeological data bearing upon the subject or referring to it only where it seems to corroborate the theories based on the linguistic evidence. This arises in part from the fact that while the archeological data relating to a large portion of the continent are few, and that archeology can not, as yet, be considered a true science; on the other hand the linguistic material, although not complete, is much more abundant, and the treatment thereof reduced to true scientific methods. As the latter field affords greater promise of reaching positive conclusions, it is more attractive to methodical students.

As the discussion of this subject from the linguistic standpoint is necessarily based upon the study of the various linguistic stocks and families of the entire continent, and, to some extent upon the migrations therein, so the discussion of the same questions from the archeological standpoint must be based upon the study of the various types and their distribution over the continent. And the same necessity for generalization and classification arises here as in the linguistic field. Although the lines of demarkation between the types and groups with which the antiquarian has to deal are apparently less distinct than those with which the philologist is concerned, yet careful study will show that this difference is not so great as at first it seems to be. The indications of comprehensive archeologic sections and also of minor

districts are too apparent to question their existence. The chief drawback in attempting to use these as evidences of ethnic distinctions
arises from three causes: First, the lack of sufficient data by which to
outline the different sections and districts; second, the overlapping and
intermingling of types in consequence of the shifting of positions by
tribes; and third, the fact that types of art and other archeologic characteristics are not governed strictly by ethnic lines, but are often the
result of environment, materials, and contact with other tribes. Nevertheless race characteristics and tribal customs impress themselves to a
certain extent under all variations in locations and conditions so long
as the identity of the race or tribe is maintained. There is no difficulty
in distinguishing the Mexican and Central American antiquities as a
whole from those of the mound area of the eastern half of the United
States, yet the geographical boundaries of these sections can, with our
present knowledge, only be determined approximately. If, however,
we move from the Mexican district southward or northward along the
western side of the continent we shall find the distinguishing features
less marked than when compared with the types of the mound area.
There is no difficulty in distinguishing the types of the Huron-Iroquois
district from the works of the Dakotan area (Wisconsin, Minnesota,
and the Dakotas), and we can point out some specimens of the former
types within the latter area, yet, where not fixed by natural conditions,
it is impossible with present data to draw a definite boundary to either
district.

Although we meet with this difficulty in defining geographically the
boundaries of the districts and more comprehensive sections it does not
prevent us from drawing correct conclusions from their general positions and peculiar types. That all the distinguishing types of a district
or section can not be attributed to the peculiar physical features of such
districts or sections must be admitted. Will any one claim that the
vast difference between the archeologic types of Mexico and Wisconsin
have resulted wholly from the physical differences of the two areas?
If not, it follows that so much as has not resulted from physical peculiarities must be attributed to racial or tribal customs.

It is necessary at this point, in order to present the thought in view,
to repeat a few sentences given in the previous part of the volume
relating to "Archeological Areas and Distribution of Types."

A careful examination of what has been ascertained in regard to North
American archeology; with special reference to the question of archeologic sections, leads in the first place to the conclusion that the
ancient remains belong in a broad and comprehensive sense to two
general classes. One of these classes is limited geographically to the
Atlantic slope, the other chiefly to the Pacific slope, the eastern or
Rocky mountain range of the great continental mountain belt to the
Rio Grande, forming approximately the dividing line between the two
areas. According to this division the Atlantic section includes that

part of the continent east of the Rocky mountains and north of the Gulf of Mexico, and the Pacific section the remainder from Alaska to the isthmus of Panama. The arctic regions, except Alaska, are not taken into consideration.

While there are manifest and marked differences in the types and characters of the ancient works and remains of different areas within each of these two comprehensive sections, yet when those of the Pacific slope as a whole are compared with those of the Atlantic slope, there is a dissimilarity which marks them as the products of different races or as the result of different race influences.

If this division into two great archeologic sections is based on sufficiently reliable data to justify its adoption, it will form a very important landmark in the discussion of the chief problems of the prehistoric times of our continent. Reference to some, only of the evidences bearing upon this point, is made here to show their character, as it would not be possible to present them in detail in a short chapter.

One of the first impressions made upon the mind of the student of North American ethnology is the resemblance in a broad and general sense of the features, customs, arts, and archeological remains of the west coast to those of the islands in and countries bordering on the Pacific ocean, while on the other hand there is no such resemblance between them and those of the Atlantic slope. In other words, the types when classified in the broadest sense appear to arrange themselves in two general divisions—those belonging to the Pacific slope and those confined to the Atlantic slope.

Although this classification in express words has not been made, yet we see a tendency in the works relating to the west coast ethnology toward such a classification and a disposition to form what may be termed the Pacific types. This is perhaps most clearly indicated by Prof. W. H. Dall, in his paper on "Masks, labrets and certain aboriginal customs," published in the Third Annual Report of the Bureau of Ethnology. Referring to this subject in his summary, he says:

The original population of America is too distant to form the subject of discussion. There can be no doubt that America was populated in some way by people of an extremely low grade of culture at a period even geologically remote. There is no reason for supposing, however, that immigration ceased with these original people. Analogy would suggest that from time to time accessions were received from other regions of people who had risen somewhat in the scale elsewhere, while the inchoate American population had been doing the same thing on their own ground. Be this as it may, we find certain remarkable customs or characteristics geographically spread north and south along the western slope of the continent in a natural line of migration with overflows eastward in convenient localities. These are not primitive customs, but things which appertain to a point considerably above the lowest scale of development in culture.

Some are customs pure and simple; e. g., labretifery; tattooing the chin of adult females; certain uses of masks, etc.

Some are characteristics of culture, e. g., a certain style of conventionalizing natural objects, and, in a higher stage, the use of conventional signs in a hieroglyphic way; a disposition to, and peculiar facility in, certain arts, such as carvings in wood, etc.

Some are details of art related to religious or mythological ideas, such as the repetition of elaborate forms in a certain attitude, with relation to myths therefore presumably similar in form or origin.

Some are similar myths themselves, a step further in the retrospect.

If these were of natural American growth, stages in development out of a uniform state of culture, it might fairly be expected that we should find them either sporadically distributed without order or relation as between family and family wherever a certain stage of culture had been reached or distributed in certain families wherever their branches were to be found. This we do not find.

The only other alternative which occurs to me is that these features have been impressed upon the American aboriginal world from without. If so, whence?

Northern Asia gives us no help whatever. The characteristics referred to are all foreign to that region.

If nations from the eastern shores of the Atlantic were responsible, we should expect the Atlantic shores of America to show the results of the influence most clearly. This is not the case, but the very reverse of the case.

We are then obliged to turn toward the region of the Pacific.

The great congeries of islands known to geographers as Polynesia and Melanesia stretch toward South America in latitude 25° south, as in no other direction. Here we have a stream of islands from Papua to the Paumotus, dwindling at last to single islets with wide gaps between, Elizabeth, Ducie, Easter Island, Sala-y-Gomez, San Felix, St. Ambrose, from which comparatively it is but a step, swept by the northerly current to the Peruvian coast. We observe also that these islands lie south from the westerly south equatorial current, in the slack water between it and an easterly current and in a region of winds blowing toward the east.

Here, then, is a possible way.

I have stated how the peculiar and remarkable identity of certain carvings associated with religious rites turned my attention to the Melanesian islands.

The customs, etc., I have called attention to are, particularly, the use of masks and carvings to a more than ordinary degree, labretifery, human-head preserving; identity of myths. [1]

Prof. Dall calls attention to the singular form of carving, representing a figure with the tongue hanging out, and usually communicating with a frog, otter, bird, snake, or fish, observed on the northwest coast from Oregon to Prince William sound and also in Mexico and Nicaragua. We may add that this feature is found in numerous instances in statues and bas-reliefs from Mexico to the Isthmus, also in the codices of Mexico and Central America, but seldom if ever appears in the antiquities of the Atlantic division.

The prominent Tlaloc nose of Mexican and Central American figures, of which the supposed elephant proboscis is but one form, and the bird bill (thunder bird) of the northwest coast are but different methods of representing the same idea, and one is undoubtedly an outgrowth of the other. The method of superimposing, in totem posts and statues, one figure upon another, usually combining human and animal, is found, except in California, from Alaska to the Isthmus, and is a true Pacific type, being almost unknown in the Atlantic division.

The angular designs on the pottery and basketry are another marked

---

[1] Pp. 146. 147.

feature of the west coast division. And thus we might, if this were the proper place to enter into details, go on enumerating marked distinctions between these two primary ethnological sections. As evidence of the fact stated let any one compare the figures in Ensign Albert P. Niblack's excellent work on The Coast Indians of Southern Alaska and Northern British Columbia,[1] with the Mexican and Central American monuments and figures. The marked resemblance in many of the designs will probably be sufficient to convince him of some relation between the peoples of the two sections or derivation from some common source; for example, the headdress, Pl. IX, with the headdresses of the Copan statues; the superimposed heads on the skirt, No. 34, Pl. X, with the similar series of ornaments on the façade of the Casa de Monjas of Uxmal[2] and on other structures, and the general designs of the totem posts and mortuary columns shown therein with statues of Nicaragua. There is, however, a somewhat remarkable break in the continuity of types along the western coast of upper California.

How are we to explain this? That the spread of particular types over such a vast extent of country varies with environment and local conditions, must be admitted. We must, therefore, consider these types as ethnic peculiarities, having a common origin, or adopt the theory of Prof. Dall that "they have been impressed upon the American aboriginal world from without," for which influence we must, beyond question, look to the region of the Pacific.[3] But the somewhat distinct limits to which some of the more marked of these types are confined, especially as we find them on the most ancient monuments, must be considered ethnic, as pertaining to particular stocks or tribes. Prof. Dall's theory is, after all, but a different method of expressing substantially the same idea. To impress peculiar characteristics in prehistoric times required long contact or intermingling, hence by settlement on the continent. Are we to presume from the differences between western and eastern types that the latter are due to immigration on the Atlantic side?

The general tendency of the more recent opinions in regard to the peopling of the continent is that it was at least partly from the Atlantic side. This is shown by the fact that some recent authorities, abandoning the more generally received theory that the original population came from the Pacific side, are inclined to look to Europe as the original source. For example, Dr. Brinton remarks in his " Races and Peoples:" "These knotty points I treat in another course of lectures, where I marshal sufficient arguments, I think, to show satisfactorily that America was peopled during if not before the great ice age; that its first settlers probably came from Europe by way of a land connection which once existed over the northern Atlantic." But he does not stop here, as he adds, "and that their long and isolated residence in this

---

[1] Published by the Smithsonian Institution, 1890.   [3] Third Ann. Rep. Bureau Ethn., p. 147.
[2] Bancroft's Native Races, vol. 4, p. 185.

continent has molded them all into a singularly homogeneous race, which varies but slightly anywhere on the continent, and has maintained its type unimpaired for countless generations. Never at any time before Columbus was it influenced in blood, language, or culture by any other race." Dr. Horatio Hale is inclined to substantially the same view, though somewhat reserved. The theory certainly does not require the molding process referred to, as the settlers, according to his belief, were of one race and received thereafter no intrusive element.

It is evident that this idea of a migration on the Atlantic side reached by linguists after a study of the large amount of data which has been collected, is to be attributed largely to the unsatisfactory results obtained in attempting to trace out the links in the other direction. But the important fact is to be borne in mind that those who reach this conclusion have prosecuted their studies on the Atlantic slope, while the more recent authors who have carried on their studies on the Pacific slope have reached an exactly opposite conclusion. It is therefore highly probable that a more thorough and comprehensive study of all the data bearing on the question will show, as appears to be indicated by the archeology, that the truth lies between these opposite views; in other words, will lead to the conclusion that the continent was peopled from two sources, one part coming to the Atlantic coast, the other to the Pacific side. Some of the Central American traditions correspond with this view, but traditions purporting to reach back so far in the past are of course worthless. This conclusion is not incompatible with the fact that the aborigines of America form a comparatively homogeneous race. As remarked somewhere by Prof. Dall, even though derived from different sources, the long continental isolation and molding influence would have brought about this condition. But it does not follow that there would have necessarily been a unification of customs, habits, and religious beliefs.

The spread of types of custom and art would be governed in part by several influences, as ethnic lines, migrations, contact, and physical conditions. Where we find those of a character which do not depend upon physical conditions, but upon superstitious notions, following a given line without spreading out indefinitely, we may assume, until satisfactory evidence of another cause is given, that they mark a line of migration and are largely ethnic. It is in this light we are inclined to view the coast-line extension of the types peculiar to the Pacific slope.

It is somewhat significant that Dr. Brinton should, notwithstanding the views he advances in regard to the origin and homogeneity of the American race, arrange his linguistic groups geographically by substantially the same dividing lines as those we have indicated as separating the archeological divisions. His "North Atlantic Group," omitting the Eskimos, corresponds geographically with our Atlantic divisions, and his "North Pacific" and "Central" groups combined, with our Pacific division. This arrangement, as he admits, is not one of convenience only, as he attaches certain ethnographic importance to it. "There is," he continues, "a distinct resemblance between the two Atlantic groups, and an equally distinct contrast between them and the Pacific groups, extending to temperament, culture, and physical traits. Each of the groups has mingled extensively within its own limits and but slightly outside of them." [1] Elsewhere he remarks that "a few of the eastern stocks, the Athabascan and the Shoshonian, have sent out colonies who have settled on the banks of the Pacific; but as a rule the tribes of the western coast are not connected with any east of the mountains. What is more singular, although they differ surprisingly among themselves in language, they have marked anthropological similarities, physical and psychical. Virchow has emphasized the fact that the skulls from the northern point of Vancouver Island reveal an unmistakable analogy to those of southern California. *   *   *   There are many other physical similarities which mark the Pacific Indians and contrast them with those east of the mountains." [2]

In his "Races and Peoples" Brinton emphasizes this eastern and western division still more pointedly: "All the higher civilizations are contained in the Pacific group, the Mexican really belonging to it by derivation and original location. Between the members of the Pacific and Atlantic groups there was very little communication at any period, the high Sierras walling them apart." [3] This view, which is based on abundant linguistic, archæologic, and custom data, and seems to be supported by the mass of evidence, is, however, at variance with Dr. Brinton's theory in regard to the original populating of the continent, as advanced in his "American Race."

As this separation is shown to have existed as far back as we are able to trace customs by the archeological indications, is there not in this fact a valid reason for believing that the original peopling of the continent was from two different sections? Not necessarily from the distant shores of the opposite oceans, for the characteristics of the race, taken as a whole, as remarked by Nadaillac, and, we may add, as shown by the archeologic remains, point toward affinities with people belonging to the Pacific region rather than with those bordering the opposite coasts of the Atlantic basin.

But to pursue this line of thought would carry us farther into the field of speculation than is consistent with the object of this work. Our only object in view in touching upon the subject was to show that, taking the more comprehensive view of the ethnology of North America, we reach the same conclusion as that arrived at by a study of the archeologic details, viz, that the supposed relation between the mound-builders and the civilized nations of Mexico and Central America is not

---

[1] American Race, p. 58.   [2] Op. cit., pp. 103, 104.   [3] P. 248.

sustained. The peoples of the two sections have been too long separated from each other to render such a supposition admissible.

Linguistic evidence leads to the same conclusion. Time is an element in the development of languages that can not be overlooked, notwithstanding the widely different views entertained in regard to it. Even accepting the views of those assigning the most limited period to the formation of languages and adopting the theory of more than one original migration, the time required for the differentiation into the numerous stocks and dialects of the different sections of the North American continent must have been very great. That the various stocks and dialects of the Mexican and Central American section, as also of the Atlantic section or mound area, have been differentiated since separation from the main stock, if ever they were united, must be admitted; and that this development took place chiefly in their respective areas may be safely assumed from the respective positions of the branches. This must have required a long period of time and presents a very formidable obstacle to any other view than that the Indians of the mound area were the authors of the ancient works found therein.

Analogy also leads to the same conclusion. The ancient remains of other sections of North America and also of South America are traceable in most cases to the races found inhabiting those sections when first discovered by Europeans. Few if any students of American archeology entertain any longer a doubt that the monuments of Mexico and Central America are attributable to the direct ancestors of the people found occupying those countries at the time of the Spanish conquest. Hubert H. Bancroft, speaking of the remaining evidences of Central American civilization, remarks as follows: " I deem the grounds sufficient therefore for accepting this Central American civilization of the past as a fact, referring it not to an extinct ancient race, but to the direct ancestors of the people still occupying the country with the Spaniards."[1] Dr. D. G. Brinton, in his work entitled "The American Race," makes the following statement: " We can not identify the builders of the ruined cities of Palenque in Tobasco and Copan in Honduras with the ancestors of any known tribe, but the archeological evidence is conclusive that whoever they were they belonged to this stock (the Maya) and spoke one of its dialects."[2] A little further on he adds: "At the time of the conquest the stately structures of Copan, Palenque T'Ho and many other cities were deserted and covered with an apparently primitive forest; but others not inferior to them, Uxmal, Chichen-Itza, Peten, etc., were the centers of dense population, proving that the builders of both were identical."[3] Marquis de Nadaillac, who embraces the Mayas, Aztecs, and other Central American stocks in the " Nahautl race," says that " it is to various branches of this conquering race that we owe the ruined monuments still scattered over Mexico, Yucatan, Honduras,

---

[1] Native Races. vol. II, p. 117.   [2] P. 153.   [3] P. 155.

Guatemala and Nicaragua and found, as far as the Isthmus of Tehuantepec.[1]

This view coincides with the conclusion of all the leading archeologists of the present day. Nor could they reach any other decision if led by the data which is conclusive on this point.

That the ruined pueblos of New Mexico and Arizona are attributable to the ancestors of the sedentary tribes of those sections is not questioned. It is also now conceded that the cave and cliff dwellings and other remains of that region are attributable to the ancestors of the present Pueblo tribes.

While it does not necessarily follow that because this is true in regard to some sections it must be true in reference to all, yet it furnishes a reason for concluding that the remains of the mound section are due to the ancestors of the Indians of that section, especially as they are the only pre-Columbian inhabitants of that region of which we have any knowledge.

---

[1] L'Amérique Prehistorique, p. 264.

INDEX.

A.

o